Public Papers of
the Secretaries-General of
the United Nations

VOLUME III

DAG
HAMMARSKJÖLD

1956–1957

Public Papers of

the Secretaries-General of

the United Nations

VOLUME III

DAG HAMMARSKJÖLD

1956–1957

Selected and Edited with Commentary by

ANDREW W. CORDIER

AND

WILDER FOOTE

COLUMBIA UNIVERSITY PRESS

1973

NEW YORK AND LONDON

ANDREW W. CORDIER has served as Dean of the School of International Affairs at Columbia University 1962–1972 and as President of the University 1968–1970. From the beginning of the United Nations until 1962 Dr. Cordier was Executive Assistant to the Secretary-General with the rank of Under-Secretary. During the entire period he also had the top Secretariat responsibility for General Assembly affairs.

WILDER FOOTE served in the United Nations Secretariat from its early days until December 1960 as Director of Press and Publications and acted as spokesman to the press for Secretaries-General Trygve Lie and Dag Hammarskjöld. Later he was a Research Associate in the School of International Affairs, Columbia University.

Library of Congress Cataloging in Publication Data
Cordier, Andrew Wellington, 1901–   comp.
  Public papers of the Secretaries-General of the
United Nations.
  Bibliographical footnotes.
  CONTENTS: v. 1. Trygve Lie, 1946–53.—
v. 3. Dag Hammarskjöld, 1956–1957
  1. United Nations—Collections.   I. Lie, Trygve,
1896–   II. Foote, Wilder, joint comp.   III. Title.
JX1977.C62   341.23′08   68-8873
ISBN 0-231-03735-X

Editors' Note on the Series

THE ROLE OF THE Secretary-General in the political life and constitutional development of the United Nations since 1945 has far exceeded the expectations of those who wrote the Charter. This has enhanced the historical significance of their public papers. These include many texts that are valuable and often indispensable as source materials in study of the Organization as a whole, of the office of Secretary-General in particular, and of the place of both in world affairs.

It is important that such papers be readily available to scholars and specialists in international affairs. In practice their accessibility has been severely limited. Some of the public papers of the Secretaries-General are included in the official documentation and some are not. In the former category are periodic and special reports to United Nations organs, proposals, and statements at meetings of the General Assembly, the Security Council, the other councils, committees, and commissions, and certain communications to governments. Not included in the official records are various other communications to governments, the Secretary-General's addresses outside the United Nations, statements to the press, press conference transcripts, radio and television broadcasts, contributions to magazines and books. Most of the texts in this second category were issued as press releases, none as official documents.

More or less comprehensive collections of the official documents are maintained by depository libraries designated by the United Nations and located in most of the countries of the world. After more than twenty-five years it is not surprising that the volume of this documentation is immense. The record of what successive Secretaries-General have spoken or written in the official proceedings is widely dispersed throughout a great mass of records. Furthermore, it is necessary to go to the press releases for the public papers in the second category described above. The Dag Hammarskjöld Library at United Nations Headquarters maintains a comprehensive collection of press releases but it has not been the practice to include them in the deposit

of official documentation in the depository libraries. Yet the press releases are usually the only source of a very important part of the public
record—the Secretary-General's speeches to other groups and organizations and his press statements and press conferences. Successive
Secretaries-General have frequently used these for historically significant and revealing statements.

Thus the present series of volumes of the public papers of the Secretaries-General has been undertaken to meet a real need. The project
has been made possible by a grant from the Ford Foundation to the
School of International Affairs of Columbia University. The series will
include all texts believed by the editors to be essential or most likely
to be useful in study and research about the United Nations. These
have been assembled from official, semiofficial, and nonofficial sources.
The texts selected for the printed series are reproduced in full except
where otherwise indicated. The styles of spelling and capitalization,
which were variable in the official documents and press releases, have
generally been reproduced as they were in the originals. Dates have
been conformed throughout to the month-day-year style. The texts are
arranged for the most part in chronological order corresponding to the
sequence of events to which they are related. Commentary recalling
the contemporary context and giving other background for the texts
is provided whenever this seems useful. The full collections at Columbia University and the Dag Hammarskjöld Library are open to scholars
wishing to consult them.

It should also be explained that the official records of the United
Nations include many reports issued in the name of the Secretary-
General that may more correctly be classified with the records of the
organs requesting them. Such reports are factual accounts of developments or programs without personal commitments of policy or principle by the Secretary-General. There are a few borderline cases, but
in general, reports of this nature have not been considered as belonging
with the public papers of the Secretaries-General.

Acknowledgments

THE SERIES of volumes of *Public Papers of the Secretaries-General of the United Nations* has been made possible by a grant from the Ford Foundation to the School of International Affairs of Columbia University. The project has also benefited from a generous provision in the will of the late Julian Clarence Levi and from a grant by the Blaustein Foundation. The editors are deeply grateful for this financial assistance.

The task of assembling the texts has been greatly facilitated by various officers serving in the United Nations Secretariat, especially those in the Dag Hammarskjöld Library and in the Public Inquiries Unit at United Nations Headquarters. Their willing cooperation is much appreciated.

Our editorial and research assistant, Miss Alice Smith, has rendered indispensable and devoted service in assembling texts, researching the background of events for use in the commentary, finding and checking sources and references, reading proof, and supervising the transcription and reproduction of both texts and commentary. In this last respect a special word of appreciation is also due to the School of International Affairs' very helpful and efficient Xeroxing service.

Finally, the editors are grateful to Brian Urquhart, United Nations Assistant Secretary-General, and Max Harrelson, chief of the United Nations bureau of the Associated Press from 1950 to 1972 and at present a Research Associate in the School of International Affairs, who read the manuscript of Volume III and made a number of helpful comments.

Contents

Contents

Contents

1957

Contents

Public Papers of
the Secretaries-General of
the United Nations

VOLUME III

DAG HAMMARSKJÖLD

1956–1957

Note to the Reader

---

*The unnumbered footnote at the bottom of the
page beginning each titled section gives the
source of the text matter in that section.*

Introduction to This Volume of
the Public Papers of Dag Hammarskjöld

I

THIS VOLUME OF THE public papers of Dag Hammarskjöld begins on March 7, 1956, and concludes at the end of December 1957. It is the second of four volumes in the series of *Public Papers of the Secretaries-General of the United Nations* in which are collected Hammarskjöld's reports, statements, addresses, diplomatic communications, verbatim press transcripts, and other documentary and press material of public record from the time of his election as Secretary-General in 1953 until his death in 1961.

The period with which the texts and accompanying commentary in this volume are concerned was a watershed in the uses of international organization. It began with Hammarskjöld's cease-fire mission to the Middle East and continued through the dispute over nationalization of the Suez Canal, the surprise attack on Egypt mounted by Israel, France, and the United Kingdom, the creation of the United Nations Emergency Force, the withdrawal of the invaders from Egyptian soil, and the United Nations clearance of the Suez Canal.

In these developments the Secretary-General served the Member governments as constitutional innovator and chief negotiator and was entrusted, besides, with executive responsibilities of unprecedented scope. The results demonstrated how effective a contribution could be made by the Secretary-General and his international staff, working together with representatives of Member nations, when the balance of power and policies among the great nations gave them the chance. Such circumstances applied in the Middle East, but not to the simultaneous Hungarian affair, to which we shall recur later.

II

At the beginning of 1956 the situation in the Middle East was evolving in ways that tended further to sharpen the tensions and complicate the problems by which the area was so heavily beset.

The painful retreat of Britain and France from domination of the Arab world had continued, despite efforts to stem or slow the process. Having experienced Western imperialism, but not the Soviet variety, the Arab nationalists directed their hostility against the remaining centers of Western power and influence. As Moslems most of them rejected Communist ideology but they saw the Soviet Union as a powerful counterweight to the Western Big Three. The Soviet government moved to take advantage of the opportunities thus offered in an area where the West had succeeded in blocking all earlier efforts at penetration by both Czarist and Communist Russia.

From 1950 until the latter part of 1955 Britain, France, and the United States had for the most part effectively controlled and rationed the flow of arms to the Arab states and to Israel. Then, after the United States and Britain had twice refused Egypt's requests in 1955 for more arms, Gamal Abdel Nasser turned to the Soviet Union. This resulted in the Czech-Egyptian arms agreement announced in the fall of 1955. The new weapons began arriving as the evacuation of the last British troops from the Suez Canal Zone entered its final stage, in accordance with the terms of the 1954 Anglo-Egyptian treaty.

Another blow to Britain—and to the United States—came at the end of 1955 when Jordan decided against joining the Baghdad Pact. This left Iraq, then ruled by King Faisal and Prime Minister Nuri es-Said, as the only Arab member of the Middle East alliance to defend against Soviet expansion. Nasser and the Arab nationalists generally were committed to a policy of nonalignment in the cold war, and a strong campaign against the Baghdad Pact led by Cairo finally prevailed everywhere in the Arab world outside Iraq. Furthermore, despite all Nuri es-Said's schemes to the contrary, the unstable Syrian régimes were turning more and more to Nasser's leadership and in October 1955 formation of a joint Egyptian-Syrian command of the armed forces of the two countries was announced.

These setbacks caused concern and frustration in the United States and British governments. Nevertheless they decided to confirm their offer to join with the International Bank in underwriting the costs of the first stages of the great Aswan Dam project, which was the most ambitious of Nasser's plans for transforming Egypt's economy. Both in Washington and London there continued to be doubts about the financial soundness of investing in so vast a venture. Nasser had also amply demonstrated a prickly independence and unwillingness to pay any political price for such assistance. But the United States and British governments, with the Czech arms agreement still fresh in their minds, thought it best at the time to maintain the prospect of Western financing as against the possibility of another Soviet investment in Egypt.

Unlike Britain and the United States, France did not like the Baghdad Pact, which it viewed as a scheme perpetuating the exclusion of French influence from parts of an area where France had been an important factor before World War II. But France had its own reasons for quarreling with Arab nationalism and with its leader, Nasser. France had lost Indo-China in 1954. Now, in North Africa, after many painful episodes, Morocco and Tunisia were in the process of gaining their independence, with French agreement. France, however, was determined to hold on in Algeria, an integral part of the French republic, and was locked in a bloody struggle with the nationalist rebellion led by the National Liberation Front. Cairo was a center of vocal Arab support for the rebel cause as well as of more concrete forms of assistance.

In the area of Arab-Israeli relations, where the United Nations carried a major responsibility, there had been during 1955 a further deterioration of the armistice régime and a sharpening of tensions. The tendency had grown to justify violation by one side of one provision of the armistice agreements by claiming that the other side was violating another provision, and the list of longstanding violations by both sides was lengthening. If this process were permitted to continue unchecked it could only lead to a complete breakdown of the armistice régime.

During 1955 Israel also executed with increased severity its policy of exacting retribution for Arab incursions. Especially heavy casualties were inflicted in two retaliatory raids on Egyptian posts in Gaza and a third on Syrian posts near Lake Tiberias. These raids were carried out by regular Israeli army units, while the Arab incursions were generally carried out by Palestinian Arabs, usually as individual marauders, but sometimes organized in the clandestine guerrilla bands of "fedayeen."

The Security Council, while recognizing the provocation, repeatedly and unanimously condemned the retaliatory raids as clear violations of its 1948 cease-fire order and the armistice agreements, but it did not act to compel compliance. Israel claimed that retaliation was a legitimate form of self-defense. The theory seemed to be that the Arab governments, knowing the superior fighting capacity of Israel's army, could be frightened by such punishing blows into acting to prevent the Palestinian Arab incursions from their territory. The effect, however, was

somewhat different, especially in Egypt. Instead of discouraging fedayeen activities, Israel's policy provoked increased support for them. A
guerrilla-type response to the humiliation of the Israeli raids was safer
than the use of regular forces and better in Arab eyes than no response
at all. Thus, as 1956 began, the Palestine cease-fire, which was the key-
stone of the armistice agreements, was increasingly threatened by the
interaction of Israel's policy of retaliation and Arab encouragement of
the fedayeen.

Meanwhile the fundamental conflict between Jewish and Arab claims
in Palestine had become more intractable with each passing year, as
Jewish immigration continued to fill up Israel while the Palestinian
Arabs who had lost their homes watched in bitterness from the other
side of the armistice demarcation lines. Israel's ardent desire for peace,
so frequently voiced, required Arab recognition of Israel as the Jewish
homeland. The Arab states refused to consider peace or recognition unless the right of the Palestinian Arabs to return to their homes—if they
chose—was accepted, and this was a demand Israel found quite impossible to meet. Continuing Arab resentment and hostility were expressed
in the economic boycott of Israel, the blockade against Israeli shipping
through both the Suez Canal and the Gulf of Aqaba, violent speeches,
press and radio propaganda threatening Israel's destruction, as well as
in the marauding and incursions by Palestinian Arabs across the armistice demarcation lines.

In sum, the Middle East provided more than enough reasons for the
gloom, alarm, and dire predictions that were being reported from national capitals both inside and outside the region. Hammarskjöld saw
these realities as clearly as anyone, but he also perceived other realities
that he thought might provide a precarious foothold for a limited but
confidence-building turn for the better.

III

During the Secretary-General's travels to Middle Eastern and Asian
Member states early in 1956, Anthony Eden had visited Washington
and had urged Eisenhower to take some action "to put teeth" into the
1950 Tripartite Agreement in order to counter further Soviet penetration of the Middle East and prevent an Arab-Israeli war. Among his
ideas was a buildup—in the Eastern Mediterranean area by the Western Big Three—of military reserves that would be ready for forceful intervention in case of an outbreak, but Eisenhower and Dulles drew back

from any such open-ended commitment to military involvement in the quicksands of the Middle East.[1]

Another suggestion was to reinforce the United Nations Truce Supervision Organization with a United States–United Kingdom–French contingent that would be big enough to guard the armistice lines and empowered to use force against violations from either direction. In the prevailing circumstances, this idea was unrealistic. It would have required the negotiated consent of Israel and the Arab states and a new decision by the Security Council or, perhaps, the General Assembly. Israel, with memory still fresh of the British military presence in the final years of the Mandate, adamantly opposed the presence on its territory of any outside force with such powers, whether under the UN flag or not. Arab nationalism, led by Nasser, was equally opposed to any move tending to restore the Western European military presence—and so, of course, was the Soviet Union.

Hammarskjöld considered projects for an outside military response to Middle Eastern problems to be wrong in principle and folly in practice. He did not believe the United Nations should attempt to impose solutions and he deplored talk of great-power intervention from either side in the cold war. The proper role of the United Nations was to be quietly helpful to both sides as a friendly third party in an effort to keep the tensions of a presently intractable conflict within bounds, and to seek at every turn to find the greatest common denominator in the positions of the two sides. Reconciliation between the aspirations of Zionism and the Arab awakening was not now within reach. Meaningful progress toward solutions required the freely given acceptance of both sides. Much more time, perhaps a generation or more, would have to be allowed for the slow and necessary processes of adjustment and accommodation.

During his trip the Secretary-General had been impressed by the intellectual capacity, maturity, and strong character of men like Ben-Gurion and Nasser and some others of the leadership in that part of the world. After his return he insisted to skeptical correspondents (and skeptical delegates also) on the "will to peace" and "sense of responsibility" he said he had found. What he meant, and could not spell out in public, was this.

On the one hand Israel's leaders knew that the ultimate goal of peace

---

[1] For Eden's account see *Full Circle: The Memoirs of Anthony Eden,* Houghton Mifflin Company, 1960, p. 372.

with its Arab neighbors was not yet within reach. In the meantime Israel needed surcease from Palestinian harassments on its borders and release from the blockades against Israeli shipping which Egypt had imposed on the excuse of belligerent rights. Despite Israel's growing strength and high morale, continuing use of force over these issues would block progress toward that reconciliation that would in the end be essential to Israel's future.

On the other side Arab leaders such as Nasser, despite their violent rhetoric and sense of injustice at Israel's hands, drew back from the risks of a military confrontation which their comparative weakness would entail. They would not now accept peace with Israel, but the restoration of a fully effective armistice régime, provided the violations on each side were corrected in an equitable manner, was something else again.

Finally, Israel and the Arabs agreed in one respect at least. Both were strongly opposed to attempts from outside to impose solutions to their conflicts. These were factors that led Hammarskjöld to believe the leadership of both sides might recognize that a restoration of the armistice régime, which would end the present state of partial belligerency, was a better and safer course than the continuing drift toward war. At the end of Volume II of the *Public Papers of the Secretaries-General* and at the beginning of this volume (see pages 37–58) the Secretary-General explained his attitude, and the basis for it, as fully as he felt he could in public.

After consultations with the great powers and other Members, during March, the Secretary-General's view prevailed, with powerful assistance from the United States. On March 21 the latter proposed that the Security Council adopt a resolution requesting him urgently to survey the state of compliance with the armistice agreements and to "arrange" with Israel and the Arab states for measures to reduce tensions along the armistice lines. The resolution was adopted unanimously on April 4 after a debate during which Israel and the Arab states all found the resolution acceptable and agreed in principle to cooperate, although with various reservations.

The Council's action provided Hammarskjöld with valuable diplomatic support for his mission, but he also used the opportunity to place on record with the Council his views that the assignment was one that he could, under the Charter, have assumed on his own responsibility. He then took off for a month of intensive discussions during which he shuttled back and forth among Jerusalem, Cairo, Amman, Damascus, and Beirut. He aimed first for new commitments—made this time directly to the United Nations—to observe the basic cease-fire clauses in the various armistice agreements. He secured these new commitments, subject only to reserves for self-defense. In the correspondence that formed part of his reports to the Security Council he put on record, from the United Nations side, that the reserve for self-defense could not, under the terms of the armistice agreements and the Charter, permit retaliation, either of the Israeli kind or by the fedayeen, and none of the governments formally challenged that interpretation in their replies (pages 76–83).

As to violations of various other clauses of the armistice agreements, Hammarskjöld reported that all the governments wished for a return to a state of full compliance. The difficulty was to maintain a balance between the remedial action required of one side and that required of the other. Since the negotiation of explicit two-sided agreements was not feasible, the way forward lay in related unilateral moves "inspired by greater confidence in the possibility of a peaceful development." For this the new cease-fire commitments were the essential first step. The initiative for the next steps now lay with the governments party to the armistice agreements.

In his May 9 report the Secretary-General did not spell out the related unilateral moves he had in mind, though the Israel and Arab governments well knew what they were. Months later, however, in his September 27 report to the Council, he wrote that he had had in mind "such steps" as restoration of the demilitarized character of the El Auja zone and freedom of navigation for Israeli ships in the Suez Canal (page 250). The Secretary-General concluded his cease-fire report by expressing his firm belief that reestablishment of full compliance with the armistice agreements represented "a stage which has to be passed in order to make progress possible on the main issues. . . ." And he put the essence of what he hoped his mission had accomplished in the following words: "If we have previously experienced chain reactions leading to a continuous deterioration of the situation, we may now have the possibility of starting a chain of reactions in the opposite direction" (pages 84–111).

The Council was pleased with the Secretary-General's work, unanimously endorsed his report, and called upon Israel and the Arab states to cooperate with him and with Major General E. L. M. Burns, Chief of Staff of the UN Truce Supervision Organization (UNTSO), in the steps necessary to "establish full compliance with the Armistice Agreements" (pages 125–26).

IV

For about three months, from the middle of April until the latter part of July, the cease-fire held up quite well and there were no serious incidents. However, neither Israel nor the Arab governments undertook any of the confidence-building unilateral moves for which Hammarskjöld laid the groundwork. Nor did General Burns receive in practice the cooperation that had been promised in various measures to reduce the danger of incidents along the armistice lines. A combination of developments outside the region was generating pressures for belligerency and a hardening of positions that soon proved far stronger than the influences toward moderation and conciliation that Hammarskjöld had sought to nurture.

In France the government of Premier Guy Mollet, unable to pacify Algeria, turned more and more strongly against Nasser, who gave aid and encouragement to the Algerian rebellion. At the same time Israel found in France a ready source of arms to offset the weapons being sent by the Soviet to Egypt. During the winter of 1956 Washington and London had maintained strict limits on additional arms for Israel, considering that the new Soviet weapons in poorly trained Egyptian hands could not for some time pose any military threat to Israel. By June France had become Israel's principal arms supplier, but only a small part of the flow of sophisticated weaponry—including many *Mystères*—was reported to France's allies in accordance with the provisions of the Tripartite Pact. The extent of this largely clandestine traffic, which increased throughout the summer, remained a well-kept secret from the rest of the world until the October 29 invasion of Egypt.

The British attitude toward Nasser also hardened during the spring of 1956. King Hussein's sudden dismissal of General Sir John Glubb, commander since 1939 of the British-trained Arab Legion in Jordan, and the withdrawal from the Suez Canal Zone of the last of the British occupation forces, which had been in Egypt since 1882, were strong psychological factors in the growing conviction of the Eden cabinet that conciliation would not work with Nasser and he must be taught a lesson.

It was true that Nasser was not directly responsible for General Glubb's dismissal, which came about because the young King Hussein had finally had enough of being told what to do and what not to do by this successor of Lawrence of Arabia. It was also true that the final withdrawal from Suez was by previous agreement with Egypt, to which Winston Churchill had reluctantly consented in his final months as Prime Minister. But Eden had memories. He was Churchill's personally chosen successor and Churchill had once said that he had not become the King's first minister to preside over the liquidation of the British Empire. And there was Eden's own reputation as the opponent of appeasement late in the 1930s. Increasingly Eden perceived Nasser as an Arab "Hitler," as members of the Mollet government in France were also already doing—or at least pretending to.

Meanwhile negotiations on the terms for the loans and credits for the Aswan Dam project had dragged on month after month. Nasser feared that the financial guarantees that London, Washington, and the International Bank thought necessary would give the West a controlling voice in Egypt's economy. He was stubborn and believed that the prospect of turning to the Soviet Union instead would in the end win him better terms. This proved to be a mistake. Earlier Western doubts over the financial soundness of so vast a project in a poor country had increased as a substantial share of Egypt's limited resources was mortgaged to paying for Soviet arms and would thus not be available for Egypt's share of the Aswan Dam costs. Both the British and United States governments became thoroughly irked by Nasser's attitude and came to the conclusion about the middle of July that they would gain little or nothing politically by going through with the project. In the United States Egypt's recognition of the People's Republic of China a month before had caused an additional problem. The combined opposition of the "China Lobby" and the "Israel Lobby" did not make a request for an appropriation for Aswan an attractive political prospect in an election year.

On July 19, with an Egyptian delegation in Washington hoping to complete negotiations with the International Bank and the United States government, Secretary of State Dulles rather abruptly decided to end the matter there and then. He told the Egyptian ambassador that the United States' offer was withdrawn. This made impossible the projected loan from the International Bank as well, and the British offer was formally withdrawn two days later. Nasser was meeting in Brioni with Tito and Nehru when the news came. On July 26, soon after his return to

Egypt, he announced without warning the immediate nationalization of the Universal Suez Canal Company and his intention (soon abandoned) of using Canal tolls to help replace the credits for the Aswan Dam that had been denied him.

The British and French governments reacted by openly threatening to use force unless negotiations led promptly to the return of the Canal to international management, and early in August they began the joint planning and the buildup of their forces in the Eastern Mediterranean that would be required for an attack on Egypt if talks failed.

Hammarskjöld was in the Middle East for talks with the Israeli, Egyptian, and Jordanian government leaders as a follow-up to his cease-fire mission when Dulles announced the decision to withdraw the Aswan Dam offer. The Secretary-General had been concerned that not one of the unilateral moves toward restoring full compliance with the armistice agreements for which he had hoped had been undertaken, but he was still hopeful that the new cease-fire commitments might be maintained and he planned another follow-up visit in October (page 180). Indeed, just after his departure from the area Ben-Gurion had responded to his appeal and withheld retaliation against Jordan after two incidents in the sensitive Jerusalem–Mount Scopus area. Then came nationalization of the Suez Canal and the militant hostility toward Nasser with which the British and French governments reacted.

Israel already had in France a resolute ally and a clandestine source of arms. Great Britain, though anxious to maintain its Arab friendships, also joined in enmity to Nasser and now spoke openly of using force against him. Of the Tripartite Powers only the United States remained committed against any resort to force in the Middle East. Hammarskjöld's advocacy of restraint and strengthening of the armistice régime as a wiser and safer road to peace for Israel was undermined. If the opportunity came to join France and Britain in an operation likely to secure, without undue risk, the destruction of Israel's most powerful and militant enemy in the Arab world, the temptation would be very strong indeed.

We now know that during August and September, while efforts for a negotiated settlement of the Suez Canal dispute were being pursued without result, French and Israeli military planners were meeting secretly. The French did not even tell the British—with whom they were engaged in parallel joint planning for a possible attack on Egypt—until later.

Though Hammarskjöld was unaware of these clandestine preparations, the effect of the Franco-British attitude in the Suez Canal dispute upon Israeli policy toward its Arab neighbors and the armistice régime became quickly apparent. In the middle of August, Israel resumed its policy of organized military reprisals for Arab incursions, acts of sabotage, or shooting across the line. Reprisals were first visited against Egyptian forces in Gaza and then against Jordan. Three raids against Jordan in September and early October were particularly severe and caused heavy casualties. Cooperation with General Burns in efforts to carry out various measures to strengthen the UN deterrent capacity along the armistice lines was evaded or refused. Instead further restrictions on the freedom of movement of the UN observers were progressively imposed.

Hammarskjöld issued a series of notes and statements reaffirming the obligations of the cease-fire and armistice agreements and warning both sides of the consequences of further deterioration. He also sent a report to the Security Council recounting developments since July (pages 246–63). On September 26, in a letter addressed to the Council's president, he contemplated the possibility of action under Chapter VII when he wrote that "if the Governments concerned, in cooperation with the Truce Supervision Organization, do not bring the situation rapidly under control, I submit that the Security Council should take the matter up in order to reaffirm its policy, as established in previous resolutions, and, were the Council to find the continued deterioration to constitute a threat to peace, to decide what further measures may be indicated" (pages 243–44).

The Secretary-General was well aware, however, that hope for reversing the downward trend in Palestine depended first of all on the success of efforts to bring the Suez Canal dispute under control.

V

In Hammarskjöld's Introduction to the Eleventh Annual Report of the Secretary-General, completed just before the Security Council began consideration of the Suez Canal dispute, he reiterated his belief that Member governments had tended to emphasize the role of public debate of issues at the expense of the "resources for reconciliation" that the United Nations could also provide. "The tensions of our time are too severe," he wrote, "to permit us to neglect these resources and should impel us to use the United Nations in such a manner as to widen the possibilities for constructive negotiation" (page 270). He now devoted all his powers of persuasion and private diplomatic skills toward turning the Council's consideration of the Canal dispute from confrontation to "constructive negotiation." The obstacles were formidable. The British and French governments continued to insist that Egypt must accept as the basis for a negotiated settlement the return of the Suez Canal to international operation in accordance with the 18-Power proposals drawn up in London in August. The Egyptian government had already flatly rejected this demand; nationalization was Egypt's sovereign right and was not negotiable, even though other questions were.

The British and French brought to the Security Council a resolution reaffirming the 18-Power call for international management and sharply condemning Egypt for the act of nationalization, although the resolution was certain to be rejected by Egypt and vetoed by the Soviet Union. Egypt meanwhile brought to the Council a countercomplaint charging Britain and France with endangering peace by their military preparations and threats against Egypt. The Council inscribed both complaints on its agenda for September 26 but postponed debate until October 5, when the foreign ministers could be present.

Against these prospects for confrontation there were some positive factors with which the Secretary-General could work. The United States government preferred the 18-Power proposals, which Dulles had helped to draw up, but it was willing to settle for something less than international management of the Canal, provided the international interest could be protected in other ways. The United States was, furthermore, firmly opposed to any resort to force against Egypt under the present circumstances. Its influence, therefore, was strongly on the side of further negotiation. Simultaneously, India was urging the Egyptian government toward a more moderate posture.

The Egyptian government itself had already declared its willingness to negotiate with the user nations on matters other than national operation of the Canal and continued to reaffirm its intention to compensate the shareholders of the Suez Canal Company and to uphold the international guarantees of the Constantinople Convention of 1888. In the meantime the Egyptians were proving quite competent to operate the Canal despite dire predictions to the contrary following the withdrawal of the British and French pilots. Ships passed through the Canal at least as rapidly and safely as before. There were no incidents, no breakdowns, and the users, except for Israel, had no cause to complain of Egypt's performance. This record tended to cool the highly charged emotions that Nasser's abrupt action had evoked.

Hammarskjöld's aim was to persuade the parties to try private negotiations within the Security Council framework. In this he succeeded. When the Council met on October 5 none other than Selwyn Lloyd, who opened the debate, suggested that the Council meet in private after the opening round of statements. Mahmoud Fawzi was quite willing for Egypt, and Christian Pineau, somewhat grudgingly, concurred for France. At the first private Council session it was agreed that Lloyd, Pineau, and Fawzi would go one step further and engage in private talks with Hammarskjöld in the latter's office. These talks produced agreement on six "principles," or "requirements," as the basis for a peaceful settlement. These principles were then approved unanimously by the Council on October 13. There also was progress in preliminary discussion of the concrete arrangements that might be negotiated to meet the requirements.

Despite this progress the British and French governments insisted on pressing to a vote a modified version of the part of their original resolution that endorsed the 18-Power proposals for return of the Canal to international management, although this time the way was opened to consider counterproposals by Egypt providing equivalent "guarantees" to the users. These paragraphs were vetoed by the Soviet Union. However, the Council adjourned with the understanding that the foreign ministers, with the Secretary-General's continued assistance, would pursue the private talks that had produced so promising a start.

Lloyd had originally intended to explore further the possibilities for progress before leaving New York, but he was suddenly recalled to London by Eden. Fawzi did stay on for several days of further talks. Afterward, Hammarskjöld put down on paper in outline form his own impressions and conclusions about a way forward that could be acceptable to both sides. On October 24 he sent this outline privately to Fawzi in Cairo for his reactions, informing Lloyd and Pineau at the same time. Fawzi replied on November 2—fairly promptly but too late—that Hammarskjöld's letter provided an acceptable framework for a negotiated settlement (for commentary and texts on the Suez Canal negotiations, see pages 292–303).

In the light of subsequent revelations it is clear that the dispute over operation of the Suez Canal could have been resolved fairly, and without bloodshed, if the Eden and Mollet governments had not already de-cided to use force. Only a pretext for attack was needed and it was se-cretly arranged that Israel should provide this pretext at the very time Hammarskjöld was registering progress toward a peaceful settlement.

Between October 13 and October 29 enough adverse developments were visible at the United Nations, in Washington, and in other capitals hoping for a peaceful way forward to cause continued worry. But the truly decisive developments were veiled from view and the combined at-tack on Egypt thus came as a stunning shock.

Quite visible were the Anglo-French military and naval buildups at Cyprus and Malta, the increasingly belligerent words and reprisal raids from Israel, and the complete absence of any sign of interest in London or Paris in pursuing the Suez talks with Hammarskjöld and Fawzi. In Washington, after October 16 the Eisenhower administration noted a drying up of diplomatic and intelligence information from Britain and France and discovered at the same time that the French had secretly sent to Israel many times the admitted number of *Mystère* fighters and other equipment.

Unknown to all except the few participants in the scheme was the fact that on the day after the Security Council adopted the Six Princi-ples, the French had approached Eden with a plan for an Israeli attack on Egypt across the Sinai, to which the British and French would re-spond by seizing the Suez Canal Zone, thus "protecting" the waterway and "separating" the combatants. Here was the long-sought pretext, and it seemed to Eden an ideal one, for Britain and France could present themselves as both saviors of the Canal and preservers of the peace. This was why Eden had so suddenly recalled Lloyd from New York. By October 25, the day after Hammarskjöld sent his letter to Fawzi, all had been arranged in a series of clandestine meetings in Paris that included at the last the presence of Ben-Gurion himself to seal the bargain (see commentary pages 304–305). Among those kept in the dark, besides the Secretary-General, were the governments of the United States, the Com-monwealth countries, most of Western Europe, the British Labor party leadership, and Britain's own ambassadors.

VI

Israel's invasion of Egypt on October 29 was the first in a series of un-expected developments that evoked consternation at the United Nations, in Washington, and in many other capitals. In New York on October 30

Britain and France resorted to the veto to defeat a United States resolution calling upon Israel to withdraw forthwith behind the armistice lines. On the same day the British-French twelve-hour ultimatum was delivered to Egypt and Israel, demanding evacuation of the Suez Canal Zone in favor of a Franco-British force with the supposed mission of "protecting" the Canal and "separating" the combatants.

The next day, after Egypt's rejection of the ultimatum, British and French planes began dropping bombs on Egyptian airfields and other military targets, and thousands of leaflets calling for Nasser's overthrow upon the civil populace. The Egyptians responded by sinking dozens of small vessels to block the Suez Canal and sought to regroup their defenses in the face of the second invasion that now impended, by sea from Malta and by air from Cyprus. At this time most of the Israeli army was still well back in the Sinai, a long way from the Canal from which the ultimatum had called upon them to "withdraw."

When the Security Council met again on October 31 to consider and then approve a Yugoslav proposal to convoke an emergency special session of the General Assembly, Hammarskjöld presented the members with a declaration of conscience that also posed a question of confidence.

Like the great majority of the Member governments, he had been deeply shocked by acts of force that were clearly in violation of Charter obligations and treaty commitments. When Israel invaded Egypt, he told the Council, he would have acted under Article 99 had not the United States moved first. He would have done so again when news came of the Anglo-French ultimatum if the matter had not already been under consideration in the Council. "The discretion and impartiality" required of the Secretary-General, he said, "may not degenerate into a policy of expediency," and he continued: "He [the Secretary-General] must also be a servant of the principles of the Charter, and its aims must ultimately determine what for him is right and wrong. For that he must stand. A Secretary-General cannot serve on any other assumption than that—within the necessary limits of human frailty and honest differences of opinion—all Member nations honour their pledge to observe all Articles of the Charter. . . ."

He concluded with the following sentence: "Were the Members to consider that another view of the duties of the Secretary-General than the one here stated would better serve the interests of the Organization, it is their obvious right to act accordingly" (pages 304–13).

Despite the clear evidence in this declaration of where Hammarskjöld stood on the actions of their governments, the British and French delegates joined the representatives of the United States, the Soviet Union, and other members in expressions of confidence and personal regard that strengthened his position to meet the tests that were to follow. Four days later, after the Soviet Union vetoed a resolution calling for withdrawal of its forces from Hungary, Hammarskjöld placed on record in the Council that what he had said on October 31 about the duties of the Secretary-General and his understanding of the stands he must take applied also in that situation.

The sixty days from November 2 to December 31, 1956, were the most innovative and fruitful two months in the first twenty-five years of the history of the United Nations. This was the time when the attack on Egypt was halted, the United Nations Emergency Force (UNEF) was created and began its deployment, the British and French withdrew their troops, and the Suez Canal clearance operation was organized and launched. The constitutional, political, and administrative achievements crowded into this very short time were all the more remarkable because they were brought about when the simultaneous Hungarian crisis was demanding much time and attention from delegates and Secretariat alike.

With the New Year, 1957, there followed another three months offering severe diplomatic challenges and political trials before Israel finally, and much against its will, withdrew the last of its troops and UNEF was established on the Egyptian side of the armistice line and at Sharm el-Sheikh. Early in April the UN Suez clearance operation was completed and the Canal was restored to full traffic.

The texts and commentary in the main part of this book provide, if read together, a fairly full chronological account of these many developments: for the first Middle East period, pages 304–411; for Hungary, pages 412–52; for the spring of 1957, pages 453–601. Here the editors will touch briefly on some of the more significant aspects and decisions in each of these three groups.

VII

When the emergency special session of the General Assembly began its meetings on November 1, Britain, France, and Israel found that an overwhelming majority of the membership opposed the course of action they had taken. The United States was the leader of a coalition including the Soviet bloc, the Afro-Asian and Latin American states, most of the Commonwealth, and a majority of the smaller Western European Members. Within a few hours a United States resolution calling for an immediate cease-fire, a halt to the impending Franco-British invasion, and Israeli withdrawal behind the armistice line was adopted 64 to 5 with 6 abstentions.

This was a stunning rebuke. More significant even than the size of the vote was the unequivocal position of the United States as the leader of the majority. The Eden, Mollet, and Ben-Gurion governments had expected from the Eisenhower administration disapproval and even some anger over being deceived by two close allies and a friend, but the speed and strength of the reaction at a time when the presidential election was supposed to monopolize the national attention came as a blow and foreboded further difficulties for their enterprise. In London the impact was made more severe by the furious opposition of the Labour party, whose leaders were already convinced that the pretext of separating the combatants was a sham but did not yet have the evidence to prove it.

The Canadian government had disapproved of Britain's action but was anxious to help Eden find a way to draw back and to heal the breach between Britain and the United States. In Parliament Eden had claimed that "police action" by Britain and France was necessary because their forces were immediately available and the United Nations had no force of its own. Lester B. Pearson, then Canada's Foreign Minister, had long advocated some means of providing the United Nations with military capacity for peace-keeping. He now proposed that the General Assembly establish such a force and send it to the Middle East "to keep these borders at peace while a political settlement is being worked out" for Suez and Palestine.

This was the origin of the United Nations Emergency Force, but there were basic questions of principle, of constitutionality, and of political viability to be settled before the Force could become a reality. The Assembly handed to the Secretary-General the main responsibility for producing acceptable answers to these questions. That he was able to do so within the forty-eight–hour time limit set for him—and with no applicable precedents to work from—still seems, many years later, as it did at the time, an almost miraculous achievement. He had indispensable support from Ambassador Lodge for the United States and the cooperation and advice of a nuclear group of able and widely representative delegates, especially Pearson himself, Arthur Lall of India, Hans Engen of Norway, and Francisco Urrutia of Colombia. However, Hammarskjöld was the helmsman who steered the enterprise safely and rapidly among the many dangerous reefs upon which it could so easily have been wrecked.

The special session of the Assembly was the first to be convened under the Uniting-for-Peace resolution adopted in the fall of 1950. The United Nations action in Korea had been undertaken by the United States, assisted by fifteen other Members, in response to a recommendation of the Security Council that they aid South Korea to repel the attack launched by North Korea. The Council had acted in the temporary absence of the Soviet delegate and the principal purpose of the Uniting for Peace resolution had been to establish a procedure by which the Assembly could act in future cases of armed aggression should the Council be paralyzed by use of the veto.

The situation in November 1956 was not what the authors of the Uniting-for-Peace resolution had had in mind six years before. Indeed it was one of those ironies of history that John Foster Dulles, the principal author of 1950, now found himself applying the resolution against Britain and France, America's principal NATO allies, instead of against a Communist power; and that Arkady Sobolev, the Soviet delegate, provided the necessary seventh affirmative vote in the Council to invoke a resolution that the Soviet Union had always denounced as unconstitutional under the Charter.

There was a variety of views about what should be done. At one extreme the Eden and Mollet governments had welcomed Pearson's suggestion but their idea was a UN force with a mandate to carry on what they had begun—occupation of the Canal Zone until the Arab-Israeli and Suez Canal questions were settled to their satisfaction. At the other extreme were calls for forceful sanctions if Britain, France, and Israel did not immediately agree to a cease-fire and a withdrawal. Nehru suggested that the U.S. Sixth Fleet be deployed to halt the Anglo-French armada approaching Port Said. When the British and French persisted, the Soviet government even proposed to the Security Council joint United States–Soviet intervention, under Chapter VII of the Charter, to enforce compliance.

The Eisenhower administration flatly rejected such proposals as unthinkable. Its goal was to secure a cease-fire and a withdrawal as quickly as possible by a combination of peaceful pressures and persuasions, thus averting demands for military sanctions and the danger of Soviet intervention, or of some other move that might cause the conflict to spread beyond control. It was prepared to—and did—apply economic and financial pressures in support of a cease-fire and withdrawal and was firm in the stand that these must be unconditional and that Britain, France, and Israel should not gain any political advantage from their illegal use of force.

This stand was wholly in accord with the Secretary-General's own approach and was a decisive factor in forging and holding together the majority that made possible the creation and deployment of the United Nations Emergency Force. Arab-Asian suspicions that the Force might be turned into an instrument of pressure against them had some basis. In addition to the views expressed by the British and French on Pearson's suggestion, there were some others in the Western camp whose sympathies leaned in a similar direction or who tended to wobble on the issue of principle. The clear-cut position of the United States as the Western leader helped both to allay Arab-Asian suspicions and to stiffen some backbones on the Western side.

The decision to limit the mandate of UNEF to securing and supervising the cease-fire and withdrawal of the invaders and to divorce it from political objectives was the first to be made. This decision was reflected in the wording of Pearson's first resolution of November 3 requesting the Secretary-General to produce a plan for the Force within forty-eight hours. Answers to other questions followed in rapid succession as the Secretary-General developed his plan, consulting for political viability at each step along the way.

Because of the limitations imposed by the Charter on the powers of the Assembly, UNEF would require the consent of the nations participating in it and the consent of Egypt to operate on Egyptian territory. Though composed of soldiers it would be a nonfighting force, yet more than an observer corps. Its function would not be to impose a cessation of hostilities and withdrawal of forces but to supervise and to help secure by its presence the fulfillment of negotiated agreements to these ends.

It was decided very early not to include the big powers in UNEF. This shut the door to British and French hopes for inclusion and also avoided complications involving the United States and the Soviet Union. The nonfighting nature of UNEF made it politically possible for governments of smaller countries to come forward right away with offers of contingents and made it practicable to put together quickly from such sources a Force that would be competent to fulfill its limited mandate.

Perhaps the most interesting of many innovations was the command structure of UNEF. In Korea the Security Council delegated (or confirmed) to the United States the command of the United Nations forces. The Chapter VII forces intended by the Charter would have been directed by the chiefs of staff of the Big Five. Hammarskjöld proposed that the Assembly itself appoint the commander—General Burns, then the UNTSO chief of staff. The chain of command would thus extend from the General Assembly to the Secretary-General to UNEF's commander instead of being delegated to one or more national governments. It would make UNEF the first force in history under a command with purely international responsibilities.

This proposal was approved by the Assembly on November 5 as a preliminary step in the creation of UNEF. Its genuinely international character undoubtedly helped to win the prompt agreement to UNEF of the suspicious and beleaguered Egyptian government and this, in turn, was a decisive factor in achieving a cease-fire before it was too late (pages 329–35).

There was no precedent for such a setup but it is interesting—and also just—to recall the words of Trygve Lie at Harvard in 1948, after regretting the failure of the permanent members of the Security Council to agree on the UN forces that had been intended by the Charter:

It is possible that a beginning could be made now through the establishment of a comparatively small guard force, as distinct from a striking force. Such a force could be recruited by the Secretary-General and placed at the disposal of the Security Council. Such a force would have been extremely valuable to us in the past and it would undoubtedly be very valuable in the future. Even a small United Nations force would command respect, for it would have all the authority of the United Nations behind it. I do not think of a single case that has been dealt with by the Security Council so far in which a large force would have been needed to act for the United Nations, provided that a small United Nations guard force of some kind had been available for immediate duty at the proper time. I include Palestine.[2]

Lie's trial balloon had failed to produce the response he had hoped for and differed in several respects from the plan adopted for UNEF but there were also similarities in concept and purpose.

---

[2] Trygve Lie, *Public Papers of the Secretaries-General of the United Nations,* Volume I, Columbia University Press, 1969, pp. 134–135.

In his second and final UNEF report on November 6 Hammarskjöld proposed, and the Assembly accepted, a small Advisory Committee of representatives of Members which would be chaired by the Secretary-General and would serve a continuing consultative function between the executive and legislative organs as questions of policy and political tactics arose in connection with the deployment and operations of the Force. Hammarskjöld's experience with the Atomic Advisory Committee had been a happy one and the UNEF Advisory Committee proved to be especially useful in the many politically sensitive and difficult moments encountered in the first six months of UNEF's existence. It was composed of representatives of Brazil, Canada, Ceylon, Colombia, India, Norway, and Pakistan and thus included delegates who had the most to do with planning the Force—Pearson, Urrutia, Lall, and Engen—as well as members of every major voting bloc in the Assembly except the Soviet bloc.

Despite Hammarskjöld's extremely rapid pace, at dawn on November 6 it still remained doubtful whether UNEF could be established in time. The British and French proceeded at that hour with their invasion at Port Said, still holding to their resolve to try to complete seizure of the Suez Canal Zone before agreeing to a cease-fire. There was grave danger that this defiance would provoke reactions inflaming and spreading the conflict out of control.

The Egyptian government had cabled its acceptance of the UN Command resolution on November 5, after the first British-French paratroop landings that morning. However, when the invasion fleet arrived and the attack on Port Said was pursued in full force the next day, the Egyptian response was to broadcast an emotional worldwide appeal for volunteers and arms to help fight the invaders.

Later in the morning, fortunately, the Eden government finally gave way to the combination of pressures upon it. The text of Hammarskjöld's second and final UNEF report had just arrived and could be used as a reason for calling a halt to the invasion. The severity of the economic and financial consequences of continued defiance was now all too apparent, with Middle East oil supplies cut off, a run on the pound, and the United States prepared to block all needed credits until there was compliance with United Nations resolutions. Finally the tide of opposition in the United Nations, the Commonwealth, and the House of Commons was stronger than ever. All this had a heavy cumulative effect.

Eden decided to order a cease-fire effective at midnight November 6, and the French, confronted with a *fait accompli,* perforce concurred. Before the cease-fire went into effect Port Said and Port Fuad were occupied and an armored column proceeded a few miles down the Canal but that was all. Hostilities between Israeli and Egyptian forces had ceased the day before. On November 7 the Assembly adopted a resolution endorsing Hammarskjöld's second report in all respects. The UN Command resolution of November 5 had been approved 57 to 0 with 19 abstentions. This time the vote was 64 to 0 with 12 abstentions. Britain and France now voted in the affirmative, ignoring the fact that UNEF's mandate and composition did not at all correspond to their wishes (pages 340–56).

By another overwhelming vote, 65 to 1 with 10 abstentions, the Assembly also approved a resolution calling for "immediate" withdrawal by British, French, and Israeli forces. Israel's was the only negative vote while Britain and France abstained. The resolution was so worded that the demand for Israel's withdrawal to behind the armistice lines was clearly unconditional while the "immediate" withdrawal of the British and French could be interpreted as being related in some way to UNEF's deployment.

Israel's initial reaction had been that it would have nothing to do with UNEF. In response to strong pressures from all sides, however, it agreed on November 8 to "withdraw its forces from Egypt immediately upon the conclusion of satisfactory arrangements with the United Nations in connection with the emergency international force." All three invaders had now committed themselves to withdraw from Egypt but the timing of the British and French withdrawals was made to depend in their replies on the arrival and deployment of UNEF, and Israel's withdrawal was made to depend in its reply also on "satisfactory arrangements" that were later defined to be such as to ensure Israel's security against the threat of attack or "acts of belligerency by land or sea." All three sought to use delays for further attempts to salvage some political gain from their illegal use of force.

On November 7 UNEF did not exist as a force in being. There were only the Assembly's favorable votes on Hammarskjöld's plan, the offers of various contingents and other assistance, and the appointment of General Burns as the commander. Eight days later the first advance units flew into Egypt. To accomplish so much so quickly required not only a dazzling succession of improvised arrangements for UNEF's recruitment, assembly, transport, and supply, but difficult and delicate negotiations with the Egyptian government, whose consent was required for the entry and deployment of UNEF on its soil. A full account of day-by-day developments on both counts will be found on pages 360–76. Here a few words should be said about the basic understandings Hammarskjöld reached with Nasser and Fawzi after he flew in with the second group of UN soldiers on November 16.

Egypt had accepted the UN Command resolution of November 5 but UNEF was a brand new international instrument whose like had never before been seen. Nasser's government was concerned, with good reason, about present or prospective British, French, and Israeli maneuvers for advantage and was highly sensitive, as always, about Egypt's sovereign rights. It sought assurances and clarifications about the extent of the commitments being asked of it.

The choice of the national contingents composing UNEF was the occasion for quite a brouhaha at first, but was quickly resolved. Hammarskjöld considered that international law and the Charter required Egypt's consent to the admission of each national contingent on its territory but, at the same time, firmly upheld his own responsibility for determining the composition of the Force. This stand amounted to negotiating the agreement of Egypt to the nationalities the Secretary-General planned to include in the Force. When Egypt raised preliminary objections to the participation of Canada, Norway, and Denmark because they belonged to NATO, Hammarskjöld flatly rejected the argument and Egypt—after some delay in Canada's case—yielded. Canada was briefly embarrassed because its politically unwise first choice of "The Queen's Own Rifles" had to be withdrawn in favor of various transport, signal, ordnance, and other specialist units needed by General Burns, but the Canadian contingent soon became the largest in UNEF. At its full strength of 6,000 men, UNEF included contingents from Brazil, Canada, Colombia, Denmark, Finland, India, Indonesia, Norway, Sweden, and Yugoslavia.

On the question of UNEF's deployment inside Egypt the Secretary-General reassured Nasser that the legislative record made clear the Assembly's intention that after the British and French withdrew UNEF would have no further function in the Suez Canal Zone, except possibly for a staging area. Its mandate then would be to follow the Israeli withdrawal and end up at the armistice demarcation line, where the positions it occupied would, as elsewhere in Egypt, be subject to Egyptian consent.

The Egyptian government asked for an unconditional United Nations commitment that UNEF would leave whenever Egypt might decide to withdraw consent to its continued presence. In terms of the law of the Charter the Egyptian position was correct. However, Hammarskjöld was able to negotiate what amounted to a political limitation on Egypt's future freedom of action in this respect. He managed this by the terms of the "good faith" agreement of November 20 between the United Nations and Egypt on the presence and functioning of UNEF in Egypt. When exercising "its sovereign rights" (which included the right to withdraw consent) Egypt would "be guided, in good faith, by its acceptance" of the General Assembly's UN Command resolution of November 5. On its side the United Nations would "be guided, in good faith, by the task established for the Force" in its November 5 and 7 UNEF resolutions; "in particular, the United Nations, understanding this to correspond to the wishes of the Government of Egypt, reaffirms its willingness to maintain UNEF until its task is completed." Thus if Egypt were to withdraw consent before the United Nations considered that UNEF's task was completed, Egypt would place itself in conflict with the General Assembly.

When the British and French governments agreed to stop military operations on November 6 they proposed that they should nevertheless be given the job of clearing the Suez Canal. Hammarskjöld had coolly replied that he was exploring possibilities for undertaking the task "through agents from nations not engaged in the present conflict." While in Cairo he was assured of Egyptian cooperation with such a United Nations enterprise as soon as the British-French evacuation was complete and Israeli forces had withdrawn from the vicinity of the Canal.

Meanwhile the British and French governments had met à series of rebuffs in their efforts to delay withdrawal. Right after the cease-fire Eden and Mollet had proposed coming to Washington for talks with Eisenhower from which they hoped to gain some salvage at least, but they were politely informed the visit was not timely. The United States government thought withdrawal should be completed before any such meeting. Later in the month Selwyn Lloyd came over. He lobbied vigorously in New York and Washington for using the Anglo-French salvage fleet to clear the Canal, asserting that the United Nations could not possibly find the skills and resources anywhere else to do the job. But Hammarskjöld had already succeeded in that task and the Egyptian reaction to any prospect of the invaders working down the Canal was obvious. In Washington it was made plain that complete withdrawal was a necessary condition for American help with Britain's balance-of-payments crisis and for the provision of oil to Europe from the Western Hemisphere. In New York the General Assembly approved by overwhelming votes Hammarskjöld's proposals for organizing the Canal clearance operation and the "good faith" agreement with Egypt. Another resolution, calling for withdrawal "forthwith," was also adopted by 63 to 5 with 10 abstentions after an attempt by Paul-Henri Spaak and Pearson to ease the pressure on Britain, France, and Israel had failed because the United States withheld its support.

The game of delay was now ended for London and Paris. On December 3 they informed the Secretary-General of their decision to complete their withdrawal promptly. Hammarskjöld had just given them face-saving assistance by announcing that UNEF's strength in Egypt would be over 4,000 men by mid-December. The evacuation was completed on December 21. Ten days later a United Nations salvage fleet began clearance work in the Canal proper. It was agreed that British and French vessels should complete salvage operations already under way in Port Said harbor and then be phased out. UNEF detachments began moving out into the Sinai following the first stage of the Israeli withdrawal.

VIII

The Soviet military intervention in Hungary coincided with the military intervention in Egypt by Britain, France, and Israel. A second special emergency session of the General Assembly was convened on November 4 to deal with the question. For the next two months delegates and Secretariat alike were confronted simultaneously by the two issues, shifting their attention back and forth between the Middle East and Hungary from day to day and week to week. In this volume, however, the editors have grouped most of the commentary and texts on Hungary separately from those on the Middle East in order to provide a more orderly account of the sequence of developments in each case. The documents and background on the Hungarian question will be found on pages 412–52.

In contrast to results in the Middle East, attempts through the United Nations to stop the Soviet military intervention and bring about a Soviet withdrawal from Hungary were ineffective. It is important to be clear about the reasons for the difference—because, in the case of Hungary, the dichotomy between the realities of power and policy on the one hand and emotional and ideological engagement on the other tended to confuse matters.

The circumstances that resulted in the Soviet intervention in Hungary may be recalled. Widespread unrest in Poland and Hungary led to the accession to power in October 1956 of more nationally minded Communist governments. Both countries had been firmly within the Soviet Union's East European system since 1945 and Soviet troops were stationed in both under the terms of the Warsaw Pact.

In Poland the Soviet leaders withheld a threatened military intervention when they concluded that the new Gomulka government was strong enough to maintain Communist party rule intact and would remain completely loyal to the Soviet bloc. In Hungary the Soviet at first hesitated when Imre Nagy became Premier and János Kádár First Party Secretary, but the new Communist leadership proved unable to cope with riots and uprisings spreading like wildfire through the country.

The Nagy government was then reorganized to include non-Communists and Nagy, who had at first opposed bringing the situation to the United Nations, announced on November 1 that Hungary would repudiate the Warsaw Pact in favor of a neutral foreign policy, demanded the withdrawal of all Soviet troops from the country, and asked for United Nations help.

Western and Soviet perceptions of the trend in Hungary at this point were alike in one respect. Both saw that a national uprising threatened to end Communist rule and take the country out of the Soviet bloc. This was welcomed in the West but the Soviet Union saw its East European security system gravely menaced. The Soviet reaction was a massive military intervention to crush the revolt. Nagy was overthrown and Kádár, having been persuaded that Soviet troops were necessary to restore Communist party control of his country, headed a new Communist government. This was the situation when the Hungarian question was brought to the General Assembly on November 4 after a Soviet "veto" prevented adoption of a withdrawal resolution by the Security Council.

In most of the non-Communist world, especially in the West, there was a wave of sympathy for the Hungarian uprising and indignation against the Soviet Union. Both emotions were deeply felt and found strong verbal expression in Assembly resolutions and in the reactions from many capitals. But the question of adopting countermeasures of a more concrete kind received a very different kind of response.

All the Western governments ruled out from the start any thought of the threat or use of military sanctions in a situation where their use would have meant going to war with the Soviet Union. Also, unlike Britain, France, and Israel, the Soviet Union was not vulnerable to economic and financial sanctions, and diplomatic sanctions were not considered. This left as leverage only the condemnation of majority public opinion as reflected in the world organization and elsewhere. That sanction was fully employed, and with some damaging effect upon the Soviet Union, though it was of no help to the rebels in Hungary. Soviet standing, especially in the West, was hurt and Western Communist parties also suffered damage, though in both respects the penalty was a minor price to pay, in Soviet eyes, compared to the loss of Hungary.

The majority approach was fair enough, given the realities of power and the prevailing public judgment. Unfortunately it was thought necessary, or expedient, to express the judgment in successive resolutions making demands with which the majority well knew it would not win compliance. Thus the Assembly called upon the Soviet Union to withdraw "forthwith," called upon the Hungarian government of János Kádár to admit UN observers to check on compliance, and called for free elections under UN auspices to establish a new government.

The majority doubtless considered that the expected rejection of these demands would sharpen the image of Soviet defiance of world opinion, but the manner of the exercise also reflected a bad habit in which Member governments have too often indulged throughout the history of the United Nations: When there are no workable answers to a problem, bring it to the United Nations and thus shift—or at least spread—the blame for failure.

As we have seen from the Middle East affair, the United Nations can be an essential vehicle for rallying support for viable policies to which a sufficient number of governments are able and willing to commit their power and influence; it can also be vital to the successful execution of these policies. In the Hungarian situation the constitutional, political, and military realities left no room for such results. Since resolutions can serve but cannot substitute for policy, and the United Nations can serve but cannot substitute itself for the power of governments, it would seem better to avoid pretenses when the necessary conjunction of power and policy is not present.

Despite the very different circumstances the resolutions on Hungary were so worded as to hand responsibilities to the Secretary-General that were seemingly as broad as those given to him in the Middle East. He was to appoint observers, arrange for their admission to Hungary, investigate and report to the Assembly. Having failed to find any answers themselves, the majority even addressed to him the fantastic request "as soon as possible to suggest methods to bring an end to the foreign intervention in Hungary."

Hammarskjöld's great skills and dedication did not include the capacity to produce a miracle out of nothing more substantial than wishful thinking. His room for diplomatic maneuver and persuasion was also severely restricted. Soviet withdrawal and the admission of UN observers were promptly refused. He then sought to arrange a personal journey to Budapest, reverting to the formula he had used for his mission to Peking two years before. He would go in his own right as Secretary-General under the Charter. For a while it seemed that the visit might be arranged. The Hungarian government never did say "no" but it evaded and postponed setting a date until it was too late for such a mission to serve any purpose.

It took the Soviet troops some weeks to complete the task of crushing the insurrection but after November 4 the outcome was never in doubt. The Hungarian people received no help in their uprising but were aided through a hard winter by a relief program in which the United Nations and the Red Cross collaborated. In addition, the great numbers of Hungarian refugees were given a generous welcome by many Member countries. Early in January 1957, at Hammarskjöld's suggestion, the Assembly established a special committee of Members to investigate the circumstances of the Hungarian revolt and the Soviet intervention. Some months later this committee produced a carefully documented report that presented a powerful indictment of the Soviet intervention. It was endorsed by the Assembly in September 1957 by a vote of 60 to 10 with 10 abstentions.

IX

More than two months elapsed after the last British and French troops left Port Said before the Israeli withdrawal from Egypt was completed. The Israeli government remained determined to gain something substantial from its invasion. It therefore resorted to delaying tactics while it sought with great tenacity to weaken the resolve of the majority of United Nations Members against rewarding the illegal use of force. The texts and background commentary on pages 466–533 provide quite a full account of the course of developments. Here it will suffice to consider briefly some significant aspects.

On January 14 Israel informed the Secretary-General that its withdrawal from the Sinai would be completed by January 22, except for the Sharm el-Sheikh area, on which it was ready to enter into discussions. No commitment was made on the Gaza Strip. On January 19 by a vote of 74 to 2 (Israel and France) with 2 abstentions, the Assembly responded by adopting a resolution reaffirming that withdrawal must be complete and unconditional and requesting the Secretary-General to report on the results within five days.

Four days later Israel made known its terms on both Sharm el-Sheikh and Gaza. It would withdraw from the former if UNEF remained there to prevent any interference with freedom of navigation until a peace settlement—or equivalent international guarantee—was reached. Israel's army would withdraw from the Gaza Strip but its administration and police would remain. No return of Egypt in any form would be permitted and UNEF itself was also to stay out. There could be no return to the Armistice Agreement, for it had been violated and broken "beyond repair." This stand was accompanied by a well-organized and effective campaign conducted through the mass media and the lobbying of parliamentary bodies in important Western countries—especially the United States—and aimed at arousing sympathy and gaining political support.

Israel's position defied the Assembly's repeated affirmations that withdrawal must be unconditional and provoked renewed and increasingly impatient calls for imposing sanctions from Arab and Asian states and the Soviet bloc. Unless Israel could be persuaded to give way the final stage of the long effort to liquidate the invasion of Egypt by the peaceful means of negotiation and the presence of UNEF would be placed in grave jeopardy.

Hammarskjöld's reports of January 15 and 24, 1957, especially the latter, gave the lead for a United Nations response upholding the constitutional position but also suggesting steps to be taken after withdrawal toward meeting Israel's legitimate security concerns—effective measures to prevent raids across the armistice line and to permit freedom of passage through the Straits of Tiran. The Secretary-General consulted closely with the UNEF Advisory Committee, Lodge, and other delegates before writing these reports, for it was a delicate matter to stake out a course of action that would be acceptable to all factions in the majority coalition.

His reasoning and recommendations are fully set forth in the texts and commentary (pages 466–86) and need not be recapitulated in detail here. In essence, he felt that the aim, after Israeli withdrawal, should be to restore the armistice régime to its full integrity, using the presence of UNEF at the demarcation line as an important new support for such a course. UNEF might also be deployed on the Israeli side of the line as well as on the Egyptian side. This action would require Israel's consent, but it would strengthen UNEF's ability to stop incursions from either direction and should make it easier for both sides to agree to correct long-standing violations of various provisions of the Armistice Agreement.

As to the administration of Gaza the Secretary-General pointed out that this belonged to Egypt under international law and any change would require Egypt's consent. As to Sharm el-Sheikh, UNEF might stay on there with Egypt's agreement after Israel's withdrawal, but the terms demanded by Israel would violate the principle approved by the Assembly that UNEF should not be used to influence the settlement of political or legal issues in dispute.

On February 2 the Assembly fully endorsed the Secretary-General's line in two resolutions. One reaffirmed the call for unconditional withdrawal "without further delay" and was approved by the same 74 to 2 vote as before. The second endorsed the subsequent course of action he had proposed, including deployment of UNEF on both sides of the demarcation line and full compliance by both sides with the Armistice Agreement. This resolution carried 55 to 0 with 22 abstentions, the latter including the Arab and Soviet blocs as well as France and Israel.

Some statements in the debate from the Western side had revived Arab suspicions about the uses to which UNEF might be put. The West generally agreed that Israeli shipping should have freedom of passage through the Straits of Tiran. Also, although Israel gained no support for remaining in Gaza, the West showed considerable sympathy for the idea of a United Nations administration of the Strip, and one of those who expressed this view was Lester Pearson. Thus, despite the strong Assembly votes, Israel was encouraged to hold out for the same reasons that had caused uneasiness among the Arabs.

During February the struggle over the Israeli withdrawal was waged in both New York and Washington. At the United Nations Israel evaded giving replies to the Secretary-General's questions on its intentions with respect to the Assembly's February 2 resolutions, including the proposed deployment of UNEF on its side of the demarcation line. There was a stalemate here, but Hammarskjöld won Fawzi's agreement to the inclusion in reports to the Assembly of affirmations of Egypt's commitment to observe all articles of the Armistice Agreement, provided Israel also observed them, and of its willingness to give the United Nations a stronger role in the Gaza Strip in order to help end raids across the armistice line and thereby secure peaceful conditions (pages 489 and 505).

In Washington the Eisenhower administration assured the Israeli government that it was ready to join with other maritime powers in upholding freedom of passage through the Straits of Tiran. This assurance was coupled with public and private warnings that Israel would face trade and financial sanctions unless it withdrew behind the armistice line without further delay. Israel's lobby sought to counter the threat of sanctions by enlisting strong Congressional opposition to such a course, including statements by both Republican and Democratic Senate leaders, William F. Knowland and Lyndon B. Johnson. Eisenhower stood firm, however, and on February 22 went to the people in a nationally televised address that fully committed his great personal prestige. He also cabled another private warning and appeal to Ben-Gurion (pages 501–504).

That same day Lebanon and five other Asian-African Members submitted a resolution to the General Assembly calling upon "all States to deny all military, economic or financial assistance and facilities to Israel." Debate was put off from day to day, however, while a formula to cover Israel's retreat was devised in talks at Washington which were joined by Israel's faithful friends, Mollet and Pineau, who had arrived on a mission of reconciliation with Eisenhower and Dulles.

On March 1, Mrs. Golda Meir, Israel's Foreign Minister, announced to the Assembly Israel's "plans for full and prompt withdrawal" in compliance with the February 2 withdrawal resolution. She then proceeded to set forth various "expectations" and "assumptions" as the basis for Israel's decision. Lodge followed with a statement of the United States' position during which he characterized Israel's expectations as "for the most part . . . not unreasonable." In fact, though the two statements had been drafted and compared during the Washington talks, they only thinly papered over some continuing basic differences, especially on the future status of Gaza. This is evident in the analysis and comparison of these and other texts comprising the record of the agreed withdrawal procedure, which will be found on pages 511–22. Here a prime example concerning Gaza may be noted.

Hammarskjöld's February 22 statement of Egypt's intentions on Gaza had spoken of three stages, all within the context of continued Egyptian administration: (*a*) the take-over from Israel, "which, as has been the case [i.e., Port Said and the Sinai—EDITORS], in the first instance would be exclusively by UNEF"; (*b*) the period of transition during which reference was made to UN help in providing good civilian administration and police protection; (*c*) for the longer term, special and helpful arrangements using UNEF to put "a definite end to all incursions and raids across the border from either side."

On March 1 Mrs. Meir said that Israel expected the take-over of Gaza would be exclusively by UNEF, omitting the qualifying phrases "as has been the case" and "in the first instance." She then proceeded to quote the Secretary-General's references to UN police and administrative functions during the period of transition before the return of Egypt, but in her version the period of transition would continue until a peace settlement or other definitive agreement had been finally concluded and the United Nations would be *the* agency of administration until that distant day, thus excluding a return of Egypt.

Lodge, by quoting Hammarskjöld's February 22 statement in full, set the record straight in that respect, and he reaffirmed United States recognition of Egypt's right to retain administration of the Gaza Strip. However, he also expressed the "hope" that the arrangements mentioned in Hammarskjöld's statement might continue until a peace settlement and he failed to specify exactly which set of arrangements he was referring to—those for the transition, or those for the longer range.

Similar examples of ambiguity and quoting out of context were widespread in the discussions that followed both inside and outside the United Nations. These served further to confuse and muddy the record. Meanwhile the Israeli withdrawal was carried out and UNEF took over in Gaza on March 7 and in Sharm el-Sheikh on March 8.

The Secretary-General had counted on at least a fortnight for the period of transition in order to give him time to negotiate in Cairo the "special and helpful" arrangements envisaged in his February 22 statement. However, Nasser suddenly decided to send in an Egyptian administrative team before instead of after his talks with Hammarskjöld, moved apparently by a combination of Israel's reiterated "expectation" that Egypt would not return, various expressions in the Assembly debate of Western sympathy for that stance, and an incident in Gaza involving a clash between a UNEF patrol and Palestinian Arab demonstrators.

Nasser's move provoked another brief crisis. Israel protested loudly about being misled, yet as we have just noted Israel had contributed its full share to the misleading ambiguities and barely concealed contradictions involved in the March 1 procedure for agreed withdrawal. Certainly it could never have been in any doubt on where Hammarskjöld stood. As for the United States, it is difficult not to conclude that any misunderstandings were entered into with open eyes on both sides in order to complete the turn around a very difficult corner. In any event Israel's protests, having been registered for the record, quickly subsided.

A few days later the Secretary-General negotiated with Nasser the special arrangements for UNEF in the Gaza area and elsewhere that had been promised for the longer pull. These proved sufficient in the months ahead (and for ten years thereafter) to make UNEF an effective instrument for the preservation of peaceful conditions on the line between Israel and Egypt, while UNEF remained at Sharm el-Sheikh and Israeli shipping passed undisturbed through the Straits of Tiran.

Hammarskjöld had taken care that his understandings with Nasser should not be contingent upon reciprocal commitments from Israel. This proved to be of vital importance, for Israel never did consent either to return to the procedures of the Armistice Agreement or to the deployment of UNEF on its side of the line. At the end of March Hammarskjöld made an unpublicized try to break out of the stalemate caused by

Israel's insistence that an Egyptian commitment to full nonbelligerency must precede any response by Israel to his questions on the Armistice Agreement and UNEF deployment. To both Egypt and Israel he put three questions of his own, aimed at eliciting reaffirmations of the non-aggression provisions of Article I of the Armistice Agreement.

Neither side was willing to make the first move and the questions remained unanswered. Thus Israel continued in a state of noncompliance with the Assembly's second February 2 resolution both with respect to the Armistice Agreement and to the deployment of UNEF. Despite Hammarskjöld's urgings, Egypt, when the Suez Canal was reopened to traffic in April, resumed its own noncompliance with the Security Council's 1951 resolution in support of the rights of passage for Israeli ships through the Canal. Whether a moderation of position by either Israel or Egypt might have led to a series of reciprocal steps toward a fully effective armistice régime as envisaged by Hammarskjöld is a question to which no definitive reply is possible. One thing is evident, however. If UNEF had been established on both sides of the line, the inhibiting effect of its presence upon a renewal of hostilities from either direction would have been greatly enhanced.

Later in the spring the Secretary-General decided that the time was not ripe to press such issues further. The Middle East needed a period of convalescence during which recent wounds might have a chance to heal. The UNEF arrangements with Egypt were working well enough to support such a period of quiet even though Israel's cooperation in UNEF's deployment was incomplete. Hammarskjöld shaped his own actions accordingly and used his influence with the governments before and during the next Assembly session to work against a reopening of debates on the unresolved controversies in the Middle East. His twelfth Annual Report in August, his report on UNEF in October, and his final report on clearance of the Suez Canal in November, all reviewed developments of the past year in the least controversial manner possible.

The only decisions requested of the Assembly concerned financing for UNEF and the clearance operation. His proposal that the costs of the latter be met by a temporary 3 percent surcharge on Canal tolls was approved without difficulty. There continued to be strong minority resistance to meeting the costs of UNEF by assessments on the regular scale but the principle, which was supported by Hammarskjöld, was reaffirmed after the United States and United Kingdom made special voluntary contributions of $12 million and $1 million, respectively. This reduced the impact for the smaller Members. Nevertheless the arrears in the peace-keeping account began at this time and mounted cumulatively each year thereafter. Some Members, such as the Soviet bloc, the Arab states, and a few Latin Americans, refused to pay on principle; others simply failed to pay.

The final acts in the dispute over operation of the Suez Canal began soon after the Canal was reopened to traffic in April. Through the winter and early spring Hammarskjöld had sought to persuade Egypt to resume negotiation of a multilateral agreement based on the Six Principles and his talks with Fawzi. The British-French resort to force had changed Nasser's mind, however, and he adamantly refused.

The best that could be managed was a unilateral declaration by Egypt reaffirming the obligations of the Constantinople Convention of 1888, and committing itself to arbitration of disputes with the users and compensation to the old Canal Company. This was registered with the United Nations as "an engagement of an international character" under Article 102 of the Charter, which provides for the registration of all treaties and international agreements. The unilateral nature of the commitment and the absence of any provision for organized cooperation with the users at first caused concern. However, the new operating arrangements proved satisfactory in practice, except for Israel's long-standing grievance.

It was in large part owing to the quiet good offices of the Secretary-General and of Eugene Black, President of the International Bank, that an equitable compensation agreement between Egypt and the shareholders of the old Canal Company was reached a year later, in April 1958, without having to resort to arbitration procedures (see Volume IV).

X

On September 26, 1957, the Security Council unanimously recommended the appointment of Dag Hammarskjöld to a second five-year term as Secretary-General and the Assembly immediately accepted the recommendation by a vote of 80 to 0. His second term actually began on April 10, 1958. During the twenty-two months covered by this volume he had lifted to new heights the influence of his office in international life and the respect of the governments for his personal capacity and character.

Several texts in particular give valuable insights on how Hammarskjöld viewed the world, the Organization, and his own role at this time. Among them are his address to the American Jewish Committee on April 10, 1957; the opening pages of the Introduction to his twelfth Annual Report on August 22, 1957; his acceptance speech in the Assembly of September 26, 1957; and several paragraphs near the end of his presidential address on Linnaeus to the Swedish Academy on December 20, 1957.

At the end of their introduction to Volume II the editors mentioned that Joseph P. Lash's brief study, *Dag Hammarskjöld,*[3] completed only a few months after the Secretary-General's death, remained a reliable, well-informed, and perceptive biographical source despite the limitations of time, space, and circumstance under which the author worked. That judgment stands but we must now add mention of a new book, Brian Urquhart's *Hammarskjold,*[4] which provides a much more comprehensive and detailed account of Hammarskjöld's years as Secretary-General. Urquhart is a valued former colleague of the editors in the United Nations Secretariat. Naturally there are a few places where the editors, on the basis of their own personal experience and understanding, differ somewhat from Urquhart in his interpretation or evaluation of events, but on the whole Urquhart's book provides an invaluable complement to the *Public Papers* series for all those seriously interested in the full story of the struggle for international order in our time.

The next volume (Volume IV of this series) will begin with January 1958 and will include the Lebanon-Jordan affair and other international developments in which the Secretary-General had a role before the 1960–1961 crisis for the Congo and the United Nations, which will be the subject of Volume V.

ANDREW W. CORDIER
and WILDER FOOTE

December 1972

---

[3] Joseph P. Lash, *Dag Hammarskjold—Custodian of the Brushfire Peace,* Doubleday and Company, 1961.
[4] Brian Urquhart, *Hammarskjold,* Alfred A. Knopf, 1972.

❧ 1956 ❧

Transcript of Canadian Broadcasting
Corporation Television Program, "Press Conference"
NEW YORK   MARCH 7, 1956

IN THIS televised question-and-answer program with four well-informed correspondents Hammarskjöld replied to questions concerning the Middle East, economic development, Asian attitudes, cooperation in the peaceful uses of atomic energy, and the seating of Communist China. His responses for the most part were clear and interesting formulations of his political judgments and diplomatic method.

ANNOUNCER: This is "Press Conference," a CBC affairs program in which the men who report the news meet the men who make the news. This week again "Press Conference" is coming to you from the United Nations in New York, and our guest is the United Nations Secretary-General, Dag Hammarskjöld. To question Mr. Hammarskjöld we have a panel of distinguished correspondents, members of the international press corps covering the United Nations: first, William R. Frye, of *The Christian Science Monitor;* next to him, Simon Malley, of *Le Progrès Egyptien;* then Eric Britter, of *The Times* of London.

And now here is this week's Chairman of "Press Conference," Peter Stursberg, of the CBC.

THE CHAIRMAN: Now for our first question, I will call on the Egyptian correspondent, Simon Malley.

MR. MALLEY: Mr. Hammarskjöld, tension has suddenly increased in the Middle East and there is a growing feeling in many capitals of the world that war between Israel and the Arab states is nearer today than when you visited the area a few weeks ago. Now, sir, I would like to

UN Note to Correspondents No. 1248, March 7, 1956.

say that during your trip in the Middle East you had been looked upon as a man dedicated to the principles and aims of the United Nations, unbiased and impartial. Thus my question: Do you share this concern of the world capitals and do you feel, sir, that the United Nations or you personally should consider any direct action to prevent a flare-up from turning into a real explosion?

THE SECRETARY-GENERAL: First of all, I would like to say that I share concern about the situation. However, I do regret, and I have regretted, the tone struck in some comments. After all, tension is high, but I do believe that the people in the area fully recognize that war is never inevitable. We must not develop into a state of mind where we believe that we are drifting without will and direction toward war. I do not believe that is true, and I believe so even less after having met the leading personalities of the Arab countries and of Israel. We have, of course, continuous frictions; we have borderline incidents which are extremely regrettable also in their repercussions. We have underlying basic problems which are very difficult to solve indeed, and we have all over the area a fear of war. All that, of course, builds up a picture which, I can understand, may lead people to feel pessimistic and sometimes even very pessimistic. But I think that we add to the tension by talking glibly about the danger of war. If we talk about the danger of war, we should do so with the full understanding of the underlying circumstances and of the explanations, and with a very clear demonstration of our will to tackle impartially those underlying difficulties in a way that will reduce the temperature to a more reasonable level and to show the people the possibilities of progress toward peace.

I must say that I believe firmly in the existence of such possibilities and, in fact, I have stressed, and I want to stress again, that we are facing a situation where on all sides we have to count on responsible leaders, realistic leaders, who know what they are talking about and who know what the risks are. I must say that I have enough confidence in human wisdom to believe that, that being the case, we also will be able to master the present situation.

I have partly given you a reply to the role of the United Nations by what I have said, because it is obvious that if this attitude of mine is correct—and I believe it to be correct—the role of the United Nations should be to help those who are responsible, all of whom want peace, to work toward peace. They can do that by introducing whatever means they have at their disposal to reduce borderline tensions, to engage in intelligent discussion of the major underlying problems and to help in keeping down the temperature by as realistic an appraisal of the situation as possible. I think that is a fairly complete reply.

THE CHAIRMAN: I should like to explain that the Secretary-General has just returned from a six-weeks' tour of the Middle East and the Far East—I think he spent more time in the Far East. But I think we should try to deal with one subject at a time. Is there any other question on the Middle East?

MR. FRYE: Mr. Secretary-General, I wonder if you would be willing to be a bit more specific about your approach to some of these specific problems. Last August, I remember, Secretary Dulles put forward a plan to meet what he said were the three principal problems of the area: borders, refugees, and this fear of war. You said at that time, I believe, that you hoped the Secretary's ideas would become the basis for a settlement. Well, now that you have had a chance to talk with the key men in the area face to face, do you still think that the outline plan put forward by the Secretary of State is a good basis for a settlement of those major problems?

THE SECRETARY-GENERAL: I cannot, of course, speak in any way for Secretary of State Dulles, but I believe that he himself would recognize that it is more a contribution to a plan than a full plan for a settlement. I welcomed on that occasion last August especially the first part in which Mr. Dulles indicated the willingness of the United States—and he certainly spoke for a large part of the so-called West—to contribute the funds necessary if we are ever to get a solution of the refugee problem.

May I be explicit on that point? As concerns the refugee problem, which is a very burning one indeed both politically and from a humanitarian point of view, I think money is necessary but money is not the reply. That is to say, I still regard the Secretary's proposal as an extremely interesting and valuable contribution. I do not regard it—and I do not think it should be regarded—as a full reply to the problem.

THE CHAIRMAN: Simon Malley, of *Le Progrès Egyptien,* has another question on the Middle East.

MR. MALLEY: Mr. Hammarskjöld, I would like to come back to my previous question and ask you, if direct and immediate action is not being contemplated by the United Nations or by you personally regarding the tense situation in the Middle East, what is your personal opinion and how do you feel about the reported intention of some Western

Powers to intervene outside the United Nations in order to prevent a war?

THE SECRETARY-GENERAL: First of all, I would like to correct an impression that I may have given. I do envisage regular United Nations action and direct United Nations action, but along what I might call conventional lines, although with an intensified effort to get somewhere. You know, a solid basis has been laid by various decisions of the Security Council. The powers and the authority given to General Burns and myself are, I believe, sufficient for us to go ahead with various things which are essential and which may prove helpful. To that extent we are active and we are increasingly active.

But the question you raise is a delicate one partly because I do not know exactly what the three powers had in mind in talking about it. I refused the other day in a press conference to comment on it, and I think that is understandable due to the lack of information. On the other hand, I guess that a proper interpretation would be that such action could be taken only provided that it could be said that the United Nations had failed, that is to say that it would be an emergency and nothing else, and, I take it also, an emergency directed by the very principles which should guide United Nations activities. However, that is purely hypothetical, as I am not properly informed.

THE CHAIRMAN: I think that Eric Britter, of *The Times* of London, has a question on this subject.

MR. BRITTER: Mr. Hammarskjöld, do you believe that the prospects of peace in the Middle East have been dimmed by the dismissal of Glubb Pasha by the King of Jordan?

THE SECRETARY-GENERAL: Again you raise a question which is extremely difficult to treat for the simple reason that I again know too little. Of course, this is a remarkable fact and a fact to be noted, but I would rather like to wait with my reply until I know what events led up to the dismissal.

MR. FRYE: Do you think it would increase or decrease the danger of war if Israel were allowed to buy jet fighter planes and antitank guns from the United States?

THE SECRETARY-GENERAL: You are very precise in your questions. I can understand that because you come down to the heart of really interesting issues. You may well guess that there again you find a somewhat reluctant opposite number on this side of the table. It all is a question of what is defense and what is not defense, when you come to questions of this and that type of arms. I think that I should leave the reply to those who have the decision to make.

THE CHAIRMAN: You are asking the head of a peace organization to recommend arms shipments. Well, have you got another question on the Middle East?

MR. MALLEY: Sir, there is a general feeling in many Arab countries that you have just visited that the Western Powers seem to take a kind of exclusive right in deciding about the issues of the Middle East. In your capacity as Secretary-General of the United Nations, which includes seventy-six Members including the Soviet bloc, do you feel that the Middle Eastern question should be limited to the Western Powers in any way?

THE SECRETARY-GENERAL: Well, my feeling as Secretary-General of the United Nations is rather obvious. My feeling is that a question which is already of major United Nations concern should remain a United Nations concern. On the other hand, that does not exclude others from taking a very active interest in the developments. But I want to point out that neither can any other action exclude the United Nations from what is a United Nations responsibility.

THE CHAIRMAN: Well, I think that we have dealt with the Middle East now and as a transition I should like to ask you a question, sir, which applies both to the Middle East and to the Far East. When you returned here from your tour of the Middle East and the Far East, you spoke of the imperative challenge to live up to the economic needs of the vast majority of mankind. Now, sir, my question is: How can we meet this imperative challenge that you spoke of?

THE SECRETARY-GENERAL: The very first step is, of course, that we recognize the needs and that we recognize our own interest in meeting the needs. We have tended, I think, to regard this question a little bit from the point of view of, let us say, handing out a contribution, charity. It is nothing of the kind. As I see it, it is much more a question of sharing, because once we have joint responsibility for the future—and we have very much so in this case—we must cooperate. We can contribute some things, like money, experts, know-how, and what-not; on the other hand, the real work will be done by the countries themselves in their rehabilitation, their reconstruction, their social reform work, and so on. From that point of view, this is a joint operation and we must understand it as a joint operation, and not as any kind of high-handed contribution which we make to something which is really not our interest.

Once that is properly understood, my own feeling is that we would reach the conclusion that much more is needed than we have so far been able to put out. It is a heavy burden on the taxpayers all over the West, but I think that it is a burden that we should shoulder for the reasons that I gave. Once we do that, on the other hand, we should do it in such forms so that the funds and the know-how will be put to their greatest possible usefulness. In order to achieve that, I think that we should recognize a few psychological and political facts which seem to me to be essential.

First of all, such an operation should be run in such a way so as to give the initiative of the peoples and the governments themselves full swing. It should be their responsibility; in a sense it should be their show. Secondly, and it does follow, we should accept in the Organization, the United Nations, and in other ways, a somewhat more modest role than we have sometimes assumed. That is to say, we are assistants integrated into a major effort, and not in any way all-informed guides who can take the lead and master the situation.

Having reached that point, I think that another conclusion follows. It is easier to run this kind of operation within the framework of an international organization than on any other basis. I would not for that reason say that I have any clear-cut proposals to make concerning the part to be played by the United Nations, and so forth. I do not want to make any specific recommendation. I repeat what I said: I believe that it is easier to run an operation on the basis of an international organization and, for that reason, I think that by sheer force of circumstance we will find international assistance more and more internationalized and a greater and greater responsibility devolving upon the United Nations.

THE CHAIRMAN: Now that we have passed to the Far East, I see that we have a number of questions. Simon Malley, our Egyptian correspondent.

MR. MALLEY: During your press conference last week, sir, you told us about the very high standing that the United Nations enjoys in Asia, and you spoke of the man in the street, who sometimes considers the United Nations as a bulwark against tyranny and exploitation. Is there any way that this feeling which you gathered during your trip could be conveyed to the developed nations of the world, where sometimes, as we all know, the United Nations is thought of as a poor relation?

THE SECRETARY-GENERAL: I think we must look at this in the light of historical developments, and I should like to put my answer in a somewhat paradoxical way. It is natural for old and well-established countries to see in the United Nations a limitation on their sovereignty. It is just as natural that a young country, a country emerging on the world stage, should find in the United Nations an addition to its sovereignty, an added means of speaking to the world. That difference between the two approaches is basic and is easily explained, I think, by historical circumstances and present political problems.

You complain indirectly of the somewhat high-handed way in which perhaps the United Nations is sometimes treated and discussed in some countries. I would not complain about it, because I think it is perfectly natural—just as I regard the reaction of many countries in the East as being natural. But I think that to whatever extent Asian people and, to some degree, I myself, as a kind of indirect spokesman for Asian people, can make it clearer to the Western countries that the United Nations comes into the picture in this way in a very great part of the world, to that extent we will smooth out this curious difference and at the same time bring about a realistic appraisal of the United Nations in political terms, so that you will reach your result in the long run. But I would not like to preach to the Western countries that you are criticizing. I would just like to bring home to them the natural difference of view which is represented by the Asian countries.

THE CHAIRMAN: Eric Britter, of *The Times* of London, has a question.

MR. BRITTER: I hope this is a realistic question, sir. As you know, the admission of Communist China to the United Nations is a hot potato which has been taken up and dropped by the General Assembly and the Security Council several times. As a matter of practical politics, do you favor postponing the next session of the Assembly until November, when the American presidential election is over, and then tackling the problem of the representation of China in a realistic way?

THE SECRETARY-GENERAL: Those are two rather different questions. As concerns the postponement of the General Assembly session, I think that for practical reasons—and without any political overtones—I would personally be in favor of postponement. I think it would be wise.

I think it would speed up our work—and that is sufficient reason for us to consider postponement. Of course, the matter is in the hands of the delegations and of the governments, and we will see what comes out of their deliberations.

As for the other question, it is, as you say, a rather burning one, and the United Nations has approached it several times without really bringing its solution any closer. I hate to guess about the situation which may prevail some ten or twelve months from now, and for that reason I would not give any advice in any direction. I think that this is a problem which should not be brought up while it is still too controversial. Whatever solution is found for the problem, I hope it will be a solution which will not continue to split the United Nations but which may represent a joint approach—with greater or lesser feelings of happiness but, in any event, a joint approach, with joint recognition of what is wise in the political situation.

THE CHAIRMAN: May I put in reverse that question which Mr. Britter put to you. You spoke, when you returned from your trip, of the United Nations being a symbol and a guarantee of equity, and I think it is true that this Organization depends more than any other on moral force. And I think that you, too, spoke of the moral responsibility of the United Nations. Now, do you think it does the United Nations any good to pretend that the Nationalists, who represent no more than Formosa, represent China?

THE SECRETARY-GENERAL: What my feelings and views are on that score you may guess from various actions and statements of mine. I do not feel that I would help the discussion of the question in any way by putting publicly on record my reactions, in whatever direction they may lie.

THE CHAIRMAN: Mr. Frye, of *The Christian Science Monitor,* has a question.

MR. FRYE: Just a little over a year ago, sir, you took another important trip to the Far East on a somewhat similar peace mission. I wonder whether you would care to tell us just how dangerous you think that situation is now and what the prospects of war are. And, supposing that such a war were to come, do you think the United Nations should fight to keep Quemoy and Matsu or Formosa out of Communist China's hands?

THE SECRETARY-GENERAL: You are embarking on rather hypothetical questions. Let me skip the latter part of your question and address myself to the first part. On that first part, I would only like to note that, apart from this and that kind of incident—occasional shooting—we have had a long period of reasonable quiet in that area.

(*Inaudible remark by member of panel.*)

THE SECRETARY-GENERAL: No, no, no, no, I don't claim any merit in that connection. But, anyway, let us hope that that is significant and that it indicates what we may expect for some time to come.

THE CHAIRMAN: And now Eric Britter, of *The Times* of London.

MR. BRITTER: I read recently in the newspapers that when you arrived in Karachi, the capital of Pakistan, on your recent trip around the world, you ran into a mob demonstration about Kashmir, that lovely mountain paradise which is a bone of contention between India and Pakistan. As this issue has been before the United Nations for the last eight years and continues to divide these two countries, do you think it is possible for the United Nations to do anything practical to resolve it, such as proposing that Kashmir be made an independent and neutral country in its own right?

THE SECRETARY-GENERAL: You know, there is a defined United Nations stand on the question and, although it is difficult to be sure, I would rather guess that if the matter were brought up again that stand would be reaffirmed. Whether the United Nations can do something in the direction you indicate is a matter which I find it extremely difficult to talk about because, as long as there is a United Nations stand, I think we should stick by it.

THE CHAIRMAN: And now Simon Malley, our Egyptian correspondent.

MR. MALLEY: The idea of war today, in the atomic age, seems to be becoming obsolete, and it also seems to many of us that no national leader appears to be ready to take a decisive step toward disarmament. In your capacity of Secretary-General of the United Nations, do you feel that, where peace is at stake, the Secretary-General can take a direct action in order to break the present deadlock?

THE SECRETARY-GENERAL: If, by "direct action," you mean public action, I do not think that it would be a good idea at all. On the other hand, if you mean continuing direct discussions with the delegations most deeply involved in order to try to find certain paths and to try to influence them in a direction which may give some promise of more tangible results, I think such contacts are most useful and certainly, on my side, they will be continued to whatever extent I find a basis for continuing them.

THE CHAIRMAN: William Frye, of *The Christian Science Monitor.*

MR. FRYE: Do you think that under international law it is legal and proper to send (*a*) reconnaissance balloons and/or (*b*) weather balloons over the territory of another country?

THE SECRETARY-GENERAL: We seem to be approaching a rather esoteric field of discussion.

(*Inaudible remark by member of panel.*)

THE SECRETARY-GENERAL: I know that is very practical but, for the time being, I would abstain from any comment on it. We may have the question in the United Nations, and that would be the right time for me to look into it—in another way. Pending that development, I would not care to comment.

THE CHAIRMAN: There is a very important conference going on now, the conference on atomic energy which is meeting in Washington—a United Nations conference—and I believe that William Frye, of *The Christian Science Monitor,* has a question to ask you on that subject.

MR. FRYE: You have already commented quite extensively on the United Nations' efforts to meet the challenge of poverty and ignorance throughout the world. To what extent do you think the United Nations should lead and guide the atomic revolution, as it might be called? How much influence should the United Nations have, and how much should be left for bilateral atomic technical assistance?

THE SECRETARY-GENERAL: The questions are closely related, as you have indicated—the question of technical assistance in the economic and social fields, on the one side, and technical assistance in the atomic field, on the other. My reply would be very much the same. I believe in the growing tendency to keep this field of atomic energy internationalized. With such internationalization, the role of the United Nations will probably be growing. I do not believe that the United Nations should try to run the affair. The United Nations is mainly a service organization, an organization which can see to it that matters which should not be controversial do not become controversial. It may maintain it on the open ground between the fighting camps, so to speak. I think that is a major service the United Nations can render. And I hope that, if and when the discussions now taking place in Washington result in the establishment of this agency, the relationship between the agency and the United Nations will be so organized as to give the United Nations just that role of seeing to it that politically the question is in the middle of the stream and is not caught in any of the whirlpools on either side.

THE CHAIRMAN: Eric Britter, of *The Times* of London.

MR. BRITTER: This raises the principles of noninvolvement, doesn't it? Or what we might call nonalignment in controversial affairs? As a result of your trip to India, do you have the feeling that India and countries with a position like hers are right and sensible in following a policy of noninvolvement in the ideological war of East and West?

THE SECRETARY-GENERAL: I do not think that primarily it is a question of right and wrong, because right and wrong, of course, are to be considered mainly in the light of one's own interests in the political field. I think it is much more a question of seeing what is a natural reaction in the light of the historical situation and political balance. From that point of view, I think we should recognize that the great ideological conflict which is splitting our world is a conflict which is a little bit extraneous from the point of view of the many Asian countries. It is really a conflict between two big groups in the West. The East has a tradition of its own. If, for that reason, they look at these ideological developments from some distance and find it natural, first of all, to develop their own approach, whatever it may be, I consider that to be a political fact about which it does not make much sense to say that it is right or that it is wrong. It is a political fact which I think we simply have to recognize, and with which we have to live, and which we have to take into account also in discussing the problems of the historical West, including the Soviet Union and its collaborating countries.

You talked about freedom from alignments. Of course, in a peculiar sense, that is the specific problem also of the Secretary-General. Whatever my personal ideology may be, I have certain obligations in relation to all the Member Nations, and one primary obligation, of course, is to understand—without approval or disapproval—what the facts are and how they fit into the picture.

It is in that light that I give these comments on the developments in Asia—very much the same kind of light in which I would comment on something said or done in the historical West.

THE CHAIRMAN: And now, Simon Malley, of *Le Progrès Egyptien*.

MR. MALLEY: A few days ago, Mr. Pineau, the Foreign Minister of France, aroused widespread criticism around the world because he had criticized the military emphasis of the alliances in the world and had urged an economic emphasis. Could you please tell us how you personally feel about that problem?

THE SECRETARY-GENERAL: My reply must be very much in the terms I used in my reply to Mr. Britter. For the Secretary-General, this is really a question of nonalignment. That is to say, I can note that a majority view expressed in the West is in another direction. These issues are rather controversial, and my main problem is necessarily to understand how this policy has come about, how it influences the present world situation, and what adjustments would be in the interests of mankind as a whole, as represented by the United Nations.

THE CHAIRMAN: Thank you very much, sir. I am afraid that is all the time we have.

From Transcript of Remarks
at UN Correspondents Luncheon
NEW YORK   MARCH 8, 1956

THE SECRETARY-GENERAL began his remarks at the UN Correspondents luncheon with an appeal to the press. The mass media's built-in tendency to play up conflicts and bad news was, he believed, one of the factors undercutting UN efforts to lower the temperature in the tense Palestine situation. He asked the correspondents for their help in working for a better balance between the reporting of good and bad developments without, as he put it, "departing from what you think is realism or what you think is truth, but avoiding a dramatization in the direction of the devils and give God something." Unhappily his auditors worked for a system that defined news in a way that gave them little room for an affirmative response.

Most of the questions and answers again concerned Palestine. Hammarskjöld had met with Dulles in Washington on February 29. After the conference he had issued the following statement: "I came to Washington today at the invitation of Secretary Dulles to discuss with him and members of his staff some of the impressions which I carried away with me as a result of my visit to the Middle East and other Asian countries. During our conversation at luncheon we discussed among other things the role the United Nations might usefully play in helping resolve some of the problems which face the world today." [1] Now a correspondent, remarking that there had been no further talk since then of the Tripartite Powers proceeding outside the United Nations, asked if the Secretary-General had "played his role" in this development. Hammarskjöld's response went further than usual in confirming the correspondent's surmise: "I think the Secretary-General has played his role. What that role is I leave to you to guess." Once again, it may be noted, Hammarskjöld doubted the utility of bringing the Security Council into the picture at this time. Less than two weeks later the United States would propose that the Security Council send the Secretary-General on an urgent mission to the Middle East (see page 69).

THE SECRETARY-GENERAL: . . . . this being not a press conference but a gathering where you have very kindly arranged for a very nice

UN Note to Correspondents No. 1249, March 8, 1956.

[1] UN Press Release SG/466, February 29, 1956.

meal, I may perhaps strike a slightly different note, a note which I would never dare to strike at Headquarters, a note on your part in our work and your part in my job, if I may put it that way. It sounds very pretentious but it really is not so.

It is a question on which it would make sense if sometimes I said one or two words. You see, as I look at the activities at Headquarters, we have three groups in a curious kind of cooperation—delegates, Secretariat, and you ladies and gentlemen of the press. I must say that much as I appreciate the cooperation we have with the delegations, I appreciate in no way less the cooperation which we have with you. That is not in any way a mere courtesy or sweet words. It is something very solid because I do feel, and feel strongly, that you carry a very large part of the burden in the United Nations operation, as I look at it.

After all, we are many things, but we are also a kind of body or organ where opinions are formed and where things are explained to the world, where we try to the best of our understanding to give guidance. That is an activity in which we in the Secretariat have only a very limited access to the public. You have an access which is very much more important in many ways. I am not very helpful in giving you stuff, either in the form of news, statements, or considered opinions, and whatnot. I try to be helpful in other ways by explaining as well as I can on this or that point how I really do look at this or that problem, and you on your side are infinitely helpful because I must say, and I have said it before, that from my point of view, by and large, the way in which you bring to the notice of the public the problems in which we are engaged is very helpful to the public, and for that very reason very helpful to us.

I would like to enlist you as a part of the United Nations, and a part of the United Nations which works with very much the same aims in mind, apart from your professional viewpoints which must come into play, as they do in the Secretariat. I would like to add one word more, and that is that I have been struck by the reactions on many occasions from many of you, both publicly and privately to me, and in questions, reactions, which have revealed how deeply you feel for the purposes of the United Nations, how deeply you feel yourselves engaged in that venture in your activities as individuals. To use the word "heartening" would be sentimental. I think it, after all, from my point of view, has been registered as something indicating deep solidarity, which does explain that to such a large extent what you do and what we are trying to do seems to be mutually supporting to a degree which is really extremely valuable from the point of view of the Organization.

These general observations have a special application these very days. You have seen, you have heard, and you have sensed that I have taken in many respects a somewhat critical attitude to the trend of public debate on certain very burning issues. I have done so because I felt that really the trend of that discussion in its somewhat heated forms worked against not only our purposes but against what probably are the purposes which you want to serve yourselves. I am not criticizing any of you or the press in general. I just refer to the reactions and attitudes which you know just as well as I, and which are easily explained from my point of view.

The fact is this, and I would like to go back for a second to our last press conference and what has been said concerning the Middle East and my own attitude to it. The fact is, in a situation like this one, which is tense, which does involve all sorts of risks—who could deny it— what is said in the press has an impact on the very situation. We should never, and I do not think anybody for a second would like to, depart from what we consider to be realistic and true. I would never try to approach a problem of that seriousness either in a frivolous spirit of smoothing out difficulties or in a spirit of fooling you and the public as to what I feel about it. But I do feel that, on the other hand, it is our duty—I look at it from my angle, but I think it is true about you too —to approach the facts of the situation in this spirit, to avoid squeezing the last possible drop of venom out of bad news. On the other hand, when something is said which is constructive, which is positive, which does indicate responsibility and perspective, one should give that, although it is good news and not bad news, just as much of a display as the bad news.

From my point of view, that is to say, it is not a question of truthfulness and realism, it is all a question of emphasis and of avoiding interpretations which brush aside everything that seems to indicate hope and enlarge everything that may be bad. It is really not for a slant in an optimistic direction, but for a very careful balance between good and bad news. I say that in the way I do here because I do feel that the impact of comments on the situation in the Middle East is so important in the present situation, and I think that by these very simple means which are under our control, we can help those who work for peace, on this side or that side in the area, while, on the other hand, by taking another line we do help the destructive forces, which is so very much against what we want to do.

So my simple conclusion is that, with reference to the way in which I

know you look at these problems and United Nations operations generally, I would not explain the approach I have had personally and publicly to these problems, but go a little bit beyond that and appeal to you
not only to understand the spirit in which I approach these problems,
but also to see to it if you cannot in your work help us in the United
Nations in that very direction, without, and I repeat it, departing
from what you think is realism or what you think is truth, but avoiding a dramatization in the direction of the devils and give God something.

That is what I would like to say in general terms, and with that background I would like to invite those questions which your Chairman
promised, on my behalf.

QUESTION: I listened carefully to your appeal against overdramatizing
the Middle East situation. Since your last press conference there have
been four people killed on Lake Tiberias. There has been an incursion
into Israel by Egyptian scouts. Many of us have not been able to see
the basis on which you have been optimistic about a solution, nor have
we been able to see what the United Nations could do in this situation
or that it was doing anything in this situation. I therefore welcome this
opportunity to hear if there is anything being done.

THE SECRETARY-GENERAL: I will try to reply to your various questions. First of all as to the first question—and I am not being polemical
in any way—I just want to speak freely—did you see war round the
corner at the time of the Qibya incident, the Nahallin incident, or the
Gaza story? No, you did not. This is bad, it is very bad, but it is not a
new phase in the development. It is extremely regrettable and I need
not in any way explain to you how you react to it. But you should not
in this case give recent current events a different implication from the
one you have given similar events of the same type, or sometimes perhaps even more threatening, in the past.

In your second question, you asked on what I based my so-called optimism. I may have been misunderstood, using the word optimism, in
the sense that it has been understood as indicating that I think that
everything will go well. I have no reason to know how it will turn out.
Nobody knows. But what I have said and what I want to stick to is another matter. If you analyze the situation at the present moment, you
can see that people who are animated by such and such motives which are
the guiding motives of the forces of the nations involved, serving their
own interests, must arrive at conclusions which exclude the initiative of

war. If on the other hand you find that the people who, like—for example Ben-Gurion the other day—have the right to speak for the people, themselves publicly discard such possibilities, I for one give credence to what is said if what is said does correspond to what makes sense. I prefer to believe them, not to disbelieve them. I agree that that is always a hypothesis and everyone knows how minds may change. Nobody knows how the situation may develop, but you see in a case like this one might have to choose a line, in the sense you have to believe in possibilities or exclude possibilities. And what I have called, perhaps lightly, "optimism," and what you have interpreted as an anticipation of a certain outcome, it is not optimism in that sense. It is the firm belief that I and we all have to base our reactions on the possibility of a good outcome and work in that direction, and not accept the other stand, the inevitability of a bad outcome. My reason for this, why I consider that to be a realistic attitude, is that the declared attitudes of those responsible is in line with what I have said and is supported by what common sense indicates.

Finally, you asked what the United Nations can do about it. If you mean what the United Nations can do by way of resolutions, I understand your question very well—what can the United Nations do about it—but if you mean what can the United Nations do about it from day to day, or even from hour to hour, I think there is no need for very great imagination to see it does quite a lot. It does quite a lot directly in current negotiations concerning small matters and major matters. It does quite a lot to bridge the gulfs, to act as a lightning conductor service for bringing high tensions down by explanations. It does a current operation from day to day, and even from hour to hour. It cannot and it will never make news because no single piece of it is news, and the whole thing, the continuous operation, should not be news, because it is a matter of course. But it is an operation; it is very much like the constant attendance of a good nurse, which may be just as important as the operation itself. Surgeons' operations are news, the work of nurses is not.

. . . . QUESTION: I asked a question at the last press conference which you were unable to answer. My question concerned action outside the United Nations. Since your visit to Washington and your conference with Mr. Dulles, and at the last press conference of the President, we have heard no mention of any action outside the United Nations. What I should like to know is whether the Secretary-General played his role in convincing the three from going outside United Nations action.

THE SECRETARY-GENERAL: I think the Secretary-General has played his role. What the role is I leave to you to guess.

QUESTION: As part of the work of a good nurse, do you expect that the United Nations Observer Corps and General Burns' team will be increased?

THE SECRETARY-GENERAL: That will depend entirely on the conclusions of General Burns. I said at a press conference that there is a standing agreement between us that he gets whatever people he feels he wants. I want to stress that it is not a political issue. It is house business. I can very well see from the present situation that he may feel his observers are too thinly spread to do what they have to do under their present terms of reference. If he feels that he wants the addition because of a greater frequency of clashes and so on, in my view he should have them. I regard that as entirely within the limits of what he and I are entitled to agree upon, and I am sure I will get support when I ask for the people from those governments that can provide them.

So let us put it in this way. A difficult patient may need more than one nurse, and the head nurse has to see to it that it is attended to all the time as it should be.

QUESTION: There has been no request as yet?

THE SECRETARY-GENERAL: No. There has not.

QUESTION: I should like to ask two questions within the framework set by our Chairman at the beginning. One is purely geographical, and I take it that mountain climbers are familiar with geography. Have you received any reports about the allegations made by both Syria and Israel to the effect that, on the one hand, Israeli troops are massing on the Syrian border and, on the other hand, that Egyptian troops are massing on the Israeli border?

The other question is literary. There was a piece of prose delivered by Mr. Eisenhower yesterday, who said that it is all up to the United Nations. Could the Secretary-General tell us whether the United States has indicated in any way to the United Nations exactly how it is up to the United Nations?

THE SECRETARY-GENERAL: On the first point, we have so far no reports from our people in the field on the specific aspect of the story to which you refer. Reports always take time because it is a very careful checking that comes into play in such a case as this one.

On the other point, this piece of literature, as you call it, of course it is up to the United Nations. But the United Nations is composed of Member governments; that is to say, in the United Nations, it is up to the Member governments. Apart from that, of course, the United Nations is something which is I would say not in any way lifted outside the context of the Member governments—that is, the Secretariat and the Secretary-General. But at all events, it is something which is free to take action to quite a considerable extent independently of initiative from Member governments. If you interpret an appeal to the United Nations for action in this limited sense where it is not a question for Member governments but for the Secretary-General, all I can tell you is that anything that from my point of view and from the point of view of my collaborators does make sense within the limits of the legal rights of the Secretary-General, is being done.

QUESTION: I should like to address a question to the Secretary-General as a traveler. You have recently undertaken a long trip during which you visited fifteen or sixteen or maybe seventeen Member countries. Could you tell us if you have any more plans to visit other Member governments?

THE SECRETARY-GENERAL: Yes, I have. It is of course a little bit early to be precise about it because with developments such as those to which reference has been made frequently in this discussion, I have to keep my travel plans and all sorts of plans very open.

It is also from here that normally things can be run, and when I am away there are limitations which are unavoidable. With that reserve, however, for this year I have in mind something like three more trips. One would cover countries in Eastern Europe, one would cover some of the new Member countries and old Member countries in Southeastern Europe, and the third one would cover some of the countries in Latin America, further south than I have ever been. In other words, one would cover cities like Helsinki, Moscow, Warsaw, and Prague; that is the one possible plan. Another one would cover cities like Vienna, Belgrade, and Rome, where I have not been while in this office. And a third one would, if time permits and the situation makes it reasonable, cover countries in Latin America, where I have not been.

So much for this year, and I think it is very wise not to talk about the next one.

QUESTION: You have been asked about traveling and even about literature. I think it is up to me to ask you about mountaineering, not only because I am a Swiss correspondent but because during this period of my life people are faced with the idea that they have reached the summit where they can look down and see the things more simply than they are recognized generally with complicated and subtle interpretations. So in my simple spirit, I think there is a situation which is extremely easy. There are Arab states which do not like Israel. If they were strong enough, they would like to expel it from Palestine. If this is the situation, what is the problem? What can the United Nations do, what will they do in order to reconcile the traditional Arab world with the existence of Israel?

THE SECRETARY-GENERAL: You indicated at least that it was a very difficult plan. I think that the question really indicates a kind of somewhat exaggerated view of the height of this political Mount Everest.

I think that in this, as in many cases, time is one factor and the common sense of man is far greater than you believe. I do not think we are so far withdrawn from a conviction that, as the world is, whatever they feel about the past and the wisdom of certain actions and decisions in the past, they know there is a stage where you cannot go back and nobody can go back on these decisions. Such recognition of facts grows with time and grows with new generations growing up. I have seen it at close quarters in Europe and I do not know why we should not be able to trust to such a development here.

My reply to your question is simply that first of all we have to maneuver the current situation in such a way as to give free swing to those forces which are constructive and conciliatory. And if we can do that, we shall do well enough. Nature has a certain healing quality and ability which is likely to bring us to a state of affairs where people may still be grudging and unhappy but where they see what is irreversible.

QUESTION: Would you speak to us for a moment about the approaching disarmament conversations in London? If I must ask a specific question, do you see any prospects of agreement or even of progress?

THE SECRETARY-GENERAL: Well, I do. You feel that I am a blue-eyed fool believing in all sorts of things that you, by the implications that your question carries, do not believe in. I do believe in possibilities. I will give you the reason in order to forestall a question from you on what basis I am an optimist.

It seems to me that statements made from various quarters indicate a few changes in the approach. One is that there is a greater willingness to consider, let us say, partial solutions. Previously, it has always been a question of some kind of total solution. I do not believe in that kind of package deal. I do not think that that ever works out in a situation so complicated as this one. So we must get to the stage where it is a recognized possibility to approach it pragmatically and step by step.

I think there is a growing awareness of such a step-by-step approach as something which is not unreasonable, to try out, so to say, this and that in order to find a ground which may be common.

The second reason for my feeling that something may come after London is that it seems to me that the statements concerning the attitudes which have proved unacceptable to the other party have been less absolute recently. That concerns all the main parties. With regard to very recent developments, for example, the important addition concerning the production of fissionable material in the statement of the President of the United States the other day is such an indication. Attitudes are certainly basically unchanged. But in detail, they may be open to certain discussions which may in turn open the road to some kind of partial agreement.

For these reasons I feel that the situation is more fluid than it has been, and not in a bad sense. If that is so, it is very much worth while trying to see how far we can get. Frankly, this sounds rather flat, but I really do mean it. Once people recognize that there is a real need, once there is some margin for negotiation operations, I do believe in the ability of extremely able and intelligent people to get something, if not on paper, at least orally understood between them which will move us forward.

After what happened last fall, most of us would have said, "Well, there is no chance with this atmosphere to get anywhere in a spring meeting at London." I think you will not say that I am wrong in the indications I have given about the situation which today has certain elements of greater possibility and greater mobility than before. It could not have been foreseen at that stage to show that we were too pessimistic because we looked at it that way last fall. . . . In fact the discussions going on in New York both in the Disarmament Commission, the Subcommittee, and the General Assembly served to prepare the ground for progress, which now is more obvious than it was at that stage.

In the same way, I would not be surprised to see the London meeting wind up on a note which did not give any clear indication of progress but where, a few months hence, we would find after all that something had happened in London.

That is the very moderate way in which I am an optimist concerning the London meetings. Those are also the reasons for which I am optimistic.

. . . . QUESTION: Mr. Hammarskjöld, to go back to your travels for a moment, considering how many young and small nations there are in Africa in the Trust Territories and so on, do you not think it would be useful if you could include Africa in some of these trips? It would be very wonderful for them and perhaps very rewarding in many ways.

THE SECRETARY-GENERAL: There was a reply which you could not possibly guess in what I said before because I said that it was better not to speak about next year. I can tell you that one of the two plans formed for next year is Africa, nothing but Africa.

QUESTION: In view of what you said about the Middle East situation, you do not seem to agree with the various Washington reports and other reports that the Security Council will have to be called into session.

THE SECRETARY-GENERAL: I do not know. It may be that the Security Council will be called to meet on those incidents which have recently taken place. In that case, those would be meetings in a long chain of similar meetings, as you know. That is one question. With respect to that question, I just do not know how to reply because it depends on the parties.

On the wider question, my question to you would be: At this specific juncture, what can the Security Council usefully contribute to a solution? That, I think, is the key to the problem. People may have different views on it, all of them within the margin of legitimate differences of opinion. Personally, I would not feel that the immediate contribution of the Security Council would be likely to add very much to the picture.

. . . . QUESTION: A propos of the Middle East, you mentioned that we should give free swing to forces which are constructive and conciliatory. Could you be more explicit about the conciliatory forces, if there are any? What do you think them to be?

THE SECRETARY-GENERAL: The main conciliatory force is the recognition of quite a few people in the area, irrespective of nationality, of the wisdom of even the slowest and most—for the time being—unrewarding efforts to work toward peace. That conviction does exist. I have experienced it myself, and I know it is sincere. That is what I call a conciliatory force, and I think it is a matter of course that that should be given as much encouragement in action as we can give.

Remarks at the Metropolitan Museum of Art on the Occasion of the Opening of a Special Loan Exhibition, "Asian Artists in Crystal"

NEW YORK   MARCH 8, 1956

The designer of one of the glasses here exhibited has given it a form vaguely reminiscent of the bold lines of the great Pagoda in Rangoon. The giant golden stupa of the Shwedagon Pagoda rises like a flame over the lowlands around the city. It may stand as a symbol for essential features of the Asian world: a deep spirituality, an exuberant artistic instinct, challengingly independent in its ultimate manifestations, a dynamism which never loses its roots in an ancient past. The Pagoda is a living shrine, focusing the deep religious life of the people as you meet them today, but the stupa—the beauty of which reveals itself fully only when your mind has opened itself to its new melody—dates back 1,000 years, and the tradition of the temple takes us back to the days of the Buddha, 2,500 years ago.

We talk these days much about the renaissance of Asia and the Asian peoples. We talk about a new nationalism, about the urge for independence and wider political influence for the peoples of Asia. I am afraid that in doing so we are sometimes so preoccupied with the specific problems and interests of what history calls "the West" that we view these developments less in the light of what they contribute to the growth of all humanity than in the light of what they may detract from the predominance of Western peoples. We see what we may lose. We do not realize what we are gaining.

In the history of Western civilization we meet again and again influences of Eastern religion, philosophy or art. Mostly it has been a question of treasures brought back from Asia by Westerners who, filtering their experiences through their own minds, have managed to infuse them into Western life. It is not until recently that the peoples of Asia have won the possibility of speaking with the West as equals. It is

UN Press Release SG/468, March 8, 1956.

therefore not until now that we could hope to see the civilization of mankind develop through a truly free interplay of the traditions of these two great parts of the world. It is my conviction that when Asia can speak—as Asia—to the West, and when the West learns to listen and to respond in the spirit of a new and equal relationship, mankind all over the world will profit by it.

Asian nationalism, Asian dynamism and traditionalism—as I said, we often tend to overlook the positive elements in these manifestations of the Asian spirit. Partly we do so because we give to these attitudes interpretations molded on the pattern of our own history, without an ear sufficiently sensitive to the special accent of Asian reactions. We tend to judge the attitudes in terms of our own values or in terms reflecting inherited standards, typical of our special traditions. Our conclusions as to what is right and what is wrong are no more generally valid than similar judgments of what is good and what is bad in the field of arts. A true interchange of ideas and a fruitful collaboration requires that we accept what *is*—is, in its own right—without narrowing our ability to comprehend and appreciate by rigid ideas about what *should be*. This is neither weak acquiescence nor unprincipled tolerance, but a constructive acceptance of the fact that conformity is no more an ideal in international life than it is so within a people, and that there are many equally valid standards for the measurement of human achievement.

This exhibition represents an unconventional and interesting approach to the problem of Asia and the West. Designs by a number of Asian artists have been projected on glass formed by craftsmen of the West. We are confronted with an attempt to marry Asian sense of line with Western technique and sense of material and form. If continued, a venture like this one day may create a basis for such a joint approach as would make the resulting work of art reflect a unity of spirit, the Western artist acquiring a deeper sense for the Eastern approach to design, and the Eastern artist acquiring a deeper sense for the form and materials used by the West. The results that this cooperation has already yielded are interesting and encouraging.

As Secretary-General of the United Nations I have recently traveled through a great number of Asian countries. I have returned with strengthened appreciation for the importance of efforts for which this exhibition may stand as a symbol, efforts to work hand in hand, each one bringing to the joint task the best of his skill and of his spiritual heritage. May the frail and subtle works of art which have grown out of these efforts, and are exhibited here, be followed by acts blending as happily the spirit of the East with forms of the West.

Remarks at Flag-Raising Ceremony
at UN Headquarters
NEW YORK   MARCH 9, 1956

This occasion is symbolic confirmation of a significant event in the history of the United Nations.

From this day on the flags of the sixteen nations admitted to the United Nations last December will fly side by side with those of the other sixty Member countries.

We welcome them, as we shall welcome others who will follow them in due course.

Albania, Jordan, Ireland, Portugal, Hungary, Italy, Austria, Romania, Bulgaria, Finland, Ceylon, Nepal, Libya, Cambodia, Laos, and Spain—they all belong here, for all are members of the world community of nations.

With these new Members the United Nations has been strengthened in its capacity to serve the most essential purposes of world organization because it has taken a long step toward universality. In the midst of the many forces that make for difference and conflict in the world, the universal goals of the Charter and the institutions of the United Nations engage the highest purposes and best hopes of all mankind.

These flags symbolize this uniting force—this affirmation of belief that there can be brotherhood in diversity, that constructive cooperation for the common benefit is an attainable alternative to war. As they fly side by side in front of these buildings, may they be a constant reminder—alike in times of disappointment and of achievement—of this engagement to which men of goodwill of every nation, race, and culture are called upon to give their faith, their courage, and their loyalty.

UN Press Release SG/469, March 9, 1956.

From Toast Proposed at Dinner in Honor of
President Giovanni Gronchi of the Republic of Italy
NEW YORK   MARCH 12, 1956

Your presence in this house would, in any circumstances, have been a signal honor for those who are its custodians. Today, we experience the added joy of welcoming here the head of a state newly admitted to the Organization. The decision of the Assembly corrected an anomaly. You are the first of the chiefs of state of the new member countries to visit us at United Nations Headquarters and, in welcoming you here today, I pay tribute to all those nations who have just taken their place in this family of peoples.

Few destinies have been as brilliant and rich in experience as that of your people. To speak of this past is necessarily to do it less than justice, but here we cannot forget that your history has contributed, perhaps more than any other, to the growth of those concepts which are the basis of our Organization. It is from Rome that the *prisca fides* come to us and the first attempt to inscribe a respect for contracts in a coherent body of institutions. It is also from Rome that we have received through the *jus gentium* the first application of a system of private international law. Again, it is in Rome, at the center of a mosaic of kingdoms, duchies, principalities, and republics, and in a confusion of divisions and internecine wars, that there was protected and preserved over the centuries one of the most fertile expressions of the principle of universality.

As Secretary-General, I cannot but make special mention here of Italy's unique contribution to diplomacy. Because your country was split and divided into so many political units, separate and often hostile, your statesmen and your thinkers were led sooner than those elsewhere to discover the technique of international relations. It is in the Italy of the fifteenth century that we find the origin of an art and of practices which have developed in the course of history to the foundation of the United Nations. It was there that was first established the practice of negotiating treaties, the forerunner of the technique of diplomatic con-

UN Note to Correspondents No. 1253, March 12, 1956.

ferences, and that the first rules governing diplomatic procedure were framed. Perhaps the most important development has been the role of accredited representatives. When the Duke of Milan sent a diplomatic representative to Cosmo de Medici, he established, in your native Tuscany, the first permanent diplomatic mission. In less than fifteen years, the practice had spread throughout Europe. Speaking at the Headquarters of the United Nations, I would like to mention in passing that, at first, the title of these representatives was not "Ambassador" but "Resident Orator."

Naturally, I would not push the comparison too far. Diplomacy at that time, in Italy as elsewhere, was based on a political philosophy certain elements of which would with difficulty find a place within the framework of our Charter. But even the much decried principles of Machiavelli can from time to time give us useful lessons because they teach us to recognize and measure our illusions, and that is a discipline we can hardly neglect in the midst of the dangers of the atomic age. . . .

Question of the Relationship of the International Atomic Energy Agency to the United Nations: Study Prepared by the Secretary-General

NEW YORK   APRIL 20, 1956

THE SECRETARY-GENERAL had consulted with the Atomic Advisory Committee in March on the basic principles that should be included in an agreement establishing the relationship of the International Atomic Energy Agency (IAEA) with the United Nations. On April 8 a revised draft statute for the IAEA had been unanimously approved in Washington by the twelve sponsoring governments (see Volume II, page 628). The draft statute and the Secretary-General's study were then circulated to Member states of the United Nations and to the specialized agencies (see also pages 264–66).

Introduction

1. This study has been prepared and is circulated in response to the request made by the General Assembly in its resolution 912 (X), on the peaceful uses of atomic energy, adopted at its 550th plenary meeting on December 3, 1955. In Section II of that resolution, entitled "Concerning an International Atomic Energy Agency," the Secretary-General, in consultation with the Advisory Committee on the Peaceful Uses of Atomic Energy, was requested "to study the question of the relationship of the International Atomic Energy Agency to the United Nations. . . ." The resolution provided that the results of this study by the Secretary-General and the Advisory Committee were to be transmitted to the "Governments concerned" prior to the conference on the final text of the statute of the Agency, to be convened by the Governments sponsoring it.

2. The study is presented in the form of those basic principles which should be included in the agreement to be entered into between the United Nations and the International Atomic Energy Agency (IAEA).

General Assembly Official Records, Eleventh Session, Annexes, agenda item 69, Document A/3122, April 20, 1956.

These principles are fully consistent with the provisions of the Charter of the United Nations and of the proposed statute of the Agency. They also take into account certain unusual features which are involved in the relationship between the United Nations and the Agency.

Principles

3. The agreement bringing the Agency into relationship with the United Nations, which will be entered into by the General Assembly on behalf of the United Nations and by the General Conference on behalf of the Agency, should be based on the Charter of the United Nations and the relevant articles of the statute of the IAEA, and should contain provisions covering the following points.

4. Recognition by the United Nations of the IAEA as the agency which, under the aegis of the United Nations as specified in the following paragraphs, is responsible for taking action under its statute for the accomplishment of the objectives set forth therein, and recognition that by virtue of its intergovernmental character and international responsibilities, the IAEA should function as an autonomous international organization under its statute, and in the working relationship with the United Nations and the specialized agencies set out in the agreement.

5. Recognition by the Agency of the responsibilities of the United Nations in the fields of international peace and security and economic and social development, and accordingly, assumption by the Agency of the obligation to keep the United Nations informed of its activities. The Agency should be required to submit reports on its activities to the General Assembly at its regular sessions, to the Security Council when appropriate, and to the Economic and Social Council and to other organs of the United Nations on matters within the competence of these organs.

6. The Secretary-General of the United Nations should report to the United Nations as appropriate on the development of the relations and on the common activities of the United Nations and the Agency.

7. The Agency should be required to consider resolutions relating to the Agency adopted by the General Assembly or any of the Councils of the United Nations and, when requested, to submit reports on action taken by the Agency or by its members, in accordance with the statute, as a result of such consideration.

8. The Agency should cooperate with the Security Council in fur-

nishing to it such information and assistance as may be required for the maintenance and restoration of international peace and security.

9. The Agency should undertake to cooperate, in accordance with its statute, in whatever measures may be recommended by the United Nations in order to ensure effective coordination of its activities with those of the United Nations and of the specialized agencies. Coordination should aim at avoiding overlapping and duplication of activities. The Agency furthermore should participate in such bodies as the Administrative Committee on Coordination and should maintain close working relationships with the secretariats of the United Nations and of the specialized agencies.

10. The Secretary-General of the United Nations or his representative should be entitled to attend and to participate without vote on matters of common interest in sessions of the General Conference of the Agency and of the Board of Governors. He also should be invited as appropriate to such other meetings as the Agency may convene at which matters of interest to the United Nations are under consideration. Representatives of the Agency should be entitled to attend, and participate without vote in, meetings of the General Assembly and its committees, meetings of the Economic and Social Council and the Trusteeship Council, and of their respective subsidiary bodies. At the invitation of the Security Council, representatives of the Agency may attend its meetings to supply it with information or give it other assistance with regard to matters within the competence of the Agency.

11. The Agency should include in the agendas of the General Conference or the Board of Governors items proposed by the United Nations. The Agency should have the right to bring questions before the United Nations in the following manner: the Secretary-General, in accordance with his authority, should bring to the attention of the General Assembly, the Security Council, the Economic and Social Council or the Trusteeship Council, as appropriate, questions proposed for their consideration by the Agency.

12. The United Nations and the Agency should arrange for the fullest and most prompt exchange of appropriate information and documents between the Agency and the United Nations.

13. The Agency should undertake to consult from time to time with the United Nations concerning administrative matters of mutual interest, particularly the most efficient use of facilities, staff, and services, and with a view to securing, within the limits of the pertinent provisions

of the statutes of the two organizations, as much uniformity in these matters as shall be found practicable. These consultations shall cover the most equitable manner in which special services furnished by one organization to the other should be financed.

14. The General Assembly, the Economic and Social Council, or the Secretary-General, as may be appropriate, should take action as necessary to extend to the Agency the various administration rights and facilities enjoyed by other organizations within the United Nations system.

15. The General Assembly should take action in each case to enable a legal question arising within the scope of the activities of the Agency to be submitted, at the request of the Board of Governors of the Agency in accordance with its statute, to the International Court of Justice for an advisory opinion.

MISSION TO THE MIDDLE EAST

APRIL—JUNE 1956

As LATE AS March 8 Hammarskjöld had continued to express doubt to the UN correspondents concerning the utility of a new move at this time by the Security Council on the Palestine question. During the next ten days, however, the outlines of a plan he could welcome were worked out in consultations among governments and with him. On March 20 the United States requested an early meeting of the Council to consider the "status of compliance given to the General Armistice Agreements and the resolutions of the Security Council during the past year." On the next day the United States submitted the following draft resolution:

The *Security Council,*

Recalling its resolutions of March 30, 1955, September 8, 1955, and January 19, 1956,

Recalling that in each of these resolutions the Chief of Staff of the United Nations Truce Supervision Organization and the parties to the General Armistice Agreements concerned were requested by the Council to undertake certain specific steps for the purpose of ensuring that the tensions along the armistice demarcation lines should be reduced,

Noting with grave concern that despite the efforts of the Chief of Staff the proposed steps have not been carried out,

1. *Considers* that the situation now prevaling between the parties concerning the enforcement of the armistice agreements and the compliance given to the above-mentioned resolutions of the Council is such that its continuance is likely to endanger the maintenance of international peace and security;

2. *Requests* the Secretary-General to undertake, as a matter of urgent concern, a survey of the various aspects of enforcement of and compliance with the four General Armistice Agreements and the Council's resolutions under reference;

3. *Requests* the Secretary-General to arrange with the parties for the adoption of any measures which, after discussions with the parties and with the Chief of Staff, he considers would reduce existing tensions along the armistice demarcation lines, including the following points:

(*a*) Withdrawal of their forces from the armistice demarcation lines;

(*b*) Full freedom of movement for observers along the armistice demarcation lines, in the demilitarized zones and in the defensive areas;

(*c*) Establishment of local arrangements for the prevention of incidents and the prompt detection of any violations of the armistice agreements;

4. *Calls upon* the parties to the general armistice agreements to co-op-

erate with the Secretary-General in the implementation of this resolution;

5. *Requests* the Secretary-General to report to the Council in his discretion but not later than one month from this date on the implementation given to this resolution in order to assist the Council in considering what further action may be required.[1]

Between March 26 and April 4, the resolution was discussed at six meetings of the Council—during which representatives of Egypt, Israel, Jordan, Lebanon, and Syria were invited to express their views. The background diplomatic preparation for the public debate was well and carefully done. The United Kingdom, France, and other Western members of course supported the resolution. The United States emphasized that the request to the Secretary-General did not derogate in any way from the responsibilities of the Security Council. The USSR did not object, provided the proposal was basically acceptable to all the parties concerned and that all measures to relieve tensions were carried out with their agreement. The Arab states welcomed the proposal, provided it was strictly limited to measures agreed to by the parties and within the purview of the armistice machinery and the Truce Supervision Organization. The United States reassured them on these points. Israel thought the resolution was valuable, although it complained that it did not go far enough. The USSR introduced some amendments, which were rejected, but on April 4 the Council acted unanimously in adopting the resolution.

The first of the following texts gives the Secretary-General's statement in the Council after the vote. In this statement he placed on record his view of his own constitutional authority in relation to his mandate and asked for cooperation from the governments with which he would be negotiating as well as from those outside the region, requesting "restraint in word and action." This latter request was directed at the intensifying competition between the Soviet Union and the Western Big Three for influence in the Middle East. The second text following gives excerpts from his April 5 press conference transcript in which he elaborates on his Council statement.

[1] Security Council Official Records, Eleventh Year, Supplement for January-February-March 1956, Document S/3575, Resolution 113 (1956).

1. *Statement in the Security Council*

NEW YORK   APRIL 4, 1956

I have listened with great attention to the discussion. The grave concern about the problems of the Middle East, which has been reflected in the debate, has prompted a unanimous decision of the Council. I share personally this concern and I feel that in the circumstances I should not hesitate to assume the responsibility which the Council has wished to put on my office. The scope of the Security Council's request is well indicated and it has been clarified further in the course of the debate. The specific responsibility which this request puts on the Secretary-General is entirely in line with the character and obligations of his office. It is obvious that this request neither detracts from nor adds to the authority of the Secretary-General under the Charter.

I note that the Council wants me to explore possible ways of reducing tension along the demarcation lines. The extent to which such an exploration is possible and likely to yield lasting results depends necessarily on the willingness of all the parties concerned to cooperate fully with the Secretary-General in a joint effort inspired by mutual confidence. Assuming the task which the Council has desired me to assume, I trust that I can count on such collaboration.

I also trust that all those who are interested in a successful outcome of the efforts, but who are not parties to the conflict, will assist the parties and me by restraint in word and action, as without this the difficulties would be unnecessarily increased.

Security Council Official Records, Eleventh Year, 722nd Meeting, April 4, 1956.

2. From Press Conference Transcript
NEW YORK   APRIL 5, 1956

THE SECRETARY-GENERAL: Now that your colleagues, the photographers, have tried to find out how I look, you may try to find out what I think. I believe that you are likely to be less successful. I have really said what I feel I should say about the decision taken yesterday by the Security Council and, as a matter of course, this is not the time nor the place for me to go into questions of substance. You saw my statement yesterday in which I indicated that, as I shared the concern about the situation in the Middle East, I felt that I should not hesitate to assume the responsibilities which the Council wished to put on the office of the Secretary-General.

Of course, I would not take that stand unless I felt that something could be done, and that something useful could be done—and I am encouraged by a feeling that this view of mine is shared by the parties. In meeting with you from time to time, I have perhaps disappointed you a little by striking a note which you have characterized as optimistic—I would not perhaps have used that word myself in the same sense—and that note which I have struck reflects the kind of attitude which I now take. It reflects the view that, where there is a will, there is a way—and I do know that there is a will all through the region to which I am going. As to my own intention of putting into the scales, with all possible energy and with all possible devotion to the task of the United Nations, whatever my office and the Secretariat can contribute in help and assistance and advice, I think that you need have no doubts. . . .

QUESTION: Would it help you in your mission if the big powers on both sides, the Western nations and Russia, were to declare a kind of holiday on military help to both sides during this period?

THE SECRETARY-GENERAL: I would not like to be more specific than I was yesterday when I used the phrase you certainly observed asking for restraint on all sides. This is a situation which presents difficulties for

UN Note to Correspondents No. 1265, April 5, 1956.

the parties, and it presents difficulties for me, and I trust the judgment of not only the big powers but all powers in their action and words so that they will try to avoid whatever might render more difficult a task which in itself already presents certain difficulties.

QUESTION: If in your observation in the Middle East you were to conclude that the flow of arms into the area was a basic unsettling factor there, would you feel that it was within the competence of your mission, as you see it, to make recommendations in that regard?

THE SECRETARY-GENERAL: Your question gives me reason to explain perhaps a little bit more fully how I regard my own relationship, as Secretary-General, to the special mission. The special mission, I think, is very clear in its indication of limits. A question of the type you refer to here is outside the field of the mission, undoubtedly. On the other hand, you must not forget that the Secretary-General remains the Secretary-General, and—something quite apart from the Security Council action, where I represent the Security Council—I have, of course, unlimited, my regular right to bring up with governments points which I think are worth consideration because they tend to complicate matters or increase tension. From that point of view—not because of this mandate, but in my regular capacity without anything having been added by the decision yesterday by the Security Council—a problem of the type you indicate is not outside the scope of my interests. To what extent I would consider it appropriate or wise, as Secretary-General, to go into such problems is an entirely different matter.

. . . . QUESTION: You have already hinted partly at this, but I wonder if you might care to enlarge just a little on that part of your statement yesterday to the Council in which you pointed out that the resolution neither limits nor enlarges the scope of the Secretary-General's duties?

THE SECRETARY-GENERAL: I think it is self-explanatory. Part of what I wanted to say I have already repeated here. It is just that it is quite obvious that this is an operation in its own right—a Security Council operation with the Secretary-General as the agent of the Security Council. I keep apart from that the fact that the Secretary-General has duties and rights under the Charter, and they coexist, so to say, with this special request and the mandate which is implied in the request. That is really the main point I had in mind.

The other point which is, I think, rather obvious—I need not emphasize it in any way—is that an exploration by the Secretary-General of this and that situation is something which, in this and that form, happens again and again. There is no need for an authorization for the Secretary-General to undertake such an exploration. On the other hand, of course, it is perfectly proper and, from the point of view of the Secretary-General, most useful if, in a specific case such as this one, there is a formal request to him to undertake such an exploration, because it means that it will be a joint operation where he can speak with the added authority of an implied mandate from the Security Council. Nothing more than that is to be found in my words.

QUESTION: Will you tell us when you come back what proposals you have made to the parties that have been rejected, as well as the ones that have been accepted?

THE SECRETARY-GENERAL: You look very far ahead. Let us hope that all my proposals will be accepted.

QUESTION: There exists, if I may say so, an opinion that if you failed in your mission it would be justifiable to take some action outside the United Nations. Do you think that your mission is some kind of "test" of the United Nations' effectiveness?

THE SECRETARY-GENERAL: No. I am very sorry that, again and again, things which we have to undertake and which I have to try to do myself are regarded as tests of the United Nations. They are not. They may be tests of me, but that is another matter. In this specific case we have been engaged for eight years in a long-haul operation, and certainly there will be quite some time yet before we reach the state of affairs where everybody can feel happy. This is just an episode on the long road. I think that I can trust that that much will be achieved, even if it will not be publicized, which will fully justify the operation, and if that is so I think that the United Nations will have done what the United Nations should do. Failure in the outward sense of the word—I do not see why there should be one, unless you expect dramatic results which are not warranted by anything that has been said or done or intended in this case. Even if there were what you would regard as an outward failure I would be most happy if you would regard it as something which is not in any way sensational in an operation of the kind in which the United Nations is engaged. The United Nations would certainly survive it, and it would not even prove that the United Nations in this specific case is no good, because even an Organization like this one—I say "even an Organization like this one"—cannot work miracles.

QUESTION: Mr. Hammarskjöld, your going to the Middle East is a sort of a climax to many months of expressions of fears that a regional or even global conflict might break out in the area. I want to ask you this difficult question because you never seem to be stumped by difficult questions. Are you going there with any fear in your heart or any apprehension that such a conflict, either regional or global, is possible? Or could it be said that your mere going there already constitutes oil on the troubled waters, that it will have a pacifying influence on the general crisis and hysteria which have marked that situation?

THE SECRETARY-GENERAL: We all know that nobody can foretell the future and nobody can say in what direction a development may turn. I have already indicated how I feel about this problem. I feel that as long as something useful can be done it should be done. As long as that is the case, there is no reason for us to talk in a desperate mood about this and that kind of risk.

I would like to add this. If I believed in the risk, it would add a reason for me to go.

. . . . QUESTION: You spoke of the duties and rights of the Secretary-General as extending beyond the specific scope of the resolution. Do you feel that these duties and rights authorize an effort to explore the possibilities of a settlement of the Palestine refugee problem? If so, do you feel that you would be authorized to include such recommendations in a report to the Security Council?

THE SECRETARY-GENERAL: First of all, do not misunderstand me. I said what I said in explanation of my statement yesterday. I think it is a truism, if anything, that this is a mandate in its own right. Whatever rights the Secretary-General may have would coexist with it. But I do not want you to have any impression that the two things would be mixed in any way. I will not use my mandate here as a vehicle to bring out viewpoints which I may have as Secretary-General in the other capacity. It follows that if I felt that, as Secretary-General, I should go into broader problems or if broader problems are brought up outside the mandate, outside the request of the Security Council, they would not come into the report and they would not be covered by my reply to the Security Council. They belong to the same sphere as all the talks which I have practically daily with the parties or representatives of the parties.

As to the concrete problem of whether or not the Secretary-General should bring those issues up, I think I can give you a very clear reply. What can be done and what should be done within the framework of the Security Council's decision is so important, so urgent, and probably in some respects so time-consuming that I would not like in any sense to muddle the issue by straying into wider fields.

. . . . QUESTION: As we understand it basically, the bread and butter of the mission concerns the armistice agreements—I think that was very well nailed down in almost all clarifying statements in the Council—but at this stage I should like to ask you the question that has perennially come up many years before this climax: Can the armistice agreements be indefinitely prolonged without a basic peace settlement and have any other than tenuous significance for the security of the world?

THE SECRETARY-GENERAL: There are quite a few situations where we must live and learn to live with provisional arrangements, because there is no solution to the long-range problem which we can find overnight. We must simply grow into the solution. In the meanwhile the very best thing you can do is to consolidate and keep clean the lines within the framework of the provisional solution. I think that for the time being if we can get compliance with the armistice agreements in their integrity, we should be quite happy and not too impatient.

. . . .

---

3. Communications Circulated by the President of the Security Council at the Request of the Secretary-General

NEW YORK   APRIL 12, 1956

THE SECRETARY-GENERAL left New York for Rome on his way to the Middle East on April 6. Just before his departure there was a new and serious outbreak of violence in the Gaza area. Egypt accused Israel of shelling cities in the Gaza Strip on April 5, killing several score civilians, including women and children. Israel charged Egyptian units with killing four Israelis by machine gun or mortar fire in a series of prior incidents and declared that Gaza was shelled to silence Egyptian batteries.

In Rome on April 8 Hammarskjöld received from General Burns a cabled

Security Council Official Records, Eleventh Year, Supplement for April-May-June 1956, Document S/3584, April 12, 1956.

report of a conversation earlier that day with Prime Minister David Ben-Gurion of Israel. General Burns reported that Ben-Gurion had requested him to obtain from Prime Minister Nasser of Egypt an unconditional undertaking to observe Article II, paragraph 2 (the cease-fire clause), of the Armistice Agreement (see page 89 for text of this clause). The Secretary-General acted immediately. He cabled requests not only to Nasser for such assurances but also to Ben-Gurion himself, including a pointed reminder to the latter that compliance with the cease-fire clause was incompatible with a policy of retaliation. Ben-Gurion's assurance, with reserves only for reciprocity and self-defense, was handed to General Burns on April 9. Hammarskjöld flew to Cairo on April 10 for talks with Nasser and Foreign Minister Mahmoud Fawzi and obtained Egypt's corresponding pledge.

The Secretary-General put on record with both governments his understanding that the reserves for self-defense had to be in conformity with the cease-fire clause. Hammarskjöld then cabled the texts of these exchanges to the President of the Security Council for immediate circulation and publication, thus nailing down the key commitments he had secured at the very beginning of his mission. The texts follow.

1. *Letter from the Secretary-General to the Prime Minister of Israel—Rome, April 8, 1956*

I have received General Burns' report on his conversation with you on Sunday at 16.00 h. I note that you requested him to obtain from the Prime Minister of Egypt an unconditional undertaking to observe Article II, paragraph 2, of the General Armistice Agreement in its entirety.

Endorsing such a request from General Burns to the Government of Egypt, I must, in the light of the most recent developments and several preceding occurrences, address the same request to the Government of Israel. I do so also under my recent mandate from the Security Council. You are undoubtedly aware of the limits this paragraph of the said article puts on your freedom of action.

Changing my previous plans, I count now on arriving in Lydda Tuesday morning at 10.00 h., intending to spend some time in Tel Aviv for an exchange of views with General Burns. If possible, he should go with me to Cairo the same afternoon. Under other circumstances we will have to consider what further United Nations action should be taken.

I am personally informing Ambassador Lodge, as President of the Security Council, about these latest developments.

DAG HAMMARSKJÖLD
Secretary-General

2. Letter from the Secretary-General to the Prime Minister of Egypt—Rome, April 8, 1956

I learn that General Burns has requested the Government of Egypt to give an undertaking to observe Article II, paragraph 2, of the General Armistice Agreement in its entirety. Deeply disturbed by the most recent developments in the Gaza area which, unless brought under control, may lead to a breakdown of the armistice; and concerned also about the impact on joint efforts to reduce tension along the demarcation lines, I wish to draw your attention to the vital need of breaking the present chain of actions and reactions. For that reason, strongly endorsing General Burns' stand, I address to the Government of Egypt, as I am simultaneously doing to the Government of Israel, a request for strict compliance with paragraph 2 of the said article.

With a change of my plans I now intend to arrive in Cairo Tuesday night, after a stop-over in Lydda, where I hope to pick up General Burns.

In view of the recent Security Council decision, I am informing personally Ambassador Lodge, as President of the Security Council, about these latest developments.

DAG HAMMARSKJÖLD
Secretary-General

3. Reply from the Prime Minister of Israel to the Chief of Staff of the United Nations Truce Supervision Organization— Jerusalem, April 9, 1956

Further to our conversation today, the following is the Prime Minister's reply to your letter of April 9, 1956, enclosing the Secretary-General's letter to the Prime Minister, dated April 8, 1956.

We agree unconditionally to comply fully with the provisions of Article II, paragraph 2, of the Israel-Egyptian General Armistice Agreement, it being understood that Egypt will do likewise. As I stated in my conversation with General Burns yesterday, if Egypt does not comply with Article II, paragraph 2, and continues her warlike acts against Israel, we must reserve our freedom to act in self-defence.

Y. TEKOAH
Director of Armistice Affairs

4. *Aide-mémoire from the Government of Egypt to the Secretary-General—Cairo, April 11, 1956*

The Government of Egypt, while reserving the right of self-defence as stipulated in the Charter of the United Nations, reiterate the expression of their unconditional acceptance of Article II, paragraph 2, of the Egyptian-Israel Armistice Agreement.

5. *Extract from Aide-mémoire from the Secretary-General to the Prime Minister of Israel—Tel Aviv, April 10, 1956*

The Secretary-General expresses his gratitude for the reply he has received to his recent message to Mr. Ben-Gurion. He notes that the Government of Israel reserves its freedom to act in self-defence. He understands that that reservation does in no way detract from the unconditional undertaking to observe Article II, paragraph 2, of the General Armistice Agreement, and that, therefore, the words "in self-defence" have to be interpreted in conformity with the stipulations of the said paragraph.

6. *Aide-mémoire from the Secretary-General to the Prime Minister of Egypt—Cairo, April 11, 1956*

The Secretary-General notes with appreciation the statement of the Government of Egypt. He notes that the Government of Egypt reserves the rights to self-defence as stipulated in the Charter of the United Nations and he understands that that reservation does in no way detract from the unconditional undertaking to observe Article II, paragraph 2, of the General Armistice Agreement and that, therefore, the words "in self-defence" have to be interpreted in conformity with the stipulations of the said paragraph and the Charter of the United Nations.

BEFORE LEAVING Cairo on April 14 the Secretary-General secured assurances from the Egyptian government that orders would be issued to its forces in the Gaza area prohibiting shooting across or crossing of the armistice demarcation line, or permitting patrols to approach the line. Israel sent assurances only on the last point. There had been new infiltration incidents costing several Israeli lives. Ben-Gurion and his Foreign Minister Moshe

Sharett sent messages questioning the worth of Egypt's assurances and also requesting the Secretary-General to take up the closing of the Suez Canal to Israeli ships, a question Hammarskjöld considered outside his Security Council mandate (see page 108). The Secretary-General pointed out that orders to the troops to carry into effect the new cease-fire pledges required mutuality of timing, but Ben-Gurion preferred to wait until Hammarskjöld came to Jerusalem for talks with him on April 17 and 18. The cease-fire agreement was then cemented and the following statement issued on April 19:

> At the request of the Secretary-General of the United Nations, the Governments of Israel and Egypt have notified him that as of 6 P.M., April 18, and from that time on, orders are in force to the effect that in implementation of assurances to observe Article II, paragraph 2 of the Armistice Agreement, no military or paramilitary forces, including non-regular forces, may shoot across the demarcation line or pass over that line for any purpose whatsoever.[1]

---

4. Letter from the Secretary-General to the President of the Security Council

JERUSALEM   MAY 2, 1956

DURING HIS Middle East mission the Secretary-General used Beirut, headquarters of the UN Relief and Works Agency for Palestine Refugees, as his base of operations. After his talks in Cairo and Jerusalem he shuttled back and forth among Beirut and Damascus, Amman, Jerusalem and Cairo. From Lebanon, Syria, and Jordan on the one side and Israel on the other he secured cease-fire commitments similar to those between Egypt and Israel but he was unable to complete his negotiations until May 3. Since the Security Council had requested a report in a month's time he sent the progress report that follows, in the form of a letter to the President of the Council. (Ambassador Josa Brilej of Yugoslavia had succeeded Ambassador Lodge for the month of May.) His final report followed on May 9.

Security Council Official Records, Eleventh Year, Supplement for April-May-June 1956, Document S/3594.

[1] UN Note to Correspondents No. 1282, April 19, 1956.

The Security Council resolution of April 4, 1956 on the Palestine question (S/3575) requested the Secretary-General to report to the Council in his discretion but not later than one month from the date of the resolution on the implementation given to the resolution.

On April 6 I left for the Middle East for consultations with the governments concerned on the questions raised in the Security Council resolution. My discussions have been going on since arrival in the region and will not be concluded until May 3. As under such circumstances it is not possible for me to complete my report by the date set, I would ask you to circulate to the members of the Security Council this letter as a progress report explaining my approach to the assignment and giving the reasons for the delay in my final report, which I hope to submit in the course of next week.

The Security Council requested the Secretary-General to undertake a survey of the various aspects of enforcement of and compliance with the four general armistice agreements and the Council's resolutions under reference in the resolution of April 4. The Council further requested the Secretary-General to arrange with the parties for the adoption of any measures which, after discussion with the parties and the Chief of Staff, he considered would reduce existing tensions along the armistice demarcation lines. Thus, the scope of the Security Council resolution was set by the general armistice agreements and certain previous resolutions under reference. The aim of the Security Council action was, on the one hand, to get a picture of the state of compliance, and, on the other, to further the adoption of certain local arrangements in support of compliance.

In carrying out my mandate, I have stayed strictly within the scope set by the Security Council resolution. I have considered it appropriate to give the aim of the resolution an interpretation according to which I should not merely survey and report on the state of compliance which existed at the time of my arrival in the region, but also try to get the parties to re-establish compliance to the greatest extent possible. Thus I have felt free to read into the Security Council resolution a mandate to negotiate for such re-establishment of compliance. In that spirit, I have regarded the question of local arrangements as subordinate to the general effort. I have submitted proposals for such specific arrangements as could serve to support and protect the degree of compliance achieved.

I have considered the basic clauses of the general armistice agreements to be those which establish a general cease-fire. It has, to me, been obvious that no measures for establishing full compliance with procedural or substantive clauses of the general armistice agreements would be fruitful and lasting unless firmly anchored in a reaffirmation of the duty of all parties concerned to observe a cease-fire.

You have already circulated documents indicating that, at an early stage, I received such assurances from the governments of Egypt and Israel. These reciprocal assurances served to relieve the threatening situation in the Gaza area, where conditions have since considerably improved as a result of strict orders issued by the two governments. I have already informed you that I received notification that such orders were in force as of 18.00 h., on April 18, 1956, and from that time on.

Negotiations for similar reciprocal assurances unconditionally to observe a cease-fire, with a reservation as to self-defence, have been conducted with the parties to the other three armistice agreements. The negotiations have in all cases been concluded with positive results. The texts of the messages exchanged will be annexed to my final report.

I wish to draw attention to the difference in character between previous cease-fires, which have been established locally, or between military commanders, and a cease-fire of the character envisaged in my negotiations. The cease-fire I have aimed at under my mandate from the Security Council is one governed by a reaffirmation by the governments, given to the United Nations, to comply unconditionally with the fundamental clause of the various armistice agreements and establishes anew the legal situation on which the armistice régime was to be founded. It furthermore expresses a recognition in this particular situation of the obligation to observe a fundamental principle of the United Nations Charter.

With the intended background of such reaffirmations of a cease-fire covering the whole region, I have studied with the Governments concerned the possibility of re-establishing full compliance with the various other clauses of the general armistice agreements. The wish to reach such full compliance has been shared by all parties. The problems presenting themselves have been of three main kinds. One is the difficulty of maintaining a balance between the remedial action required of one party and that required of the other in a gradual approach to full compliance. Another difficulty arises from the necessary and natural relation in time between the reestablishment of compliance with the several clauses. Other difficulties have their origin in differences of opinion as to the interpretation of various obligations, or their mutual relationship.

As a third stage in the approach to the task set by the Council for the Secretary-General, I have, together with the Chief of Staff, Major-General Burns, put before the governments proposals for local arrangements within the framework of the armistice agreements and the relevant Security Council resolutions. In important cases agreement has been reached with the parties concerned. In other cases negotiations are still continuing. In still other cases the final decisions should be postponed.

Finally, I have considered the problem of possible procedural measures aiming at the strengthening of the legal framework for the armistice régime established by the four agreements.

The wide field of study and consultation resulting from my interpretation of the aim of the Security Council mandate, and the difficulties of several of the problems, together with the fact that no less than five member nations are party to the consultations, explain why these have been more time-consuming than anticipated. A further reason why it has proved impossible fully to observe the time limit set by the Security Council has been the need first of all to try to stop the dangerous developments which dominated the situation in the region on my arrival.

5. *Statement at Idlewild Airport on His Return from the Middle East*

NEW YORK   MAY 6, 1956

The assignment from which I return is so far unique in the development of the United Nations. It is for others to evaluate the result, and only the future can show what, thanks to the goodwill of the governments concerned, may grow out of it. However—and that I want to stress— the assignment has shown that the United Nations can be directly helpful to Member governments in their wish to reestablish order and maintain peace; helpful, not by imposing its will, but by bringing out what is common ground for agreement to the parties in a conflict and

UN Press Release SG/478, May 6, 1956.

crystallizing it in a way which gives the governments a firm point from which they can move forward.

---

6. Report to the Security Council Pursuant to the Council's Resolution of April 4, 1956, on the Palestine Question

NEW YORK   MAY 9, 1956

The text of the Secretary-General's report to the Security Council is given below in full, with the exception of the annexes. The first four of these consisted of the cease-fire correspondence between the Secretary-General and the governments of Israel, Lebanon, Syria, and Jordan and followed the pattern established in the Secretary-General's earlier correspondence with Egypt and Israel given on pages 76–80. The next three annexes were memoranda from General Burns to the Secretary-General on the El Auja demilitarized zone, complaints by Israel against Jordan and by Syria against Israel. The final annex consisted of notes on the status of compliance with the Security Council's resolutions of March 30, 1955, September 8, 1955, and January 19, 1956. All are included in the Security Council Official Records, Eleventh Year, Supplement for April-May-June 1956.

I. The Security Council Resolution, April 4, 1956

1. The terms of my mandate are set forth in the Security Council resolution of April 4, 1956 (S/3575) which makes reference to the resolutions of March 30, 1955, of September 8, 1955, and of January 19, 1956. Also of basic importance is the resolution of August 11, 1949 which took note of the coming into effect of the armistice agreements between the parties concerned in the Palestine conflict and reaffirmed the cease-fire order under Article 40 of the Charter contained in the Security Council's resolution of July 15, 1948. The resolution of August

Security Council Official Records, Eleventh Year, Supplement for April-May-June 1956, Document S/3596.

11, 1949 constitutes the legal basis for the functions of the United Nations Truce Supervision Organization and the Chief of Staff in relation to the cease-fire order. In pursuance of my mandate, I have taken account of this resolution for the reasons and in the manner explained later in this report.

2. The Security Council resolution of April 4, 1956 which set forth the terms of my mandate is as follows: [For the text of this resolution see page 69.—EDITORS]

3. The resolution of March 30, 1955 requested the Chief of Staff to continue his consultations with the Governments of Egypt and Israel with a view to the introduction of practical measures to preserve security in the area of the armistice demarcation line between Egypt and Israel. It also called upon the Governments of Egypt and Israel to cooperate with the Chief of Staff with regard to his proposals, bearing in mind that in the opinion of the Chief of Staff infiltration could be reduced to an occasional nuisance if the agreement were effected between the parties along the lines he had proposed.

4. In its resolution of September 8, 1955, the Security Council called upon both parties to the Egypt-Israel General Armistice Agreement to take all necessary steps to bring about order and tranquillity and, in particular, to desist from further acts of violence. It endorsed the view of the Chief of Staff that the armed forces of both parties should be clearly and effectively separated by measures such as those which he had proposed. It declared that freedom of movement must be afforded to United Nations observers in the area to enable them to fulfill their functions. It called upon both parties to appoint representatives to meet with the Chief of Staff and to cooperate fully with him to these ends, and it requested the Chief of Staff to report to the Security Council on the action taken to carry out the resolution.

5. In its resolution of January 19, 1956, the Security Council called upon the Government of Israel to comply in future with its obligations under the cease-fire provisions of the resolution of July 15, 1948 under the terms of the General Armistice Agreement between Israel and Syria and under the Charter. It called upon both parties to the General Armistice Agreement between Israel and Syria to comply with the obligations under Article V of the General Armistice Agreement, to respect the armistice demarcation line and the demilitarized zone defined therein. It also requested the Chief of Staff to pursue his suggestions for improving the situation in the area of Lake Tiberias without prejudice

to the rights, claims, and positions of the parties and to report to the Council as appropriate on the success of his efforts. It called upon the parties to arrange with the Chief of Staff for an immediate exchange of all military prisoners and also called upon them to cooperate with the Chief of Staff in this and all other respects to carry out the provisions of the General Armistice Agreement in good faith, and in particular to make full use of the Mixed Armistice Commission's machinery in the interpretation and application of its provisions.

6. In its resolution of August 11, 1949, the Security Council took note with satisfaction of the conclusion of the armistice agreements between the parties to the Palestine conflict. While finding that the armistice agreements constitute an important step toward the establishment of permanent peace in Palestine, the Security Council at the same time reaffirmed, pending the final peace settlement, "the order contained in its resolution of July 15, 1948 to the governments and authorities concerned, pursuant to Article 40 of the Charter of the United Nations to observe an unconditional cease-fire." It also requested the Secretary-General "to arrange for the continued service of such of the personnel of the present Truce Supervision Organization as may be required in observing and maintaining the cease-fire, and as may be necessary in assisting the parties to the armistice agreements in the supervision of the application and observance of the terms of those agreements." It further requested the Chief of Staff of the Truce Supervision Organization to report to the Security Council on the observance of the cease-fire in Palestine. Notes on previous compliance with the Security Council resolutions of March 30, 1955, September 8, 1955, and January 19, 1956, are annexed to this report (annex 8).

II. General Observations

7. In the Security Council resolution of April 4, 1956, operative paragraph 1 requests the Secretary-General to undertake, as a matter of urgent concern, a survey of the various aspects of enforcement of and compliance with the four general armistice agreements and the Council's resolutions under reference in the resolution. In operative paragraph 4, the Secretary-General is further requested to report to the Council on the implementation given to the resolution.

8. In fulfillment of the Security Council request, I have, during visits to the countries concerned, from April 10 to May 3, 1956, explored

the current situation. In a letter to the President of the Security Council, May 2, 1956 (S/3594), I have given an interim report, mainly explaining how I have interpreted the scope and aim of the resolution of April 4, 1956, and how I have approached my task.

9. My talks with the governments concerned have, without exception, been conducted on the basis of agreement that their purpose was to explore the possibility of reestablishing the full implementation of the armistice agreements. It should follow that the cause for the present state of noncompliance is not to be found in an unwillingness on the side of the governments to carry out their obligations under the various agreements.

10. The disquieting situation which prevailed when the Security Council adopted its resolution, and which was characterized by widespread noncompliance with the stipulations of the agreements, both by standing departures from the agreed rules and by temporary infringements of those rules, is in the first place explained by political and practical circumstances. However, uncertainty as to the scope of the obligations has also played a part.

11. The development in the area which, step by step, has led to the situation prevailing until now, has in its political and practical aspects often been considered by the Council. There is no reason here to recapitulate the various stages or incidents in the history. However, attention should be drawn to some circumstances, without which this development cannot be fully understood.

12. The demarcation lines established by the armistice agreements were based on the existing truce lines. They had, in many cases, no basis in history or in the distribution of population or private property. They had to be observed in a situation of great political tension, coloured by the memories of conflict. When in such a situation people from the two sides of the demarcation lines, whether civilians or military, were brought in close contact, frictions had to be foreseen. As incidents continued and their frequency increased this, together with the strained political atmosphere, tended to give the individual occurrences wider implications than certainly in most cases were justified. The development led to explosions, sometimes of great bitterness and causing great suffering. Thus, a chain of actions and reactions was created which, unless broken, is bound finally to constitute a threat to peace and security.

13. The development could have taken another turn, if the government and citizens of one country had felt able to assume that transgres-

sors from the other country—in violation of the provisions of the armistice agreement—had acted without any instigation or approval by the authorities and that the authorities had taken active countermeasures, including appropriate punishment for transgressions. No reason would then have existed for acts of reprisal which might be considered by the country taking action as acts in self-defence: instead, a complaint to the other party would have been the natural outlet for reactions.

14. This last pattern is obviously the new state of affairs towards which any effort to reestablish the full and integral implementation of the armistice agreements must aim. The target can be reached on two conditions: the first one being the reestablishment, as a starting point for a new development, of full compliance with the armistice agreements; the second being efforts towards an improvement of the general political relations between the parties concerned and, thereby, the creation of a spirit of less distrust. In both these respects, the United Nations has a contribution to make, not only at the initial stage but also by the continued assistance it can render to Member governments in order to facilitate compliance with the relevant rules and in putting prevailing general conflicts under the discipline of the armistice agreements and the United Nations Charter.

15. I have already indicated that some uncertainty concerning the scope of the obligations of the armistice agreements has, in my view, served to contribute to the unfortunate development. I consider it essential that in the present effort of the Security Council this uncertainty be, to all possible extent, eliminated. It has therefore formed a necessary part of my study.

16. As a matter of course, each party considers its compliance with the stipulations of an armistice agreement as conditioned by compliance of the other party to the agreement. Should such a stand be given the interpretation that any one infringement of the provisions of the agreement by one party justifies reactions by the other party which, in their turn, are breaches of the armistice agreement, without any limitation as to the field within which reciprocity is considered to prevail, it would in fact mean that the armistice régime could be nullified by a single infringement by one of the parties. Although such an interpretation has never been given from responsible quarters, it appears to me that a lack of clarity has prevailed. From no side has it been said that a breach of an armistice agreement, to whatever clause it may refer, gives the other party a free hand concerning the agreement as a whole; but a tendency

to regard the agreements, including the cease-fire clauses, as entities may explain a feeling that in fact, due to infringements of this or that clause, the obligations are no longer in a strict sense fully binding, and specifically that a breach of one of the clauses, other than the cease-fire clause, may justify action in contravention of that clause.

17. Obviously, therefore, the question of reciprocity must be given serious consideration and full clarity sought. The point of greatest significance in this context is: to what extent can an infringement of one or several of the other clauses of an armistice agreement by one party be considered as entitling the other party to act against the cease-fire clause which is to be found in all the armistice agreements [1] and which, in the Egypt-Israel Armistice Agreement, reads as follows:

No element of the land, sea, or air military or paramilitary forces of either party, including nonregular forces, shall commit any warlike or hostile act against the military or paramilitary forces of the other party, or against civilians in territory under the control of that party; or shall advance beyond or pass over for any purpose whatsoever the armistice demarcation line set forth in Article VI of this Agreement except as provided in Article III of this Agreement; and elsewhere shall not violate the international frontier; or enter into or pass through the air space of the other party or through the waters within three miles of the coastline of the other party.[2]

18. The very logic of the armistice agreements shows that infringements of other articles cannot serve as a justification for an infringement of the cease-fire article. If that were not recognized, it would mean that any one of such infringements might not only nullify the armistice régime, but in fact, put in jeopardy the cease-fire itself. For that reason alone, it is clear that compliance with the said article can be conditioned only by similar compliance of the other party.

19. The stand that the cease-fire article can be conditioned only by reciprocity so far as it concerns the implementation of the same article and that, thus, the cease-fire is a stipulation in the Agreement independent of the other articles, is supported by the fact that it restates an obligation on all Members of the United Nations whose position in this respect can in no way have been changed by the Armistice Agreement; that, further, the article only states, though in more clear terms, the

[1] Article II, paragraph 2, of the General Armistice Agreement between Egypt and Israel, and Article III, paragraph 2, of the General Armistice Agreements between Israel and Jordan, Israel and Lebanon, and Israel and Syria.

[2] See Security Council Official Records, Fourth Year, Special Supplement No. 3, or United Nations Treaty Series, Volume 42, 1949.

reaffirmation by the Security Council, in its resolution of August 11, 1949, of the order contained in its resolution of July 15, 1948, to the governments and authorities concerned to observe an unconditional cease-fire; and, finally, that in the various agreements the said stipulation is eliminated from the field where the agreements can be changed by mutual consent.

20. It should be stressed that the Security Council's reaffirmation of the cease-fire order in the resolution of August 11, 1949, followed the "noting" by the Security Council, in the same resolution, of the conclusion of the several armistice agreements and thus co-exists with the armistice agreements; from this it follows that even if it were not to be recognized that the said clause has an independent status in the armistice agreements and cannot be conditioned by reciprocity as concerns compliance with other clauses, the parties to the agreements, in accordance with the Security Council decision of August 11, 1949, would nevertheless be under the substantive obligation contained in that clause.

21. As reported already in my letter to the President of the Security Council, May 2, 1956, I have, in my contacts with the governments concerned, asked them for their assurance that they will observe the obligations under the said clause unconditionally, provided the other party complies with that same clause, reserving only their right to self-defence under Article 51 of the Charter. The messages exchanged as a result of this initiative have, in the case of the General Armistice Agreement between Egypt and Israel, already been circulated under the symbol S/3584. The messages exchanged concerning the other three armistice agreements will be annexed to this report. I refer to the next section for my observations on the result achieved.

22. With an agreement with all parties that the target for the present effort should be general and full compliance with the armistice agreements in their entirety, and with, further, the acceptance of the cease-fire clauses as establishing independent obligations within the framework of the various agreements, a basis was laid for a study of how best to arrange for a balanced return to the full implementation of other clauses, and—through that process and thereafter—how best to protect compliance. Later in this report, I shall revert to the specific problems to which consideration of these two questions gives rise. In this introductory part I wish, however, first to treat two other subjects of general significance.

23. In the Security Council resolution of August 11, 1949, to which

reference has already been made, the Security Council requested the Secretary-General to arrange for the continued service of such of the personnel of the then already established Truce Supervision Organization as might be required in observing and maintaining the cease-fire, and as might be necessary in assisting the parties to the armistice agreements in the supervision of the application and observance of the terms of those agreements.

24. This decision of the Security Council, in the resolution in which the Council took note of the armistice agreements, establishes the Truce Supervision Organization as having a position independent of the armistice agreements, with the positive task of helping in continued observation and maintenance of the cease-fire. At the same time, however, the observers of the Truce Supervision Organization are requested to serve the mixed armistice commissions as provided in the armistice agreements.

25. In the later development, some confusion has arisen concerning both the status of the Truce Supervision Organization and its functions. A tendency has emerged to regard the United Nations observers, serving in that Organization, merely as impartial investigators charged with the task of presenting the mixed armistice commissions with reports on facts, in cases in which complaints had been made to the commissions. This tendency obviously represents a departure from the legal stand taken by the Security Council in two respects. It subordinates the Truce Supervision Organization exclusively to the mixed armistice commissions, and it limits, or eliminates, the function which the observers should fulfill in protecting, together with the authorities concerned, compliance with the cease-fire clauses of the armistice agreements by the prevention of incidents.

26. The question has been studied with all the governments concerned. As a result, they have all stated that, on the basis of the general armistice agreements and the Security Council resolution of August 11, 1949, it is their intention to consider favourably proposals by the Chief of Staff of the United Nations Truce Supervision Organization concerning the activities of the observers aiming at facilitating compliance with the general armistice agreements.

27. This stand, which recognizes the observer organization as, in its essential functions in relation to the cease-fire, based on the resolution of the Security Council of August 11, 1949, and which promises full cooperation with the organization in its positive and preventive task of

facilitating compliance, should render possible such freedom of action and movement for the observers as lies, in my view, within the terms of the general armistice agreements and Security Council decisions. It is my opinion that, given the good will of the parties, this freedom should prove sufficient for the proper functioning of the Truce Supervision Organization.

28. In specific cases and for specific regions, concrete and detailed arrangements must supplement the general statements just referred to. Such arrangements have been agreed upon with the governments concerned. An account of the substance of those agreements will be given later in this report.

29. The Security Council, in its resolution of April 4, 1956, referring to special arrangements for easing the tension along the demarcation lines, mentioned not only "freedom of movement" for observers along the demarcation lines, in the demilitarized zone and in the defensive areas, but also "local arrangements" and "withdrawal of their forces" from the armistice demarcation lines.

30. A withdrawal of troops, to the extent that it would not follow from compliance with explicit stipulations in the armistice agreements, may serve a useful purpose in special sectors along the demarcation lines, and from that viewpoint represents a special type of local arrangements. It has been agreed with the governments concerned that they will favourably consider proposals by the Chief of Staff of the United Nations Truce Supervision Organization for local arrangements —including separation of forces—where and when he considers such arrangements to be called for.

31. The framework for various kinds of local arrangements established already by previous proposals from the Chief of Staff and decisions in the Security Council has been discussed. Apart from a local separation of the parties' forces in the field, it covers the following possible measures:

(a) Erection of physical obstacles;

(b) Marking of demarcation lines and international frontiers;

(c) Local commanders' agreements;

(d) Joint patrols.

32. The governments concerned have declared that they have no objection in principle to any of these measures, reserving their right for a final decision if and when concrete proposals in case of need are made by the Chief of Staff.

III. The Cease-Fire

33. As appears from documents already circulated, the governments of Egypt and Israel gave unconditional assurances to observe a cease-fire—under the terms of Article II, paragraph 2, of the Egypt-Israel General Armistice Agreement, with a reserve only as to self-defence—at a stage when these assurances gave a basis for strict orders which served to relieve the situation along the Gaza armistice demarcation line. The orders—of which I was notified April 18, 1956—were not limited to that specific situation or any specific area. Nor were they qualified either by requests for compliance by the other party with any other clauses of the Armistice Agreement, or by requests for certain measures by the other party based on the agreements or for compliance with resolutions of the General Assembly or the Security Council, relating to the Agreement.

34. In negotiating with the governments parties to the general armistice agreements between Jordan and Israel, Lebanon and Israel, and Syria and Israel, I have presented the reasons for a separate treatment of the cease-fire clause given in the previous section of this report, and requested the governments for unconditional assurances, identical to the one given by Egypt.

35. At the end of my conversations with the Government of Jordan, in Amman, Mr. Samir Rifa'i, Prime Minister of Jordan, April 26, 1956, agreed on behalf of the Government of Jordan to the requested assurance, as well as on several other points raised by me, subject to confirmation after report to the appropriate authorities. I received such confirmation by letter, dated April 29. The letter from Mr. Rifa'i and my reply are annexed to this report (annex 1).

36. At the end of my conversations in Beirut, Mr. Lahoud, Foreign Minister of Lebanon, gave me orally on April 27, 1956, on behalf of the Lebanese Government, the requested assurance, to be put formally on record in a letter to me. I received, in a letter dated May 1 an official declaration from the Government of Lebanon which is annexed to this report together with a covering letter and a letter with general observations. The declaration gives the requested unconditional assurance, with the reserve for self-defence common to all the assurances. It is annexed to this report (annex 2) together with the two other letters mentioned, and my own reply.

37. Finally, at a meeting in Damascus with representatives of the Government of Syria, under the chairmanship of Mr. Ghazzi, Prime Minister of Syria, I received on May 2 the requested assurance from the Government, together with a covering letter indicating the framework within which the action was taken. The declaration, the covering letter, and my reply are annexed to this report (annex 3).

38. From the Government of Israel I received the required cease-fire assurances relating to the armistice agreements between Israel, on the one side, and Jordan, Lebanon, and Syria on the other side, by letters April 26, 1956. The assurances were, after receipt of the replies from the three last-mentioned nations, repeated in a letter of May 3, 1956. This letter and my reply are annexed to the report (annex 4).

39. In my contacts with the governments I made it clear that the giving of an unconditional assurance could not be subject to any condition without contradiction of the very declaration itself. As the declaration is the legally decisive document, no conditions for compliance with the assurance can be established or recognized, which are not covered by the text of the assurance.

40. The assurances, given to me as representative of the Security Council by the several Member states concerned, are all given within the general framework of the Charter. I have obviously considered compliance with the provisions of the Charter as a basic assumption for the discussion which did not need any explicit confirmation. The immediate relation between the assurances and the Charter is established by the reserve for self-defence to be found in all the assurances. This reserve is the only restriction on the unconditional nature of the assurances put by the text of the declarations and, therefore, the only link through which compliance with the various articles of the Charter can constitute a condition for the validity of the cease-fire assurances. In other words, a party which has given an unconditional assurance to observe the cease-fire clause, with reserve only as to self-defence under the Charter, is covered by its reserve for self-defence in cases of noncompliance by the other party with its obligations under the Charter, or under the Armistice Agreement, only if and when such noncompliance is found to be a reason for the exertion of the right of self-defence as recognized in Article 51 of the Charter. The Security Council alone can decide whether this is the case or not. The reserve for self-defence in the several cease-fire assurances and the significance it may give to compliance with the Charter, other clauses in the Armistice Agreement, or relevant Security

Council decisions, is thus under the sole jurisdiction of the Security Council, in accordance with the rules established.

41. In this context it has been asked what would happen in case of different views between the parties as to the interpretation, or the validity, of the legal obligations established in the Charter, in the armistice agreements, and by Security Council resolutions referring thereto. I have no reason here to go into this question as regards the Charter. I hold that an assurance to comply with the various clauses of the Armistice Agreement implies also an assurance to comply with the results of such authoritative interpretation of the clauses of the Armistice Agreement as may be given under international law, the Charter, or the provisions of the agreements. Finally, I have consistently stated that the Security Council alone, in cases of doubt, can interpret its own resolutions.

42. The messages exchanged concerning the cease-fire, together with the comments given here, should fully clarify the legal situation which has resulted from my request to all the governments concerned to give, unconditionally, cease-fire assurances, with a reserve only for self-defence.

43. In general terms I have described the legal character of the cease-fire I have been aiming at in the interim report, circulated to the Security Council on May 2, 1956 (S/3594). It remains for me to give my comments on where, in my view, we now stand in substance. In doing so I will not attempt any evaluation. Such an evaluation, if made, would have to take into account not only the effect of the cease-fire on current developments but also the significance of the cease-fire as a newly established firm point in the discipline under which these developments should be brought. This significance of the cease-fire, which is to be found on the level of principle and law, cannot be judged solely —or even primarily—in terms of its immediate influence on the situation in the field.

44. I have had to accept reservations as to self-defence, which, according to Article 51 of the Charter is an "inherent right." However, such a reservation is necessarily of an indeterminate nature. As already indicated, its meaning in a concrete situation can be determined only by the Security Council as established in the Charter.

45. The limit set to the effect of the cease-fire assurances by the reservation as to self-defence should, in my view, be so understood as not to bring the reservation into conflict with the substance of the cease-fire

assurances themselves. In my replies to the governments I have thus taken the stand that the reservation could not derogate from the obligations assumed under Article II, paragraph 2, of the General Armistice Agreement between Egypt and Israel, or in Article III, paragraph 2, of the other armistice agreements.

46. This qualification also gives rise to questions which it is difficult to answer in hypothetical cases. However, my interpretation makes it clear that the reservation as to self-defence does not permit acts of retaliation, which repeatedly have been condemned by the Security Council.

47. More important than the legal uncertainties is the dependence of the cease-fire arrangement on the general situation. Strains may develop which will put the arrangement to a test for which the reestablished legal obligations prove too weak. It is first of all a question of the general atmosphere in which the cease-fire is implemented. With fears of attack widely spread among the peoples, even developments without any direct political significance may be so interpreted or release such reactions as to break through the safeguards introduced. I need not go into the question of which actions and events may have such an effect; they are well known from previous developments in the region. Anything which gives the other party a feeling that it is exposed to increased risks may represent a threat to the cease-fire, and any single incident, whatever its background, may, in a situation which is still far from stable, have the same effect.

48. I shall, in the next section, discuss the question of crossings of the demarcation line and acts of violence in connection therewith. In this context I have only to draw attention to the risk they represent, as well as to the well-known fact that the situation prevailing along some parts of the demarcation lines is such that, even with active measures to prevent incidents, they still may happen. It is for that reason that the governments concerned should do all they can to keep the situation under such control as to minimize or eliminate the risk of further incidents. But it is also for the governments, for the public, and for world opinion, to avoid giving such interpretation to incidents as would weaken, without justification, faith in the cease-fire or discredit the goodwill of the other party.

IV. The Question of General Compliance

49. I have already stated that the talks with the governments concerned were, without exception, conducted on the basis of an agreement that their purpose was to explore the possibility of reestablishing full implementation of the armistice agreements. I have received from all governments assurances of their will fully to comply with all clauses of the armistice agreements, on the basis of reciprocity, but recognizing the independent position of the cease-fire clause.

50. It has been made clear that the special assurances given concerning compliance with the cease-fire clauses in no way derogate from the obligation to comply with the other clauses of the armistice agreements. This obvious fact is of special significance in the case of clauses, to be found in several but not all of the armistice agreements, which widen the scope of the cease-fire clauses to cover also occurrences related to but not explicitly covered by those clauses.

51. The general assurance about the will fully to comply with the armistice agreements has been specifically covered in the contacts with the governments of Israel and Egypt, who both have put on record their readiness to observe not only Article II, paragraph 2, but the Armistice Agreement in its entirety and, apart from paragraph 2 of Article II, regarded as an entity.

52. In its declaration that it sees the entire agreement, with the exception of Article II, paragraph 2, as an entity, the Government of Israel has stated that without observance of Article I of the agreement they cannot acknowledge that the Armistice Agreement is observed and that the principle of reciprocity has been maintained.

53. While regarding the Armistice Agreement in the sense indicated as an entity, covered by a general assurance of compliance, the governments of Israel and Egypt have given me specific assurances on two points within the framework of the Armistice Agreement between the two countries. In doing so I understand them not to have wished to give these points an independent status similar or equal to the one recognized for the cease-fire clause. The purpose has been to reenforce the general assurance of compliance on points of high importance.

54. The first point covers cases of crossings of the demarcation line and acts of violence in connection therewith. The second point refers to

the state of standing noncompliance from both sides, which is to be found in the so-called El Auja area and the defensive areas, the status of which is established by Articles VII and VIII of the Armistice Agreement. I will revert to this second point in the next section, but wish here to cover the first one.

55. The development of the cease-fire has drawn attention to the necessity of active measures against all crossings of the demarcation line and acts of violence in connection therewith. If not covered by Article II, paragraph 2, crossings of the line are prohibited in consequence of Article V, paragraph 4, which reads as follows: "Rules and regulations of the armed forces of the parties which prohibit civilians from crossing the fighting lines or entering the area between the lines, shall remain in effect after the signing of this Agreement with application to the armistice demarcation line defined in Article VI." [3]

56. Uncertainty may be felt concerning the exact limits for the application of Article II, paragraph 2, and for the application of Article V, paragraph 4. This uncertainty represents a weakness in the sense that it may be held that cases of the kind I have in mind are not always unequivocally covered by the clauses of the Armistice Agreement, or, specifically, by Article II, paragraph 2. Without raising the legal issues involved I have, in these circumstances, considered it essential to get assurances concerning certain measures essential for the support of the cease-fire.

57. I have, thus, felt that a request should be addressed to the parties for active measures against occurrences which, although they may perhaps not be regarded as in contravention of Article II, paragraph 2, nevertheless must be considered as being in contravention of the spirit of the cease-fire assurance if the government concerned has omitted to take appropriate active steps to prevent them.

58. In reply to my requests, I have received assurances to the said effect from the governments of Egypt and Israel. I consider that the attitudes of the two governments, as clarified through these assurances, provide a basis for the necessary support of the cease-fire by prevention to all possible extent of occurrences at the demarcation lines which might endanger it.

59. I understand the assurances referred to as extending the moral obligations under the cease-fire assurances, if need be, beyond the legal

[3] *Ibid.*

scope of Article II, paragraph 2, in the sense that they involve a recognition of the obligation to take active measures against all crossings of the demarcation line and acts of violence in connection therewith, irrespective of the interpretation given to the explicit provisions of Article II, paragraph 2.

60. The problem to which, in the case of the General Armistice Agreement between Egypt and Israel, I have tried to find a solution in the way just indicated may in the other armistice agreements be considered as covered by Article III, paragraph 3. During my discussions in Amman special attention was given to the implementation of this paragraph. I was assured by the Government of Jordan of its intention to enforce active measures to prevent all crossings of the demarcation line and actions of violence connected therewith.

61. The time sequence between various steps in the direction of full compliance with the armistice agreements has been carefully studied and the main questions arising discussed with the Governments. This problem cannot be solved by any explicit agreements with any two parties because it is essentially a question of coordinated unilateral moves inspired by greater confidence in the possibility of a peaceful development, each of them provoked by and, maybe, provoking similar unilateral moves on the other side. In these circumstances I find it impossible to put on record any specific results of the discussions to which I have referred. Once the cease-fire has proved effective, and as the stands of all sides have been clarified, the road should be open for the achievement of full implementation by related unilateral moves.

62. It may be felt that I should give, in this report, a survey of the various temporary infringements of the several clauses of the armistice agreements which have occurred, as well as of standing cases of noncompliance. I refrain from doing so, although the field has been fully reviewed. In the first place most of the cases of temporary infringements are now brought into a new perspective by the cease-fire arrangements and related settlements; the main cases of real or presumed standing noncompliance are brought to the attention of the Security Council in Parts V and VII of this report. Another reason for not giving a summary of the state of affairs which prevailed when the Security Council adopted its resolution of April 4, 1956, or of later infringements, is that this could be done by me only to a most limited extent without raising questions which are under the jurisdiction of other United Nations organs or organs established by the armistice agreements. Finally I find

that this is the occasion, not for a recapitulation of past failures, but for a constructive forward look from the vantage point reached.

63. In my letter of May 2 to the President I indicated that I had given consideration to procedural questions arising out of a study of the possibilities of supporting full compliance with the armistice agreements.

64. There is not in all cases an adequate functioning machinery for resolving disputes concerning the interpretation, or implementation, of the obligations assumed by the parties under the agreements. Obviously an assurance to comply with the armistice agreements has little practical bearing on the situation to the extent that any party can reserve for itself the right to give to the obligations its own interpretation, which may be different from the one which in good faith is maintained by the other party.

65. A further weakness is that no procedure has been established for the handling of conflicts covered by the general clauses in the armistice agreements. For example, the first article of the several agreements establishes a right to security and freedom from fear of attack. The parties have in many cases complained of actions from the other side as being in conflict with this stipulation. Were diplomatic relations maintained, such complaints would undoubtedly be handled through normal diplomatic channels and might in that way to a large extent be resolved. For cases of this kind which the party may not wish to bring to the Security Council, there is at present no such possibility available within the framework of the armistice régime as applied.

66. I have drawn the attention of the parties to these problems, indicating my conviction that until and unless procedures provided for in the armistice agreements could be put more fully into operation—and perhaps even when that has happened—it would be worth considering whether procedural arrangements could not be elaborated, which would meet the difficulties. I have not found it appropriate or, indeed, been in a position to make any proposals. I have only indicated that I feel that whatever solution may be considered, it is desirable to avoid organizational innovations and to work within the framework of the United Nations. The governments, while taking note of my observations concerning the procedural weaknesses indicated, have not gone further into the matter.

V. Compliance with Articles VII and VIII
of the General Armistice Agreement between Egypt and Israel

67. Article VIII, paragraphs 1 and 2, of the Egypt-Israel General Armistice Agreement establishes a demilitarized zone centred on El Auja and forbids the presence of the armed forces of the parties therein. Israel has had elements of armed forces in the demilitarized zone since the beginning of November 1955, and these at present are of the order of three companies of infantry. The three proposals put forward by the Secretary-General in a letter dated November 3, 1955, which *inter alia* provided for the withdrawal of this force, were accepted in principle by the Government of Israel, but not implemented because Israel took the stand that its national security would be imperilled if it did so while Egypt continued to occupy defensive positions in the area between the line El Quseima–Abu Aweigila and the demilitarized zone in violation of Article VIII, paragraph 3, and also had prohibited arms and an excess of troops in the defensive zone of the western front established by Article VII.

68. Egypt has refused to permit investigation of Israeli complaints to the Mixed Armistice Commission of the violations alleged above, and it may therefore be presumed that the violations in fact exist. In turn Egypt has complained on several occasions of Israeli violations of Article VII, particularly as regards the presence of armoured vehicles and heavy mortars in the defensive zone, which is prohibited.

69. The establishment by Israel of a kibbutz in the demilitarized zone in September 1953 caused the Egyptian government on October 6 of the same year to bring a complaint to the attention of the Security Council charging its establishment as a violation by Israel of Article IV, paragraph 1, and Article VIII of the General Armistice Agreement. At the request of Egypt on February 3, 1954, the Security Council placed upon its agenda an item covering this complaint but the matter has never been discussed.

70. Therefore the position is that both parties are or must be presumed to be, to a greater or lesser extent, violating Articles VII and VIII.

71. I have specific assurances from both sides of their willingness to establish full compliance with Articles VII and VIII, within the frame-

work of a full return to the state of affairs envisaged in the Armistice Agreement. A plan for the reestablishment of compliance with the two articles has been prepared by the Chief of Staff. The plan, which as such has not met with any objections from the governments, is annexed to this report (annex 5).

72. I have found that I should give a high priority to the implementation of the two articles both because of their immediate significance and because of my conviction that a return to the state of affairs they envisage, would be a major contribution in allaying fears of attack now to be found on both sides. I note, however, the view that such implementation has to find its place in relation to other steps in fulfillment of the aims of the Armistice Agreement.

VI. Local Arrangements

A

73. The basic principles and decisions governing the freedom of movement of observers and the status of the United Nations Truce Supervision Organization under the Chief of Staff have been set forth elsewhere in this report. The practical measures now needed to observe and assist compliance with the substantive provisions of the general armistice agreements have been carefully considered by the Chief of Staff who has made a number of proposals which are described below. These proposals are not far-reaching, but in the view of the Chief of Staff, they are adequate if fully implemented, and he has no further proposals to make for the present. After study of the problems involved during my visit to the region, I endorse this view of the Chief of Staff.

74. These proposals of the Chief of Staff have, in considerable measure, been accepted by the governments concerned. They involve, as already indicated, application of the principle of freedom of movement for observers, and local arrangements such as local commanders' agreements, separation of forces and marking of boundaries—all measures endorsed in principle by the Security Council in its resolutions under reference. These measures provide the practical means by which, in given situations, compliance with the basic provisions of the General Armistice Agreement, and in particular of the cease-fire clauses, may be protected and strengthened. The present proposals of the Chief of

Staff are immediately important mainly in three areas, namely along the demarcation line in the Gaza area, the El Auja demilitarized zone and the defensive areas of the western front, and Lake Tiberias.

The Gaza demarcation line

75. In order to observe and assist compliance with the cease-fire assurances along the Gaza demarcation line, arrangements proposed by the Chief of Staff for the establishment of an equal number of fixed United Nations observer posts on each side of the line have been accepted by the governments of Egypt and Israel. The activities of United Nations military observers covered by these arrangements are, of course, additional to those provided for in the general armistice agreements.

76. In accepting this arrangement the Government of Israel set a time limit of six months (until October 31, 1956) for its operation. It is understood, however, that the Government of Israel will consider proposals from the Chief of Staff for the continuance of this arrangement after October 31, if, in his view, the situation at that time calls for it. The Government of Egypt, for its part, sets no time limit on its adherence to the arrangement.

77. The arrangement as negotiated in the terms set out below will be formally adopted in the Mixed Armistice Commission to meet a request of the Government of Israel that the arrangement be tied in with procedure under the General Armistice Agreement.

The arrangement is as follows:

(*a*) The location and number of the observation posts on the Egyptian side of the demarcation line shall be agreed with Egypt and of those on the Israeli side with Israel. There shall be an equal number of observation posts established on each side. It is the intention of the Chief of Staff to arrange for the establishment of six such posts on each side of the line;

(*b*) United Nations observers shall have free access to those positions at any time;

(*c*) If so desired by the party concerned, they shall be accompanied on their way to and during their stay at the observation posts by an officer of the party on whose side of the demarcation line the observation post is situated;

(*d*) Before proceeding to any of the observation posts, the United

Nations observer shall notify the senior Israel (senior Egyptian) delegate, or his representative, to arrange that the party's forces allow passage to the posts;

(*e*) The reports of United Nations observers stationed in observation posts shall cover violations of Article II, paragraph 2, of the General Armistice Agreement, shall be directed to the Mixed Armistice Commission, and shall be used in the examination of complaints in the Commission;

(*f*) The parties shall designate a route which the United Nations observers shall follow to the observation posts;

(*g*) The United Nations Truce Supervision Organization may send patrols along the demarcation line between the observation posts when required, arrangements being made beforehand with senior delegates to the Mixed Armistice Commission. The aforesaid provisions in (*c*), (*d*), (*e*), and (*f*) shall apply to the patrols.

78. As regards proposals for local arrangements in the Gaza area, or outside of it, referred to in paragraph 3 (*c*) of the Security Council resolution of April 4, 1956, their present status and the attitude of the parties towards them is as follows:

(*a*) *Separation of parties' forces in the field*

79. The proposal that the parties should withdraw their armed forces, especially patrols, observation posts, and defensive positions, back from the demarcation line to a distance sufficient to eliminate or greatly reduce provocation which might induce undisciplined individuals to open fire leading to extensive breaches of Article II, paragraph 2, of the General Armistice Agreement has been accepted by Egypt without reservations. The intentions of Israel are understood to be that they would refrain from sending patrols up to the demarcation line except when it proved essential to do so in order to protect agricultural operations of their settlers or to prevent incursions by persons from Egyptian-controlled territory. If supported by an effective observer arrangement, the line taken by Israel may prove adequate, although it falls short of the firmer arrangements proposed by the Chief of Staff and endorsed by the Security Council and by me. Should the line now taken not meet the needs of the situation, I would find it necessary to bring the matter up for new consideration.

(*b*) *Erection of a physical obstacle along the demarcation line*

80. Israel is prepared to consider a proposal for the erection of a physical obstacle along the demarcation line by the Truce Supervision

Organization when and if such a proposal is submitted by the Chief of Staff. Egypt agrees to the erection of obstacles along selected portions of the demarcation line, subject to discussion with the Chief of Staff. In the present circumstances and until the situation has remained stable for a reasonable period, the Chief of Staff does not propose to submit any specific proposals to this end.

(c) *Marking of the demarcation line*

81. Both parties have agreed to the placing by the United Nations Truce Supervision Organization of conspicuous markers along the demarcation line surrounding the Gaza Strip. The Chief of Staff proposes to make a beginning on this work as soon as possible.

(d) *Local commanders' agreement*

82. The negotiations to effect an arrangement including a local commanders' agreement between the parties for maintaining security along the demarcation line of the Gaza Strip have been at a standstill since August 1955. After a sufficient period of tranquillity the Chief of Staff proposes to suggest to the parties that these negotiations be resumed.

(e) *Joint patrols*

83. It does not now appear opportune to establish joint patrols nor does it seem likely that they would be accepted by either party. Moreover, the proposal for joint patrols is in effect superseded by the agreement for the separation of the parties' forces and the agreement to allow United Nations military observers to patrol along the demarcation line accompanied by an officer of the party concerned.

The El Auja demilitarized zone and defensive areas of the western front

84. Proposals for the free movement of United Nations observers for the purpose of certifying compliance with the provisions of Article VII of the Egyptian-Israel General Armistice Agreement were put before the parties. No objections were raised to them and they should go into effect as soon as reciprocal action is taken by both parties to establish compliance with Articles VII and VIII.

Lake Tiberias

85. In order to facilitate compliance with the General Armistice Agreement and with the special arrangements made in regard to the eastern shore of Lake Tiberias, proposals were made both to Syria and to Israel for the placing of fixed observation posts manned by United

Nations observers on the eastern and northeastern shore of the lake. Approximately two such posts would be on Syrian-controlled territory and one in territory controlled by Israel. In addition observers should have the right to move to these posts and to any point where difficulties requiring their intervention might arise in a special United Nations boat.

86. Syria accepted these proposals and, in regard to the movement of a United Nations boat on the lake, expressed the view that as the greater portion of the lake lies in the defensive zone provided for in Article V, paragraph 6, and annex 3 of the General Armistice Agreement,[4] United Nations observers should have complete freedom of movement thereon.

87. Israel does not agree to the movement of a United Nations military observer boat on Lake Tiberias nor to the establishment of a military observer post on Israel territory, considering these measures uncalled for and as derogating from the rights which she claims over the whole extent of the lake and the territory to the north thereof and as far east as the old Palestine-Syrian boundary. Israel would, nevertheless, be prepared, after the lapse of a month, to consider a proposal by the Chief of Staff for the establishment of a United Nations military observer post should he then consider it desirable.

88. I have declared that I find it necessary to maintain the proposal both for a police boat and for a post on Israel territory. Short of these arrangements, I can scarcely find that the patrolling arrangements, mentioned below under (d), provide adequate safeguards.

89. It will be recalled that in its resolution of January 19, 1956, the Security Council endorsed five proposals in regard to Lake Tiberias which had been made by the Chief of Staff. The present status of these proposals is as follows:

(a) The request to refrain from firing in contravention of Article III, paragraph 2, of the Israel-Syrian General Armistice Agreement is covered by the cease-fire assurances referred to earlier in this report.

(b) The Syrian authorities have agreed to prevent the inhabitants of Syria from fishing in the lake pending a solution of the problem of fishing permits. The Israelis have agreed to grant fishing permits to inhabitants of villages in Syria and the demilitarized zone near the lake. As

---

[4] See Security Council Official Records, Fourth Year, Special Supplement No. 2, or United Nations Treaty Series, Volume 42, 1949.

the Israelis hold that they alone can issue permits to fish in the lake, application must be made through the Syrian representative on the Mixed Armistice Commission to the Israeli representative. The Syrian government, on the other hand, considers that permits should be issued by the Chairman of the Mixed Armistice Commission.

(c) The Israeli authorities have agreed not to interfere with the inhabitants of Syria who water their cattle in or draw water from Lake Tiberias, provided that water is drawn for domestic purposes only. The Syrian authorities have agreed not to interfere with Israeli fishing in Lake Tiberias.

(d) Israel has agreed to adopt a policy to keep their police boats back from the eastern shore of the lake, except when it is necessary to approach it "for security purposes." I understand this latter phrase to refer only to measures for the preservation of order and the protection of Israeli fishermen. As to my evaluation of the stated Israeli patrolling policy on Lake Tiberias, I refer to my observations on the corresponding problem in the Gaza area.

B

90. In other areas, the Chief of Staff does not at present propose to suggest to the parties that they put into effect any special arrangements of the type referred to in connection with Gaza and Lake Tiberias, with the one exception that a local commanders' agreement should be negotiated between Jordan and Israel. Negotiations to establish such local commanders' agreements covering the whole of the demarcation line between Jordan and Israel reached an advanced stage in the autumn of 1955. No agreement was reached, however, because of differences in view on a clause specifying that when desired by either party a United Nations observer should be present at meetings between local commanders and area commanders of the two parties. Both the parties concerned have now signified, however, that they are prepared to agree to a clause worded in the above sense. The Chief of Staff consequently proposes to invite the parties to resume negotiations in the near future.

C

91. Apart from the special arrangements for the establishment of fixed observation posts and for the free movement of United Nations

observers referred to in relation to the El Auja, Gaza, and Lake Tiberias areas, it was proposed to all five governments concerned that in implementation of the recognition of the status and functions of the Chief of Staff and observers, a specific assurance should be given that the principle of freedom of movement within the relevant areas should be freely recognized. Such assurances were given by Egypt, Jordan, Syria, and Lebanon. The position of the Government of Israel is that they will continue to afford to United Nations observers the same degree of freedom of movement inside Israel which all residents or visitors to Israel normally enjoy, and also such freedom of movement as may be required in respect to specific posts and patrols around the Gaza area referred to above.

VII. Special Questions

92. In letters to the Secretary-General of April 13 and 14, 1956, circulated as Security Council Document S/3587 of April 16, 1956, the Government of Israel raised the question of the Egyptian interference with Israeli shipping through the Suez Canal as treated by the Security Council in a resolution of September 1, 1951.[5] In the discussion the viewpoint expressed in the letters was elaborated and attention drawn also to interference in the Straits of Tiran.

93. My attitude has been that the Suez question as adjudicated by the Security Council, is not a question of compliance with the Armistice Agreement in the sense of my mandate. For that reason I have not, within the framework of my mandate, discussed the issue with the Egyptian government. For the same reason I have found that I should not in this report evaluate the legal reasons presented by Israel in support of the view that the blockade represents a case of standing noncompliance with Article I of the Armistice Agreement.

94. My mandate, as evidenced also by the choice of previous Security Council resolutions to which reference is made in the resolution of April 4, 1956, is directly concerned with the state of tension along the armistice demarcation lines and the state of compliance or noncompliance with the armistice agreements as a cause of such tension. In an approach looking beyond the immediate problems which, as I understand the resolution of April 4, 1956, the Security Council had in mind, it is

---

[5] Security Council Resolution 95 (1951).

obvious that the question raised by the Government of Israel should come under consideration in the light of the Council's finding in its resolution of September 1, 1951, that the blockade is incompatible with the armistice régime, as this régime put an end to a state in which Egypt could avail itself of belligerent rights.

95. In the letters with which the governments of Jordan and Lebanon transmitted their cease-fire assurances, they called attention to the Jordan River diversion scheme of Israel, repeatedly discussed at an earlier stage by the Security Council.

96. A judgment on legal grounds about the question raised by the governments of Jordan and Lebanon has to take into consideration the status of the demilitarized zone as established by Article V in the General Armistice Agreement between Syria and Israel, the effect of the diversion scheme in the light of the rules relevant to the demilitarized zone as interpreted by the Chief of Staff, and, finally, the situation created by the Security Council resolution of October 27, 1953.[6]

97. Under these circumstances I have found that my formal stand under the terms of my mandate must be to request the parties to abide by decisions concerning the matter taken by the Security Council or under the armistice agreements, and as indicated in a previous section, to underline that in cases where different views are held as to the interpretation of a resolution of the Security Council, the Security Council alone can interpret its resolution. A departure on my side from the stand thus taken would have meant that I interfered with the jurisdiction of the Council or of the Chief of Staff. Such interference would have been objectionable not only as leading to confusion, but also as going beyond the terms of my mandate.

98. The question how a resumption of work by Israel on the diversion scheme would influence the situation along the demarcation line, is obviously separate from the legal questions to which I have referred. It appears from the letters from the governments of Jordan and Lebanon that the two governments consider that a resumption of the work might put the situation along the demarcation line under an undue strain. This view has been expressed to me also by the other governments of the Arab countries. I have given this aspect of the question my most serious attention. I find that the strain feared in case of a resumption of the work should not be permitted to endanger the cease-fire, but as stated during

[6] Security Council Resolution 100 (1953).

my negotiations, I feel, with equal strength, that, legal considerations apart, it is the duty of all parties to the present effort to reduce tensions to avoid any action that may create an added strain.

99. Article VIII of the General Armistice Agreement between Jordan and Israel [7] establishes a procedure for the implementation of certain arrangements concerning which the same article states that an agreement in principle was reached at the armistice. It has so far not proved possible, through the machinery established, to reach agreements on methods for implementation. The Israeli government considers this to be a case of standing noncompliance from the side of Jordan. The matters involved have been discussed in substance with both governments. However, I do not feel that I should in this report go into the questions to which the article gives rise, as the judgment as to the state of compliance is primarily dependent on the jurisdiction of the Chief of Staff or on negotiations to be conducted by him. A memorandum submitted to me by the Chief of Staff on this subject is annexed to the report (annex 6).

100. For the same reasons I have not felt that I should in this report discuss issues covered by Article V of the Armistice Agreement between Syria and Israel. The matter has been discussed and the Syrian government has claimed noncompliance by Israel with the provisions of the article. A memorandum submitted to me by the Chief of Staff is also in this case annexed to the report (annex 7).

VIII. Conclusions

101. In the letter dated May 2, 1956, to the President of the Security Council, in which I presented an interim report, I restated the scope of the Security Council mandate as defined in its resolution of April 4, and indicated my interpretation of the mandate as permitting me to negotiate for the fullest possible compliance with the armistice agreements.

102. I said in my report that I had stayed strictly within the scope of my mandate. This means that I have left aside those fundamental issues which so deeply influence the present situation, and that I have devoted all my attention to the limited task of reestablishing first of all a cease-fire, and, based on the cease-fire, a state of full compliance with the armistice agreements.

[7] Security Council Official Records, Fourth Year, Special Supplement No. 1, or United Nations Treaty Series, Volume 42, 1949.

103. It may be said that this does not meet the needs of the situation. In my own view, confirmed by the frank and full discussions I have had with the leaders in the Middle East, I feel that the reestablishment of full compliance with the armistice agreements represents a stage which has to be passed in order to make progress possible on the main issues which I have considered to be outside my mandate.

104. It is still too early to say what has been achieved in substance, but the efforts made, in my view, were necessary as an initial step. Their value and effect will depend first of all on the good will and the actions taken by the governments directly concerned, in the second place on the support given to those governments by others and by the world community, as represented by the United Nations.

105. What has been done may open the door to new fruitful developments. The initiative is now in the hands of the governments parties to the armistice agreements. It is my feeling that there is a general will to peace, and that this will should be fostered and encouraged, not by attempts to impose from outside solutions to problems of vital significance to everyone in the region, but by a cooperation which facilitates for the governments concerned the taking unilaterally of steps to increase confidence and to demonstrate their wish for peaceful conditions.

106. I believe that the present situation offers unique possibilities. If we have previously experienced chain reactions leading to a continuous deterioration of the situation, we may now have the possibility of starting a chain of reactions in the opposite direction.

107. The final settlement is probably still far off, but even partial solutions to the harassing problems of the region would be a contribution to the welfare of the peoples concerned and to the peace of the world.

---

7. *Transcript of Press Conference*
NEW YORK   MAY 11, 1956

THE SECRETARY-GENERAL: Ladies and gentlemen, it is good to meet you again. I have fresh greetings from your colleagues on the other side of the Atlantic or even the Mediterranean. I think they matched you in pa-

UN Note to Correspondents No. 1303, May 11, 1956.

tience and sometimes surpassed you in imagination, and that is said in full knowledge of the fact that sometimes you are not very bad either. Anyway, I think that we can go straight ahead. As to what should have been or could have been a kind of initial statement, you have it already in writing in the report to the Security Council. For that reason, may I just invite you to start with your questions.

QUESTION: Mr. Hammarskjöld, now that we have read the report and we are all set on it, what is the next step? Where do we go from here? Does the Council meet? Do you make further recommendations? Do you go back to the Middle East maybe this summer? Could you enlarge a little bit on what we do now?

THE SECRETARY-GENERAL: Frank [Francis Carpenter, *Associated Press*], I praised you all for patience, but I must say that somehow you start off showing I was wrong. This is, as I call it, the first step. I think that the next step, humanly speaking, must be for the governments, for delegations here and for us all, to digest the result a little bit to see where we stand and not to rush on without having formed a balanced and considered opinion.

In my own view, that is a matter which will necessarily require some time and pending the result of such considerations I would not like to be specific about so-called next steps. It is for the Security Council to decide when or whether they will meet. It is for them to decide what line they want to take. As to the general philosophy within which I feel that the operation should continue, the next steps should be taken, you will find it in my conclusions, with a strong emphasis on the governments, the governments in the region in the first place, and necessarily all interested and friendly governments. I say there that "the initiative is in the hands of the governments." The phrase never satisfied me because it is not a question of initiative. We are in a long run, and it is not anything new that I am, so to say, waiting for; it is just the follow-up which is natural after the present effort, the present effort in which all governments have cooperated fully and which for that reason, I believe, may serve for the governments as a starting point for new considerations in their own policy-making.

Trying to sum up what I said, I think it is quite clear that I am not willing myself to recommend any next steps. I feel strongly that that, more than ever, is in the hands of the governments in the region and it is my natural hope that what has been begun in cooperation will continue in cooperation.

As to the question of whether or not I would go back, I would say this much: I have no such plan. I do not see any reason for me to take any initiative in that direction.

QUESTION: In your report, you referred to the unwisdom of imposing solutions from outside. Does this mean that you would like the Security Council to let these governments work out a solution themselves?

THE SECRETARY-GENERAL: I have not referred to it as "unwisdom." It may sometimes be very wise. What I have said is another matter, namely that the best way to encourage and to foster the general will to peace is to lend friendly cooperation to the governments; that is to say, I give a priority to that point. Under that point, to what extent things said more or less authoritatively by outside governments or by the Security Council serve the same purpose, I shall regard as an open question. I have not advised against it, but I have advised in favor of another approach, namely the one of cooperation indicated in the report.

QUESTION: To follow that up, you said in your statement that this should not be done by attempts to impose solutions from outside but by helping Arabs and Israelis to take their own steps toward a settlement. Does this mean that you would not oppose Security Council action recommending that the parties concerned get together as soon as possible with a view to discussing their differences and reaching some sort of a permanent settlement?

THE SECRETARY-GENERAL: I think that my position is quite clear from what I have already said to Mr. Balaraman [*The Hindu*] and from what appears in the report. I do not oppose this position or that position; I do not criticize this line or that line—I spell out in positive terms what I think is the most helpful approach for the time being. I also state in the final paragraph, as you will recall, that final settlement is probably still far off. When you combine these two points, you can easily see what I mean when I spoke previously about the philosophy in which I think this cooperation can continue. It is one in which we recognize that solutions which are accepted happily and with satisfaction by the parties are solutions which grow out of the thinking of those parties themselves. We can help the parties in that rather delicate process, and I do not think that we help parties by telling them from the outside what they should do.

QUESTION: Mr. Hammarskjöld, in your report you speak of the initiative being in the hands of the parties concerned. On the basis of your talks there, do you feel that these parties will seize this initiative and do anything more than they have done in recent years?

THE SECRETARY-GENERAL: I think that if you read my conclusions carefully you will find the reply. I have already restated it to Mr. Carpenter in somewhat different terms. With the experience of the not only friendly but constructive cooperation which I have had, it seems to me natural that the various governments will continue along the lines that were reflected in their attitude to my mission. That being so, I do not see any reason why they should not, separately or groupwise or in whatever way, explore how to get on from this vantage point. Again, I would not think it appropriate for me to try to say what they should do. I feel that there is quite a lot that can be done, and I would say this much: Between the basic steps taken as reflected in the report, that is to say the sanctifying of the general cease-fire and the reaffirmation of the armistice agreements, and what has been referred to here as a definite settlement, there is not only a very long road but there is very much that can be done on specific points which, in the words of the report, would increase confidence and would demonstrate the wish for peaceful conditions.

I think that the second stage—if we are to talk in such terms in an operation like this one—once we have the armistice agreements solidly anchored in a cease-fire and fully applied, would be to do all those things which do not préjudge longer development but which would create an atmosphere in which the approach to long-term problems would be more promising than it is today.

QUESTION: Mr. Secretary-General, I wonder whether you have any indication or assurance at this time that the powers outside the disputants are willing to restrain themselves for the time being, as you put it?

THE SECRETARY-GENERAL: I have not discussed it with them.

QUESTION: Mr. Secretary-General, in connection with the resumption of work on the B'noth Yaakov Canal in Israel, to which Syria, Jordan, and Lebanon have objected, and, in the same context, in connection with Israel's reminder that Egypt has not followed through on the Security Council resolution on freedom of shipping through the Suez Canal, I wonder whether you foresee a possible warning to Egypt that it is straining armistice compliance in the same way that Israel was reminded in your report that it may strain the armistice agreements by resuming work on the B'noth Yaakov Canal?

THE SECRETARY-GENERAL: I think that there are reminders in both directions in the report. Both questions lie within the orbit of such things which are definitely interesting when you come to that intermediary step about which I have spoken, namely the intermediary step between the reestablishment of the armistice agreements and the approach to the major problems. Both questions belong to that in-between group. I think I have made my stand clear on both. In one case I have made direct reference to the Security Council decision, and in the other case I have expressed the general view of the application of what I think is a sound principle, namely that all parties at this stage in the present efforts should avoid any action that might lead to added strain.

QUESTION: May I come back to this most important sentence in your conclusions about the steps to be taken by the five governments themselves "to increase confidence and to demonstrate their wish for peaceful conditions." Do you not think that in order to do so these governments will need the continuous cooperation of the Secretary-General, this cooperation which we feel was so successful during the last months?

THE SECRETARY-GENERAL: They will have it if they want it.

QUESTION: Sir, I am unclear after reading your report whether you regard continuing the present situation in the Suez Canal as being compatible with full compliance with the armistice agreements.

THE SECRETARY-GENERAL: The matter has been adjudicated by the Security Council, and the Secretary-General, on legal issues, unless he is willing to bring up an entirely new case and argue for it, follows the adjudication of the Security Council. The Security Council said that it found the present interference incompatible with an armistice régime, but it did not refer to any specific clause in the Armistice Agreement. You will see in my report that I have said that I found that it was not a question of compliance within the terms of my mandate; that is to say, there is a subtle legal question involved. I had first of all to decide what was the desire of the Security Council in this context. It seemed from the resolution and from the history of the resolution quite clear that the Security Council did not expect me to deal with this question. From that point of view the matter is decided for me in this special operation. Whether or not it is a lack of compliance with a specific clause in the Armistice Agreement is a controversial point. It may be said that the Security Council decision is not quite clear, but its indication is that it refers to the general state of affairs to be achieved through the armistice agreements, but not through any specific clause. I am sorry that I have to give you a bit of a lawyer's reply, but on this question I think that I have to act a little bit like a lawyer because the political aspects are so closely tied in with legal questions.

QUESTION: May I just follow that up in the hope of clarifying your answer? I was not speaking with respect to the mission that you have just completed. My question is whether you would regard the armistice agreements as being fully complied with if the present situation continued in the Suez Canal.

THE SECRETARY-GENERAL: My reply would be a direct quotation from the Security Council resolution of 1951, wherein the Security Council cites that specific legal issue by referring its judgment to the armistice régime as established by the armistice agreements, but it did not refer to any specific clause. I do not think that I should go beyond what the Security Council has said, and I have not done so on the legal issue in my talks.

QUESTION: In the light of what you have said here and of what you have said in your report, I think it might be helpful if you would clarify the relationship, as you see it, of the present recommendations with the Tripartite Declaration, which makes some recommendations.

THE SECRETARY-GENERAL: I have no basis, really, for entering into a discussion of the Tripartite Declaration. It is a question of a joint policy of three Member governments, and you know that I have stuck firmly to the rule in every case not to comment upon governmental policies in relation to United Nations questions. For that reason, I would not like to go into your question.

QUESTION: Before you left, you told us, as you had previously told the Security Council, that the resolution of April 4 did not either limit or enlarge upon your powers as Secretary-General. We got the feeling that you expected to act in your capacity as Secretary-General, in addition to carrying out your mandate. Would you tell us whether you had an opportunity of thus acting as Secretary-General beyond your mandate?

THE SECRETARY-GENERAL: I acted as Secretary-General in exactly the same way as I am acting here, that is to say, I used these opportunities to discuss very broadly in some cases problems which are of concern to me as Secretary-General, but on exactly the same basis and in exactly the same spirit in which they would have been discussed here with the main delegates. In some ways it helped me to get a more clear background for what I had to do under the Security Council's mandate. In no case did it broaden the mandate.

QUESTION: It seems to me, from the report and from what you have said here, that the armistice is the main point. From your analysis of the juridical implications of the cease-fire provisions—and it appears to me they become more like "no-fire" provisions—is there any possible reason in the world that you can think of that could possibly justify violence? I speak of violence, of course, in terms of the cease-fire provisions.

THE SECRETARY-GENERAL: I could give you replies on many different levels. On the formal level, I have to refer you to the texts which, in their turn, refer to Article 51 of the Charter.

QUESTION: As there are no possible reasons, I cannot think of any . . .

THE SECRETARY-GENERAL: As I said, I can reply on different levels. May I forget entirely my position as Secretary-General for the present, and speak as a human being? Then my reply would be: "No, I cannot."

QUESTION: Well, then, if there are no possible reasons, and I anticipated that there would be no possible reasons, are there possibly some valid excuses—such as self-defense—that any party can invoke? I ask this because it is your letters in the annex rather than the letters of the Foreign Ministers to you which delimit self-defense under Article 51 of the Charter.

THE SECRETARY-GENERAL: The first part of your question, with due respect, strikes me a little bit as metaphysical. The second question is a real one. It is a real one in the sense that I had to be specific in all these various declarations. The term "self-defense," as you have seen, was introduced in the first two letters, the Egyptian and the Israeli letters. It was in a situation of some heat and urgency, and for that reason I do not think any of us at that stage was very careful in the legal drafting, although we knew very well what we meant. At a later stage it was obviously necessary to be specific. The term "self-defense," in my view, has to be qualified in two ways in order to avoid ambiguity. One is with reference to the Charter. That follows from the fact that the Secretary-General cannot possibly be supposed to have discussions with Member nations on any other basis than that of the Charter. If the term "self-defense" is used, it is used in the sense of the Charter. But I had to go one step further, and that was to say that even if I admit it—without any interpretation, by the way, of that very difficult clause "the right of self-defense as established in the Charter"—I could not see how such a reservation could derogate from the cease-fire clause itself. That is to say, I had to introduce two limits in order to know where I stood, as these are legal terms, but they were in the very nature of the thing and they never gave rise to any discussion.

QUESTION: I wonder if the incidents reported during the past few days—minor ones, to be sure,—are consistent with the spirit of incentive toward peace, of which you speak.

THE SECRETARY-GENERAL: My reply cannot be a definite one until I have had full reports of them, but I think I would like on this score to refer you to a couple of statements which really do bring out what I feel about the present developments. One is in para. 43 of my report, where I say:

In doing so I will not attempt any evaluation. Such an evaluation, if made, would have to take into account not only the effect of the cease-fire on current developments but also the significance of the cease-fire as a newly established firm point in the discipline under which these developments should be brought. This significance of the cease-fire, which is to be found on the level of principle and law, cannot be judged solely—or even primarily—in terms of its immediate influence on the situation in the field.

To that should be added a quotation from para. 48 in which I state:

I shall, in the next section, discuss the question of crossings of the demarcation line and acts of violence in connection therewith. In this context I have only to draw attention to the risk they represent, as well as to the well-known fact that the situation prevailing along some parts of the demarcation lines is such that even with active measures to prevent incidents, they still may happen. It is for that reason that the governments concerned should do all they can to keep the situation under such control as to minimize or eliminate the risk of further incidents. But it is also for the governments, for the public, and for world opinion, to avoid giving such interpretation to incidents as would weaken, without justification, faith in the cease-fire or discredit the goodwill of the other party.

The direct reply to your question is, so to say, complete if I add to that another thing which is quite important. You may have seen in my report that I have negotiated with the governments of Egypt and Israel a kind of extension of the cease-fire to cover active measures against all crossings, and I said that "I understand the assurances referred to as extending the moral obligations under the cease-fire assurances, if need be, beyond the legal scope" of the article in question "in the sense that they involve a recognition of the obligation to take active measures against all crossings of the demarcation line and acts of violence in connection therewith." My conclusion from these various quotations is this simple one. If a government has given orders, and firm orders, to its military units, whatever type they might be, if it has taken all reasonable measures to keep civilians under control, it has lived up to its assurances. Things may still happen, and it is extremely tragic that they will, but they will not prove anything as to the failure of the cease-fire until, and unless, you are entitled to conclude from them that the governments concerned have not stuck to their orders or have not taken the appropriate active measures. If they have, the cease-fire sticks.

There is one thing I should like to add on this point. It is something you know, but it is something which is very sharply brought home to anyone who visits the region and who goes, for example, to Gaza, which of course is the most difficult spot. This is crop time. The demarcation line is, as you know, a line imposed by political decision and agreement.

We have had the most extraordinary movements of population. We have a big pile-up of refugees in the Gaza Strip. Well, all this is no excuse for any transgressions, and they do not in any way lessen the importance of keeping them under control, or their significance for the possible repercussions on the atmosphere. But they do give us food for thought in the sense that they do indicate that, even with active measures, it may be very difficult to get to a full stop.

I would also add one other observation which I think is essential. One of the leading men—a man of very great wisdom and quality— said to me, "You know, a cease-fire and what happens the week after a cease-fire, or even during the months after a cease-fire, is a little bit like the stopping of a motor. You know that immediately you stop a motor the temperature rises."

QUESTION: To follow that, may I ask whether you would care to divulge the name of this individual?

THE SECRETARY-GENERAL: No, I would not.

QUESTION: You spoke of the excellence of the imagination of our colleagues across the seas. That probably is so. But you also spoke in your piece of the will to peace of all the parties, and my imagination is not good enough to see that will to peace from here in all the parties. Could you expand on it a little bit?

THE SECRETARY-GENERAL: If you sit for four weeks together with these various gentlemen in rather searching discussions you will have your convictions of what are their guiding motives, but I cannot put them on the table any more than you can put on the table, although you have great journalistic skill, your analysis of my mentality and my way of reacting.

QUESTION: Do you expect, personally, that Israel will engage in any efforts to continue its work toward a diversion of the Jordan River?

THE SECRETARY-GENERAL: I would not like to comment on their stand.

QUESTION: A great many of us have felt that great-power rivalry in the area was one of the major factors in bringing about the recent explosive situation. Is it realistic to think that you can bring about a reversal of that situation without great-power agreement, and is not that great-power agreement to be achieved here in the Security Council?

THE SECRETARY-GENERAL: I think that it is impossible to turn the tide in the direction I indicate as a possibility in my report without that operation's being supported by all the major powers. That far, I agree with you. For that reason I believe that this is a matter which requires study and consultation also from my side with the representatives of these various powers. You say that the best place might be the Security Council. Yes, maybe. I will not have any judgment concerning that, but the Security Council is a living body, both in the sense that operations, discussions, consultations may take place backstage, and in some stages of development this may be the more fruitful approach, especially when interests of countries which are not at the Council table are deeply involved.

QUESTION: On this matter, in para. 65 you say that in the absence of diplomatic relations no procedure has been established for the handling of conflicts covered by the general clauses of the Armistice Agreement, and you go on to say that you think it is desirable to avoid organizational innovations and to work within the framework of the United Nations. Do I understand from that that you anticipate that, through talks in the field conducted by the officers of the Truce Supervision Organization and here at headquarters, these differences may eventually be resolved regarding the general clauses and scope of the Armistice Agreement?

THE SECRETARY-GENERAL: No, you see I am rather noncommittal here, though less noncommittal than the governments—because concerning the governments I just say nothing. I am rather noncommittal here because I have no proposals to make; but, studying the question of compliance with the Armistice Agreement, anybody who goes deeply into the matter cannot but be struck by two factors. There is no method, so to say, of arbitration for various cases, and there is no method by which complaints can easily be thrashed out in some rather important cases. I consider those two points as points of weakness, as I say. I am sorry I have no proposal to make, and I think that for initiative to be taken there must be initiatives which either come from or, at all events, have the very full support of, the governments in the region. What I could do on that score was just to draw attention to these two weaknesses for their consideration. They have not, obviously, so far given very much thought to that aspect of it, and for that reason I find it very natural that they would like to have a look at it. Whether something will come out of it or not I do not know.

QUESTION: As far as concerns that question of some kind of diplomatic representation procedures which is contained in the report of yesterday, is it to be taken that you envisage the possibility of having diplomatic representation between Israel and the Arab States without a proper bridge of peace?

THE SECRETARY-GENERAL: No, sir, you read it in a slightly . . .

QUESTION: A hint of peace?

THE SECRETARY-GENERAL: No, it is not even a hint. It is a *constatation de fait.* I just note that there is none; and, when there is none and yet there is a need for it, we must see if there is any way in which you can substitute for it. And then I say, concerning that, that I do not see any way, whatever it may be, which could be outside the United Nations.

QUESTION: Have you obtained an extension for General Burns—a stay of expiration [of his term] from Canada?

THE SECRETARY-GENERAL: I think I can say this much—that, although he has already overstayed by far his promise to me, he will stay on as long as the present situation is what it is and we are engaged together in this work.

QUESTION: I believe everyone is aware of the great importance of the cease-fire doctrine you are proclaiming in your report—that is to say, first, that the cease-fire must be respected independently of all other armistice clauses, and, secondly, that self-defense falls under the definition of the Charter, Article 51. Now, at the beginning of this press conference you said that it was for the Security Council to decide whether and when it will meet—whether. Do you not think it would be of great importance if the Security Council strongly and solemnly would endorse your doctrine?

THE SECRETARY-GENERAL: You mean, Dr. Beer [*Neue Zürcher Zeitung*], endorse publicly?

QUESTION: Publicly.

THE SECRETARY-GENERAL: Of course; I think that is a full reply, because I do not think there is any doubt that that doctrine is endorsed.

QUESTION: I am sure of it, but with respect to public opinion in the Middle East . . .

THE SECRETARY-GENERAL: I leave that to the distinguished members of the Security Council.

QUESTION: May I ask, in that regard, do the parties you have consulted with accept the doctrine as you have laid it down here? I am speaking now of the parties in the area.

THE SECRETARY-GENERAL: Well, read the correspondence and read my report. I think that gives a full reply. This is not a way of being in any way haughty, sir. I do not want to be harsh, but really I would not like to expand on what follows from this correspondence.

QUESTION: What is your opinion about the armaments race in the Middle East? Is it really the greatest danger which threatens the area now? In that case, would it be a good idea to obtain an embargo on arms, for instance, through the channel of the Security Council?

THE SECRETARY-GENERAL: At a previous press conference, I think I said that I do regard what you call an arms race—a potential arms race, I may perhaps add—as a symptom and not as a cause. For that reason, my reply to your question as to whether or not it is the greatest danger would be in the negative. The greatest danger is a situation, with very many component parts, which opens the door to the possibility and even the wish for what you call an arms race. That being so, my view of how these matters should be tackled gives priority to measures of a different type.

QUESTION: In para. 12 of your report, in speaking of the truce lines, you say that in many cases those truce lines had no basis in history or distribution of population or private property. We were speaking of hints a little while ago. Is there a hint there of the possibility of revising those demarcation lines because of that thinking?

THE SECRETARY-GENERAL: None whatsoever. There is no hint. It is again a *constatation de fait.*

QUESTION: Mr. Hammarskjöld, I wonder whether you would care to comment on the trip as a whole in regard to the situation there, whether it has given you a better picture of the problem involving the Arab-Israel struggle?

THE SECRETARY-GENERAL: For the first time in my life, I believe that I understand it.

QUESTION: Did you speak to the Pope about Jerusalem?

THE SECRETARY-GENERAL: No, we did not discuss Jerusalem.

QUESTION: Some time ago, you spoke about possibly going to Moscow. That was before your trip. Have you still any such plans in mind?

THE SECRETARY-GENERAL: I have had to revise my plans, but not in that respect. I stick to it.

QUESTION: Do you have a departure date in mind?

THE SECRETARY-GENERAL: I cannot say anything about the date. I have to tie it in with my visit to Europe.

QUESTION: When you arrive there, will you continue your private backstage consultations to which you referred a while ago?

THE SECRETARY-GENERAL: Where?

QUESTION: Moscow.

THE SECRETARY-GENERAL: With Moscow being just a line on the calendar, I think it is a little premature to talk about what should come up and what sort of meetings should be held. It is a natural visit in the line of visits I pay to Member countries, and, of course, we should not go outside the frame of the type of meetings I have had with other governments. What, under such circumstances, may be discussed will naturally depend on the United Nations situation at that stage.

QUESTION: Do I understand from the report that you did not go at all into the question of refugees or that you have no opinions or feelings now as to how that problem may be solved or whether there is any less inflexibility regarding it?

THE SECRETARY-GENERAL: I have certain personal views on that problem, but they are strictly outside my mandate.

---

8. *Statement in the Security Council*
NEW YORK   MAY 29, 1956

THE SECURITY COUNCIL did not meet on the Secretary-General's report until May 29. The United Kingdom had circulated a draft resolution welcoming the progress made, endorsing the Secretary-General's views, requesting him to continue his good offices and to report to the Council as appropriate.

Security Council Official Records, Eleventh Year, 723rd Meeting, May 29, 1956.

Hammarskjöld opened the discussion with the brief statement that follows. As he had done in the concluding paragraphs of his report he stressed that the need now was for unilateral steps by the parties to the armistice agreements aimed at increasing confidence on each side in the intentions of the other and at breaking the chain of violent actions and reactions.

I thank the President for inviting me to introduce my report on the Palestine question. I also thank him for his kind words of appreciation.

Hoping that the report is self-explanatory, I have indeed very few words to say. I wish first of all, on this occasion, to pay a tribute to the governments of the five Member states, parties to the armistice agreements, for their unfailing cooperation with me as the agent of the Security Council. Fully recognizing the difficulties with which some of those governments were and are faced, I appreciate their efforts to facilitate my task.

In the conclusions to my report I have indicated my feeling that we are at present in a situation where we may break the previous chain of events. Behind this statement lie many experiences during the time I spent in the region, among them the cooperation to which I have just referred.

I trust that all the parties will try to see what contributions they can now make unilaterally in order to reestablish and maintain the quiet and order so strongly needed as a background for successful efforts to cope with the great practical tasks to be tackled within all the countries concerned. Each step taken in the right direction may call forward similar steps from other sides, and thus may start and give direction to a development bringing us farther and farther from the risk of conflict. There is wide scope for such related unilateral actions in the spirit of cooperation evidenced by the Member states in the course of my negotiations.

I trust that the parties will know that they can always count on the sympathetic and impartial assistance of the Secretary-General, within the framework set by what they consider possible and desirable in their efforts to make further progress.

THE COUNCIL met six times between May 29 and June 4 on the Secretary-General's report and the United Kingdom resolution. Several provisions in the resolution met with criticism from the Arab states as going beyond the limits of the Council's April 4 resolution and the Secretary-General's mandate. In particular they disliked a paragraph in the preamble which noted the need to create conditions in which a peaceful settlement "on a mutually acceptable basis" could be made. They saw this wording as an opening to eventual peace negotiations that might depart from previous Council and Assembly decisions affirming among other things the right of the Palestinian Arab refugees to repatriation if they chose.

They also objected to wording in some of the operative paragraphs as going beyond the April 4 resolution. Finally they stressed the importance of reservations for self-defense in their cease-fire pledges in case Israel should resume work on its Jordan River diversion scheme. Israel rejected this stand and insisted that full compliance with the armistice agreements required ending the state of belligerence and opening negotiations for a mutually acceptable peaceful settlement.

In the end the United Kingdom's representative made or accepted amendments that met most of the Arab objections, including deletion of the preambular paragraph on peaceful settlement. The resolution was adopted unanimously on June 4, but the debate both before and after the vote gave sharp and emotional expression once again to the deep division between the two sides and the mutual fears and hostility born of a reciprocal sense of wrongs committed and injustice done.

Hammarskjöld's statement at the end of the meeting is given below, following the text of the resolution itself, and refers to this atmosphere. Three days later, when he met the press, most of the questions and answers were concerned with the Security Council meetings and their outcome. In the excerpts from the transcript included in the second following text (number 10, June 7) the Secretary-General gave his reactions and views on next steps at greater length.

The text of the resolution (S/3600/Rev. 2) was as follows:

The Security Council,

Recalling its resolutions of April 4, 1956, and August 11, 1949,

Having received the report of the Secretary-General on his recent mission on behalf of the Security Council,

Noting those passages of the report (Section III and annexes 1–4) which refer to the assurances given to the Secretary-General by all the parties to the general armistice agreements unconditionally to observe the cease-fire,

Noting also that progress has been made toward the adoption of the specific measures set out in operative paragraph 3 of the Security Council's resolution of April 4, 1956,

Noting however that full compliance with the general armistice agreements and with the Council's resolutions of March 30, 1955, September 8, 1955, and January 19, 1956, is not yet effected, and that the measures called for in operative paragraph 3 of its resolution of April

4, 1956, have been neither completely agreed upon nor put fully into effect,

Believing that further progress should now be made in consolidating the gains resulting from the Secretary-General's mission and toward full implementation by the parties of the armistice agreements,

1. *Commends* the Secretary-General and the parties on the progress already achieved;

2. *Declares* that the parties to the armistice agreements should speedily carry out the measures already agreed upon with the Secretary-General, and should cooperate with the Secretary-General and the Chief of Staff of the United Nations Truce Supervision Organization to put into effect their further practical proposals, pursuant to the resolution of April 4, 1956, with a view to full implementation of that resolution and full compliance with the armistice agreements;

3. *Declares* that full freedom of movement of United Nations observers must be respected along the armistice demarcation lines, in the demilitarized zones and in the defensive areas, as defined in the armistice agreements, to enable them to fulfill their functions:

4. *Endorses* the Secretary-General's view that the reestablishment of full compliance with the armistice agreements represents a stage which has to be passed in order to make progress possible on the main issues between the parties;

5. *Requests* the Chief of Staff to continue to carry out his observation of the cease-fire pursuant to the Security Council's resolution of August 11, 1949, and to report to the Council whenever any action undertaken by one party to an armistice agreement constitutes a serious violation of that agreement or of the cease-fire, which in his opinion requires immediate consideration by the Council;

6. *Calls upon* the parties to the armistice agreements to take the steps necessary to carry out this resolution, thereby increasing confidence and demonstrating their wish for peaceful conditions;

7. *Requests* the Secretary-General to continue his good offices with the parties, with a view to full implementation of the Council's resolution of April 4, 1956, and full compliance with the armistice agreements, and to report to the Security Council as appropriate.

9. *Statement in the Security Council*
NEW YORK   JUNE 4, 1956

The mandate given to the Secretary-General by the Security Council in the resolution of April 4, 1956 is well known. There is certainly no reason for me to recapitulate the terms of reference. In the resolution passed by the Council this afternoon, the Council has requested me to continue my good offices with the parties in pursuance of the said resolution and with a view to the full implementation of the armistice agreements.

I wish to say that it is with the best hopes that I shall try to meet this request of the Security Council. The decision of the Security Council gives me the privilege to continue in the spirit in which the work has been begun, thanks largely to the cooperative attitude of all the parties concerned. The analysis of the problems and the reactions to the difficulties and possibilities which I will take as the frame for my work are fully explained in my report to the Security Council on the first part of the Middle East assignment. The debate following the vote of the Council has highlighted points on which deep differences of view exist. It is my firm hope that neither these differences nor any of the expressions they have found here will be permitted to harm the effort on which the United Nations, in cooperation with the parties, has embarked.

Security Council Official Records, Eleventh Year, 728th Meeting, June 4, 1956.

10. *From Transcript of Press Conference*
NEW YORK   JUNE 7, 1956

THE SECRETARY-GENERAL: I have no introductory statement to make, ladies and gentlemen, and therefore I should like to invite you to proceed at once to put your questions and start the discussion.

QUESTION: By courtesy of Mr. Freuchen [*Politiken,* Copenhagen] here, this may be designated as the $64,000 question. When you returned from the Middle East, you intimated that on the broader issues of the Palestine case, beyond the armistice problems, you were open to the parties whenever they might be disposed to come to you. Do you feel that your position in this respect has changed following the meetings of the Security Council?

THE SECRETARY-GENERAL: To reply quite simply: No.

QUESTION: I wonder whether you could help to straighten out our thinking, in your capacity of Secretary-General, regarding certain tendencies that seem to have developed in the United Nations. What I am referring to specifically is this: More and more in the last two years, or perhaps two and a half, the Security Council has tended to adopt the doctrine of unanimity, evidently on the assumption that, unless a resolution which really says something is unanimous, it would be meaningless. The result, some people feel, is that the resolutions have become largely perfunctory; that they have skirted the basic issues, as this last one did when the Council seemed to have come to the brink of peace and then looked down and saw some horrible dissensions and shied away, because the doctrine of unanimity seemed to take precedence over everything else. From now on, would that affect other organs of the United Nations and would it continue to have an effect upon the Security Council itself?

THE SECRETARY-GENERAL: Your question as to whether or not it will affect other organs is also a very easy one for me to answer, because I challenge the truth of your basic analysis. I do not think that you char-

UN Note to Correspondents No. 1318, June 7, 1956.

acterized the situation in the Security Council correctly, and therefore I do not think that there is a disease of any kind that can spread through the Organization. As far as the Security Council is concerned, there is no doctrine of unanimity which is so important, as you state, as to make people give up anything that they consider essential. I have seen no signs of that, and I think that any statement to that effect is unjust and unjustified. In this special case, I think you should remember that there is a time and a setting for everything. It is not necessarily true that a man does not hold a certain view because he does not express it on a particular occasion. For example, I may find it unwise to give a straight reply to a question you put, although I may have made up my mind on that point very firmly, and I may find it unwise because it is not the right time. If, in an operation like the one which you see in the Security Council, whether on this occasion or another occasion, some people feel that there is a line forward and that we should see how far we can go and other people feel that we should not go that far now, that does not necessarily mean a compromise with principle, and does not in any way necessarily mean giving up something, if the distance covered on the road is a distance which makes sense and is in the right direction.

I would say that, if you read the operative paragraphs of the Security Council resolution, you will find that it is quite a step in some respects, and definitely in the right direction. Whether or not you go one step further in the preamble is a question, if not of taste, at least of judgment. And if, in the name of unanimity, one takes, not the least common denominator, but an understanding attitude as to how far one should go in the elaboration of a thesis in a special resolution, I do not think that that is an unsound practice in any sense, or in any way a new practice.

To sum up what I am saying: I think that perhaps you should take a new look at the somewhat disturbed view which was reflected in your question and see whether there is not a more understanding and more constructive and more encouraging interpretation to be given to the phenomenon to which you have referred. At all events, I must say that I do not think that there is any doctrine of unanimity which is applied by any United Nations organ in the sense that people give up their convictions if they feel that it is definitely the right time to express those convictions.

QUESTION: In your report to the Security Council, in Chapter VIII, "Conclusions," you stated that there is a general will to peace. Do you think that this statement still holds true after the speech of Ambassador Shukairy in which he said that the establishment of Israel, its membership in the United Nations, and all other resolutions will have to be revoked?

THE SECRETARY-GENERAL: I have no reason to comment on any specific statements made by any of the parties in the recent debates. As to my own statement I repeat it emphatically: I am firmly convinced of the will to peace of all the parties in the area. A will to peace is one thing; a will to peace-making on certain conditions, at a certain time, is necessarily another matter. Peace is a fact; peace-making is a legal process.

QUESTION: Following that question, could we ask whether, in Syria, you heard substantially the same thing that we heard from Mr. Shukairy here?

THE SECRETARY-GENERAL: If you read the Middle Eastern press, if you listen to spokesmen, if you read, for example, a column by Joseph Alsop yesterday after having visited a refugee camp, I think that you will find one thing. There may be differences of expression, differences of tone, and differences of choice of occasion to express views, but there are certain hard basic facts which are very much in people's minds, and those hard basic facts are very much the same as those which you get to hear about and read on all these various occasions. In that sense, I would say that substantive views expressed at the Security Council table should not be any surprise to you or any surprise to me. Basically, we have in the background the fact that we have 900,000 people at present who are outside the borders of Israel and who, until not too many years ago, were in other places. As you know, the refugees do represent the basic problem of the region in human terms and, for that reason also, necessarily partly in political terms. That basic fact is very much in everybody's mind in the region. It was very much in the air behind the words spoken here a few days ago.

QUESTION: The Security Council resolution asked you to continue your efforts. How would you envisage the continuation of your efforts?

THE SECRETARY-GENERAL: I think you mean, first of all, in technical terms—how I have to run it. In that respect I have nothing to add to what I said namely, that I do not think that this is a time when it would make very much sense to desert from my job here and to go to the region. On the other hand, I have a continuous contact not only with the representatives of the countries concerned here in New York, in America, in the United Nations, but also, to the extent necessary, with responsible people in the region. That is to say, the whole machinery necessary for the follow-up is there. You know that the previous discussions covered the ground which was not, so to say, fully mapped out in the way it should be fully mapped out. It covered the ground of full compliance with the armistice agreements, and there are assurances as to full compliance from all the parties concerned. What remain are questions of implementation. Such questions, in some cases, are quite complicated and will necessarily take some time. When I say that we covered a broader ground than was mapped out in detail it does mean that the ground is prepared for continued operation, continued discussion, continued negotiation, so as to take us closer and closer to full compliance, full implementation of the armistice agreements. That sets, so to say, the natural framework for the immediate efforts, and those immediate efforts have a solid basis in the preparatory work done while I was in the region.

What should be done and how things should be arranged at a somewhat later stage, when we, as I hope, reach full compliance, and when we, as we hope—all of us, certainly, during all the time which has passed since I was in the region—have managed to maintain quiet, is another matter which I find it a little bit difficult to go into both as to how to proceed and as to what ground to cover. I have my own ideas, but it is just one of those typical cases where I think that what I said to you about time and setting some time ago does apply. I do not think this is the time for me, nor the setting for me, in which to look beyond the area where the ground has been properly prepared already in the talks in April.

QUESTION: In your own statement before the Security Council at its last meeting you spoke of certain differences which you hoped would not be permitted to harm the efforts on which the United Nations, in cooperation with the parties, had embarked. Am I to interpret this statement of yours as meaning that the meetings of the Security Council did not in any way enhance the efforts of your mission which you embarked upon in accordance with the resolution of April 4?

THE SECRETARY-GENERAL: The Security Council development certainly had positive effects in a most desirable direction. I think that it could not leave any doubts in the mind of anybody who listened to the proceedings that the Security Council was behind not only the stand—the result—but also behind the philosophy of the report I put on the table. That is not only encouraging; it is definitely most helpful. The divergencies of views among the members of the Council which were reflected in the debate do not in any way mean reserves as to the report as such, as you may have noted. For that reason I feel that the ground which was, so to say, tentatively covered by me is now definitely covered in the sense that the Security Council has put its hallmark on the map I tried to produce. For that reason it has provided me with a firmer basis and background than we had before, and that definitely is helpful. It also indicates acceptance by the Security Council of—I would say—the expectations which are reflected in the report. I would not like to use the word "optimism" or the word "hope," and so on and so forth. They are all so faded and misused. I prefer to say "expectations"—that is to say, the expectation that further progess can be made in the right direction, and not exactly at a turtle's pace.

On the other hand, you remember that in my own conclusions I said that a final settlement is probably far off. That specific point was not discussed by the Security Council as such, but certainly the debate between the parties, or the views expressed by the parties, did indicate that on several issues the stands are very far apart indeed. There are deep differences of view, as I said in what I stated, and I think that from that you draw the same conclusion that I draw, that is to say that with such deep differences of view held after such a long time it is necessary to recognize that the road toward acceptance on various sides of agreed solutions of some kind may be, and probably is, a long one.

Now what I wanted to say in my final words was that the fact that there may be a long road to travel in order to arrive at settlement does not in any way, and should not in any way, be permitted to discourage us in our immediate effort: nor should it be used by any party as an excuse not to cooperate with us. That is what I meant.

. . . . QUESTION: Mr. Secretary-General, could you tell us whether you believe that a settlement of the Palestine question should be on a "mutually acceptable" basis?

THE SECRETARY-GENERAL: There are various approaches to your terminology, Mr. Hamilton [*The New York Times*]. As you well know, it lent itself to many interpretations, that very phrase. On one basis—the interpretation given by Sir Pierson Dixon—I think that the reply is obviously "yes." Sir Pierson Dixon, as you remember, said that he considered that it was obvious that there is no settlement unless there is an acceptance by the parties to the settlement. That was what he wanted to express. I think he himself said more or less that he considered it to be a truism, and it certainly is a truism.

Let me express it in somewhat different terms. I do not think that any settlement is lasting unless it is accepted by the parties to whom it is to apply.

. . . . QUESTION: Mr. Hammarskjöld, in your report on the cease-fire, there is a reservation on the question of self-defense which has disturbed quite a number of observers as to the exact definition of self-defense. I wonder if you would care to comment on this phrase "self-defense"; whether you would accept as self-defense a defensive method in keeping infiltrators from entering one land or the other and in driving them back to their borders—whether driving them back to their borders would also be within the scope of self-defense, or whether they should limit themselves to keeping infiltrators and marauders out?

THE SECRETARY-GENERAL: As you know, the question you raise is one of the most delicate ones in international law. That is the reason why I have not gone beyond a few negative statements in the report. One of them is that retaliation is most certainly not self-defense in the technical sense of the word. Whether a certain action is justified as self-defense or not is something which under United Nations legislation can only be decided by the Security Council. I may have my views on the concrete cases, but they would not be binding on anybody. They would just be my private views, and from that point of view they may be of interest but not of significance.

QUESTION: Mr. Secretary-General, may I come back to your answer to a previous question. You said there is no agreement possible unless both parties agree. That is a truism, as you said, but it is a far cry from both parties being satisfied. An agreement satisfactory to both parties is not necessarily—let me put it the other way—an agreement accepted by both parties is not necessarily satisfactory to both parties, so we come to this point which was raised before. Do you think it is necessary to have a peace settlement where both parties are actually satisfied?

THE SECRETARY-GENERAL: I should like to broaden that question into a much wider field in human life. In your own agreements with your landlord or whoever it may be I guess it quite often happens after all to you, as it does happen everywhere, that you cannot reach the ideal, you cannot get what you really want. Social life is a life of compromise in the sense that you have to accept what is reasonable as an outcome of the balance of interests. In that sense, I think that the word "accepted," as I used it, is a proper term. If it is agreeable and is exactly what we want, then it is certainly most satisfactory. But I do not believe in that kind of settlement, practically ever, because we never get it that way.

    . . . . QUESTION: May I go back to Palestine for one moment. Your report is based on the doctrine, endorsed I think by the Security Council, that the cease-fire is unconditional with only one exception, self-defense, and that is the definition of the Charter. In the Council meeting the representative of Syria introduced another exception, continuation of the work of the Israelis on the Jordan River. Do you consider this unilateral statement as endangering your doctrine?

    THE SECRETARY-GENERAL: No, it does not; it is entirely covered by the report in fact. He did not introduce a new condition. He gave an interpretation to what he considered to be legitimate self-defense. Let us look at a hypothetical case, I hope purely hypothetical in all respects. A situation arises which one considers to be a situation which entitles him to action. That action must be considered then as self-defense but the matter necessarily is automatically brought to the Security Council under Article 51. The Security Council may say, "this is not self-defense," and then their word counts.

    Then if action is continued, they are up against a binding decision under Chapter VII. If, on the other hand, it is considered to be self-defense, then it is self-defense. That is to say, what was said by the representative in question did not introduce any new condition. It introduced a one-sided unilateral interpretation of the reserve of self-defense in a given hypothetical situation. That is what happened.

    . . . . QUESTION: I gather that your aim now is for full implementation of the armistice agreements. Would that include what I would call corollary points that were not covered because they were not foreseen at that time, like the blockade of the Suez or other things which we may call irritants? Would you aim at solving those problems too as part of the stabilization of the situation in the Middle East?

    THE SECRETARY-GENERAL: I think that in a long-haul operation of this type it is obvious that nobody starts out with excluding anything which is essential to the solution of the problem. Another thing is that you must always argue and plan in stages, and to what stage—and what special time in the long-haul operation—points to which you refer belong is something I would not like to take up or to decide here and now. I think it is a little bit sterile because there is so much that has to be done in this tidying-up operation, which is close at hand, which is duly prepared, and so on. For that reason I stick to what I can see, what is, so to say, within reach, within the grasp. That is my reply. Beyond that, however, I repeat what I said: Nobody approaching this problem is, in my view, entitled to exclude any of the causes of friction from his thinking as to the future.

QUESTION: Mr. Secretary-General, you say that there is so much to be done, and certainly there is. We have heard so much about politics and amendments and explanations of vote, and so on. But 900,000 refugees are sitting there and suffering every day. They seem to be forgotten and we never hear anybody in the press say anything about it. Why is it that they are not put forward before anything else. We are handling people there. The Suez Canal and all those things represent money, but those are people.

THE SECRETARY-GENERAL: I happen to feel very much the way you do, Dr. Freuchen. The reason why they are not put forward is that they are tied up with the so-called main issues, and you know that all the parties, when they come to the main issues in this conflict, are inclined, and for good reason, to take an approach which is determined by long-term political considerations; that is to say, the humanitarian aspect may be quite as close to their hearts as it is to yours, and certainly to mine, and all the same they may find that they cannot bring this issue up for public debate, or with any kind of pressure, without bringing up other issues at the same time, because they would not get anywhere and they do not find that this is the time to bring them up. It is a long story, but really it is one of those cases where a clash between the humanitarian viewpoint and political planning is obvious, and I would not exculpate any of us or any of those concerned, certainly not myself. I feel unhappy about the fact that we cannot in the United Nations do more for them either practically—partly because of a shortage of funds—or politically, because of the way in which this question is linked up with other problems which we must have just as much in view in the attempt to get somewhere, on the whole, in the region.

. . . . QUESTION: In your report you stated that the solution for some outstanding problems should be found in unilateral actions by either party. Would you care to elaborate on this point?

THE SECRETARY-GENERAL: I would not care to elaborate because I think that would be more embarrassing than helpful to the governments concerned, but I think I may say one very general thing, and that is that

I think it would be a very good idea if we could get a somewhat lower tone in the public approach to these problems. That is also a question of unilateral action. It does not raise any question of principle, but it certainly would be more helpful as a demonstration of the peaceful intentions—I think that was my phrase in the report—of which I am convinced.

. . . .

Address at Celebration of the 180th Anniversary
of the Virginia Declaration of Rights
WILLIAMSBURG, VIRGINIA   MAY 15, 1956

HAMMARSKJÖLD spoke on the anniversary of the Virginia Declaration of Rights soon after his return from his Middle East cease-fire mission. His reflections in the concluding paragraphs on the problem of fear for men and nations and his call for the courage to take positive action to break the spell of fear were prompted by this experience.

His address five days later at the ceremony in honor of Woodrow Wilson (the next following text) recalled, among other quotations, Wilson's words when proposing creation of the League of Nations at the Paris Peace Conference in 1919: "It should be the eye of the nations to keep watch upon the common interest, an eye that does not slumber, an eye that is everywhere watchful and attentive." The words were prophetic of the manner in which Hammarskjöld carried out his own responsibilities as Secretary-General.

My first words must be words of gratitude for your invitation to address this distinguished gathering in Colonial Williamsburg on the occasion of the 180th anniversary of the Virginia Declaration of Rights.

The Virginia Declaration of Rights may be considered to mark the beginning of a series of declarations of human rights leading up to the Universal Declaration proclaimed in 1948 by the General Assembly of the United Nations. The United Nations Declaration is the most comprehensive in the whole long line of such attempts to crystallize our faith in the dignity of man. It reflects what has been acknowledged as one of the main purposes of the United Nations.

Who can trace the first sources of a great idea? Such ideas are brought to our awareness when they break through the inertia of human minds and of social institutions, but their antecedents, we find, generally go far back into the past. Early American political philosophy and American liberties were rooted in European theory and in British traditions that dated back in outward expressions to the Great Revolution of

UN Press Release SG/479, May 14, 1956.

1688. But behind those European theories and behind the British traditions, we find the same ideas, and the prophets for those ideas, in the distant past of our civilization.

Although justice requires that we recognize the heritage, it would, however, be unjust to belittle the significance of the act through which ideas break through the barriers and become an active factor in the life of the community. The Virginia Declaration of Rights is older by thirteen years than the French Declaration of the Rights of Man and of the Citizen of 1789. Your country can take just pride in being the one where this historically significant affirmation of human rights was given.

What was new in the Virginia Declaration of Rights was the formal recognition of human rights as part of written constitutional law. This recognition introduced a technique for the protection of the people not only against the tyranny of monarchs, but also against the intolerance and tyranny of majorities.

There is an intellectual freshness and clarity of thought about the period in American political history to which this day draws our attention, that cannot fail to attract everybody interested in a sound development of modern society. The Virginia Declaration bears testimony to this constructive state of mind.

In every society there is a tendency, as time passes, to lose dynamism and to seek protection behind time-honored formulae, protection against the law of change which is basic to all growth. "Whenever any government," the Virginia Declaration says, "shall be found inadequate or contrary to those purposes, the majority hath an indubitable, inalienable, and indefeasible right to reform, alter, or abolish it." This is the voice of self-confidence. This is the voice of trust. This is the voice which should always speak in favor of evolution in the interest of man.

The questions about the relationship of the individual to the state as they presented themselves in the eighteenth century, seem to us still to be within human perspective. There was at that time a kind of balance in the relationship of the individual to organized society. If a man were dissatisfied, he still had plenty of ways in which he might, as an individual, expect to influence the course of events.

Today, on the 180th anniversary of the Virginia Declaration, the perspective is different. The development of society is such that, in the very interest of the individual, the organized collectivity can no longer give the same scope to individual action and influences as was possible in a smaller and less developed community. Modern man seldom acts alone. He is integrated in a series of collectivities which together form our society. In almost every phase of his life and work he feels the necessity of organizing his activities in common with others whether through trade unions, cooperatives, other economic organizations, or public associations, or enterprises. Over and above these various collectivities, the individual meets the state, which is their general framework, and beyond the state there is the international community of nations with its necessarily ever widening influence.

It would take me too far to raise here the very important issues of principle, philosophy, and law involved. I cannot do so without getting deep into questions which are at the very root of the major conflicts of our time and which should not be discussed on this occasion. What I have said should suffice as an indication of the setting in which we, children of the twentieth century, have to keep alive and to apply the old ideas based on the recognition of the dignity of the human being which found a first constitutional expression in the Virginia Declaration of Rights.

The series of declarations of rights, from the Virginia Declaration to the Universal Declaration proclaimed by the United Nations, reflects indirectly the change of setting to which I have referred. At one end of the chain we have a declaration by a group of far-sighted men, framing the life of a new small community. At the other end of the chain we have a statement by the first international organization that can claim to speak for the world.

An optimist might be led to believe that this same development reflects not only the growth of society from the small national unit to the organized collectivity of nations, but also a growth of the recognition of human rights. Such an optimist would be right in the sense that ideas which seemed revolutionary, when crystallized in legal form, a couple of hundred years ago, today are so generally recognized as to make it seem improper to question them. But he would be wrong if he meant that the forces against which human rights have to be defended are less strong or less complicated than at earlier times. On the contrary, the complications have grown in manifold ways, while the resistance which arises from certain tendencies in the behavior of both the individual and the masses has certainly not lessened. We need only to remember what circumstances forced on the United Nations the problem of human rights, to understand that my pessimistic words about human nature are not unfounded. What happened in the forties may happen again. And the complications we are meeting in the fifties will still be there in the sixties.

The Charter of the United Nations calls for international cooperation in "promoting and encouraging respect for human rights and for fundamental freedoms for all without distinction as to race, sex, language, or religion." At the San Francisco Conference eleven years ago, a determined effort was made to incorporate a Bill of Rights in the Charter. However, it was realized that the task was beyond the capacity of a relatively short conference. It was therefore decided that it would not be done until the international organization had been established.

Three years later the Universal Declaration of Human Rights was a fact. This Declaration enunciates not only all the traditional political rights and civil liberties, but also economic, social, and cultural rights. It is an international synthesis of the thinking of our generation on these questions. Unlike the Virginia Declaration, which was drawn up by George Mason, there is no one person who can be identified as the principal draftsman of the Universal Declaration. The Declaration is anonymous in its character, and back of it we find literally thousands of people who directly and indirectly participated actively in its drafting. Also for that reason it may be called the universal expression in the field of human rights of the aims of our world of today, a world where the memory is still fresh of some of the worst infringements of human rights ever experienced in history, and a world which is also facing the problem of human rights in new and increasingly complicated forms.

The Universal Declaration is not, of course, a treaty and has, in itself, no force in law. But, as "a common standard of achievement for all peoples and all nations," it not only crystallizes the political thought of our times on these matters, but it has also influenced the thinking of legislators all over the world. It is in this sense a worthy successor to the long line of affirmations of human liberties which began here in Williamsburg, though it is not and cannot be the final word in these questions, which by their very nature are as dynamic as life itself.

The relationship of man to society is a relationship for which every generation must seek to find the proper form. But, just as ideas far back in the past gave direction to the efforts for the best in former times, so this declaration should give direction to those who now carry the responsibility for a sound development of society.

As it stands, the Universal Declaration of Human Rights is both a symbol of the magnitude of the problem of human rights in our century and a measure of the concern with the problem which is shared by the governments and peoples represented in the United Nations. But it is also, in words for our time, a reminder of what must be the goal for the individual as well as for governments; the recognition in action of the dignity of man and of the sanctity of those freedoms which follow from such recognition.

Some days ago I returned from an assignment in the Middle East. I had to negotiate questions connected with the implementation of the armistice agreements between Israel and her Arab neighbor states. In their first articles those armistice agreements establish the right of each party "to its security and freedom from fear of attack." In a political context of the utmost significance, this clause recognizes a human right which, in a broad sense, may be said to sum up the whole philosophy of human rights.

What is the right to security? Is it not the right to the free development of individual and national life within the limits set by the right of other parties to the same security? What is the right to freedom from attack? Is it not the right to freedom from fear?

Thus we see how close the links are between the philosophy reflected in the recognition of the rights of individuals and the basic principles which may decide the issue of war and peace.

We all know how, when moved by fear, people may act against what others see as their own best interest. We know how, when people are afraid, they may act even against their own fundamental will. We have seen how, when influenced by such actions, the course of events may take on aspects of inexorable fatality up to the point where, out of sheer weariness, no resistance to the gravitation into open conflict any longer seems possible. This is a constantly repeated pattern of tragedy.

Why is war and fear of war in the headlines of every daily paper, if not because man fears man and nation, nation? Could there be a more eloquent sign of how far we are from recognition of the philosophy behind the principles of human rights on which alone peace can be built? Can there be a greater challenge for us to work for such a recognition of the dignity of man as would eliminate the fear which is eating our world like a cancer?

I have moved on from talking about the principles of human rights to touch upon the spirit behind those principles. That brings me to the point where our concern is no longer with social philosophy, or with political action, but with individual life. If, at long last, the recognition of human dignity means to give others freedom from fear, then that recognition cannot be simply a question of passive acceptance. It is a question of the positive action that must be taken in order to kill fear.

This is not a question of abstract ethical principles. I state conclusions from some very concrete recent experiences. It is when we all play safe that we create a world of the utmost insecurity. It is when we all play safe that fatality will lead us to our doom. It is "in the dark shade of courage" [1] alone, that the spell can be broken.

[1] From Ezra Pound, *The Cantos* "Canto XC," New Directions, 1970.

Address at New York University Hall of Fame Ceremony on the Unveiling of the Bust and Tablet for Woodrow Wilson

NEW YORK   MAY 20, 1956

May I first of all thank you for inviting me to join in this ceremony. An occasion such as this in the Hall of Fame for Great Americans belongs in a very special way to the American people. This is a national shrine. The men who are honored here have helped to make the history which is your national heritage. They are bone of your bones and flesh of your flesh.

In asking an international official—the Secretary-General of the United Nations—to speak on this occasion, you have, I am told, broken a precedent of long standing. I am deeply grateful for the generous thought which prompted your invitation. You have done so because of Woodrow Wilson's pioneering leadership in the struggle to achieve a just and peaceful international order.

Woodrow Wilson came to that leadership as an authentic and eloquent spokesman to the world of the spirit of American idealism. That spirit, expressed anew from generation to generation, is deeply rooted in your own national culture. But because it also reflects and shares ideals that are universal, it has often been an inspiring and enriching influence for all mankind.

This is the case with the great idealists of any age and culture. This was the case with Woodrow Wilson's advocacy of world organization. From the very first, he spoke in terms of universal ideals and of the common interest. His first public commitment to the idea of a League of Nations was made just forty years ago this month. It was made when he spoke on May 27, 1916, to a meeting of a group of world-minded Americans who had banded together as The League to Enforce Peace.

UN Press Release SG/480, May 18, 1956.

Why was an association of nations needed? Because, he said, "the peace of the world must henceforth depend upon a new and more wholesome diplomacy"; because "the principle of public right must henceforth take precedence over the individual interests of particular nations"; because "the nations of the world must in some way band themselves together to see that that right prevails as against any sort of selfish aggression"; because "there must be a common agreement for a common object" and "at the heart of that common object must lie the inviolable rights of peoples and of mankind."

In this same speech he defined some of these rights: the right of every people "to choose the sovereignty under which they shall live"; the right of small states "to enjoy the same respect for their sovereignty and territorial integrity as the great nations" and the right to be free from every disturbance of the peace "that has its origin in aggression and disregard of the rights of peoples and nations."

These statements of the reasons for, and purposes of, world organization are as much to the point today as when they were made forty years ago. In his stress upon the precedence of "public right" over "the individual interests of particular nations" and upon "common agreement for a common object"—that is for the rights of peoples—Woodrow Wilson went to the heart of the matter.

As he so clearly understood, the international interest had to be institutionalized if it were to have a reasonable hope of prevailing in the course of time. No matter how solemn the engagement to common purposes and universal aims, whether expressed in a Covenant for a League of Nations or in a Charter for the United Nations, institutions functioning continuously in the service of these purposes would be needed to give them effect. When he opened discussion of plans for a League of Nations at the Paris Peace Conference in January 1919, Wilson called for the creation of an organization that should, he stressed, be "not merely a formal thing, not an occasional thing, not a thing sometimes called into life to meet an exigency" but that should have a "vital continuity" of function. He summed it up in these expressive words: "It should be the eye of the nations to keep watch upon the common interest, an eye that does not slumber, an eye that is everywhere watchful and attentive."

Forty years after Woodrow Wilson first uttered these words, the idea of world organization is far more firmly established than it ever was in the years of the League of Nations. The mere fact that the United Nations, unlike the League, has never lost a Member state, and now, with seventy-six Members, seems to be moving inexorably toward true universality, speaks for this. But we are still seeking ways to make our international institutions fulfill more effectively the fundamental purpose expressed in Woodrow Wilson's words—"to be the eye of the nations to keep watch upon the common interest."

I have no doubt that forty years from now we shall also be engaged in the same pursuit. How could we expect otherwise? World organization is still a new adventure in human history. It needs much perfecting in the crucible of experience and there is no substitute for time in that respect.

Two of our most common human failings, indeed, seem to be our disrespect for the slow processes of time and our tendency to shift responsibility from ourselves to our institutions. It is too often our habit to see the goal, to declare it and, in declaring it, to assume that we shall automatically achieve it. This leads us to confuse ends with means, to label as failure what is in fact an historic step forward, and in general to mistake the lesser for the greater thing.

Thus Woodrow Wilson, in the years between the wars, was commonly considered to have failed because the United States refused to join the League of Nations. Yet, in fact, he had made history, great history, by being the principal founder of the first world organization.

The League itself was labeled a failure because its existence did not prevent a second World War. Yet the failure lay not in the League, but in the nations which failed to live up to their pledged word and also failed to infuse into the League as an institution the vitality and strength that Wilson had pleaded for in 1919.

In our day, too, we often hear it said that the United Nations has succeeded here, or has failed there. What do we mean? Do we refer to the purposes of the Charter? They are expressions of universally shared ideals which cannot fail us, though we, alas, often fail them. Or do we think of the institutions of the United Nations? They are our tools. We fashioned them. We use them. It is our responsibility to remedy any flaws there may be in them. It is our responsibility to correct any failures in our use of them. And we must expect the responsibility for remedying the flaws and correcting the failures to go on and on, as long as human beings are imperfect and human institutions likewise.

This is a difficult lesson for both idealists and realists, though for different reasons. I suppose that, just as the first temptation of the realist is the illusion of cynicism, so the first temptation of the idealist is the illusion of Utopia. As an idealist, it was natural that Woodrow Wilson also did not entirely escape his temptation, any more than have most of the idealists of history. In his valiant fight for the cause of the League of Nations, he went beyond the concept of an institution acting for the common interest of the peoples of the world. He visualized the establishment of the League as ending the old system of the balance of power and substituting what he called a "community of power."

The creation of a true community of power to serve the common interest is, indeed, the goal—now as it was in Woodrow Wilson's day. But the establishment of the League of Nations did not, and could not, of itself bring such a community of power into being. It did not, nor could it, end at one stroke the system of the balance of power in international affairs.

The League was an association of sovereign nation-states, just as the United Nations is today. In such an association, the play of the balance of power is inevitable. And it should be said that one of the most serious remaining obstacles in the way of public understanding of the true role of the United Nations today results from a similar tendency to picture the United Nations of 1945 as establishing collective security for the world.

Now, as then, it is important for all of us to understand that true collective security, in the sense of an international police power engaged to defend the peace of the world, is to be found at the end, not at the beginning, of the effort to create and use world institutions that are effective in the service of the common interest.

The spirit and practice of world community must first gain in strength and custom by processes of organic growth. It is to the helping along of these processes of growth that we should devote all our ingenuity and our effort. To the extent that we are able to increase the weight of the common interest as against the weight of special interests, and therefore of the power of the whole community to guide the course of events, we shall be approaching that much nearer to the goal.

This is, in fact, the most essential message of the career of Woodrow Wilson for the present day, whether we think of him as educator, as President of the United States, or as the pioneer of world organization.

Throughout his life he was the eloquent spokesman and dedicated champion of the general welfare both within his nation and among the nations of the world. Though his hopes for the enforcement of peace through collective security were ahead of the times, he also saw that international organization should rely primarily upon moral force, because—in his words—it was "intended as a constitution of peace, not as a league of war."

He understood very well what was at the root of the difficulty with making world organization work more effectively in the common interest and he expressed it in words that we would do well to turn into the first person plural and repeat to ourselves in our own times: "They have thought too much of the interests that were near them and they have not listened to the voices of their neighbors."

Woodrow Wilson could denounce such selfishness, as powerfully as he could evoke a vision of "pastures of quietness and peace such as the world never dreamed of before." He could also give movingly human expressions to his deep-seated faith in the processes of democracy. Just before he died in 1924, he told a friend: "I am not sorry I broke down. As it is coming now, the American people are thinking their way through and reaching their own decision, and that is the better way for it to come."

It is not only the American people, of course, but the peoples of many nations, who have been thinking their way through and reaching their own decision since Woodrow Wilson first showed the way. The United Nations stands as evidence of the direction of their thinking and of their decision.

How would Woodrow Wilson have reacted to the recent developments in the life of the United Nations?

Would he not have hailed the atomic conference at Geneva last summer as evidence of the possibilities of cooperation even in a divided world, when a major interest common to all is at stake? Would he not have been happy that this cooperation developed within the framework of an organization owing so much to his original conception?

Would he not have hailed the development of the membership, which shows the vitality of the concept of universality at the present juncture in the growth of internationalism?

And, although he certainly would have been deeply worried by the underlying problems, would he not have been happy to see how in the Middle East the United Nations machinery could help Member governments in crystallizing their wish to reestablish order?

I think he would, but I think he also would have found reason for criticism. He would have been surprised to see how far we have yet failed to bring international conflicts effectively under the rule of law.

Although the spokesman for "open covenants openly arrived at"— for democracy in international negotiation—he would also, I think, not have approved all of the applications given to that sound principle. Knowing too well the ways of man to believe in his ability to resist selfish or short-sighted public pressures, he would certainly have found it appropriate to plead for a combination of the new methods of diplomacy, of which he was in favor, with such of those time-honored political techniques as would give us the result best serving the interests of peace.

It is a true measure of the leadership and idealism of Woodrow Wilson that it is not a vain pastime in this way to give some thought to the question of how he would have looked at our endeavors, our failures, and our successes, in the fields to which he devoted the best of his life. He is not only the first and foremost spokesman for true international organization. He is one of those who helped to create an international conscience which is, and will remain, a living force in all attempts to build a world of order.

AN INTERNATIONAL ADMINISTRATIVE
SERVICE

1. Address before the International Law Association
at McGill University

MONTREAL   MAY 30, 1956

IN THIS ADDRESS Hammarskjöld proposed a new form of expert assistance by
international organization to the new countries of Asia and Africa, most of
which suffered (and still suffer) from a severe shortage of the administrators
and trained civil servants needed for their development programs. This
would be a career service in which qualified international officials would, in
effect, be seconded to serve inside national administrations in an executive
capacity rather than as technical advisers for specific projects. The concept
was bold and imaginative. As will be seen in later texts (pages 184,
185, 210, 217, and 225), it soon met with skeptical reception from both
industrially advanced countries and some of the underdeveloped nations.
The former feared the additional costs of a new and untried international
program and preferred to continue putting most of their dollars and effort
into bilateral aid. The new nations, on the other hand, were highly sensitive
about keeping their independence from old masters and some feared the
proposed program might become a vehicle for a new form of "neocoloni-
alism." Eventually Hammarskjöld succeeded in winning enough support to
launch the program but it was kept to a very modest, experimental scale.

It may be appropriate for me on this occasion to share with you some
thoughts about one of the greatest international problems which face
our postwar world.

It has often been pointed out that two of the major revolutionary developments of our time are aimed, on the one side, at realizing the principle of self-determination and, on the other hand, at improving the

UN Press Release SG/482, May 29, 1956; *United Nations Review,* Vol. III,
No. 1, July 1956.

economic and social conditions of life of that vast majority of mankind which, so far, have not shared in the advantages of modern technology.

These trends are closely related. A new national state needs a fair chance to develop its own economic and social life in such a way as to give a stable basis for its new position in the world community. On the other hand, when peoples who have been held back by poverty experience an improvement of economic and social conditions, the demand for self-determination will gain added strength.

Both of these developments—and the problems they present to statesmanship—are quite generally recognized. But, I fear, we must also recognize that, so far, the efforts made to deal with them have not been equal either to the scope or to the character of the problems. What we have done so far has been on the margin of the real difficulties. The time has come, I think, for us to reconsider our position.

Whatever may be our political philosophy we all recognize that it is impossible within any nation today to defend for long an inequality of economic conditions which the majority of the people believe to be unjust. This is true even when the average standard of living is so high that those who are less well off also have the possibility of a decent life. It is all the more true when conditions are such that the poorer people cannot meet the most elementary needs. Such differences render impossible the sound life of a nation.

What is a cause for unrest within a nation may become just as much a cause of unrest and instability in the international community. The problem has to be tackled. Neither its formidable dimensions, nor the fact that it has been with us for so long, is in any way an excuse for escapism.

In the beginning, I referred to two revolutionary tendencies: one in response to the economic problem just mentioned, the other one in the direction of self-determination. I pointed out the links between the two trends and how they mutually conditioned each other. The problem of self-determination with its deep roots in newly developed national feelings and the wider recognition of fundamental human rights is not less formidable nor in any lesser need of constructive solution than the economic problem. In fact, because of the relationship, the two problems must be tackled together and within the framework of a consistent philosophy.

Within a nation the natural solution to the problem of how to achieve a satisfactory income structure is to be found through efforts to improve the mechanisms of economic and social life so that the result is a more desirable balance. To keep the major part of the population on what amounts to a dole can never be a lasting solution, nor indeed is it even a sound, short-term approach except in a situation of acute emergency. One part of society should not live on gifts from the other part any more than one part of society should live on the exploitation of others.

Again there is no difference in this respect between the life of the international community and the life of the nation. Our ultimate aim must be to level off the dangerous and unacceptable differences between the standard of living and of economic development in various countries by means integrated in and natural to the normal working of the mechanisms of international economic life. It is only as an emergency measure that the industrially developed countries can or should be asked to help the others by assistance decided upon as a measure of political policy.

In the international sphere, the development of economic mechanisms removing the need for such direct assistance is difficult and time-consuming. It is enough to recall that the techniques which have been widely adopted for such purposes within nations during the last decades include elements which could have no application in the international community. In the international field we must rely exclusively on measures to promote and accelerate the advancement of the poorest. When trying to level out prevailing differences in standards of living it is, of course, not our task to lower the ceiling. The aim is to raise the floor.

The period during which international political measures for transfer of capital from the more developed countries to the countries in need of it will be necessary, is likely to be longer than would be tolerable within a national state. Whatever the time we may have to wait, we should never lose sight of the fact that until the free flow of capital, skills, commodities, and people can itself maintain the necessary economic balance between various countries, we shall not have solved our problem. We must likewise remember that whatever political arrangements we may choose, they should always be such as to lead as rapidly as possible in the direction of an economically self-sustaining solution.

It would take me too far to attempt to discuss here tonight why the international economy does not at present function in a way which gives promise of a speedy solution of the problem of unequal distribution of wealth in the world community. It would take me too far into the history of the last hundred years and, in particular, the disruption of previous patterns of trade and capital movements caused by more recent

political events. Let us, instead, simply note the fact that whatever international economic machinery there may once have been, it has broken down and that, short of a major effort, new mechanisms necessary
in order to safeguard the general interest in stability are not likely to
come into being. Let me also repeat that as this process will be a time-
consuming one, even if we devote to it our best efforts, we have for a
period of some length to take upon ourselves the burden of seeking to
cope by extraordinary means with the dangerous situation.

In the last few years a lot has been done on a multilateral basis
through international organizations like the United Nations or in the
forms of which the Colombo Plan offers an example, or on a bilateral
basis, as is the case with the United States' technical assistance, internationally most often referred to as the Point Four Program. When I said
that what has been done so far is not adequate, this does not imply that
I would in any way belittle the wisdom and the generosity shown by
those who have initiated and carried through such activities. On the
contrary, what has been done has been pioneer work deserving of the
highest praise. It has given us valuable experience. It has demonstrated
to the economically underdeveloped countries the sense of responsibility
of the industrially developed countries. It has laid the foundation on
which all further efforts must build.

The present pattern is one of mixed bilateral and multilateral approaches. For reasons which are natural in the light of national politics,
there has been a strong emphasis in practice upon a bilateral approach
while, at the same time, the advantages of the multilateral approach
have been recognized in principle.

The advantages of a bilateral approach to the problem of economic
assistance are obvious to all and need no elaboration. The disadvantages
seem to be less fully recognized. For the assisting country it is of course
an advantage to fly its flag, but it is a disadvantage when this leads to a
competition with other countries that only too easily takes on strong political overtones. It is a disadvantage also when, in a way only too well
known from individual life, it puts a strain on the relationship between
the giving and receiving countries. We should not forget that it may be
more difficult to live on the dole than to pay it. Few friendships survive
a long-drawn-out economic dependency of one upon the other. Gratitude is a good link only when it can be given and received without an
overtone of humiliation.

If we recognize that the question of how to level out the economic differences which endanger the stability of our world is of equal importance to all parties, there should, in fact, be no question of either generosity or gratitude. We face a situation where an improvement of present conditions is clearly in the common interest. Again I am tempted to draw a parallel with national life. Private benevolence and generosity have a part to play, but it is not until we move on from these to forms of assistance which are regarded as a necessary part of sound social organization that we reap the full benefits of what is being done.

The disadvantages of bilateral aid give also the chief reasons in favor of a greater internationalization of aid. In a body like the United Nations, or its sister agencies, we have institutions in which all members share the responsibility. Assistance rendered through such organizations is free from most of the weaknesses attached to bilateral aid, without eliminating the chief benefit to be reaped by those who contribute—that is, a more stable world for which such gratitude and pride as belong to any partner in a great constructive undertaking will be forthcoming.

The two approaches to international assistance, thus, have both advantages and disadvantages. However, there is no basic conflict between them and they should not be permitted to compete. As pointed out by, among others, the Canadian Secretary of State for External Affairs, Mr. Lester B. Pearson, they can and should be coordinated and mutually support each other. On this point I believe it is necessary for the governments and the peoples to review the position and to find a sound basis for the reconciliation of the natural national interest with those international considerations which also come into play.

I have linked the question of assistance for economic development, as a tiding-over operation pending a more normal solution, to the parallel problem of the emergence—or reemergence—into self-determination of a great number of peoples and nations. To a large extent, although not fully, the two problems cover basically the same regions of the world. Apart from the mutual relationship which exists between the two problems, they have one factor in common to which we should give special attention. This is a factor which, in my view, presents the greatest difficulty, though so far it is the least discussed and least recognized aspect.

Nations emerging from long foreign rule generally lack an independent administrative tradition and a social structure within which it is easy to build up a class of national administrators. This is a major problem not only for such nations, but also for many other countries which seek to achieve a major economic and social reconstruction and to use international economic assistance in the best possible way for this end.

It may be said that this question of administration, linked as it is to the related question of the social structure, constitutes the main bottleneck which must be broken in any soundly conceived policy aimed at solving the problems of self-determination and economic balance.

Nearly all the nations whose independence as modern states is of recent date are to be found in the economically underdeveloped areas of Asia and Africa. Their social organization and, in many cases, their administrative arrangements and the available trained personnel fall far short of their needs. No one who has spent even a short time in any of those lands can fail to have been impressed by the magnitude of the task with which the new leaders are grappling, or by the truly heroic character of the effort which some of them are making to establish more secure foundations for their country.

While the need for an expansion of economic aid is now generally recognized and the debate has, by and large, turned from questions of principle to a discussion of ways and means, insufficient attention has, I think, been given to this administrative difficulty in the path of economic development. The capacity of a country to absorb large-scale economic assistance or to make the best use of its domestic resources is in no small measure determined by its administrative arrangements. It is significant, for example, that in every one of the reports of the economic survey missions sent out by the United Nations and the International Bank, some reference has been made to the handicap imposed by poorly developed public administration and the shortage of competent officials. It is no disparagement of any of the countries concerned to note that the existing governmental organization is insufficient to carry out the greatly expanded public investment and development programs that are needed. Most of these countries have had only a short period to replace the arrangements of the former administering power with their own organization and to create a public service at once efficient and responsive to their will.

It is true that in some of the countries concerned, the former administering authority has bequeathed a valuable legacy in the form of an efficient administrative apparatus and sizable cadres of experienced local officials at many levels. But this is by no means generally so. Even where it is, it does not meet the needs of peoples whose awakening has stirred far deeper feelings of hope and endeavor than were felt under the most enlightened colonial régime. Great economic development programs have béen planned which are held back more by lack of men to direct them than by lack of capital. Great national programs of social welfare are failing to move forward primarily for lack of experienced officials to undertake the manifold administrative tasks which they entail.

In the long run national training programs for officials and workers will doubtless meet the needs of the new nations for administration of their development plans. But the long run may be very long and the need is urgent. It is for this reason that I welcome the suggestion of the Canadian Secretary of State for External Affairs, Mr. Pearson, that we should consider establishing what he describes as "an international professional and technical civil service of the United Nations with experts especially trained for work in the underdeveloped areas." This farsighted proposal stands, I feel, side by side in importance with the proposal recently made by the French Foreign Minister M. Pineau, who has called for the establishment of a new United Nations agency for world economic development.

Mr. Pearson's proposal might seem, at first glance, to call for no more than an extension of existing technical assistance activities of the United Nations. To my mind, however, it should, in the light of the immensity of the problems we are facing, imply a new departure along lines rather different from those we have hitherto followed. An essential feature of a new international service adequate for the task would be this: It would be a career service under international responsibility for qualified men and women of any nationality, who were prepared to devote a significant part of their lives to work in the less-developed countries of the world as public officials integrated in the national administrations of these countries while maintaining their international status. (In fact, such an arrangement was foreshadowed as early as 1951 in the Report of the United Nations Technical Assistance Mission to Bolivia, where it was proposed that "the United Nations assist the Bolivian Government in obtaining the services of a number of experienced and competent administrative officials of unquestioned integrity drawn from a variety of countries, and that the Bolivian Government appoint these officials on a temporary basis to positions of influence and authority as integral members of the Bolivian civil service.")

The highest standard of selection would rightly be demanded for such a service with special emphasis on quality of character and social outlook as well as upon intellectual background. Can it be imagined, though, that there would be any lack of candidates, well qualified and eager to take part in such an absorbing, so worthwhile a venture?

Before an international service of this kind on anything like the scale needed could be established, it would be necessary to clarify the principles which would govern its operation and to examine a number of legal and practical considerations to which such a program would give rise. Above all, it would be essential to remove any latent ambiguities in the relationships which will come into being between such officials enjoying the special responsibilities and status of an international official and the governments to which their loyal and devoted service would be due.

Quite apart from the other considerations which prompted M. Pineau to put forward his proposal for a new world economic development agency, the task of establishing and administering an international professional and technical civil service of the kind here envisaged seems to call for a reconsideration of our organizational approach to international aid and technical assistance. From such a reconsideration it may well emerge as M. Pineau assumes that these questions cannot be tackled in a satisfactory manner and on a sufficient scale without the establishment of a special administration.

A new agency, if established, would have to be brought into a relationship with the United Nations itself so close as to permit continued, intimate cooperation. Its main task would be a new one. It would place heavy emphasis on the strictly administrative problem of how best to establish, maintain, and run an international service which, on a secondment basis, could meet the need for qualified experts and officials in those countries which now have to develop independently their national life and, with international assistance, to build up a strong and sound economy.

In the present world situation, we have had a tendency to give much attention to the need for a wider movement of capital to areas in need of economic development. We are right in doing so. The needs are enormous. But even more important than the money are the skills. The greatest contribution to the creation of the world we want to see come into being is to put at the disposal of the less-developed countries our own human resources. Fundamentally, man is the key to our problems, not money. Funds are valuable only when used by trained, experienced, and devoted men and women. Such people, on the other hand, can work miracles even with small resources and draw wealth out of a barren land.

It should not be overlooked that even with the best of men half-hearted and timid measures will lead nowhere. The dynamic forces of history will overtake us unless we are willing to think in categories on a level with the problem. That is why we must be prepared to envisage such departures into new fields as those which have been suggested by the two distinguished political leaders to whom I have referred, proposals which I have permitted myself to link together and to develop somewhat further here tonight in a way which should not seem radical to those who have measured the full dimensions of the problem.

2. From Transcript of Press Conference Held at the Headquarters of the International Civil Aviation Organization

MONTREAL   MAY 30, 1956

. . . . QUESTION: Do you envision an international civil service pool from which countries could draw? Or do you see countries asking the United Nations for help and the United Nations going out and asking for, you might say, volunteers?

SECRETARY-GENERAL: I envisage a pool. My feeling is that the administrative problem which we are facing is so big that, the very moment the various governments most directly interested get down to it and find that there is such a possibility, there will be a very great demand indeed. Of course, today there is no possibility, really. Technical assistance experts are all right but they are international civil servants; they cannot be integrated into the home organization. If the United Nations family could meet that demand, I think we would render those countries and the world as a whole a very great service. But for that reason we have to do that in a pool, and a pool which I would guess would have to be of very considerable size. However, before building up the pool, as I indicated, I feel that we must solve some rather touchy problems because this will be a completely new kind of international administration. You see, on the one side, they will have the international loyalty

UN Note to Correspondents No. 1319, June 8, 1956.

under regular United Nations Charter oath of service—I will get back to that. On the other hand, they will be integrated in a national administration and, of course, being integrated, they should be 100 percent loyal servants of that administration. What we achieve is really for underdeveloped countries if this is realized—to get administrative help which is integrated in their own home service without in any way getting that unpleasant overtone of dependence on any one country or any risk of dual loyalty. You can well see that that is something which has to be thought out very carefully, and in consultation with countries likely to be interested. You see the present oath of service of a technical assistance man, an ICAO man or a UN man, is that he should not take or seek advice from any government. Well, in this case, of course, that should apply in the same way with one major exception—that he should be under the discipline and instructions of one Member government on the basis of some kind of contract between that Member government and whoever will administer it, the United Nations or a specialized agency or what not.

. . . . QUESTION: This United Nations agency, to begin with, is it proposed to supplement agencies like the Colombo Plan?

SECRETARY-GENERAL: Well, you see the Colombo Plan has a relation to the United Nations operations, and by UN operations I do not mean United Nations Organization operations—I mean operations by every single agency of the United Nations: ICAO, FAO, World Health, and so on, the whole family of UN organizations, on an equal level; we are all equals in that respect. The Colombo Plan is something different, of course. It is basically, after all, a kind of regional arrangement and it is a regional arrangement with somewhat of a bilateral accent in its operations. It is not fully internationalized in the sense that technical assistance operations are within the UN family. For that reason I would say that the relationship between whatever new administrative arrangements might come into being and the Colombo Plan would be exactly the same as those between any member agency of the United Nations family and the Colombo Plan. That is to say, there is no competition; they supplement each other in a certain way. There is a basic difference of approach in the sense that the United Nations family approach is in the most strict sense of the word fully internationalized, while the other one has certain elements which I wouldn't say narrow the basis but give it a character of being closer to group and bilateral approaches than you find in the United Nations family.

I should perhaps add one word about this business and its relation to the present operations in the United Nations. Probably you know very little about the organization of economic assistance as it is run at present in the United Nations family. The United Nations itself and the various specialized agencies run in principle their own technical assistance and their own economic assistance to the various countries. It is a series of autonomous operations coordinated at various levels.

Now I haven't raised, and I wouldn't like to raise, the question of how this new activity, which I would like to have considered as a purely administrative one, would fit into the picture. One possibility, of course, is just to add it and to coordinate it with the rest of the activities in the way ICAO activities are coordinated with United Nations activities. That is one possibility and that is perfectly natural.

On the other hand, there is the other possibility, and that is that the various governing bodies of the several specialized agencies would find that, with such a body, if created—I say again, if created—it might be a good idea to put on the shoulders of that organization certain of the activities which we run at present in the United Nations or which are run at present in the various specialized agencies. I wouldn't like to pre-judge that at all, because we are very far indeed from seeing such proposals as these put into effect. My main purpose has been not to try to tell how the problem should be solved, especially in relation to the United Nations family, but to try to point out that there is a problem which we haven't even really seriously discussed so far and which cannot be solved, as I see it, on the present basis without fairly far-reaching innovations.

I am quite sure that the United Nations itself, the General Assembly and governing bodies of the specialized agencies would like to have a very careful look at the impact of consequences of a departure in this new direction, and out of that would grow whatever may be the consensus on the right way to coordinate those new activities with the old ones, with or without the taking over of certain functions of the United Nations and specialized agencies. But as I say, this is a problem somewhat separate from the one of the Colombo Plan. We certainly wouldn't feel in any way embarrassed by this or in conflict or competition with it. We just could note that here is a new element which certainly is likely to prove most useful if it comes into being.

Basically, you know, in all these cases it is a question for very much the same group, the same Member governments—the governments are members of these various organizations and they have to make up their minds how best to tackle the practical problem. I repeat what I said, that my main purpose in this operation, or rather in this statement which I make today, is to bring sharply into focus the existence of the major problem.

. . . . QUESTION: Do you envisage, in this personnel pool that may be set up some time in the future, any particular problem insofar as the breakdown of national groups is concerned?

SECRETARY-GENERAL: Well, we will certainly run into problems there as we have done in all the international secretariats, and perhaps more here than anywhere else because it will be necessarily rather a touchy problem. My own feeling is that it should be very much on the same basis as you find, under the Charter terms, in the United Nations and other organizations in the United Nations family—that is to say, with so-called wide geographic distribution. But, on the other hand, the question of competence, experience, and so on will necessarily come in as a very major consideration. You are likely to need a certain kind of people having a certain professional training, and they are not to be found all over the world. Then I happen to have a personal view in this case, and that is that on the whole the more we mix people the better it is. That is to say, I would not favor very much having, in this special context, "Asia for the Asians." I do not think it would be a good idea. I think that it is good for Westerners, whether it is from this or that part of the Western Hemisphere or from Europe or from other parts, to get a more intimate inside knowledge of the Asian world in the same way. Mind you, it is not only in the Asian or African world that you find countries in need of this kind of help. I would, on the other hand, be very happy to see Asians with very fine administrative and technical experience—of whom we find quite a few—take part and help on the Western side.

But it is quite obvious that, as in this case the national viewpoints—the national government viewpoints—must come heavily into play, they should fit them into their own pattern. The recruitment problem will be more difficult than it has been in an international secretariat where they are, so to say, behind the fence in the sense that they are working together inside the framework of one unit. Here they will be split up in very many units, and very many units spread all over the world. So you can easily see, with some imagination, that that, too, is a question to which we will have to give quite a lot of thought. But that should not stop us.

.... QUESTION: Do you suggest that it would be an ideal state to have these underdeveloped countries have their problems administered by people of their own nationality and language, and I believe you suggest that this might be some time in coming? To your mind, what might be a major danger that could arise before this ideal situation is arrived at?

SECRETARY-GENERAL: Well, you see, we are in a certain sense in a hurry. The newly awakened national feelings—and very sound national feelings—which you find reflected in the demands for self-determination, and all that, have also their reflection in the demand—and I think basically a justified demand—for an improvement of living conditions. As you know, these are incredibly low in some places. Now, as I see the danger and the difficulty, they are as follows. To administer a major social and economic operation of the kind necessary in order to raise the economic standard and the standards of living in a reasonable time, you need fairly experienced administration. Some countries have got it, and some countries are likely to be quite successful in that effort. They can, so to say, absorb the capital which will flow their way. In other cases—and I could give you examples—with a very qualified central group in and behind the government they are at the same time short of people down the line; in those cases you have the situation of a very qualified top group, enormous economic needs, the economic means available, but no possibility for the top group to use the means for the needs because there is this gap in the administrative structure down the line.

That is the sort of case where I do feel that the international community has a responsibility which it could fill. But, as you stressed very, very rightly, I feel that it is a temporary solution because, of course, every major economic and social operation for the lifting of people necessarily is and should be the nation's own show; if you will permit a somewhat vulgar term, it should be the nation's show also in the sense that it is run to the fullest possible extent by a national administration. For that reason, this international assistance with experts, technicians, administrators, and so on and so forth is just something you have to use for a while. But the real reason I consider this to be pressing and urgent is that, even with the best will in the world, and even with the most qualified and far-sighted governments in charge, you just cannot use the means unless you have people down the line. A national administration is something that goes straight through society, as we know, and there you need people. The reason it takes some time to build it up is, first of all, that it does require tradition and experience, but, secondly, something which you realize, namely, that a good administration must have a kind of substratum from which to recruit.

The question of good administration is related to the question of social structure, and if you take some countries in Africa or Asia you find a curious structure. You find an extremely poor farmer class, which is the great majority of the people; you find a small commercial class, for example; and you find a small, leading group—intellectual, and very often with Western training and so on. But you have not got what we in the West would call the fairly broad and solid middle class. You have not got this in-between group from which, I think, the universities and colleges in the West and the administrations in the West recruit most of their people. You just have not got it. That will come the very moment we get the proper kind of economic and social development. It will grow naturally, as it has grown in the West. But, waiting for that, we will be in a vicious circle, because you cannot get the proper substratum from which to recruit an administration without an economic improvement, and you cannot get economic improvement without having the people you can recruit from such a class. That is to say, we are in a kind of deadlock, and it seems to me that a good way out would be to offer our services.

Now I should add one thing, and that is, of course, that in this case as in other cases I would warn personally very strongly against the idea that we should go in in any, let us say, paternal way and push this or that kind of proposal. An idea like this one, or a development like this one, is something which has to be asked for, properly understood, and sponsored primarily by the countries in need—not by the countries which wish to render services. That is to say, if I may go back to the phrase I used in reply to the representative of *The New York Times,* it is again a question of making an international service available. It is not a question of forcing an international service on these countries.

QUESTION: Is it your suggestion that there is an imbalance between the technical and the economic facilities being offered these underdeveloped countries by the United Nations or by the West?

SECRETARY-GENERAL: In very many cases, yes. In very many cases we are more advanced on the economic side than on the administrative side. Now, it so happens that I do not consider that we, either, are sufficiently advanced on the economic side. So you can easily see that what I am trying to do is also to reestablish a little bit more of the balance.

People are asking and asking and asking the political leaders—and, also the Secretary-General—for more money for technical assistance and economic assistance. But what's the use of asking for money unless you can take care of it in the proper way and use it in the right way?

QUESTION: Do you advocate any particular system which might be better than another to bring all this about—whether it's free enterprise, Communism, Socialism, Social Credit?

SECRETARY-GENERAL: I think it has very little to do with ideologies or principles. Every country will find its own way, its own balance, its own form. This is a case where I personally happen to hope that private initiative will take all possible responsibility. I think that is a sound thing. And you will find in the text of what I say that I stress very strongly that we should get into a system where economic life, so to say, is self-sustaining, without any policy measures and introduction of foreign elements of this kind. In that sense, you may find it rather liberal in its ideology, and it certainly is in its intentions.

On the other hand, I think that even the most staunch liberals will have to recognize that sometimes private initiative falls short of the need—and, in this case, a need with considerable risk-taking. This is not an income-yielding enterprise at all. The common sense and responsibility which you can mobilize, in political terms, in most countries has to come into play to supplement—at least while waiting for the initiatives—and, in a certain sense, to prepare the ground for the initiatives. If I happened to be an investor, I would be rather reluctant to get going on investments in certain regions—unnamed—until we had got this further development which is not likely to come about without international cooperation. So it's "both-and" and it's a question of the time sequence. . . .

On the Uppsala Tradition—
From Address after Receiving Honorary Degree
at Upsala College

EAST ORANGE, N. J.   JUNE 4, 1956

. . . . The name of this college carries with it a responsibility—not because the name is shared with the great sister institution in Sweden —but because of what the name symbolizes of human endeavor, of ideals, and of their realization. The name carries with it memories from what is known to us as the first religious shrine in the North to which people from all over Scandinavia found their way. It carries memories of the birth of the national state we today call Sweden. It reminds us of great Roman Catholic archbishops and, later, of the Reformation and the Thirty Years War. Its history as a center of learning is marked by names such as Rudbeck and Linné.

A name with such traditions is a challenge. But it can rightly be for us also a source of pride only when we, in our own efforts, live up to the standard it sets for us.

The Uppsala tradition reflects, within its limited sphere, a heritage which I feel has something to give to our world of today. It may, therefore, be justified to say a few words about what this heritage means. In doing so I am not referring to any country or people but to a spiritual legacy beyond such boundaries.

At their best the representatives of this legacy show the quiet self-assurance of people firmly rooted in their own world, but they are, at the same time and for that very reason, able to accept and develop a true world citizenship. At their best they are not afraid to like the man in their enemy and they know that such liking gives an insight which is a source of strength. They have learned patience in dealings with mightier powers. They know that their only hope is that justice will prevail and for that reason they like to speak for justice. However, they also know the dangers and temptations of somebody speaking for justice without

UN Press Release SG/484/Rev. 1, June 4, 1956.

humility. They have learned that they can stand strong only if faithful to their own ideals, and they have shown the courage to follow the guidance of those ideals to ends which sometimes, temporarily, have been very bitter. And, finally, their spirit is one of peace. . . .

FROM TRANSCRIPTS OF
PRESS CONFERENCES
JUNE—JULY 1956

THE SECRETARY-GENERAL left New York on June 27 for official visits to Warsaw, Helsinki, Moscow, Prague, Belgrade, and Vienna, ending with his usual summer stay at Geneva. The trip brought him to the Soviet Union and its Eastern European allies for the first time. In Moscow he talked with Bulganin and Khrushchev, then respectively Premier and Communist party First Secretary, and with the new Soviet Foreign Minister Dmitri T. Shepilov who had replaced Molotov a few weeks before. Shepilov was just back from a ten-day visit to Arab countries in the Middle East.

Hammarskjöld told the press in New York on June 22 (first following text) that he had no plan to return to the Middle East while in Europe, though he did not exclude the possibility. A few days later he changed his mind and on June 26 wrote privately to David Ben-Gurion proposing a visit with him on July 19 and 20. This was agreed to during his Eastern European tour, and was to be followed by a visit to Amman and Cairo on July 21 and 22. To the correspondents in Geneva on July 24 (fifth following text) he described this trip as "just a check-up visit, without any agenda" but he was obviously concerned by the lack of progress toward converting "the legal cease-fire . . . into a state of mind," as he had put it at his June 22 press conference. His careful replies to questions on the Middle East at his Moscow press conference and at Vienna may also be noted (second and fourth following texts).

1. From Transcript of Press Conference
UN HEADQUARTERS NEW YORK   JUNE 22, 1956

. . . . QUESTION: Are you planning, by any chance, within this summer, to go back to the Middle East?

THE SECRETARY-GENERAL: I have no plans at all. You see, the Middle East necessarily has a kind of first priority in my working plans at pre-

UN Note to Correspondents No. 1327, June 22, 1956.

sent. For that reason I never exclude anything. On the other hand, I have so far not included anything of that kind. I would, however, perhaps, because of your question, go on a little beyond this immediate journey and look ahead because that leads to a somewhat fuller reply to what you have in mind.

In August, still under the assumption that circumstances are favorable, I would make an attempt, at the end of the month, to go to a few of the Latin American countries which I have so far not been able to visit. It is again just an attempt to establish a somewhat closer personal contact; there is no specific political purpose behind this. That would bring us up to some time in September. In September we are likely to have the atomic agency conference here at Headquarters, which I should attend, at least at the beginning. Further, we shall have, of course, the preparation of the General Assembly. When the Assembly gets started, as you know, for something like three or four months I shall be practically tied to Headquarters, which will make it impossible for me to go out on any travels or negotiations. For that reason, I have reserved time in October for a visit to the Middle East. Mind you, I phrase it with care—I have reserved time for it. I think that it would be desirable for me to maintain as close a personal contact with the situation as I can, and this would be the last opportune moment before the General Assembly. For that reason, I wish to keep the possibility open. This does not necessarily mean that I will go. I have not discussed it with the countries in the region. But you can certainly see that in this kind of longer-term planning it is wise for me to keep such a possibility open and time reserved. That does not necessarily mean that I may not go earlier. That obviously depends both on the possibility of my getting away and my feeling as to the usefulness of such an expedition. If I go earlier, it is only too likely that the October plan will be changed—that the earlier trip will be made instead of the later one. There is nothing which is hard and fast in the plan apart from the atomic conference here at Headquarters, which is a conference I should like to attend.

QUESTION: Could you tell us anything about any contacts that you have had since the Security Council resolution was adopted by way of its implementation?

THE SECRETARY-GENERAL: The implementation of the resolution in the first instance, as you know, just means a follow-up of previous contacts—to get on with it, to get the practical local arrangements carried through, and to widen the field in which we get the situation under control. I think I have mentioned to a few of you—it was not a press conference—that in fact I use practically daily one or another of the possible means of contact—direct communication with the governments, contact with the delegations here, or contact via the Chief of Staff or his representative in Jerusalem. The scope of those contacts is described fully by what I have said.

As a matter of course we here on the inside think a little bit ahead, but I do not think it would be useful in any way to get into that thinking ahead. What is essential is that the follow-up activity is going on without interruption. I will have a gap now for a fortnight when I am traveling around. It is just as easy for me to run this special part of my job from Geneva as it is from here.

. . . . QUESTION: Mr. Secretary-General, we always switch back to the Near East. I have here a clipping that quotes an Arab paper of Lebanon, *Al Goumhouria*. It states: "On the basis of informed sources, Mr. Hammarskjöld is proposing or will propose a new approach to the solution of the Palestine problem in this manner: that Egypt remove the blockade of the Suez Canal; that Israel return immediately 100,000 Arab refugees on condition that the rest of the refugees be settled elsewhere, with the help of $200 million from the United States." This is quoted in your name in this newspaper of Beirut. I wonder if you can tell us anything about it.

THE SECRETARY-GENERAL: I can indeed. I can tell you that one of my greatest delights during the last few months has been to read what I am supposed to have said. In this case I have to extend the tribute I have paid to the imagination of the press to the imagination of that informed source, whoever it may be. He has certainly cooked up something where he has pieced together elements from my report, where I mentioned the Suez story, and elements from the Conciliation Commission protocols of a few years back, and elements of the Dulles Plan of August 1955. But this special cocktail, the combination, is his own invention. It is an unusual cocktail.

QUESTION: Since you just mentioned Mr. Dulles, may I ask whether in your conversation with Mr. Dulles last week the question of forwarding his plan in the next few months figured in terms of your visit to Moscow?

THE SECRETARY-GENERAL: As a matter of course, I cannot go into the substance of my talk with Secretary Dulles in any way. We more or less covered the waterfront on those matters which have come up here as important issues since we met the last time.

QUESTION: The Visiting Mission has reported to the Trusteeship Council on its visit to the Pacific Islands. The Mission brought back the news that the [radiation] dosage to which people in the Marshall Islands have been subjected has been sometimes ten times as much as the permissible radiation dose suggested by the report of the National Academy of Sciences, which was distributed by the United States Mission the other day. Similarly that report says that Bikini and Eniwetok will not be habitable for a long time to come, if ever. I should like to ask you if you have any observations on weapons testing in Trust Territories that would enhance our thinking on this subject.

THE SECRETARY-GENERAL: When I saw this information, my own feeling was that it was very good that the last General Assembly established a highly qualified committee which covers a much broader subject, of course, but which is able to speak with some knowledge of the facts and problems on these issues. I find myself in what I guess is roughly your situation—knowing too little about it to feel that it makes any sense to me to express my view before I have heard the comments of people who are more informed about these matters than I am.

QUESTION: I am particularly interested in the role of the Trusteeship Council, on which we should have some opinions. At least I have some.

THE SECRETARY-GENERAL: I cannot anticipate what kind of stand or line the Trusteeship Council may take on these issues. It is in their hands to decide whether and to what extent this is within their competence and for me to express views on what is the right procedure would certainly cause the Trusteeship Council some surprise. I do feel that once we have the Committee on Atomic Radiation, it will be very natural to rely heavily on it for its conclusions, which I would consider to be valuable and a solid guidance for us as laymen. I guess that the Trusteeship Council, wise people that they are, also know that they know very little about this whole matter before they have heard expert opinions on a broad front, experts from different schools and different countries.

. . . . QUESTION: Are you planning to discuss Austria's obligation under the Charter in view of its declared neutrality?

THE SECRETARY-GENERAL: No, I do not see any reason to do that. You will remember that I come myself from a country which is representative of one type of neutrality. I spend very much of my time in Geneva. Switzerland is another type of neutrality. I have never found any reason to discuss the possibility of reconciling Sweden's position within the United Nations, nor have I found any reason to go into Swiss neutrality as a reason for staying out of the United Nations. It is just something which is part of our political map today, and I do not think, in the light of that, that it is very likely that this matter will come up in any form.

QUESTION: This is a very interesting course of discussion here, because there is a great debate now on types of neutrality. Would you care to enlarge just a little bit on what type of neutrality Sweden has, for instance, or would you not want to get into that debate?

THE SECRETARY-GENERAL: From my examples you have gathered that I do not know of any encyclopedia definition of neutrality, which I consider very interesting politically. I really do regard every single case as a case in its own right, with its own specific problems, and to start out discussing any one of those specific problems—well, I would with pleasure do it one evening with you, Frank [Francis Carpenter, *Associated Press*], but I do not think we should take up time with it here.

QUESTIONER: I shall look forward to that.

QUESTION: Do you agree that neutrality is immoral—end of quotation?

THE SECRETARY-GENERAL: Well, gentlemen, we are coming very quickly to, so to say, the free-lance part of the press conference. That is all right. For my own part, I think that neutrality may be moral, that neutrality may be immoral, that lack of neutrality may be moral, that lack of neutrality may be immoral—it all depends on factors which are not strictly linked to the definition.

. . . . QUESTION: Coming back to what you said about your contacts with the countries of the Middle East, would you say that any progress has been made since the last Security Council meeting?

THE SECRETARY-GENERAL: I would say "yes," and I would say so for a reason which I think is obvious to you. An operation such as this is one in which the general rule that, if you do not make progress, you slip back, does not apply. This is an operation in which, as I see it, if you have made progress in the initial stage and managed to maintain it, you should be quite satisfied. My dream is, so to speak, to see the legal cease-fire converted into a state of mind. I firmly hope that that process is going on—at least, I have no clear indication that it is not—and I would consider that this very early stage of convalescence warrants a reasonably favorable doctor's report.

QUESTION: In connection with the great tidal wave which we are now witnessing for the establishment of a sizable international fund for the economic development of the underprivileged areas, there appears to be a school of thought which is arising as the primary formidable argument against it, to the effect that some big power—the Soviet Union has been named—might control such a fund in such a way as to serve its national policies, or some other big power perhaps might do so. What is your opinion? On the basis of past experience here in technical assistance, is it possible for any such international fund to be kidnapped by some big power, or little power, or any combination of powers, in such a way that the baby would disappear?

THE SECRETARY-GENERAL: If that happened, I would say that we were running the show very badly from the Secretariat's side. Another observation is that the kind of risk you have in mind is something that should be thought of when we frame the statute and set up the rules of the game for such a fund. Once we have done that—and if we have done it with reasonable wisdom—I would be very sorry indeed if we indulged in that favorite game of this age, to fear big ghosts and all sorts of risks, and for that reason shied away from what we should do.

QUESTION: We are approaching the eleventh anniversary of the signing of the Charter. At the tenth anniversary meetings in San Francisco, there seemed to be a sudden reversal from the old deadlock that occurred so many times in the first ten years of the United Nations, and a new sense of cooperation was evident. How would you evaluate this last year that has passed?

THE SECRETARY-GENERAL: I think that the last year, from that point of view, has been a reasonably good one, don't you? We have not lost ground, at all events, and I think we have gained some—in rather unexpected directions at times, but anyway we have gained it.

QUESTION: What do you think the chances for world peace are today as compared with a year ago?

THE SECRETARY-GENERAL: That is an impossible question to answer. I do not believe that world peace is threatened, nor did I so believe one year ago. That does not mean, of course, that we may not have a mess. But that is an entirely different story.

. . . . QUESTION: While you are in Geneva, will you see any Red Chinese? Have you heard anything from the Red Chinese since our last press conference?

THE SECRETARY-GENERAL: I have no reason to get in touch with either Ambassador Wang Ping-nan or Ambassador Johnson. There is nothing special in my mind which would cause such an approach on my part.

QUESTION: Is anything being done further with regard to the Americans who are still left in China?

THE SECRETARY-GENERAL: I believe that, as I have already told you, from my point of view, as long as the Geneva discussion is continuing, it has a natural priority. I do not consider that any initiative on my part would be in any way helpful. It might even introduce a risk of some kind of crossing of wires.

.   .   .   .

---

2. From Transcript of Press Conference
MOSCOW   JULY 5, 1956

THE SECRETARY-GENERAL: Gentlemen, I think there is no need for me to introduce myself, as I take it that you all know who I am. I will therefore confine myself to two general observations.

In the first place, I should like to say how pleased I am to have met you, to have met this gathering of press representatives, this being my first experience here of the kind. In the second place, I would point out that you are accustomed to interviewing politicians. But I regard myself as a little different from ordinary politicians, as I am the servant of seventy-six nations representing the most varied political philosophies and outlooks. This does not of course mean that I am completely neutral and have no point of view of my own. But my position is nevertheless affected by this fact. I should therefore also like to say that I am afraid my answers will perhaps strike you as rather general.

This is really all I had to say.

And now the floor is yours.

QUESTION: To the best of my knowledge, this is Mr. Hammarskjöld's first visit to the Soviet Union. In view of this, I should like to know what impressions he has gained from his stay in our country.

THE SECRETARY-GENERAL: It is correct that this is my first visit to the USSR. However, I had previously studied Russian affairs in the United

Unnumbered mimeographed press note, July 5, 1956.

Nations and so what I have seen in the USSR has served to fill in the general picture I already had.

I have met and talked to the people I wanted to meet and have seen what I wanted to see. I am very grateful for the hospitality I have received and for the confidence placed in me during my talks.

I have seen interesting examples of construction work in the USSR, such as the building of the Moscow State University. I have also acquainted myself with the great art treasures in the country.

Unfortunately, I have not been able to meet the general public and my impressions are therefore to some extent incomplete. But I am extremely satisfied with my visit and am only sorry that I came to the USSR so late and that my visit has been so brief.

QUESTION: You recently visited the countries of the Near East. Would you be good enough to give us your views on a peace settlement in this area?

THE SECRETARY-GENERAL: The situation in the Middle East is a very large question and my answer may sound a little general.

I must state that both the parties to this conflict unquestionably desire peace. It may then be asked why, if this is so, does such a situation exist. The cause lies partly in historical circumstances, partly in the manner in which the question was settled before and after the Armistice, and partly in a variety of psychological factors.

In my view, the period of the greatest complexity in this area after the conclusion of the Armistice has been the last eighteen months or two years. I consider it necessary that efforts should be made to restore normal conditions along the lines laid down in the Armistice Agreement and on the basis of the existing demarcation lines.

In this connection, I should like to refer to the Soviet Government's declaration of April 17, according to which an attempt should be made to find a settlement in the area of the Near East on a mutually acceptable basis. If we succeed in stabilizing the situation on the basis of the Armistice Agreement, our first object will have been accomplished. Unquestionably, no settlement is feasible in the Near East except as a result of agreement between the interested parties. I doubt whether it can be said that any type of mediation is now possible there. I believe that agreement can be reached only as a result of a direct contact between the governments concerned. In this matter, in my view, the governments must have the last word.

QUESTION: Has Mr. Hammarskjöld anything to say about his talks with Mr. Shepilov, who has also recently returned from a visit to the Middle and Near East?

THE SECRETARY-GENERAL: I usually decline to answer such questions. On this occasion, however, I might briefly say that we exchanged information on the question under discussion and acquainted each other with our respective points of view.

. . . . QUESTION: Mr. Hammarskjöld said that he would like to discuss a number of questions affecting the Near East with the governments concerned. Does he regard the Soviet Government as one of the governments concerned?

THE SECRETARY-GENERAL: I should like to say that the term "governments concerned" is not altogether appropriate in this context; the term used in this connection should be the "governments directly concerned," i.e., the governments in the region with whom it is necessary to maintain contact with a view to the settlement of these problems. Where the Government of the Soviet Union is concerned, my aim was a mutual clarification of views.

As regards the question of tension in the area of the demarcation line, I have discussed here questions connected with operation of the cease-fire in practice and my own appraisal of the situation. The settlement of the conflict is solely a matter for the governments directly concerned, i.e., the Governments of the Arab states and the Government of Israel. At the present stage, we should seek to promote a settlement on the basis of the foundation which has already been laid.

. . . . QUESTION: We are aware of the statements you have made regarding the universality of the United Nations. Could you please tell us what you think would be the best means of rectifying the present inequitable situation in which the People's Republic of China is still deprived of its legal rights in the United Nations?

THE SECRETARY-GENERAL: You are quite correct in saying that I have expressed myself in favor of universality for the United Nations. The United Nations made definite progress in that direction with the decisions taken last year. Where the question of the Chinese People's Republic in the United Nations is concerned, this has long been a subject of heated discussion in the United Nations. The Secretary-General cannot determine the views of the members of the United Nations, with whom alone a decision on this question rests. I would therefore prefer not to go into the question at the present time.

. . . . QUESTION: The United States press reports that one of the purposes of your visit to the Soviet Union is to attempt to organize a further meeting of the Foreign Ministers of the four powers late this year or early next year. Have you anything to say on this subject?

THE SECRETARY-GENERAL: I must ascribe statements of this kind to the imagination of certain representatives of the press. Any such purpose would, I consider, to be outside my sphere of competence and activity.

. . . .

3. From Transcript of Press Conference

PRAGUE　　　JULY 7, 1956

. . . . QUESTION: As is well known, the Disarmament Commission has now been in session in New York for a week. The readers of the *Rude Pravo* would greatly appreciate it if you could give your views on the course and on the outlook of the work of this Disarmament Commission.

THE SECRETARY-GENERAL: As you understand, during the last few days I have found it very difficult, indeed impossible, to follow the day-to-day work of the Disarmament Commission as I have traveled around, and even the most frequent reports never cover the ground in the way one wishes. However, by tomorrow I will have a very full report as the Principal Secretary of the Disarmament Commission will join my party for a few days, and he has with him such a report of what has happened during the last week. For that reason, I have to limit my reply to my own judgment on the chances as they look to me, with a reserve for whatever developments may have taken place without my knowledge.

You have to realize one thing, and that is that I seem to belong to an optimistic minority. I do not in any way feel ashamed of the fact that I find myself in such a minority because I feel that I have good reasons for my belief. First of all, the experience so far of disarmament work has been that we cannot evaluate it on its face value. At face value, the various debates in the Sub-Committee have always seemed rather disap-

Unnumbered mimeographed press note, July 7, 1956.

pointing. But it has always emerged—and I have tried to explain this impression of mine to your colleagues a few times—that when one meets again a few things have happened. After all, the debates are perhaps not so much negotiations intended to lead to hard and fast results at a table, as the sounding out of possibilities and opinions which later on are digested by the governments and on which they act. So that when the governments meet the next time, they have tried to all extent possible to adjust their thinking and their approach in order to make the most constructive possible approach.

The result has been that we have proceeded, so to say, by jumps from one meeting to the next of the various organs on disarmament, and the silent period between the meetings seems in a certain sense to have been more productive as the period of gestation than the discussions immediately seem to warrant. I firmly hope that the same will prove true in the case of the Disarmament Commission.

Then there is a recent very important added element; that is, in the Disarmament Commission there is an additional number of countries around the table as compared with the Sub-Committee, and we all know the constructive fertilizing influence that the addition of new voices may have on the debate. A further observation is that interest in disarmament is especially pronounced in small countries. For that reason, although they have no decisive voice and they are not parties concerned in the first instance, it is not unlikely that the debate with broader representation would show a greater intensity and eagerness than you might feel has been found in the discussions so far.

There is one thing I should like to stress in this context: What we are aiming at is, of course, agreed steps toward disarmament. That should not in any way exclude unilateral steps. On the contrary, I believe that unilateral steps may give quite some momentum to efforts toward an agreed solution. But I think one should never forget that until and unless we get an agreed solution we have not really achieved what we are aiming at. This is a case where we must show quite some patience because very serious security, psychological, and technical problems are involved. It is definitely a field where progress at the very best is slow, until you have got considerable improvement of the international atmosphere. Now there is, of course, a kind of shuttle traffic between the improvement in the international atmosphere and disarmament. On the one hand, as I said, disarmament is not likely to come about in an efficient, effective way short of a further improvement in the international situation. On the other hand, I do not think any single policy move will contribute more to an improvement in the international atmosphere than an agreement on even the most modest step in the direction of disarmament.

QUESTION: Mr. Secretary-General, I understand that during your stay here you had talks with President Zapotocky, also the Deputy Prime Minister, the Chairman of the National Assembly, and other officials. Could you perhaps tell us some details of the subjects you discussed, and in particular whether the question of the supplying of Czechoslovak arms to Egypt and other Arab countries was touched upon?

THE SECRETARY-GENERAL: It is right that I have paid a call on the President; it is right that I had even a long discussion with the Acting Prime Minister, the Foreign Minister, and others of the political leaders and members of the government here in Prague. The discussions have been of a very general nature, only an exchange of information concerning such matters which represented a special area or, rather, in which both the Czechoslovak government and I myself had special interest within the sphere of the General Assembly agenda and my own competence. As to details, I simply have to follow the rule, which I think you fully understand, that I am not free to discuss my discussions. In general terms I may, perhaps, say, without any indiscretion in relation to the Czechoslovak government, that the discussion has brought out the strong wish of the Czechoslovak government to support the UN efforts in general.

. . . .

---

4. From Transcript of Press Conference

VIENNA   JULY 10, 1956

. . . . QUESTION: I should like to ask two questions. The first is this: What significance do you attach to the forthcoming Tito-Nasser meeting? In other words, what do you think is to be anticipated from this meeting? The second question is: Now that Austria is a member of the

Unnumbered mimeographed press note, July 10, 1956.

United Nations, is there a prospect that Austrians will be appointed to the staff of the United Nations?

THE SECRETARY-GENERAL: On the first point, I may be included among those who believe that direct contacts between the leading states-men are in most cases extremely useful. We live in a world with too many misunderstandings and in which all sorts of clarifications certainly are necessary. To go beyond that in making any comments on the meet-ing between Marshal Tito and Colonel Nasser would be, for obvious reasons, impossible.

As regards the other question, I hope that now that Austria is a Member of the United Nations, we shall find possibilities to open the doors for Austrians to all types of cooperation within the Secretariat or in special committees of the Organization. It is necessarily a somewhat time-consuming process, because there are sixteen or seventeen new Members and they have entered when everything has already been set up. But I can assure you that not only among the other Member Na-tions but also in the Secretariat and among those I have to represent, there is the strongest wish to open possibilities to active cooperation for Austrians in all respects.

QUESTION: While you were at Moscow did you touch on the Middle East question, and were you given any promises which you could tell us about? I should like to ask one further question. According to reports in the press, shortly after your stay you are to leave for Jerusalem. You already know the area; you were there a short time ago and were very successful. Have you a clear-cut plan for settling the situation between Israel and Jordan and for reducing tension as was done in the case of Israel and Egypt?

THE SECRETARY-GENERAL: As to the first question, what I have al-ready said does apply. I should not like to say which questions were discussed in Moscow. But I have already said to your colleagues in Moscow that all those matters within the Secretary-General's compe-tence which were of mutual interest were on the table before us. You can easily guess where you have to put the question of the Middle East. The discussion was not especially for the Middle East in any way. We just covered the ground—the waterfront, as it is said in America.

As regards the other question, when I go back now it is just because, as the press communiqué stated, I do find the time, being in Geneva, to make new personal contacts. It is not for any specific purpose. It is just that this affair is now one of very close cooperation between the governments in the region and the Secretariat. For that reason I should take every opportunity available to keep that contact alive through personal visits also.

I have no ready-made plan for solving anything in the region. I do not think that anybody, in fact, has one. That does not mean that I do not have certain ideas about the direction in which things should go. I feel, however, that such ideas should first of all be aired and tried out with the governments in the region. In that light I can only say now that my firm plans do not extend beyond making the present cease-fire as much of a reality as possible—to make the change, as I said in a press conference in New York, from a legal concept to a state of mind.

QUESTION: On your visit to Moscow, did you get the impression that the change of course in the Soviet Union might really provide the basis for a genuine rapprochement?

THE SECRETARY-GENERAL: You have asked me for very much. I do not think that I could reply to that question on any basis with any meaning. I would certainly find it a bit difficult to discuss a question of that type. I do want to say that, as Secretary-General of the United Nations, I have been pleased already to note in New York—and that was confirmed in Moscow—that representatives of the Soviet government are very much in support of some of the things which I have to do in fulfilling my duties as Secretary-General; that is to say, some of the specific efforts in which I am engaged have their support.

. . . .

5. *From Transcript of Press Conference*

GENEVA   JULY 24, 1956

THE SECRETARY-GENERAL: It is with great pleasure that I am once more here in Geneva meeting with you. I fear perhaps that on this occasion you will talk less about the reasons why I am in Geneva than about the reasons why I was away from Geneva. On that score I would like to say just one word, and that is that this special operation in the Middle East

Unnumbered mimeographed press note, July 24, 1956.

is one in which you will find me rather impossible, because it is one which definitely prospers in what I would call fertile darkness and is not furthered by premature or immature comments from my side. So for that reason, although of course I will try and do my best to reply to questions concerning Middle East affairs, I warn you beforehand that I will be, as you say in newspaper language, secretive. With those few warning words I would like to invite you to put whatever questions you have in mind.

QUESTION: Can you make any very general comments about whether or not you found any new developments in the Middle East? I realize that it will have to be pretty general, but I wonder if you can tell us anything?

THE SECRETARY-GENERAL: We have not lost any ground, and this is an operation where I think that this is a reasonably positive statement. We are in the middle of a run where we do something which is rather unusual—or rather we *try* to do something which is rather unusual in diplomatic and political history—and that is to change the direction of a stream. If in such a situation you manage to keep your stand and, so to say, to consolidate it, I wouldn't exactly call it progress but I am not unhappy to be able to know that that much is a fact. On the other hand I would add that there are obviously—and anybody who reads the press can see that—points on which things are not the way I would like them to be at all. But to throw the cards on the table for such a reason as that we haven't reached anything like perfection, seems to me to be a very unwise, impatient policy.

QUESTION: Have you any present plans to go back there?

THE SECRETARY-GENERAL: I have already announced that I will reserve time in October for a kind of half-year "check-up." Whether or not that trip will come about will depend of course very much on how the governments themselves feel about it and how it looks from my angle, whether it is useful or not. I must say that my recent experience, which was just a check-up visit, without any agenda, without any specific questions to negotiate, in order so to say to deepen the groove in which we are playing this melody, indicated that my own reaction in October is likely to be that I should go. But of course the final decision should be in the hands of the governments—I am just their servant and not their master.

. . . . QUESTION: This is taking you back a little farther in your travels, but I saw it stated at the time you were in Moscow, or perhaps shortly afterward, you paid a visit to the department or bureau or at any rate administration that has been set up in the Soviet Union to handle technical assistance to underdeveloped countries. Now I myself have heard nothing about that and I wondered if you could tell us something about how they have set it up. Perhaps this is old stuff. I just don't happen to have seen it and I wondered if you could tell us a little bit. What sort of . . . I take it this was new machinery, a new department, and I wonder if you can tell us anything about it?

THE SECRETARY-GENERAL: As sometimes happens when the Secretary-General visits a ministerial department they put more questions to him than he puts to them. I frankly spent most of the time in replying to questions and learned very little about their specific way of operation. It was from my point of view—and there I speak without specific knowledge—very much a departmental bureau of the type we can meet in any foreign office, both in its approach and the problems they have to meet. From my angle the major part of the time was taken up by an attempt to explain what I had in mind with the new proposals I made concerning extended administrative services.

QUESTION: I think you heard Lord John Hope today give rather a grave warning against further expenditure by the United Nations and the specialized agencies and I wonder if you would like to make some comment on that speech?

THE SECRETARY-GENERAL: Well, it's . . . I don't know. I can't, so to say, interpret what he said without having discussed it with him, but my own interpretation was that his emphasis was upon what I myself consider to be good economy, that is to say on a choice of program and activities, a selection which, so to say, gets the maximum out of the money put into the machine. I felt that his criticism was directed against something which I myself criticize, that is to say the spreading of our effort over such a broad field that the marginal yield is sometimes very low indeed. When he spoke about the financial burdens of governments, I interpreted it as an indication of financial burdens for matters of the value of which they were not convinced. Interpreted in that way he is very much in line with what I in various ways have been trying to say myself, so far without, perhaps, always very intense response for the very reason he indicated himself, that is to say that there is always some kind of interest in every single project and the minority—which sometimes happens to be the countries who are the largest contributors—is therefore overridden at the vote. That is a very natural situation which is unavoidable in an organization with the setup we have, with the political decisions taken on the strict basis of voting majorities. Basically, if I interpret him correctly, I am agreed with the philosophy. If it had meant or if it does mean feeling that, irrespective of the needs we have to fill, we should stop short because of international budget considerations, I think we are brought to the point where an intense and deepened study is necessary, because it is my own personal conviction that there are aims to be filled, needs to be met by the United Nations, which should warrant even further financial contributions from Member governments. That is to say I look on the question as one not of quantity, but quality in what we are doing. . . .

I think I would like to add as background observation that the problem raised is not a new one. It has been raised again and again more or less pointedly, and I think it does direct attention to what is a very serious question, that is to say that without the conviction that the purpose for which we spend the money is of high international value and priority we will have rather unhappy feelings from quite a few ministers of finance. Perhaps have we sinned not only in that respect but we have failed also in the respect that sufficient information about needs and sufficient information about what the UN and its agencies can do has not always been given.

QUESTION: Since the Secretary-General more or less implies that there may possibly be some—well, I would not say waste—but some reproaches made, what measures does he propose to take to eliminate waste and to streamline United Nations efforts?

THE SECRETARY-GENERAL: A couple of years ago I had a survey made within the United Nations, where we suggested the shelving, or even the killing, of quite a few so-called projects. As a result of this we had a debate here in ECOSOC, and later in the General Assembly, which accepted some of the proposals but not all of them. I do not think there is any other way to do this than to be rather watchful and, on the inner lines, quite outspoken about our own feelings in the Secretariat about the usefulness of this or that project. Necessarily, doing so we may run into conflict with such and such interests, but I think that is natural and inevitable in this kind of process. But anyway, I think I have no bigger and more revolutionary suggestion to make than that we look after ourselves within the Secretariat and speak out.

QUESTION: Concerning your preceding remark as to the vote which took place concerning the program, can we believe that a vote which would take into consideration the amount of contribution of each country would lead us to a more realistic program?

THE SECRETARY-GENERAL: In my view, without any official tie on, for there is no official line here, that would be to pay too high a price because after all what I call the democratic principle of voting by majority without weighted votes, is rather essential if we are to maintain some characteristics of this Organization which I think are vital for a sound development. If we introduce weighted votes it would tip the balance very very heavily in favor of a few countries and that would necessarily lead to reactions by one part of the world which would cease feeling that the United Nations is just as much their organization and their platform as it is the platform of any other nation. So for that reason I do not believe that we are in any way ripe for weighted voting, certainly not on the basis of any kind of contribution scale at present.

QUESTION: Lord John Hope this morning developed a certain theory in planning the functions of the Council and of the United Nations in general, especially with reference to planning for regions and countries. Would you agree that there is such a thing?

THE SECRETARY-GENERAL: It is difficult for me to comment on interventions of members in the Council when the Council is in session; I made an exception on the first point because I felt that I was basically in agreement and it was the same old line which was expressed again on this point. The line Lord Hope took on the points now raised is one which I would consider it quite difficult to argue. It is a question, as I see it, largely of the maturing of international cooperation. You know there are all shades in the world in this cooperation, and in different fields within the United Nations, as to the degree in which the United Nations represents, certainly not a super nation, but let us say a crystallized consensus of opinion which for that reason has a specific impact on national politics. To try and lay down principles on those points is difficult for me. I think that it is a field where different views can and naturally will be held, and that the reply will come from the process of development within the organization. We start out with a very wide independence of nations and we have then seen, in various fields, a growing central influence developing, not in the sense that any directives are given to tie the hands of the nations, but in the sense that the consensus in the United Nations will come to carry an increasing weight in national politics. This is a natural organic development. It does not come into being unless it is acceptable to the countries concerned—it is not enforced.

. . . . QUESTION: Have you made any progress with your idea of an international civil service to help underdeveloped countries?

THE SECRETARY-GENERAL: Yes, in the sense that quite a few people are critical of it, and that is a good beginning. That is one way of getting interest up to the point where a real study is made, and what I want is a real study, not necessarily acceptance of this or that idea. I should perhaps add that there are those who are in favor of it too, but I think the majority is so far on the side of the question mark.

. . . .

STATEMENTS TO THE ECONOMIC AND SOCIAL COUNCIL

TWENTY-SECOND SESSION, 1956

IN THE SECOND of the following texts, which was circulated as a written statement a month before discussions in the Council, the Secretary-General placed before the members (paragraph 22 of the text) the suggestion he had made at Montreal on May 20 for an international administrative service (page 149). The idea had encountered criticism and skepticism, as he noted at the end of his July 24 press conference. Hammarskjöld dealt with the main questions that had been raised in his fourth and fifth statements in the Council's debate on development and coordination. No action on the suggestion was taken until a year later (page 602).

1. Statement in the Economic and Social Council Introducing Debate on the World Economic Situation

GENEVA   JULY 16, 1956

Ten years ago the Council embarked on the tasks laid down in the Charter: To promote "higher standards of living, full employment, and conditions of economic and social progress and development." How far can we, here and now, report success in the advance toward these goals?

The World Economic Survey which we have set before the Council is, in part, an attempt to evaluate the economic successes and failures of the postwar period. There is much in the record of the past ten years providing legitimate grounds for satisfaction, but some of the most important problems confronting the world are almost as far from solution as they were when the Council began its work.

I do not propose to say more than a few words concerning the

UN Press Release SG/493, July 16, 1956. The summary record is given in Economic and Social Council Official Records, Twenty-second Session, 934th Meeting, July 16, 1956.

achievements of the first postwar decade—they are documented in the World Economic Survey and the regional economic surveys which are before the Council. Our responsibility is to build for the future rather than to congratulate ourselves upon successes of the past.

It is, nevertheless, appropriate to recall that both in the developed enterprise economies and in the centrally planned economies, prewar levels of per capita production and trade have by now been left far behind; and that, while part of the rise in output has been sidetracked into armaments, a substantial margin has nevertheless been available in many areas for improvement in present and future levels of living.

In the centrally planned economies, highest priority has been given to investment in heavy industry as against light and consumer goods industries and—until recently—also agriculture. The level of living has thus risen much less than has output. With the growing attention now being given to agriculture, however, the lag between the rates of growth in production and consumption is expected to diminish.

In the private enterprise developed economies, a significant measure of both economic progress and security has been achieved. Defenses have been built against the waste and misery of economic depressions, and ways and means have been found in many countries of mitigating economic insecurity. It is true that the strength of these defenses has yet to be seriously tested, but the widespread consciousness of a need in this area, and the deeper understanding of the economic forces which give rise to this need, in themselves represent an impressive advance on the groping in the dark of the interwar years.

It is, I think, fair to say that the Council has a record of positive achievement in this area. The Council has defined the manner in which the full employment obligation to which all nations subscribed in the Charter is to be understood, and the nature of the responsibilities which governments have thereby assumed—namely to make legislative and administrative provisions adequate for the attainment of the national full employment goals.

Moreover, the Council has proclaimed the international, as well as national, character of the full employment obligation; it has helped toward securing recognition of the principle that any country which fails to maintain full employment within its own borders by that very fact makes it more difficult for other countries to do so. If international division of labor lifts the productivity of the world community, it also increases the mutual interdependence of its several parts; the economic health of each comes to depend in significant measure upon the well-being of all.

When one Member contracts the disease of unemployment it threatens all others, not only because the circulation of international trade becomes constricted but also because so close is the attunement between Members that palpitation in one may set off sympathetic vibrations in the others. The Council has therefore rightly emphasized the principle that each Member country has not only an internal but also an international responsibility to maintain conditions conducive to good economic health of the world community. It must be admitted that we are far from agreement on the practical implications of this principle.

The prolonged success in the industrially developed countries of national full employment policies, combined with the unexpected mild international repercussions of the United States recession of 1953–1954, has perhaps encouraged us to feel more complacent in this area than we should. Nevertheless, it seems safe to say that over a substantial portion of the earth's surface man has tasted the benefits of rising levels of material welfare, and has even succeeded in harnessing, to a greater or lesser extent, economic forces hitherto regarded as beyond his control.

There are those who feared, and perhaps still fear, that security may be inimical to progress—that the whiplash of insecurity is needed to spur mankind on to increased effort. No more convincing refutation of this thesis is required than has been provided by the experience of the past decade. With levels of unemployment that in the 1930s would have been regarded as incredibly low, economic growth has been accelerated, rather than stifled. Never in the history of man has his economic pulse been so quick, never has he shown so great a degree of flexibility or so rapid and continuous an increase in work efficiency.

Unfortunately, the achievement in stabilizing the national economies of the developed countries finds no parallel in the stabilization of the national economies of the underdeveloped countries. Nor has sufficient progress been made in stabilizing and integrating the world economy as a whole. The world continues to be divided into two economic regions with only marginal trade relations between them. While world trade has grown significantly, the flow of international capital has never regained its importance of only a generation ago, either in relation to trade or to income and investment. I have dealt with these problems on past occasions and they are fully documented in the surveys which are before the Council. Rather than summarize all that has been discussed under these topics, I shall confine my words at this point to only one aspect which troubles me greatly. I refer to the problem of commodity stabilization.

While unemployment has long ceased to be acceptable as the price for keeping an industrial economy in balance, the world still does not seem to recognize that violent price fluctuations are not essential to maintaining economic balance in farm and mining economies. Of course, some degree of price flexibility is necessary to permit adjustment of commodity markets to changing demand and supply conditions. In similar fashion, some degree of flexibility of manpower and resources is required to adjust to changing conditions in the economy at large.

But just as we know that mass unemployment introduces not flexibility but economic paralysis, so we must come to realize that the violent price fluctuations which have characterized commodity markets are not productive of economic balance but rather of economic chaos. One searches in vain for any economic purpose served by the price gyrations in coffee and cocoa in recent years. And surely whatever adjustment in demand and supply was achieved during the Korean boom and collapse of raw material prices could have been accomplished with price movements only a fraction of those actually experienced.

At one time it seemed to many economists that if the problem of stabilizing aggregate effective demand in the developed countries could be solved, the task of achieving stability in commodity markets would thereby be reduced to manageable proportions. Eloquent testimony of the secondary importance attached to the problem of commodity stability may be found in the economics curriculum of every university. Whereas the study of effective demand and employment has everywhere become the central theme of general economic analysis, the broad problem of commodity stabilization has for the most part received relatively marginal attention.

One of the most fundamental of the lessons we have to learn from the economic developments of the past ten years is that economic stability in the highly developed countries is by no means a sufficient condition for stability in the demand of these countries for primary products. Despite full employment and rapid growth in industrial countries, few underdeveloped countries know from year to year where they stand regarding their export incomes and their supply of disposable foreign exchange.

An inventory shift in a particular commodity may be of small moment in relation to the total inventory movement of a major developed country, and insignificant in relation to the aggregate production of that country; but it may spell disaster for the short-term, and perhaps even long-term, plans of the underdeveloped countries dependent upon that commodity for the bulk of their foreign exchange incomes, and hence for their capacity to import development goods. Any unevenness in the advance of, say, heavy and light industries, such as we have witnessed recently in the developed countries, may mean windfall gains for some primary producers and extraordinary losses for others.

Nor can the gains of the fat years always be offset against the losses of the lean years. The lean years are likely to bring difficulties and discouragement, and impede the drawing up of development plans and programs, both private and public. In that case, the advent of better times may find countries ill equipped and ill prepared to take advantage of the improvement in their situation, and the new resources may be dissipated on luxury imports.

Moreover, the cycle of commodity prices is not necessarily superimposed upon any stable long-term trend; fluctuations in commodity prices are so irregular that there can be no assurance that the gains will cancel out the losses over any reasonable period. Indeed, as is noted in the survey, violent price fluctuations in themselves exert an adverse long-term effect upon commodity markets; the fat years may be swallowed up by the increasingly lean years as the gyrations in prices encourage industrial countries to strive for growing self-sufficiency.

There is no magic formula for solving the problem of commodity price stability. The search for such a formula will not yield a simple result, applicable in all circumstances. But there seems to me no doubt that our inability to make any serious headway with this problem constitutes one of the greatest weaknesses in the fabric of international economic cooperation at the present time. This is a weakness which we cannot afford to overlook.

While the commodity problem may be ancillary to the broad problem of economic stability in the highly developed countries, it cannot be considered as of secondary importance from the standpoint of the world at large; the vast majority of mankind still earns its living in primary rather than industrial production. It would be dangerous to underestimate the difficulties attached to the problem of commodity stabilization.

The root of the difficulties is clear enough—it lies in the wide fluctuations in demand, especially for inventories and in the yield of agricultural production, coupled with the extremely low price elasticities of both demand and supply for most primary products. Despite all efforts, both national and international, the practical means for increasing these elasticities, or offsetting their effects on prices, remain a baffling puzzle.

In important respects the problem is even more difficult than is that of stabilizing employment. Since the labor market is predominantly national in character, the main requirement for implementation is appropriate national policy for full employment; what is required at the international level is that each country keep reasonably in step with the others and not seek to solve its unemployment problem at the expense of others. Provided this is done there is no conflict of national interests regarding the maintenance of full employment; all countries share a common interest in its maintenance all over the world.

Commodity markets, however, are in essence international rather than national; no nation, no matter how strong, is likely to prove adequate by itself in the task of price stabilization. National action must therefore be supplemented by and indeed undertaken in a framework of international policy if it is really to succeed at the international level. However, the difficulties of reconciling the short-term interests of producing and consuming nations have proved a powerful obstacle to action, despite the long-term benefits to be derived by all nations alike.

This is not, of course, to overlook the fact that intergovernmental arrangements with limited price ranges are now in operation for wheat, sugar, and tin and that price fluctuations in these commodities have been reduced in more recent years. It is also pleasing to note that an agreement has been made on olive oil, thereby demonstrating that the present machinery can be used effectively for commodities of lesser importance in total world trade but of vital concern to particular regions; however, this agreement awaits the signature of sufficient governments to bring it into force. Even so it has taken almost a decade to arrive at only these four agreements. Surely greater interest must be shown if substantial progress is to be made through the commodity-by-commodity approach which so many governments have favored.

It is the absence of a framework of international policy that compels the underdeveloped countries each to seek its own salvation in its own way without reference to wider horizons. How often have we not heard the voices of those who bewail the fact that this underdeveloped country is moving along the slippery path to autarky, that that country is neglecting its exports, whether agricultural or mineral, or that yet a third country is manipulating its exchange rates in a manner contrary to the letter and spirit of the Bretton Woods agreements? And yet how many of those who belabor the underdeveloped countries in this fashion have given adequate thought to the structure of world economic relationships which has forced these countries into unorthodox patterns of behavior?

The Council is at this session debating one notable proposal with a significant bearing on commodity stabilization—the World Food Reserve proposal on which the FAO has just submitted its report—and it has in the past ranged over the whole gamut of international measures from individual commodity agreements through buffer stocks to commodity currency proposals. Thus far, however, disappointingly little progress has been recorded.

I do not wish to minimize the difficulties and complexities in this area, but I must, nevertheless, express my firm conviction that much more can be done than has thus far been accomplished. Surely a great deal more has been achieved in other directions—no less difficult— toward economic development. Who could have envisaged, only a generation ago, that the nations of the world would embark upon a collective program of technical and financial assistance to underdeveloped countries! Yet this program is today a living reality. What goodwill and understanding have accomplished in establishing a foundation for international aid, they also can achieve in laying the groundwork for stabilizing the trade of underdeveloped countries.

If peoples and governments will once come to understand that commodity stabilization is not merely a narrow matter of price haggling between producers and consumers, but is a problem of eliminating the wild fluctuations which beset the economies of underdeveloped countries—problems of as grave import to them and to the world as depressions in the developed countries—then I have no doubt that ways and means will be found for its solution.

In the light of the fact that both the FAO and the Contracting Parties of GATT are working in this field and that we have a special Commission on International Commodity Trade as well as an Interim Commodity Committee of the Council, it seems to me that it is not so much new machinery or new gadgets that are required; what is necessary is proper education and goodwill, both of the public and of governments to coordinate and utilize more effectively the machinery which already exists.

Of course, I do not wish to imply that commodity stabilization is an all-sufficient answer to economic development. No matter what our success may be in stabilizing commodity earnings, we cannot rely upon primary production alone to close the gap in per capita incomes between the developed and underdeveloped areas. This is not simply because the gap partly depends upon the long-run terms of trade and not merely on the fluctuations around the trend. The problem lies deeper than this; it has its roots in the world structure of demand.

It is true that with the growth of output and incomes of the industrial countries, the demand for primary production may be expected to rise, but experience over a long period shows that this rise is far from proportional. Even if supplies of primary products were to keep pace with the demand and the terms of trade were to remain unchanged, the growth of income earned in primary production would lag considerably behind the growth in income of industrial countries.

As is demonstrated in the World Economic Survey, the growth of total output in the underdeveloped countries has lagged behind that of the developed countries, not because of lesser progress in each of the major sectors of production taken separately, but because agriculture, which accounts for a much higher proportion of the total in underdeveloped countries, almost everywhere has expanded at a much lower rate than manufacturing.

If the underdeveloped countries are even to maintain, let alone increase, their relative share of the world's total output, they cannot rely exclusively on expanded exports of primary products to industrial countries, but must embark upon a program of broad economic development. Of course, the underdeveloped countries with their very low productive capacities cannot hope to match the absolute growth of the developed countries; in absolute terms the gap in per capita incomes between them must be expected to continue to widen in the foreseeable future.

What is disappointing, however, is that even in percentage terms the underdeveloped countries should have failed to match the rate of growth in per capita incomes of the industrial countries since before the war. In view of the very much lower levels from which the percentage changes are calculated in the case of the underdeveloped countries, a reasonable target for economic development should at least provide for a higher percentage rate of growth in the underdeveloped than in the developed countries; otherwise, it would be impossible ever to increase the share of the underdeveloped countries in the distribution of the per capita income of the world. That we have thus far fallen short of the target only dramatizes how great is the need to intensify our efforts, both national and international, to speed the process of economic development.

If I do not speak about international aid here, it is only because in this area the Council has at least laid a foundation on which we can build. A proper perspective requires us to bear in mind that international aid—however generous and unselfish it may be—can never be an adequate substitute for stable and growing export earnings. Even in highly prosperous times, the year-to-year fluctuations in commodity earnings frequently cancel out several times over the total international assistance which a country may be receiving from all sources.

It is enough to realize that a change of only 5 percent in average export prices is approximately equivalent to the entire annual inflow of private and public capital and government grants to underdeveloped countries. Essential as it is to expand international financial aid in all its forms—private and public, bilateral and multilateral—highest priority must surely be given to stable and expanding trade of the underdeveloped countries, not only because of its sheer size, but because trade is after all the best form of aid.

---

2. Introductory Statement for the Economic and Social Council's General Review at Its Twenty-second Session of the Development and Coordination of the Economic, Social, and Human Rights Programmes and Activities of the United Nations and the Specialized Agencies as a Whole

JUNE 14, 1956

---

1. At this twenty-second session, the Council will be celebrating its tenth anniversary and, in order the better to plan for the future, it may wish to use the occasion to survey the experience of the past ten years.

Economic and Social Council Official Records, Twenty-second Session, Annexes, agenda item 3, Document E/2894/Rev. 1, June 14, 1956.

Under the second item on its agenda, the salient developments in the world economic situation since 1946 will be brought to its attention. Under the third item, which deals with the development and coordination of the activities of the United Nations and specialized agencies in the economic and social fields, it would be fitting to refer to the Council's own accomplishments in that period, to the remarkable expansion in the scope of international action, and, more generally, to the contribution of what we have come to call the United Nations family to the fulfillment of the objectives of Article 55 of the Charter.

2. In the present introductory statement, I shall confine myself to making a few brief comments on this theme. In the first place, there has been welcome progress towards universality in the programmes and the membership of the various international organizations. Their activities have spread to every part of the world; in respect of membership, the goal of universality has been steadily approached by many of the specialized agencies, and now, with the admission of sixteen new Members last December, by the United Nations itself. Since the Second World War some twenty states have been created, almost all of them economically underdeveloped and eager to build up their resources. These states have been active participants in the drive towards economic development which has been so sharply reflected in the debates of the Council and has contributed to the strengthening of the economic and social work of the United Nations and the specialized agencies.

3. In the second place, important new institutions affecting the welfare and even the lives of millions have been created, either as parts of the United Nations Organization itself (Technical Assistance Administration [TAA], United Nations International Children's Fund [UNICEF], the Office of the High Commissioner for Refugees, the Council's own regional economic commissions and its functional commissions), or as specialized agencies (the World Health Organization [WHO], the temporary International Refugee Organization, the Interim Commission for the International Trade Organization and the Preparatory Committee of the International Maritime Consultative Organization). In addition, organizations created earlier—the International Labour Organisation (ILO), dating from 1919, the Food and Agriculture Organization of the United Nations (FAO), the United Nations Educational, Scientific and Cultural Organization (UNESCO), the International Bank for Reconstruction and Development (Bank), the International Monetary Fund, the International Civil Aviation Organiza-

tion, dating from 1944–1946, the International Telecommunication Union, the Universal Postal Union, and the World Meteorological Organization (WMO),[1] dating from the nineteenth century—have been brought as specialized agencies within the United Nations framework. The new or expanded international institutions have played a significant role, both as vehicles for the efforts of governments and through the work performed by their secretariats, in shaping the postwar world.

4. International action has developed new methods and forms, as witness the "sharing of skills" in the programme of technical assistance for economic development, and it has extended to new fields, including the peaceful uses of atomic energy, the provision of supplies and equipment for programmes benefiting children, the use and conservation of water, and community development. It has become more systematic and comprehensive and forward looking. Nor has it been confined to the promotion of material and social welfare: it has also been consciously directed towards the promotion of human dignity and equality through the United Nations programme of human rights.

5. If, therefore, international economic and social action after the war was built largely on the basis laid by the League of Nations, not only its scale and range, but also its methods and approaches and its very spirit have undergone far-reaching changes; the responsibilities of the international organs are far more "operational" and there are greater resources to enable these responsibilities to be carried out. However difficult it is to appraise the precise influence of international action on economic and social progress since the Second World War, it is certain that such action has proved itself effective over a wide field and in many countries. One must be on guard against claiming too much credit for the international organizations themselves, which represent a collective expression of the policies and attitudes of governments. Nevertheless, if economic and social progress in the last decade appears to be more solidly based, and more in harmony with new forces than the progress achieved in the 1920s now seems in retrospect, part of the difference must be ascribed to action through international organizations. The experience of the 1930s, the experience of the war, the new techniques taught and learned in both periods, the emergence of the underdeveloped countries and their "revolution of rising expectations"—

---

[1] By the 1947 Washington Convention, the WMO superseded the former International Meteorological Organization, a semigovernmental body.

all these together have obviously provided a new and stimulating setting, in which the international organizations have been directed and encouraged by governments to do their work. The international work which falls within the Council's purview has affected almost every phase of economic and social life, from full employment policies to the removal of the remaining vestiges of slavery, from the strengthening of public administration to the protection of refugees, from the financing of economic development to the promotion of political rights of women. It has already left its mark on the history of our time.

6. The deliberate decentralization of international economic and social action reflected in Articles 57 and 63 of the Charter raised the problem of how to ensure coordination among the United Nations and the various autonomous agencies brought into relationship with it. This problem was on the one hand a matter for appropriate arrangements within the administrations of the Member states, but it was also a matter for international action under the supervision of the Council, and a matter to which the Council has in fact devoted a great deal of time and attention. One of the Council's major concerns has been, of course, to ensure the establishment of appropriate coordinating machinery and procedures. One may recall in this connection the negotiation of the relationship agreements with the specialized agencies in 1946 and subsequent years; the setting up in 1946 of the Administrative Committee on Coordination (ACC) under the chairmanship of the Secretary-General "to ensure the fullest and most effective implementation" of these agreements; [2] the establishment, through ACC, of the Technical Assistance Board (TAB) when the Expanded Programme of Technical Assistance was initiated in 1950; [3] the drawing up in 1950 and 1951 of criteria for priorities and procedures for the application of these criteria; the adoption in 1952 of a schedule of United Nations priority programmes. One may recall, too, the careful consideration devoted year by year by the Council, in plenary session, in its Coordination Committee and Technical Assistance Committee and in other Committees, to the promotion of coordination and cooperation among the United Nations organizations in specific fields, in respect of the Expanded Programme of Technical Assistance as well as the regular programmes, and in respect of regional as well as Headquarters activities. It would be

[2] Economic and Social Council Resolution 13 (III).
[3] Economic and Social Council Resolution 22 A (IX).

wrong to conceal or minimize the difficulties of the task of ensuring good coordination among dynamic and independent organizations with wide, and in some areas, overlapping interests. Certain of these difficulties are indeed mentioned later in this statement. At the same time, important positive results have been achieved, as reflected in the recent reports of ACC.

7. Let us now shift our gaze from the horizons of ten years' accomplishments to the nearer vista of the past twelve months. I shall say nothing of the work falling mainly within the competence of the specialized agencies, for this work has been summarized for the Council in the agencies' annual reports and will, no doubt, be commented on by the Directors-General themselves in the Council's debate. Among the major problems and tasks with which the United Nations itself, or in association with the specialized agencies, has been closely concerned must be mentioned the peaceful uses of atomic energy; the financing of economic development; the annual reporting to the Council on world economic conditions; the promotion of industrialization and productivity, water utilization and conservation, and community development; the problems of urbanization and demographic problems; and international measures for further advancing the cause of human rights. Most of these subjects have been fully reported on to the twenty-first or twenty-second session of the Council,[4] and I shall consequently confine myself to commenting on a few which have not been the subject of such reports.

8. First, the peaceful use of atomic energy, a subject eminently suited for exploration on an international basis, and one which may appropriately be given pride of place because of its dramatic possibilities for human betterment. A preliminary survey of this vast field of knowledge was made in Geneva in August 1955 at the International Conference on the Peaceful Uses of Atomic Energy, whose proceedings have now been published by the United Nations in sixteen volumes. The Conference, while predominantly scientific and technical, opened with a detailed discussion of the possibilities of utilizing nuclear energy as a source of

[4] See, for example, the reports entitled Survey of Current Work on Industrialization and Productivity (E/2816), International Cooperation with Respect to Water Resource Development (E/2827), *World Economic Survey, 1955* (E/2864 —UN Sales No.: 1956. II. C.1), Interim Report of the *Ad Hoc* Committee on the Question of the Establishment of a Special United Nations Fund for Economic Development (E/2896), Advisory Services in the Field of Human Rights (E/2825 and E/2839), and Report of the Twelfth Session of the Commission on Human Rights (E/2844 and Add. 1).

power in the context of increasing demands for a new source of energy for the nations of the world. From the detailed consideration, both scientific and economic, of various types of reactors, it became clear that the use of nuclear reactors as a source of power, while as yet largely in the experimental stage and unable to compete economically with conventional sources of power, except in areas where the cost of those fuels is abnormally high, was rapidly becoming a factor to be considered in future economic development. In addition to its uses as a source of power, many applications of nuclear energy or its by-products are already being made to industry, agriculture, medicine, forestry, transportation, etc. The need for personnel trained in physics, engineering, chemistry, metallurgy, etc., and for stringent safety regulations and codes of practice in nuclear plants are among the key problems in this field towards the solution of which international action can and must contribute. On the question of the effects of radiation on man and his environment, the General Assembly has established a scientific committee whose long-term studies will, it is hoped, provide the knowledge essential for the safe operation of nuclear plants and the use of radioactive materials throughout the world. For certain of these studies the Committee will rely on the cooperation of specialized agencies, more specifically WHO, UNESCO, the ILO, and FAO.

9. It is encouraging that, in the early years of a great development of science, the groundwork has already been laid for a responsible international approach to its practical applications. As reported by ACC, a subcommittee of that body has been set up under my chairmanship to help coordinate the work of the United Nations organizations, several of which are already dealing with aspects of the problem within their respective fields; and emphasis has rightly been laid on the necessity for the closest cooperation between our existing United Nations organizations and the proposed international atomic energy agency, the establishment of which will doubtless lead to a considerable extension of international cooperation in the whole field. The study of the application of atomic energy to economic development in respect of power, industry, and agriculture, which the Council has requested the Secretariat to make in cooperation with the interested specialized agencies, will no doubt be a useful preliminary step in orienting the international programme of work on the peaceful uses of atomic energy towards the greatest benefit for all nations. Such a study is moreover to be complemented very appropriately by the exploratory studies likewise requested on the

practical possibilities of utilizing other nonconventional sources of energy.

10. Like atomic energy, the field of water control and utilization has many implications for economic development, particularly for the development of arid lands. Special studies on various aspects of water development are in preparation at United Nations Headquarters, in the secretariats of the regional commissions and in the specialized agencies. One of the Headquarters studies—on water problems in Africa—is before the Council at this session.[5] A handbook on watershed management is being prepared by FAO and UNESCO. A basic inquiry into existing hydrologic services has been started in cooperation with WMO and other agencies. The importance of such services in any long-term plan for water development, whether for irrigation, for hydroelectric power, or for navigation, is obvious.

11. The development of atomic energy for peaceful purposes and the development of water resources are in many areas an essential condition of any significant acceleration of the rate of industrialization. The initiative shown by the Council in the field of industrialization has stimulated great interest amongst underdeveloped countries; it has also begun to have a far-reaching influence on the orientation of the Secretariat's work. For example, in working out the programme for the expansion of economic studies in the Middle East which was approved by the Assembly last year, it seemed appropriate to begin with a special study of the problems of industrialization in the Middle East and a good deal of the necessary work on this subject will be done on the spot this year. Much useful work has of course already been done by the regional economic commissions in respect of industrialization in other regions.

12. Industrialization is not simply a tool that can be handed over from one society to another. It is also a way of life, with implications beyond the economic field and with potentialities for harm as well as good. Due attention must therefore be given in our work to the social aspects of the industrialization process—to questions of housing, labour, migration, social services, education, and the various other social problems that become particularly urgent during the transition from one type of economy to another.

13. Furthermore, it is proper that our work on industrialization

[5] Aspects of Water Development in Africa (E/2882)—UN Sales No.: 1956. II. C. 3.

should be complemented by a programme in the field of urbanization. The process of industrialization has usually been accompanied by the rapid growth of cities, although other factors besides industry have led to urban growth. Urbanization is not necessarily a goal to be universally sought today, at least not in the chaotic form in which it so often appears. In fact, for many who live in modern cities, Rousseau's vision of man in his natural state still has great appeal, but it has less appeal for those inhabitants of rural areas who live amid disease, ignorance, and boredom and who eagerly flock to cities. In any case, the process of urbanization must be faced and dealt with, through coordinated study and action. It may perhaps be tempered by measures such as decentralization of industry and careful town planning; nevertheless, it will without question be a major social fact in the future of the economically underdeveloped countries. Throughout these countries today, the cities are growing with startling rapidity and a large part of their growth is caused by migration from rural areas. The actual numbers, characteristics, and needs of the city dwellers who were peasants yesterday are known very imperfectly, but it is clear that their adaptation to city life is difficult, that they suffer from appalling deficiencies of housing, health, and diet, and that they pose new problems for all categories of social programmes. One year ago, the United Nations and the specialized agencies agreed to cooperate in developing a long-range plan for concerted action in this field,[6] and plans for jointly sponsored seminars on urbanization in the regions of the Economic Commission for Asia and the Far East and the Economic Commission for Latin America are now well under way.

14. From my remarks above, it will be evident to members of the Council that I view the process of development as one requiring balanced and coordinated action in a variety of fields, that is, one of organic growth of a total society. This implies coordination in the fullest and deepest sense—a continuous search for balanced and integrated action and a recognition of the necessity for accompanying action in one field with supporting and complementary action in other fields.

15. This necessity has been made into a virtue in the case of what is known today as "community development." It emerged as an empirical principle from efforts at development in rural areas. Experience from many countries showed that whether one's goal was increased agricul-

[6] Economic and Social Council Resolution 585 C (XX).

tural production, improved health, extension of education, better homes, or some other objective, successful pursuit of a single goal was, in general, not possible without simultaneous action towards other goals.

16. It may be worthwhile, at this stage, for me to stress two points in connection with community development, which is now a major focus of United Nations activity in the social field. Firstly, in using this phrase as a generic description for organized self-help measures for the growth of communities, we must recognize that there can be no uniform action pattern for all cases; various types of programmes with different titles are, in fact, under way in different countries and, sometimes, within the same country, but they have the same general purpose. While the methods of community development need continuous clarification through evaluation of new experiences, variety of expression is itself a quality to be especially cherished in this field, and it would be a mistake to try and fit every programme into the same mould. Secondly, whatever particular aspect of a community development programme may be stressed at the start—e.g., health, education, agriculture—the compulsion of circumstances will eventually engage other related aspects of growth. One aspect which has been neglected in the rural areas is the improvement of craft production and small-scale industries which, in countries where the pressure of population on resources is high, may be vital for sustained progress in agriculture and other sectors of the economy. The problem of exploring methods of strengthening the artisan class without creating vested interests in inefficient production is one that has to be squarely faced. We may be called upon to revise many preconceptions expressed in theory and in practice and should be prepared to make a bold experimental approach to this problem.

17. Community development has the advantage that it sets forth certain general guiding principles and at the same time allows for adaptation and uniqueness of approach in the different localities with their varying economic, social, and cultural circumstances. Experience has taught us, and wise observers have informed us, that, in other fields of activity as well, the transfer of modern techniques from one society to another, cannot be an automatic and routine procedure. Assimilation and adaptation are the essence of effective aid. This may not be so important in certain cases where the treatment of biological ills is involved and where the existence of common biological processes permits an easy transfer of techniques, but it is of extreme importance in a field such as social welfare where the variety of human societies and cultures

requires a highly adaptive and flexible approach in technical assistance. The United Nations is currently working in cooperation with the ILO on the question of the most appropriate measures for maintenance of family levels of living in countries at varying levels of economic development and with varying social and cultural backgrounds.

18. I have, in previous reports, emphasized the need for more adequate quantitative information, particularly concerning less-developed countries. The dependence of many of these countries on the production of food and raw materials and on the maintenance of a high level of international trade, together with the pressure of population on resources which they continue to feel, make it desirable that their economic and social policies should be based on the fullest possible statistical information. It is clearly important that the United Nations should seek means of bringing to such countries some of the advantages which the developed countries possess in the form of comprehensive statistical information about their economies. The Statistical Commission, in its report which is before you, recommends the establishment of a small group of statistical experts to assist the less-developed countries to this end.[7]

19. The Statistical Commission is also concerned that population censuses should be taken around the year 1960 on as nearly as possible a worldwide basis,[8] in order to provide the demographic data which are of especial importance to less-developed countries. During the past year our activities intended to help these countries to obtain such information have made steady progress. Of particular importance were the two regional seminars held at Bandung and Rio de Janeiro, the principal aim of which was to determine the demographic statistics most needed for the study of problems of economic and social development and the best means of obtaining and using these statistics. The United Nations is now well advanced in preparations for the establishment of a Latin American regional centre for demographic research and training. It is expected that a similar centre will be created in the Far East near the end of this year.

20. The evolution of United Nations work in several of the fields mentioned above illustrates the trend noted last year towards the formulation and carrying out, under the leadership of the United Nations it-

[7] Economic and Social Council Official Records, Twenty-second Session, Supplement No. 7, paragraph 25, Resolution 1 (IX).
[8] *Ibid.*, p. 24, draft resolution for action by the Economic and Social Council.

self, of broad programmes, aspects of which fall within the specialized competence of the sister agencies. This trend, reflecting as it does a new conception of the role of international action in the central issues of economic and social policy, is certainly a welcome and important one. I must, at the same time, call attention to one of its administrative consequences, namely the tremendous increase in the extent of consultation with the specialized agencies which the United Nations Secretariat is called upon to undertake. In view particularly of the volume of work to be undertaken, this is beginning to place a serious strain on the existing arrangements for coordination. A choice indeed has sometimes to be made between full consultations and meeting the deadlines. I for my part will do everything possible to avoid having to make this invidious choice, and I feel sure that I can count on the understanding cooperation of my colleagues in the specialized agencies. The steps which some of them have recently taken to strengthen their offices at United Nations Headquarters have already proved helpful in this connection. In the interest of minimizing delay, moreover, it would seem better to avoid where possible joint reporting and joint responsibilities and to assign full responsibility for particular segments of work to one agency. The Council will note that in several of the documents before this session, which the Secretary-General was asked to prepare in cooperation (or in consultation) with the specialized agencies, contributions submitted by the specialized agencies have been directly incorporated.

21. There is no doubt that, as a result of measures taken by the Council, international efforts and resources are now far better concentrated on objectives of major importance than in the early years. Papers on the implementation of priorities under the programme of concerted practical action in the social field of the United Nations and the specialized agencies (E/2890) and on coordination of UNICEF programmes with the regular and technical assistance programmes of the United Nations and the specialized agencies (E/2892) are before the Council at this session. On the economic side, the discussions under many of the major items—the world economic situation, industrialization, the financing of economic development, and the technical assistance programme —represent in themselves an exercise in the determination of priorities. There are, however, certain priorities of an institutional character to which it would be appropriate for me to refer. I welcome the early prospect of the establishment of an International Finance Corporation which, through the Bank, will seek relationship with the United Nations

as a specialized agency. The Corporation should contribute notably to the process of industrialization in underdeveloped countries. At the close of the debate on the "general review" item last summer (agenda item 4) at the Council's twentieth session, I made some general observations (882nd meeting) on the problem of international trade, stressing that the promotion of international trade is one of the Council's priority programmes and that a central review and coordination of work in this, as in other fields of international endeavour, are essential. I sincerely trust that appropriate international arrangements in this field may shortly be made so as to fill a gap that has too long existed in the machinery for international cooperation.

22. In order that the United Nations may more effectively pursue its overriding programme priority, namely, the development of underdeveloped countries, I have recently had occasion to stress the difficulties created by the absence of proper administrative machinery to handle the problems of economic and social development. In this connection, I have suggested consideration of a new long-term approach to the organization of international service to assist governments in this tremendous problem of administration. This would be a career service under international responsibility open to qualified men and women of any nationality who would work as officials in the national administrations of underdeveloped countries. It might be difficult to organize such a service adequately without establishing a new international agency for the purpose. In the meantime, I hope that the building up of public administration—which ACC brought forward in 1950 as the main immediate objective of the technical assistance programme—may claim the attention it deserves in national and international plans for economic development. In this connection, it should be noted that since the funds allotted under the regular United Nations programme for assistance in public administration are so out of proportion to the urgent needs, a modest increase in these funds will certainly be necessary. I am anxious that, whatever changes in the structure of international aid may seem desirable over the larger area, no opportunity should be lost to improve the operation of the United Nations machinery that now exists.

23. In this same field, I commend to the Council's attention the report of TAB entitled A Forward Look, and ACC's comments on it (E/2885), with which I am in general agreement. I am impressed by the Board's presentation of a wide range of technical assistance projects which in many cases represent a logical and necessary extension of

work already being done. The importance attached to scientific surveys of basic resources and to training and research institutes, amongst the many projects envisaged by the Board, strikes me as well justified. I am particularly interested in the emphasis placed on helping the governments of underdeveloped countries to develop their civil services and their administrative machinery along sound lines; the lack of adequate government machinery to administer ambitious economic development plans often threatens the success of such plans.

24. As regards the United Nations Secretariat itself, I proposed to the tenth session of the General Assembly certain limited measures designed to ensure an improved use of the combined staff resources of TAA and the Department of Economic and Social Affairs,[9] including the secretariats of the regional economic commissions. Consideration of these proposals—which I had foreshadowed in a statement to the Council at the 879th meeting of its twentieth session last summer—was deferred until the eleventh session of the General Assembly with the understanding that I would post to Latin America certain Technical Assistance Programme officers on an experimental basis in 1956. Four officers have in fact now been assigned to Santiago and two to Mexico City; all of them will be able to draw upon the services of the ECLA secretariat. I shall make an interim report on these arrangements to the eleventh session of the General Assembly. At this stage I would merely like to stress that what they are intended to secure for our Technical Assistance Programme is the benefit of the special—and indeed unique —knowledge of the economic problems of the countries of the region accumulated by the staff of the regional commissions. But such an arrangement does not alter the responsibility of the New York Headquarters for the administrative and substantive aspects of the programme. To a considerable extent, the preparatory work and the channels of communication will differ from previous practice, but the final decisions will, as before, be taken in New York.

25. At the same time, I have changed the duty stations of four social affairs officers from Headquarters to Bangkok, Santiago, and Beirut to strengthen direct advisory services to governments in the social field and to accomplish a better integration of the economic and social development programmes of the United Nations. The Social Commission gave

[9] See General Assembly Official Records, Tenth Session, Annexes, agenda item 38, Document A/3041.

full support to the plan which was reported to it in the spring of 1955 before it was incorporated in my report to the General Assembly. As in the case of the experimental arrangements regarding TAA in Latin America, the movement of these social affairs officers in no way modifies the responsibilities of the Headquarters Secretariat toward the Council and its Social Commission. Recent experience in planning the work programmes of these officers confirms my view that we can achieve a reasonable degree of "regionalization" of the social affairs programme without diminishing Headquarters control.

26. I said earlier that the United Nations and the specialized agencies had achieved a gratifying degree of universality in their programmes. That is true, but there is one great continent, Africa, where the need for international economic and social assistance is immense and to which—as I reported to the General Assembly last year—too little attention has as yet been paid. Some excellent work has, it is true, already been done. Several specialized agencies are well established in Africa, and UNICEF in particular has greatly expanded its work there during the past year. In the past year also, a United Nations–led survey mission on community development visited a number of African territories, and the Secretariat has produced a study on African water problems [10] which is before the Council at this session. But all this represents little more than the beginnings of effective international action by the United Nations organizations, and in my view concerted efforts on a far greater scale than heretofore are imperative.

27. The Middle East is also an area which is at present, in my view, not being adequately served in the economic and social fields by the United Nations, although considerable aid has been given by UNICEF and under the Technical Assistance Programme. It is true that, as I mentioned previously, more of the Secretariat's Middle East economic work will be done this year on the spot. But this means merely giving facilities to a few staff members to make direct observations in Middle East countries on an experimental basis. In the future we shall need much better and more numerous connections, and my own hope is, as I explained to the General Assembly last year [in Document A/C. 5/646, November 23, 1955] that in due course it will be possible for the United Nations Department of Economic and Social Affairs and TAA to have a combined office in the Middle East served by staff permanently resident there.

---

[10] *Op. cit.* (E/2882).

28. The claims of the whole so-called underdeveloped world to rapidly improved standards of life and a removal of inequalities, and their demand for help in creating the conditions that make this possible are insistent, and it is in the interest of the whole world that they be met generously. One great lesson of the past ten years is that they can in large measure be met, and met efficiently and effectively, through international action. In respect of international technical assistance activities alone, as TAB has brought out, resources many times the size of those now available are called for. I hope it may now be possible to consider the problem of international aid from a broader angle such as I have tried to indicate, and to reappraise the whole scale of the action that should be undertaken through the United Nations organizations in favour of the economic and social development of the underdeveloped countries.

---

3. From Statement in the Economic and Social Council Opening Debate on Item 3: General Review of the Development and Coordination of the Economic, Social, and Human Rights Program and Activities of the United Nations and the Specialized Agencies as a Whole

GENEVA   JULY 24, 1956

My statement introducing this item has been circulated to the Council in Document E/2894/Rev. 1, and there is, I think, little that I need add at this stage.

Some reference must, however, be made to the meeting of the Administrative Committee on Coordination (ACC) which took place since that statement was issued. While that meeting was largely concerned with problems of administration, it reviewed in a preliminary way (and

UN Press Release SG/494, July 24, 1956. The summary record is given in Economic and Social Council Official Records, Twenty-second Session, 942nd Meeting, July 24, 1956.

subject to further consideration in October) the results of a series of recent intersecretariat consultations on social programs; and it set in motion a number of informal consultations, which have since taken place in Geneva, on various economic as well as social activities.

While the results of these consultations will be incorporated in the report which the ACC will issue in the autumn, special mention should at this stage be made of a welcome clarification that has been reached on concepts, and of the respective roles of the various organizations, in the important field of community development.

To quote a provisionally agreed text on this question: "The term 'community development' has come into international usage to connote the processes by which the efforts of the people themselves are united with those of governmental authorities to improve the economic, social, and cultural conditions of communities, to integrate these communities into the life of the nation, and to enable them to contribute fully to national progress.

"This complex of processes is then made up of two essential elements: the participation by the people themselves in efforts to improve their level of living with as much reliance as possible on their own initiative; and the provision of technical and other services in ways which encourage initiative, self-help, and mutual help and make these more effective. It is expressed in programs designed to achieve a wide variety of specific improvements."

As the comprehensive character of community development has become apparent, the necessity has arisen to define more specifically its component services, such as fundamental education and agricultural extension and their respective relationships with community development. In the field of fundamental education this redefinition has made great progress.

It is now recognized that fundamental education is not synonymous with community development, but that the term covers a range of educational activities essential to community development. Dr. Evans [Dr. Luther Evans, Director-General of UNESCO] or his representative may wish to elaborate on this point in the course of this debate. In addition to community development, the recent intersecretariat consultations have covered *inter alia* questions relating to long-range programs for children, and work in the field of housing, industrialization, urbanization, social policies for indigenous peoples, commodity questions, and land reform.

They have included a review of the main elements in the social programs of the five organizations principally concerned and in programs in the field of atomic energy. They have represented a joint effort of the international staffs concerned to plan together at the earliest stage in programs of common interest, to clarify concepts, methods, and responsibilities, to adjust existing plans changing emphases and conditions, to remove misunderstandings or points of friction, and to find the most practicable working arrangements in cases where competences overlap.

Consultations for just such purposes are, I need hardly say, a daily occurrence between departmental officials in every capital city, the normal routine indeed of modern governmental processes. If those held under the auspices of ACC deserve mention, it is because the peculiar features of our system of international cooperation—namely, decentralization of authority and geographic dispersal—accentuate the problems of coordination found in every national service and the cost and effort required to solve them.

Every summer, advantage is taken of the presence of senior officials in Geneva from United Nations Headquarters and the specialized agencies to arrange personal consultations of this kind. This year the scope of the consultations has been wider than in the past and this, it may frankly be said, has reflected the increased strains to which our international system of cooperation has recently been subjected.

As I said in my introductory statement [Document E/2894/Rev. 1], certain developments in United Nations work, and in particular the trend toward the formulation and execution of broad programs covering fields which are within the competence of the specialized agencies, do raise new and difficult problems of coordination. On certain of these relating in particular to the ways in which the resources of all agencies within the United Nations family can be more fully mobilized in relation to such comprehensive programs, studies have been initiated by ACC, the results of which will be duly brought to the Council's attention.

Other problems are of a different character. I myself have suggested, in my written introductory statement, that to help meet one of the central conditions of economic development, namely the building up of adequate national administrations in the less-developed countries, there is need for a new organizational approach at the international level.

Two years ago I summarized in the words "unity within freedom" the principle that in my view should guide the relationships between the various organizations within the United Nations system. I pointed out that the application of that principle should provide in considerable measure the advantages of a closely unified system without the disadvantages of rigid centralization; that this required the development of a spirit of mutual confidence, directed toward common aims; and that this in turn required constant consultation and unremitting efforts among the permanent staffs not only at the technical level but also—indeed I would say above all—among the heads of the organizations themselves.

The contacts which my colleagues and I have developed, including the occasional and increasingly informal meetings which are perhaps rather misleadingly formalized by the term "sessions of the ACC," have indeed become a rather vital element in making the system work. Interorganizational relationship and cooperation still has many interpretations. Its most encouraging element, in my view, is the growing awareness at the most responsible level of the need for close collaboration over and outside stiffly formal arrangements. This human element, which I consider vital, can never be laid down in rules, nor enforced. It is a fact, or it is not a fact. As a fact it is tied to personalities. . . .

4. Further Statement in Economic and Social Council on Proposed International Administrative Service

GENEVA   JULY 24, 1956

[SUMMARY RECORD]

The Secretary-General said that he appreciated the opportunity of clarifying certain points which had been raised in the debate, concerning his proposal for the creation of an international service to assist governments of underdeveloped countries in their task of administration.

The Chinese representative had asked what kind of international civil

Economic and Social Council Official Records, Twenty-second Session, 943rd Meeting, July 24, 1956. No verbatim text of this statement was issued.

servants he had had in mind when he had spoken about the need for a new approach, and had very rightly made a distinction between two types, one of which was approximately of the present kind—consultants, experts, and the like—and another consisting of people who would actually form part of the national administration of the country concerned. The first line of action—namely, the provision of assistance to countries by expert advice and putting consultants at their disposal was—as had been pointed out in the debate by the representatives of the specialized agencies—a procedure which had already been tried and had been developing favourably. He had had in mind the second type, an arrangement by which people might be attached to national administrations, not as consultants, but as members of the actual administration.

The reason why he considered that that was needed was that very many countries which had recently emerged as independent modern states had previously had a foreign administration, or at least strong foreign elements in the national administration, which had provided a considerable part of the machinery needed to run the country, but had now lost that assistance. At the same time, they were confronted with major social and economic problems which certainly required the greatest efficiency and maturity in administration.

Another factor was that those countries usually lacked what might be called a social infrastructure which would enable them to recruit within a reasonable time, and build up, a national civil administration capable of coping with the enormous problems now arising. He had felt that it was the duty of the international community, of the United Nations and all its organs, and of the specialized agencies, to consider that need very carefully.

He did not think there could be any doubt about the existence of the need, and he felt that all who had been working with the so-called underdeveloped countries and looking at the problems from under their skin, must recognize it. That need could not be filled by the speedy development of national administrations. It could not be filled by consultants and experts put at the disposal of the governments in an international capacity, but not integrated in the national administration; such consultants remained, and should remain, outside the national administration, and could not, for that reason, fill the same needs as those who could be integrated in, and brought under the discipline of, the government concerned. On the other hand, it must be recognized that the countries concerned were faced with considerable difficulties in recruiting people from other nations. They might have connections with some other governments enabling them to receive assistance from them and the proper kind of recruitment, but all the same there would be the difficulty that people thus recruited would virtually have dual nationality. Even if country A were to second a good man to the civil service of country B, he would always carry with him too much of the nationality of, and of special duties and relations to, country A to make it very easy for country B to absorb him and use him as one of their own.

The proper role of the international family of organizations would therefore be to provide forums in which the national governments could recruit the necessary people for its administration, in the first place to make sure that they got the right people and, secondly, to avoid the complications inherent in using in their national service people who were also under the discipline of another government. That could be done; if an international organization—the United Nations or the specialized agencies or a new agency—established working relations with governments so as to be able to draw from the national civil service people of the right quality, the type needed in those countries which had to build up an administration, and could at the same time change them into international civil servants—that is, denationalize them to the extent that (for example, he [Dag Hammarskjöld] himself was denationalized) it would certainly be of very great help to the country in need. Such countries would thus have the assistance of an international body in finding the people they needed, and the people they obtained could be incorporated in the national administration without any feeling of dependence on any other country.

Such people who were integrated with the national administration would obviously not be under any instructions from their own government, nor under any instructions at all from the international organizations, which would serve as a kind of labour exchange. They would be independent administrative servants under the rules and laws of the country concerned, under orders from the government concerned, on a secondment basis, and only with the additional responsibility typical of an international civil servant, which meant, in fact, an added demand for integrity and for the observance of certain rules of the game.

He thought that there seemed to have been one other misunderstanding in the discussion, and that was that he had proposed, and considered necessary, the creation of a new specialized agency. He felt that it might well be that the problem could not be solved without establishing a new specialized agency, but he had a completely open mind on the point. What he had felt to be his duty had been to draw the attention to the basic need in a number of countries in order that it might be properly considered and studied, and then it might be seen what kind of response should be given.

The matter had a very close relationship with the questions of self-determination on the one hand and of financial assistance on the other. The United Nations had become the foremost spokesman for the self-determination of new nations and of older nations which had newly acquired statehood. Self-determination was a question of political maturity, but, even if there was full political maturity, there was not necessarily the necessary equipment economically or administratively. He would say that the very opposite was often the truth.

In many cases it was felt by the Trusteeship Council and the General Assembly that a nation was ripe for self-determination, although there was neither adequate administrative machinery nor the necessary economic basis for a happy life as an independent nation. He felt that once the consequences of the policy of self-determination—which, he thought, was one of the main lines in present international politics—were accepted, it must be recognized that the two subordinated aspects referred to had to be covered: assistance in the establishment of a national administration and assistance in the creation of the necessary financial and economic basis for a happy life as an independent nation. Thus, from his point of view, the proposal for a civil service of a new type—about the need for which he had spoken—was closely related to the major issue of self-determination and closely related, too, to the question of the financing of the independent life of those new nations.

In the last-mentioned respect he would go very far, and would indeed say that he could, with good conscience, propose to Member nations to give much-needed international assistance to such countries only if he felt that they had an administration of sufficient strength to put such financial assistance to the best use.

Summing up, he would just repeat that he had wished to point out the existence of a need. He was not ready to say that this or that was the answer, but he felt it to be essential to look with open eyes as early as possible at that major difficulty, which had so far not been met by any of the arrangements made within the United Nations family.

5. Statement in Economic and Social Council Concluding Debate on Development and Coordination

GENEVA   JULY 25, 1956

[SUMMARY RECORD]

The Secretary-General said he had followed the debate with the greatest interest. Of the many issues that had been raised there were one or two to which he would like to address himself.

The first was, in a sense, a marginal point that had arisen in the debate on economy. In fact, the discussion of economy and the relation between coordination and economy had reminded him of the debate which had taken place in the Council at its eighteenth session. At the 796th meeting he had then placed before the Council the far-reaching findings of a survey undertaken, by the Secretariat itself, on the manning and the tasks of the United Nations Secretariat. Those findings had gone so far as to cause obvious concern, not only in the Council, but also, and especially, in some of its subordinate organs. It had been felt that the cut-down of the Secretariat might jeopardize the efficiency of United Nations operations and had perhaps been rather too sharp with regard to certain social projects.

The broad lines of the proposals had, however, been approved both by the Council and, subsequently, by the General Assembly. Unfortunately, in later developments, part of the results had been lost, owing to the attitude taken in various United Nations organs, reflecting the majority views of Member governments.

He had had in mind at that time two main kinds of savings: administrative, and the reduction of tasks and projects undertaken. On the first score, the strength of the Secretariat had been reduced by 15 percent within two years; and, as many members would know from experience in national administrations, such a reduction could not be undertaken without certain consequences, not so much on morale as on tranquil and

Economic and Social Council Official Records, Twenty-second Session, 945th Meeting, July 25, 1956. No verbatim text of this statement was issued.

regular working. He would strongly advise against a speedy repetition of an operation of that kind, although, in his view, further cuts were possible both in principle and in practice. He would advise against it because it was bad economy to submit an administration to continuous reviews and surveys and studies. There must be a period in which it could work on its main tasks; and, after all, a considerable cut in the budget over two years, for the first time in the history of any of the international organizations, was something which might give cause for reasonable satisfaction.

With regard to work programmes and the possibility of making savings thereon, he would repeat only what some representatives had already said. It must be remembered that while the Secretariat had responsibilities in the various international organizations, the primary responsibility lay with the governments. The Council might recall what had happened when economy proposals had been put forward in the Secretariat which went further than the governments represented in the Council and in the General Assembly had been willing to accept. The fact was that the work programme of the United Nations was decided by Member governments, and, on practically all points, represented the approval by Member governments of proposals which themselves had been made by Member governments. In such circumstances, it was one of the Secretariat's main functions to warn. It might be that it had not warned enough. But it might also be that its warnings had not been sufficiently heeded. For that reason, he could not but welcome most strongly the expressions in the Council of the determined will of governments to look at the matter seriously, and he hoped that would be reflected also in support for the Secretariat when it proposed cuts in the working programme.

He should say a word in defence of the Secretariat. There had been references in the debate to what he thought had been called the Parkinson's disease of international administration—the self-protecting, sometimes empire-building, attitude of civil servants. Nobody denied it; everybody knew it from his home field and from international organizations. There was another disease, if they were to enter upon the pathology of international organizations, the kind of schizophrenia reflected in the fact that the same governments took opposite views in different organs. That was a major complication from the point of view of the Secretariat and of cooperation among the international organizations. He hoped nobody would regard it as improper or going beyond what was justified by facts if he were to say that coordination began at home.

It had been proposed that a committee should be set up to overhaul the programme. He must strongly warn against it. A committee for that purpose would be a good thing only if one condition were met: that it would not show the same weaknesses as were shown by most collective international organs, and would not tend, like them, more or less to follow the law of the highest common denominator when it came to programmes, and the lowest common denominator when it came to the budget. That put the secretariats in a position where, sometimes, frankly, it was not possible to operate in a rational way. Before embarking on such an attempt it was necessary to be quite sure that there was behind the creation of such a committee the full and unreserved willingness of all governments to put into effect the desires for a reduction or streamlining, or better selection of projects.

Reference had been made to ACC and to the possible contribution of ACC to coordination. He had already had the opportunity at the 943rd meeting to say how much emphasis should, in his opinion, be placed on the factor of personality in the development of coordination among the autonomous bodies which made up the United Nations family. There was one fact which was sometimes overlooked: that there were limits to the extent to which the members of ACC could establish coordination. Apart, perhaps, from the Secretary-General himself, all the members of ACC had behind them a governing body representing a certain number of Member governments. They had no freedom to reach agreement in ACC which might run counter to the authority, and perhaps the wishes, of their own governing bodies. All of them must act within the limits of their constitutional competence. To change that would require a change in the constitutions of most of the international organizations, and that was something that nobody contemplated. They could, up to the precise point set by the terms of reference given them under the constitutional terms of the various organizations, achieve cooperation by further development of personal contacts, inspired by common aims; but, there again, there was a point where government responsibility came heavily into play and where coordination at government level was a prerequisite.

The Canadian and other representatives had raised the question of longer terms of office for those excellent, but not too numerous, international experts who combined high *expertise* with broad background knowledge and the right kind of spirit in the field of technical assistance. That proposal indicated a direction in which much indeed could be done. He was already aware of various possibilities, which had been tried fairly fully, but certainly further improvements were possible in that direction and a hard core of more or less permanent civil servants of that type might finally be built up which would definitely meet in one way the needs to which he had referred at the 943rd meeting.

He would, however, like to point out again, in order to avoid misunderstanding, that there was a fundamental and definite difference between an expert placed at the disposal of a government—that was to say an expert who advised and had no executive responsibility—and a man seconded to a government, who acted on behalf of a government and with executive responsibility. It was the latter type he had in mind, and it was the latter type that was certainly needed in certain countries. It went without saying that in that, as in other cases, the demand should determine the supply. There had never been, and there certainly was not now, any idea in anybody's mind, certainly not in his own, that countries should be forced to take administrators whom they themselves did not feel that they needed. But he was quite sure that the longer present developments continued, the more aware a number of countries would become that they could not meet their own basic administrative needs without some kind of assistance. When that point came, he believed they would rightly ask the world community for assistance of the type he had indicated, and it was to be hoped that by that time it could be supplied.

It would be unwise for the United Nations to shut its eyes to needs or, out of consideration for administratively desirable arrangements, to forget what was the main duty, not only of the Organization, but of the governments themselves. The test of organizations and governments alike was, of course, what they achieved, and he personally was convinced that with full and unreserved devotion to the task which was theirs, they would find that questions of coordination would solve themselves automatically.

Statement on Incidents on Jordanian-Israeli Demarcation Line

GENEVA   JULY 26, 1956

THE INCIDENTS to which the following statement refers were as follows: First, after exchanges of fire across the Jordan-Israeli demarcation line in an area close to the main Jerusalem—Tel Aviv highway, investigating UN military observers had been attacked and two had been wounded by armed Palestinian Arab villagers; second, three more UN military observers had been seriously wounded by a land mine in the demilitarized zone on Mount Scopus. The Secretary-General feared the incidents might set off a chain reaction of reprisals that would undermine the cease-fire.

I deeply regret the incidents which have recently taken place on the Jordanian-Israeli demarcation line. I am grieved by the injuries suffered and I extend my warm sympathy to the United Nations observers who have been seriously injured while on duty in the cause of peace.

The incidents were unexpected, as I felt entitled to count on the most rigorous measures in implementation of the general cease-fire. They are expressions of the deeply disturbed conditions which still prevail and which render it imperative for all concerned to impose the discipline which alone can preserve peace and order.

I have directed a new strong appeal to those concerned to take all measures necessary for the protection of the cease-fire to which they are bound by solemn undertakings to the United Nations. I trust that these appeals will be heeded.

The obligations remain, and failures to live up to them do not mean that these obligations are reduced to empty words. It is my conviction that the governments will be faithful to and put into action their responsibilities so as to help the United Nations to develop the cease-fire into a generally accepted state of mind in which a repetition of what has just happened is excluded.

UN Press Release SG/495, July 26, 1956.

I now return to New York where, at Headquarters, I will do my utmost on the basis of my recent experiences in the region and in the light of the latest developments to see to it that the cease-fire is followed through. My return should not give rise to any impression that I consider us to face an emergency where we are in danger of losing what in past months has so painstakingly been built up. It is motivated by my conviction of the usefulness of continued and intensified efforts along the lines on which we have embarked.

From Transcript of Press Conference

UN HEADQUARTERS, NEW YORK   AUGUST 2, 1956

ON JULY 19 the United States had abruptly withdrawn its offer to help finance the Aswan Dam project. Nasser had reacted a week later by nationalizing the Suez Canal Company with the announced intention of using Canal tolls for the dam instead. His move had provoked an extremely hostile response from Great Britain and France, with threats of force unless Egypt backed down and agreed to restore operation of the Canal to international control. Dulles had flown to London and was conferring with the Eden and Mollet governments on a plan to call a conference of signatories of the Constantinople Convention and other major users of the Canal when Hammarskjöld met the press on August 2. In response to questions the Secretary-General answered that he found it would be quite appropriate if the United Nations were to be given some kind of responsibility in the matter, although he emphasized that this was not a proposal. He also made clear that he had not yet been consulted by any of the powers.

Other questions at this conference concerned the Palestine situation, the attitude of the USSR toward United Nations operations, multilateral aid for economic development, and Hammarskjöld's proposal for an international administrative service.

. . . . QUESTION: In your capacity as Secretary-General of the United Nations, which includes among its duties to see to it that international law is respected, do you believe that the act of the Egyptian government in nationalizing the Suez Canal, which is operated by an Egyptian company, is a violation of that law? If not, do you not believe that the hysteria created in some Western Powers has increased world tension?

THE SECRETARY-GENERAL: That is really what I would call a leading question, and for that reason, if there is no other reason to give for it, I would prefer to give no comment at all.

QUESTION: I wonder if you would care to shed a little light on your all-day session with Premier Ben-Gurion.

THE SECRETARY-GENERAL: I do not understand why there is any need

UN Note to Correspondents No. 1354, August 2, 1956.

to throw light on it. I remember, to go back to Egypt, that when I came out from the talk with President Nasser I was asked why I had had a talk with Colonel Nasser. I said, "Why are you always asking why things are done? Is nothing natural? Is it not natural that I am in Cairo, and, being in Cairo, that I should have a talk with Colonel Nasser?" At the same time, I consider my long talks with Premier Ben-Gurion to be something completely natural which does not need any explanation and on which I have no reason to throw any light. I think you all saw the press statement. We reviewed the situation fully and fruitfully, as we said; we reviewed what had happened in the past and we looked a little bit on what could be done in order to get closer to full compliance with the armistice agreements. I have really nothing to add to the communiqué.[1]

. . . . QUESTION: I have been reading in the newspapers about the internationalization of waterways, and I know there are some views in the United Nations on that. Could you give us your views on how, under the aegis of the United Nations, a waterway could be internationalized?

THE SECRETARY-GENERAL: That would take us very far, and I have not briefed myself properly on it, and I would hate to indulge in some kind of loose talk. But this much I think I can say: that, to the extent that countries and the international community would feel that this or that waterway has such general international significance as to warrant some kind of guarantee for all parties concerned and, on that very basis, arrive at the conclusion that the United Nations should assume some kind of responsibility, I would find such a development perfectly natural.

QUESTION: Direct United Nations responsibility?

THE SECRETARY-GENERAL: I am not making any suggestions here. I am just saying, hypothetically, that, if the community of nations felt that a reasonable way of guaranteeing an international waterway would be for the United Nations to assume some kind of responsibility, I would

---

[1] The communiqué was released jointly in Jerusalem by the Prime Minister of Israel and the Secretary-General following the conclusion of their discussions in the afternoon of July 20, 1956, and read as follows: "The Secretary-General of the United Nations, Mr. Dag Hammarskjöld, and Prime Minister David Ben-Gurion had a full and fruitful review of the developments in this area since the last visit of the Secretary-General, and they discussed ways and means to establish the state of affairs envisaged in the Armistice Agreements between Israel and her neighbors." (Issued at UN Headquarters the same day as UN Press Release Note No. 1344.)

myself not consider such a development out of line with what I consider to be natural United Nations functions.

QUESTION: May I ask you what, according to your information and your judgment, is the situation now between Jordan and Israel?

THE SECRETARY-GENERAL: On the situation in general terms, I do not think that there is any need for comment. It is a situation we have had and which we have known very well for a long time. What you have in mind is, of course, the acute development there. The situation is that we had last week a couple of incidents which I personally regret very much. They might have touched off some rather disturbing developments, but they did not. The development stopped short of any more dangerous turn, and for that reason I think that we are now in a position where we can put into the archives the records, the findings, and the protocols concerning these incidents. They indicate definitely that the situation is strained, I would not say politically, but strained in the sense that in some quarters nerves are a little bit on edge. For that reason, an accident may develop into an incident. In the past few months, several things have happened along that demarcation line which I also regret. On the other hand, so far nothing has happened which has created in my mind any doubt as to the seriousness of the intention of the governments concerned to follow up the previous efforts and the assurances they have given to the United Nations.

To sum up, I would say that this and that has happened, which is regrettable, but I would warn against drawing any far-reaching conclusions, either as concerns the relations between the countries—that these relations have been changed—or as concerns the attitude of any of the governments concerned.

QUESTION: You have been in Moscow and Eastern Europe. I would like to ask you this three-part question. As a result of your visit there —which, I understand, was the first visit in your life, to Moscow at any rate—have you discerned (a) a tendency which would reaffirm your faith in the continued peace of the world; (b) whether these tendencies would also contribute to the strengthening of the United Nations; and (c) whether we should pack our bags and prepare to go to Moscow for our 1957 session of the General Assembly?

THE SECRETARY-GENERAL: On the last point, I think you can wait with the packing. On the other points, I should like to combine your (a) and your (b) and say that my impressions in Moscow and my talks in Moscow very definitely confirmed an impression which I already had, and that is the interest of the people in Moscow in the United Nations, the United Nations operations, and, I would also say, in the success of the United Nations operations. To talk the way you do about tendencies is something which I always hesitate to do, because that is projecting a direct impression into the future. I think it is enough to know where we stand for the moment, and I can only say what I have said: My impressions and my discussions confirmed this impression which I had before of Soviet Union support for the present United Nations efforts.

QUESTION: My question is divided into two parts: One, Prime Minister Nehru, in the recent past, has been suggesting the desirability of major powers channeling their economic and technical aid to the so-called underdeveloped countries through the United Nations. Are there any indications on the part of the major powers to use the United Nations machinery for this? Out of nearly $4 billion foreign aid voted by the United States Congress, it would appear that only $15 million was intended for the United Nations technical activities. Is this an improvement, or otherwise, on similar contributions in the past years?

Part two of my question—we of India are very much interested in this. You spoke at the recent Economic and Social Council session at Geneva of the need for a separate international civil service to give assistance in the administration of newly independent countries. As we understand it, even at this time, similar assistance is being given by the United Nations through the Technical Assistance Administration, which employs experts on public administration. Will the new service which you contemplate be merely an expansion of the present expert service, or will it be an altogether separate service under a new agency?

THE SECRETARY-GENERAL: Your first question, as to the channeling of international aid through the United Nations and other international agencies, does raise a very broad problem as you know. My own feeling is that, after all, not only the United Nations, but internationalism as such, is a fairly young phenomenon in its modern form, and for that reason there is necessarily a question of testing out ways and means of education and of demonstration of possibilities.

We are still certainly in a state of affairs where a preference in many countries is given to bilateral aid; that is to say, they still feel that the advantages attached to bilateral aid are such as to make them prefer to avoid the other channel.

However, there is another aspect to the problem, and that is that, in a certain sense, we have not convinced them sufficiently either of the efficiency or of the advantages of an internationalized aid. That is to say, instead of directing criticism to various governments for the fact that, so far, international aid has been only to a slight extent internationalized, I direct the criticism a little bit against ourselves. I do not think we have failed, but we have not so far demonstrated clearly enough both the advantages and what we can do. I think those governments, and those who, obviously, like you, feel that an internationalization of aid is desirable, can help us considerably in demonstrating the advantages from the point of view both of the donor country and of the receiving country, and by highlighting a little bit too that, after all, the job done has been a reasonably good one. My own efforts in this respect go in the direction of trying to demonstrate these advantages, these possibilities, without in any way denying that there are situations where very much can be said for bilateral aid. However, where there is bilateral aid, I would like to see it brought into its proper context in relation to international aid. We have not only not enough internationalization of aid, but I think we also lack a little bit the coordination between various bilateral schemes and the international schemes.

To your second point, the reply simply is that what I have in mind is something qualitatively different from the technical assistance in administration which is given now. The technical assistance now given in the field of administration is given by sending experts and consultants, and they remain just experts and consultants; that is to say, they are on our payroll, they are under our instructions, or discipline, and so on and so forth. They have no direct responsibility in relation to the government in the country where they serve. They cannot take orders from that government. They have no executive functions for that government. The experts we send out, I think, do a good job and they certainly are appreciated by the men in the governments with whom they serve; but a consultant is a consultant. He can say his word, but he says his word, so to say, from the outside, without sharing the same responsibilities and without, on the other hand, the same possibilities of action that a man would have who would be in the service of the government.

The basic difficulty, as I see it, is that governments which have not been able so far to build up their administration are not properly served by having people in this way, halfway between them and the outside world—people who are outside consultants. What they would need would be people with the same expert knowledge, serving them under their instructions, carrying responsibility and with executive functions.

What I had in mind when I put forward this proposal was to try and find the forms in which the world community could assist governments —if they wanted to have that kind of assistance—by giving them people who could be integrated in their civil service, who could carry executive functions; that is to say, who were no longer experts, although they should have the same expert knowledge, but under the rules of the very country where they serve.

That is definitely an innovation and, if you please, a radical one. Whether it is a good idea will be decided, I think, mainly by the reaction of the countries which would receive such help. If they feel they want it, if they feel they can receive it under sufficient guarantees, then the idea is good and sound. If they do not, well, of course then it is just something we would have to shelve. However, when I have taken it up, and when I was pushing it lately—in Geneva for example—it has been with a view to the fact that such a demand, such a need, is likely to be felt, and that we would close our eyes to realities if we did not make preparations and from our side did try to find out what could be done if and when such a need arises, if and when such a demand is put to us.

We should not meet such a demand unprepared. Whether or not such an arrangement requires a new agency is a question on which I have an open mind. If it takes on the proportions which are possible, it might be such a heavy administrative burden that we would find it rather difficult to run it from here, and then I think that no other agency would be in a better position; that is to say, then it should be made some kind of independent operation under its own leadership. But on that score I have an open mind. I think the decisive point will be what size this operation will take.

. . . . QUESTION: Have you been having any discussions with any delegations here on the Suez Canal question, and have any delegations sought your advice in the matter?

THE SECRETARY-GENERAL: No, my advice has not been considered that interesting on this question. I have been informed about certain aspects by the Permanent Representative of Egypt. That is all. We have not discussed it.

. . . . QUESTION: Would you be prepared, if called upon, to place the facilities of the United Nations site in Geneva at the disposal of the proposed international conference on the Suez Canal? Secondly, would you be willing, if called upon, to act as host to, or even chairman of, that conference?

THE SECRETARY-GENERAL: That is a very hypothetical question. I think we have to leave the second part of it completely aside.

As regards the first part of the question, I would say this: If the conference developed into a general one, I think that you yourself can see that it would be in line with my previous policy concerning the United Nations headquarters in Geneva to take a very favorable look at the possibility you have suggested. Of course, it is not only a question of principle, but also a question of what we can do in a practical way. As for the question of principle, I would certainly judge that question in the light of the same considerations as those which decided in favor of holding the Indo-China conference and the summit meeting last year in Geneva.

QUESTION: Last week, the Government of Israel gave the Security Council notice that that Government considered it useless to present any further statements of censure to the Mixed Armistice Commission on the Jordan-Israel border incidents. In the light of that fact, just how could any incidents be handled, if not through that machinery? Furthermore, does the obligation remain for both parties to use that machinery?

THE SECRETARY-GENERAL: In the first place, I do not share the view that it is useless to go to the Mixed Armistice Commission. I think that that is a good procedure, which should be followed.

In the second place, I would say this: Of course, any party can stay away; that is his right. Such a course, however, will necessarily have its impact on the outcome, because only one party will have been represented. In that way, the operations of the MAC machinery could be stymied.

In the third place, we all have reactions this or that way, and I think that we all also feel that such reactions may be changed in the light of later experiences and developments. For that reason, I would not myself give any kind of permanency to the declaration which has just been mentioned. I think that it is more a statement of frustration than a statement of policy.

QUESTION: My question also has two parts. The first refers to the answer which you gave Mr. Huss [Pierre Huss, *International News Service*] about the international conference on the Suez Canal and the Geneva headquarters of the United Nations. Would your answer be the same if, by any chance, Egypt and the Soviet Union refused to participate in such a conference?

The second part of my question is as follows: We have been watching with great interest all your efforts to reduce world tension. Could you tell us what the Secretary-General of the United Nations has done with regard to the Suez Canal question to reduce the tension which has been created?

THE SECRETARY-GENERAL: As regards the first point, I would say this: When United Nations Headquarters are opened for a conference, they are opened only for a truly international conference. That has been the case in the past; it will be the case in the future.

As regards the second point, we are still, as you know, at a very early stage in the development of this story. We are at the stage of very acute negotiations. At this stage I think it would be premature for me to intervene. The water must be a little bit clearer before I can see if I have any platform at all that would make it appropriate for me to go into the matter. And, if I saw that it was appropriate, I would like to have sufficient background to form a personal opinion.

QUESTION: You have just returned from attending meetings of the Economic and Social Council in Geneva. The paramount question at that session of the Economic and Social Council seems to be the perennial one of stepped-up economic aid to the underdeveloped areas of the world. In line with the many questions that are being asked about the Suez Canal, I should like to ask this question: Do we not have in the Suez Canal matter a very clear example of the economic roots of war tensions that could arise in the future, after the cold war of the big powers has somewhat subsided?

I do not get the impression from the reports of the Economic and Social Council session that the big industrial powers are as yet fully aware of the great urgency, from the standpoint of war and peace, of making very clear what their contributions are going to be to the development of the economically underdeveloped areas—especially the new nations which are arising and which have new responsibilities. What was your impression in Geneva? Was it your impression that these big powers were still procrastinating and temporizing? Or was it your impression that some real, definite, muscular, energetic steps were being taken to make the United Nations contribute vitally to peace through economic assistance?

THE SECRETARY-GENERAL: I have, in fact, already replied in part to your question in speaking of the internationalization of aid; the arguments which I used in that context also apply to the question of the extent to which various Member countries are willing to engage in economic aid. I would say generally—and this goes far beyond governments and down to public opinion—that the view which you seem to hold and which I certainly share—that is, the view that there is a very vital link between economic assistance, or, as it were, the sharing of wealth in this sense with the underdeveloped countries, and the question of war and peace—is not yet common property. I am very sorry that that is so, because it means that when you talk about it and when I talk about it and when the underdeveloped countries talk about it, too many regard it as a curious kind of devious blackmail: "Unless we get the money, we shall make trouble and war." That is a completely false presentation of the facts, as we all know; but it is a natural misunderstanding in the light of the circumstance that, so far, people have not seen the links between these troublesome economic conditions and the political equilibrium of the world.

QUESTION: Do you think the current session of the Economic and Social Council is showing the proper awareness of this matter—or, at least, that the big powers which are members of the Council are showing the proper awareness? Without designating myself as a one-man collection agency for the United Nations, I have in mind this, for instance: We hear irresponsible speeches at the United Nations to the effect that certain savings from disarmament will go toward the financing of this economic assistance program—which is essentially a program of money—and yet armies are being reduced unilaterally and bilaterally, and no one in the Economic and Social Council, so far as I have been able to see from the records, has said one word about these promissory notes which the big powers have written out verbally here at the United Nations, which they are not making good and which seem to be just so many words.

I wonder whether you do not feel that the United Nations and the United Nations press must become conscious of the fact that this is becoming a vital issue. I think that the Suez Canal really erupted out of an economic issue, the Aswan Dam, and I feel that similar incidents could arise in the future.

THE SECRETARY-GENERAL: Let us stick to facts. I am not willing to pass any judgment either on the Council or on the governments which are represented on the Council. As to the result, I can say that it will not mark any considerable progress in the direction in which I myself show a certain impatience. That much I would say, but that is an evaluation of the possible outcome—nothing else. For the rest, I think we should be a little cautious because the very argument which you brought out, and which I endorse, can of course be overplayed. It can be overplayed to the extent that it becomes quite natural if people sit back and feel very, very hesitant.

. . . . QUESTION: Mr. Secretary-General, when you were in Geneva you made a statement, as far as we could understand from the report in the newspapers here, saying that you had a promise from the parties concerned in the Middle East that they would not do anything to endanger the armistice agreements for a duration of three months. I doubt whether you said it that way because this did not make a very hopeful impression.

THE SECRETARY-GENERAL: No, I have no idea how that rumor came about because I remember only one public statement concerning these matters, and that was in a released statement, which you probably recieved. I said there that I felt disappointed in the somewhat unexpected turn events took in the middle of last week—thank God, it is now a thing of the past—because I felt entitled, in the light of the previous discussions, to expect the strictest discipline. I did not make any other statement in Geneva as to what you mentioned. I would agree with you not only that it would be discouraging, but I will go one step further: I would say that it is nonsensical.

. . . .

STATEMENTS
ON FURTHER PALESTINE INCIDENTS

UN HEADQUARTERS, NEW YORK   AUGUST 16–17, 1956

DURING HIS August 2 press conference Hammarskjöld had expressed relief
that the dangers for the Israeli-Jordan cease-fire created by the incidents of
July 24–26 had been contained, at least for the time being. Now, two serious breaches of the cease-fire on the Israeli-Egyptian demarcation line occurred in rapid succession, the second one clearly a retaliatory raid by Israel. Once again he resorted to public statements as part of his effort to
prevent further deterioration of the situation.

1. Statement of August 16

I have learned with great regret about two serious incidents today in
which, according to present information, four Israeli citizens have been
killed and eight wounded. The first incident took place when a civilian
vehicle was blown up by a mine—16 kilometers south of Sede Boker
where an incident took place August 14 in which a truck was blown up
by a mine. In the second incident a bus and jeep were attacked on the
way to Elath. I wish to express my deep sympathy for those stricken by
these irresponsible actions.

In my report to the Security Council of May 9, 1956, I pointed out
the duty of the governments in the region to observe strictly the military
cease-fire, and also their obligation "to take active measures against all
crossings of the demarcation line and acts of violence in connection
therewith." This, in my view, is a most serious moral obligation on
which the maintenance of the cease-fire may ultimately depend. Pending
an investigation of today's incidents, which would make it possible to
clarify the full responsibility, I must, with all possible emphasis, renew
my appeal for measures against infiltration and acts of violence, such as
these—so contrary to the conditions of peace and order which it must
be of vital interest for all to maintain.

UN Press Release SG/496, August 16, 1956.

In the light of the results of the investigations it will be decided what action should be taken by me because of these most serious acts of violence, including requests for punishment of the transgressors.

2. Statement of August 17

In a statement yesterday I expressed my deep concern for two serious incidents which had just taken place in Israel, and I extended my sympathy to those stricken by the actions. I also pointed out the danger which such acts of violence represented to the maintenance of the cease-fire. Today two new incidents have been reported in which nine Egyptians have been killed. In the second one of these incidents an Egyptian car with medical personnel was ambushed. Both these incidents are still being investigated. What I said in my statement yesterday applies with equal strength to these new incidents.

Whatever the sequence of cause and effect, and whatever the arguments which might be brought out as a reason for acts of violence, the one who resorts to such acts, whether starting or prolonging a chain of disturbances, takes on himself a very great responsibility for the final development in the area. The difference in the degree of responsibility borne by those found to have initiated such a chain of disturbances and by the other party does not remove the grave responsibility of the latter for a resort to acts of violence in contravention of the rules of the Charter. This, apart from all legal considerations, is the uncontradictable thought behind the repeated condemnations by the United Nations of acts of violence, understood to have been in retaliation, and the view that such acts cannot be considered as acts of self-defense in the sense of the UN Charter. I strongly urge the governments concerned to avoid and prevent any actions in violation of the cease-fire because of the events of the last two days.

I have requested the Chief of Staff to transmit to me a report on the developments of August 16 and 17 for presentation to the Security Council.

UN Press Release SG/497, August 17, 1956.

From Transcript of Press Conference

UN HEADQUARTERS, NEW YORK   AUGUST 23, 1956

MOST OF THE questions at this conference concerned the Suez Canal dispute and how Hammarskjöld viewed the status of the cease-fire on the armistice demarcation lines between Israel and Jordan and Egypt after the serious incidents of July and August. When the Secretary-General met the press, the London conference of maritime nations was about to end with an 18-Power proposal for creation of an international Suez Canal Board, including the principal users of the Canal, which was to have the responsibility for operation of the Canal. The proposal was opposed by the Soviet Union, India, Indonesia, and Ceylon. It would have assured control of management of the Canal by the Western Powers and Nasser turned it down early in September when Sir Robert Menzies, the Australian Prime Minister, came to Cairo in a futile effort to persuade him to accept it.

. . . . QUESTION: Should the Suez dispute come to the United Nations, what do you think would be the most suitable forum in which it might be discussed—the Security Council, or a special session of the General Assembly, or the regular session of the Assembly?

THE SECRETARY-GENERAL: That is a rather hypothetical question because there are very many forms in which the problem can be presented. It depends on the angle from which it comes up—as a question of certain practical arrangements, as a question of open conflict, as a question of approval of things already done, and so on and so forth. The Suez question is so diversified and has so many aspects that for that very reason it is impossible to say what would be an adequate forum in the United Nations. However, we may get some guidance from what has emerged from the London conference. I think that all speakers at the London conference have made some kind of reference to an association with the United Nations. If such an association were to develop and be the result of forthcoming negotiations, I think that is something which would require some kind of approval from the United Nations; and, if

UN Note to Correspondents No. 1378, August 23, 1956.

so, I think that the proper forum would be likely to be the General Assembly in regular session. But that is a reply given on the basis of a hypothesis—that is to say, that this association with the United Nations develops into an agreed plan for some kind of United Nations responsibility in the matter.

QUESTION: I wonder whether you think that your cease-fire arrangements in the Middle East have broken down, and also whether you have any hopes that the current visit of Mr. Cordier may help restore those cease-fire arrangements.

THE SECRETARY-GENERAL: First of all, let me dispose of the part of your question concerning Mr. Cordier. His visit has nothing to do with this at all, and he probably will not have any discussions which will cover this kind of ground either with Israeli authorities or with Jordanian authorities. So we can leave that aside.

As to the question of the cease-fire, I think it is essential to be quite clear on the point. The cease-fire in April was, first of all, a legal fact. You know that there was a cease-fire clause in the armistice agreements which somehow had been put in jeopardy just because it was mixed with all sorts of other stipulations in the armistice agreements, and it was an open question whether lack of compliance with those other stipulations in the armistice agreements had not given a legal basis for non-observance also of the cease-fire. For that reason, I considered it essential to lift the cease-fire out, to give it its own legal status as something independent of the Armistice and representing an obligation in relation to the United Nations itself. That was done, and that is something which has created in some respects a clearer legal situation than we had before. And no lack of observance, no failure to comply with this cease-fire, can, so to speak, undo the fact that the cease-fire now is an independent obligation for all the parties in relation to the United Nations. It can be a case of violation; it cannot be a case of breakdown until this obligation is canceled by any of the parties—and, as you know, nothing of that kind has happened. So that result remains.

What you have in mind is, of course, how the situation is in practice. In practice, I think we must recognize that, quite apart from the fact that we have had various incidents in all sorts of directions with varying responsibilities which are impossible to reconcile with a strict observance of the cease-fire, and apart from the fact that we have had on at least two occasions—late July and last week—major incidents which, as I have said in my reports, at least had clear elements of a breach of the cease-fire obligations, we cannot in any way find that what is happening in the field indicates that the governments consider themselves *de facto* as freed from the cease-fire obligations. On the contrary, I must say that in these various cases, in my direct and indirect contacts with the governments, they make it perfectly obvious that they wish to pay not only lip service but real service, allegiance, to their obligations under the cease-fire undertakings of last spring. For that reason, I refuse to draw any conclusions from even the graver incidents in the direction you may have in mind; that is to say, that they are incidents indicating that the governments wish to disregard or have brushed aside their legal obligations as recently established. I do not find that I have any right to draw such a conclusion as matters stand.

On the other hand, I do recognize—and I think I made it perfectly clear in my statements—that on different levels and in different directions what happened on the sixteenth and seventeenth are things which put the cease-fire in a very discouraging light. Whatever the explanations are of things such as those which occurred last week, it is unavoidable that they do contribute to undermining the feeling of sanctity of the cease-fire obligations in public opinion not only here but in the region. You cannot sin too often and still hope that a commandment will be generally regarded as a commandment in the sacred sense of the word. For that reason, coming back to your question, I would say that what has happened so far—the incidents to which I have reacted—does represent a danger to the cease-fire in the practical sense, not in the legal sense. These incidents represent a danger but they do not mean that the cease-fire, even *de facto,* has broken down.

As I wish to be rather clear on this point, you may perhaps excuse me for trying to sum up. The legal obligation established in April is there until it is canceled or openly challenged by any government. That has not happened. The legal situation is stable. *De facto,* things have happened which seem to put the application of these obligations in doubt. I do not think we are entitled to say that they have been put in doubt by what has happened, but I do feel that a repetition of things like those that have happened will create a most unhealthy and a most unhappy psychological atmosphere, and will demoralize public opinion with respect to the sanctity of the obligations to observe the cease-fire. For that reason, what we can do to forestall any repetition of such incidents we will do and we are doing. I hope that such efforts will be successful. The reason for this hopefulness is that I do believe that all these governments recognize that they have a vital interest in the maintenance of the cease-fire.

QUESTION: In your statement of August 16, I think, you indicated something about the punishment of the people who carried out the raids. If you catch them, who will do the punishing?

THE SECRETARY-GENERAL: The government in the country of which the criminals are citizens.

QUESTION: The United Nations, therefore, is bringing rather strongly to those governments that punishment is expected?

THE SECRETARY-GENERAL: It was brought very forcefully, I think, to their attention by a public statement. I do not know of any sharper form in which I can possibly bring it to the attention of governments. On the other hand, to follow up this intention, I need to know a little more about the facts than I know so far.

QUESTION: I wish to go back to Mr. Heffernan's [Reuters] question on the Suez. I see that Mr. Dulles in Point D stated the provision for appropriate association with the United Nations, and for review as may be necessary. Many of us have wondered whether this association will be directly under United Nations control or whether it will be an independent organ indirectly associated with the United Nations. I wonder if you would care to explain this?

THE SECRETARY-GENERAL: I cannot clarify that point at all. I have understood the declaration to be a declaration of principles and a declaration of principles intended to be the basis for discussions. I guess that every single technical arrangement which falls within the framework of the principles, for that reason, is a possibility. You mentioned two possibilities: there may be others. For my part, I do believe that they are reasonably within the limits of the principles stated—both of them— but I have no indication as to the direction in which the thing has been moving.

QUESTION: Coming back to your comments on the cease-fire, do I understand you correctly to mean that in your opinion the events of August 16 and 17 did not occur with the knowledge of the governments concerned and, therefore, that the legal obligation of the cease-fire was not violated?

THE SECRETARY-GENERAL: Let me put it in a more precise form. I must on these issues be very strict, as you understand. I have no right to conclude from either of the two incidents an intention on the side of the two governments to break the cease-fire. I have no right to conclude; I have no evidence which would lead me to such a conclusion.

. . . . QUESTION: You have been good enough to answer several questions related to the Suez matter. Your comment has not been asked yet on an action that followed hard on the heels of the Suez action and that, in the opinion of the Netherlands government, was inspired by it —namely, the repudiation of the Indonesian debts to the Netherlands. According to press reports, the people and the press in Holland are wondering what the United Nations is going to do about it. In view of the fact that the amount of the debt was fixed voluntarily by the round-table conference under the auspices of UNCI, the United Nations Commission for Indonesia, is there anything you can say on this subject? For instance, does UNCI still exist, and, if so, is it within its or anybody else's purview to look after the implementation of those accords?

THE SECRETARY-GENERAL: I find it rather difficult to give any precise reply to your question today. I know very little about this story beyond what I have read in the papers, and my intention has been, at a somewhat later stage when I will have an opportunity, to inform myself informally from the two delegations directly concerned about the matter. Before having done so, I find it difficult to say anything.

QUESTION: To put the question, perhaps, in a more general light, would you like to comment on what may be the effect of an action such as the nationalization of the Suez Canal on the discussions that have been going on within the United Nations for special funds for economic development?

THE SECRETARY-GENERAL: I hope that a solution to the Suez problem will be found in harmony, through negotiation. I therefore hope that, once this episode has come to an end, the situation will be such that there will be no reactions in the field to which you have referred. On the other hand, we all know that every major conflict involving these various parts of the world has at least psychological repercussions on the discussions related to assistance to underdeveloped countries. It is obvious that, if the governments engaged in the present operation do not find a way out, an accent will be added to the discussions on assistance to underdeveloped countries, an accent which may render more difficult the achievement of the progress for which all of us in this room are hoping. I repeat, however, that that would be the case only if there were to be an unhappy outcome of the present efforts.

QUESTION: A number of Security Council resolutions are pending with respect to the Suez Canal. Do you think it would be appropriate, once the international board has been finally created, with the indicated association with the United Nations, for these pending resolutions to receive some consideration by the board and the United Nations?

THE SECRETARY-GENERAL: I do not think that the United Nations has ever forgotten those resolutions—at least I have not. I do not know what the competence and functions of this proposed organ would be, and it is therefore difficult for me to say what would be the proper form for handling this specific issue to which you have referred, if the organ were established. But these resolutions have never been shelved; they are part of United Nations legal history, and, for that reason, they are part of the background of whatever I am doing.

QUESTION: Since the Suez issue is being discussed, I should like to ask you this: Did not the United Nations perhaps become the most important party to the incident when the United Kingdom government saw fit to inaugurate a virtual national mobilization of force and a disposition of naval strength in a manner which appears to me—I may be wrong—to constitute one of the most complete and flagrant violations of the spirit of the Preamble to the United Nations Charter? The Charter is very definite on this point, that nations—especially Member Nations—must not resort to force or even the threat or show of force without first attempting to negotiate a dispute. I realize that the question has never been raised and that there have been all kinds of diversions concerning boards, dividends, and so forth. It does seem to me, however—and I would appreciate it if you would tell me whether I am wrong—that this action by the United Kingdom Government was in many ways one of the most grave and serious challenges to the spirit of the United Nations. If a nation can take such action, what are we sitting here for anyway?

THE SECRETARY-GENERAL: Other persons may ask themselves that same question, for other reasons; I do not think that we should take it too seriously.

On this issue, however, which is a serious one, I think that we have every reason in the world to make a difference, before we consider the issue, between comments and interpretations given in public debate, in newspapers, and in other ways, and the interpretations given by those directly responsible for the actions we are considering. In that respect, we have an authoritative explanation—the one given by the Foreign

Secretary of the United Kingdom, Mr. Selwyn Lloyd, in his first speech to the London conference. I think that you should consider your question in the light of the explanation which Mr. Lloyd gave. If you did that, I do not think you would need to feel quite so disturbed by the situation as you seem to be.

. . . . QUESTION: At the last press conference you said that your advice had not been sought by anyone on the Suez question. I wonder if that still holds true?

THE SECRETARY-GENERAL: If you take the words I used literally— "advice being sought"—it still holds true. If you give it a wider interpretation, if people or delegations or governments have shown interest in how I analyze the situation and what I feel about it, it does not hold true because the question has come up quite a few times.

QUESTION: I believe that Mr. Dulles did discuss it with you. Could you tell us who else has been discussing it?

THE SECRETARY-GENERAL: No, I would not go into that.

. . . .

ON FURTHER PALESTINE INCIDENTS
SEPTEMBER 1956

A T THE TIME of the Secretary-General's Middle East report of May 9 (page 84), Israel had not placed on record any dissent from his view that the reservations for self-defense in the new cease-fire agreements could not be used to justify reprisal raids, which the Security Council had repeatedly condemned.

Israel had not, however, abandoned its long-standing policy of retaliation. It had withheld its hand late in July following the incidents on the Israeli-Jordan line, but had retaliated sharply against the Egyptians in mid-August. Now it was Jordan's turn. After several Israelis had been killed by fire from Jordan across the demarcation line, or by infiltrators, Israel launched two major midnight reprisal raids in rapid succession on September 10 and 12, blowing up two Jordanian police posts and two school buildings, one of them recently built with UNRWA funds. Thirty Jordanian soldiers and police were killed.

The press statement and the *notes verbales* to Israel and Jordan which are the first three following texts refer to these incidents, to the arguments advanced by Israel in justification for its actions, and to the failures of the Jordan Government to exercise effective control on its side of the line. Hammarskjöld used strong language in these diplomatic notes, which he immediately made public, contrary to his usual custom. Both refer to private notes of appeal and warning he had sent two days earlier. Israel's response had been the September 13 reprisal raid by its armed forces. On the Jordan side marauders had crossed into the Negev desert and killed three guards at an oil-drilling camp. The difference in circumstances accounts for the difference in tone of the two notes.

---

1. Statement Concerning Further Palestine Incidents
UN HEADQUARTERS, NEW YORK   SEPTEMBER 13, 1956

The very serious incidents which have taken place during the last few days in the Middle East, raise the question of the continued validity of

UN Press Release SG/502, September 13, 1956.

the cease-fire arrangement agreed upon in April. I consider it for that reason appropriate to make the following comments.

The armistice agreements between Israel and its Arab neighbors contain, all of them, an article prohibiting the use of the military or para-military forces of one party, including nonregular forces, for warlike or hostile acts against the other party. The same articles stipulate, further, that such forces may not advance beyond or pass over for any purpose whatsoever the armistice demarcation lines. Thus, the cease-fire forms part of the armistice régime itself, as established by the armistice agreements.

The arrangements made in April gave to these clauses an independent status so that a breach of the cease-fire could no longer be justified by a violation by the other parties of other clauses of the armistice agreements than the one establishing a cease-fire. The new arrangement also made the United Nations a direct party to the cease-fire as the cease-fire obligation was reaffirmed in assurances given to the Organization. The cease-fire, as established in the armistice agreements and reaffirmed as an independent obligation to the United Nations, in fact reflects a basic duty of all Member Nations of the United Nations under the Charter.

The establishment in April of a general cease-fire of this legal nature served to alleviate the very tense situation prevailing at that time. It was, on the whole, observed until late in July. From that time on we have witnessed a mounting series of incidents, followed by counter-moves, the most serious of which took place on September 10 and 12.

Established as an independent legal obligation in relation to the United Nations the cease-fire obviously remains fully valid as such, irrespective of the incidents that may occur. As reflecting a *general* obligation under the Charter, it can never cease to bind a Member of the United Nations. As a *formal* obligation, accepted independently of the Charter and binding on the nations, party to the armistice régime in Palestine, it can be put out of existence only if formally repealed by one of the governments concerned, or if challenged by actions clearly indicating that the government does not consider itself as any longer bound by the obligation.

It may be felt that the cease-fire, through the serious violations which have occurred, has been brought to an end. One could just as well say that the fact that all parties in the region, in varying degrees, are violating the armistice agreements, has annulled the armistice régime. If a government, or the United Nations, were to accept such interpretations, it would amount to saying that they, because of various incidents, considered that a state of war had been reestablished. This is obviously unjustifiable. I am sure that no one in a responsible position would endorse such a stand. Neither the armistice agreements nor the cease-fire obligations have been repealed by any of the parties concerned, and to say that the cease-fire obligation has been annulled by the violations it has suffered, would be incorrect as well as irresponsible.

---

2. *Press Release on* Note Verbale *to Government of* Israel

NEW YORK   SEPTEMBER 14, 1956

Following is the text of a *note verbale* handed today by Secretary-General Dag Hammarskjöld to Ambassador Abba Eban, Permanent Representative of Israel to the United Nations:

In a *note verbale* dated September 12 I called to the attention of the Government of Israel its solemn undertakings and the serious consequences that might come about if the current chain of events was not brought to an end immediately by careful avoidance of all further acts of violence. In spite of this appeal, and in disregard of the obligations undertaken in the armistice agreements and under the cease-fire assurance, a report of the United Nations Observers on an incident on September 13 indicates that Israeli forces have engaged in a new extensive action leading to heavy casualties. It may be supposed that this action is considered to be justified as an act "in self-defense." However, the action now undertaken cannot be considered as within the limits of legitimate self-defense in face of the acts of violence because of which it may be supposed to have been undertaken. In discussions with representatives of the Government of Israel I have repeatedly emphasized that, legal obligations apart, a policy like the one now pursued defeats its own purpose by leading to further tension and highly increasing the risk

UN Press Release SG/503, September 14, 1956.

for acts of violence directed against Israeli persons or territory. In my view events amply demonstrate the utter futility of actions such as those of which the incident of September 13 offers a new example, as actions aimed at protecting Israel's security.

The disregard both of the appeals from the United Nations and of the obligations under the armistice agreements, specifically the cease-fire obligation, means that Israel must be held fully accountable for its actions.

3. *Press Release on* Note Verbale *to Government of Jordan*

NEW YORK   SEPTEMBER 14, 1956

Following is the text of a *note verbale* handed today by Secretary-General Dag Hammarskjöld to Thabet Khalidi, Acting Permanent Representative of Jordan to the United Nations:

In a *note verbale* dated September 12 I called to the attention of the Government of the Hashimite Kingdom of Jordan the serious consequences that might come about if the current chain of events was not brought to an end immediately by careful avoidance of all further acts of violence. A further incident on September 12, which is still being investigated, suggests the possibility of a crossing of the demarcation line from the Jordan side, which led to new casualties.

I note with great concern that acts of violence have continued. I repeat my appeal to the Government to take all measures possible in order to forestall a repetition of such occurrences. I likewise appeal to the Government to show restraint and to abstain from all actions that would prolong the present serious unrest. It is my firm conviction that such actions would militate against Jordan's own interests in a quick reestablishment of order in the region.

For actions in disregard of the appeals of the United Nations and of the obligations under the armistice agreements, specifically the cease-fire

UN Press Release SG/504, September 14, 1956.

obligation, the Hashimite Kingdom of Jordan would have to be held fully accountable.

---

4. Letter to President of Security Council, Dr. Emilio Nunez Portuondo

SEPTEMBER 26

THIS LETTER was prompted by another massive Israeli reprisal raid during the night of September 25. A few days before, an Arab legionnaire, apparently suddenly gone berserk, had opened fire on members of an archeological congress examining recent excavations right at the armistice line and had killed four persons. He was quickly disarmed and arrested by his superiors and Jordan offered to have him examined for insanity by a neutral psychiatrist but Israel rejected the plea. Then on September 24 a Palestinian infiltrator had shot an Israeli girl picking olives, and a tractor driver was murdered in a separate incident. Israel's reprisal was to kill thirty-nine Jordanian legionnaires and national guardsmen and to blow up another police post and school building.

Mr. President,

I consider it my duty to draw the attention of the Security Council to the latest development along the Jordan-Israel Armistice demarcation line. As soon as possible I will, under my mandate from the Security Council, report on the whole development in Palestine up to the present time, to the extent that it has not been covered by previous reports to the Council. My reporting will have to cover not only the Jordan-Israel situation, but also the situation along the Israel-Egypt demarcation line and developments in general in the respects covered by the Security Council resolutions of April 4 and June 4, 1956.

The most recent events at the Jordan-Israel demarcation line have brought to a culmination a development which has been progressing for a few months. I have, so far, not found that I should ask the Security

UN Press Release SG / 506, September 26, 1956.

Council to take the situation up for active consideration. However, if the governments concerned, in cooperation with the Truce Supervision Organization, do not bring the situation rapidly under control, I submit that the Security Council should take the matter up in order to reaffirm its policy, as established in previous resolutions, and, were the Council to find the continued deterioration to constitute a threat to peace, to decide on what further measures may be indicated.

Accept, Mr. President, the assurances of my high regard,

DAG HAMMARSKJÖLD

THE REPORT which the Secretary-General had mentioned in his letter of September 26 to the President of the Security Council was issued the next day. It was, however, dated as of September 12, thus cutting off his account just before the latest and alarming incidents that had evoked his *notes verbales* to Israel and Jordan and his letter to the Council President. The report was a registration for the record of disappointed hopes.

Hammarskjöld had seen the new cease-fire arrangements he had negotiated in the spring as providing a more favorable atmosphere for unilateral steps by Israel and the Arab states to lessen their mutual fears and perhaps to start a chain reaction toward more peaceful conditions. For two and a half months the cease-fire held up quite well, but not one of the initiatives Hammarskjöld had hoped for and encouraged was undertaken by any of the governments concerned. Israel maintained and even strengthened its military occupation of the strategic El Auja demilitarized zone on the Egyptian frontier. Egypt maintained its refusal to permit Israeli ships to use the Suez Canal. Infiltration by Palestinian Arabs from Gaza and Jordan and shooting incidents across the line began to increase again.

After the end of July Israel's attitude toward its Arab neighbors and the UN armistice machinery became progressively tougher. It refused or evaded cooperation with General Burns' efforts to strengthen the UN position on the demarcation lines and further restricted movements of the UN military observers. It returned to its policy of reprisal raids against Egypt and Jordan on an even more massive scale. It justified its own violations of the armistice agreements by charging continued violation by the Arab states of Article I of the agreements and invoking the doctrine of "indivisibility" which the Secretary-General discusses in the report that follows.

The world did not then know the extent of the clandestine flow of French planes and arms to Israel during the summer and knew nothing at all of the secret planning in Paris and Tel Aviv for joint military operations against Egypt. The French government, which was simultaneously working with the

British on a separate contingent plan to attack Egypt and seize the Suez Canal, did not let even the Eden government in on their secret planning with Israel until mid-October. Nevertheless, the danger was apparent that Israel might strike if Britain and France decided to use the force they had been threatening all summer, should they fail to win a satisfactory settlement of the Suez Canal issue by negotiation. General Burns sent a private memorandum to Hammarskjöld on September 14 expressing the opinion "that if hostilities between the disputants in the Suez Canal question should break out, Israel might try to settle some accounts with the Egyptians." [1]

The Security Council had met the day before the Secretary-General's Palstine report was circulated, and agreed to take up the Suez Canal question as soon as the foreign ministers of the principal parties could arrange to attend. The Anglo-French military build-up at Cyprus, Malta, and Algiers was now far advanced. It was essential that the forthcoming Security Council meetings be turned from confrontation to genuine negotiation and Hammarskjöld was already devoting all his diplomatic skills and influence toward moving things in this direction. His Palestine report did not, of course, touch on any of this background, and was strictly limited to the framework of the armistice machinery and his mandate from the Council.

[1] General Burns later published the memorandum in his book *Between Arab and Israeli,* Clarke, Irwin & Company, 1962, p. 169.

Report (Dated September 12) to the Security Council Pursuant to the Resolutions of April 4 and June 4, on the Palestine Question

UN HEADQUARTERS, NEW YORK   SEPTEMBER 27, 1956

SECTION I

1. The Security Council, in its resolution of April 4, 1956 [S/3575], noted with grave concern that despite the efforts of the Chief of Staff of the United Nations Truce Supervision Organization certain specific steps for the purpose of ensuring that the tensions along the armistice demarcation lines should be reduced had not been carried out. It requested the Secretary-General to undertake a survey of the various aspects of enforcement of and compliance with the four General Armistice Agreements in Palestine and the Council's resolutions under reference in the decision. The Council further requested the Secretary-General to arrange with the parties for the adoption of any measures which, after discussion with the parties and with the Chief of Staff, he considered would reduce existing tensions along the armistice demarcation lines, including the following points: (*a*) Withdrawal of their forces from the armistice demarcation lines; (*b*) Full freedom of movement for observers along the armistice demarcation lines, in the demilitarized zones and in the defensive areas; (*c*) Establishment of local arrangements for the prevention of incidents and prompt detection of any violations of the armistice agreements.

2. My negotiations subsequent to this decision of the Security Council were the subject of a report to the Council on May 9, 1956 [S/3596].

3. The Council, in the light of this report, on June 4, 1956, passed a second resolution [S/3605] in which it noted that while progress had been made toward the adoption of the specific decisions set out in the resolution of April 4, full compliance with the general armistice agree-

Security Council Official Records, Eleventh Year, Supplement for July-August-September 1956, Document S/3659, September 27, 1956.

ments had not yet been effected, and that the measures called for in the previous resolution had been neither completely agreed upon nor fully put into effect. On the basis of this finding the Security Council declared that the parties to the armistice agreements should speedily carry out measures already agreed upon with the Secretary-General and should cooperate with him and the Chief of Staff to put into effect their further practical proposals. Specifically, the Council declared that full freedom of movement of United Nations observers must be respected along the armistice demarcation lines, in the demilitarized zones, and in the defensive areas, as defined in the armistice agreements, to enable them to fulfill their functions. The Council finally requested the Secretary-General to continue his good offices with the parties, with a view to full implementation of the Council's resolution of April 4, 1956, and to full compliance with the armistice agreements, and to report to the Security Council as appropriate.

4. In the reports of August 3, 1956 [S/3632], and August 20, 1956 [S/3638], I have drawn attention to incidents which have taken place along the armistice demarcation lines. In view of later developments I consider it appropriate now to put before the members of the Security Council a more complete evaluation of the developments which have taken place after June 4, 1956, when the Council passed its latest resolution on the matter.

5. The immediate reason for this new report is continued incidents along the armistice demarcation lines, and the temporary suspension of the discussions which have been going on concerning such matters as various local arrangements. On both these subjects the Chief of Staff has recently submitted a report (see annex to this report).

SECTION II

6. In my report to the Security Council of May 9, 1956 [S/3596] I pointed out the complications which had arisen because of confusion concerning the extent to which compliance with the armistice agreements could be conditioned by reciprocity. I said in this context:

As a matter of course, each party considers its compliance with the stipulations of an armistice agreement as conditioned by compliance of the other party to the agreement. Should such a stand be given the interpretation that any one infringement of the provisions of the agreement by one party justifies reactions by the other party which, in their turn, are breaches of the armistice agreement, without any limitation as to the field within which reciprocity is considered to prevail, it would in fact mean that the armistice régime could be nullified by a single infringement by one of the parties. Although such an interpretation has never been given from responsible quarters, it appears to me that a lack of clarity has prevailed. From no side has it been said that a breach of an armistice agreement, to whatever clause it may refer, gives the other party a free hand concerning the agreement as a whole, but a tendency to regard the agreements, including the cease-fire clauses, as entities may explain a feeling that in fact, due to infringements of this or that clause, the obligations are no longer in a strict sense fully binding, and specifically that a breach of one of the clauses, other than the cease-fire clause, may justify action in contravention of that clause [S/3596, paragraph 16].

7. In view of this lack of clarity I considered it essential to lift the cease-fire clauses out of the armistice agreements so as to give them an independent legal status as obligations, compliance with which was conditioned only by reciprocity in respect of the implementation of the same obligations by the other parties to the armistice agreements. As a result of the negotiations last spring such an independent status was established for the cease-fire obligations to be found in Article II, paragraph 2, of the Egypt-Israel Armistice Agreement, and in Article III, paragraph 2, of the Jordan-Israel, Lebanon-Israel, and Syria-Israel armistice agreements. Thus, no party could any longer justify a violation of the cease-fire by reference to an alleged noncompliance by other parties with other clauses of the General Armistice Agreements than the cease-fire clause itself, and then only if and when such noncompliance were found to be a reason for the exertion of the right of self-defence as recognized (and subject to the conditions) in Article 51 of the Charter. Any such measure must be immediately reported to the Security Council and is subject to decision by the Council. In this connection, circumstances make it necessary to emphasize again that acts of retaliation have repeatedly been condemned by the Security Council.

8. The assurances given to the United Nations of unconditional observance of the cease-fire clauses, further, made the United Nations itself a party to the cease-fire obligations. Its right to take steps for securing the implementation of these obligations was thereby again clearly established in line with the decision of the Security Council on August 11, 1949.[1]

9. The establishment of a general cease-fire of this legal nature served

---

[1] Security Council Resolution 73 (1949).

to alleviate the very tense situation prevailing in April of last spring. It helped to bring to a stop a rapidly developing deterioration of the situation along the armistice demarcation lines. Thus, the new cease-fire arrangement, at the same time as it established an additional legal basis and removed any possibility of confusion, contributed to the creation of a state of affairs in which progress might be possible toward a discussion of those fundamental issues which so deeply influence the whole situation in the Middle East, but which cannot be successfully essayed until after an improvement of the situation along the demarcation lines.

10. In my report of May 9, 1956, I gave this evaluation of the situation prevailing after the negotiations:

What has been done may open the door to new fruitful developments. The initiative is now in the hands of the governments parties to the armistice agreements. It is my feeling that there is a general will to peace, and that this will should be fostered and encouraged, not by attempts to impose from outside solutions to problems of vital significance to everyone in the region, but by a cooperation which facilitates for the governments concerned the taking unilaterally of steps to increase confidence and to demonstrate their wish for peaceful conditions.

I believe that the present situation offers unique possibilities. If we had previously experienced chain reactions leading to a continuous deterioration of the situation, we may now have the possibility of starting a chain of reactions in the opposite direction [S/3596, paragraphs 105 and 106].

11. Recent discussions have underscored the significance of the reestablishment of a general and independent cease-fire obligation. It should, thus, be mentioned that added stress has recently been put on the argument that the armistice agreements, apart from the cease-fire clauses, are "indivisible." This theory—especially when broadly interpreted—is destructive enough when applied to the armistice agreements in general. If permitted to apply to the cease-fire obligation as well, it would obviously lead to a complete collapse of order and security in the area.

12. In other respects, too, I still believe the previous evaluation to have been essentially correct. Experiences after the submission of my first report have confirmed the impression that the parties in the region all have a wish to establish peaceful conditions. And my conviction stands firm that the quiet prevailing after the agreements on the cease-fire arrangements offered them unique possibilities to give such expressions to this will as might have started a chain of reactions in a positive direction. However, I must now register, with regret, that, so far, none

of the parties concerned has used the opportunities thus offered and that, in consequence, the quiet established has not had the much needed support from developments toward a better general atmosphere which positive initiatives taken by the parties would have helped to bring about.

SECTION III

13. When in the report of May 9, 1956 [S/3596], I discussed unilateral, though related, moves serving to increase confidence and leading to an improvement of the general conditions, I had in mind such steps of a general nature as abstention from repeated threats, and specifically, compliance from both sides with Articles VII and VIII of the Egypt-Israel General Armistice Agreement and the reestablishment of freedom of navigation for Israel ships in the Suez Canal in accordance with the resolution of the Security Council of September 1, 1951 [S/2322]. Common to all countries was, of course, the possibility to demonstrate their wish for better conditions in the region by a strict adherence to the reconfirmed cease-fire obligations, covering also active measures against crossings of the armistice demarcation lines and acts of violence in connection therewith.

14. Obviously, possibilities remain open for constructive steps on these various points, as well as in, for example, the fields of repatriation and resettlement of refugees or the utilization of Jordan waters where decisions by the United Nations have for long been neglected or even challenged. However, the urgency of the matter is great. Lacking such steps the serious deterioration of conditions likely to develop again might lead to the loss for an indefinite time of most of what was gained in the course of last spring in cooperation between the governments and the United Nations. The responsibility rests on the governments in the region. The United Nations can—as last spring—make a contribution by helping to stop a dangerous sequence of incidents. But the United Nations cannot take over the role of the governments in efforts to turn the tide.

15. The governments in the region have so far not only not taken any initiatives which could help to start the necessary developments in a positive direction, but also, while in many cases they have made energetic efforts to support the cease-fire by appropriate instructions to their forces, they have, seen in retrospect, failed to carry through a discipline

sufficiently firm to forestall incidents which, step by step, must necessarily undermine the ceasefire. Established as an independent obligation in relation to the United Nations, the cease-fire remains, of course, fully valid as such, irrespective of the incidents that may occur. As reflecting a general obligation under the Charter it can never cease to bind a Member of the United Nations in a general sense. As a formal obligation, accepted independently of the Charter and binding on a specific group of states in a specific situation, it can cease to be binding on a given state, only if there is a formal release from the obligation by all parties concerned, including the United Nations, or if the actions of one of the other states concerned, or all of them, clearly indicate that it *de facto* has repudiated the obligation.

16. However, if the cease-fire is permitted continuously to be challenged by actual events, it will lose its sanctity and become a dead letter which is not respected by any of the parties although still existing as a legal obligation. This will happen even when these events cannot be interpreted as indicating an intention of a government to repudiate its cease-fire assurance, for example because the government contends that it has acted "in self-defence."

17. Repeated incidents, which have taken place in the latter half of the summer, have brought us close to a point where facts, in a most dangerous way, undermine the law. The occurrences along the Egypt-Israel demarcation line on which the Chief of Staff reports in the annex to this paper, present several typical cases. Acts of violence, supposed to have been staged by one party, have been immediately followed by acts of violence which must be supposed to have been staged by persons on the other side "in self-defence," as part of a policy of retaliation.

18. Similar developments of equal seriousness have taken place between Jordan and Israel. To be properly understood, these incidents—and especially the motives behind acts of so-called retaliation—must, of course, be viewed in the light of the whole previous development of the situation along the demarcation lines, characterized by repeated waves of serious unrest against which the means at the disposal of the United Nations were not considered to provide sufficient safeguards.

19. The present state of affairs is deeply disturbing. Even to the extent that the acts of violence may have seemed to be limited to a pattern of what might be called "short-term reciprocity," this may well be explained by temporary circumstances. There is a permanent risk that the incidents release a chain of events, such as that prevailing at the time of

the cease-fire arrangement in the middle of April. Apart from legal considerations this fact in itself fully justifies the stand of the Security Council on *all* acts of violence including those which reflect a policy of retaliation.

SECTION IV

20. Short of full and earnest cooperation from the governments in the region, consistently reflecting a will to maintain peaceful conditions, it is impossible to bring the disturbances along the armistice demarcation lines to an end. However, much can be done for a reduction of risks and an easing of pressures by proper local arrangements and by observers' activities in support of the cease-fire. It is, therefore, a source of great concern that such arrangements have been put into effect only to a very limited extent, due to a lack of the necessary cooperation. The so-called freedom of movement of observers has even had to suffer from new restrictions and the conditions under which they have to operate have deteriorated. I refer in this context for details to the report of the Chief of Staff circulated as an annex to this paper.

21. As appears from the report of the Chief of Staff, one argument put forward by Israel against acceptance of his proposals and requests has been that each one of the armistice agreements, apart from the cease-fire clauses, is an indivisible whole. On this basis, what one party finds to be a lack of compliance by other parties to the armistice agreements, especially with their basic Article I, has been considered to give the party who finds its interests jeopardized freedom from its obligations under the agreements (apart from the cease-fire obligation), including its obligations to the United Nations in connection with the observers' operations, as envisaged in the agreements. Specifically, it is held by Israel that the lack of compliance by Egypt with the Security Council finding that the blockade of Israel shipping in the Suez Canal is incompatible with the armistice régime—which Israel considers to be a case of noncompliance with Article I of the Egypt-Israel General Armistice Agreement itself—gives Israel the right to consider Articles VII and VIII of the same Agreement as suspended, and, in consequence, to refuse the United Nations observers freedom of movement in the demilitarized zone at El Auja. Likewise, and on similar grounds, Israel refuses to assist in implementation of the armistice agreement stipulation which establishes the Mixed Armistice Commission's headquarters in El

Auja—a stand which explains why recently the Commission has not been able to meet. Attention should in this context be given also to a new case of noncompliance with Article V of the Syria-Israel Armistice Agreement.

22. The armistice agreements, it is true, are formally bilateral agreements, and the theory of "indivisibility" may well be considered as valid for most bilateral treaties under international law. However, the fact that, with the consent of the parties, the agreements have been endorsed by the Security Council—I refer specifically to the Council's decision of August 11, 1949 [2]—and that they must be considered as establishing the equivalent of an international régime, submits the application of this theory to the armistice agreements to very serious limitations. Any other view would, as appears from previous observations in this report, lead to obviously unreasonable consequences. In this connection, it may be noted that the theory of "indivisibility" is not invariably applied to contracts of a bilateral nature under national law, and it is for the courts, not for one of the parties acting unilaterally, to decide whether and in what way the clauses shall be treated as indivisible or separable.

23. However, the theory to which I have just referred will not be properly understood, in its application to the Middle East, if considered merely as an abstract principle of law. In essence, it reflects factors underlying the whole tragic situation in the region.

24. Article I of the various armistice agreements establishes, "with a view to promoting the return to permanent peace in Palestine," the following principles "to be fully observed by the parties during the armistice":

1. The injunction of the Security Council against resort to military force in the settlement of the Palestine question shall henceforth be scrupulously respected by both parties;
2. No aggressive action by the armed forces—land, sea, or air—of either party shall be undertaken, planned, or threatened against the people or the armed forces of the other; it being understood that the use of the term *planned* in this context has no bearing on normal staff planning as generally practised in military organizations;
3. The right of each party to its security and freedom from fear of attack by the armed forces of the other shall be fully respected;
4. The establishment of an armistice between the armed forces of the two

[2] *Ibid.*

parties is accepted as an indispensable step toward the liquidation of armed conflict and the restoration of peace in Palestine.

25. When the "indivisibility" of the armistice agreements is invoked by Israel, this reflects the view that these principles are not observed by the other parties which, in Israel's view, in word and deed maintain—and for years have maintained—a threat against Israel and, therefore, must be considered as challenging the very armistice. In this situation Israel considers itself obligated to comply with the articles of the General Armistice Agreements only to the extent that this can be done without prejudicing its security in face of such threats.

26. The view of the other parties is a similar one in the sense that it is held in many responsible quarters that Israel maintains a policy which constitutes a threat to its neighbours in violation of the basic principles of the armistice.

27. When deadlocks develop on such a basis on all such questions on which positive steps could have been taken, and when for the same reasons the efforts of the United Nations, through the Truce Supervision Organization, to stabilize conditions do not meet with the necessary co-operation, the fears to which I have just referred will become strengthened and entrenched.

SECTION V

28. I have wished to bring what has been reported here to the attention of the Security Council in order to emphasize my concern for the lack of positive initiatives, shown by all the governments in the region, the unsatisfactory implementation of the cease-fire, the obstructions to improving the status and efficiency of the observer organization, and new serious departures from compliance with the armistice agreements.

29. These matters may well be a source of great concern, but they can in no way excuse the United Nations from resolutely pursuing its efforts. However, the efforts of the United Nations, whatever the resources used, can never be of appropriate effectiveness without the cooperation of the sovereign governments directly concerned. As already stated, I have found no reason to doubt the view formed in April that there is a general will to peace in the region, nor that the state of affairs which we have had during part of this year has been one which has offered unique possibilities for improvements of the situation. However, later developments have indicated that the will to establish peaceful

conditions had not grown strong enough for any of those concerned to take the risks necessary for a use of existing opportunities.

30. The possibilities are still there, and the United Nations must continue to impress on the governments in the region their serious duty to use them.

ANNEX

Report of the Chief of Staff of the United Nations Truce Supervision Organization

Jerusalem, September 5, 1956

I have the honour to report on the current situation in the El Auja and Gaza areas and on negotiations as to the following matters:

(*a*) Freedom of movement of United Nations military observers in the El Auja demilitarized zone;

(*b*) Resumption of the meetings of the Egypt–Israel Mixed Armistice Commission;

(*c*) Marking of the demarcation line of the Gaza Strip: Withdrawal of forces of both parties 500 metres from the same demarcation line;

(*d*) Dismantling of fortifications constructed in the demilitarized zone created by the Israel-Syrian General Armistice Agreement;

(*e*) Establishing of United Nations observation posts on the northern shore of Lake Tiberias.

SECTION I

Developments in the El Auja demilitarized zone

1. The Israel Army continues to occupy the El Auja demilitarized zone created by Article VIII, paragraph 1, of the Egypt-Israel General Armistice Agreement. The Israel settlement of the area which began with the establishment of *kibbutz* Qetsi'ot in September 1953, is also being expanded. Israel has further decided considerably to limit the freedom of movement and access of United Nations military observers in the demilitarized zone.

2. On July 5, 1956 the Chairman of the Egypt–Israel Mixed Armistice Commission was informed by the Senior Israel Delegate that movement of United Nations military observers in the El Auja demili-

tarized zone would be restricted to the use of the road from Beersheba, through the demilitarized zone, to the Mixed Armistice Commission headquarters; and that no movement on other roads would be allowed in the demilitarized zone, and radio messages sent would be restricted to administrative reports.

3. The Chief of Staff protested against this decision to the Minister for Foreign Affairs, pointing out that "in its resolution of June 4, 1956 [S/3605], the Security Council has declared 'that full freedom of movement of United Nations observers must be respected along the armistice demarcation lines, in the demilitarized zones and in the defensive areas, as defined in the armistice agreements, to enable them to fulfill their functions.' " The Chief of Staff requested the Israel government to reconsider its decision, as an action of this kind would constitute a further step in the process of noncompliance with the provisions of Article VIII relating to the demilitarized zone and the duties of United Nations military observers in that zone.

4. On July 17, 1956, the Chief of Staff received a reply from the Ministry for Foreign Affairs of Israel contending that in their conversations with the Secretary-General (in the month of April) it was recognized that Articles VII and VIII of the General Armistice Agreement were not operative as long as Egypt did not implement Article I in all four of its sections, and that in default of such implementation, Israel did not regard itself as bound by Article VIII. Therefore, the presence of United Nations observers in the Nitzana (El Auja) area was, in the view of the Israel government, altogether superfluous.

5. The letter also referred to the refusal of the Egyptian authorities to allow United Nations military observers to investigate complaints of the infringement of Article VIII, paragraph 3, in the area between the line El Qusaima—Abu'Aweig'ila and the international frontier, implying that the restrictions imposed by the two parties were on a par. In fact, Article VIII, paragraph 1, gives the Chairman and observers of the Egyptian-Israel Mixed Armistice Commission a responsibility in regard to the demilitarized zone which they do not have in regard to the area on the other side of the international frontier.

6. The view was further expressed that "Israel cannot be regarded as an 'extra-territorial' area where United Nations observers are not subject to the laws of the state. Outside of the duties they are required to discharge under the armistice agreement, they should not claim any special rights." This presumably refers to paragraph 5 of the Security Council resolution of June 4, 1956 [S/3605].

7. The matter was discussed during the talks between the Prime Minister and Foreign Minister of Israel and the Secretary-General and the Chief of Staff on July 20, 1956. Finally, at a meeting with the Chief of Staff on September 3, 1956, the Prime Minister of Israel maintained the viewpoints set forth above. He indicated that since the demilitarized zone was now occupied by Israel military forces, it served no purpose to have United Nations military observers there.

8. In the view of the Chief of Staff, irrespective of the lack of compliance with Articles VII and VIII of the General Armistice Agreement by both Egypt and Israel (see annex 5 to the Secretary-General's report of May 9, 1956 [S/3596]), the maintenance of observers in the El Auja demilitarized zone, with freedom of movement and to transmit messages to the Chairman of the Egypt–Israel Mixed Armistice Commission and the United Nations Truce Supervision Organization by the speediest means, is essential in order to fulfill the duties imposed on the United Nations Truce Supervision Organization by paragraphs 3 and 5 of the Security Council resolution of June 4, 1956 [S/3605]. The strategic importance of the roads radiating from El Auja is such that if one side or the other should contemplate aggression on a large scale against the territory of the other, primary or secondary lines of operations would certainly be established through the demilitarized zone. If either side entered the demilitarized zone with forces on an offensive scale, this would be *prima facie* evidence of aggression. The presence of United Nations military observers, therefore, is a deterrent against aggression and their withdrawal from the area would be a removal of this deterrent.

Meetings of the Egyptian-Israel Mixed Armistice Commission

9. El Auja is not only the centre of the demilitarized zone, as defined in Article VIII, paragraph 2, of the Armistice Agreement. It is also, under Article X, paragraph 2, the headquarters of the Mixed Armistice Commission. Because of her military occupation of the demilitarized zone, Israel refuses access to El Auja to the Egyptian members of the Mixed Armistice Commission. Article X, paragraph 2, also stipulates that the Mixed Armistice Commission shall hold its meetings at such places and such times as it may deem necessary for the effective conduct of its work. The Egyptian authorities have not accepted the Israel refusal to allow the Mixed Armistice Commission to hold meetings at

its headquarters. They have proposed that the Mixed Armistice Commission should hold every other meeting at El Auja. Meetings of the Mixed Armistice Commission—ordinary or emergency—have not been resumed. Complaints by either party are being investigated when an investigation is requested. The fact that the complaints are no longer considered in the Mixed Armistice Commission greatly increases the responsibility of the United Nations Truce Supervision Organization Chief of Staff and his representative, the Chairman of the Mixed Armistice Commission, for observing the maintenance of the cease-fire by the two parties.

10. At his meeting with the Chief of Staff on September 3, 1956, Mr. Ben-Gurion repeated his refusal to allow meetings of the Mixed Armistice Commission at El Auja, stating that Article VIII of the General Armistice Agreement and the provision in Article X, paragraph 2, relating to the headquarters of the Mixed Armistice Commission, were in suspension owing to Egypt's noncompliance with Article I and the Security Council resolution of September 1, 1951, concerning interference with the passage through the Suez Canal of shipping bound for Israel. No Egyptians could now be allowed in the El Auja area for security reasons. He was willing, however, to have the Mixed Armistice Commission meet at other places.

SECTION II

*Situation along the demarcation line
bounding the Gaza Strip*

11. Following the cease-fire assurances by Egypt and Israel to the Secretary-General late in April as set forth in Section III of his report of May 9, 1956 [S/3596], conditions along the demarcation line surrounding the Gaza Strip were stable for a period of nearly two and a half months. Commencing about the middle of July, however, they began to deteriorate and tension increased markedly. Neither side is adhering to its undertaking to strictly observe Article II, paragraph 2, of the General Armistice Agreement. Attached as appendix A [3] are statistics and abbreviated accounts of the most serious incidents which were complained of by the parties.

12. The observation posts referred to in Section VI of the Secretary-

[3] The appendixes have not been included.

General's report [S/3596, paragraphs 75 to 77] have been established and five to seven posts are manned daily. As will be seen from the account of the incidents in appendix A the presence of these observers has not always deterred the parties from opening fire across the demarcation line, nor from crossing the demarcation line. Whenever such incidents have been observed, protests to the party which has violated the armistice agreement have been made but these protests have not prevented further incidents from occurring.

13. In the view of the Chief of Staff the failure to mark the demarcation line clearly, as provided in paragraph 81 of the Secretary-General's report, and the failure to accept the proposals for the separation of the parties' forces referred to in paragraph 79, of the Secretary-General's report, and also paragraph 3 (a) of the Security Council's resolution of April 4, 1956 [S/3575], are regrettable, as they might have gone far toward preventing the occurrence of so many breaches of the cease-fire.

14. The adoption of these two measures at the present time might give a concrete evidence of the parties' desire to stabilize the situation along the demarcation line and help to prevent further incidents.

Marking of the demarcation line

15. On June 19, 1956, the Chairman of the Egyptian–Israel Mixed Armistice Commission was informed by the Senior Israel Delegate that Israel did not agree to United Nations military observers marking the demarcation line surrounding the Gaza Strip by placing barrels in certain areas. The work had been arranged to commence on June 20. The Chief of Staff drew the attention of the Ministry for Foreign Affairs to the relevant passage in the Secretary-General's report [S/3696, paragraph 81]. However, the Israel government maintained that they had not agreed to this particular proposal.

16. In subsequent conversations they suggested that it would be better if the barrels were placed by the Egyptians just on their own side of the demarcation line, or by the Israelis on their side.

17. This suggestion was referred to the Egyptian government which saw no reason for changing the arrangement to which they had agreed and which, as had been stated in the report to the Security Council, had been accepted by both parties. No objection to this statement had been raised by Israel at the time.

18. On June 28, Mr. Ben-Gurion informed the Chief of Staff that the matter could be further considered. Inquiries were made from time to

time, but no decision was given on the matter until Mr. Ben-Gurion told the Chief of Staff at their meeting on September 3 that Israel would not agree to the marking of the demarcation line by the United Nations Truce Supervision Organization. However, he was ready to have a line marked on the Israel side at some distance from the armistice demarcation line with United Nations military observers and Egyptian representatives present. The Egyptians, if they so desired, could also mark a line on their side.

19. This proposal has not yet been communicated to the Egyptian government.

Withdrawal of forces 500 metres
from the demarcation line

20. The Chief of Staff proposed at his meeting with Mr. Ben-Gurion on September 3, 1956 that during daylight both sides should withdraw any defensive or observation posts from the zone 500 metres on each side of the demarcation line and should refrain from sending patrols into this zone.

21. This is the same proposal as that referred to in paragraph 79 of the Secretary-General's report [S/3596]. Mr. Ben-Gurion maintained the stand cited in that paragraph, i.e., that Israel will refrain from sending patrols up to the demarcation line except when it is necessary to do so to protect settlers working on their lands or to prevent people crossing from Egyptian-controlled territory. It will be seen from the accounts of several of the incidents given in appendix A that in practice this arrangement has not proven sufficiently firm. Some of the patrols which United Nations military observers have seen approaching the demarcation line were neither protecting settlers working in the fields, nor were there any infiltrators to be prevented from crossing.

SECTION III

Questions relating to the demilitarized zone
created by the Israel-Syrian General
Armistice Agreement and to Lake Tiberias

22. In the demilitarized zone created by Article V of the Israel-Syria Armistice Agreement, the question of permanent fortifications at the Is-

rael settlement of Hagovrim, in the central sector of the zone, and at Susita, in the southern sector, has given rise to a controversy and the Chairman of the Mixed Armistice Commission has been prevented from exercising his responsibility in the demilitarized zone. Annex II, paragraph 3, to the General Armistice Agreement provided for the destruction or removal of permanent fortifications in the demilitarized zone after the signature of the armistice. Annex II, paragraph 4, entitled the Chairman to order the destruction of such permanent fortifications, which, in his view, ought not to remain in the demilitarized zone. The destruction of permanent fortifications according to annex II, was a part of the demilitarization of the zone. Construction of permanent fortifications under the armistice régime may be considered as being, in some degree, a remilitarization of the zone. (See appendix B which deals with the legal aspect of this problem generally, and especially paragraph 5 in this particular connection.)

23. The Chairman may, however, rule that certain works are permissible for the protection of civilian life referred to in Article V, paragraph 5 (*e*), of the General Armistice Agreement and in Dr. Bunche's authoritative comment quoted in full in the resolution adopted by the Security Council on May 18, 1951 [S/2157]. The Government of Israel has maintained that Israel settlers may construct permanent fortifications in the demilitarized zone, as they do along the armistice lines. In the opinion of the Chief of Staff, certain fortifications which the United Nations observers have seen at Hagovrim and Susita go beyond what is required for the protection of civilian life. The Chief of Staff, accordingly, requested the dismantling of the fortifications in question. The reply received from the Israel Foreign Ministry argued that the Chief of Staff should permit these works as necessary for the protection of civilians. Meanwhile, in spite of the Chief of Staff's request, Israel continued to extend the fortifications in this area.

24. The Israel delegation has, on the other hand, complained about the fact that certain Syrian fortifications in the north encroached upon the demilitarized zone. Investigation by United Nations military observers showed that some minor Syrian works of fortification were encroaching upon the demilitarized zone. Syrian authorities, when requested by the Chief of Staff to demolish these works, replied they were ready to do so when the Israelis demolished the permanent fortifications in and near Hagovrim and Susita.

25. At the meeting on September 3, 1956, when the Chief of Staff

asked for a definitive answer of the Government of Israel to his request for the dismantling and demolition of the above-mentioned permanent fortifications in and near Hagovrim and Susita, Mr. Ben-Gurion said that, apart from the legal position concerning fortifications in the demilitarized zone about which the Israel Foreign Ministry and the Chief of Staff disagreed (see appendix B), Israel could not comply with the Chief of Staff's request. This he justified by the statement that Syria was violating Article I of the armistice agreement by threatening Israel. Furthermore, the recent acquisition of a considerable quantity of offensive armament by Syria placed the Israel settlements in the demilitarized zone in considerable danger. In his view it was unreasonable to leave these settlements without the protection of fortifications. He inquired whether the Chief of Staff would be willing to give an unqualified assurance that the settlements were in no danger of attack.

26. It is the view of the Chief of Staff that the extensive works consisting of both fire and shelter trenches, concrete bunkers, and barbed wire entanglements, which are located at Hagovrim and nearby, constitute a type of fortification which might be described as a company strong point and which goes beyond that which is needed for the protection of the civilian population.

Observation posts on the Israel side of the demarcation line near Lake Tiberias

27. In paragraph 85 of the Secretary-General's report of May 9, 1956 [S/3596], proposals for establishing observation posts on the eastern and northeastern shores of Lake Tiberias are referred to. The proposals were accepted by Syria and an observation post has been established on the Syrian side, near Buteiha Farm. The report further refers to Israel's refusal to allow the establishment of an observation post on their side and states that "Israel would nevertheless be prepared after the lapse of a month, to consider a proposal by the Chief of Staff" [S/3596, paragraph 87]. The Chief of Staff made such a proposal in a letter to the Israel Minister for Foreign Affairs dated June 19, 1956. On June 28, Mr. Ben-Gurion, while maintaining his opposition to the use of a United Nations boat on Lake Tiberias, told the Chief of Staff that the proposal for an observation post on the shore would be considered.

28. The question was taken up from time to time with the Israel For-

eign Office, but no answer was received until, at his meeting with the Chief of Staff on September 3, 1956, Mr. Ben-Gurion stated that he saw no need for an observation post on the Israel side. He said, however, that if the need arose, the matter could be discussed again.

29. Practically no fishing is going on in the lake at present, but when the fishing season begins, there may be a repetition of the incidents and troubles which the placing of United Nations military observers in fixed observation posts along the lake was intended to prevent. In the view of the Chief of Staff, it is necessary that both sides should agree to this system and that the observation post arrangements should now be settled, so that the system would be in working order and understood by both sides when the need for it arose.

Statement on the Question of the Relationship of the International Atomic Energy Agency to the United Nations, before the Conference on the Statute of the Agency

UN HEADQUARTERS, NEW YORK   OCTOBER 2, 1956

THE FOUNDING conference on the draft statute for the International Atomic Energy Agency (IAEA) met at UN Headquarters from September 20 to October 26, 1956, with eighty-one states represented. The study on the relationship of IAEA with the United Nations to which the Secretary-General refers in the following text had been prepared and circulated in April 1956 (page 65). It was endorsed unanimously by the conference as the basis for an agreement to be negotiated with the United Nations. On January 11, 1957, the UN General Assembly also unanimously approved the paper and authorized the Atomic Advisory Committee to negotiate the draft agreement with the Preparatory Commission of IAEA. The agreement came into force November 14, 1957, after approval by the General Conference of IAEA and the UN Assembly.

Since for the duration of this conference I must wear two hats—and I take this first opportunity to thank you for the honor of serving as the Secretary-General of the conference—I should inform you that while speaking very briefly this morning I do so as Secretary-General of the United Nations.

I do not propose to speak generally about the statute of the projected new atomic agency, although in the nature of its function it will be dealing regularly with matters of quite obvious importance to the United Nations, not the least of which will be the promotion of economic development. But having in mind the objective of the General Assembly in directing me, as Secretary-General of the United Nations, to prepare the paper which has been distributed to you, I would wish now to call specifically to your attention—and to say a few words in explanation of—

UN Press Release SG/507, October 2, 1956.

Document IAEA/CS/5, the study of the question of the relationship of the International Atomic Energy Agency to the United Nations.

I have prepared this study in consultation and agreement with the Advisory Committee on the Peaceful Uses of Atomic Energy established by the General Assembly and consisting of representatives of Brazil, Canada, France, India, the United Kingdom, the USSR, and the United States. Moreover, I take it, the principles set forth in the study have been found generally acceptable by the twelve members of the sponsoring group which formulated the draft statute now before this conference, and are, in fact, reflected in some measure in the relevant articles of that statute, notably Articles III, V, XVI, and XVII.

In response to questions already raised and in anticipation of others, I take the liberty of indicating how, in my view, this study might usefully be treated by the conference.

If in the course of its deliberations, these principles are found to be favorably regarded by this conference, as I trust will be the case, they will, I assume, find more specific and detailed expression in the agreement to be entered into between the United Nations and the new International Atomic Energy Agency. The conference, no doubt, will wish to authorize the Preparatory Commission of the agency to undertake the groundwork for such an agreement.

It is my hope, of course, that this study will be borne in mind when relevant articles of the draft statute are under consideration. There is, however, no intent or desire to suggest possible amendments to the statute but rather to look ahead to the ultimate agreement defining the relationship between the two bodies. In this regard, it occurs to me that adequate conference endorsement of the guiding principles might be achieved through their inclusion in whatever guidance the conference may finally give to the Preparatory Commission.

The study itself being sufficiently explicit, it is not necessary here to review the basic principles which it expounds. But I should like to stress that what is sought is a relationship designed to meet as well as possible all of the new needs created by a unique international agency, and sufficiently close in a working sense to ensure maximum coordination and cooperation, and the most efficient use of facilities, staff, and services.

I may add, without venturing into the realm of controversy over the subject, that the United Nations, inevitably, will have a deep and continuing interest in the system of safeguards and controls foreseen for the agency. In fact, it is recognized that no such system is likely to be found satisfactory unless balanced by certain arrangements made by the United Nations within the field for which it is responsible. It may be appropriate, in this context, to draw attention also to another question concerning the relations between the agency and the United Nations which, as falling outside the framework of the arrangements treated in the memorandum on relationship, is not covered by the paper before you. Within the United Nations a special committee has been established, originally for the preparation of the first conference on peaceful uses of atomic energy, but later for the preparation of a second conference and for questions of coordination of the activities of the various agencies and the United Nations within the field of peaceful uses of atomic energy. It may be worth considering that this committee, which is of the highest scientific standard and the record of which demonstrates the value of its advice, might be used for consultations by those responsible for the activities of the new atomic agency.

The principles set forth in the study, taken as a whole and as they presumably will be expressed in the agreement defining the relationship between the two organizations, will, I am confident, provide a sound and workable basis for attaining a mutually satisfactory and helpful relationship between the United Nations and the new agency. The principles are no more than a foundation, however. Upon them there will have to be carefully and skillfully erected a structure of daily cooperation, regular consultation, personal contact, and routine interchange which alone can give meaning to the principles. Furthermore, in working out the relationship in practice, much will depend upon considerations which cannot be written into an agreement—the spirit in which it is carried out, a reciprocally earnest desire to collaborate, and the help of governments in ensuring that the work of the organizations concerned is complementary and not overlapping.

I may assure you that insofar as the United Nations Secretariat is concerned every effort will be bent to achieve a close, harmonious, and mutually beneficial working relationship with the new agency.

Introduction to the Eleventh Annual Report

OCTOBER 4, 1956

WHEN THE Secretary-General completed the Introduction to his Annual Report the Security Council was about to begin consideration of the Suez Canal dispute. The Introduction would not be distributed to Member governments and made public until October 22 and Hammarskjöld limited his comments to a general discussion of conflicts involving such issues of self-determination. In the paragraphs that follow the subheading "The role of the United Nations in a changing world" in the text below, he presented a cogent case for greater use of the United Nations as an instrument for really negotiating just and peaceful settlements of such conflicts, not just debating them. The paragraphs' applicability to both sides in the Suez dispute was quite apparent.

In this report the Secretary-General also turned his attention to Africa's "crucial stage of transition," to problems of economic development, and to questions of administration and budget.

When I submitted the eleventh annual report of the Secretary-General on the work of the United Nations, for the period June 16, 1955, to June 15, 1956, I informed the Member states that the review of the role of the Organization in world affairs usually included as an introduction to the report would be transmitted at a later date, closer to the postponed opening of the eleventh regular session of the General Assembly on November 12, 1956.

Universality and its consequences

In the period under review the most important development bearing upon the future role of the United Nations in world affairs is the decisive step that has been taken toward universality of membership.

When the General Assembly convenes next month, sixteen new Member states will be represented and the Assembly will have before it the unanimous recommendation of the Security Council for the admis-

General Assembly Official Records, Eleventh Session, Supplement No. 1A (A/3137/Add. 1).

sion of three additional new Members. Thus, after many years of deadlock, the United Nations will have increased its membership within a single year by approximately one-third. Furthermore, important additions have been made to the membership of the specialized agencies. The whole United Nations system, therefore, enters its second decade far closer than before to becoming, in fact, a system fully representative of the diversity of the world community.

The new Members of the United Nations will be welcomed in their own right. Their admission, and the admission of other nations which may be expected to follow in due course, will also be welcomed because of the opportunities for more effective service to the purposes of the Charter that the wider membership will give to the Organization.

We live in a period of fundamental and rapid changes in the relationship of nations and peoples having differing cultures and social systems. The new age that is emerging is an age of promise. It could also become one of disaster. We are seeking to cope with world issues of great difficulty but equally of high challenge. The hope of finding peaceful, just, and constructive solutions of these issues rests upon our ability to foster the growth of understanding, cooperation, and mutual accommodation of interests among all the nations.

Because its Charter is a world Charter, the United Nations is a unifying force in a divided world. Because its institutions are world institutions, they are fitted to determine the common interest and enlarge the area of common grounds. This applies in full measure, I believe, to three great challenges of our times. These are: first, the relationship of the peoples of Asia and Africa with the peoples of Western traditions; second, economic development for that majority of mankind which has so far shared so little in the fruits of the industrial age; third, the unresolved conflict between the ideologies that divide the world. Because the United Nations is now becoming more widely representative, its capacity to serve as an influence for peace and constructive progress in meeting these great challenges has been increased.

To make good use of this increased capacity for service presents, in itself, a challenge of considerable difficulty. The admission of many new Members creates new constitutional, political, and organizational problems for the United Nations. There are such constitutional questions as those raised by proposals to enlarge the membership of the Security Council and of the Economic and Social Council. There are problems of political adjustment to the fact that changes in world relationships will henceforth be more fully reflected in the debates and decisions of the United Nations. There are procedural problems relating to the orderly, responsible, and expeditious conduct of business which increased membership inevitably brings and there are, for the Secretariat, organizational and administrative problems to which I shall refer later. These problems are, however, far outweighed by the opportunity to build a more effective world organization.

The United Nations can grow in real strength only to the extent that ways are found to use the Organization to full advantage for the purposes it was created to serve. The events of the past year have in some respects given encouraging evidence of such growth.

The role of the United Nations in a changing world

Article 1 of the United Nations Charter states that one of the main purposes of the United Nations is "to develop friendly relations among nations based on respect for the principle of equal rights and self-determination of peoples." This recognition of the principle of self-determination as a basis for friendly relations among nations means that democratic ideals, which have carried many peoples to new heights, are given a worldwide application. The governments signatories to the Charter have formulated here a policy which, in the light of history, may well come to be regarded as one of the most significant landmarks of our times.

The United Nations, of course, is not the cause of the great change through which more than half of mankind, for centuries voiceless, has grown into or is now moving toward membership of the world community as citizens of independent national states. But the Organization is inevitably a focal point for efforts so to guide the difficult and delicate development that this progress may be achieved in peace and become a means to reinforce peace.

To say this is not to overlook that, in many cases, other procedures than those created by the Charter may provide possibilities of working out fundamental elements of the new relationship. The Charter itself foresees negotiations between parties as an initial step in the solution of conflicts which are unavoidable during a period of fundamental change. But I believe that such negotiations gain by being conducted against the background of the purposes and principles of the Charter and that the results can usefully be brought within the framework of the United Nations. If the negotiations prove unsuccessful, they should then be followed up on the basis laid down and in the forms prescribed by the Charter.

It is important to remember that the Charter endorses self-determination as a basis for friendly relations among nations. Both unrealistic impatience in the movement toward self-determination and wasteful resistance to it would contradict this philosophy of the Charter by leading to conflicts which might threaten peace. Under the Charter, the nations concerned are therefore called upon to further the movement toward self-determination in such a manner as to strengthen the bonds of world community instead of weakening them.

Forces that stimulate this movement have also led to the emergence of a new nationalism. This nationalism can be a constructive element, raising the dignity and stature of peoples and mobilizing their best moral resources. But, in a period of severe emotional strains, it may also find expressions which are in fact hostile to the steady growth of the very national life it aims to serve. The United Nations may help in avoiding such a self-defeating development.

Within the community of nations, so great a change in the political relationships must arouse deep emotions on all sides. Positions long vital to great nations are involved. And on the other side the intensity of aspirations for equal status creates pressures for extreme action. I am convinced that in this situation the United Nations could be a source of greater assistance to governments than it has so far been. The give and take of public debate has been firmly established within the Organization and plays a valuable role in the determination of the common interest, but the resources for reconciliation, which the Organization can also provide, have not received equal recognition. The tensions of our time are too severe to permit us to neglect these resources and should impel us to use the United Nations in such a manner as to widen the possibilities for constructive negotiation which are inherent in the nature of the Organization.

We should, I believe, seek a development which would give greater emphasis to the United Nations as an instrument for negotiation of settlements, as distinct from the mere debate of issues. The Charter does not envisage settlements imposed by force. But the obligation of states to settle their disputes by peaceful methods does not mean that principles of justice and international law may be disregarded. The Charter reconciles the obligation of peaceful settlement with the objective of justice and equity through its emphasis on peaceful negotiation in which the full weight of the world community, as organized in the United Nations under the principles of the Charter, is brought to bear on the issue at stake.

The preceding observations have, in varying degree, a bearing on several problems which will come up for consideration in the forthcoming session of the General Assembly. What has been said about the role of the United Nations also has a bearing on the Suez problem which, when this is written, is before the Security Council. I shall make no further comment on any of these problems here.

The Palestine question has a position more independent of the general development to which I have referred, but it is not unrelated in certain of its aspects. Since I have recently submitted several reports to the Security Council on the situation in Palestine, I do not consider it necessary to give here any further summary of developments since the last session of the Assembly. It may, however, be appropriate to stress my continuing belief, in spite of the difficulties and disappointments encountered, that the approach chosen by the Security Council last spring is one that should be followed up with all possible energy. I believe that the Council has improved the chances of developing a policy helpful to the governments and peoples working for peace in the area, by adding to its public debate of the issues involved a direct diplomatic approach to the governments in the region, along the lines of its resolutions of last spring.

Atomic energy

Since my last report, much progress has been made toward building a worldwide partnership in the development of atomic energy for peaceful purposes which will place the common interest above political differences.

The International Atomic Energy Conference convened by the United Nations in the summer of 1955 at Geneva proved to be an important turning point in this direction. At this Conference, channels for the free exchange of peaceful atomic knowledge, which had been closed, were opened wide. The Conference resulted in a sharing of scientific and engineering knowledge of unprecedented scope in this field. This, in itself, will benefit the world for years to come. It laid the foundation for further and more rapid progress toward mastery of the practical applications of this new source of energy. But the Conference did more than this. It was a successful reassertion of faith in international cooperation for the common benefit. In a time of tension and anxiety, it gave evidence that our generation was capable of a political initiative worthy of its scientific and technical achievements.

The spirit of cooperation was evident also in the successful outcome of the discussions and negotiations on a new International Atomic Energy Agency, culminating in the conference of eighty-two nations on the draft statute now in session at United Nations Headquarters. It was equally evident in the unanimous decisions of the General Assembly last year to hold a second United Nations conference for the exchange of technical information on peaceful uses and to establish the fifteen-member Scientific Committee on the Effects of Atomic Radiation. The Advisory Committee to the Secretary-General on atomic matters has recommended that the second conference should take place on or about September 1, 1958. The Radiation Committee has made a good start upon its important work of assembling and evaluating available information in this field and will hold its second meeting later this month. Finally, on the basis of the progress made during the past year, there is good reason to hope that the International Atomic Energy Agency will come into being next year, and that it will function in close relationship with the United Nations and with the specialized agencies, in accordance with the recommendations of the General Assembly. Such a relationship will undoubtedly be to the mutual benefit of the organizations and safeguard that unity of action, with freedom of initiative, which is essential for the success of this new development.

Our knowledge points to the probability that atomic energy will become in the not too distant future a major new source of power for a second industrial revolution. The new capacity for economic expansion that will be ours when this time comes can be turned to the support of economic progress in all countries. It can, in particular, facilitate a faster rate of economic development in those parts of the world where the standard of living continues to lag dangerously far behind the industrialized areas. It can also help our efforts to reduce tensions and conflicts by removing some of their economic and social causes. It can do so, and the inequities and weaknesses which marred the industrial revolution of the last century can be avoided, under one condition. We must continue to guide the development in the same spirit of cooperation that has marked its beginnings. And we must entrust to the new International Atomic Energy Agency and other United Nations activities in this field responsibilities commensurate with the central role of world organization in matters which vitally concern the common welfare of all nations.

Disarmament

The past year has been a time of reassessment of the problem of disarmament in the nuclear age. Strong evidence has been given of the growing mutual recognition that the immensely destructive power of the new weapons has made another world war incompatible with national survival on both sides. This, in itself, should help to pave the road toward agreement on a system for the international control and reduction of armaments. Also, the advances in and wider sharing of atomic knowledge and technology, together with the evolution that is under way in international political affairs, are leading governments to rethink and reexamine the problems of effective controls.

The main new proposals that have emerged in the disarmament discussions during the past year have been advanced primarily as partial or limited steps of a confidence-building nature. There have been the proposals of the United States and of the USSR aimed at preventing a surprise attack, the proposals of the Western Powers and of the USSR for a limited initial reduction of armed forces, the proposal of France for the publication of military budgets, the proposal of the United Kingdom to try out inspection and control in a limited area, and the proposal of India to end experimental explosions of nuclear weapons.

Little, if any, progress toward the necessary measure of agreement on any of these proposals has been evident in the disarmament discussions that have taken place since the last session of the General Assembly. This should not, however, discourage renewed efforts to further an atmosphere of greater mutual confidence. If the nations have found it possible to join together in a constructive programme to use atomic energy for man's peaceful progress, they should also be able to find a way in time to join together in a disarmament programme that will provide them all with safeguards against destruction.

Africa

It becomes steadily more significant to the rest of the world that the continent of Africa, with some two hundred million inhabitants, is in a crucial state of transition. Changes in political, economic, and social

ways are taking place in much of the continent, at times perhaps with a
rapidity too great for proper assimilation. On the other hand, there is a
growing restiveness, born of impatient nationalism, racial handicaps,
and frustrated aspirations, that is virtually endemic to some areas. The
urgency of the time factor in seeking peaceful and orderly solutions for
Africa's basic problems has become even more evident in the year
under review than before.

It is quite clearly in prospect that the voices of Africa which will be
heard henceforth in the United Nations will be increasingly those of the
Africans themselves. Morocco, Sudan, and Tunisia, having achieved independence, are in process of admission to membership. This will expand to eight the number of Member states in the African continent.
The Gold Coast is well on the way to becoming a fully sovereign
member of the British Commonwealth under the name of Ghana, and
may be seeking membership within the coming year. Nigeria is advancing rapidly along the same road. The independence promised by the
General Assembly to Somaliland under Italian administration becomes
due in 1960.

In the interest of the common good, the United Nations must seek to
be as helpful as possible to this continent in transition—to its independent and dependent areas alike. Last May, the United Nations supervised the plebiscite in the Trust Territory of Togoland under United
Kingdom administration, in which a majority of Togolese voters fa-
voured union with an independent Gold Coast. Subsequently, the Trusteeship Council recommended to the General Assembly termination of
the trusteeship when the Gold Coast attains independence within the
British Commonwealth. These were precedent-making and historic
steps toward fulfillment of the Charter objectives for dependent peoples.

There are clear constitutional limitations to the extent of other
United Nations contributions to orderly progress in Africa. Nevertheless, even within these limitations, the United Nations can, I believe, be
more helpful than it has been. Its necessarily modest efforts can be undertaken on a wider basis and possibly in some new directions.

The broad assurances of the United Nations Charter might be spelled
out more specifically in their application to individual territories. The
question of the course of development that a people may anticipate is
no less valid for the peoples of Africa than for any other peoples. It
would seem to be in the best interest of all the nations concerned with

Africa and its future that Africans should be as fully advised as possible on this score.

It is evident that in the immediate future the pace of economic, social, and political development in many places will have to be substantially accelerated if serious stresses are to be averted. The pace in the past, when confronted with the new demands and pressures of this day, inevitably appears too casual and leisurely. The international community, through its various channels of technical aid, affords, upon call, a ready means of assistance toward more rapid development, whatever the existing status of the people and territory concerned. A preliminary United Nations technical assistance mission is about to visit Morocco and Tunisia at the request of the governments of these two countries. The need being so large, there is a sound basis for expecting more requests for such assistance. The United Nations should be prepared to meet these growing needs.

As concerns those economic and social programmes and activities relating to Africa which are undertaken within the United Nations family, there is undoubtedly a need for further efforts toward developing effective coordination and a common perspective. I shall, in due course, offer some suggestions in this direction within the area of Secretariat responsibilities.

Economic and social questions—
the economic situation

At its summer session this year the Economic and Social Council marked its tenth anniversary by reviewing the main economic trends of the past ten years and the development of international action during that period in support of the objectives of Article 55 of the Charter. The United Nations economic surveys and the statements of representatives of Member governments pointed to many positive achievements, both national and international, which provide good foundations for further progress. They also made clear that some of the most important economic and social problems confronting the world are almost as far from solution as they were ten years ago.

Most serious is the continued widening of the gap between the industrially advanced countries and the underindustrialized countries in the relative rate of growth of *per capita* incomes since before the war. This has occurred in spite of all the effort and attention that have been directed over the past decade in national, bilateral, regional, and United Nations programmes toward the economic development of those vast areas of the world where poverty continues to be the law of life for the great majority of mankind.

While we have not yet succeeded in bridging the gap between economically developed and underdeveloped countries, we have come to understand better that the problem has roots in the world structure of demand.

With the growth of output and income in most of the industrial countries, it is true that the demand for primary production may be expected to rise, but experience over a long period has shown that this rise is far from proportional. Even if supplies of primary products were to keep pace with the demand and the terms of trade were to remain unchanged, the growth of income earned in primary production would lag considerably behind the growth in income of industrial countries.

As is demonstrated in the *World Economic Survey, 1955,* the growth of total output in the economically underdeveloped countries has lagged behind that of the developed countries, not so much because of lesser progress in each of the major sectors of production taken separately, but because agriculture, which accounts for a much higher proportion of the total in these countries, almost everywhere has expanded at a much lower rate than has industrial production.

If the economically underdeveloped countries are even to maintain, let alone increase, their relative share of the world's total output, they cannot rely exclusively on expanded exports of primary products to industrial countries, but must embark upon a programme of broad economic development. It is true that, because of the great difference in their productive capacity, the economically underdeveloped countries cannot hope for many years to come to match in absolute terms the rate of growth in the economically advanced countries. Unless, however, at least a higher percentage rate of growth in the economically underdeveloped countries than in the developed countries can be achieved, it will be impossible ever to increase the share of the less developed countries in the distribution of the *per capita* income of the world. This should be a reasonable and attainable target for economic development. So far, this target has not been reached and the trend persists in the other direction. Even in percentage terms, the poor have become relatively poorer.

Put this way, it is easy to see how wrong and how dangerous it would be to permit such a trend to continue. The political, economic, and social consequences of failure to take adequate and timely remedial action upon the hopes of all nations for peace and a better life are only too apparent. We must intensify our efforts, both national and international, to reverse the trend by stepping up, on a considerable scale, the processes of economic development.

I would be the last to minimize the difficulties and complexities that confront the nations in this field. The many-sided character of the problem of economic development is abundantly clear; we have grown increasingly aware not only of its economic dimensions but also of its diverse social ramifications. The goal of economic development implies for many countries a concerted undertaking to set up an industrial revolution more rapid than that which transformed Western European civilization, and yet does not involve the extreme social costs which were then incurred. It is self-evident that the primary responsibility for such an undertaking must rest with the underdeveloped countries themselves. Nevertheless, I believe there are several areas open to more effective international action which would contribute to the ends we seek.

Stabilization of commodity prices

There is, first, the problem of attenuating fluctuations in commodity markets upon which the economically underdeveloped countries are so heavily dependent both for their income and their foreign exchange requirements. To the extent that we can progress toward a solution of this problem we shall be better able to place the problem of assistance through the flow of international capital in proper perspective.

Since the economically underdeveloped countries depend to so large an extent upon exports of primary products for their export earnings, they are especially vulnerable to the extreme price fluctuations that have continued to characterize the world commodity markets. As I pointed out to the Economic and Social Council last July, the vital importance of stabilization of commodity prices to economic development is shown by the fact that even in highly prosperous times fluctuations in commodity earnings frequently cancel out several times over the international assistance a country may be receiving from all sources. Furthermore, a change of only 5 percent in average export prices is approximately equivalent to the entire annual inflow of private and public capital and government grants to underdeveloped countries.

The stabilization of the prices of primary products should, I believe, have a high priority in an intensified programme for economic development. I do not suggest new international machinery for this purpose. What is needed is greater understanding and goodwill on the part of both governments and people in using the machinery that already exists. We have long ceased to accept unemployment as the price for keeping an industrial economy in balance. We have also accepted full employment as an international as well as a national obligation. Equally, we must come to realize that violent price fluctuations in the commodity markets are not productive of economic balance in the world, but of economic chaos with all its political and social consequences in the underdeveloped countries. And we must learn to accept commodity price stabilization as an international obligation inseparable from the increasing economic interdependence of the world community. A more stable and expanding foreign trade is the most essential economic condition of, and will supply the greatest financial resources for, the necessary acceleration of the processes of economic development.

International capital for economic development

We have also to face the fact that the flow of international capital has failed in the past ten years even to regain its importance of only a generation ago; this is the case in relation both to trade and to income and investment. It is evident that we must seek ways to increase the supply of foreign investment capital, both public and private, available for economic development. The past several years have witnessed an increase in governmental action, both in capital-exporting and capital-importing countries, designed to promote the international flow of private capital, but the results have thus far been rather limited. Recent events have once again brought to the forefront the importance of international confidence for the flow of private capital.

In the field of international organization, the International Finance Corporation is now in being and is a step in the right direction. So would be the establishment of the proposed Special United Nations Fund for Economic Development. But an adequate solution of the problem involves, of course, considerations much wider than can be answered by new institutions alone.

It has often been said that heavy expenditures for armaments to defend national security make it difficult to increase the flow of capital for economic development. However true this may be, to make adequate progress in economic development dependent upon disarmament is to put the cart before the horse. We need a wider understanding and acceptance of the fact that a successful programme of economic development is one of the most necessary elements in building up the conditions of stability and confidence which will make possible real progress toward disarmament. Such a programme would be one of the greatest and most lasting contributions we could make toward strengthening the security of all nations.

The technical assistance programme

In addition to new measures for stabilizing the foreign trade of the economically underdeveloped countries and in other ways increasing the financial resources available for economic development it is evident that we need also to increase the flow of skills and experts.

This year's review of the United Nations Expanded Programme of Technical Assistance has confirmed the growing usefulness of the programme. In the political sense, it is a living demonstration that it is possible for diverse and differing nations to work effectively together for the common good. It has shown itself to be well adapted to the requirements of the countries seeking help. On the other hand, it is also clear that the technical assistance needs of those countries far exceed the present financial resources of the programme. A realistic reappraisal of the role of multilateral technical assistance in economic development will lead, I believe, to the conclusion that the resources available to the programme should be increased in order to enable it to respond more fully to the needs that are so evident.

The administrative gap in national development programmes

The administrative problem confronting nations which are entering the industrial age for the first time deserves more attention than it has received. The lack of a sufficient number of experienced officials to administer national economic development plans is common to most of these countries. In the long run, as a social structure better adapted to the requirements of modern technology is built up, they will develop a class of national administrators adequate to their needs. But for many years the shortage of such a class will be strongly felt.

In the short run there is, for many of these countries, no way to fill the administrative gap without outside help. It is for this reason that I have suggested consideration of creating a new type of international civil service, whose members would be seconded for duty as administrators to governments needing them for their national development programmes. As distinct from experts under the technical assistance programme, who give advice but are not normally entrusted with executive responsibilities, such officials would be expected to serve in an executive capacity the governments to which they were seconded. They would, at the same time, help the governments to build up more rapidly the trained personnel needed for their national administrations, both by their contribution to "on-the-job" training and by service in administrative training programmes such as those to which the United Nations Technical Assistance Administration is giving increasing aid.

I recognize, of course, that there are many legal and organizational questions that require study and clarification before an international service of this kind could be established. The creation of such a service should, of course, be attempted only if it would be welcomed by the interested countries themselves. But there is evidence that the urgency of the need is becoming ever more apparent to governments now struggling, with insufficiently manned administrations, to cope with the complex and difficult problems that confront them. I also believe that the political circumstances which dominate our age point to the world community as the best source of outside assistance of this kind. The world community should be prepared to respond to this need.

Community development

Four years ago, the first United Nations World Social Report found that the people of the villages were the forgotten men of economic development. While their problems remain far from solution it is fair to say that today most governments are undertaking in some degree the extension to its rural population of technical services in agriculture, health, education, and welfare. This extension has been most effective in countries which have undertaken these programmes with full attention to the importance of community participation. We have witnessed a real surge of interest in many Member states in these community development programmes. The results are not always spectacular in physical terms, the improvements effected are small in themselves, but they are clearly expressive of a new spirit of self-confidence which has started people on a forward move. We shall be mistaken if we lose sight of the great potential for contributing to material advancement through the voluntary mobilization of individual human resources and the awakening of dormant incentives. This has a special significance for development in those areas where scarcities of capital, skills, and managerial competence now operate as inhibiting factors.

The difficulties attendant upon social and institutional changes at both national and local levels are only too evident. It seems to me that the United Nations can make a constructive contribution in assisting governments to achieve this new orientation, which holds such great promise not only for economic development but also for enhancing the "dignity and worth of the human person."

Other practical steps

The international community can also help to strengthen economic and social development programmes in two areas where knowledge of the basic facts is frequently insufficient for sound planning. Intensified efforts are required to assist many countries in improving the content and methodology of national statistics and in training statisticians. And we need to know more about the relation of population growth and other demographic problems to development, particularly with respect to internal migration from rural areas to the cities. I hope to give to the Economic and Social Council an analysis of these problems in the forthcoming World Social Report.

We should, I feel, take further steps to encourage the development of regional economic cooperation within the United Nations framework. The work of the Economic Commissions for Europe, for Asia and the Far East, and for Latin America provides one of the most promising avenues open to the Member governments for common action leading to more effective results in programmes of economic and social development.

Aid to children and refugees

The United Nations programmes for children and for refugees were established by the Member Nations as responses of conscience by the international community to clearly felt needs. The United Nations Children's Fund is increasingly effective in its work because of the support that Members are rightly providing in growing measure. But support for the programmes of aid to refugees continues to lag far behind despite repeated appeals. Surely it is incumbent upon all concerned that the comparatively small amounts needed for these victims of war and political upheaval should be forthcoming.

Human rights

The Organization has continued to deal with some human rights questions in the traditional manner—that is to say, through the preparation of international conventions on particular aspects of human rights. During the past year agreement was reached on the substantive provisions of the Convention on the Nationality of Married Women, and a United Nations conference, attended by representatives of over fifty states, approved and opened for signature an international instrument outlawing debt bondage, serfdom, and other forms of servile status. This Supplementary Convention on the Abolition of Slavery, the Slave Trade and Institutions and Practices Similar to Slavery, also includes an agreed solution of a problem which has long preoccupied the United Nations, namely, the question of the application of United Nations conventions to Trust and Non-Self-Governing Territories. The compromise solution reached at this conference might help in removing one of the obstacles to an agreement on the covenants on human rights.

The United Nations will soon be engaged in studying developments in the observance of human rights throughout the world by means of a periodic reporting system which may prove to be of considerable significance. Combined with this system there will be a series of intensive studies of the evolution and application of specific rights or groups of rights, including a series of studies of discrimination in various fields. An encouraging development during the past year has been the willingness of nearly all governments to cooperate with the United Nations in the preparation of such global studies as a prelude to further action. This reporting system should not be allowed to develop into a vehicle for the criticism of Member states, and the studies of particular rights should not become mere catalogues of instances in which those rights have been violated or denied. The purpose of these activities should be to share experiences and techniques that may help us to make more progress in promoting human rights.

In response to government requests, preparations are going forward to develop the programme of advisory services in the field of human rights which the General Assembly authorized at its last session. When addressing the Commission on Human Rights earlier this year, I confessed to some scepticism about applying in this area certain methods usually associated with technical assistance programmes. Since then proposals have emerged which, I now believe, may well contribute to the clarification of some human rights problems. I refer particularly to the sharing of experience through seminars under the new programme of advisory services.

Budget and administration—
economy and concentration of effort

The need to devote additional resources to the most urgent of the tasks which the United Nations system exists to serve underlines the importance of economy in the allocation and use of the total resources that can be made available. On the administrative side, Member governments are familiar with the views of the Secretary-General and the steps he has taken toward reducing administrative costs. But economy is also, and primarily, a question of the number and scope of programmes that Member governments ask the United Nations to undertake. Many efforts have been exerted over the past three years—in the specialized agencies as well as in the United Nations itself—by representatives of governments and by the Secretariat to achieve a greater measure of concentration upon major tasks. Nevertheless, the tendency still persists to proliferate programmes which are then frequently endowed with inadequate resources.

This dichotomy has proved to be one of the most stubborn ailments afflicting the participation by Member governments in international organization. So long as it continues the capacity of the world community to respond adequately to the really great needs of our time will be impaired. Economy must not be achieved at the expense of effective performance of the major tasks which are rightly entrusted to the United Nations. But economy by concentration of resources upon these tasks is an objective greatly to be desired. I warmly welcome the resolution recently adopted on this subject by the Economic and Social Council.

Internal organizational questions

As already indicated, the wider membership and the growing responsibilities of the Organization create problems also of an administrative nature. Within a framework set by the greatest possible economy, the main task of those responsible for the administration of the Secretariat is to see to it that the personnel resources are so utilized and coordinated as to provide for the highest efficiency. In the reorganization which has been put into effect over the last few years, considerable attention was given to the question of the balance between officials on the most senior level and the rest of the staff. It was pointed out that a streamlining operation reducing the total number of staff necessarily must increase the responsibilities for leadership on high levels and that, therefore, a reduction of the senior posts could never be expected to be proportionate to the general reduction of the staff. In spite of that, the reorganization led to a reduction of the total cost for officials on the top level of close to 25 percent.

The lack of necessary experience with the new arrangements and certain adjustments made in order to facilitate the transition from the older system, gave to the new organization on the senior levels a tentative character, and it was my declared intention to submit for the approval of the General Assembly such definite proposals concerning arrangements on the senior level as might emerge from the experiences gained during a trial period. I hope to present at the twelfth session of the General Assembly a report containing such proposals. However, it may be appropriate for me, in anticipation of that report, to give a brief evaluation of the situation as it appears now.

The whole question of the organization at the senior level is closely related to the development of the position and functions of the Secretary-General himself. In the administrative field, an important element in the reorganization was that the previous arrangement by which an Assitant Secretary-General was the normal link between the Secretary-General and the Principal Directors in charge of personnel problems and budgetary questions was abandoned so that, instead, a Director of Personnel and a Controller, both with rank of Under-Secretary, would report directly to the Secretary-General. It was then assumed that close cooperation should be established between the two officials just mentioned, but that they would both have such access to the Secretary-General as would render it possible for him to exert a direct and personal leadership in the two main administrative fields. It is my experience, from the two years that this new system has been functioning, that it has led to increased efficiency and smoothness of operation without in any way increasing the burden on the Secretary-General personally. It has recently been suggested that it might be advisable to revert to the previous arrangement, presumably because of a feeling that the other responsibilities of the Secretary-General would render it difficult for him also to put his full weight behind administrative policies, especially the important activities pursued by the Director of Personnel and the Controller. As indicated, experience so far does not lead me to believe that such a reversal of the present arrangement would be to the advantage of the Administration. I would, however, like to postpone my final judgment. Next year the longer experience gathered would also make it easier for Member governments to reach a definite conclusion.

The suggestion referred to above draws attention to the increased responsibilities which the Secretary-General has had to shoulder in recent times. These responsibilities have, especially in the course of 1956, made it necessary for the Secretary-General to be absent from Headquarters for considerable periods and have engaged an increasing part of his time when at Headquarters. This development has been linked primarily to the special tasks entrusted to the Secretary-General by the Security Council in relation to the Palestine problem. It is, of course, too early to say to what extent such special tasks may indicate a continuing trend in the development of the functions of the Secretary-General. In any event, they have demonstrated the desirability of a system sufficiently flexible to enable the Secretary-General to devote a major part of his time to specific political problems. Although, in the light of experience, I would consider it premature to put forward any proposals now which would help to increase this flexibility, I feel that the Organization is facing here a question which merits attention on a long-term basis.

With a Secretariat whose executive head under the Charter is the only elected officer, and who, for that reason, can delegate his responsibilities only to a limited extent, the possibilities of creating such a flexibility are necessarily restricted. One is indicated by the proposal to reintroduce a senior post above the posts of Director of Personnel and Controller. Other possibilities might be to regularize a system by which part of the specific responsibilities of the Secretary-General are delegated for longer periods, for example one year, in rotation among the senior officials. Still another possibility would be to create an intermediary post of Deputy Secretary-General either elected by the General Assembly or appointed by the Secretary-General himself as his personal representative for all questions which he, because of his other duties, might not be able to follow in the way and to the extent which is desirable. None of these possible solutions is free from serious objections. So far I do not consider that the responsibilities of the Secretary-General have been such as to overburden him personally or to restrict his possibilities of fulfilling his various functions. Were it to become necessary, it might be possible to overcome temporary difficulties by an *ad hoc* arrangement, covering, for example, such a special assignment as the one the Secretary-General now has in relation to the Palestine problem. In a final consideration of the question raised here no innovations should, of couse, be made which might weaken the unity of policy and introduce elements of political controversy or lead to administrative inadvertencies.

Belonging to the same category of problems is the question of the proper number of Under-Secretaries and other officials on the most senior level of equal rank. The view has been expressed that the number of officials on this level at present is unduly large. It has been felt that this represented a lack of economy, was bound to lead to difficulties in the coordination of the various activities, and might put the Secretary-General under an unnecessary pressure in his efforts to maintain current contact with all the senior officials. In part, the present number of senior officials is explained by historical circumstances; it is my hope that, at the end of the trial period, the proposals put forward can be framed independently of such considerations. I have given the matter constant and careful thought and my conclusion is that, even on a purely rational basis, only a minor reduction of the present number of senior officials is possible. To some extent that is explained by the need to provide for a wide geographical distribution. The main reason, however, is of another character. It should not be overlooked that the Secretariat has to cover a field not much less diversified than that of a national cabinet and that, therefore, specialization on the top level must be pushed fairly far. A simple enumeration will indicate what I have in mind. Senior officials are necessary for all the three Councils and for servicing the General Assembly and its committees. Such officials are likewise necessary for public information and for legal matters. In the purely administrative field, it is necessary to have special senior officials in charge of the Executive Office of the Secretary-General, of the Office of Personnel, of the Office of the Controller, and of the very numerous problems relating to the administration of the buildings and technical services of the Organization. Likewise, a senior official must be in charge of the administration of technical assistance. Finally, there are three regional commissions and the European Office. In at least one of the Departments—the Department of Economic and Social Affairs—there is, further, an undeniable need for a deputy with responsibility also for relationships with the specialized agencies. In the special case of the Technical Assistance Board, which has an interagency secretariat, there must be a senior official, appointed by the Secretary-General in consultation with the heads of the organizations participating in the Expanded Programme of Technical Assistance, to serve as Executive Chairman. This enumeration, which represents the number of specialized responsibilities requiring the leadership of a senior official reporting directly to the Secretary-General, already amounts to seventeen different posts. When attention is paid also to a reasonable geographical distribution and certain vital needs which may be expected to arise from time to time, such as the atoms for peace programme, it is difficult not to exceed this figure, which differs from the present number of senior posts only by four.

For a comparison it may be pointed out that, in the system prevailing before the present reorganization, the number of posts of Assistant Secretaries-General and Principal Directors, taken together, was higher than the present number of posts on the present unified Under-Secretary level. This is explained mainly by the fact that, in the earlier system, in a number of the enumerated cases, both an Assitant Secretary-General and a Principal Director functioned—all of them reporting to the Secretary-General—where now only an Under-Secretary is in charge. I have already mentioned that this simplification, which in my view has functioned well, has reduced the impact on the Secretary-General, has led to better coordination, and has likewise rendered possible considerable savings. One consequence of the change, which in my view later experience has fully borne out, is that the officials on the new Under-Secretary level all carry greater responsibilities than the previous Principal Directors, together with responsibilities which although slightly different in direction, are at least comparable in importance to those previously exercised in theory by the Assistant Secretaries-General. The change is characteristic of what is a general trend in foreign service from what might be called political diplomacy to diplomatic administration of a policy-making type.

My justification for raising in this Introduction in a preliminary way these various organizational problems, which may seem peripheral and too technical properly to be included, is the considerable interest attached to them by governments at the present juncture when, more than ever, the highest standards must be requested, not only of the individual members of the Secretariat, but also of the organization of the Secretariat if it is to meet the increasing demands that justly are put on it in face of the growing responsibilities of the United Nations.

DAG HAMMARSKJÖLD
Secretary-General

October 4, 1956

Letter to the President of the Security Council
Following Israeli Attack on Qalqiliya, Jordan
UN HEADQUARTERS, NEW YORK   OCTOBER 18, 1956

DURING THE night of October 10 to 11, 1956, Israeli armed forces staged another major retaliatory raid on a Jordanian police post at Qalqiliya in which forty-eight Jordanian police, soldiers, and civilians were killed. On October 15, Jordan asked for a Security Council meeting and two days later Israel filed a countercomplaint against Jordanian violations of the Armistice Agreement.

The Secretary-General's letter of October 18 transmitted General Burns' report on the Israeli raid and also called attention to his report of a week earlier that Israel was now refusing to permit UN observers to investigate incidents on its side of the Israel-Jordan armistice line. This was a further move to limit UNTSO's ability to function and was soon applied also on the demarcation line with Egypt.

General Burns' report also included an appendix listing casualties suffered by Israel and its four Arab neighbors during 1955 and the first nine months of 1956. The number of Israelis killed totaled 121, of Arabs 496. Some years later General Burns recalled these figures in his book, commenting that "Israel's retaliatory policy had piled up an impressive balance of corpses in her favour." [1]

By letter dated September 26, 1956 (S/3658), I drew the attention of the Security Council to the latest developments along the Jordan-Israel armistice demarcation line. I indicated that, if the situation were not rapidly brought under control, the Security Council might have to take the matter up in order to reaffirm its policy as established in previous resolutions and, were the Council to find the continued deterioration to constitute a threat to peace, to decide on what further measures might be indicated.

On September 27, 1956, I submitted to the Security Council a report

Security Council Official Records, Eleventh Year, Supplement for October-November-December 1956, Document S/3685, October 18, 1956.

[1] Burns, *Between Arab and Israeli*, p. 174.

dated September 12 (S/3659) with a general evaluation of the situation. To this report were annexed reports from the Chief of Staff covering *inter alia* freedom of movement of United Nations observers, and related matters, and the developments in the area surrounding the Gaza Strip. The same day I also circulated to the Security Council a report from the Chief of Staff concerning incidents on the Jordan-Israel armistice demarcation line (S/3660).

Following up the aforementioned reports and my previous letter I submit, annexed to this letter, a report of the Chief of Staff, dated October 17, 1956, on the incident which took place on the night of October 10 to 11 and which reflects a further deterioration of the situation.

I wish in this context to draw attention also to the report to the Secretary-General by the Chief of Staff dated October 11, 1956, circulated as document S/3670. In this document the Chief of Staff, referring also to incidents which preceded the incident of October 10 to 11, states that, at present, the situation is that one of the parties to the General Armistice Agreement makes it own investigations, which are not—and cannot be made—subject to check or confirmation by the United Nations observers, publishes the results of such investigations, draws its own conclusions from them, and undertakes actions by its military forces on that basis. I endorse the view of the Chief of Staff that this is a dangerous negation of vital elements of the Armistice Agreement. It represents a further step in the direction of a limitation of the functions of the United Nations Truce Supervision Organization, indicated already in my report of September 12, circulated on September 27, 1956 (S/3659).

Beyond drawing again the attention of the Security Council to these various developments which, in my view, require the most serious consideration by the Council, I would, for the present, limit myself to noting that clear and firm lines are established by the Council in respect of, on the one side, the need for an efficient observer organization, and, on the other side, the condemnation of all acts of violence, with the single exception of such acts as constitute acts of self-defence under Article 51 of the Charter.

DAG HAMMARSKJÖLD
Secretary-General
of the United Nations

THE SECURITY COUNCIL took up both Jordan's and Israel's complaints in meetings on October 19 and 25. Jordan's representative, Abdel Monem Rifa'i, declared the attack on Qalqiliya was no border incident but part of a policy of aggression, of "actual war." For Israel, Abba Eban responded by charging Jordan and Egypt with encouraging and assisting repeated fedayeen raids on Israel to which it was necessary to react. He declared: "The Government of Israel . . . will faithfully observe the cease-fire so long as the cease-fire is faithfully observed by the other side. It will start no war. It will initiate no violence." [2]

The Security Council had intended to continue its consideration of the case on Tuesday, October 29. On that day Israel launched its full-scale attack on Egypt across the Sinai. In the Council on October 30 Eban termed the Israeli action an exercise of "our sovereign rights of self-defence" and declared "Israel is not out to conquer any new territory, but is determined to wipe out the bases in the Sinai wilderness from which murder and death and destruction are launched against it." [3]

---

[2] Security Council Official Records, Eleventh Year, 745th Meeting, October 25, 1956.

[3] *Ibid.,* 749th Meeting, October 30, 1956.

SETTLEMENT
OF THE SUEZ CANAL DISPUTE

WHEN THE Security Council met to discuss the Suez Canal dispute on October 5, seven foreign ministers were at the table—John Foster Dulles, Selwyn Lloyd, Christian Pineau, and Dmitri T. Shepilov for the Big Four, Koca Popovic of Yugoslavia, and Paul-Henri Spaak of Belgium among the nonpermanent members, and Mahmoud Fawzi, representing Egypt as a party to the dispute.

Was this to be a confrontation setting the stage for a military "crunch," or could it become a genuine effort to negotiate the basis for a peaceful solution in the manner Hammarskjöld had urged in his yet to be published annual report (pages 270–71)?

Threatening words had been coming from the British and French governments all summer. Both had refused to rule out the use of force if Nasser did not promptly return the Canal to international management and a good deal was known about the continuing buildup of their military forces in the Mediterranean. The United States government, on the other hand, had consistently opposed resort to force both in public statements and private advice. It continued to support the 18-Power proposal for international operation that Nasser had rejected—and Dulles himself was the author of the supplementary Suez Canal Users Association (SCUA) plan—but it was committed to seeking a settlement with Egypt by negotiation.

The United States had refused to join Britain and France in bringing the dispute to the Security Council because it privately suspected the British and French purpose. Eisenhower wrote in his memoirs that late in September he and Dulles wondered whether it was "a sincere desire to negotiate a satisfactory settlement . . . or was this merely a setting of the stage for the eventual use of force in Suez? We were apprehensive." He also recalls that their apprehensions were reinforced on October 5, the day the Security Council began its deliberations, when Pineau told Dulles that Britain and France "did not believe that any peaceful way existed . . . that only through capitulation by Nasser could the Western standing in Africa and the Middle East be restored," adding "Foster disagreed vehemently." [1]

Later revelations of the development of the Suez conspiracy indicate that Pineau's remark accurately described French intentions at this time but that the British government was not yet irrevocably committed to force, although it was leaning strongly in the same direction. Britain and France in-

[1] Dwight D. Eisenhower, *Waging Peace,* Doubleday & Company, 1965, pp. 52–53.

troduced in the Security Council a draft resolution sharply condemning Egypt and standing pat on the 18-Power proposals which Nasser had already rejected. This would clearly be unacceptable to both Egypt and the Soviet Union. However, when Selwyn Lloyd opened the debate on October 5, he suggested private meetings of the Council as soon as the opening statements had been concluded, stressed Britain's desire to seek a peaceful solution by negotiation, and described the 18-Power proposals as *"a* basis for negotiation which we believe to be just" instead of the draft resolution's take it or leave it phrasing *"the* basis" [emphasis added—EDITORS].

Ever since the decision to bring the dispute to the Council, Hammarskjöld had been working to encourage private discussions between the two sides at the foreign ministers' level within the Council framework. In this effort he had the backing of the United States. Lloyd had arrived in New York three days in advance of the Council meeting and had been persuaded at least to explore the possibilities of arriving at a compromise satisfactory to Britain.

Fawzi also had come early. In a letter to the President of the Security Council on September 17 Egypt had reaffirmed its intention to pay "full and equitable compensation" to the shareholders of the nationalized Suez Canal Company and "to continue to guarantee the freedom of passage through the Canal in conformity with the 1888 Convention." Though opposed to the SCUA plan, Egypt had also placed on record its willingness to negotiate with users of the Canal solutions for questions relating to freedom and safety of navigation in the Canal, its development to meet future navigation requirements, and the establishment of just and equitable tolls.[2]

Now, when Fawzi's turn in the opening round of statements came on October 8, he went further. "It is probably advisable," he said, "to establish a negotiating body of reasonable size, and more important still, to put for the guidance of that body a set of principles to work by and objectives to keep in mind and attain." While rejecting a return to international management of the Canal, he emphasized that one of the main objectives would be to establish "a system of cooperation" between the Egyptian operating authority and the users of the Canal.[3]

The United States had agreed in advance to vote for the Anglo-French resolution, though it would not join in sponsoring it. Dulles had delayed his opening statement until the end of the opening round. He now proceeded to welcome Fawzi's suggestion of a set of principles to guide negotiation, spoke of the "four basic principles" stated in the 18-Power proposals, and passed lightly over the demand for handing the Canal back to an international operating authority. The four principles, Dulles said, were efficient operation and maintenance, insulation from the politics of any nation, a fair return for Egypt, and tolls as low as consistent with these requirements. "If, as the

[2] Security Council Official Records, Eleventh Year, Supplement for July-August-September 1956, Document S/3650.

[3] *Ibid.,* 736th Meeting, October 8, 1956.

Charter commands, we are to seek justice," he emphasized, "we must agree that the operation of this international utility shall be insulated from the politics of any nation."[4]

With this statement the Security Council moved from public to private sessions. At the first of these, after Pineau had been persuaded, it was agreed that he and Lloyd and Fawzi would meet with Hammarskjöld in his thirty-eighth floor office. They held six meetings from October 9 to 12. Hammarskjöld's part was to act as a catalyst, noting points where agreements seemed within reach and suggesting formulations that both sides could accept. The Secretary-General was able to record agreement on six principles, or "requirements," for a settlement, including the principles on which Dulles and Lloyd had put so much weight, that "the operation of the Canal shall be insulated from the politics of any country" and "the manner of fixing tolls and charges shall be decided by agreement between Egypt and the users."

When the results were reported to the Council at a private meeting October 12, Hammarskjöld informed the members that some progress had also been made in preliminary discussion of questions relating to practical application of the principles, though further exploration would be required. In sum it appeared that a decisive turn toward a negotiated settlement had been taken. Selwyn Lloyd himself seemed to think there had been a significant advance, but his Prime Minister was unhappy and so, of course, were the French. Anthony Nutting, Minister of State, recalls in his memoir on the Suez affair trying in vain to persuade Eden that the Six Principles provided a basis for negotiating an agreement with Egypt that would give the maritime powers the substance of the guarantees they had been asking for, though conceding Egyptian management of the Canal. Eden did not agree and instructed Lloyd to join with France in forcing a vote on the question of endorsing the 18-Power demand that the Canal be returned to international management.[5]

As a result, when the Security Council resumed its public sessions on October 13, it was presented with a revised Anglo-French resolution which began with the agreed Six Principles or "requirements" as the resolution termed them, and then proceeded to reaffirm the 18-Power plan as corresponding to the requirements. The condemnation of Egypt in the original resolution of October 5 was dropped entirely, room was left for further consideration of counterproposals to the 18-Power plan, and Egypt, France, and the United Kingdom were invited "to continue their interchanges." But the resolution explicitly placed the onus on Egypt to produce promptly more precise proposals "providing guarantees to the users not less effective than those sought by the proposals of the 18 Powers."[6]

During the debate Fawzi put on public record that he had already gone further in the private talks toward an accommodation than was implied in

---

[4] Ibid., 738th Meeting, October 9, 1956.
[5] Anthony Nutting, No End of a Lesson, Clarkson Potter, 1967, pp. 77–79.
[6] Security Council Official Records, Eleventh Year, Supplement for October-November-December 1956, Document S/3671.

the language of the second part of the resolution and in the statements by Lloyd and Pineau. He was conciliatory but hoped the Council would not adopt the second part of the resolution with its endorsement of international management and payment of tolls to the Suez Canal Users Association.

For the United States Dulles gave his support to the resolution as a whole but put the emphasis on continued negotiation on the basis of the Six Principles. Now that the principle of insulating the Canal from the politics of any country had been accepted, he said, the United States was confident that the remaining problems could be resolved.

The two parts of the resolution were put to the vote separately. The first part—the Six Principles—was adopted unanimously. The second part received nine affirmative votes but was vetoed by the Soviet Union. While regretting that only the Six Principles had been approved, Dulles said he considered that the Council remained seized of the question and the Secretary-General could continue to encourage further discussions among the governments of Egypt, France, and the United Kingdom. After the Council adjourned Hammarskjöld promptly issued the following statement:

> The resolution passed by the Security Council reflects the agreement on principles reached in the private talks between the foreign ministers of Egypt, France, and the United Kingdom. It provides a valuable starting point for a further exploration of existing possibilities to find a just and peaceful solution to the Suez problem.
> My own efforts to be of assistance will be pursued as indicated by Secretary of State Dulles.[7]

Despite the loss of the second part of the resolution, the United States government was much relieved by the progress registered. To President Eisenhower it appeared that "a very great crisis . . . is behind us."[8]

But on the same day that the Security Council adopted the Six Principles Anthony Eden told the Conservative Party Conference that the United Kingdom would continue its military buildup in the Eastern Mediterranean, adding that "we have always said that with us force is the last resort, but it cannot be excluded."[9] Fawzi lost no time in placing on record with the President of the Security Council Egypt's regret and alarm at the harmful effect of such statements upon efforts to create an atmosphere more favorable to peaceful negotiation. Egypt, he noted in his letter, had just agreed in the interests of conciliation not to press for Security Council consideration of its pending countercomplaint against Britain and France for their threats and pressures against Egypt.[10]

Fawzi and Selwyn Lloyd had agreed to stay on for a few days after Octo-

[7] UN Press Release SG/510, October 13, 1956.

[8] *Public Papers of the Presidents of the United States, Eisenhower, 1956,* television broadcast on October 12, 1956, Government Printing Office, Washington, D.C., p. 241.

[9] Eden, *Full Circle,* p. 567.

[10] Security Council Official Records, Eleventh Year, Supplement for October-November-December 1956, Document S/3679, October 15, 1956.

ber 13 to explore with Hammarskjöld further arrangements that might be acceptable to both sides in giving effect to the Six Principles. If sufficient progress were registered it was hoped that the foreign ministers might meet for further discussions toward the end of the month, probably in Geneva.

Now, however, Eden abruptly recalled Lloyd to London on Monday, October 15, for an urgent meeting of the inner cabinet. Years later, Anthony Nutting, his Minister of State, wrote that this was because the French had just sent secret emissaries to inform Eden of the French-Israeli plans and to invite Britain to join in a combined attack on Egypt. Eden's reaction had been favorable (see also page 304).[11] At the time this was not known, of course, to anyone outside the few who were privy to the project. Hammarskjöld hoped Lloyd's account of the progress in New York would help steer Eden and the Cabinet war hawks like Harold Macmillan toward a more moderate course.

After Lloyd left, Hammarskjöld continued his talks with Fawzi until the latter's departure on October 19. Eden and Lloyd flew to Paris on October 16 for a meeting with Mollet and Pineau. When the meeting ended a *communiqué* was issued reaffirming British and French resolve to stand firm on the 18-Power proposals, including international operation of the Canal "unless the Egyptian government produce other proposals for a system meeting the requirements (Six Principles) and affording equivalent guarantees to the users."[12] The tone was discouragingly rigid but gave no hint of the commitment to the plan for a combined attack on Egypt that appears to have been agreed at this meeting (see page 304).

Despite their anxiety, neither at United Nations Headquarters nor in Washington did it seem believable in the circumstances that Eden, veteran of the League of Nations, cofounder of the United Nations, careful diplomat, and trusted friend of the United States and of Eisenhower personally, would choose in the end the path he followed.

The hardening of the British and French position had undercut prospects for continuing discussions in Geneva before the end of the month. London and Paris were now making further talks conditional on additional commitments from Egypt, and their renewed threats were hardly calculated to make the latter more forthcoming. Meanwhile word of the original understanding about Geneva had leaked to the press. This caused a spokesman for the Secretary-General to issue a statement on October 20 confirming that Hammarskjöld had "remained in touch with the parties" but adding that "speculations about new developments and proposals for resumption of the talks which have appeared in the press are unfounded."[13]

As the situation stood on October 20, this was true enough, but four days later Hammarskjöld made a move which he hoped would put the negotiations back on the rails. He sent Fawzi a carefully worded confidential letter (second following text) in which he put on record his own "conclusions"

[11] Nutting, pp. 90–95.   [12] Eden, p. 573.
[13] UN Note to Correspondents No. 1420, October 20, 1956.

and "understandings" based on the sense of his discussions with Fawzi and the earlier talks with Lloyd and Pineau.

As will be seen in the text these went quite far in spelling out the scope of arrangements that might be agreed upon for implementing the principle of organized cooperation between Egypt and the users, including ample safeguards for the latter in case of disputes. At the same time Lloyd and Pineau were informed. On November 2, three days after the attack on Egypt began, Fawzi's response was to endorse Hammarakjöld's letter with the single and quite understandable exception of his reference to the right of the aggrieved party to "limited 'police action' " in case of noncompliance with an arbitral award. The Secretary-General immediately put on public record as a Security Council document his letter and Fawzi's reply.

Eisenhower recalls receiving on October 30 a report from the U.S. Ambassador to Egypt, Raymond A. Hare, that Fawzi had told him he would have gone to Geneva if the British and French had not made unreasonable and coercive demands.[14] If Britain and France had not already decided on force, Hammarskjöld's letter would have provided a basis for resuming the talks that promised a good deal more in safeguards for the users than they were eventually to receive.

---

1. Six Principles for Settlement of the Suez Canal Dispute

UN HEADQUARTERS, NEW YORK   OCTOBER 13, 1956

THE SECRETARY-GENERAL reported to a private meeting of the Security Council on October 12 on the agreement of the foreign ministers of Egypt, France, and the United Kingdom to the Six Principles. These were then incorporated, with only minor stylistic changes, in the resolution unanimously adopted by the Council the next day. The text that follows is as presented in the resolution.

Security Council Official Records, Eleventh Year, Supplement for October-November-December 1956, Document S/3675.

[14] Eisenhower, *Waging Peace*, p. 75.

The Security Council,

Noting the declarations made before it and the accounts of the development of the exploratory conversations on the Suez question given by the Secretary-General of the United Nations and the foreign ministers of Egypt, France, and the United Kingdom,

Agrees that any settlement of the Suez question should meet the following requirements:

1. There should be free and open transit through the Canal without discrimination, overt or covert—this covers both political and technical aspects;

2. The sovereignty of Egypt should be respected;

3. The operation of the Canal should be insulated from the politics of any country;

4. The manner of fixing tolls and charges should be decided by agreement between Egypt and the users;

5. A fair proportion of the dues should be allotted to development;

6. In case of disputes, unresolved affairs between the Universal Suez Maritime Canal Company and the Egyptian government should be settled by arbitration with suitable terms of reference and suitable provisions for the payment of sums found to be due.

2. Exchange of Correspondence on Steps toward a Settlement of the Suez Canal Question with the Foreign Minister of Egypt

UN HEADQUARTERS, NEW YORK   NOVEMBER 3, 1956

NOTE: The Secretary-General refers to the question entitled: "Situation created by the unilateral action of the Egyptian government in bringing to an end the system of international operation of the Suez Canal, which was confirmed and completed by the Suez Canal Convention of

Security Council Official Records, Eleventh Year, Supplement for October-November-December 1956, Document S/3728, November 3, 1956.

1888," pending before the Security Council. At the end of the deliberations of the Council, on October 13, 1956 (743rd meeting), it was indicated that the Secretary-General might continue his good offices.

In the week following the consideration of the question in the Council and until the departure of Dr. Fawzi, Foreign Minister of Egypt, on October 19, 1956, the Secretary-General had several discussions with him in order further to explore and clarify existing possibilities to find a solution to the Suez problem, meeting the requirements approved by the Security Council. Later, on October 24, the Secretary-General sent a letter to the Foreign Minister of Egypt in which he tried to set out his conclusions from the observations made in the series of private talks which had taken place up to October 19. He informed the foreign ministers of France and the United Kingdom of this move.

The Secretary-General has now received a reply from the Foreign Minister of Egypt to his letter of October 24, 1956. As this reply, together with the letter from the Secretary-General, seem to him to represent a significant further development in the consideration of the matter as initiated by the Security Council, he has considered it his duty to circulate the two letters to the members of the Security Council.

1. Letter Dated October 24
from the Secretary-General to the Minister
for Foreign Affairs of Egypt

(Personal and Strictly Confidential)

Dear Dr. Fawzi,

You will remember that at the end of the private talks on Suez, trying to sum up what I understood as being the sense of the discussion, I covered not only the "requirements," later approved by the Security Council, but also, in a summary form, arrangements that had been discussed as possible means of meeting those requirements. However, time then proved insufficient for a satisfactory exploration of those arrangements.

Before you left New York I raised with you the question of time and place for a resumption of the exploratory talks, in case the three governments directly concerned would find that such further talks should be tried. As a follow-up to these observations to which, so far, I have had no reactions either from you or from Mr. Selwyn Lloyd or Mr. Pineau,

I would, for my own sake, wish to put on paper how I envisage the situation that would have to be studied at resumed exploratory talks, if they were to come about.

Again, what I do is not to put out any proposals of my own, nor to try to formulate proposals made by you or any of the others. Just as I did at the end of the private talks in New York, I just wish, in my own words, to try and spell out what are my conclusions from the—entirely noncommittal—observations made in the course of the private talks, adding to some points in the light of my interpretation of the sense of the talks where they did not fully cover the ground. Whether you approve of my phrasing or not, I feel that it would be valuable to know if, in your view, I have correctly interpreted the conclusions from the tentative thinking which would provide the background for further explorations.

1. From the discussions I understood that the legal reaffirmation of all the obligations under the Constantinople Convention should not present any difficulty; this is a question of form, not of substance. I further understood that it would not present any difficulties to widen the obligations under the Convention to cover the questions of maximum of tolls (as at present); maintenance and development; reporting to the United Nations.

2. Nor should, if I understood the sense of the discussions correctly, the questions of the Canal code and the regulations present any difficulties of substance, as I understood the situation to be that no revision of the code or the regulations was envisaged which would lead to rules less adequate than the present rules. I further understood that revisions would be subject to consultation.

3. Nor, in my understanding, should the question of tolls and charges present any difficulties, as, according to what emerged in the discussions, the manner of fixing tolls and charges would be subject to agreement, as also the reservation of a certain part of the dues for development purposes would be subject to agreement.

4. Nor, in my understanding, should the *principle* of organized cooperation between an Egyptian authority and the users give rise to any differences of views, while, on the other hand, it obviously represents a field where the arrangements to be made call for careful exploration in order to make sure that they would meet the three first requirements approved by the Security Council (S/3675). The following points in the

summing up of my understanding of the sense of the discussions refer to this question of implementation of an organized cooperation:

A. The cooperation requires obviously an organ on the Egyptian side (the authority in charge of the operation of the Canal), and a representation of the users, recognized by the Canal authority (and the Egyptian government) and entitled to speak for the users.

B. Provisions should be made for joint meetings between the authority and the representation to all the extent necessary to effect the agreed cooperation.

C. Within the framework of the cooperation, the representation should be entitled to raise all matters affecting the users' rights or interests, for discussion and consultation or by way of complaint. The representation should, on the other hand, of course not, in exercising its functions, do this in such a way as to interfere with the administrative functions of the operating organ.

D. The cooperation which would develop on the basis of points A–C would not give satisfaction to the three first requirements approved by the Security Council unless completed with arrangements for fact-finding, reconciliation, recourse to appropriate juridical settlement of possible disputes, and guarantees for execution of the results of reconciliation or juridical settlements of disputes.

E. (*a*) Fact-finding can be provided for by direct access for the party concerned to a checking of relevant facts, or by a standing (joint) organ, with appropriate representation for both parties;

(*b*) A standing (joint) organ might also be considered for reconciliation;

(*c*) In case of unresolved differences, as to facts or other relevant questions, not resolved by the arrangements so far mentioned, recourse should be possible—as the case may be—to a standing local organ for arbitration, set up in accordance with common practices, *or* to whatever other arbitration organ found necessary in the light of a further study of the character of the conflicts that may arise, *or* to the International Court of Justice (whose jurisdiction in this case of course should be mandatory), *or* to the Security Council (or whatever other organ of the United Nations that may be established under the rules of the Charter);

(*d*) Concerning the implementation of findings by the United Nations organ, normal rules should apply. In respect of the implementation of awards made by a standing organ for arbitration, or by whatever other organ may be established for similar purposes, the parties should undertake to recognize the awards as binding, when rendered, and undertake to carry them out in good faith. In case of a complaint because of alleged noncompliance with an award the same arbitration organ which gave the award should register the fact of noncompliance. Such a "constatation" would give the complaining party access to all normal forms of redress, but also the right to certain steps in self-protection, the possible scope of which should be subject to an agreement in principle; both sides, thus, in case of a "constatation," should be entitled to certain limited "police action," even without recourse to further juridical procedures.

5. It was, finally, my understanding that the question covered by the requirement in point 6 of the Security Council resolution (S/3675) would not give rise to special difficulties, as the subject seems fairly well covered by the formulation of the principle itself.

Whether or not a set of arrangements will meet the three first requirements approved by the Security Council, will, according to my understanding of the situation, depend on the reply to the questions under point 4 above. That is true not only with an arrangement starting from the assumption of operation of the Canal by an Egyptian authority, but also on the assumption that the operation of the Canal (in the narrow sense of the word) is organized in another way. If I have rightly interpreted the sense of the discussions as concerns specifically the questions of verification, recourse, and enforcement (point 4,E) and if, thus, no objection in principle is made *a priori* against arrangements as set down above, I would, from a legal and technical point of view—without raising here the political considerations which come into play—consider the framework sufficiently wide to make a further exploration of a possible basis for negotiations along the lines indicated worth trying.

I am sure you appreciate that whatever clarification you may give of your reaction to this interpretation of mine of the possibilities would be helpful for me in contacts with the other parties—of the reactions of which I likewise need a more complete picture—and might smooth the way to progress beyond the point reached in the private talks.

DAG HAMMARSKJÖLD
Secretary-General
of the United Nations

2. *Letter Dated November 2 from the Representative of Egypt Transmitting a Communication from the Minister for Foreign Affairs of Egypt to the Secretary-General*

(*Strictly Confidential*)

Excellency,

I have the honour to transmit to you the following communication which I have just received from Dr. Mahmoud Fawzi:

"Dear Mr. Hammarskjöld,

"I have the honour to refer to your letter of October 24, 1956. You will recall that on October 29, I informed you through the Permanent Representative of Egypt, Ambassador Omar Loutfi, that it was under careful consideration and that I shall convey to you the result as soon as possible.

"I am now doing this; and am pleased to be able to tell you that, with the exception of the latter part of 'd' of subparagraph 'E' of paragraph 4, we share with you the view that the framework you have outlined in your letter is sufficiently wide to make a further exploration for a possible basis for negotiations along the lines indicated in it worth trying.

Mahmoud Fawzi

OMAR LOUTFI
Permanent Representative of
Egypt to the United Nations

STATEMENTS IN THE SECURITY COUNCIL ON THE DUTIES OF THE SECRETARY-GENERAL AT THE TIME OF THE SUEZ AND HUNGARIAN CRISES

THE REVELATIONS of later years seem to confirm that Eden committed himself at the October 16 meeting in Paris with Mollet and Pineau (pages 296–97) to the French plan for coordinating an Anglo-French attack on the Suez Canal Zone with an Israeli invasion of Egypt across the Sinai. Israel would strike first in the direction of the Canal. Britain and France would then issue ultimatums to both sides to pull back from the Canal and demand that Egypt permit Anglo-French occupation of the Canal Zone, ostensibly to separate the combatants and to keep the Canal functioning. When Egypt, as was to be expected, refused, a combined air- and sea-borne operation would seize key points by force and, hopefully, topple Nasser as well.

The plan would provide the pretext for using force to regain control of the Canal that Britain and France had been seeking since July. They had expected in the beginning that the Egyptians would show themselves incompetent to keep the Canal functioning. On their insistence most of the pilots who had worked for the Universal Suez Canal Company had therefore been withdrawn to help prove the point. But the move had failed. Egyptian management had proved quite competent, replacement pilots were promptly recruited, and in September more ships than ever had passed quickly and safely through the Canal.

In his memoir on the Suez affair Nutting recalls that Lloyd's first reaction on hearing from him of the French plan, on his arrival from New York on October 16, was "We must have nothing to do" with it, but he was promptly swept along by Eden and others in the inner Cabinet group determined to teach Nasser a lesson.[1] The day after the Paris meeting Nutting had warned Lloyd he would be forced to resign as Minister of State if the government went through with "this sordid conspiracy." The Foreign Minister himself, though perhaps plagued by inner qualms and doubts, played a key role in completing arrangements for the operation.

During the next week Lloyd returned to Paris secretly for clandestine talks with Ben-Gurion and the French on the timing and final arrangements.

[1] Nutting, p. 97. See also Hugh Thomas, *Suez,* Harper & Row, 1967, pp. 105–106.

It was agreed that Israel would attack on October 29. A twelve-hour Anglo-French ultimatum to both sides would follow the next day. Israel was assured that as soon as Egypt refused to accept the ultimatum, as expected, British bombers would attack Egyptian airfields and prevent Egypt from using its Russian-made bombers to retaliate on Israel. On October 25 the British Cabinet gave its approval to this response to an Israeli attack, though some ministers apparently considered this a contingency plan and were not aware that a date for the attack had been prearranged.[2]

The strictest secrecy cloaked these commitments. After the October 16 Paris meeting the United States government noted a drying up of diplomatic and intelligence information from Britain and France. "From about this time on," Eisenhower recalled in his memoirs, "we had the uneasy feeling we were cut off from our allies." [3]

Hammarskjöld heard nothing more from Lloyd and Pineau. Britain's own ambassadors were kept in the dark—including in Paris Sir Gladwyn Jebb, former Executive Secretary of the UN Preparatory Commission and long-time United Kingdom representative to the United Nations, and in Cairo, Sir Humphrey Trevelyan. In Washington, the British Embassy, then without an ambassador, was told nothing.

On October 15, U.S. intelligence discovered that France had clandestinely sent Israel sixty *Mystère* jets, not just the twelve it had earlier reported to its tripartite allies. There were also signs that Israeli reserves were being called up. Eisenhower immediately sent to Ben-Gurion the first of several warnings against resort to force.[4] On October 17 Ben-Gurion made a major speech to the Knesset in which he declared that the gravest danger facing Israel was of attack by the "Egyptian fascist dictator." [5]

At the same time, however, Israel was threatening to attack Jordan if Iraq sent troops to bolster King Hussein's shaky régime. After the massive October 11 reprisal raid on Qalqiliya the King had feared Israel was preparing to launch a full-scale invasion and had asked for help under the terms of the Anglo-Jordanian defense treaty. Iraq was then still ruled by the pro-Western government of Nuri es-Said and was a member of the Baghdad Pact. At Britain's request Nuri agreed to send an Iraqi brigade to Jordan, but Eden quickly backed off when Israel insisted such a move would be considered a *casus belli*. Britain could hardly risk becoming involved in war against Israel as Jordan's ally at the very moment it was preparing to attack Egypt in concert with Israel. In desperation Hussein now turned to Nasser for help. On October 25 Jordan joined Egypt and Syria in a combined military command under an Egyptian Commander in Chief.[6]

By October 28 Israel was fully mobilized. Ambassador Eban continued to insist the mobilization was purely defensive but Eisenhower sent two more urgent pleas against the use of force to Ben-Gurion. It seems that the U.S.

---

[2] Nutting, pp. 104–105; Thomas, p. 116; Eden, p. 581.
[3] Eisenhower, *Waging Peace*, p. 56.   [4] *Ibid.*, p. 56.
[5] Thomas, pp. 107–108.   [6] Nutting, pp. 85–87, 103.

State Department still thought an attack, if made, would more likely be against Jordan than Egypt.[7]

Israel launched its surprise Sinai campaign on October 29. Within hours the United States moved for immediate Security Council action ordering Israeli forces to withdraw behind the armistice line. This was in full accord with United Nations policy, repeatedly affirmed over the years since 1949 in a succession of unanimous Security Council resolutions. It was also in full accord with the 1950 Tripartite Declaration pledging Britain, France, and the United States to immediate action against attacks across the armistice lines by the regular armed forces of either Israel or the Arab states.

However, when Ambassador Lodge approached Sir Pierson Dixon the evening of the twenty-ninth to ask him to join the United States move, he was told, according to Eisenhower, that the United Kingdom would not join in any action against Israel and that it considered the Tripartite Declaration ancient history and without validity in the present situation. "We were astonished," wrote Eisenhower in a private cable to Eden the next morning.[8] Evidently instructions from London to follow a brand new policy had reached Dixon promptly.

The Security Council met at 11:00 A.M. on October 30. Lodge spoke first, declaring Israel had committed a breach of the peace and that he would introduce a resolution at the afternoon meeting calling on Israel to stop military action and withdraw its forces behind the armistice lines. Hammarskjöld spoke next and confined himself at this stage to telling the Council what General Burns had so far reported. The latter had already requested Israel to withdraw its troops and to agree to an immediate cease-fire, had informed the Egyptian government of his action and asked Egyptian concurrence to a cease-fire. No information on the replies, if any, had so far been received.

General Burns had also reported that a UN military observer and radio officer had been expelled from the El Auja demilitarized zone the afternoon of October 29 at 3:30 P.M. local time. The Secretary-General concluded by reminding the Council that UNTSO had not been permitted by Israel to investigate any of the incidents of alleged Arab infiltration in recent days.[9]

With reference to the expulsion of the UN military observer from El Auja, it is interesting to recall General Burns' comments included in the Secretary-General's report to the Security Council dated September 12 (page 257), though Hammarskjöld did not refer to them in his brief statement on October 30. General Burns had tried in vain all summer to persuade Israel to lift the restrictions it had imposed in El Auja on the freedom of movement of UN observers, which were in direct violation of the Security Council resolutions. Finally, on September 3 Ben-Gurion "indicated

---

[7] Eisenhower, pp. 68–72.

[8] *Ibid.*, p. 75. The full text of the cable is given in the appendices, pp. 678–679.

[9] Security Council Official Records, Eleventh Year, 748th Meeting, October 30, 1956.

that since the demilitarized zone was now occupied by Israel military forces, it served no purpose to have United Nations military observers there." General Burns then commented that "the strategic importance of the roads radiating from El Auja is such that if one side or the other should contemplate aggression on a large scale against the territory of the other, primary or secondary lines of operations would certainly be established through the demilitarized zone." And so, indeed, it happened. The UN observer had been forcibly ejected just before the Israeli invasion began.

After Hammarskjöld's brief report from General Burns only Ambassadors Brilej of Yugoslavia and Entezam of Iran had spoken, both in support of the United States initiative, when Arkady Sobolev of the USSR electrified the Council by reading a wire agency dispatch from London just handed to him that brought the first report of the Anglo-French ultimatum declaring their intention to occupy key positions in the Suez Canal Zone. A short time later an embarrassed Sir Pierson Dixon learned enough from London to tell the Council his Prime Minister had just made an important statement in Parliament and the text would soon be coming. He and Sobolev were by no means the only ones to receive from news wires first word of the ultimatum. President Eisenhower, Britain's Commonwealth partners, her ambassadors, including Trevelyan in Cairo, had the same experience. This happened because Eden had gone directly to the House of Commons to make his announcement as soon as the ultimatum had been handed to the Egyptian and Israeli envoys in London and messages had been approved for dispatch to Eisenhower and the Commonwealth governments. News agency reports of his speech traveled faster than his diplomatic cables.

Eden's excuse at the time was that the emergency gave him no chance to consult in a situation of imminent danger to the Canal and of wider war in the Middle East. Later he was to give a more candid explanation: ". . . There would be attempts to modify our proposals, to reach some compromise. . . . This was the last thing in the world we wanted, because we knew quite well that once palavers began, no effective action would be possible." [10] Or as Mollet was to put it with admirable succinctness to the Americans: "If your government was not informed of the final developments, the reason . . . was our fear that if we had consulted it, it would have prevented us from acting." [11]

When the Security Council met again in the afternoon of October 30 the text of Eden's House of Commons speech was distributed and Dixon urged the United States not to press its resolution. Lodge was unmoved and formally presented the U.S. draft resolution calling upon Israel "immediately to withdraw its armed forces behind the established armistice lines" and upon all United Nations Members to refrain "from the use of force or threat of force in the area" and "from giving any military, economic, or financial assistance to Israel." The Secretary-General was requested to report on compliance and "to make whatever recommendations he deems appropriate for the

[10] Eden, p. 588.   [11] Eisenhower, p. 77.

maintenance of international peace and security in the area." [12] Lodge accepted an amendment, inserting a paragraph calling upon "Israel and Egypt immediately to cease fire." The resolution was then pressed to a vote over British and French protests. It received seven affirmative votes but was vetoed by Britain and France. Australia and Belgium abstained.

Sobolev immediately proposed a substitute resolution. It omitted the paragraphs directed at Britain and France and retained those calling for immediate cease-fire, Israeli withdrawal, and reporting by the Secretary-General. Sir Pierson Dixon and the French representative at that meeting, Louis de Guiringaud, found the new proposal interesting and requested and received a brief adjournment so they might consult their governments on how to vote.

Their instructions were not changed and when the Council reconvened late in the evening of October 30, they cast their second pair of vetoes against the USSR resolution. With the twelve-hour Anglo-French ultimatum about to expire the Council then adjourned to the next day to consider a suggestion by Brilej of Yugoslavia that, since the Security Council had been rendered powerless to act by the vetoes, the General Assembly be called into emergency session under the 1950 Uniting-for-Peace resolution.

Hammarskjöld had been deeply shocked by the successive violations of the Charter during the past two days—first by Israel, then by Britain and France, two nations for whom he had always had a special affinity and admiration. The blow was all the more severe because it came just after negotiations, in which the Secretary-General played the central role, had seemed to be opening the way to a fair and peaceful settlement of the Canal question.

He decided that he must promptly declare his stand and define the principles under which he could continue to serve as Secretary-General. He read his statement at the beginning of the next Security Council meeting in the afternoon of October 31. It confronted the members with a question of confidence. If they disagreed with his view of his duties he clearly implied he was ready to resign. The text follows.

---

[12] Security Council Official Records Eleventh Year, Supplement for October-November-December 1956, Document S/3710.

1. *Suez Crisis*

NEW YORK   OCTOBER 31, 1956

Yesterday morning—on the basis of the information then available—I would have used my right to call for an immediate meeting of the Security Council, had not the United States government in the course of the night taken the initiative.

Yesterday afternoon—on the basis of reports of the Anglo-French ultimatum to Egypt—I would have acted likewise, had not the substance of the matter already been under consideration as one new aspect of the item proposed by the United States.

This morning, under my special mandate from the Security Council, which still is formally valid, I would have directed an appeal to the governments of Israel and Egypt to the effect of the second draft resolution of yesterday, had not the most recent developments rendered my mandate and such an initiative pointless.

This afternoon I wish to make the following declaration: The principles of the Charter are, by far, greater than the Organization in which they are embodied, and the aims which they are to safeguard are holier than the policies of any single nation or people. As a servant of the Organization, the Secretary-General has the duty to maintain his usefulness by avoiding public stands on conflicts between Member Nations unless and until such an action might help to resolve the conflict. However, the discretion and impartiality thus imposed on the Secretary-General by the character of his immediate task, may not degenerate into a policy of expediency. He must also be a servant of the principles of the Charter, and its aims must ultimately determine what for him is right and wrong. For that he must stand. A Secretary-General cannot serve on any other assumption than that—within the necessary limits of human frailty and honest differences of opinion—all Member Nations honor their pledge to observe all articles of the Charter. He should also

Security Council Official Records, Eleventh Year, 751st Meeting, October 31, 1956.

be able to assume that those organs which are charged with the task of upholding the Charter will be in a position to fulfill their task.

The bearing of what I have just said must be obvious to all without any elaboration from my side. Were the Members to consider that another view of the duties of the Secretary-General than the one here stated would better serve the interests of the Organization, it is their obvious right to act accordingly.

HAMMARSKJOLD'S statement evoked the following expressions of confidence in him from all sides during the ensuing debate: [1]

Henry Cabot Lodge, Jr., of the United States: "The United States thinks highly of the Secretary-General, of his mind and of his character. We regard him as being both able and fair. We share the opinions that he has just expressed and his concept of his duties. If there were a vote of confidence in him here this afternoon, we would unhesitatingly vote our confidence in him."

Louis de Guiringaud, of France: "I wish to associate myself with what the representative of the United States has just said, and I believe I can say the same thing in my capacity as President."

Arkady A. Sobolev, of the USSR: "The Soviet delegation has confidence in the Secretary-General of the United Nations and lends him its support."

Dr. Joza Brilej, of Yugoslavia: "The views expressed here by the Secretary-General have the full support of my government. On behalf of my government, I should like to reiterate our appreciation for the efforts he has always tirelessly deployed in the cause of peace."

Nasrollah Entezam, of Iran: "I was deeply moved by the Secretary-General's statement. I should like to tell Mr. Hammarskjöld that he has always enjoyed the full confidence of my delegation, a confidence which the courageous stand he has just taken has only served to increase. By this I mean that he will have the unreserved support of the delegation of Iran and—I think I would not be going too far in saying—the support of all peace-loving nations."

Sir Pierson Dixon, of the United Kingdom: "I should like to associate myself with the expressions of regard for the Secretary-General which have been voiced by various members of the Council. We have the highest regard for the integrity and impartiality of Mr. Hammarskjöld."

Dr. Victor A. Belaúnde, of Peru: "The delegation of Peru has had no occasion to voice anything but approval—indeed, nothing but enthusiastic endorsement—for the conduct of the Secretary-General not only as the

[1] Security Council Official Records, Eleventh Year, 751st Meeting, October 31, 1956.

chief executive officer of an efficient administration but also as the secretary of an Assembly deeply imbued with the spirit and purposes of the Charter.

"It is most gratifying to my delegation to note that the Secretary-General regards himself not only as the efficient head of an administration but also as the man who has received the mandate of seventy-six nations to watch over the observance of the Charter. . . ."

Dr. E. Ronald Walker, of Australia: "The Australian government, like the other governments represented around this table, has the fullest confidence in the Secretary-General and the greatest respect for the devoted and extremely able efforts that he has deployed in carrying out the tasks assigned to him by the Council in connection with the conflict in the Middle East."

Despite the Secretary-General's unequivocal stand on their resort to force, the representatives of Britain and France thus associated themselves with Lodge and other delegates in accepting his concept of the duties of his office, and Sobolev placed the USSR on record, too. Hammarskjöld emerged from this test in a stronger position to meet the new and great responsibilities which were soon to be placed in his hands.

Most of the discussion at this Council meeting concerned the Yugoslav proposal to call an emergency special session of the Assembly. This was the first occasion on which the Uniting-for-Peace resolution had been invoked. Dixon and Guiringaud resorted to legal technicalities in attempts to prevent a vote, but the resolution received the necessary seven affirmative votes, including that of the Soviet Union. The General Assembly convened the next day.

* * *

The Soviet intervention in Hungary engaged the attention of the United Nations at the same time as the Middle East crisis. In Poland on October 20 Wladyslaw Gomulka, a nationalist Communist, had successfully defied the Soviet leadership and won control of the Polish government and party on his terms. Three days later, after demonstrations and riots in Hungary, Imre Nagy, also a nationalist Communist, became premier. In Poland Gomulka and his associates kept the country firmly under control; there was no question of renouncing the alliance with Russia or loosening the grip of the Communist party on the life of the nation. In Hungary, on the other hand, matters quickly got out of hand. Riots and disorders spread throughout the country, Soviet troops and tanks were heavily engaged in Budapest, there were defections in the Hungarian Army and disarray in the Communist party leadership as it struggled to reestablish control.

On October 27 the United States, Britain, and France brought the situation to the Security Council, which began on October 28 a series of four meetings on the question. At first the Nagy government protested any Council consideration on the grounds of domestic jurisdiction and this stand was, of course, supported by the Soviet Union. However, the Council proceeded and the Western delegates called upon the Soviet Union to end the intervention of its troops in Hungary's internal affairs. The Soviet Union maintained that its forces, which were stationed in Hungary in accordance with the

Warsaw Pact, had responded to the Hungarian government's appeal for help in putting down counterrevolutionary elements which sought to exploit the "democratic movement." On October 30 a USSR government statement declared the Soviet Union would withdraw its forces from Budapest as soon as the Hungarian government thought it necessary and was also willing to negotiate on the presence of its troops in Hungary.

Two days later, after his government had been reorganized to include non-Communists, Nagy addressed an urgent appeal to the Secretary-General. More Soviet units were entering the country. Nagy had not only protested but had informed the Soviet Union that Hungary was immediately repudiating the Warsaw Pact and declaring its neutrality as of November 1. He requested the Secretary-General to place the question of Hungary's neutrality and the defense of that neutrality by the four great powers on the agenda of the forthcoming session of the General Assembly. The next day Nagy sent a further message stating he had proposed negotiations for the withdrawal of Soviet troops and requesting the Security Council to instruct the Soviet and Hungarian governments to start negotiations immediately.

On November 3 Lodge submitted a draft resolution calling upon the USSR to end its intervention in Hungary's internal affairs and expressing the hope it would withdraw its forces without delay. At this meeting the representative of Hungary, János Szábo, informed the Council that meetings were being held between representatives of the Soviet and Hungarian armed forces on questions of withdrawal and Sobolev confirmed for the USSR that negotiations were in progress.

During the night of November 3/4, however, reports poured in of new and massive attacks by Soviet forces in Budapest and elsewhere in Hungary. The Security Council was summoned to an urgent session at 3:00 A.M. on November 4. A revised U.S. resolution calling upon the USSR to withdraw all its forces from Hungary without delay received nine affirmative votes but was vetoed by the Soviet Union. The Council then voted to call another emergency special session of the Assembly to consider the situation in Hungary. Before the Council adjourned the Secretary-General, in the brief statement that follows, stated that his declaration of October 31 also applied to the Hungarian situation.

2. Hungarian Crisis
NEW YORK   NOVEMBER 4, 1956

Last Wednesday I had the honor to make before this Council the dec-laration concerning the views I hold on the duties of the Secretary-Gen-eral and my understanding of the stands that he has to take. It is certainly not necessary, but all the same I would like to put on record that the observations I made on that occasion obviously apply also to the present situation.

Security Council Official Records, Eleventh Year, 754th Meeting, Novem-ber 4, 1956.

BIRTH OF THE UNITED NATIONS
EMERGENCY FORCE

WHEN THE Assembly met in its first emergency special session at five in the afternoon of November 1, the Anglo-French aerial bombardment of Egyptian airfields had been underway for twenty-four hours and the Egyptian air force had been knocked out of action on the ground. Leaflets by the tens of thousands had been dropped over Cairo and other cities warning civilians to stay away from military targets and urging them to join in overthrowing "the dictator" Nasser. The latter had ordered most of his forces to withdraw from the Sinai to help in defense against the coming invasion by British and French troops and the Suez Canal was promptly blocked by sinking ships in the channel.

The United States was determined to press for immediate action by the Assembly, although this involved leading the way against its two closest allies, Britain and France, as well as Israel. The Eisenhower administration was unhappy about this aspect, but it considered their action a serious mistake and illegal under the Charter. It had also now concluded that there must have been advance collusion between Britain, France, and Israel about which the United States had been kept deliberately in the dark.[1]

Secretary of State Dulles personally presented the U.S. draft resolution to the Assembly and asked for action on it that night. The text was as follows:

The General Assembly,

Noting the disregard on many occasions by parties to the Israel-Arab armistice agreements of 1949 of the terms of such agreements, and that the armed forces of Israel have penetrated deeply into Egyptian territory in violation of the General Armistice Agreement between Egypt and Israel of February 24, 1949,

Noting that armed forces of France and the United Kingdom of Great Britain and Northern Ireland are conducting military operations against Egyptian territory,

Noting that traffic through the Suez Canal is now interrupted to the serious prejudice of many nations,

Expressing its grave concern over these developments,

1. *Urges* as a matter of priority that all parties now involved in hostilities in the area agree to an immediate cease-fire and, as part thereof, halt the movement of military forces and arms into the area;

2. *Urges* the parties to the armistice agreements promptly to withdraw all forces behind the armistice lines, to desist from raids across

---

[1] See, for example, Eisenhower, *Waging Peace*, p. 82.

the armistice lines into neighboring territory, and to observe scrupulously the provisions of the armistice agreements;

   3. *Recommends* that all Member states refrain from introducing military goods in the area of hostilities and in general refrain from any
acts which would delay or prevent the implementation of the present
resolution;

   4. *Urges* that, upon the cease-fire being effective, steps be taken to
reopen the Suez Canal and restore secure freedom of navigation;

   5. *Requests* the Secretary-General to observe and report promptly on
the compliance with the present resolution to the Security Council and
to the General Assembly, for such further action as they may deem appropriate in accordance with the Charter;

   6. *Decides* to remain in emergency session pending compliance with
the present resolution." [2]

In its description of what had happened the resolution, it may be noted,
used mild terms, carefully avoiding the words "invasion" or "aggression": Israeli forces had "penetrated deeply" after many previous violations of the
armistice agreements by both sides; Britain and France were "conducting
military operations against Egyptian territory." But the operative paragraphs
were unequivocal. There should be an immediate cease-fire (which would include stopping the aerial bombardment of Egypt), the French and British armada now approaching the coast should be halted, the Israeli forces
"promptly" withdrawn behind the armistice lines and other States (which
would include the Soviet Union and Egypt's Arab allies) should not intervene on their own.

There was overwhelming support for the resolution and for completing
action on it before the night was over. Tabling of amendments was successfully discouraged and a proposal to limit debate accepted. Soon after midnight the resolution was adopted by 64 to 5 with 6 abstentions. Only Australia and New Zealand voted with the United Kingdom, France, and Israel
against the resolution. Canada, Belgium, the Netherlands, Portugal, South
Africa, and Laos abstained. Thus Britain found itself opposed by most of
the Commonwealth countries, and Britain and France together by most of
Western Europe, in addition to the United States, all of Latin America, the
Soviet bloc, and the Asian and African states.

Canada's position was a special one, with its Commonwealth ties to Britain on the one hand, its unique relationship with the United States on the
other, and a measure of independence traditionally exercised toward both in
its conduct of foreign policy. In addition its Foreign Minister, Lester B. Pearson, had worked consistently over the years to strengthen the influence of
the United Nations and had been a Western favorite for election as Secre-

---

[2] General Assembly Official Records, First Emergency Special Session, Annexes, Document A/3256, subsequently Resolution 997 (ES-I), November 2,
1956.

tary-General in both 1946 and 1953. Especially since the United Nations action in Korea, to which Canada had contributed a brigade, Pearson had supported proposals to provide the United Nations with a police and peace-keeping capacity.

The Canadian government strongly disapproved of the way first Israel, and then Britain and France, had taken the law into their own hands. It also had sympathy for the grievances and frustrations which had prompted their action and it was dismayed by the extent of the break in relations between Britain and the United States. Pearson came to New York for the emergency Assembly session determined to work for a United Nations response of a kind that might bring a prompt end to the military intervention by opening to the offenders an acceptable line of retreat from their mistaken course.

A few hours before the Assembly began its debate on the U.S. cease-fire and withdrawal resolution on November 1, the Eden government had been under heavy attack in the House of Commons by the Labour opposition for resorting to force in defiance of the United Nations. In the course of defending himself Eden had asserted that immediate "police action" was necessary to separate Israeli and Egyptian forces and safeguard the Canal Zone, that British and French forces were "available" and the United Nations did not have the means to do the job. Once this was accomplished, he added, "If the United Nations were then willing to take over the physical task of maintaining peace in that area, no one would be better pleased than we." [3]

Soon after the Assembly debate began Sir Pierson Dixon repeated these words in the course of a speech urging a conference to bring about a lasting settlement in the Middle East. Dulles, when he introduced the U.S. resolution, agreed that "there needs to be something better than the uneasy armistices . . . there needs to be a greater sense of confidence and sense of security in the free and equal operation of the Canal." [4] But the first step must be the call for unconditional cease-fire and withdrawal as provided in his resolution.

Pearson did not speak before the vote, but privately he sought to persuade Dulles to include in the resolution some reference to a political settlement and to creating a UN force. When he failed he decided to abstain and afterward explained his abstention. Pearson summed it up in the words, "Surely we should have used this opportunity to link a cease-fire to the absolute necessity of a political settlement in Palestine and for the Suez." He also regretted that the resolution did not authorize the Secretary-General to start making "arrangements with Member states for a United Nations force large enough to keep these borders at peace while a political settlement is being worked out," and hoped that "it may not be too late to give consideration to this matter." His government would recommend Canada's participation in such a force.[5]

[3] Eden, p. 599.
[4] General Assembly, First Emergency Special Session, 561st Plenary Meeting.
[5] *Ibid.*, 562nd Plenary Meeting.

Before the Assembly adjourned at 4:20 A.M. on November 2, Dulles returned to the rostrum to express his agreement with Pearson on the importance of encouraging a constructive and positive development of the situation. President Eisenhower felt the same way, he said, and the United States would be very happy if the Canadian delegation would formulate and introduce a concrete proposal along the lines suggested by Pearson.

Shortly after the Assembly's adjournment on November 2 Hammarskjöld issued the press statement that follows. It welcomed "concrete proposals" but spelled out the Secretary-General's view of "the conditions under which they may prove useful" and made no mention of a United Nations force.

---

1. Statement to the Press
after General Assembly's
First Cease-fire Resolution on Middle East

UN HEADQUARTERS, NEW YORK   NOVEMBER 2, 1956

I see in yesterday's resolution, supported by the greatest number of votes ever registered in the United Nations, an event strengthening the Organization and giving new significance to its principles and purposes. I share the hope of the Assembly that a cease-fire, a halting of the movement of military forces into the area, and a withdrawal of all forces behind the armistice lines will promptly be effected.

I noted with great interest the many interventions in which suggestions were made for a fresh, positive approach to the problems of the Middle East, and hope that concrete proposals, aiming at progress toward peace with justice for all of the harassed peoples in the region, will be brought before the Emergency Special Assembly.

However, in considering those proposals, we must have a clear view of the conditions under which they may prove useful. I do not believe that propaganda is the way to friendship. I do not believe that it is by invoking the letter while forgetting the spirit of the law that you build a future of peace. I do not believe that acts of violence, whatever the reason, lead to cooperation. I do not believe that victories, bought at the

UN Press Release SG/515, November 2, 1956.

price of violations of treaty obligations, create confidence among neighbors. But I do believe that respect for decisions of the United Nations earns those concerned the support from the world community which every nation needs.

IN LONDON the Eden government had been badly shaken by the overwhelming rebuff administered by the General Assembly under United States leadership. It was still committed to a military operation that would take about a week to complete, but it sought to avoid making a wholly negative response to the United Nations call for an immediate cease-fire. Pearson's words about arranging a United Nations force, and the subsequent encouragement given to the idea by Dulles, seemed to suggest a way out of a very tight corner and perhaps a way to salvage an enterprise threatened by disaster.

Pineau flew over to London the afternoon of November 2 (London time) and a joint reply to the Secretary-General was agreed upon that evening. The United Kingdom and France would stop military action on the following conditions:

(a) Both the Egyptian and the Israel governments agree to accept a United Nations force to keep the peace;
(b) The United Nations decides to constitute and maintain such a force until an Arab-Israel peace settlement is reached and until satisfactory arrangements have been agreed in regard to the Suez Canal, both agreements to be guaranteed by the United Nations;
(c) In the meantime, until the United Nations force is constituted, both combatants agree to accept forthwith limited detachments of Anglo-French troops to be stationed between the combatants.[1]

This was in line with Eden's House of Commons statement on November 1. If accepted, it would have conferred legitimacy on the use of force by Britain, France, and Israel and sanctioned a political settlement influenced by the military advantage they had gained. It is true that Pearson's language in his Assembly speech had not been quite clear on this central question of principle—he had spoken of "the opportunity to link a cease-fire to the absolute necessity of a political settlement" and of "a United Nations force large enough to keep these borders at peace while a political settlement is being worked out." But Pearson's objective was quite different from Eden's. It was to persuade Britain and France to stop the bombing and to call off their projected landings in favor of the United Nations. And the concept of a United Nations force was to evolve over the next thirty-six hours in a manner far removed from that conceived in the Anglo-French reply.

[1] General Assembly Official Records, First Emergency Special Session, Annexes, Document A/3267, November 3, 1956.

As he had indicated in his November 2 statement, Hammarskjöld did not consider that bombardment and invasion provided a propitious atmosphere for progress toward lasting settlements in the Middle East. He also had some initial doubts about attempting to create suddenly and out of nothing a United Nations force. However, as he explored the constitutional, political, and practical aspects in talks with Lodge, Pearson, and others, he soon decided that the idea was not only feasible, but perhaps an essential key to a solution of the crisis and that a plan could be worked out that would win the necessary degree of support in the Assembly.

The mission of the force would be divorced from political objectives and would serve solely the Assembly's call for cease-fire and withdrawal. The restrictions of the Charter on the powers of the Assembly would be strictly honored by requiring Egypt's consent to its presence. Contingents from Britain and France could not participate in the force. This was the concensus that developed during the crowded hours of November 2 and 3.

Throughout it all Lodge gave unwavering and powerful support to Hammarskjöld's stand that force contrary to the Charter should not be rewarded directly or indirectly. Pearson accepted Hammarskjöld's judgment of what was necessary politically to win acceptance by the Assembly of a United Nations force and also concurred, subject to some reservation, with his constitutional stand. Hans Engen of Norway, for the Nordic States, Arthur Lall of India for the Arab-Asians, and Francisco Urrutia of Colombia for the Latin Americans were brought into the discussions at an early stage and played key roles in the preparatory work. The Secretary-General circulated his first report on compliance with the cease-fire resolution, with the reply from the United Kingdom and France that was quoted above, early in the afternoon of November 3. Word had been received the previous evening from the Egyptian government accepting the resolution "on the condition of course that it could not implement the resolution in case attacking armies continue their aggression." [2]

No reply had been received from Israel at the time Hammarskjöld's report was issued. Anglo-French bombing attacks on Egyptian military targets had continued without interruption and Israeli forces had occupied the Gaza Strip and seized control of the Straits of Tiran at the mouth of the Gulf of Aqaba. Later on November 3 the Government of Israel sent the Secretary-General a defiant "declaration." Having achieved all its military objectives it agreed "to an immediate cease-fire provided a similar answer is forthcoming from Egypt," but it categorically rejected paragraph 2 of the resolution calling for withdrawal behind the armistice lines and reestablishment of the armistice régime. Egypt's policies had "destroyed the Armistice Agreement," the reply declared. Instead, Israel asked the Assembly "to lend its entire authority to the establishment of a freely [*sic!*] negotiated peace between the governments and peoples of the Middle East." [3]

---

[2] *Ibid.*, Document A/3266, November 2, 1956.
[3] *Ibid.*, Document A/3279, November 3, 1956.

With the Anglo-French air attacks continuing, Egypt now requested an immediate meeting of the General Assembly "to take the actions it pledged itself to undertake in order to uphold the principles of law and order and to stop the unprovoked attack." [4] The Assembly met late in the evening of November 3 after the Security Council had temporarily suspended its discussion of the simultaneous Hungarian crisis when it was informed by both the Soviet and Hungarian representatives that discussions on the question of withdrawal of Soviet troops were in progress in Budapest (see page 312).

The somewhat shaky alliance between the Arab-Asians and most of the Western nations prevailed at this third meeting of the emergency special session. The Arab-Asians wanted a new and stronger cease-fire resolution setting a deadline for compliance. They needed the support of those Western nations more interested in pressing through the proposal for a UN force, while the West needed Arab-Asian backing for Pearson's initiative. The consultations on mutually acceptable language in the two draft resolutions which had begun earlier in the day continued during the night session as the debate proceeded.

Canada's resolution on a United Nations force was as follows:

The General Assembly,

Bearing in mind the urgent necessity of facilitating compliance with resolution 997 (ES-I) of November 2, 1956,

Requests, as a matter of priority, the Secretary-General to submit to it within forty-eight hours a plan for the setting up, with the consent of the nations concerned, of an emergency international United Nations force to secure and supervise the cessation of hostilities in accordance with all [5] the terms of the aforementioned resolution.[6]

India and eighteen other Asian-African nations submitted a new and tougher cease-fire resolution with a twelve-hour time-limit, which read as follows:

The General Assembly,

Noting with regret that not all the parties concerned have yet agreed to comply with the provisions of its resolution 997 (ES-I) of November 2, 1956,

Noting the special priority given in that resolution to an immediate cease-fire and, as part thereof, to the halting of the movement of military forces and arms into the area,

Noting further that the resolution urged the parties to the armistice agreements promptly to withdraw all forces behind the armistice lines,

---

[4] *Ibid.,* Document A/3270, November 3, 1956.

[5] The word "all" was inserted by Pearson in the text during the debate in response to a request by Lall of India. See below.

[6] General Assembly Official Records, First Emergency Special Session, Annexes, Document A/3276, subsequently General Assembly Resolution 998 (ES-I), November 3, 1956.

to desist from raids across the armistice lines into neighbouring territory, and to observe scrupulously the provisions of the armistice agreements,

1. *Reaffirms* its resolution 997 (ES-I) of November 2, 1956, and once again calls upon the parties immediately to comply with the provisions of the said resolution;

2. *Authorizes* the Secretary-General immediately to arrange with the parties concerned for the implementation of the cease-fire and the halting of the movement of military forces and arms into the area and requests him to report compliance forthwith and, in any case, not later than twelve hours from the time of adoption of the present resolution;

3. *Requests* the Secretary-General, with the assistance of the Chief of Staff and the members of the United Nations Truce Supervision Organization, to obtain compliance of the withdrawal of all forces behind the armistice lines;

4. *Decides* to meet again immediately on receipt of the Secretary-General's report referred to in operative paragraph 2 of the present resolution.[7]

The United States had earlier introduced two draft resolutions proposing new machinery for negotiations aiming toward final settlements of the Palestine question and the Suez Canal dispute, but consideration of them was deferred when Ambassador Lodge requested that priority be given to Canada's resolution. The U.S. resolutions, Lodge said, concerned the longer range and could wait, but he hoped Pearson's resolution would be acted on that night "because it contains a real hope of meeting the very grave emergency that confronts the world." [8] As matters developed, both United States resolutions were to remain on the shelf and were never taken up by the Assembly. It is of interest to note, however, that the United States resolution on the Suez dispute mentioned as the framework for a settlement: the Constantinople Convention of 1888; the Six Principles; and the Hammarskjöld-Fawzi exchange which the Secretary-General had placed on public record earlier that same day (page 298). Omitted was mention of both the London 18-Power proposals and the SCUA plan for which the United States had earlier voted in the Security Council.

Pearson did not present his resolution as an alternative to the new Asian-African cease-fire resolution but as a necessary complement to it in order to facilitate prompt compliance. The Canadian resolution explicitly defined and delimited the mandate of the proposed UN force as being "to secure and supervise the cessation of hostilities" in accordance with the Assembly's November 2 resolution. Pearson, when he introduced it, emphasized this limited purpose and dropped his earlier suggestion that the mandate of the force be linked to settlement of the Suez and Palestine questions.

[7] *Ibid.,* Document A/3275, subsequently General Assembly Resolution 999 (ES-I), November 3, 1956.
[8] *Ibid.,* 563rd Plenary Meeting, November 3, 1956.

Early in the debate there were calls from several of the Arab delegates for sanctions and collective measures under Chapter VII of the Charter, but the language of the resolution introduced by Ambassador Lall for the Arab-Asians, though firm in its call for compliance, was as moderate in tone as the November 2 cease-fire resolution that had been sponsored by the United States forty-eight hours before.

Lall agreed that the Canadian resolution should be given priority in the voting over his own resolution after first securing clarifications from Pearson of language in the resolution that nailed down its meaning about both the mandate and the composition of the proposed force. Just before the vote he stated India's understanding that the phrase "with the consent of the nations concerned" referred to nations which would contribute to the force, and that these would not include Britain or France. He also understood that "all" the terms of the November 2 resolution would apply to the mandate of the proposed force. Pearson confirmed this understanding from the rostrum and agreed to insert the word "all" in his resolution.

The vote was 57 to 0 with 19 abstentions. All the Afro-Asians, with the exception of Egypt, voted in favor and Latin America was solidly on the affirmative side, as were Belgium, Greece, Italy, Ireland, Spain, Yugoslavia, and the four Nordic states from Europe. The abstainers included the Soviet bloc, Egypt, Britain, France, Israel, Austria, Laos, Portugal, South Africa, Australia, and New Zealand. These last two Commonwealth countries supported a UN force but with a mandate corresponding to that urged by Britain and France.

The new Afro-Asian cease-fire resolution was then approved 59 to 5 with 12 abstentions. Those opposed were Britain, France, Israel, Australia, and New Zealand. The Nordic states, which had voted for the November 2 resolution, abstained on this one while Canada, which had abstained on the earlier cease-fire resolution, voted affirmatively this time.

During the meeting news had come in of a new and massive attack by Soviet troops and tanks in Budapest and the Security Council reassembled as soon as the Assembly adjourned shortly after three o'clock in the morning of November 4.

(To make it easier to follow the sequence of events in each of the crises which confronted the United Nations simultaneously—in the Middle East and in Hungary—texts and commentary for the critical days of November and December are grouped separately from this point on. Material concerning Hungary begins on page 412. It should be borne in mind, however, that in fact delegates and the Secretariat alike had to move back and forth between the Middle East and Hungary throughout this period.)

2. From Report on Implementation
of General Assembly's Cease-Fire Resolutions
of November 2 and 4, 1956

NOVEMBER 4

THE ASSEMBLY convened in emergency special session on Hungary during the afternoon of Sunday November 4 and adopted a United States resolution calling on the Soviet Union to withdraw its forces from Hungary and requesting the Secretary-General to observe and report on the situation (for texts and commentary see page 412). It then reconvened on the Middle East at 9:45 P.M. Hammarskjöld had meanwhile prepared and circulated reports on his discharge of the tasks assigned to him under the Afro-Asian cease-fire and Canadian UN force resolutions which the Assembly had adopted early in the morning of the same day.

When Hammarskjöld introduced his cease-fire report in the Assembly, only Egypt had accepted the resolution and agreed to cease fire. France and the United Kingdom had acknowledged receipt of his cables and promised replies after they had consulted together. There had been no reply from Israel. In his brief introductory remarks on the situation from the rostrum the Secretary-General limited himself to the following comment: "We are now less than two hours from the time set for an agreed cease-fire. Without commitments from the three governments which so far have not indicated their acceptance, the time left is scarcely sufficient for the further contacts necessary if we are to meet the target. The Assembly may wish to consider this situation." [9]

The first of the following texts includes Hammarskjöld's cables to Egypt, Israel, and the United Kingdom, which were annexed to his report. His cable to France, which was identical to that sent to the United Kingdom, is not reproduced. In his messages to the United Kingdom and France, it should be noted, the Secretary-General correctly interpreted the Assembly's action as rejecting the Anglo-French declaration of the day before that a cease-fire should be conditional upon the establishment of a UN force and that in the meantime their troops should be stationed in the Canal Zone. He also pointed out that Israel had earlier agreed to accept a cease-fire if Egypt would, and Egypt had agreed to accept if military actions against her were

[9] General Assembly Official Records, First Emergency Special Session, 565th Plenary Meeting, November 4, 1956.

stopped. Thus achievement of a cease-fire between Israel and Egypt now depended on Britain and France stopping their bombing raids and calling off the imminent landing of their troops.

---

1. In its resolution 999 (ES-I) of November 4, 1956, the General Assembly authorized the Secretary-General immediately to arrange with the parties concerned for implementation of the cease-fire and the halting of the movement of military forces and arms into the area as requested in its resolution 997 (ES-I) of November 2, 1956. The General Assembly also requested him to report on compliance forthwith and in any case not later than twelve hours from the time of adoption of the resolution.

2. In fulfillment of the task thus entrusted to him, the Secretary-General addressed communications to the four governments directly concerned. These communications, the texts of which are annexed (annexes 1 to 4), were sent directly by cable a few hours after the adoption of the resolution.

3. Taking into account the practical difficulties which were bound to arise in the course of the operation, both for the Governments and for the Secretary-General, the latter felt entitled to suggest as the time for a cease-fire 20.00 GMT (15.00 New York time). This proposal made it obviously impossible for him to report within twelve hours as requested. However, in order to increase the chances for a successful outcome and in the light of observations made by a sponsor of the resolution of November 4, 1956, the Secretary-General followed this course, which would still enable the General Assembly to take the matter up for renewed consideration during the evening of November 4.

4. In the course of his contacts with governments, the Secretary-General's attention has been drawn to difficulties which would follow from the very narrow margin allowed in the time limit which had been set. In the light of these difficulties, which it would have been harmful to the operation not to take fully into account, the Secretary-General later addressed to the four governments identical cables, stating that the time limit set for the cease-fire was changed from 20.00 GMT, November 4, 1956, to 05.00 GMT, November 5, 1956 (24.00 November 4, 1956, New York time). The text of these identical cables is annexed (annex 5). The extension of the time limit does not, of course, in any way influ-

ence the request made to the four governments for the earliest possible reply.

5. At the time of the preparation of the present report (16.00, November 4, 1956) the Secretary-General has received a reply to the questions raised in his cables to the four governments early this morning only from the Government of Egypt. The message from this government is annexed (annex 6). Communications received later will be circulated as separate documents.

ANNEX 1

Cablegram Dated November 4, 1956, Addressed to the Minister for Foreign Affairs of Egypt

1. The first emergency special session of the General Assembly at its meeting of November 3–4, 1956 adopted the following resolution [for this text, see page 320]:

2. In this regard, I note the information conveyed in the *aide-mémoire* of November 2 transmitted to the Secretary-General by the permanent representative of Egypt to the United Nations (A/3266) to the effect that the Egyptian government accepts the resolution of November 2 "on the condition . . . that it could not implement the resolution in case attacking armies continue their aggression."

3. In connection with my responsibilities under the above-mentioned resolution of November 4, I trust that the acceptance by the Government of Egypt of the resolution of November 2, subject to the condition stated, applies equally to the resolution of November 4.

4. In pursuance of the provision in operative paragraph 2 of the resolution (999 (ES-I)) authorizing the Secretary-General "immediately to arrange with the parties concerned for the implementation of the cease-fire and the halting of the movement of military forces and arms into the area," I am notifying the other three parties now involved in hostilities in the area of Egypt's acceptance, as stated, of the resolution of November 2, and am requesting all four parties, which of course include Egypt, to bring to a halt all hostile military actions in the area by 20.00 GMT Sunday, November 4, 1956. May I further request that your government's decision in this matter be communicated to me at the

General Assembly Official Records, First Emergency Special Session, Annexes, agenda item 5, Document A/3287, November 4, 1956.

earliest possible moment, and at all events so early as to render it possible to inform the other parties concerned about your decision prior to the said hour. The decisions of the other parties in this regard will be transmitted to the Government of Egypt without delay.

5. In pursuance of operative paragraph 2 of the resolution of November 2 and operative paragraph 3 of the resolution of November 4, the Government of Israel is being requested promptly to withdraw its forces behind the armistice demarcation lines.

6. In view of the urgency of the situation, which accounts for the short time limit fixed in the resolution of November 4, I request again that a definitive reply be given at the earliest possible hour.

[ANNEX 2 OMITTED]

DAG HAMMARSKJÖLD
Secretary-General

ANNEX 3

Cablegram Dated November 4, 1956, Addressed to the Minister of Foreign Affairs of Israel

1. The first emergency special session of the General Assembly at its meeting of November 3–4, 1956 adopted the following resolution [for this text, see page 320]:

2. In this regard, I note the statement conveyed in the *aide-mémoire* of November 4, 1956 (A/3279), to the effect that "Israel agrees to an immediate cease-fire provided a similar answer is forthcoming from Egypt."

3. It is noted from the *aide-mémoire,* November 4, 1956, that the Government of Israel has not stated its acceptance of the implementation of operative paragraph 2 of the resolution (999 (ES-I)) of November 2, urging the parties to the armistice agreements "promptly to withdraw all forces behind the armistice lines, to desist from raids across the armistice lines into neighbouring territory, and to observe scrupulously the provision of the armistice agreements."

4. I may call to your attention that the Government of Egypt had, before the meeting of the Assembly of November 3–4, accepted the resolution of November 2, "on the condition . . . that it could not implement the resolution in case attacking armies continue their aggression."

5. In connection with my responsibilities under the above-mentioned

resolution of November 4, I trust that the statement by the Government of Israel concerning a cease-fire applies to the resolution of November 4.

6. In pursuance of the provision in operative paragraph 2 of the resolution (999 (ES-I)) of November 4 authorizing the Secretary-General "immediately to arrange with the parties concerned for the implementation of the cease-fire and the halting of the movement of military forces and arms into the area," I am requesting all four parties, which of course includes Israel, to bring to a halt all hostile, military actions in the area by 20.00 GMT, Sunday November 4, 1956. May I further request that your government's decision in this matter be communicated to me at the earliest possible moment, and at all events so early as to render it possible to inform the other parties concerned about your decision prior to the said hour. The decisions of the other parties in this regard will be transmitted to the Government of Israel without delay.

7. In view of the urgency of the situation, which accounts for the short time limit fixed in the resolution of November 4, I request again that a definitive reply be given at the earliest possible hour.

8. In pursuance of the function entrusted to me by operative paragraph 2 of the resolution of November 4, and in view of the provisions of operative paragraph 2 of the resolution of November 2 and operative paragraph 3 of the resolution of November 4, I must inquire whether the Government of Israel will accept these provisions and accordingly will be willing to make arrangements with the Secretary-General, assisted by the Chief of Staff and the members of the United Nations Truce Supervision Organization, for the withdrawal of the armed forces of Israel behind the armistice lines.

DAG HAMMARSKJÖLD
Secretary-General

ANNEX 4

Cablegram Dated November 4, 1956, Addressed to the
Secretary of State for Foreign Affairs of the
United Kingdom of Great Britain
and Northern Ireland

1. The first emergency special session of the General Assembly at its meeting of November 3–4, 1956, adopted the following resolution [for this text, see page 320]:

2. In this regard, I note the information conveyed in the letter of November 3 addressed to the Secretary-General by the permanent representative of the United Kingdom of Great Britain and Northern Ireland to the United Nations (A/3269), and particularly the conditions under which military action would be stopped.

3. I wish to make the following comments on the three conditions established by your government for a cessation of your action. (*a*) In the voting on the resolution contained in document A/3276 requesting the Secretary-General to submit within forty-eight hours a plan for the setting up of an emergency international United Nations force, the delegations of Egypt and Israel abstained. (*b*) The request to which I have just referred, and which was approved by the Assembly, establishes that the Secretary-General should submit his proposal within forty-eight hours. In a separate resolution at the same meeting the Assembly established a time limit of twelve hours for a report on the cease-fire. It thus follows that the General Assembly did not accept the decision on the establishment of a United Nations force as a condition for the cease-fire. (*c*) The statements made prior to the adoption of the resolution on the United Nations force made it clear that it was a widespread view that none of the parties engaged in the present operations in the area should participate in the force. This has a direct and obvious bearing on any possibility of stationing Anglo-French troops between the combatants, pending the establishment of a United Nations force. I must assume the decision in question to have been taken on the basis of an interpretation which if maintained would exclude such an arrangement as a possible condition for a cease-fire.

4. In pursuance of the functions entrusted to me by operative paragraph 2 of the resolution of November 4, quoted above; in view of the provision in paragraph 2 of the resolution of November 2 and operative paragraph 3 of the resolution of November 4; and in view, further, of the Canadian-sponsored resolution, also adopted on November 4, concerning the plan for a United Nations force, and the indications it gives as to the attitude of the General Assembly to the three conditions established by your government, I must inquire whether the Government of the United Kingdom will accept the provisions set forth in operative paragraphs 1 and 3 of the resolution of November 2 and will be willing to make arrangements with the Secretary-General for the implementation of the cease-fire and the halting of the movement of military forces and arms into the area, in accordance with operative paragraph 2 of the resolution of November 4.

5. I wish to draw to your attention that the Government of Israel has accepted the cease-fire on the condition of reciprocal acceptance by Egypt, while Egypt has accepted the cease-fire provided that military actions against Egypt are stopped. With the stands thus taken by Israel and Egypt, it is obvious that the position of your government and the Government of France will determine whether or not it will be possible to achieve a cease-fire between Egypt and Israel.

6. In pursuance of the provision in operative paragraph 2 of the resolution (999 (ES-I)) of November 4 authorizing the Secretary-General "immediately to arrange with the parties concerned for the implementation of the cease-fire and the halting of the movement of military forces and arms into the area," I am requesting all four parties, which of course includes the United Kingdom, to bring to a halt all hostile military actions in the area by 20.00 GMT, Sunday, November 4, 1956. May I further request that your government's decision in this matter be communicated to me at the earliest possible moment, and at all events so early as to render it possible to inform the other parties concerned about your decision prior to the said hour. The decisions of the other parties in this regard will be transmitted to the Government of the United Kingdom without delay.

7. In view of the urgency of the situation, which accounts for the short time limit fixed in the resolution of November 4, I request again that a definitive reply be given at the earliest possible hour.

[ANNEX 5 OMITTED]

DAG HAMMARSKJÖLD
Secretary-General

UNDER THE Canadian resolution Hammarskjöld had another thirty-six hours in which to submit his plan for a United Nations emergency force. During the day, however, it was decided to proceed at once with the first stage of the plan—establishment of a United Nations Command. Consulting closely along the way with Pearson, Engen, Lodge, Urrutia, and Lall, Hammarskjöld prepared and submitted the "First Report" which is the first following text. He proposed that the Assembly immediately appoint General Burns, the Chief of Staff of the UN Truce Supervision Organization, as Chief of the United Nations Command and authorize him to recruit first a nucleus of officers drawn from the UNTSO military observer corps and later directly from Member states, with the proviso that none of the latter should be nationals of the permanent members of the Security Council. A draft resolution to this effect jointly sponsored by Canada, Colombia, and Norway was submitted by Pearson, Urrutia, and Engen and distributed to members by the time the Assembly convened.

The text was as follows:

The General Assembly,

Having requested the Secretary-General, in its resolution 998(ES-I) of November 4, 1956, to submit to it a plan for an emergency international United Nations force, for the purposes stated,

Noting with satisfaction the first report of the Secretary-General on the plan, and having in mind particularly paragraph 4 of that report,

1. *Establishes* a United Nations Command for an emergency international force to secure and supervise the cessation of hostilities in accordance with all the terms of General Assembly resolution 997(ES-I) of November 2, 1956;

2. *Appoints,* on an emergency basis, the Chief of Staff of the United Nations Truce Supervision Organization, Major-General E. L. M. Burns, as Chief of the Command;

3. *Authorizes* the Chief of the Command immediately to recruit, from the observer corps of the United Nations Truce Supervision Organization, a limited number of officers who shall be nationals of countries other than those having permanent membership in the Security Council, and further authorizes him, in consultation with the Secretary-General, to undertake the recruitment directly, from various Member states other than the permanent members of the Security Council, of the additional number of officers needed;

4. *Invites* the Secretary-General to take such administrative measures as may be necessary for the prompt execution of the actions envisaged in the present resolution.[1]

There were good reasons for urgent action by the Assembly. Britain and France had not acceded to either of the Assembly's cease-and-desist resolutions, their bombing of Egypt continued without interruption during the day, and their invasion fleet was approaching Port Said. Sentiment for sanctions was rising among the Arab and Asian nations, encouraged and supported by the Soviet bloc. Broadcasts from Moscow and Peking reported calls for volunteers to come to Egypt's aid. Nehru hoped that elements of the U.S. Sixth Fleet might be assigned under UN auspices to stop the threatened Anglo-French invasion. This idea attracted considerable Arab-Asian support but was quickly rejected by the Eisenhower administration as impossible.

Ever since the Anglo-French ultimatum the Canadian government had been trying to persuade London to call off its own intervention and accept instead a UN force. If the UN Command resolution could be approved that

[1] *Ibid.,* Document A/3290, subsequently General Assembly Resolution 1000 (ES-I), November 5, 1956.

night it was hoped this might be in time, combined with all the other pressures at work, to cause the British and French governments to call off, or at least suspend, the landing of their troops.

Hammarskjöld's discussions earlier in the day with such men as Pearson, Lodge, Lall, Engen, and Urrutia, and the work of this nuclear group of delegates among their colleagues, assured a strong majority for the UN Command resolution and quick action that night in the Assembly. In his introductory remarks the Secretary-General had only this to say about the UN Command report: "In this report, I put before the Assembly certain preliminary proposals which I recommend for its serious consideration. I believe that the report is self-explanatory and therefore I do not wish to take up the time of the Assembly with any special comments." [2]

Despite the lack of compliance with the November 2 and 4 cease-fire resolutions, no new resolution calling for immediate compliance was introduced, though Sobolev of the USSR urged such action, adding: "The implementation of such a decision would not require any supervision machinery or any UN command." [3]

When he took the floor as a cosponsor of the resolution Pearson spoke of it as "designed to implement the first stage of this task of ours to bring about a cessation of hostilities," but he then reverted to the necessity for prompt action aimed at a peace settlement.

"To find a way out of our present tragic dilemma," he said, "that is our immediate responsibility and our immediate task; but to seek a lasting settlement is our next and greater task. So, as the Secretary-General has shown us how to proceed with energy and dispatch by producing a report within twenty-four hours of the passing of resolution 998 (ES-I), I hope that we shall be able to proceed with equal energy and dispatch in our consideration of the draft resolutions that deal with the larger question [i.e., settlements for Palestine and the Suez Canal] and which have been submitted by the United States delegation." [4]

For the United States Lodge was firm and unequivocal. The Assembly's call for a cease-fire was unconditional and must be accepted. "Silencing of the guns," he said, "is the necessary prelude to solution of any—I repeat—*any* of the problems which beset the Middle East." He moved for closure of the debate and immediate adoption of the UN Command resolution "to permit the Secretary-General and the Governments with which he is consulting to proceed at full speed in making plans for the emergency international force."

Sir Pierson Dixon protested that the Assembly should wait for the expected reply from Britain to the Secretary-General's messages, since this was likely to have "a considerable bearing on this conception of an international force," but the Assembly voted closure by 50 to 6 with 16 abstentions and then adopted the resolution, just after midnight, by 57 to 0 with 19 abstentions. The vote was identical to that for Canada's resolution at the previous

---

[2] *Ibid.*, 565th Plenary Meeting, November 4, 1956.   [3] *Ibid.*   [4] *Ibid.*

meeting, except that Austria shifted to the affirmative from abstention, while Turkey abstained instead of voting "yes."

Bulletins reporting the dawn landing of British and French parachute troops on Port Said and Port Fuad came in over the news wires at UN Headquarters soon after the Assembly adjourned at 12:25 A.M. (New York time), November 5. Somewhat later the Secretary-General received identical replies from the British and French governments to his November 4 communication. The text [5] of the British note was as follows:

I have the honour on instructions from Her Majesty's Government in the United Kingdom to transmit the following reply to your communication of November 4, 1956 (A/3287, annex 4).

1. The governments of the United Kingdom and France have studied carefully the resolutions of the United Nations General Assembly passed on November 4. They warmly welcome the idea, which seems to underlie the request to the Secretary-General in the resolution sponsored by Canada and adopted by the Assembly at its 563rd meeting, that an international force should be interpolated as a shield between Israel and Egypt, pending a Palestine settlement and a settlement of the question of the Suez Canal. But, according to their information, neither the Israeli nor the Egyptian government has accepted such a proposal. Nor has any plan for an international force been accepted by the General Assembly or endorsed by the Security Council.

2. The composition of the staff and contingents of the international force would be a matter for discussion.

3. The two governments continue to believe that it is necessary to interpose an international force to prevent the continuance of hostilities between Egypt and Israel, to secure the speedy withdrawal of Israeli forces, to take the necessary measures to remove obstructions and restore traffic through the Suez Canal, and to promote a settlement of the problems of the area.

4. Certain Anglo-French operations with strictly limited objectives are continuing. But as soon as the Israeli and Egyptian governments signify acceptance of, and the United Nations endorses a plan for, an international force with the above functions, the two governments will cease all military action.

5. In thus stating their views, the United Kingdom and French governments would like to express their firm conviction that their action is justified. To return deliberately to the system which has produced continuing deadlock and chaos in the Middle East is now not only undesirable but impossible. A new constructive solution is required. To this end they suggest that an early Security Council meeting at the ministerial level should be called in order to work out an international settlement which would be likely to endure, together with the means to enforce it.

[5] *Ibid.*, Annexes, Document A/3293, November 5, 1956.

I request you to be so good as to circulate this reply to all Members of the United Nations.

PIERSON DIXON

Soon afterward other messages arrived. Fawzi cabled Egypt's acceptance of the UN Command resolution (1000 (ES-I)). Israel's reply to the Secretary-General's message of the day before consisted of five questions: Was Egypt's agreement to a cease-fire "clear and unequivocal"; Did Egypt continue to maintain that "she is in a state of war with Israel"; Is Egypt ready to enter immediately into peace negotiations with Israel; Does Egypt agree to cease its economic boycott of Israel and open the Suez Canal to Israeli shipping; Does Egypt "undertake to recall fedayeen gangs under her control in other Arab countries"? [6]

Eban later in the day made clear that Israel's readiness to agree to cease-fire was not conditional on replies to these questions. Sir Pierson Dixon informed the Secretary-General that a cease-fire had been ordered at Port Said and, as a consequence, "orders have been given that all bombing should cease forthwith throughout Egypt. Any other form of air action as opposed to bombing will be confined to the support of any necessary operation in the Canal area." [7] [The Port Said cease-fire report proved to be premature, as the local Egyptian commander was ordered by Nasser to continue resistance.—EDITORS]

Hammarskjöld pressed ahead with planning for the UN Force, consulting delegates and working toward completion of his second report, spelling out the nature, mandate, functions, and organization of the Force. By the end of the day he had more or less firm offers to contribute units from Canada, Colombia, Denmark, Norway, Pakistan, and Sweden, and discussions about an Indian contribution were well advanced. Norway acted with the greatest dispatch. A special bill was rushed through Parliament during the day authorizing the government to provide an infantry company and Engen informed the Secretary-General that soldiers were "ready for dispatch to the area tonight." In the Assembly Ambassador Lodge had already offered United States assistance with airlifts, shipping, transportation, and supplies.

Late in the afternoon, after he had received Israel's confirmation of its agreement to a cease-fire, the Secretary-General sent an *aide-mémoire* to the governments of France and the United Kingdom. He pointed out that if Israel would now accept the Assembly's UN Command resolution, as Egypt had, and if France and the United Kingdom would recognize that resolution as meeting the condition about a UN force which they had advanced, the remaining obstacles to agreement on a general cease-fire would be removed. The text of this *aide-mémoire* is the second of the following texts. It remained confidential until after the United Kingdom and France had replied the next day.

[6] *Ibid.,* Document A/3291, November 5, 1956.
[7] *Ibid.,* Document A/3299, November 5, 1956.

3. First Report on the Plan for an Emergency International United Nations Force

UN HEADQUARTERS, NEW YORK　　　　　NOVEMBER 4, 1956

1. In resolution 998 (ES-I) of November 4, 1956, concerning an emergency international United Nations force, the General Assembly requested the Secretary-General, as a matter of priority, to submit to it within forty-eight hours a plan for the setting up, with the consent of the nations concerned, of such a force, in order to secure and supervise the cessation of hostilities in accordance with all the terms of resolution 997 (ES-I) of November 2, 1956. In pursuance of this request I have the honour to submit this first report.

2. In the course of the day I consulted the representatives of various Member states in order to explore the possibility of assistance from those countries in the setting up of a United Nations force. The contacts will be continued, and the Assembly will be informed about the results in my final report. I am, however, in a position to state that, among the representatives so far consulted, the representatives of Colombia and Norway have, on behalf of their governments, accepted participation in the projected force. The representative of New Zealand has confirmed the declaration to the same effect that he made in the Assembly debate during the 563rd plenary meeting. Other representatives have submitted the question to their governments with their recommendation.

3. In the course of my consideration of the matter I have arrived at the conclusion that a step which should be taken immediately is the setting up of a United Nations Command for the purpose in question. The first elements of such a Command can be drawn from the staff of the United Nations Truce Supervision Organization. If the General Assembly were to decide on the immediate establishment of a United Nations Command, the decision, therefore, could be put partially into effect without any delay.

General Assembly Official Records, First Emergency Special Session, Annexes, agenda item 5, Document A/3289, November 4, 1956.

4. In accordance with the view just expressed, I submit that the General Assembly, without waiting for my final report, should now decide that a United Nations Command for "an emergency international United Nations force to secure and supervise the cessation of hostilities in accordance with all the terms" of its resolution 997 (ES-I) of November 2, 1956, be established; that the Assembly should further appoint, on an emergency basis, General Burns, at present Chief of Staff of the United Nations Truce Supervision Organization, to be Chief of the new Command; that General Burns, in that capacity, should be authorized immediately to organize a small staff by recruitment from the observer corps of the Truce Supervision Organization of a limited number of officers, drawn from countries which are not permanent members of the Security Council; that, further, General Burns should be authorized, in consultation with the Secretary-General, to recruit directly from various Member states, with the same limitation, the additional number of officers of which he may be in need; and that the Secretary-General should be authorized to take such administrative measures as would prove necessary for the speedy implementation of this decision.

5. In the continuing consultations which, in my view, will be considerably facilitated in case the General Assembly should decide immediately on the establishment of the United Nations Command, I would try to determine from which countries the necessary troops might be drawn without delay, as well as from which countries recruitment may be possible for a somewhat later stage. For both stages I would endeavour to develop a plan where, as a matter of principle, troops should not be drawn from countries which are permanent members of the Security Council.

6. The first of the stages referred to seems in a natural way to coincide with the stage immediately envisaged in resolution 999 (ES-I) of November 4, 1956. The later stage is likely to correspond to a period where the functions would be of a somewhat different nature, and should be viewed in the light of efforts over a longer range. While mentioning this point in the present report I reserve my right to elaborate the considerations, briefly mentioned here, in my final report.

7. In keeping with the terms of the resolution, the explorations, undertaken in order to establish the requested plan, are concerned only with the situation which would follow from the implementation of General Assembly resolution 997 (ES-I).

4. Aide-Mémoire Addressed to the Governments of France and the United Kingdom

NOVEMBER 5

1. In replies received to the request for a cease-fire, effective November 4, 1956, 24.00 GMT the governments of France and the United Kingdom informed the Secretary-General (A/3293, A/3294) that as soon as the governments of Israel and Egypt signify acceptance of, and the United Nations endorses a plan for, an international force with the functions prescribed, the two governments would cease all military action.

2. By adoption of the resolution, November 5, 1956, providing for the establishment of a United Nations Command, the United Nations General Assembly has taken the first decisive step in implementation of its previous acceptance in principle of a United Nations force to secure cessation of hostilities under all the terms established in its resolution on the subject of November 2, 1956.

3. The Government of Egypt has, through a message to the Secretary-General of November 5, 1956 (A/3295), accepted the resolution of the General Assembly of November 5, 1956, and may thus be considered as having accepted the establishment of an international force under the terms fixed by the United Nations. No similar declaration is yet available from the Government of Israel.

4. The Government of Egypt has, November 4, 1956, accepted the request of the Secretary-General for a cease-fire, without any attached conditions. It is to be assumed that this acceptance (A/3287, annex 6), although referring to the time limit set in the request of the Secretary-General, is generally valid.

5. The Government of Israel has now, in a clarification (A/3297) of its first reply to the request of the Secretary-General for a cease-fire, stated that in the light of Egypt's declaration of willingness to a cease-fire Israel confirms its readiness to agree to a cease-fire.

General Assembly Official Records, First Emergency Special Session, Annexes, Document A/3310, November 7, 1956.

6. The conditions for a general cease-fire would thus seem to be established and a new request warranted, provided that the governments of France and the United Kingdom would recognize the decision of the General Assembly, establishing a United Nations Command, as meeting the condition they have made for a cessation of hostilities, and if, further, the Government of Israel were to endorse the same General Assembly decision.

7. In view of the urgent request from the General Assembly for a cease-fire, in view of the attitudes on a cease-fire taken by the governments of Egypt and Israel, in view of the General Assembly decision to establish a United Nations Command and its acceptance by the Government of Egypt, and in pursuance of the General Assembly resolution (A/3275) adopted on November 4, 1956 (resolution 999 (ES-I) operative paragraph 2), I wish to ask the governments of France and the United Kingdom whether they would recognize the decision of the General Assembly establishing a United Nations Command, as meeting their condition for a cease-fire. I likewise wish to ask the Government of Israel if it finds itself in a position to accept the General Assembly resolution on the establishment of a United Nations Command.

8. In case of affirmative replies to the questions in paragraph 7 I intend to address again the proposal for an agreed cease-fire to the four governments concerned.

AS THIS PROGRESS was being registered the Soviet government reacted to the Anglo-French airborne landings in the Canal Zone in a series of strongly worded diplomatic notes. Bulganin proposed to Eisenhower that the Soviet Union and the United States prepare to join forces to put an end to the aggression against Egypt by force if necessary. Simultaneously USSR Foreign Minister Shepilov sent a request for an immediate meeting of the Security Council and proposed a draft resolution giving the United Kingdom, France, and Israel twelve hours to accept a cease-fire and three days to withdraw. Should they fail to do so, the resolution would consider "it essential, in accordance with Article 42 of the United Nations Charter, that all states Members of the United Nations, especially the United States of America and the Union of Soviet Socialists Republics as permanent members of the Security Council having powerful air and naval forces at their disposal, should give military and other assistance to the Republic of Egypt, which has been the victim of aggression, by sending naval and air forces, military units, volunteers, military instructors and other forms of assistance. . . ." [1]

[1] Security Council Official Records, Eleventh Year, Supplement for October-November-December 1956, Document S/3736, November 5, 1956.

Bulganian also sent cables to Eden, Mollet, and Ben-Gurion threatening massive Soviet intervention. Eisenhower quickly issued a statement terming the Soviet proposal "unthinkable" and warning Bulganin that the entry of any new forces into the conflict would oblige all Members of the United Nations, including the United States, to take effective countermeasures.[2]

The Security Council met at eight o'clock the evening of November 5 in response to the Soviet request. Hammarskjöld was the first speaker and made the statement that follows on his efforts to achieve a cease-fire, excusing himself for his intervention because he felt "the progress marked in the course of the day is of significance" to the Council's "considerations."

Van Langenhove of Belgium then requested an immediate vote on the adoption of the agenda and it was defeated by 4 to 3 with 4 abstentions. (Those who voted *against* were the United States, United Kingdom, France, and Australia; those who voted *for* were the USSR, Iran, and Yugoslavia; those who abstained were Belgium, China, Cuba, and Peru.) Explanations of vote followed, during which Sobolev defended the Soviet proposal but made no serious effort to revive it.

---

5. Statement in the Security Council
on Progress toward a Cease-Fire

UN HEADQUARTERS, NEW YORK   NOVEMBER 5, 1956

I thank the President for this opportunity to inform the Security Council about the situation as I envisage it at present. The Council will remember that under the resolution adopted by the General Assembly, I am authorized to pursue efforts in order to achieve a cease-fire. That is the point on which I feel that the Council would like to be informed.

In replies received to the request for a cease-fire, effective November 4 at 2400, New York time, the governments of France and the United Kingdom informed the Secretary-General that as soon as the governments of Israel and Egypt signify acceptance of, and the United Nations endorses a plan for, an international force with the functions prescribed, the two governments would cease all military action.

Security Council Official Records, Eleventh Year, 755th Meeting, November 5, 1956.

[2] Eisenhower, *Waging Peace*, p. 90.

By the adoption of the resolution [1000(ES-I)] of November 5, 1956, providing for the establishment of a United Nations Command, the United Nations General Assembly has taken the first decisive step in the implementation of its previous acceptance in principle of a United Nations force to secure cessation of hostilities under all the terms established in the resolution [997(ES-I)] of November 2 on that subject.

The Government of Egypt has, through a message which I received today, accepted the resolution of the General Assembly of November 5, and may thus be considered as having accepted the establishment of an international force under the terms fixed by the United Nations. The Government of Egypt has further accepted yesterday the request of the Secretary-General for a cease-fire without any attached conditions. It is to be assumed that this acceptance, although referring to the time limits set in my request, is generally valid.

Today I received from the Government of Israel, in clarification of its first reply to my request for a cease-fire, a statement to the effect that in the light of Egypt's declaration of willingness to cease fire, Israel wishes to confirm its readiness to agree to a cease-fire.

The conditions for a general cease-fire would thus, it seems, depend on the possibility of an agreement concerning the plan for an international force. The Council is aware of the fact that by tomorrow, on the instructions of the General Assembly, I hope to be able to present such a plan, following up the first decision through which the United Nations Command was established. However, in view of the significance of this specific problem and the situation we are now facing in the cease-fire question and in view of the progress made, I felt that it was appropriate to seek with great urgency a further clarification in order to facilitate progress.

I have in this situation also to mention that this afternoon I received a letter from the permanent representative of the United Kingdom which I have taken the liberty of having circulated to the members of the Security Council. There is one point in that letter which is in my view of special significance for the progress report I have taken the liberty of presenting. It is the following one: the representative of the United Kingdom states that orders have been given that all bombing should cease forthwith throughout Egypt.

I beg the pardon of the Council if I have interfered in any way with a question which in a certain way may be extraneous to the proceedings of the Council, but I have done so because I feel that the progress marked in the course of the day is of significance in its considerations.

DURING THE night of November 5/6 Hammarskjöld completed his second and final report on an emergency United Nations force (page 344). Copies were immediately dispatched to London and Paris and distributed to delegates at Headquarters. A few hours earlier (dawn by Egyptian time), and after a naval bombardment, British and French troops aboard the ships of the invasion armada had landed on the beaches at Port Said and Port Fuad. They met sporadic resistance but soon consolidated their control and an armored column set off in the direction of Ismailia, halfway down the Suez Canal.

The governments in Washington, London, and Paris were all inclined to regard the Bulganin notes of the day before and the Soviet move at the United Nations as probably an exercise in propaganda aimed at winning favor among the Arabs. Nevertheless there was some apprehension about the danger that hostilities might spread to other parts of the Middle East and about the threat to send volunteers. The memory of the massive intervention of Chinese "volunteers" in Korea was still fresh. And after Bulganin's notes and the Anglo-French seaborne landings the Egyptian government itself issued a public appeal "for help by volunteers, arms or otherwise, to all those all over the world who care still for the dignity of man and the rule of law in international relations." [1] In Washington President Eisenhower ordered that the U.S. Forces should quietly and by degrees "achieve an advanced state of readiness." [2]

When the British cabinet met on the morning of November 6 Hammarskjöld's *aide-mémoire* and his second report on a UN emergency force were both on the table. These provided a line of retreat at a moment when the various pressures to halt the ill-starred military adventure had built to overwhelming proportions. On the political side the massive majority of UN Members remained firm in its demand for unconditional cease-fire and withdrawal and this majority included the United States and most of the Commonwealth. At home the Labour opposition in Parliament and even some Conservatives sided with the United Nations, not with the Eden government. Finally, a cease-fire between Israel and Egypt was now in effect and the pretext for seizing the Canal Zone to separate the combatants had been removed. On the economic side the Suez Canal was blocked, the pipeline from the Iraq oil fields was blown up, and Saudi Arabia had imposed an embargo on oil shipments to Britain and France. Oil would have to come from the Western hemisphere and this meant payment in dollars. But Britain's

[1] General Assembly Official Records, First Emergency Special Session, Annexes, Document A/3304, November 6, 1956.

[2] Eisenhower, *Waging Peace,* p. 91.

dollar reserves were dropping at an alarming rate, there was a run on the pound, and the U.S. government made it quite plain that it would itself provide no credits and would prevent any from the International Monetary Fund unless the United Kingdom accepted the United Nations resolutions. On hearing this news the Chancellor of the Exchequer, Sir Harold Macmillan, hitherto a leading Cabinet hawk, instantly became a dove and the Cabinet decided to order a cease-fire at midnight GMT. The French had wished to carry the operation through to the end but when Eden telephoned the British decision, Mollet had little choice but to concur. Shortly before noon New York time Sir Pierson Dixon delivered the following letter to Hammarskjöld:

I have the honour, on instructions from Her Majesty's Government in the United Kingdom, to inform you that they have received and most carefully considered the communication which you addressed to them yesterday evening (A/3310) and your second and final report to the General Assembly (A/3302) which was issued this morning.

I have been instructed to convey to you at once the following message from Her Majesty's Government:

"Her Majesty's Government welcome the Secretary-General's communication, while agreeing that a further clarification of certain points is necessary.

"If the Secretary-General can confirm that the Egyptian and Israeli governments have accepted an unconditional cease-fire, and that the international force to be set up will be competent to secure and supervise the attainment of the objectives set out in the operative paragraphs of the resolution passed by the General Assembly on November 2, Her Majesty's Government will agree to stop further military operations.

"They wish to point out however that the clearing of the obstructions in the Suez Canal and its approaches, which is in no sense a military operation, is a matter of great urgency in the interests of world shipping and trade. The Franco-British force is equipped to tackle this task. Her Majesty's Government therefore propose that the technicians accompanying the Franco-British force shall begin this work at once.

"Pending the confirmation of the above points, Her Majesty's Government are ordering their forces to cease fire at midnight GMT unless they are attacked."

I request you to be so good as to circulate this reply to all Members of the United Nations.

PIERSON DIXON [3]

The Assembly was not scheduled to take up the Secretary-General's second report until the next day, thus delaying a formal reply, but Hammar-

[3] General Assembly Official Records, First Emergency Special Session, Annexes, Document A/3306, November 6, 1956.

skjöld instantly decided to use the press as a vehicle to give informally, and personally, the second confirmation requested. On five minutes' notice the reporters were assembled. The transcript of what the Secretary-General said follows in the text below.

---

6. *Transcript of Remarks to the Press*

UN HEADQUARTERS, NEW YORK   NOVEMBER 6, 1956

I have an important communication to make. I received some few moments ago a letter from the British delegation, which I will read to you.

[After having read out the letter from the United Kingdom delegation, quoted above, the Secretary-General made the following remarks.]

That is the communication. Concerning it, I can only remind you of the fact that the Egyptian and Israel governments have accepted an unconditional cease-fire, and that, therefore, I can give such a confirmation.

It is also my personal conviction that if the General Assembly, as I certainly hope it will, accepts the proposals I have made in my second and final report on the international force, the force will be competent to secure and supervise the attainment of the objectives set out in the General Assembly resolution. However, it is natural that I will wait with my formal reply until the General Assembly has pronounced itself on the second and final report. This delay is of no significance as, independently of my reply, the Franco-British forces have been ordered to cease fire at midnight (GMT).

This is a letter from the British delegation. It covers, as you see, the "Franco-British forces," as has been confirmed to me.

I have one final point. As you may have observed, there is here in the text a reference to a communication which I addressed to the British government yesterday evening. It is the communication to which I referred in my statement before the Security Council last night.

Well, ladies and gentlemen, that is all I have to say.

UN Note to Correspondents No. 1433/Rev. 1, November 6, 1956.

THERE WAS no historical precedent for the kind of international force proposed by Hammarskjöld in his first and second reports to the General Assembly. Yet he was able, within forty-eight hours, to produce documents providing answers to the main questions of principle about its authority, organization, and mandate. His conclusions were soundly based, both constitutionally and politically, and were immediately accepted by the great majority of Member governments, though not always with full understanding. Delegates at the time considered it a remarkable achievement and paid repeated tribute during the Assembly debate to the intellectual capacity, integrity, tactical skill, and stamina of its author, who had been working twenty-hour days since October 29, and was to continue at this pace for some weeks to come.

Some of the conclusions in the text that follows derived from the limitations set by the Charter on the powers of the Assembly and some from the way in which the Assembly had defined and delimited the mandate of the force in its previous resolutions. Thus it would be a nonfighting force, supervising but not enforcing an agreed cease-fire and withdrawal; it would require consent both from nations contributing units and from Egypt for entry of the force and its operations on her territory; it would not be in any sense an occupation force and it would not be used to influence "the political balance affecting efforts to settle the conflict."

The most interesting innovation, however, was the internationalization of the command structure of the force. The operation would not be conducted on behalf of the United Nations by a single nation, as by the United States in Korea, or by a group of nations, as envisaged in the Charter provisions for the Military Staff Committee and in the Uniting-for-Peace resolution, but by officials with exclusively international responsibilities—the Secretary-General and the Commander of the force, whose relations to the Secretary-General "should cor.espond to those of the Chief of Staff" of UNTSO. The Secretary-General, aided by an advisory committee of delegates which he chaired, would be directly responsible to the Assembly. He would thus be the executive for the United Nations peace-keeping operation with responsibilities to the Assembly corresponding to those in a parliamentary system. This became the precedent for a similar division of responsibilities between the Secretary-General and the Security Council in later UN peace-keeping operations—the UN military observer group in Lebanon in 1958, the UN Congo force in 1960, and the UN Cyprus force in 1964.

Hammarskjöld pointed out in his report that the command structure provided a degree of independence from "national policies" [or "power politics"--EDITORS] not otherwise attainable. Though he did not directly say so, the decision not to include any contingents from the great powers in the force was also an important factor in this respect. The small and middle-sized states which would provide contingents for the force and serve on the advisory committee lacked the military and economic power of the great states and did not have spheres of influence to defend or enlarge. The United Nations as an independent influence in international life thus tended to hold a higher priority in their conduct of policy. As events were soon to demonstrate, Canada, the Nordic states, India, and many others were glad to join in strengthening the peace-keeping capacities of the United Nations when great power attitudes gave them the opportunity.

One additional point should be noted about the command structure and composition of the emergency force. Hammarskjöld touched upon it lightly in the report that follows. Though the powers of this force were constitutionally limited because of its establishment by the Assembly, such a force could also be constituted by the Security Council under Chapter VII of the Charter if the Council so decided.

7. Second and Final Report on the Plan for an Emergency International United Nations Force

UN HEADQUARTERS, NEW YORK   NOVEMBER 6, 1956

1. In resolution 998 (ES-I) of November 4, 1956, concerning an emergency international United Nations force, the General Assembly requested the Secretary-General, as a matter of priority, to submit to it within forty-eight hours a plan for the setting up, with the consent of the nations concerned, of such a force in order to secure and supervise the cessation of hostilities in accordance with all the terms of resolution 997 (ES-I) of November 2, 1956. In pursuance of this request I have the honour to submit this second and final report.

2. In my first report on this matter (A/3289), submitted on November 4, 1956, to the General Assembly, I gave an account of the initial consultations with delegations and submitted for consideration a proposal for the immediate establishment of a United Nations Command for the purpose in question. A draft resolution sponsored by Canada, Colombia, and Norway (A/3290), based on this report, was adopted by the General Assembly on November 5, 1956 (resolution 1000 (ES-I).

3. In my first report, I touched briefly on various questions which would arise in setting up the projected United Nations force. After further consideration and consultations, I have the honour to submit here-

General Assembly Official Records, First Emergency Special Session, Annexes, agenda item 5, Document A/3302, November 6, 1956.

with the conclusions which I have been able to reach within the short time at my disposal.

Questions of Principle

4. An emergency international United Nations force can be developed on the basis of three different concepts:

(*a*) It can, in the *first* place, be set up on the basis of principles reflected in the constitution of the United Nations itself. This would mean that its chief responsible officer should be appointed by the United Nations, and that he, in his functions, should be responsible ultimately to the General Assembly and/or the Security Council. His authority should be so defined as to make him fully independent of the policies of any one nation. His relations to the Secretary-General of the United Nations should correspond to those of the Chief of Staff of the United Nations Truce Supervision Organization;

(*b*) A *second* possibility is that the United Nations charge a country, or a group of countries, with the responsibility to provide independently for an emergency international force serving for purposes determined by the United Nations. In this case it would obviously be impossible to achieve the same independence in relation to national policies as would be established through the first approach;

(*c*) Finally, as a *third* possibility, an emergency international force may be set up in agreement among a group of nations, later to be brought into an appropriate relationship to the United Nations. This approach is open to the same reservation as the second one, and possibly others.

Variations of form, of course, are possible within a wide range, but the three concepts mentioned seem to circumscribe the problem.

5. In the decision on the establishment of the United Nations Command, on an emergency basis, which the General Assembly took on November 5, 1956, the Assembly chose to follow the first of the three types mentioned in paragraph 4 above. The second type was that followed in the case of the Unified Command in Korea. There is no precedent for the use of the third type, but it would seem to represent one of the possible forms for implementation of the suggestion in the replies of November 5, 1956, of the governments of France and the United Kingdom (A/3294, A/3293) to my request for a cease-fire. In attempting to work out a plan for setting up an emergency international

United Nations force, I have based my considerations on the legal situation created by the decision in principle of the General Assembly, implied in the request of the Assembly to me to submit within forty-eight hours a plan for such a force, and in its later decision to establish a United Nations Command, in implementation of this first resolution.

6. In its resolution 1000 (ES-I) on the United Nations Command, the General Assembly authorized the Chief of Command, in consultation with the Secretary-General, to recruit officers from the United Nations Truce Supervision Organization, or directly from various Member states other than the permanent members of the Security Council. This recruitment procedure affords an important indication of the character of the force to be set up. On the one hand, the independence of the Chief of Command in recruiting officers is recognized. On the other hand, the principle is established that the force should be recruited from Member states other than the permanent members of the Security Council. The first of these elements in the new approach has an important bearing on the interpretation of the status of the Chief of Command. The second point has an equally important bearing on the character of the whole Command. It may in this context be observed that the Franco-British proposal, to which I have already referred, may imply that the question of the composition of the staff and contingents should be subject to agreement by the parties involved, which it would be difficult to reconcile with the development of the international force along the course already being followed by the General Assembly.

7. Resolution 998 (ES-I), in which the General Assembly requests the Secretary-General to submit a plan for the international force, gives further guidance. Thus, it is said that the force should be set up on an "emergency" basis. The situation envisaged is more clearly defined in the terms of reference of the force (resolution 998 (ES-I)) which are "to secure and supervise the cessation of hostilities in accordance with all the terms" of the General Assembly resolution of November 2, 1956.

8. A closer analysis of the concept of the emergency international United Nations force, based on what the General Assembly has stated in its resolution on the matter, indicates that the Assembly intends that the force should be of a temporary nature, the length of its assignment being determined by the needs arising out of the present conflict. It is further clear that the General Assembly, in its resolution 1000 (ES-I) of November 5, 1956, by the reference to its resolution 997 (ES-I) of November 2, has wished to reserve for itself the full determination of the

tasks of this emergency force and of the legal basis on which it must function in fulfillment of its mission. It follows from its terms of reference that there is no intent in the establishment of the Force to influence the military balance in the present conflict and, thereby, the polical balance affecting efforts to settle the conflict. By the establishment of the force, therefore, the General Assembly has not taken a stand in relation to aims other than those clearly and fully indicated in its resolution 997 (ES-I) of November 2, 1956.

9. Functioning, as it would, on the basis of a decision reached under the terms of resolution 337 (V), Uniting for Peace, the force, if established, would be limited in its operations to the extent that consent of the parties concerned is required under generally recognized international law. While the General Assembly is enabled to establish the force with the consent of those parties which contribute units to the force, it could not request the force to be stationed or operate on the territory of a given country without the consent of the government of that country. This does not exclude the possibility that the Security Council could use such a force within the wider margins provided under Chapter VII of the United Nations Charter. I would not for the present consider it necessary to elaborate this point further, since no use of the force under Chapter VII, with the rights in relation to Member states that this would entail, has been envisaged.

10. The point just made permits the conclusion that the setting up of the force should not be guided by the needs which would have existed had the measure been considered as part of an enforcement action directed against a Member country. There is an obvious difference between establishing the force in order to secure the cessation of hostilities, with a withdrawal of forces, and establishing such a force with a view to enforcing a withdrawal of forces. It follows that while the force is different in that, as in many other respects, from the observers of the United Nations Truce Supervision Organization, it is, although paramilitary in nature, not a force with military objectives.

Questions of Functions

11. The question of determining the functions of the emergency international United Nations force has been dealt with in part in the preceding paragraphs. It is difficult in the present situation and without further study to discuss it with any degree of precision. However, the

general observations which are possible should at this stage be sufficient.

12. In the General Assembly resolution 998 (ES-I) the terms of reference are, as already stated, "to secure . . . the cessation of hostilities in accordance with all the terms" of resolution 997 (ES-I)of November 2, 1956. This resolution urges that "all parties now involved in hostilities in the area agree to an immediate cease-fire and, as part thereof, halt the movement of military forces and arms into the area"; and also "urges the parties to the armistice agreements promptly to withdraw all forces behind the armistice lines, to desist from raids across the armistice lines into neighbouring territory, and to observe scrupulously the provisions of the armistice agreements." These two provisions combined indicate that the functions of the United Nations force would be, when a cease-fire is being established, to enter Egyptian territory with the consent of the Egyptian government, in order to help maintain quiet during and after the withdrawal of non-Egyptian troops, and to secure compliance with the other terms established in the resolution of November 2, 1956. The force obviously should have no rights other than those necessary for the execution of its functions, in cooperation with local authorities. It would be more than an observers' corps, but in no way a military force temporarily controlling the territory in which it is stationed; nor, moreover, should the force have military functions exceeding those necessary to secure peaceful conditions on the assumption that the parties to the conflict take all necessary steps for compliance with the recommendations of the General Assembly. Its functions can, on this basis, be assumed to cover an area extending roughly from the Suez Canal to the armistice demarcation lines established in the armistice agreement between Egypt and Israel.

Questions of Size and Organization of the Force

13. Time has so far not permitted the necessary technical studies. It is therefore not yet possible to say what should be the size of the force. In my first report, I pointed out that the situation is likely to involve two stages: the first one when certain immediate tasks have to be fulfilled, the second one when somewhat different tasks, although within the framework set out in paragraph 12 above, will fall upon the force. It is likely that the size of the force will require some adjustment to the development of the tasks. Further study of such matters is required, and

I have invited the Chief of the United Nations Command, General Burns, to present his views urgently.

14. It is not possible at this time to make any proposals as to the general organization of the force beyond those clearly following from resolution 998 (ES-I) of November 4, 1956. General experience seems to indicate that it is desirable that countries participating in the force should provide self-contained units in order to avoid the loss of time and efficiency which is unavoidable when new units are set up through joining together small groups of different nationalities. The question requires additional study and is obviously closely linked to the condition that various Member states will provide sufficiently large units. The difficulty in presenting a detailed plan of organization need not delay the establishment of the force. It is likely that during the first period, at all events, the force would have to be composed of a few units of battalion strength, drawn from countries or groups of countries which can provide such troops without delay. It is my endeavour in the approaches to governments to build up a panel sufficiently broad to permit such a choice of units as would provide for a balanced composition in the force. Further planning and decisions on organization will to a large extent have to depend on the judgment of the Chief of Command and his staff.

Questions of Financing

15. The question of how the force should be financed likewise requires further study. A basic rule which, at least, could be applied provisionally, would be that a nation providing a unit would be responsible for all costs for equipment and salaries, while all other costs should be financed outside the normal budget of the United Nations. It is obviously impossible to make any estimate of the costs without a knowledge of the size of the corps and the length of its assignment. The only practical course, therefore, would be for the General Assembly to vote a general authorization for the cost of the force on the basis of general principles such as those here suggested.

Questions of Recruitment

16. Time permitted me to discuss the question of participation in the force with only a limited number of Member governments. Offers of as-

sistance in writing so far received are annexed to the present report. In cases other than those covered by the annexed letters, the question of participation is under consideration by the governments. It is my hope that broader participation will be possible as soon as a plan is approved, so that a more definite judgment may be possible concerning the implications of participation. The reactions so far received lead me to believe that it should be possible to meet quickly at least the most basic need for personnel. The possibilities, as finally established, may call for an adjustment later of the size and organization of the force in relation to what would in principle be the most satisfactory solution.

General Questions

17. In my first report it was stated that the later stage in the development to which I referred in paragraph 13 above "is likely to correspond to a period where the functions . . . should be viewed in the light of efforts over a longer range" (A/3289, paragraph 6). While mentioning this point I reserved my right to elaborate the consideration briefly dealt with. After further reflection, I would not for the present wish to go beyond what I have said on the subject in previous parts of the present report, especially concerning the functions of the force. It would be premature to express views on problems likely to arise after the immediate crisis is past.

18. On several matters mentioned above it has been necessary to leave the question open. This is explained in part by a lack of time and in part by the need for further study. I suggest that these open matters be submitted to exploration by a small committee of the General Assembly; this body, if established, might also serve as an advisory committee to the Secretary-General for questions relating to the operations. On the other hand, on all points where a decision of significance to the further development of the plan seems possible now, the General Assembly should proceed to action forthwith.

19. I am fully aware of the exploratory character of this plan in many respects. Time is vital and this is some excuse not only for the lack of detail in this first approach but also for decisions by the General Assembly reached in more general terms than is customary. If the force is to come into being with all the speed indispensable to its success, a margin of confidence must be left to those who will carry the re-

sponsibility for putting the decisions of the General Assembly into effect.

[ANNEXES OMITTED]

THE GENERAL ASSEMBLY discussed the Secretary-General's UN emergency force proposals in morning and afternoon meetings on November 7. The British and French had ceased fire the midnight before. They were in control of Port Said and Port Fuad and continued to land additional troops but they had stopped their advance only twenty miles down the Canal Zone at El Cap.

There were two resolutions before the Assembly. The first, sponsored by Argentina, Burma, Ceylon, Denmark, Ecuador, Ethiopia, and Sweden, endorsed the Secretary-General's report in every respect, named an advisory committee of seven representatives, and urged full speed ahead with organization of the force (the text as amended is given in commentary on pages 355–56). The second resolution was sponsored by nineteen Asian-African States. It reaffirmed the Assembly's previous resolutions on cease-fire, withdrawal, and the UN Command and called upon Israel, France, and the United Kingdom "immediately to withdraw" all their forces (text page 357).

The Secretary-General opened the debate with a brief statement informing the Assembly of arrangements under way for General Burns and ten UNTSO military observers to proceed at once to Cairo (first of following texts). For Egypt Ambassador Loutfi flatly rejected the proposal of France and the United Kingdom to start clearing the Suez Canal. Egypt would never agree that "the aggressors" should play any part in this work and nothing could be done until evacuation took place. Egypt had accepted the UN Command resolution but Britain and France had advanced many unacceptable conditions.

Several of the Arab delegates were concerned about going ahead with the deployment of a UN force without enforcement powers in the absence of any commitment to withdraw from Israel and with only conditional commitments from Britain and France. The Secretary-General's second intervention was concerned with these and related questions (second following text).

8. Statement in the General Assembly Introducing Second Report on UN Emergency Force

UN HEADQUARTERS, NEW YORK   NOVEMBER 7, 1956

I do not think that many words are needed in the introduction of my second and final report on the United Nations force. I have put the main document before the Members. I only wish to express my earnest hope that a decision in line with my proposals will be taken promptly so as to permit us to get going. There should not be left in the minds of people any uncertainty about the determination of the United Nations.

I would like to announce that last night I sent instructions to the Chief of the United Nations Command, after agreement with the Egyptian government, to proceed forthwith to Cairo for the first contacts. I have now received the first reply from the Chief of Command in which he informs me that Egyptian authorities agreed in principle to his flying to Cairo, but that detailed arrangements cannot be made before today.

The Chief of Command has established direct radio contact with allied forces in Cyprus, which will be necessary for clearance and aircraft passage and, later, for other purposes. Egyptian authorities agreed this morning also, in principle, to accept ten observers at once in Cairo. These observers will need jeeps and radios. Therefore the Chief of Command will try to send these by road to Egypt. The Israel government has been requested to allow passage. That is the announcement I feel I should make as the first progress report on the setting up of the force in the area.

General Assembly Official Records, First Emergency Special Session, 566th Plenary Meeting, November 7, 1956.

9. *Further Statement in the General Assembly during Debate on UN Emergency Force*

UN HEADQUARTERS, NEW YORK   NOVEMBER 7, 1956

In the course of the debate certain requests for clarifications have been directed to me. I felt that at this stage of the discussion it might be useful if I gave a reply.

At the 566th meeting, the representative of Syria expressed the fear that in case of noncompliance by Israel with the request for the withdrawal of forces behind the armistice demarcation lines, there would arise, on the basis of the position taken in my report, a situation where Egypt would be presented with a *fait accompli,* as the United Nations force is not at present established with a view to enforcing the withdrawal of forces. The representative of Syria said that he could not but feel the deepest misgivings concerning this situation.

My reply is simple. Were the unfortunate situation envisaged by the representative of Syria to arise, I would consider it my duty to bring it at once to the attention of the General Assembly or of the Security Council for such measures as those two main organs of the United Nations might decide upon. Egypt would thus not be faced with a *fait accompli* but could resort to the means provided for in the Charter. My position as to the functions of the United Nations force in no way limits the right in these respects. I consider the definition of those functions in the report to be sound as a basis for this first stage in the setting up of the force.

Another question which has been directed to me concerns the interpretation of the legal situation in respect of withdrawal of non-Egyptian forces other than the Israel forces. In my view, it follows from resolution 997 (ES-I) that all non-Egyptian forces—with the obvious exception of the United Nations force which will be there with the consent of the Egyptian government—have to withdraw from Egyptian territory. It

General Assembly Official Records, First Emergency Special Session, 567th Plenary Meeting, November 7, 1956.

goes without saying that "Egyptian territory" in this context must be understood in the sense which follows from international law and the Armistice Agreement.

Still another question which I should like to clarify concerns the interpretation of my indication that the United Nations Force will have to operate within a region extending from the Suez Canal to the armistice demarcation line as established in the Egyptian-Israel General Armistice Agreement. What I intended to say was entirely directed to the situation with which we are faced. The United Nations force will have to come in at what is at present the dividing line between the Egyptian and Israel forces. It is at whatever may come to be the dividing line that it will have to function. As the situation is, that means that United Nations activities will have to start close to the Suez Canal, but that after the expected compliance with the recommendations of the General Assembly they would end up at the armistice demarcation line.

Other points have been raised on which I find it difficult to elaborate what I have said in the report, which to me seems to be self-explanatory. For example, I have been asked for an interpretation of what I have said about the length of the assignment of the force being determined by the need arising out of the present conflict. I am sure the Members will appreciate that, in the still unclear situation, it would be premature for me to say how the needs might develop after the end of the immediate crisis. However, the force being under ultimate authority of the General Assembly, I think that this point need not give rise to worries. Likewise, I find that the interpretation of my statement concerning previous decisions, to the effect that there is no intent in the establishment of the force to influence the military balance in the present conflict and thereby the political balance affecting efforts to settle the conflict, should be evident. However, this aspect too will certainly be followed closely by the General Assembly.

AN INTERESTING development during the day had been the receipt of offers from Czechoslovakia and Romania, along with others, to contribute contingents to the UN Force. Now Ambassador Michalowski of Poland proposed an amendment to the resolution adding Czechoslovakia to the Advisory Committee so that Eastern Europe as well as the other regions of the world would be represented. The Soviet bloc had abstained on both the previous resolutions about a UN force but Sobolev of the USSR had not yet made an issue of the constitutionality of creation of such a force by the Assembly. The Polish amendment was defeated by 31 to 23 with 14 abstentions.

The Asian-African withdrawal resolution was drafted in such a way as to leave room for varying interpretations of the words "immediately to withdraw," and these were expressed during the debate. The Asian-Africans wished to maintain maximum pressure on Britain, France, and Israel to withdraw. The United States, Canada, Latin America, and the smaller Western European countries wished to help Britain and France to withdraw by providing a bridge over which to retreat. The resolution, as worded, demanded unconditional and immediate Israeli withdrawal. But Britain and France were to withdraw "immediately" in accordance with earlier resolutions which included creation of a UN force to secure and supervise the cease-fire and withdrawal. Thus Pearson could say in the debate that "in our minds there is a relationship implicit in the word 'immediately' between the withdrawal of the forces referred to in the resolution and the arrival and functioning of the UN force." [1]

In a somewhat bizarre episode, the British and French representatives were instructed to vote for the Emergency Force resolution despite the fundamental differences in its mandate and composition from what their governments had wanted. Ignoring the clear language and intent of the resolution and of Hammarskjöld's report, Sir Pierson Dixon repeated his government's conditions of the day before and declared the force should remain in the area until the Suez Canal and Palestine questions were settled. For France, de Guiringaud went all the way back to Léon Bourgeois in 1919 to claim French parentage for the idea of an international force and promised withdrawal as soon as the Emergency Force was "in a position to carry out the vital missions we are performing." [2]

When the vote came, the Emergency Force resolution was adopted 64 to 0 with 12 abstentions. The latter included only the Soviet bloc, Egypt, Israel, and South Africa. The withdrawal resolution then carried by 65 to 1 with 10 abstentions. Israel's was the only negative vote and the abstainers included Britain, France, Australia, New Zealand, Belgium, the Netherlands, Luxembourg, Portugal, Laos, and South Africa. After the vote V. V. Kuznetsov declared that creation of the Force by the Assembly was contrary to the Charter and the Soviet Union had abstained only because Egypt, the victim of aggression, had been compelled to agree to the Force. No attempt was made to reconcile this position on the constitutional issue with the Polish proposal to add Czechoslovakia to the Advisory Committee and the Czech and Romanian offers of contingents.

The texts of the two resolutions were as follows:

Resolution 1001 (ES-I) of November 7, 1956

The General Assembly,

Recalling its resolution 997 (ES-I) of November 2, 1956, concerning the cease-fire, withdrawal of troops and other matters related to the

[1] *Ibid.* [2] *Ibid.*

military operations in Egyptian territory, as well as its resolution 998 (ES-I) of November 4, 1956, concerning the request to the Secretary-General to submit a plan for an emergency international United Nations Force,

Having established by its resolution 1000 (ES-I) of November 5, 1956, a United Nations Command for an emergency international Force, having appointed the Chief of Staff of the United Nations Truce Supervision Organization as Chief of the Command with authorization to him to begin the recruitment of officers for the Command, and having invited the Secretary-General to take the administrative measures necessary for the prompt execution of that resolution,

Noting with appreciation the second and final report of the Secretary-General (A/3302) on the plan for an emergency international United Nations Force as requested in General Assembly resolution 998 (ES-I), and having examined that plan,

1. *Expresses its approval* of the guiding principles for the organization and functioning of the emergency international United Nations Force as expounded in paragraphs 6 to 9 of the Secretary-General's report;

2. *Concurs* in the definition of the functions of the Force as stated in paragraph 12 of the Secretary-General's report;

3. *Invites* the Secretary-General to continue discussions with governments of Member states concerning offers of participation in the Force, toward the objective of its balanced composition;

4. *Requests* the Chief of the Command, in consultation with the Secretary-General as regards size and composition, to proceed forthwith with the full organization of the Force;

5. *Approves provisionally* the basic rule concerning the financing of the Force laid down in paragraph 15 of the Secretary-General's report;

6. *Establishes* an Advisory Committee composed of one representative from each of the following countries: Brazil, Canada, Ceylon, Colombia, India, Norway, and Pakistan, and requests this Committee, whose Chairman shall be the Secretary-General, to undertake the development of those aspects of the planning for the Force and its operation not already dealt with by the General Assembly and which do not fall within the area of the direct responsibility of the Chief of the Command;

7. *Authorizes* the Secretary-General to issue all regulations and instructions which may be essential to the effective functioning of the Force, following consultation with the Committee aforementioned, and to take all other necessary administrative and executive action;

8. *Determines* that, following the fulfillment of the immediate responsibilities defined for it in operative paragraphs 6 and 7 above, the Advisory Committee shall continue to assist the Secretary-General in the responsibilities falling to him under the present and other relevant resolutions;

9. *Decides* that the Advisory Committee, in the performance of its duties, shall be empowered to request, through the usual procedures, the convening of the General Assembly and to report to the Assembly whenever matters arise which, in its opinion, are of such urgency and importance as to require consideration by the General Assembly itself;

10. *Requests* all Member states to afford assistance as necessary to the United Nations Command in the performance of its functioning, including arrangements for passage to and from the area involved.

Resolution 1002 (ES-I) of November 7, 1956

The General Assembly,

Recalling its resolutions 997 (ES-I) of November 2, 1956, 998 (ES-I) and 999 (ES-I) of November 4, 1956, and 1000 (ES-I) of November 5, 1956, adopted by overwhelming majorities,

Noting in particular that the General Assembly, by its resolution 1000 (ES-I), established a United Nations Command for an emergency international Force to secure and supervise the cessation of hostilities in accordance with all the terms of its resolution 997 (ES-I),

1. *Reaffirms* the above-mentioned resolutions;

2. *Calls once again upon* Israel immediately to withdraw all its forces behind the armistice lines established by the General Armistice Agreement between Egypt and Israel of February 24, 1949;

3. *Calls once again upon* the United Kingdom and France immediately to withdraw all their forces from Egyptian territory, consistently with the above-mentioned resolutions;

4. *Urges* the Secretary-General to communicate the present resolution to the parties concerned, and requests him promptly to report to the General Assembly on the compliance with this resolution.

---

10. Letter to the Secretary of State for Foreign Affairs of the United Kingdom

NOVEMBER 7, 1956

IMMEDIATELY after the Assembly had acted to carry into effect the Secretary-General's second report on the United Nations Emergency Force he addressed identical messages to the United Kingdom and France in reply to theirs of the day before. The text of the message to Selwyn Lloyd follows

General Assembly Official Records, First Emergency Special Session, Annexes, Document A/3314, November 7, 1956.

below. Hammarskjöld's pointed reference to the wholly negative and defiant attitude toward the projected Force expressed at this time by Israel, their partner in the Suez enterprise, may be especially noted. If this attitude were maintained the avenue of retreat chosen by Britain and France would be jeopardized. There were other powerful pressures at work on the Israeli government. Its had been the only negative vote on the withdrawal resolution; Britain and France both voted for the United Nations Force and Israel now found itself without any support at all for its stand on this issue. On the United States side President Eisenhower sent Ben-Gurion a very strong private message.[1]

After a nine-hour Cabinet meeting Foreign Minister Golda Meir sent word to Hammarskjöld on November 8 "that the Government of Israel will willingly withdraw its forces from Egypt immediately upon the conclusion of satisfactory arrangements with the United Nations in connection with the emergency international Force." She then repeated, "without prejudice to this undertaking," the five demands upon Egypt Israel had advanced on November 4 (page 333) and urgently requested the United Nations "to call upon Egypt" to meet these demands.[2]

As soon as he received the cable from Mrs. Meir the Secretary-General called in the correspondents to put the new commitment on public record without delay, just as he had done with the United Kingdom's message two days before (second following text).

I have the honour to acknowledge receipt, in reply to my communication, dated November 5, (A/3310), of your message dated November 6 (A/3307), transmitted to me by letter from the permanent representative of the United Kingdom the same day.

I note the wish of Her Majesty's Government to have my confirmation on three points, referred to in the letter.

Messages stating acceptance of an unconditional cease-fire have been received from the governments of Egypt and Israel. These messages have been circulated as General Assembly documents. I gave, immediately, verbal confirmation of these acceptances. The governments of Egypt and Israel were informed about the confirmation thus given. I now wish to repeat it to you in writing.

The General Assembly this afternoon approved a resolution fully implementing the recommendations in my second and final report on an

[1] Eisenhower, *Waging Peace,* p. 94.
[2] General Assembly Official Records, First Emergency Special Session, Annexes, Document A/3320, November 8, 1956.

emergency international United Nations Force (A/3302). It is my conviction, in the light of the promises of participation received from various Member governments, that the Force, when established in accordance with the General Assembly resolution now adopted, will be capable of the tasks assigned to it under the resolution of November 2.

I have in this context to draw attention to a statement of the Prime Minister of Israel, Mr. Ben-Gurion, in his address to the Knesset on November 7. According to a report received from the Chief of the United Nations Command, the Prime Minister in this statement declared that "the armistice lines between Israel and Egypt have no validity," and "on no account will Israel agree to the stationing of a foreign force, no matter how called, in her territory or in any of the areas occupied by her."

This position, if maintained in violation of the resolutions of the General Assembly on these matters, while not affecting the cease-fire arrangement, would seriously complicate the task of carrying out the resolution of November 2, 1956.

I shall as soon as possible revert to your offer to assist in the technical work to be undertaken in order to reopen the Suez Canal. At present I am exploring the possibility of undertaking this task under United Nations auspices through agents from nations not engaged in the present conflict.

DAG HAMMARSKJÖLD
Secretary-General

11. Transcript of Remarks to the Press

UN HEADQUARTERS, NEW YORK   NOVEMBER 8, 1956

THE SECRETARY-GENERAL: . . . . There are only two points I would like to draw to your attention so that there is no misunderstanding. The second half of the letter which I read to you brought again to attention certain hopes and demands of the Israeli government. But you should

UN Note to Correspondents No. 1439, November 8, 1956.

note that these viewpoints are introduced in the letter after the declaration, that it is done without prejudice to the undertaking; that is to say, there is no condition in this second part of the letter.

As to the first part of the letter, I think it is self-explanatory. I would however indicate that when you read it, you should observe that the declaration of willingness to withdraw Israeli forces from Egypt is said to be "immediately upon the conclusion of satisfactory arrangements with the United Nations in connection with the emergency international force." I read this sentence as clearly implying acceptance of that United Nations force.

That, I think, is all for today. I would, however, like to point out that with this communication on the table, and what has happened on the steps in these negotiations, we have arrived at a point where a new phase should be possible, a new phase should begin.

QUESTION: Mr. Secretary-General, how soon should the new force be arriving on the scene?

THE SECRETARY-GENERAL: I may have the pleasure of meeting you in this way again very shortly.

ISRAEL was not alone in continuing efforts to win some political advantage from the resort to force. On November 7 Eden telephoned Eisenhower proposing that he and Mollet should come at once to Washington for talks. Eisenhower was at first receptive, then pulled back after consulting his advisers. Eden's purpose, of course, was to try to salvage something, but the United States position remained firm. France and the United Kingdom must first carry out the UN resolutions, and this meant withdrawal as well as cease-fire. Until this happened the United States was equally opposed to the British-French proposal for a Security Council meeting at the foreign ministers' level to take up settlements of the Arab-Israeli and Suez Canal questions and nothing came of this proposal.

Britain and France also met a cool preliminary rebuff to their proposal to start clearing the Suez Canal in the concluding words of Hammarskjöld's November 7 letter, in which he stated that he was "exploring the possibility of undertaking this task under United Nations auspices through agents from nations not engaged in the present conflict."

* * *

The United Nations Emergency Force approved by the General Assembly would be the first of its kind in history. There was no previous experience on which to draw, all arrangements had to be improvised, commitments would be required for which there were no precedents. All this presented a host of policy questions and practical problems for the United Nations, for the Members offering contingents or other assistance, and for Egypt in admitting this brand new international presence on its territory.

In such circumstances even the fastest-paced and surest-footed leadership would need weeks to complete the necessary negotiations and the tasks of transport and organization. But it was essential to bring the first contingents of the UN Emergency Force into Egypt in a matter of days, not weeks, to start the process of withdrawal at the earliest possible moment, and to preserve the shaky cease-fire. Egypt had accepted the November 5 UN Command resolution, but the next day, when the British-French forces proceeded with the occupation of Ports Said and Fuad, its government had issued a general appeal for volunteers, arms, and other assistance to expel the invaders. Britain and France, on the other hand, while agreeing to the cease-fire, had refused to withdraw until the UN Emergency Force was in position and capable of assuming the functions assigned to it.

Beginning on November 7, the Secretary-General concentrated all the resources he could muster—his own skills and high standing with the governments, the best abilities of the Secretariat, with Ralph J. Bunche and Andrew W. Cordier assigned the leading roles, the essential aid of key delegates working with him—to start contingents on the way and to reach agreement with Egypt on their entry. As he had done in the spring of 1956 he used publicity in support of private diplomacy for the goals he sought.

His first move was a message to the Egyptian government, on which he promptly issued a press release. The press release was as follows:

> The Secretary-General announced today that he has sent a message to the Egyptian government through its Permanent Representative to the United Nations, Omar Loutfi.
>
> In his message, the Secretary-General, referring to decisions of the General Assembly and noting the acceptance by Egypt of the establishment of a United Nations force [i.e., the November 5 UN Command resolution—EDITORS], informed the Egyptian government that a decision putting the United Nations force into operation could be effected without any delay by a call on a number of governments to send contingents.
>
> The Secretary-General asked for an immediate reply to the question of whether Egypt would raise objections against participation of troops from any of the designated countries in the force to be stationed on Egyptian territory in fulfillment of the prescribed tasks.
>
> The Secretary-General asked Mr. Loutfi to transmit this message with the greatest possible urgency.
>
> In his message, the Secretary-General said that immediately on receipt of the reply of the Egyptian government he would address a request to the governments of the nations mentioned for the quickest possible execution.
>
> The Secretary-General said that he would keep the Egyptian govern-

ment informed about further developments and would appreciate an immediate planning in consultation with General E. L. M. Burns as Chief of the United Nations Command for the stationing of the projected force. He added that he would await the advice of General Burns on the size and character of the troops immediately necessary.[1]

The message itself remained confidential but the press release was a generally close paraphrase, the main difference being the omission of the names of the "designated countries." These were Canada, Colombia, Denmark, Finland, Norway, and Sweden. It was too soon to make this list public. The Secretary-General wished to give Egypt a chance to react in private and the advice of General Burns, as stated in the press release, was also awaited.

Immediately after the Assembly adjourned in the evening of November 7, the Secretary-General called the Advisory Committee together for its first meeting. It was agreed that Hammarskjöld should proceed as rapidly as possible with organizing the Force and arranging for transportation of advance units to Egypt while simultaneously pursuing his negotiations with the latter on their entry.

Over the next four days the Secretary-General, with wholehearted cooperation from governments to whom he turned for assistance, directed a dazzling demonstration of speed and improvisation in starting the UN Force on its way.

The United States was ready to assist with the airlift but a staging area where elements of the Force and supplies for them could be assembled was lacking. On November 8, Hammarskjöld turned to the Italian government, which responded within twelve hours by making available the Capodichino airport near Naples.

The Assembly had excluded the permanent members of the Security Council from UNEF (the United Nations Emergency Force) and talk of direct Soviet assistance to Egypt was still in the air. For these reasons the use of U.S. military planes and crews to fly the rest of the way to Egypt was ruled out. With the approval and assistance of the Swiss federal government the Secretary-General concluded on November 9 an agreement with Swissair to provide its DC-6's for the Naples to Egypt leg, starting November 12.

The U.S. Military Air Transport Service C-124's began arriving at Capodichino with advance UNEF contingents on November 10, first the Danes and Norwegians, then the Colombians, airlifted from Bogotá. Indian participation in UNEF was now confirmed and the United States agreed to airlift an advance unit of the Indian battalion all the way from Agra. All these developments were announced to the press as they occurred.

At Hammarskjöld's request General Burns flew to Cairo on November 8 for direct talks on the arrival of UNEF. His white-painted UN C-47 was the first plane to land since the Anglo-French bombing of Egyptian airfields.

[1] UN Press Release SG/519, November 7, 1956.

He was promptly and courteously received by Foreign Minister Fawzi and President Nasser but immediately encountered problems. The Egyptian government, always highly sensitive about the protection of Egypt's sovereignty, was all the more so since the Anglo-French-Israeli invasion. Furthermore, statements by some of the Western delegates during the Assembly's UNEF debate on November 7 had aroused fears that the Force might after all somehow be turned into an instrument of pressure against Egypt in settling the Suez Canal dispute. These fears in turn influenced the initial Egyptian attitude toward some of the national contingents proposed for the Force.

During the next three days there was an exchange of messages between the Secretary-General, General Burns, and the Egyptian leaders on the composition of the Force and on other questions concerning its deployment and the duration of its presence that troubled the Egyptians. In sharp contrast to the publicity given to each step in the assembly and transport of UNEF, the United Nations kept this exchange confidential and gave no official publicity to the difficulties encountered, though more or less well-informed rumors leaked out from other sources.

Hammarskjöld considered that decisions on establishment and organization of the Force were not subject to conditions by Egypt. On the other hand Egypt's consent was required, under international law, for the entry and stationing on its territory of each of the national contingents included in the Force. Soon after his arrival in Cairo, General Burns (himself a Canadian) reported to Hammarskjöld Nasser's unhappiness over the inclusion of Canadian soldiers in the Force, giving as his reason that they owed allegiance to the same Queen as the British invaders in Port Said and wore British-type uniforms; the Egyptian people would not understand the difference and there might be ugly incidents. A later message from Cairo gave Egypt's consent to Colombian, Swedish, and Finnish units and suggested adding Yugoslavia and Indonesia (which had offered to contribute forces on November 8 and 10 respectively) as countries not militarily allied to the Anglo-French "aggressors." This left out Norway and Denmark as well as Canada, all members of NATO.

Hammarskjöld reacted in the strongest terms. He could not possibly agree to exclude Canada, Norway, and Denmark. Membership in NATO was irrelevant, since all units of the Force would be under the exclusive authority of the General Assembly, the Secretary-General and the United Nations Commander. He warned of the serious consequences for Egypt and for the whole enterprise if he were forced to bring into the open his differences with Egypt on this matter. He agreed however, to adding Yugoslav and Indonesian units to the Force. Nasser responded on November 12 by agreeing to Norwegian and Danish units but the question of Canadian troops remained unresolved. By this time the Secretary-General had determined to go to Cairo himself with the first UNEF contingents in an effort to resolve other pending questions and he now added the Canadian issue to his list.

The exchange of private messages between November 8 and 12 also concerned three questions about United Nations intentions on the status and functions of the Force after its admission to Egypt, questions about which Nasser and Fawzi requested assurances from Hammarskjöld.

The Egyptian leaders wished to be sure that UNEF could not become an instrument of pressure in settling the dispute over operation of the Suez Canal by remaining in the Canal Zone after the British and French withdrew. The Secretary-General replied that the legislative record made clear the Assembly's intention that UNEF would follow the Israeli withdrawal to the armistice demarcation line and would have no further function in the Canal Zone except for the use of a staging area by agreement with Egypt.

Egypt also wished to be sure that the positions eventually occupied on the Egyptian side of the armistice demarcation line by UNEF would be subject to its agreement. Hammarskjöld's answer was "Yes."

The third question was more difficult: Once admitted to Egypt how long might UNEF stay there? The Egyptian government sought a flat United Nations commitment to withdraw the Force if Egypt no longer consented to its presence. Juridically Egypt was on solid ground. The Assembly had recognized that the consent of Egypt was necessary to the entry and presence of UNEF and Hammarskjöld agreed that the Force could not stay unless Egypt continued to consent. But the Secretary-General sought to link the question of withdrawal to completion of the tasks defined for the Force in the November 5 resolution which Egypt had accepted. If a difference should arise as to whether or not UNEF had completed the mission for which Egypt had consented to its entry, the matter should be negotiated with the United Nations.

By November 12 Hammarskjöld had not received any direct reaction on this proviso from the Egyptian leaders, who were standing firm on their sovereign right to withdraw consent. In the meantime the Secretary-General had sent several personal messages to Nasser and Fawzi stressing the dangers of any further delay on Egypt's part. Finally, on November 12 they sent word that Hammarskjöld could announce agreement on the arrival of the UN Force with the understanding that Egypt reserved its position on its rights concerning composition of the Force, that Egypt's consent was necessary to its entry and presence in any part of its territory, that the Force would leave if consent were withdrawn, and that the Force would have no function in the Canal area after British-French withdrawal. On the same day General Burns had brought to Cairo the UNTSO officers who were to serve as his nucleus headquarters staff and Nasser designated a high-ranking Egyptian staff officer, Brigadier Amin Helmy, to serve as chief liaison officer with UNEF. They agreed that Abu Suweir, an airfield with extensive barracks near Ismailia, bombed by the British but still serviceable, would be most suitable for the reception of UNEF.

Despite the remaining gaps between his views and Egypt's the Secretary-General decided to go ahead with the announcement. He considered it essential to get the first UN units into Egypt at once and equally essential that he go himself at the same time to talk out the unresolved problems face to face with Nasser and Fawzi. The most troublesome question, Egypt's right to withdraw consent to UNEF's presence, he had to recognize as a sovereign right, but he sent a private note to Fawzi amplifying his position that the exercise of this right, before the tasks that the Assembly had prescribed had been completed, would run counter to Egypt's acceptance of the resolution and that any differences on this point should be negotiated.

He then called the press together and read the announcement in the text that follows. He deliberately played down the subjects of his discussions in Cairo as "details," a considerable understatement. To suggest publicly that these problems were serious would only add to the hazards of a venture that already carried more than enough. His carefully worded statement, in response to a question, that the great powers, despite their differences, were "obviously" agreed "to let me try to see what I can do about it," was in the same vein.

The Secretary-General also used this press conference to announce his first appointments to the Investigation and Observer Groups under the General Assembly's November 4 resolution on Hungary. This part of the conference is covered in the grouping of texts and commentary on the Hungarian question (pages 418–24).

From Transcript of Press Conference

UN HEADQUARTERS, NEW YORK   NOVEMBER 12, 1956

THE SECRETARY-GENERAL: Well, ladies and gentlemen, I want to give you some information concerning the two major issues which the General Assembly has been discussing recently, and concerning which I have certain personal responsibilities.

Any minute now you will have in your hands a press release on which I should like to give you a few comments. I will, however, first read it, as I do not think that it has been distributed. It reads:

Agreement on the arrival in Egypt of the United Nations Force has been reached between the Secretary-General and the Egyptian government. The first groups of the United Nations Force will go to Egypt early this week. It is the intention of the Secretary-General to visit Cairo at the very first stage of the operation for discussions of details with the Egyptian government. He will also inspect the staging area for the United Nations Force in Italy.

As concerns the timetable, there is the technical possibility, which I think we will use, to send in the first contingent tomorrow afternoon. I intend myself to leave New York tomorrow afternoon and to arrive in Cairo Thursday morning for a maximum stay of two days and then to be back here on Sunday. We are revising the travel plans of General Burns so that he will meet me in Rome; we will have time for consultations. He is likely to continue after those consultations to New York for consultations with the experts over here. In this way we will manage to combine my talks in Cairo with the direct contact between General Burns and myself in Rome and his contacts here in New York without any breaking up or breaking down of the timetable.

For the rest, I do not think that I have anything to add on this issue. If you have any questions of a factual nature, I will be happy to tell you what I can tell you. I do not think that this is the proper occasion for any discussion of the very many issues of a more general nature which are implied in this operation. Anyway, for what it is worth, I give you a chance to plague me for a moment.

QUESTION: I do not know whether, historically, a newspaperman would be out of order to say what I am saying now, but I think that the

UN Note to Correspondents No. 1447, November 12, 1956.

United Nations press, no less than any other segment of the world, feels that we owe you thanks for your contribution to peace and to the life of the United Nations.

As to my question, I should like to know whether you are going to Cairo in order to clarify for Colonel Nasser the function and the purposes of the emergency force.

THE SECRETARY-GENERAL: I thank you, of course, for your generous words. Whatever has been done in this case is of course the work of very, very many, and for that reason I should like to pass your words on to all those who have cooperated.

As to the second point, I would explain it in this way. It is, as you know, the first time in history that a truly international force has been set up. Egypt is the first country with which all the technical arrangements necessary in such a case have to be made. It is but natural that in such an initial stage —which should not be experimental and which should be a success—I am rather anxious to see to it that there are no unnecessary loose ends, and for that reason you may see my going there not as an expression of any kind of uncertainties or difficulties, or of any need for explanations, but just simply to see to it that to the extent that it is in my power, this will get the start it deserves and set a precedent which the United Nations needs.

QUESTION: Are you likely during your trip to confer with other military or political leaders of the Franco-British forces on the one hand and the Israelis on the other, so as to be able to coordinate the withdrawals with the taking over by the United Nations police force?

THE SECRETARY-GENERAL: That is staff work, and for that reason is entirely under the authority of General Burns. It does not fall within the scope of what I am going to do.

QUESTION: I wonder if you can tell us what nations thus far have volunteered to serve in the United Nations police force.

THE SECRETARY-GENERAL: I think you must have a whole library of letters by this time, and I really cannot sit here and enumerate them. But you can get them from the documents, because we have circulated every single offer as a General Assembly document.

QUESTION: Will you go to Hungary at any time on this trip? We have had a dispatch from Budapest which stated that Cardinal Mindszenty had suggested you might come to Hungary?

THE SECRETARY-GENERAL: May I revert to the question of Hungary at a later stage, during the second part of this press conference?

QUESTION: Has it been agreed where the first contingent of United Nations forces will be stationed?

THE SECRETARY-GENERAL: That is a technical matter on which discussions are at a very advanced stage, but where I should not like to go into details.

QUESTION: I have one more question on the Middle East. I have a dispatch from Burma stating that their offer was not accepted and that therefore they will not contribute any men to this force. I wonder what might be the situation?

THE SECRETARY-GENERAL: I do not remember exactly if there has been any offer. At all events, I can tell you frankly there has been no refusal. I have not refused any contributions, as every offer represents that much of a moral support and for that reason is most helpful. But, on the other hand, it will be seen that there will be practical considerations coming into play. It has been said that there should be a balanced composition, and that means there must be a selection in order to arrive at a balanced composition, with a reasonably limited and, at the same time, a reasonably representative number of participants. If we had, let us say, some twenty offers, then even those of us who have only been privates can understand that the staff work would be completely impossible if we had all the twenty units mixed up. I think that Mr. Fry [*Christian Science Monitor*] had another question.

QUESTION: No, that has already been answered.

QUESTION: Will the British, French, and Israeli troops begin withdrawing tomorrow afternoon with the arrival of the first contingent of the international force?

THE SECRETARY-GENERAL: I think you should direct that question to those who are responsible for that part of the operation.

QUESTION: This international police force is a formula which I think must have the backing of all the great powers, but the great powers are divided now as they never were before. As a matter of fact, they are in war and instigating some of these tensions. Of course they are throwing everything on your lap. They are saying "Let George do it. Let Mr. Dag Hammarskjöld handle it." My questions are two. Why have not the great powers been included in the police force? It is better to keep them there so that we can watch them. The second question is: The Secretary-Generalship is getting to be more political than administrative. Of course, an American political pundit[1] has said this, and I agree with

[1] Walter Lippman.

him: "Fortunately, the management of the undertaking is in the hands of Mr. Dag Hammarskjöld, as competent, as cool, as astute, and as objective a diplomat as we have seen for many a long day."

But to me it seems that they are sort of making you, if there is a failure, a scapegoat for this whole thing.

THE SECRETARY-GENERAL: We should not be losing our time concerning what may be my personal troubles or my personal merits. I can tell you one thing, that if it would in any way help the United Nations for me to be a scapegoat, I would be quite happy to be one. The other thing I should like to point out is that you have exaggerated some of the dissent and difference of views between the big powers, because obviously they are agreed, and I can register that in the current cooperation, to let me try to see what I can do about it.

. . . .

THE NEXT DAY, November 13, the Secretary-General postponed his departure for two reasons. On November 12 the Hungarian government had cabled him rejecting the dispatch of observers to Hungary but welcoming humanitarian assistance from the United Nations. Hammarskjöld decided to act on this opening and on November 13 made an oral offer to the Hungarian Foreign Minister, Imre Horvath, who was in New York, to go personally to Budapest for discussions on the basis of United Nations humanitarian activities in the country (see page 423). It was announced to the press that he had postponed his departure in hope of an early reply.

There was a second reason, which was not announced. A cable arrived from Fawzi rejecting the Secretary-General's stand on the question of UNEF withdrawal as an infringement of Egyptian sovereignty, and suspending Egypt's agreement to the entry of UNEF until any misunderstanding was cleared up. Hammarskjöld replied immediately that Egypt had indeed misunderstood. Neither he nor the Assembly questioned Egypt's sovereign right to give or withdraw consent to the presence of UNEF. He had simply pointed out that a withdrawal of consent before the completion of the tasks set for UNEF, though within Egypt's rights, would go against its acceptance of the Assembly's resolution. If there were a difference of opinion on whether the tasks had been completed this should, in his opinion, be a matter for discussion with the Secretary-General. He had introduced no new condition to the exercise of Egypt's sovereign right but it was necessary to reserve his own freedom to react should the way in which Egypt exerted that right seem to him contrary to its acceptance of a force with the missions defined by the Assembly. He was quite willing to discuss the matter when he came to Cairo, but he would not come before Egypt gave the green light to the first UNEF contingents and he hoped this could now be done at once. If not he would have to bring the issue before the Assembly, where the political repercussions were likely to be most unfavorable to Egypt.

This explanation broke the threatening deadlock. On November 14 Fawzi sent a message reactivating Egypt's agreement to the arrival of UNEF, provided Egypt's sovereign rights were fully respected. Hammarskjöld immediately called the UNEF Advisory Committee together, reviewed with them his exchanges with the Egyptian government, and received their approval for proceeding with deployment of the Force on the basis of the understandings reached so far. By now there were 650 UNEF officers and men at Capodichino from Denmark, Norway, Colombia, and Canada, with 350 more due from India, Colombia, and Sweden by the end of the week. General Burns had flown in also for his first sight of the men he would command. He was ordered to start moving the first units to Abu Suweir and on November 15 Danish and Norwegian contingents arrived in Egypt aboard the Swissair DC-6's. Hammarskjöld flew to Capodichino, conferred with General Burns, and then flew on to Abu Suweir on November 16 with the advance Colombian contingent. General Burns proceeded to New York and the Secretary-General to Cairo for his talks with Nasser and Fawzi.

Before Hammarskjöld's departure from Headquarters it was announced that the reply from the Hungarian government to his offer to go to Budapest for talks on United Nations relief and humanitarian programs would be forwarded to him when received and that he might go to Budapest on his return journey from Cairo if the reply were favorable and arrangements could be made. The reply turned out to be an offer to meet him in Rome, not Budapest, and Hammarskjöld replied that in that case it would be better to pursue the talks in New York (see also pages 423–24).

The Secretary-General held extensive talks with Nasser and Fawzi in Cairo November 16 to 18. He had three major objectives: to win Egyptian consent to the presence in Egypt of Canadian units in UNEF; to reach an agreed basis for United Nations assistance in clearing the Suez Canal; finally, and most important, to reach an agreement in principle on the basis for the presence and functioning of UNEF in Egypt.

The Canadian Defense Ministry had chosen an infantry battalion from a famous regiment, The Queen's Own Rifles, for service with UNEF, and was preparing to send them aboard the aircraft carrier *Magnificent* from Halifax. The choice could not have been more unfortunate in view of Nasser's argument against Canadian participation because they served the same Queen as the British invaders and his people would not understand the difference. In Cairo Hammarskjöld was able to win Egyptian consent to Canadian air transport, and technical and administrative personnel, but not to infantry.

General Burns, meanwhile, had come to New York to plan organization of the Force. It was immediately evident that there was an oversupply of available infantry units while there was a severe undersupply of engineers, signal corps, transport and maintenance units, ordnance specialists, and the like, which Canada was in by far the best position to supply quickly. General Burns wrote a letter to Pearson stating his opinion as Commander that this was the most urgently required and valuable contribution Canada could make. The Queen's Own Rifles returned to base and the Canadian government was embarrassed. However, the Canadian contingent soon became the largest in UNEF and General Burns wrote later that the "supporting troops Canada provided then and subsequently were absolutely essential, and the Force could not have operated without them." [1]

Agreement with Egypt on United Nations assistance in clearing the Suez Canal was reached quickly and is dealt with on page 383.

Hammarskjöld's most difficult problem was to find a formula for the presence and functioning of UNEF in Egypt under which the Egyptian government would accept a political restriction upon the exercise of its legally unrestricted right to request and obtain withdrawal of UNEF.

At the Advisory Committee meeting on November 14, just before Hammarskjöld left for Cairo, one of the members had expressed concern over what might happen if Egypt, having admitted UNEF for the purpose of securing the peaceful withdrawal of the invaders, should then decide to change its policy and resume active resistance. The Secretary-General had responded as follows: "You touched there upon one of those things which have to be considered in thinking out the trend of this policy. If we cannot base the United Nations action on a reasonable degree of *good faith* [italics added—EDITORS] then, of course, we have embarked on an extremely dangerous adventure."

The formula Hammarskjöld decided to use consisted of interlocking "good faith" declarations by Egypt and the United Nations which committed both sides to completion of the tasks set for UNEF under the General Assembly's November 5 resolution. He sat up most of the night of November 15/16 at Capodichino drafting the "Aide-Mémoire" in the first following text, to which he won Egypt's agreement with minor changes after difficult and lengthy discussions over the next two days in Cairo.

Some eight months later—August 5, 1957—he dictated a memorandum for his private files, headed "aide-mémoire," recalling the main steps in his exchanges with the Egyptian government on the question of UNEF withdrawal and giving his interpretation of exactly what the "good faith" agreement meant for Egypt—and for the United Nations. The Secretary-General prepared this memorandum for his private use at the time because of recurrent disputes and misunderstandings over the respective rights of Egypt and the United Nations in the matter of withdrawal.

A copy was published in June 1967 after the Six Day War which followed the withdrawal of UNEF at Egypt's request.[2] It does not have the status of an agreed interpretation, of course, but it is included here as the sec-

---

[1] Burns, *Between Arab and Israeli*, p. 215.

[2] The copy had been given to Ernest A. Gross, a former deputy U.S. Representative to the United Nations, who served as a legal consultant to Hammarskjöld from time to time after his return to private law practice.

ond following text because it provides the most authoritative possible commentary on how Hammarskjöld himself viewed the "good faith" agreement in the summer of 1957. The extent of its applicability to the situation that prevailed ten years later became a matter of controversy which need not concern us here.

The Secretary-General discussed and cleared with the UNEF Advisory Committee his report on the "good faith" agreement as well as a second report on the clearance of the Suez Canal (third following text) before submitting them to the General Assembly. The clearance report was carefully framed in terms of a United Nations response to a request by Egypt for assistance in reopening the Canal and of the wish of the Egyptian government that the work begin immediately after the British and French had withdrawn from Port Said and the Canal area. To get going, the Secretary-General proposed requesting the General Assembly to adopt a procedure inverting the usual order. Before any estimate of the cost could be made the Assembly would authorize him, in consultation with the UNEF Advisory Committee, to conclude preliminary agreements for the undertaking with salvage firms, including such financial commitments as were unavoidable. Only later, after a survey had been made of the extent of the damage and the probable costs, would he return to the Assembly for the necessary financial decisions. The question of how the costs should be shared, which was bound to be controversial, he would leave until then. He would approach only salvage firms in countries outside the conflict, thus ruling out putting the United Nations flag on the Anglo-French salvage fleet now assembling in Port Said, but he left the way open for taking over some of its equipment later if it were needed.

Just as with UNEF, the Assembly would thus be asked to commit the United Nations to a course of action before it knew the costs or how they would be shared. The request was bold and unorthodox and suitable only in an emergency. Hammarskjöld believed, correctly, that a large majority would support him because reopening the Canal was so important to so many and this was the only way it could be undertaken promptly, since the British and French were politically unacceptable both to Egypt and the Assembly majority. The Secretary-General was aware that the problems of financing both UNEF and the Canal clearance would be difficult at best but he believed that under the circumstances they could and should be confronted only after the United Nations was firmly committed by policy decisions to the course it had chosen. The UNEF Advisory Committee accepted his judgment.

While he was in Cairo Hammarskjöld had asked how the Egyptian government now stood on his letter of October 24 suggesting a framework within which settlement of the Suez Canal dispute might be sought. He was told that Fawzi's affirmative reply of November 2 still stood. The Secretary-General privately informed the Advisory Committee and some other delegates of this reaffirmation but made no public statement about it.

Report to the General Assembly on Basic Points for the Presence and Functioning in Egypt of the United Nations Emergency Force

UN HEADQUARTERS, NEW YORK   NOVEMBER 20, 1956

1. After the adoption, November 7, 1956, by the General Assembly of resolution 1001 (ES-I) concerning the establishment of the United Nations Emergency Force, the Government of Egypt was immediately approached by the Secretary-General through the Commander of the Force, Major General E. L. M. Burns, in order to prepare the ground for a prompt implementation of the resolution.

2. The Government of Egypt had, prior to the final decision of the General Assembly, accepted the Force in principle by formally accepting the preceding resolution 1000 (ES-I) on the establishment of a United Nations Command. Before consenting to the arrival of the Force, the Government of Egypt wished to have certain points in the resolutions of the General Assembly clarified. An exchange of views took place between the Secretary-General and the Government of Egypt in which the Secretary-General, in reply to questions addressed to him by the Government of Egypt, gave his interpretations of the relevant General Assembly resolutions, in respect of the character and functions of the Force. At the end of the exchange, he gave to the Advisory Committee set up by General Assembly resolution 1001 (ES-I), a full account of the interpretations given. Approving these interpretations, the Advisory Committee recommended that the Secretary-General should proceed to start the transfer of the United Nations Emergency Force.

3. On the basis of the resolutions, as interpreted by the Secretary-General, the Government of Egypt consented to the arrival of the United Nations Force in Egypt. The first transport of troops took place on November 15, 1956.

4. While the Secretary-General found that the exchange of views which had taken place was sufficient as a basis for the sending of the

General Assembly Official Records, Eleventh Session, Annexes, Volume II, agenda item 66, Document A / 3375, November 20, 1956.

first units, he felt, on the other hand, that a firmer foundation had to be laid for the presence and functioning of the Force in Egypt and for the continued cooperation with the Egyptian authorities. For that reason, and also because he considered it essential personally to discuss with the Egyptian authorities certain questions which flowed from the decision to send the Force, after visiting the staging area of the Force in Naples, he went to Cairo, where he stayed from November 16 until 18. On his way to Cairo he stopped briefly at the first staging area in Egypt, at Abu Suweir.

5. In Cairo he discussed with the President and the Foreign Minister of Egypt basic points for the presence and functioning of the Force in Egypt. Time obviously did not permit a detailed study of the various legal, technical, and administrative arrangements which would have to be made and the exchange of views was therefore related only to questions of principle.

6. The Secretary-General wishes to inform the General Assembly of the main results of these discussions. They are summarized in an *"Aide-mémoire* on the basis for presence and functioning of the United Nations Emergency Force in Egypt," submitted as an annex to this report.

7. The text of this *aide-mémoire,* if noted with approval by the General Assembly, with the concurrence of Egypt, would establish an understanding between the United Nations and Egypt, on which the cooperation could be developed and necessary agreements on various details be elaborated. The text, as it stands, is presented on the responsibility of the Secretary-General. It has the approval of the Government of Egypt.

8. The Secretary-General, in this context, submits below a few indications as to the numerical development of the Force.

9. As of November 20, 1956, a total number of 696 were at the staging area in Egypt at Abu Suweir. At the same time a total number of 282 were at the staging area in Italy at Naples. According to the present planning a total number of 2,241 will be transferred to Egypt in the immediate future. A further number of 1,260 are to be transferred to Naples or directly to Egypt at times still to be determined.

10. The extensive practical arrangements, necessary for a successful development of the Force and its activities, are making progress. A report on the situation in this and other technically relevant respects will be presented to the General Assembly as soon as the initial stage is passed.

11. The initial activities of the Force are determined by the fact that, as yet, no withdrawals have taken place in compliance with General Assembly resolutions 997 (ES-I) and 1002 (ES-I) of November 2 and 7, 1956. In pursuance of these two resolutions I shall report to the General Assembly on this matter as soon as I receive clarifications from the governments concerned. I am sure that the General Assembly, in view of the great urgency, will wish to give their immediate attention to the matter raised in this report so as, by consolidating the basis for the presence and functioning of the Force in Egypt, to contribute to speedy progress towards the ends it has set for the United Nations activities in the area.

ANNEX

Aide-Mémoire on the Basis for the Presence and Functioning of the United Nations Emergency Force in Egypt

Noting that by telegram of November 5, 1956, addressed to the Secretary-General the Government of Egypt, in exercise of its sovereign rights, accepted General Assembly resolution 1000 (ES-I) of the same date establishing "a United Nations Command for an emergency international Force to secure and supervise the cessation of hostilities in accordance with all the terms of resolution 997 (ES-1) of the General Assembly of November 2, 1956";

Noting that the General Assembly in its resolution 1001 (ES-I) of November 7, 1956, approved the principle that it could not request the Force "to be stationed or operate on the territory of a given country without the consent of the government of that country" (A/3302, paragraph 9);

Having agreed on the arrival in Egypt of the United Nations Emergency Force (UNEF);

Noting that advance groups of UNEF have already been received in Egypt;

The Government of Egypt and the Secretary-General of the United Nations have stated their understanding on the basic points for the presence and functioning of UNEF as follows;

1. The Government of Egypt declares that, when exercising its sovereign rights on any matter concerning the presence and functioning of UNEF, it will be guided, in good faith, by its acceptance of General Assembly resolution 1000 (ES-I) of November 5, 1956.

2. The United Nations takes note of this declaration of the Government of Egypt and declares that the activities of UNEF will be guided, in good faith, by the task established for the Force in the aforementioned resolutions; in particular, the United Nations, understanding this to correspond to the wishes of the Government of Egypt, reaffirms its willingness to maintain UNEF until its task is completed.

3. The Government of Egypt and the Secretary-General declare that it is their intention to proceed forthwith, in the light of points 1 and 2 above, to explore jointly concrete aspects of the functioning of UNEF, including its stationing and the question of its lines of communication and supply; the Government of Egypt, confirming its intention to facilitate the functioning of UNEF, and the United Nations are agreed to expedite in cooperation the implementation of guiding principles arrived at as a result of that joint exploration on the basis of the resolutions of the General Assembly.

Private Aide-Mémoire on Conditions
that Should Govern the Withdrawal
of the United Nations Emergency Force

UN HEADQUARTERS, NEW YORK   AUGUST 5, 1957

August 5, 1957

AIDE-MÉMOIRE

As the decision on UNEF was taken under Chapter VI, it was obvious from the beginning that the resolution did in no way limit the sovereignty of the host state. This was clear both from the resolution of the General Assembly and from the second and final report on the Emergency Force. Thus, neither the General Assembly nor the Secretary-General, acting for the General Assembly, created any right for Egypt, or gave any right to Egypt, in accepting consent as a condition for the presence and functioning of UNEF on Egyptian territory. Egypt had the right, and the only problem was whether that right in this context should and could in some way be limited.

My starting point in the consideration of this last mentioned problem —the limitation of Egypt's sovereign right in the interest of political balance and stability in UNEF operation—was the fact that Egypt had spontaneously endorsed the General Assembly resolution of November 5 and by endorsing that resolution had consented to the presence of UNEF for certain tasks. They could thus not ask UNEF to withdraw before the completion of the tasks without running up against their own acceptance of the resolution on the Force and its tasks.

The question arose in relation to Egypt first in a cable received November 9 from Burns, covering an interview the same day with Fawzi. In that interview Egypt had requested clarification of the question how long it was contemplated that the Force would stay in the demarcation line area. To this I replied the same day: "A definite reply is at present

Published in *International Legal Materials: Current Documents,* Vol. VI, No. 3, May–June 1967, pp. 595–602.

impossible, but the emergency character of the Force links it to the immediate crisis envisaged in the resolution of November 2 and its liquidation. In case of different views as to when the crisis does not any longer warrant the presence of the troops, the matter will have to be negotiated with the parties." In a further cable to Burns the same day I said, however, also that "as the United Nations Force would come with Egypt's consent, they cannot stay nor operate unless Egypt continues to consent."

On November 10 Ambassador Loutfi, under instruction, asked me "whether it was recognized that an agreement is necessary for their (UNEF's) remaining in the Canal area" once their task in the area had been completed. I replied that it was my view that such an agreement would then be necessary.

On November 11 Ambassador Loutfi saw me again. He then said that it must be agreed that when the Egyptian consent is no more valid, the UN Force should withdraw. To this I replied that I did not find that a withdrawal of consent could be made before the tasks which had justified the entry, had been completed; if, as might happen, different views on the degree of completion of the tasks prescribed proved to exist, the matter should be negotiated.

The view expressed by Loutfi was later embodied in an *aide-mémoire,* dated the same day, where it was said: "The Egyptian government takes note of the following: *A.* It being agreed that consent of Egypt is indispensable for entry and presence of the UN Forces in any part of its territory. If such consent no longer persists, these forces shall withdraw."

I replied to this in a memo dated November 12 in which I said: "I have received your *aide-mémoire* setting out the understanding on the basis of which the Egyptian government accepts my announcing today that agreement on the arrival in Egypt of the United Nations Force has been reached. I wish to put on record my interpretation of two of these points." Regarding the point quoted above in the Egyptian *aide-mémoire,* I then continued: "I want to put on record that the conditions which motivate the consent to entry and presence, are the very conditions to which the tasks established for the Force in the General Assembly resolution, November 4, are directed. Therefore, I assume it to be recognized that as long as the task, thus prescribed, is not completed, the reasons for the consent of the Government remain valid, and that a withdrawal of this consent before completion of the task would run counter to the acceptance by Egypt of the decision of the General Assembly. I read the statement quoted in the light of these considerations. If a difference should develop, whether or not the reasons for the arrangements are still valid, the matter should be brought up for negotiation with the United Nations."

This explanation of mine was sent to the Egyptian Mission after my telephone conversation in the morning of the twelfth with Dr. Fawzi where we agreed on publication of our agreement on the entry of UNEF into Egypt. In view of the previous exchanges, I had no reason to believe that my statement would introduce any new difficulty. I also counted on the fact that Egypt probably by then was so committed as to be rather anxious not to reopen the discussion. However, I recognized to myself that there was an element of gambling involved which I felt I simply had to take in view of the danger that further delays might cause Egypt to change its mind, accept volunteers, and throw our approaches overboard.

However, the next morning, November 13, I received a message from Dr. Fawzi to the effect that the Government of Egypt could not subscribe to my interpretation of the question of consent and withdrawal, as set out on November 12, and therefore, in the light of my communication of that date, "felt impelled to consider that the announced agreements should remain inoperative until all misunderstandings were cleared up." The government reiterated in this context its view that if its consent no longer persisted, the UNEF should withdraw.

I replied to this communication—which caused a further delay of the transportation of troops to Egypt by at least twenty-four hours—in a cable sent immediately on receipt of the communication. In drafting my reply I had a feeling that it now was a must to get the troops in and that I would be in a position to find a formula, saving the face of Egypt while protecting the UN stand, once I could discuss the matter personally with President Nasser.

In the official reply November 13 I said that my previous statement had put forward my personal opinion that "the reasons" for consent remained valid as long as the task was not completed. I also said that for that reason a withdrawal of consent leading to the withdrawal of the Force before the task was completed (as previously stated) in my view, "although within the rights of the Egyptian government would go against its acceptance of the basic resolution of the General Assembly." I continued by saying that my reference to negotiation was intended to indicate only that the question of withdrawal should be a matter of discussion to the extent that different views were held as to whether the task of the General Assembly was fulfilled or not. I referred in this respect to my stand as explained already in my message of November 9, as quoted above.

I commented upon the official reply in a special personal message to Fawzi, sent at the same time, where I said that we "both had to reserve our freedom of action, but that, all the same, we could go ahead, hoping that a controversial situation would not arise." "If arrangements would break down on this issue" (withdrawal only on completion of the tasks), "I could not avoid going to the General Assembly" (with the conflict which had developed between us on this question of principle) "putting it to their judgment to decide what could or could not be accepted as an understanding. This situation would be a most embarrassing one for all but I would fear the political repercussions, as obviously very few would find it reasonable that recognition of your freedom of action should mean that you, after having permitted the Force to come, might ask it to withdraw at a time when the very reasons which had previously prompted you to accept were still obviously valid." I ended by saying that I trusted that Fawzi on the basis of this personal message could help me by "putting the stand I had to take on my own rights, in the right perspective." The letter to Fawzi thus made it clear that if the government did not accept my stand on withdrawal as a precondition for further steps, the matter would be raised in the Assembly.

On the basis of these two final communications from me, Egypt gave green lights for the arrival of the troops, thus, in fact, accepting my stand and letting it supersede their own communication of November 13.

In my effort to follow up the situation, which prevailed after the exchange in which different stands had been maintained by Egypt and by me, I was guided by the consideration that Egypt constitutionally had an undisputed right to request the withdrawal of the troops, even if initial consent had been given, but that, on the other hand, it should be possible on the basis of my own stand as finally tacitly accepted, to force them into an agreement in which they limited their freedom of action as to withdrawal by making a request for withdrawal dependent upon the completion of the task—a question which, in the UN, obviously would have to be submitted to interpretation by the General Assembly.

The most desirable thing, of course, would have been to tie Egypt by an agreement in which they declared that withdrawal should take place only if so decided by the General Assembly. Put in this naked form, however, the problem could never have been settled. I felt that the same was true of an agreement to the effect that withdrawal should take place upon "agreement on withdrawal" between the UN and the Egyptian government. However, I found it worthwhile to try a line, very close to the second one, according to which Egypt would declare to the United Nations that it would exert all its sovereign rights with regard to the troops on the basis of a good faith interpretation of the tasks of the Force. The United Nations should make a reciprocal commitment to maintain the Force as long as the task was not completed. If such a dual statement was introduced in an agreement between the parties, it would be obvious that the procedure in case of a request from Egypt for the withdrawal of UNEF would be as follows. The matter would at once be brought before the General Assembly. If the General Assembly found that the task was completed, everything would be all right. If they found that the task was not completed and Egypt, all the same, maintained its stand and enforced the withdrawal, Egypt would break the agreement with the United Nations. Of course Egypt's freedom of action could under no circumstances be limited but by some kind of agreement. The device I used meant only that instead of limiting their rights by a basic understanding requesting an agreement *directly concerning withdrawal,* we created an obligation to reach agreement on the fact that the tasks were completed, and, thus, *the conditions for a withdrawal established.*

I elaborated a draft text for an agreement along the lines I had in mind during the night between November 15 and 16 in Capodichino. I showed the text to Fawzi at our first talk on November 16 and I discussed practically only this issue with Nasser for seven hours in the evening and night of November 17. Nasser, in this final discussion, where the text I had proposed was approved with some amendments, showed that he very fully understood that, by limiting their freedom of action in the way I proposed, they would take a very serious step, as it would mean that the question of the extent of the task would become decisive for the relations between Egypt and the United Nations and would determine Egypt's political freedom of action. He felt, not without justification, that the definition given of the task in the UN texts was very loose and that, tying the freedom of action of Egypt to the concept of the task—which had to be interpreted also by the General Assembly—and doing so in a written agreement, meant that he accepted a far-reaching and unpredictable restriction. To shoot the text through in spite of Nasser's strong wish to avoid this, and his strong suspicion of the legal construction—especially of the possible consequences of differences of views regarding the task—I felt obliged, in the course of the discussion, to threaten three times, that unless an agreement of this type was made, I would have to propose the immediate withdrawal of the troops. If any proof would be necessary for how the text of the agreement was judged by President Nasser, this last mentioned fact tells the story.

It is obvious that, with a text of the content mentioned approved by Egypt, the whole previous exchange of views was superseded by a formal and explicit recognition by Egypt of the stand I had taken all through, in particular on November 9 and 12. The previous exchange of cables cannot any longer have any interpretative value as only the text of the agreement was put before the General Assembly and approved by it with the concurrence of Egypt and as its text was self-contained and conclusive. All further discussion, therefore, has to start from the text of the agreement, which is to be found in Document A/3375. The interpretation of the text must be the one set out above.

Report to the General Assembly on the Clearing of the Suez Canal

UN HEADQUARTERS, NEW YORK   NOVEMBER 20, 1956

1. In the course of the recent hostilities in Egypt great damage was done to the Suez Canal. The Canal is now out of function, and considerable efforts of a most urgent character are needed to clear it from obstructions.

2. In its resolution 997(ES-I) of November 2, 1956, the General Assembly urged that steps be taken to re-open the Suez Canal. Immediately upon the adoption of the resolution the Secretary-General proceeded to explore the technical possibilities of engaging the services of private firms for assistance in the clearing operation. For that purpose the Secretary-General addressed himself to the governments of Denmark and of the Netherlands. On the basis of replies received, contacts were made with a number of private firms.

3. During the visit of the Secretary-General to Cairo, November 16 to 18, 1956, he had an opportunity to discuss the matter directly with the Government of Egypt. In view of the urgency of clearing the obstructions of the Suez Canal, and the scope of the task, the Government of Egypt addressed to him a request for assistance from the United Nations in arrangements for this purpose, as a matter of high priority. The Government of Egypt considered that the work should be started immediately upon withdrawal of non-Egyptian forces from Port Said and the Canal area.

4. Under the authority given to the Secretary-General under the relevant resolutions adopted by the General Assembly, the Secretary-General gave his assurance, in principle, that the United Nations would seek to provide such assistance. In pursuance of this assurance, the Secretary-General now wishes to submit the question to the General Assembly.

5. The exploration undertaken has indicated that various private enterprises, with important resources, might agree to cooperate in the

General Assembly Official Records, Eleventh Session, Annexes, Volume II, agenda item 66, Document A/3376, November 20, 1956.

clearing of the Canal. The Secretary-General would propose that the General Assembly, confirming in this respect its previous decisions, should authorize the Secretary-General to proceed with his exploration of existing possibilities and to negotiate agreements with such firms as might speedily and effectively undertake the clearing operations. As indicated above, he would, given the approval of the General Assembly to this proposal, intend to address himself to firms in countries outside the present conflict. In his contacts with the firms approached, he would try to clarify to what extent they, in turn, may need assistance from enterprises not directly approached by the United Nations.

6. At the present stage the Secretary-General is not prepared to indicate how the costs should be shared. He intends to revert to this question when the approximate costs have been estimated. He will at the proper stage of the negotiations request the necessary authority to conclude agreements concerning the operation.

7. In the course of the discussions between the Government of Egypt and the Secretary-General, the Government of Egypt expressed its wish to see the operation completed with the utmost speed. In view of the interest of the Government of Egypt, as well as of the interest of all the users of the Canal, the Secretary-General feels that the most expeditious procedure to achieve the desired results should be followed in connection with the matter. That is why he suggests to the General Assembly to authorize him, in consultation with the Advisory Committee set up under resolution 1001(ES-I) of the General Assembly of November 7, 1956, to enter into the financial commitments that are unavoidable, although he is not now in a position to indicate the size of those initial commitments.

8. As a first result of the further exploration and negotiations the Secretary-General anticipates that experts would have to be sent in order to survey the work to be undertaken. It would be his intention to use experts now employed within the United Nations Technical Assistance Programme, assisted by representatives of the firms approached.

9. Although it is not proposed that the work begin until after the withdrawal of non-Egyptian forces from Port Said and the Canal area, the Secretary-General considers it possible to pursue negotiations and, in agreement with the Government of Egypt, to arrange for the necessary survey of the conditions in the Canal without delay.

From Report to the General Assembly on Administrative and Financial Arrangements for the United Nations Emergency Force

UN HEADQUARTERS, NEW YORK   NOVEMBER 21, 1956

THE THIRD of four reports to the General Assembly tabled by the Secretary-General after his return from Cairo concerned administrative and financial arrangements for the United Nations Emergency Force. The text follows below. The first part of the report on organizational arrangements was non-controversial. The second part of the report, on methods of financing, ran into trouble. Soon after the report was circulated it became evident there was too much opposition or hesitation to permit prompt Assembly approval of Hammarskjöld's proposal in the draft resolution annexed to the report that the costs of the Force "shall be borne by the United Nations" under Article 17 of the Charter and allocated among the Members in accordance with the regular scale of assessments. He proposed an initial assessment of $10 million. The Soviet bloc thought the costs should be borne by the "aggressors"—Britain, France, and Israel. Many others among the smaller states thought a larger share of the extraordinary costs of an action upholding international peace and security should be borne by the great powers than was the case for the ordinary budget.

The Secretary-General needed immediate authority to expend funds for UNEF beyond the standing authority given him each year for unforeseen expenses. He also saw that more time was needed for consideration of how the costs should be assessed. On November 25, therefore, he revised the draft resolution in such a way as to give him authority to draw up to $10 million for a special UNEF account from the Working Capital Fund and to refer to the Fifth Committee and the Advisory Committee on Administrative and Budgetary Questions the issues of assessment and apportionment. Both the original and revised versions of the draft resolution are included in the text below, which is followed by the Secretary-General's opening statement in the Assembly's debate on November 26. In its revised form the resolution was approved, but by a smaller majority than preceding resolutions on UNEF (see also page 399).

General Assembly Official Records, Eleventh Session, Annexes, Volume II, agenda item 66, Document A/3383 and Rev. 1, November 21, 1956.

1. In accordance with the provisions of paragraph 4 of resolution 1000(ES-I) adopted by the General Assembly on November 5, 1956, and paragraph 7 of resolution 1001(ES-I) adopted on November 7, 1956, administrative and executive measures necessary for the establishment and operation of the United Nations Emergency Force have either been instituted or are in the process of being given effect to, in consultation as required, with the Advisory Committee, established under paragraph 6 of resolution 1001(ES-I). Subject to such action as the General Assembly may decide upon with respect to certain basic questions of administrative and financial policy to which attention is called in paragraphs 5 to 14 hereunder, it is the intention of the Secretary-General to issue such regulations and instructions as are necessary for the guidance of those concerned.

2. Having regard to the relevant provisions of the resolutions which the General Assembly has adopted, and following consultation with the Advisory Committee on questions left open in my report (A/3302), the organization of the Force is proceeding on the basis of the following provisional arrangements:

(*a*) All personnel assigned to the Force will be under the direct supervision of the Commander who, in consultation as required with the Secretary-General, will undertake the recruitment from Member governments of officers for his command. The Commander may hire such local personnel as he requires and arrange with the Secretary-General for such detailment of staff from the United Nations Secretariat as may be necessary.

(*b*) The Commander will have charge of the billeting and the provision of food for all personnel attached to the Force, and may negotiate with governments and private suppliers for the provision of premises and food.

(*c*) The Commander will arrange for the transportation of personnel and equipment to and from the area of operations; will make provision for local transportation within the area; and will coordinate the use of all transportation facilities furnished by governments.

(*d*) The Commander will be responsible for the procurement, storage, and issuance of supplies required by the Force.

(*e*) The Commander will make such arrangements as may be necessary for obtaining equipment required by the Force, other than the standard equipment expected to accompany national contingents.

(*f*) The Commander, in consultation with the Secretary-General, will make appropriate arrangements for the inclusion in the Force of such supporting units as may be necessary to provide for the establishment, operation, and maintenance of communications within the area of operations and with United Nations offices.

(*g*) The Commander, in consultation with the Secretary-General, will also arrange for the necessary supporting units to provide medical, dental, and sanitary services for all personnel.

(*h*) The Secretary-General, in consultation with the Advisory Committee, will have final authority for all administrative and financial operations of the Force. He will be responsible for concluding agreements or making other arrangements with contributing governments regarding the provision of troop units, supplies, or services required by the Force.

3. Arrangements have been made, pursuant to the provisional approval contained in paragraph 5 of resolution 1001(ES-I), for the finances of the Force to be handled under a Special Account outside the normal budget of the United Nations. As provided for in paragraph 7 of the draft resolution annexed to the present report, the Secretary-General will issue provisional financial rules for the operation of the Special Account as soon as the General Assembly has acted on the policy questions raised in this report. Such rules will provide *inter alia,* for audit of transactions relating to the Special Account by the United Nations Board of Auditors and for the scope of such audit to be determined by the Board in consultation with the Advisory Committee on Administrative and Budgetary Questions. Established United Nations procedures for financial control and accounting will be applied to the extent that they are appropriate.

4. The Secretary-General believes that the arrangements provide a basis for the effective functioning of the Force. There are, however, administrative and financial questions involving broad policy considerations on which the Secretary-General requests the guidance of the General Assembly. Such matters relate to the method to be adopted for allocating to Member governments the costs for the Force; the necessity of assuring necessary cash requirements; the problem of currency of payment of troops and related questions; and arrangements regarding compensation for service-incurred death or disability. The views of the Secretary-General with respect to these particular matters are set forth hereunder, and the draft resolution annexed is based on these views.

Methods of Assessment on Member States for the
Expenses in Connection with the Force

5. The Secretary-General considers it essential that the General Assembly decide at an early date on the method of allocating to Member states the costs of the Force to be financed by the United Nations.

6. In order to assist the General Assembly in considering this question, the Secretary-General recommends:

(*a*) That the expenses of the Force be allocated to Member states on the basis of the scale of assessments to be adopted for the United Nations budget for 1957.

(*b*) That the General Assembly decide now on an initial amount of assessment for the Special Account.

7. The Secretary-General is not, at this stage, in a position to inform the General Assembly of the likely total requirements. He would suggest, however, that, for the purpose of an initial assessment for the Special Account, an amount of $10 million should be approved. It would be understood that any balances ultimately remaining from assessments for the Special Account would be refunded to Member states in the same proportion as their contributions to this Account.

. . . .

ANNEX

Draft Resolution [original version—EDITORS]

The General Assembly,

Having decided, in resolutions 1000 (ES-I) and 1001 (ES-I) of November 5 and 7, 1956, to establish a United Nations international Force (hereinafter to be known as the United Nations Emergency Force), under a Chief of Command (hereinafter to be known as the Commander),

Desiring to adopt arrangements regarding the costs of maintaining the Force,

Having considered and provisionally approved the recommendations made in this respect by the Secretary-General (A/3302, paragraph 15),

1. *Decides* that expenses of the Force, other than for pay and equipment of national contingents and such other supplies, equipment, and services as may be furnished, without charge, by Member governments,

shall be borne by the United Nations; and shall be apportioned among the Member states in accordance with the scale of assessments adopted by the General Assembly for contributions to the annual budget of the Organization for the financial year 1957;

2. *Authorizes* the Secretary-General to establish a United Nations Emergency Force Special Account to which the contributions of Member states shall be credited and from which payments may be made for the purpose of meeting the expenses of the Force;

3. *Approves* an initial assessment for the Special Account in the amount of $10 million;

4. *Authorizes* the Secretary-General, pending receipt of contributions to the Special Account:

(*a*) To advance from the Working Capital Fund such sums as the Special Account may require to meet any expenses chargeable to it;

(*b*) Where necessary, to arrange for loans to the Special Account from appropriate sources, including governments and international agencies; provided that the repayment of any such advances or loans to the Special Account shall constitute a first charge against contributions as they are received;

5. *Further authorizes* the Secretary-General to treat as an advance to the Special Account, as he may deem appropriate and with the concurrence of the governments concerned, the cost of services and supplies chargeable to the Special Account which have been furnished by a Member state;

6. *Urges* all Member states to remit promptly their initial assessment under the present resolution and, to the extent possible, to make advances to the Special Account;

7. *Requests* the Secretary-General to establish such rules and procedures for the Special Account as he may consider necessary to ensure effective financial administration and control of that Account. These rules shall apply in lieu of such of the United Nations financial regulations and rules as are inconsistent with them.

Revised Version of the Draft Resolution

(*Presented in Document A/3883/Rev. 1, November 25, 1956*)

The General Assembly,

Having decided, in resolutions 1000 (ES-I) and 1001 (ES-I) of November 5 and 7, 1956, to establish an emergency international United

Nations Force (hereafter to be known as the United Nations Emergency Force), under a Chief of Command (hereafter to be known as the Commander),

Having considered and provisionally approved the recommendations made by the Secretary-General concerning the financing of the Force in paragraph 15 of his report (A/3302),

1. *Authorizes* the Secretary-General to establish a United Nations Emergency Force Special Account to which funds received by the United Nations, outside the regular budget, for the purpose of meeting the expenses of the Force shall be credited, and from which payments for this purpose shall be made;

2. *Decides* that the Special Account shall be established in an initial amount of $10 million;

3. *Authorizes* the Secretary-General, pending the receipt of funds for the Special Account, to advance from the Working Capital Fund such sums as the Special Account may require to meet any expenses chargeable to it;

4. *Requests* the Secretary-General to establish such rules and procedures for the Special Account and make such administrative arrangements as he may consider necessary to ensure effective financial administration and control of that Account;

5. *Requests* the Fifth Committee and, as appropriate, the Advisory Committee on Administrative and Budgetary Questions, to consider and as soon as possible, report on further arrangements that need to be adopted regarding the costs of maintaining the Force.

Statement in the General Assembly on Administrative and Financial Arrangements for United Nations Emergency Force

UN HEADQUARTERS, NEW YORK   NOVEMBER 26, 1956

Members of the General Assembly will have received, this morning, a revised text A/3383/Rev. 1 (annex) of the draft resolution that was appended to my report of November 21 on administrative and financial arrangements for the United Nations Emergency Force.

In order to assist the General Assembly in its consideration of the revised draft resolution, might I offer the following explanations and comments.

The draft resolution in the "stripped-down" form in which it is now presented seeks to limit the action required to be taken at this stage by the General Assembly in plenary session to some three or four basic matters on which decisions are urgently needed in order that the establishment and operations of the Force may proceed without interruption and delay.

I have accordingly considered it imperative to seek the concurrence of the General Assembly in the following matters: first, the establishment of a United Nations Emergency Force Special Account; secondly, the establishment of this Account in an initial amount of $10 million; thirdly, the authorization of advances from the Working Capital Fund for the purpose of interim financing of the Force; fourthly, authorization to establish necessary rules and procedures and to make necessary administrative arrangements for the purpose of ensuring effective financial administration and control of the Account so established.

First, let me make it abundantly clear that the draft resolution I have offered, both in its original and in its revised form, relates solely and exclusively to arrangements regarding the Emergency Force, and in no way to other responsibilities which the United Nations may acquire in the area.

General Assembly Official Records, Eleventh Session, 596th Plenary Meeting, November 26, 1956.

Secondly, I wish to make it equally clear that while funds received and payments made with respect to the Force are to be considered as coming outside the regular budget of the Organization, the operation is essentially a United Nations responsibility, and the Special Account to be established must, therefore, be construed as coming within the meaning of Article 17 of the Charter. It follows from this that the Secretary-General will be obliged to follow to a maximum degree the regular financial rules and regulations of the Organization, as well as the machinery and processes that have been laid down by the General Assembly for the purpose of financial review and control.

Having regard to the scope and complexity of the financial operations involved, it is indeed my intention to make special arrangements for a continuing independent audit to be carried out of all financial transactions concerning the Force.

Thirdly, it has been my assumption in drafting the revised text that Member states, while recognizing the need for taking certain decisions without delay, will nevertheless wish to follow established procedures to the fullest extent practicable. Accordingly, I have felt it wise to suggest that such problems as allocation of costs among Member states should be deferred temporarily, pending an opportunity of their being properly and adequately considered and discussed in the appropriate committee of the Assembly, that is, the Fifth Committee. Such action as the Assembly may see fit to take here and now in plenary session would therefore be without prejudice to subsequent decisions on other complementary and supplementary financial arrangements that need to be made. I would, however, hope that the Fifth Committee and, as necessary, the Advisory Committee on Administrative and Budgetary Questions, would give these matters priority consideration.

Report on Withdrawal in Compliance with General Assembly Resolutions 997 (ES-I) and 1002 (ES-I)

UN HEADQUARTERS, NEW YORK NOVEMBER 21, 1956

THE SECRETARY-GENERAL'S fourth report to the Assembly after his return from Cairo was on the question of compliance with the Assembly's November 2 and November 7 resolutions calling for "immediate" withdrawal of the invading forces. The report consisted mainly of annexes giving the replies to his enquiries from the British, French, and Israeli governments. These are omitted from the following text but may be briefly summarized.

The British and French remained ready to withdraw when UNEF became strong enough to carry out the tasks assigned to it by the General Assembly. In the meantime one-third of the French troops had been withdrawn and Britain had decided to withdraw "at once" one infantry battalion. Both claimed several minor violations of the cease-fire by Egyptians. Selwyn Lloyd's reply made much of plans to turn over to UNEF equipment and supplies needed by the latter. This was presented in such a way as to give an impression of continuity between the Anglo-French forces and UNEF and evoked the comment in paragraph 6 of the Secretary-General's report below. The Israeli government reported that its forces had pulled back for varying distances along the entire front and reiterated its willingness to withdraw entirely from Egypt if satisfactory arrangements were made with the United Nations, adding "the 'satisfactory arrangements' which Israel seeks are such as will ensure Israel's security against the recurrence of the threat or danger of attack, and against acts of belligerency by land or sea." Thus the Israeli government remained determined to use its occupation of Egyptian soil as a bargaining counter, despite the Assembly's reiterated calls for unconditional withdrawal behind the armistice line.

Israel's response to the Secretary-General's letter on the situation in Gaza —jammed with Palestinian Arab refugees—declared all was now peaceful there after riots "instigated by Egyptian agents" had "regrettably" resulted in casualties "among the mob." Nothing was said of UN observers, but a personal representative of the Secretary-General would be welcome to investigate and report on the situation. Hammarskjöld accepted this and immediately assigned Colonel Knut Nelson, a former UNTSO observer now on General Burns' UNEF staff, to go to Gaza.

General Assembly Official Records, Eleventh Session, Annexes, Volume II, agenda item 66, Document A/3384, November 21, 1956.

1. The General Assembly in resolutions 997 (ES-I) and 1002 (ES-I) of November 2 and 7, 1956, requested the Secretary-General to report promptly on compliance with the resolutions.

2. The Secretary-General addressed, November 19, to the governments of France, Israel, and the United Kingdom orally a request for clarification of the present state of compliance as a basis for a report to the General Assembly. The Secretary-General indicated that he would wish to be in a position to clarify to the General Assembly whether any withdrawal of forces had taken place and, if so, to what extent, whether anything could be said concerning the plans for withdrawal, what were the reasons for the fact that so far no—or no more—progress had taken place in compliance with the General Assembly resolutions, and, finally, what, in the view of the government concerned, was the state of compliance with the cease-fire.

3. A question was addressed November 20, to the Government of Egypt, whether it had any observations to offer on the last-mentioned point.

4. The Secretary-General has now received replies to his request to the governments of France, Israel and the United Kingdom. The replies are circulated as annexes to this report (annexes 1 to 3).

5. At the present stage the Secretary-General does not wish to present any observations concerning the state of compliance reflected in the replies received. Nor does he find it to the purpose now to discuss the views expressed on the circumstances under which compliance was to be established.

6. As to the part of the letter from the Government of the United Kingdom which refers to the possibility of certain facilities being made available to the United Nations Emergency Force, the Secretary-General finds it premature now to comment on questions which form part of the general problem of supplies and transport to be treated in a later report to the General Assembly. Solutions will be sought to that problem which are fully in line with the international character of the Force, as set up for the specific purposes defined in the relevant General Assembly resolutions.

7. If and when the Government of Egypt should wish to reply to the question addressed to it, the reply will be circulated separately.

8. At the same time as the replies to the request for clarification, November 19, are circulated, the Secretary-General circulates also a letter from him to the Foreign Minister of Israel, November 21, 1956, to-

gether with a preliminary reply received (annexes 4 to 5). This exchange of letters refers to the possibility of placing observers in an important part of the area from which, according to the request of the General Assembly, Israel forces should withdraw. The final reply from the Foreign Minister of Israel will be circulated separately as soon as it is received.

[ANNEXES 1 THROUGH 3 OMITTED]

ANNEX 4

Letter Dated November 21, 1956, Addressed to the Minister for Foreign Affairs of Israel

According to information received which I must consider as reliable, the situation in the Gaza Strip, in particular in Rafah, has been one giving rise to great concern. I will not here go into the question of the reasons for this unrest, nor into the information we have on the casualties ensuing. I hope that the situation has improved, and I gather from you that according to your information that is the case. However, the situation remains one which I cannot disregard in the execution of my obligations under the relevant General Assembly resolutions.

The other day I addressed to you a request that observers from the United Nations Emergency Froce be permitted to enter, to be stationed and to function within the Gaza area. I now wish to repeat this request. It seems to me that such an arrangement is the only way in which I can fulfill my obligation to assist in securing the cessation of all hostilities within the area, which, in the light of the stand taken by the General Assembly, is the area where the United Nations Emergency Force has to function in support of the cease-fire.

The steps you have taken concerning the representatives in Gaza of the United Nations Truce Supervision Organization, has seriously limited their possibilities to fulfill their functions. I will not now enter on a discussion of the questions to which this policy on your side gives rise, but I mentioned it as an added reason for my request.

I may remind you of the fact that already at an early stage British and French authorities permitted United Nations observers to enter Port Said where we have at present also units of the United Nations Emergency Force.

I would appreciate an immediate reply to this request. I would also appreciate receiving all information you can furnish about the present state of affairs in the Gaza area. I am sure that you agree that in face of the concern felt in the light of previous events, and the possibilities implicit in the situation, it should be in Israel's own interest to receive observers, even if quiet would now prevail.

DAG HAMMARSKJÖLD
Secretary-General

[ANNEX 5 OMITTED]

THE SECRETARY-GENERAL'S four reports were considered by the General Assembly at seven meetings from November 23–27. Hammarskjöld introduced his reports with a one-paragraph statement and did not intervene again in the debate, though he was as usual active behind the scenes. His statement was as follows:

The four reports I have put before the General Assembly cover the first phase of the United Nations efforts after the adoption by the General Assembly of its basic resolutions. Some progress in implementation is registered. Some new steps have to be taken. In my actions in implementation of the resolutions of the General Assembly I have, to the best of my understanding, neither added anything to the position of the General Assembly nor detracted anything from that position. I have been guided by the fact that the United Nations, in requesting a cessation of hostilities and withdrawal of foreign troops from Egypt, rejected the resort to force as a means to any of the proclaimed aims.[1]

The last two sentences were his response to those who still hoped to extract some political advantage from the invasion under cover of the United Nations flag and to those who sought to discredit, as yielding too much to Nasser, his careful respect for international law and for the limitations of the Charter upon the Assembly's powers in his negotiations with the Egyptian government.

Canada, Colombia, India, Norway, the United States and Yugoslavia joined in sponsoring the following resolution approving the "good-faith" agreement with Egypt and his proposals for clearing the Suez Canal:

The General Assembly,
  Having received the report of the Secretary-General on basic points for the presence and functioning in Egypt of the United Nations Emergency Force (A / 3375),

---

[1] *Ibid.*, 591st Plenary Meeting, November 23, 1956.

Having received also the report of the Secretary-General on arrangements for clearing the Suez Canal (A/3376),

1. *Notes with approval* the contents of the *aide-mémoire* on the basis for the presence and functioning of the United Nations Emergency Force in Egypt, as annexed to the report of the Secretary-General;

2. *Notes with approval* the progress so far made by the Secretary-General in connexion with arrangements for clearing the Suez Canal, as set forth in his report;

3. *Authorizes* the Secretary-General to proceed with the exploration of practical arrangements and the negotiation of agreements so that the clearing operations may be speedily and effectively undertaken.[2]

Twenty-one Arab-Asian nations sponsored a resolution calling once again upon Israel, France, and Britain to comply "forthwith" with its withdrawal resolutions of November 2 and 7. In its original version this resolution in its first operative paragraph noted "with grave concern that its repeated resolutions calling for the complete and immediate withdrawal of Israel, French, and United Kingdom forces have not been complied with." This language was unacceptable to most of those Western delegates who had joined the Arab-Asians in the earlier withdrawal resolutions. It did not recognize that some withdrawal had already begun. It also failed to take into account the link between British-French withdrawal and the arrival of UNEF which could be read into the language of the November 7 resolution (see page 357).

The alliance between the Arab-Asians and the majority of the Western nations which had so far assured overwhelming majorities for the Assembly's Middle East resolutions was thus threatened. After many discussions off the floor between members of the two camps the Arab-Asians introduced on November 24 a revised draft on withdrawal with a modified first operative paragraph. The revised resolution reads as follows:

The General Assembly,

Having received the report of the Secretary-General on compliance with General Assembly resolutions 997 (ES-I) and 1002 (ES-I) of November 2 and 7 (A/3384),

Recalling that its resolution 1002 (ES-I) called upon Israel immediately to withdraw its forces behind the demarcation line established by the General Armistice Agreement between Egypt and Israel of February 24, 1949,

Recalling further that the above resolution also called on France and the United Kingdom of Great Britain and Northern Ireland immediately to withdraw their forces from Egyptian territory, in conformity with previous resolutions,

[2] *Ibid.,* Annexes, agenda item 66, Document A/3386, November 23, 1956, subsequently General Assembly Resolution 1121 (XI) of November 24, 1956.

1. *Notes with regret* that, according to the communications received by the Secretary-General (A/3384), two-thirds of the French forces remain, all the United Kingdom forces remain although it has been announced that arrangements are being made for the withdrawal of one battalion, and no Israel forces have been withdrawn behind the armistice line although a considerable time has elapsed since the adoption of the relevant General Assembly resolutions;

2. *Reiterates* its call to France, Israel, and the United Kingdom of Great Britain and Northern Ireland to comply forthwith with resolutions 997 (ES-I) and 1002 (ES-I) of November 2 and 7, 1956;

3. *Requests* the Secretary-General urgently to communicate the present resolution to the parties concerned, and to report without delay to the General Assembly on the implementation thereof.[3]

This revised resolution was now too soft for Fawzi, and Egypt withdrew from the list of sponsors, though in the end it voted for the resolution. The resolution remained stronger, however, than Canada and the Western Europeans liked. Pearson had already said Canada considered another withdrawal resolution neither necessary nor helpful, now that withdrawals in compliance with the earlier resolutions had begun. The Assembly might better devote its time to "the task of bringing about a settlement, creating an atmosphere within which progress could be made to such a settlement and expediting the solution of practical problems, such as the clearing of the Suez Canal and the maintenance there of freedom and security for navigation for all countries." [4]

Statements such as this, coupled with active lobbying by Selwyn Lloyd and the desire of Britain's European friends to make retreat easier for her, rekindled Asian and Arab suspicions that the completion of withdrawal might still be made conditional on extracting some political concession from Egypt, thereby rewarding the use of force.

For the United States, however, Lodge stood firm. Although his government did not believe the withdrawal resolution to be "necessary," the United States would vote for it since it "expresses sentiments which are in every respect consistent with our policy." [5] Lodge's position was, indeed, consistent with U.S. policy, for the Eisenhower administration had once again made clear to the Eden government that it could expect no help with its balance of payments crisis until the withdrawal from Suez was completed.

Despite Lodge's stand the Western Europeans and Canada went ahead with an attempt to modify further the revised Arab-Asian resolution. Paul-Henri Spaak proposed an amendment to strike out the first two operative paragraphs and replace them with a paragraph noting the withdrawals that

[3] *Ibid.*, Annexes, agenda item 66, Document A/3385/Rev. 1, November 24, 1956, subsequently General Assembly Resolution 1120 (XI) of November 24, 1956.

[4] *Ibid.*, 592nd Plenary Meeting, November 23, 1956.

[5] *Ibid.*, 593rd Plenary Meeting, November 24, 1956.

had already taken place and stating that the Assembly considered the three powers should "expedite the application" of the resolutions of November 2 and 7 "in the spirit in which they were adopted, particularly with regard to the functions vested in the United Nations Force." [6]

Spaak made an eloquent plea for his amendment, declaring its adoption would probably enable the Assembly to come close to unanimity and thus "mark the first step—and I hope the decisive step—towards a logical, peaceful, rational and just solution of the dispute." [7]

Lloyd for Britain and Vincent Broustra for France both declared they would vote for the withdrawal resolution if the Belgian amendment were adopted. Eban, who had hastily put on record with the Secretary-General a statement that the equivalent of two brigades of Israeli soldiers had now left Egyptian territory, also spoke in support of the amendment. Israel would stand by its undertaking to withdraw, he said, but sought a "method of withdrawal" which would make a renewal of the conflict "unthinkable." [8]

Krishna Menon led the Arab-Asians in strong opposition to the amendment. He saw it as an "outflanking" move aimed at helping Britain, France, and Israel to justify and reap benefits from their "aggression." None of the twenty sponsors of the withdrawal resolution would be able to vote for it if the Belgian amendment passed. And he warned that such a result would also have a bearing on the fate of the UNEF and Suez clearance resolutions, "because, unless there is a withdrawal of troops, or at least an urging of the withdrawal of troops, it is not right to consider other questions." [9]

When the vote came the Belgian amendment was defeated 37 to 23 with 18 abstentions. Those voting for the amendment included some of UNEF's strongest supporters—Canada, Norway, Sweden, Denmark, Italy, and Brazil —as well as the Benelux countries, Britain, France and Israel, Australia and New Zealand. The United States, however, was among the 18 abstainers and this was probably decisive for the outcome, for 12 of the Latin Americans also abstained and only 4 of them voted for the amendment. The 20-Power withdrawal resolution was then adopted 63 to 5 with 10 abstentions. Canada and the Benelux countries were among the abstainers, but the Nordic bloc now moved back into line and voted in the affirmative. The five negative votes were cast, as several times before, by Britain, France, Israel, Australia, and New Zealand.

The 6-Power resolution endorsing the "good faith" agreement on UNEF and plans to clear the Suez Canal was then approved by 65 to 0 with 9 abstentions. The vote was by a show of hands.

Two days later—November 26—the Secretary-General's revised draft resolution on the financing of UNEF was approved with little debate by a vote of 52 to 9 with 13 abstentions. The Soviet bloc, which had abstained on previous UNEF resolutions, now voted "no," and the abstainers were small countries fearful of the additional costs they might be called upon to pay, most of whom had previously been in the affirmative column.

[6] *Ibid.,* Annexes, agenda item 66, Document A/L. 215, November 24, 1956.
[7] *Ibid.,* 594th Plenary Meeting, November 24, 1956.   [8] *Ibid.*   [9] *Ibid.*

Statement to the Press on the
United Nations Emergency Force

NOVEMBER 28, 1956

THE GENERAL ASSEMBLY did not resume plenary discussion of the Middle East situation until December 18. In the meantime the experience of the British and French foreign ministers during the latter part of November both at the United Nations and in Washington was decisive in bringing their governments finally to accept speedy and total withdrawal of their forces from Egypt on the terms laid down by the United Nations.

On November 28 Hammarskjöld issued as a press release the statement that follows. In form it was simply a progress report on organization and deployment of the UN Emergency Force. But it included language which would be helpful to the British and French governments in announcing a decision to complete their withdrawal without further delay. Thus the Secretary-General declared that "after a fortnight, this will be an organized military force" and that "the UNEF, in terms of potential effectiveness in performing its mission, must be rated as equivalent to a substantially larger military body."

The United Nations Emergency Force has now been in Egypt for just short of two weeks. By means of the daily airlift from Naples, first by the Swissair aircraft which were indispensable to the operation in the early days and now by the Canadian and Italian planes, the Force steadily grows both in personnel and in the vehicles, equipment and supplies available to it.

As of Tuesday, November 27, a total of approximately 4,500 officers and men have been accepted from eight of the twenty-three states which have offered military units to the Force. Of this total, on that date, 1,374 were in Egypt, of whom 1,184 were at Abu Sueir and 190 at Port Said. Most of these at Abu Sueir are scheduled to be deployed without delay to Port Said and Port Fuad (where at least a thousand will be stationed, with the Scandinavians predominating) and the El Cap-El Qantara sectors.

UN Press Release SG/540, EMF/28, November 28, 1956.

On the twenty-seventh, also, there were 514 officers and men at the Naples staging area of Capodichino, and 1,097 were en route to Naples and Port Said by air and sea. By the end of this week, that is by December 1, on the basis of the airlift schedule, which thus far has been maintained remarkably well, it is expected that close to 2,700 officers and men, well armed and equipped, will be deployed in the canal area.

Within a fortnight virtually all elements of the Force activated to date will have been lifted to Capodichino or Egypt. By that date the Force in Egypt should number approximately 4,100, with some 300 air personnel stationed at Naples.

It may be added that after a fortnight, this will be an organized military force, with a Headquarters and Staff under the command of General Burns as Commander of the Force, with two armored car companies, and with necessary supporting units, including medical, engineer, transport, signal, supply, workshop, provost, and post units and other army service elements.

This is the projection of the Force in the days immediately ahead. What size it may ultimately need to be can be better judged in the light of developments and the assessment of the Commander of the Force as to his requirements in carrying out the mandates of the General Assembly. Provisionally, our target is two combat brigades. In this regard, it may be pointed out that given the experience of the force thus far, admittedly limited though it is, and the reception it has received in the area of its operation, the UNEF, in terms of potential effectiveness in performing its mission, must be rated as equivalent to a substantially larger military body.

SELWYN LLOYD used this statement when he spoke in the House of Commons on November 29 to prepare the ground for final retreat. Over the weekend the texts of simultaneous *notes verbales* addressed to the Secretary-General from the British and French governments were drawn up in terms acceptable to Hammarskjöld. These were dispatched on December 3 and immediately circulated by the Secretary-General in the following document:

Note by the Secretary-General

The Secretary-General has the honour to transmit to the Members of the General Assembly the text of two communications which he has received from the Permanent Representatives of the United Kingdom of Great Britain and Northern Ireland and of France (see A and B below), and to call the attention of Members to an instruction issued by him to the Commander of the United Nations Emergency Force (see C below).

A. Note Verbale *Dated December 3, 1956, from the Permanent Representative of the United Kingdom of Great Britain and Northern Ireland, Addressed to the Secretary-General*

The Permanent Representative of the United Kingdom of Great Britain and Northern Ireland to the United Nations presents his compliments to the Secretary-General and has the honour to make the following communication on behalf of Her Majesty's Government in the United Kingdom.

1. Her Majesty's Government and the French Government note that:

(*a*) An effective United Nations Force is now arriving in Egypt charged with the tasks assigned to it in the Assembly resolutions of November 2, 5, and 7.

(*b*) The Secretary-General accepts the responsibility for organizing the task of clearing the Canal as expeditiously as possible.

(*c*) In accordance with the General Assembly resolution of November 2 free and secure transit will be reestablished through the Canal when it is clear.

(*d*) The Secretary-General will promote as quickly as possible negotiations with regard to the future régime of the Canal on the basis of the six requirements set out in the Security Council resolution of October 13.

2. Her Majesty's Government and the French Government confirm their decision to continue the withdrawal of their forces now in the Port Said area without delay.

3. They have accordingly instructed the Allied Commander, General Keightley, to seek agreement with the United Nations Commander, General Burns, on a timetable for the complete withdrawal, taking account of the military and practical questions involved. This timetable should be reported as quickly as possible to the Secretary-General of the United Nations.

4. In preparing these arrangements the Allied Commander will ensure:

(*a*) That the embarkations of personnel or material shall be carried out in an efficient and orderly manner;

(*b*) That proper regard will be had to the maintenance of public security in the area now under Allied control;

(*c*) That the United Nations Commander should make himself responsible for the safety of any French and British salvage resources left at the disposition of the United Nations salvage organization.

5. In communicating these conclusions Her Majesty's Government and the French Government recall the strong representations they have made regarding the treatment of their nationals in Egypt. They draw attention to the humane treatment accorded to Egyptian nationals in the United Kingdom and France. They feel entitled to demand that the position of British and French nationals in Egypt should be fully guaranteed.

B . . . . [*The text of the French note, being virtually identical to the British note, is not reproduced*—EDITORS]

C. *Instruction Issued by the Secretary-General to the Commander of the United Nations Force*

The Secretary-General has instructed the Commander of the United Nations Emergency Force, Major-General Burns, to get into immediate touch with the Anglo-French Commander with a view to working out with him arrangements for the complete withdrawal of Anglo-French forces without delay. General Burns has been further instructed to arrange for the earliest possible date for the completion of this programme, taking into account the military and practical questions involved and the need to maintain public security in the area. In view of the Secretary-General's understanding of the policy of the United Kingdom and French Governments regarding withdrawal, the attention of General Burns has been drawn to the need to ensure that the United Nations Emergency Force should be in a position to assume its responsibilities in the Port Said area by the middle of December.[1]

In the course of his speech in the House of Commons on December 3 announcing the withdrawal decision, Selwyn Lloyd expanded on the Secretary-General's commitment mentioned in paragraph 1(*d*) of the *note verbale* to promote negotiations in the Suez Canal dispute. Hammarskjöld would, Lloyd said, work on the basis of (*a*) the Six Requirements, (*b*) the October conversations between Hammarskjöld, Fawzi, Lloyd, and Pineau, and (*c*) Hammarskjöld's October 24 letter to Fawzi and the latter's response of November 2. However, Lloyd added that "Her Majesty's Government, of course, adhere to their view" in support of the London 18-Power proposals.[2] That addition was not helpful.

Once the British and French had completed their evacuation and United Nations operations to clear the Suez Canal were well launched Hammarskjöld was prepared to try to revive negotiations on the basis of points (*a*), (*b*), and (*c*). He had no commitment from the Egyptian side and would not seek one while British and French troops remained on Egyptian soil, but Fawzi's preliminary and private reactions gave him hope for a positive re-

---

[1] General Assembly Official Records, Eleventh Session, Annexes, agenda item 66, Document A/3415, December 3, 1956.

[2] Great Britain Parliamentary Debates (Hansard), Volume 561, p. 883.

sponse when the right time came. However any attempt by the British and French to revive the 18-Power approach would be likely to negate prospects for negotiating an agreed settlement.

During the latter part of November Hammarskjöld had also prodded Israel's government on arrangements for the promised withdrawal of its forces from Egypt. On December 1 he received a letter from Abba Eban declaring that "there will be no Israel forces anywhere within a wide belt of territory (about 50 kilometres) in proximity to the Suez Canal along its entire length by the morning of December 3" and agreeing to facilitate movement of UNEF units into the area between the Canal and the western limits of the Israeli positions.[3] This withdrawal, like the coming evacuation of Port Said, was a necessary prelude to commencement of United Nations clearance operations.

[3] General Assembly Official Records, Eleventh Session, Annexes, agenda item 66, Document A / 3410, December 1, 1956.

Message to the United Nations Emergency Force

UN HEADQUARTERS, NEW YORK   DECEMBER 10, 1956

THE SECRETARY-GENERAL recorded the following message on the inauguration by United Nations Radio of special programs for the men serving in the United Nations Emergency Force. By this date the strength of UNEF in Egypt had risen to over 3,500 men from eight countries: Canada, Colombia, Denmark, Finland, India, Norway, Sweden, and Yugoslavia. General Burns was establishing his headquarters at El Ballah on the Canal between Port Said and Ismailia. In Port Said–Port Fuad the area of UNEF responsibility was being steadily extended as the British and French forces pulled back toward their embarkation zones. In the Sinai, units of the Yugoslav motorized battalion, which had arrived by sea with their vehicles, were moving out into the desert between the Canal and Israeli positions.

As members of the United Nations Emergency Force you are taking part in an experience that is new in history. You are soldiers of peace in the first international force of its kind. You have come from distant homelands, not to fight a war but to serve peace and justice and order under the authority of the United Nations.

Thus the opportunity for service which is yours is not to be measured by your numbers or your armor. You are the front line of a moral force which extends around the world, and you have behind you the support of millions everywhere.

Much will depend upon the example that this Force sets. Your success can have profound effect for good, not only in the present emergency, but on future prospects for building a world order, of which we may all one day be truly proud.

I know the United Nations can count on you. I know also that in greeting you and thanking you for the part you are playing, I express good wishes and gratitude that are shared by countless others who are with you in heart and in spirit.

UN Press Release SG / 549, December 10, 1956.

Statement in the General Assembly on
Status of Israeli Withdrawal

UN HEADQUARTERS, NEW YORK   DECEMBER 21, 1956

THE GENERAL ASSEMBLY discussed during plenary meetings from December 18 to 21 British, French, and Israeli complaints that had been addressed to the Secretary-General and the President of the Assembly charging mistreatment by the Egyptian government of British and French nationals and of the Jewish community living in Egypt. Many were reported to have been arbitrarily expelled and their property seized in violation of the Charter and the Declaration of Human Rights. Egypt replied that the measures taken were for the protection of public order and security after the nation had been attacked. They were not arbitrary and were in accord with generally recognized rules of international law in such circumstances.

Britain, France, and Israel received little support for their complaints and proposed no resolution on the subject. Before the discussion ended on December 21, the representative of Jordan, Abdel Monem Rifa'i, in the course of a speech critical of delays in the withdrawals of British, French, and Israeli forces, requested the Secretary-General to give the Assembly an oral progress report before the recess for Christmas and New Year's. Hammarskjöld responded in the statement that follows. This was mostly concerned with the Israeli forces, for the British-French withdrawal from Port Said, though a week behind the target date, was now in its last twenty-four hours. On December 19 UNEF had taken over all civil affairs responsibilities in Port Said from the British, on December 20 the airport was handed over by the Anglo-French Command, and on December 21, under the supervision of UNEF, 472 British civilian internees were exchanged for 357 Egyptian service personnel and civilians. Also on December 21 UN salvage ships for the Canal clearance operation reached El Cap, the first ships to enter the Canal since hostilities had begun. The day after the Secretary-General spoke the Anglo-French evacuation was completed.

This morning [630th meeting] the representative of Jordan directed to me certain questions. To the extent that I am in a position to reply to those questions I would like to use this opportunity to do so.

The first question put to me concerned the withdrawal of Israel

General Assembly Official Records, Eleventh Session, 632nd Plenary Meeting, December 21, 1956.

armed forces behind the armistice lines. The four resolutions of the General Assembly relating to withdrawal of forces from Egypt, as the Members of the General Assembly will remember, call for the withdrawal of Israel forces behind the armistice lines. The last of these resolutions, adopted on November 24, called for compliance "forthwith" with the previous requests. As of today, the extent of Israel withdrawal, and the further withdrawal in prospect, are as follows.

On December 1, the representative of Israel informed the Secretary-General by letter that, on the morning of December 3, Israel forces would be removed from "a wide belt of territory (about 50 kilometres) in proximity to the Suez Canal along its entire length. . . ." This withdrawal has been confirmed by General Burns, and elements of the United Nations Emergency Force immediately entered this area, although progress in it has been impeded because of mine fields and destroyed roads.

On December 11, the representative of Israel informed the Secretary-General that Israel was now ready to effect further withdrawals of Israel troops in the Sinai peninsula, in order to enable the United Nations Emergency Force to extend its occupation eastwards, and invited a meeting between the Commander of the United Nations Emergency Force and the Israel General Staff to discuss arrangements to this effect.

General Burns met with General Dayan, the Israel Commander, on the morning of December 16. General Dayan informed General Burns that, according to his instructions, the Israel forces were to be withdrawn from the Sinai peninsula at the approximate rate of 25 kilometres per week during the "next few weeks." General Burns recalled to General Dayan that the Israelis were expected to withdraw behind the armistice lines as rapidly as possible. He felt sure that the rate mentioned would not be acceptable to the Secretary-General.

Specific arrangements presented at the same time provided for the withdrawal of Israel forces on December 18 to Misfaq on the El Qantara-El Arish road, and to Bir Gifgafa on the Ismailia-El Auja road. The Israelis stated that on the road from Suez to Elath they had already withdrawn to Sudr el-Heitan. In each such withdrawal, the United Nations Emergency Force contingents would advance to within 5 kilometres of the Israel positions. In the Suez Gulf coast region, the Israel forces were to withdraw from Sudr on the morning of December 19, with a UNEF detachment moving promptly forward to take over the oil-well installations at that place.

The specific withdrawal arrangements for December 18 and 19 were accepted by General Burns.

Subject to further discussion, and in addition to the aforementioned withdrawals, it was assumed as a tentative arrangement that, within a week, the United Nations Emergency Force would move forward approximately another 25 kilometres on roads eastward from the Canal, and also to Wadi Feiran on the Suez Gulf coast. It was agreed that a "reconnaissance party" of UNEF would proceed immediately to El Arish to obtain information regarding the billeting and other requirements of UNEF preparatory to its entry there.

It was estimated by my military adviser, General Martola, and his military aides, that the pace and schedule for the Israel withdrawal reported to General Burns by General Dayan on December 16 would mean that from four to six weeks might elapse before the withdrawal would bring Israel forces behind the armistice lines, as required by the resolutions of the General Assembly. The assumption by General Burns that the pace of withdrawal proposed by General Dayan would be unacceptable to me was confirmed to a member of the Israel delegation on December 17.

Specific Israel proposals for the withdrawal of its forces beyond what had been agreed upon on December 19 were presented the same day to General Burns. In substance, they provided for a further withdrawal of only some 20 kilometres along the main roads. General Burns informed General Dayan that these proposals were inadequate. On December 20, I informed the representative of Israel that this schedule of withdrawal, which had no completion date, was inconsistent with the intention of the resolutions of the General Assembly and unsatisfactory. The representative of Israel informed his government to this effect.

Today the representative of Israel has presented a new withdrawal proposal which had been received from his government and which supersedes the proposal of December 19. This envisages that the remaining Israel withdrawal will take place in two phases. In the first phase, no Israel forces would be "west of El Arish" after the first week in January, although Israel occupation of Sharm El Sheikh and Tirana would continue. The details of this phase of the withdrawal are to be worked out in another meeting between General Burns and General Dayan. The second phase would involve full Israel withdrawal, understood to mean behind the armistice lines, at an unstated date.

Despite the difficulties encountered by the United Nations Emergency

Force in its advance into the Sinai peninsula, resulting from mine fields and destroyed roads, some limitations in communications and transport, and the nature of the terrain, the Force is prepared to move forward at whatever pace may be required by a rapid Israel withdrawal behind the armistice lines, as envisaged by the General Assembly.

The second question put to me this morning concerned the withdrawal of French and British troops from Egyptian territory. The Anglo-French withdrawal from Port Said is in a very late phase, and I do not feel that it calls for any specific comments from my side.

The third question was regarding the destruction which took place in Port Said. So far, I have no specific information on that point.

Another question was to what extent there had been demolition in Sinai. On that point I wish only to refer to a letter from the Permanent Representative of Israel to me, which was circulated last week to delegations of the General Assembly, according to which the Israel government gave assurances that no demolition would take place in Sinai. As to the extent to which such demolition may have taken place, I am not in possession of any exact information.

Finally, the representative of Jordan referred to "atrocities which are practised on the Arab population in the Sinai peninsula." Again, I am not in a position to make any comments. He referred also to the Gaza Strip and the policy of Israel in that area. Shortly, the reports will be circulated on the present state of affairs of Gaza as well as the developments under the United Nations Relief and Works Agency for Palestine Refugees in the Near East in Gaza. As regards the policy of Israel in this area, I have no specific information to give to the General Assembly.

AT THE SAME meeting which heard the foregoing oral report on withdrawal by the Secretary-General, the Assembly adopted a compromise resolution recommended by the Fifth (Administrative and Budgetary) Committee on the troublesome question of how the costs of UNEF should be shared.

It will be recalled that this question had been referred on November 26 for further consideration by the Fifth Committee after the Secretary-General had proposed this procedure (see page 385). Hammarskjöld did not personally take part in the Committee's discussions, but Bruce R. Turner, the UN Controller, spoke as his representative when the Committee took up the question on December 3. He unequivocally reaffirmed the Secretary-General's opinion that the costs of UNEF were expenses of the Organization within the meaning of Article 17 of the Charter and, apart from those costs "which individual governments may themselves elect to bear," should be borne in accordance with the regular scale of assessments. The statement was as follows:

> Members will recall that in the course of the statement I made on behalf of the Secretary-General on November 27, last, it was suggested that the Committee should defer, temporarily, consideration of the method to be adopted for the allocation to Member states, of the costs for the United Nations Emergency Force which are to be financed by the United Nations. I stated that the Secretary-General would be willing, if the Committee so desired, to make a proposal in due course as to the manner in which consideration of this question might best proceed. After further reflection, however, and taking into account the views expressed informally by a number of delegations, the Secretary-General has come to the conclusion that the only practicable and equitable basis for allocating the expenses of the Force is the one which he has already recommended to the General Assembly in paragraph 6 of A/3383—namely, that such expenses should be shared by Member states in accordance with the scale of assessments to be adopted for the regular budget of the United Nations for 1957. Apart, moreover, from considerations of equity and practicality, he believes that the collective sharing of costs in this manner is the right and proper course to adopt.
>
> Since the General Assembly has established the Force as a United Nations instrument for the accomplishment of certain stated purposes, it would seem logical to follow that the United Nations must itself assume full and final responsibility for its effective functioning, including those obligations, financial and otherwise, that flow therefrom. It is relevant to call attention, in this connection, to the conceptional basis for the establishment and organization of the Force which was accepted by the General Assembly in its decision of November 5, 1956, under resolution 594 (XI). By virtue of this decision, the Force has been set up, in the first place, on the basis of principles reflected in the constitution of the United Nations itself. Consequently, its Commander is appointed by the United Nations and is ultimately responsible, in the exercise of his functions, to the General Assembly. His authority is so defined as to make him fully independent of the policies of any one nation.
>
> While, therefore, the expenses of the Force, other than those which individual governments may themselves elect to bear, may be treated from a stricly budgetary and accounting viewpoint, as separate from the regular annual appropriation voted by the General Assembly for financing the activities of the Organization, they remain, nevertheless, United Nations expenditures within the general scope and intent of Article 17 of the Charter, paragraph 2 of which reads "the expenses of the Organization shall be borne by the Members as apportioned by the General Assembly." Hence, it would seem to the Secretary-General en-

tirely appropriate that the arrangements decided upon by the General Assembly, at this session, for apportioning the expenses of the Organization, should apply also to [those] relating to the Force.

The Secretary-General wishes it to be made very clear, however, that the considerations set forth are concerned with the United Nations Emergency Force only; they should *not* be construed as necessarily relevant to other responsibilities which the United Nations has acquired or may acquire in the area. The clearance of the Suez Canal, for example, and the responsibilities that devolve upon the United Nations in connection therewith, presents, in the Secretary-General's opinion, a quite separate problem which, in its financial aspects, may conceivably need to be dealt with in a totally different manner.

The Secretary-General hopes that the views he has ventured to express concerning the method to be adopted for allocating to Member states the costs of the Force, will serve as a useful basis for consideration of this matter by the Fifth Committee. Members will appreciate his concern that there will be no avoidable delay in reaching decisions as to the manner in which necessary administrative and financial arrangements for the Force should proceed. He trusts, therefore, that the Fifth Committee will find it possible to report back to the General Assembly, on the matters referred to it, at an early date.[1]

The Committee was unable to reach a clear-cut decision in time for action by the Assembly before its Christmas–New Year's recess. The same differences prevailed in its discussions to which reference has already been made on page 385. Finally a compromise resolution was put together and presented for plenary action on December 21. The resolution provided that the first $10 million of UNEF expenses should be borne by the United Nations and apportioned according to the regular scale of assessments. However this would be without prejudice to the apportionment of expenses in excess of $10 million. That question would be considered by a committee composed of Canada, Ceylon, Chile, El Salvador, India, Liberia, Sweden, the USSR, and the United States. This committee was instructed to take into account, among other things, the differing views expressed in the General Assembly, the possibility of voluntary contributions and of a special scale of contributions different from the ordinary budget.[2] Thus a definitive stand on the issue of principle was put off once again.

This resolution was accepted by the General Assembly just before adjournment by a vote of 62 to 8 with 7 abstentions. The vote was by show of hands.

[1] General Assembly, Eleventh Session, Fifth Committee, Document A/C. 5/687, December 3, 1956 (mimeographed). The summary record is given in General Assembly Official Records, Eleventh Session, Fifth Committee, 541st Meeting.

[2] General Assembly Resolution 1089 (XI) of December 21, 1956.

MESSAGES AND STATEMENTS
ON HUNGARY

1956

WHEN THE second emergency special session of the General Assembly convened at 4:00 P.M. on Sunday, November 4, the massive Soviet military intervention in Hungary was well under way. The government of Imre Nagy, which had included for a brief moment non-Communists in its ranks, was overthrown and Nagy had taken refuge in the Yugoslav embassy. With Soviet backing, another Communist leader, János Kádár, formed a new government. He had suffered during the Stalinist purges of the early 1950s and had joined Nagy's government but switched sides when persuaded that only Soviet troops could save the party's control of his country in the face of a popular uprising so intense and widespread.

Kádár, joined by Imre Horvath, the new Foreign Minister, sent a cable to the Secretary-General declaring that Imre Nagy's requests for United Nations intervention had no legal force and that the new government "objects categorically" to any discussion of the Hungarian question by either the Security Council or the General Assembly, "because that question is within the exclusive jurisdiction of the Hungarian People's Republic." [1]

Sobolev used this message in the Assembly that afternoon to support his contention that discussion of Hungary was a violation of the domestic jurisdiction clause of the Charter (Article 2, paragraph 7). However the agenda was quickly adopted 53 to 8 (no representative of Hungary was present) with 7 abstentions. Less than four hours later, after speeches passionately denouncing the Soviet Union's intervention, the Assembly adopted a resolution introduced by the United States which follows below. The vote was 50 to 8 with 15 abstentions. The latter included India, Egypt, and eleven other Arab-Asians, together with Yugoslavia and Finland. The resolution was as follows:

The General Assembly,
Considering that the United Nations is based on the principle of the sovereign equality of all its Members,

Recalling that the enjoyment of human rights and of fundamental freedom in Hungary was specifically guaranteed by the Peace Treaty between Hungary and the Allied and Associated Powers signed at Paris on February 10, 1947, and that the general principle of these rights and this freedom is affirmed for all peoples in the Charter of the United Nations,

---

[1] General Assembly Official Records, Second Emergency Special Session, Annex, Document A/3311.

Convinced that recent events in Hungary manifest clearly the desire of the Hungarian people to exercise and to enjoy fully their fundamental rights, freedom, and independency,

Condemning the use of Soviet military forces to suppress the efforts of the Hungarian people to reassert their rights,

Noting moreover the declaration of October 30, 1956, by the Government of the Union of Soviet Socialist Republics of its avowed policy of nonintervention in the internal affairs of other States,

Noting the communication of November 1, 1956, of the Government of Hungary to the Secretary-General regarding demands made by that Government to the Government of the Union of Soviet Socialist Republics for the instant and immediate withdrawal of Soviet forces,

Noting further the communication of November 2, 1956, from the Government of Hungary to the Secretary-General asking the Security Council to instruct the Government of the Union of Soviet Socialist Republics and the Government of Hungary to start negotiations immediately on the withdrawal of Soviet forces,

Noting that the intervention of Soviet military forces in Hungary has resulted in grave loss of life and widespread bloodshed among the Hungarian people,

Taking note of the radio appeal of Prime Minister Imre Nagy of November 4, 1956,

1. *Calls upon* the Government of the Union of Soviet Socialist Republics to desist forthwith from all armed attack on the people of Hungary and from any form of intervention, in particular armed intervention, in the internal affairs of Hungary;

2. *Calls upon* the Union of Soviet Socialist Republics to cease the introduction of additional armed forces into Hungary and to withdraw all of its forces without delay from Hungarian territory;

3. *Affirms* the right of the Hungarian people to a government responsive to its national aspirations and dedicated to its independence and well-being;

4. *Requests* the Secretary-General to investigate the situation caused by foreign intervention in Hungary, to observe the situation directly through representatives named by him, and to report thereon to the General Assembly at the earliest moment, and as soon as possible to suggest methods to bring an end to the foreign intervention in Hungary in accordance with the principles of the Charter of the Union Nations;

5. *Calls upon* the Government of Hungary and the Government of the Union of Soviet Socialist Republics to permit observers designated by the Secretary-General to enter the territory of Hungary, to travel freely therein, and to report their findings to the Secretary-General;

6. *Calls upon* all Members of the United Nations to cooperate with the Secretary-General and his representatives in the execution of his functions;

7. *Requests* the Secretary-General in consultation with the heads of

appropriate specialized agencies to inquire, on an urgent basis, into the needs of the Hungarian people for food, medicine, and other similar supplies, and to report to the General Assembly as soon as possible;

8. *Requests* all Members of the United Nations, and invites national and international humanitarian organizations, to cooperate in making available such supplies as may be required by the Hungarian people.[2]

The resolution employed vigorous language, its demands upon the Soviet Union were unequivocal, and the assignment handed to the Secretary-General apparently far-reaching, but the impression of decisive action was deceptive. Strong words cloaked the weak constitutional, political, and military position of the majority. As in the Middle East the Assembly could only recommend a course of action, it could not compel. And as in the Middle East the effectiveness of its recommendation would depend on the persuasions and pressures that Member states were willing and able to put behind it. In case of noncompliance there was the theoretical possibility under the Uniting-for-Peace resolution of an Assembly recommendation to Member states to come to the aid of Hungary in expelling the invaders as the United States and others had responded to a Security Council recommendation when South Korea was invaded in 1950. The possibility of such a course of action, involving war with the Soviet Union, was ruled out from the start by the United States and its NATO allies.

Short of a military response, or the threat of it, the West was severely limited in its ability to influence the course of the Soviet Union. In the Middle East crisis the British government was faced by strong opposition at home, a threatened breakup of the Commonwealth and decisive financial sanctions by the United States. Israel, too, was dependent on financial and economic aid from the United States. No comparable political and economic pressures to which the Soviet Union would be vulnerable were available in the case of Hungary. Though resistance inside Hungary would continue for another two or three weeks, the outcome was already certain on November 4. The Soviet government had decided its vital interests required keeping Hungary in the Communist camp at all costs and it had sent in more than enough troops and armor to assure that outcome.

So the course adopted by the Assembly majority on November 4 was to put the Soviet Union in the dock, keep it there, and make it suffer as much as possible in reputation and influence. In this they were to achieve considerable success in Western Europe and Latin America, where the Communist cause received sharp setbacks. In Asia, however, the effect proved to be of less consequence. While it was thus possible to hurt the Soviet Union in this peripheral way, help to Hungary itself was beyond reach, except for relief supplies and new homes for the refugees who soon began streaming across the Austrian border.

In the light of the realities the Assembly's November 4 resolution and its

[2] General Assembly Resolution 1004 (ES-II), November 4, 1956.

successors could accomplish little more than dramatize the Soviet Union's defiance of the will of the United Nations majority. They were expressions of moral outrage and condemnation, not the vehicles for viable action in support of the stated objectives which they pretended to be. They were an embarrassment to the Soviet Union, but they were also damaging to the United Nations. The Organization was made to appear weak and ineffectual because it was asked to achieve results that were impossible short of war by Member states which had already rejected resort to force and could find no better alternative than a propaganda barrage from the General Assembly hall.

Unlike the Middle East crisis the Secretary-General had virtually no room for the exercise of his diplomatic skills in response to the requests addressed to him in paragraph 4 of the November 4 resolution. In Hungary the Nagy government which would have welcomed United Nations observers had been overthrown and the Kádár régime depended on Soviet troops to regain control of the country for the Communist party. The request that Hammarskjöld "as soon as possible . . . suggest methods to bring an end to the foreign intervention in Hungary in accordance with the principles of the Charter of the United Nations" carried confidence in him to the realm of fantasy. It was like saying: we have not been able to think of anything else to do, we can give you no tools with which to work except our indignation, so, please, pass a miracle.

This Hammarskjöld could not produce, but, within the bounds of reality, he did what he could. At the conclusion of the November 7 session of the General Assembly, which approved his second UNEF report, he spoke as follows:

> Before this meeting is adjourned, I should like to inform the Assembly that, despite the responsibilities which the Middle Eastern question has placed upon me and my staff, we are giving serious consideration to our responsibilities under resolution 1004 (ES-II) on the question of Hungary, adopted by the General Assembly on November 4. That resolution has been formally called to the attention of the two governments most directly concerned. I shall shortly be in a position to report on further steps that will be taken in implementation of the resolution. In the meantime, the Office of the United Nations High Commissioner for Refugees is working with other welfare agencies to meet the need for food, medicine, and similar supplies.[3]

On the following day, November 8, the Secretary-General addressed an *aide-mémoire* to the Hungarian government formally requesting its agreement to the admission of observers. The Assembly was meeting again on Hungary for the first time since November 4 to permit delegates to explain their votes, and Hammarskjöld called their attention to the *aide-mémoire*,

[3] General Assembly Official Records, First Emergency Special Session, 567th Plenary Meeting, November 7, 1956.

hoping the Members would "also consider it as the first progress report."
The text follows.

---

1. Aide-Mémoire to the Minister of
Foreign Affairs of Hungary

UN HEADQUARTERS, NEW YORK   NOVEMBER 8, 1956

---

1. In its resolution 1004 (ES-II) of November 4, 1956, on the situation
in Hungary, already transmitted to the Government of Hungary, the
General Assembly of the United Nations requested the Secretary-General
to observe the situation directly through representatives named by
him, and to report thereon to the General Assembly at the earliest moment. In support of this request the General Assembly called upon the
Government of Hungary and the Government of the Union of Soviet
Socialist Republics to permit observers designated by the Secretary-
General to enter the territory of Hungary, to travel freely therein, and
to report their findings to the Secretary-General.

2. Referring to the operative parts of the resolution just mentioned, I
wish to address to the Government of Hungary the question whether, in
pursuance of the demand of the General Assembly, it is willing to permit observers designated by me, as soon as possible, to enter the territory of Hungary for the purpose prescribed, to travel freely within Hungary, and to report to me on their findings.

3. I would appreciate an early reply to this question. After receipt of
the reply I shall approach the other government directly concerned.

4. I intend to proceed with a selection of observers on the
assumption that the Government of Hungary will meet the request of
the General Assembly.

5. In its resolution the General Assembly has also requested the Secretary-General to investigate the situation caused by foreign intervention in Hungary. I have taken steps for such an investigation on the
basis of available and confirmed material.

General Assembly Official Records, Second Emergency Special Session, Annex,
Document A/3315, November 8, 1956.

6. The General Assembly has, finally, requested the Secretary-General as soon as possible to "suggest methods to bring an end to the foreign intervention in Hungary in accordance with the principles of the Charter of the United Nations." This matter is under active consideration within the Secretariat. It is obviously not possible to reach a final result before the end of the investigation just referred to, and without the cooperation of the Hungarian government in the sense indicated above.

7. I finally wish to repeat once again my request, expressing at the same time my firm expectation that the request of the General Assembly will be accepted.

THE GENERAL ASSEMBLY adopted three additional resolutions on the situation in Hungary on November 9, after two days of debate. The first of these was introduced by Cuba, Ireland, Italy, Pakistan, and Peru. Besides reiterating the November 4 demand upon the Soviet Union to withdraw its forces and cease its intervention in Hungary's internal affairs, this resolution declared that the General Assembly "considers that free elections should be held in Hungary under United Nations auspices, as soon as law and order have been restored, to enable the people of Hungary to determine for themselves the form of government they wish to establish in their country." [1] This resolution was adopted by 48 to 11 with 16 abstentions. India and Yugoslavia, which had been among the abstainers on November 4, joined the Soviet bloc in voting *against*. The abstainers included most of the Arab-Asians plus Austria and Finland.

A second resolution, sponsored by the United States, accused Soviet armed forces of interfering with receipt and distribution of food and medical supplies and called for their cooperation with United Nations agencies and the Red Cross in such humanitarian assistance. It also noted the rapidly increasing flow of refugees from Hungary "as a result of the harsh and repressive action of the Soviet armed forces" and requested "the Secretary-General to call upon the United Nations High Commissioner for Refugees to consult with other appropriate international agencies and interested governments with a view to making speedy and effective arrangements for emergency assistance to refugees from Hungary." [2] This resolution was adopted by 53 to 9 with 13 abstentions.

A third resolution, urging relief measures without political overtones, was proposed by Austria and adopted by 67 to 0 with 8 abstentions. Poland left the Soviet bloc to support this resolution. Under its terms the Assembly voted to undertake immediately a large-scale relief program for the Hungar-

[1] General Assembly Resolution 1005 (ES-II), November 9, 1956.
[2] General Assembly Resolution 1006 (ES-II), November 9, 1956.

ian people, called on all Member states to participate, requested "the Secretary-General to undertake immediately the necessary measures" and "urgently" appealed "to all countries concerned to give full assistance to the Secretary-General in the implementation of this task." [3]

On November 10 the Assembly voted to transfer the Hungarian question from the emergency special session to the eleventh regular session which convened on November 12.

In the three following texts, all dated November 10, the Secretary-General (*a*) prodded the Hungarian government for a reply to his November 8 request to admit observers, (*b*) asked the Soviet government to support his request, (*c*) asked the Hungarian government for information on relief needs and proposed discussions with the government "on the best means of providing the assistance required."

Hammarskjöld also announced to the press that he had, on November 4, charged Philippe de Seynes, Under-Secretary for Economic and Social Affairs, with operating responsibility for resolutions dealing with Hungary's relief needs and had requested the United Nations Deputy High Commissioner for Refugees to coordinate and arrange emergency assistance for Hungarian refugees.

---

2. *Aide-Mémoire to the Government of Hungary*

UN HEADQUARTERS, NEW YORK   NOVEMBER 10, 1956

In an *aide-mémoire* sent to the Government of Hungary on November 8 (A/3315), I addressed to the government the question whether it is willing to permit observers, designated by me, to enter the territory of Hungary in pursuance of the resolution 1004 (ES-II) of the General Assembly of November 4. I expressed my firm expectation that the request of the General Assembly would be accepted.

It is with disappointment that I note that, so far, I have not received any reply, although the situation is one of the greatest urgency. I must therefore reiterate my request and ask the government to send me a reply without further delay. Should the reply have been held up by a consideration of the modalities for such a visit by observers, I am willing immediately to arrange for a discussion about the modalities.

General Assembly Official Records, Eleventh Session, Annexes, Volume II, agenda item 67, Document A/3335, November 11, 1956.

[3] General Assembly Resolution 1007 (ES-II), November 9, 1956.

I have given a copy of this *aide-mémoire* to the Permanent Representative of the Union of Soviet Socialist Republics, together with a request for the assistance of the Government of the USSR in the fulfillment of my mandate.

If I were not to get any reply from you shortly, I would have, under the resolution 1004 (ES-II) of November 4, to submit the situation to the General Assembly for consideration and the steps it may wish to take.

---

3. Aide-Mémoire to the Government of the Union of Soviet Socialist Republics

UN HEADQUARTERS, NEW YORK   NOVEMBER 10, 1956

Referring to the General Assembly resolution (1004 (ES-II)) of November 4 on the situation in Hungary, reaffirmed November 9 in the part relevant in this context, I wish to remind the Government of the Union of Soviet Socialist Republics of the request I addressed on November 8 to the Government of Hungary (A/3315), and to inform it about a renewed request I have addressed today in an *aide-mémoire* (A/3335) directed to the Government of Hungary.

In pursuance of my obligations under the General Assembly resolutions, I now ask the Government of the USSR to lend its assistance in the fulfillment of my mandate. Thus, I would ask the Government of the USSR to support my demand to the Government of Hungary for permission for observers, designated by me, to enter the territory of Hungary, to travel freely therein, and to report their findings to me. I likewise feel entitled to count on the assistance of the Government of the USSR to the observers, to the extent this is within its authority, in order to facilitate their work as soon as they enter the territory of Hungary.

I am convinced that the Government of the USSR is aware of the sense of urgency with which the General Assembly envisages this problem.

General Assembly Official Records, Eleventh Session, Annexes, Volume II, agenda item 67, Document A/3336, November 11, 1956.

4. Note Verbale *to the Minister of Foreign Affairs of Hungary*

UN HEADQUARTERS, NEW YORK   NOVEMBER 10, 1956

The Secretary-General presents his compliments to the Minister for Foreign Affairs of the Hungarian People's Republic and has the honour to refer to the provisions of the resolutions adopted at the second emergency special session of the General Assembly, which instruct the Secretary-General to take immediate measures to furnish medical supplies, foodstuffs, and clothes to the territories affected by the recent events in Hungary (resolutions 1006 I (ES-II) and 1007 (ES-II).

Accordingly the Secretary-General would appreciate receiving at the earliest possible date from the Government of Hungary information concerning the needs of the Hungarian people for medical supplies, foodstuffs, and clothes from abroad. Upon receipt of this information the Secretary-General would wish to discuss with the Hungarian government the best means of providing the assistance required.

DURING THE evening of November 12 the Secretary-General received the following reply, signed by Istvan Sebes, Acting Minister and Deputy Minister for Foreign Affairs of Hungary, to his communications of November 8 and 10:

In connection with the notifications of the Secretary-General of the United Nations concerning the resolutions of the General Assembly accepted on November 4 and 10, 1956, the Revolutionary Workers' and Peasants' Government of the Hungarian Peoples' Republic deems it necessary to state the following:

In the past weeks, mass demonstrations took place in Hungary, the democratic and patriotic demands of which the Revolutionary Workers' and Peasants' government has accepted as its own. From the beginning

General Assembly Official Records, Eleventh Session, Annexes, agenda item 67, Document A/3337, November 11, 1956.

the participants of these demonstrations included organized Fascist elements, and later ordinary criminals also who escaped from prison. These persons meanwhile gradually took the lead and carried off and murdered hundreds of progressive-minded people and members of their families.

In this situation, the first task was the restoration of law and order, the prevention of the danger of Fascism, which task Hungary has, in article 4 of the Treaty of Peace, also undertaken to carry out.

In the serious situation which arose, the Revolutionary Workers' and Peasants' government could restore law and order only by requesting the aid of Soviet troops. After the complete restoration of order, the Hungarian government will immediately begin negotiations with the Government of the Soviet Union for the withdrawal of these troops from Hungary.

On the basis of the foregoing, the Hungarian government most emphatically states the settlement of the situation which has arisen in Hungary lies exclusively within the internal legal competence of the Hungarian state. Therefore, any resolution of the General Assembly relating to the internal political situation of Hungary constitutes an interference in Hungarian internal affairs and is in contradiction with the provisions of Article 2, paragraph 7, of the Charter.

Accordingly,

1. The Hungarian government and the Soviet government are exclusively competent to carry on negotiations concerning the withdrawal of the Soviet troops from Hungary, which troops are here only for the purpose of restoring law and order and do not take any measures against the population which are contrary to international law and the principles of humanity.

2. In view of the fact that Soviet troops are in Hungary at the request of the Hungarian government, the Hungarian government is decidedly of the opinion that the sending of representatives to be appointed by the Secretary-General of the United Nations is not warranted.

3. The holding of elections in Hungary is entirely within the competence of the Hungarian authorities.

In connection with the resolution on Hungarian refugees, the Hungarian government states that it will make possible for Hungarian citizens who have fled abroad as a result of the battles to return freely and without harm.

The Hungarian government accepts with sincere thanks the humane resolutions of the General Assembly which are in conformity with Article 1, paragraph 3, of the United Nations Charter and aim to assist the Hungarian people; and communicates that it will facilitate with every means the receipt and distribution of food and medicine sent for the Hungarian people, and is at present also cooperating with the representatives of the International Red Cross Committee. The Soviet troops in Hungary do not hinder this relief work in any way. In carrying out this task, the Hungarian government is prepared to cooperate most fully with the agencies of the United Nations.

The assessment of damages is now proceeding. After final estimates of its needs, the Hungarian government will inform the Secretary-General of the United Nations. Meanwhile, the Hungarian government gratefully accepts all food, clothing, and medicine for Hungarian families who face a difficult winter.[1]

The next day Hammarskjöld responded in a cable urging the Hungarian government to reconsider its objection to UN observers. The text follows.

---

5. Cablegram to the Acting Minister and Deputy Minister of Foreign Affairs of Hungary

UN HEADQUARTERS, NEW YORK   NOVEMBER 13, 1956

I have the honour to acknowledge receipt of your cablegram dated November 12, 1956 (A/3341). I note with satisfaction your observations on the resolutions of the General Assembly concerning relief to Hungary, and the willingness of your government to cooperate most fully with the agencies of the United Nations for the humanitarian ends to which these resolutions are directed. I note that you will inform me of the needs as soon as final estimates have been made. In your cablegram you discuss also the previous resolution of the General Assembly of November 4, 1956 and the request for permission for observers, designated by the Secretary-General, to enter the territory of Hungary and to report to the Secretary-General. The views now expressed by the Hungarian government on this subject are noted. In my execution of the decision of the General Assembly it would not be to the purpose for me to enter upon a discussion concerning that decision. The Hungarian government concludes that it "is decidedly of the opinion that the sending of representatives to be appointed by the Secretary-General of the United Nations is not warranted." I would invite the Government of

General Assembly Official Records, Eleventh Session, Annexes, Volume II, agenda item 67, Document A/3346, November 13, 1956.

[1] *Ibid.*, Document A/3341, November 12, 1956.

Hungary to reconsider this judgment in the light of the opposite view, so widely expressed by Member governments in the General Assembly and reflected in the vote and, as a Member of the United Nations, to co-operate with the great majority in the clarification of a situation which has given rise to such concern in the General Assembly—DAG HAMMARSKJÖLD, *Secretary-General, United Nations.*

ON NOVEMBER 13 the Soviet Union, as was to be expected, turned down the Secretary-General's request for its assistance and support in arranging for UN observers to go to Hungary. In a brief *note verbale* Ambassador Sobolev reaffirmed Soviet opposition to the November 4 resolution and declared that the admission of United Nation observers was "a matter lying exclusively within the jurisdiction of the Government of the Hungarian People's Republic." [1]

However, a second cable arrived from the Acting Foreign Minister in Budapest which gave details of the most urgent relief needs and stated that the Hungarian government was prepared to discuss with the Secretary-General the best means of providing the assistance required as well as how his representatives might participate in organizing the assistance on the spot.[2] The new Hungarian Foreign Minister, Imre Horvath, had meanwhile arrived in New York for the Assembly session. Hammarskjöld promptly talked with Horvath and offered to go personally to Budapest during his imminent trip to Egypt to discuss the basis for UN humanitarian activities in Hungary. No reply had been received by the time of Hammarskjöld's departure on November 14, but the next day a cable arrived from the Deputy Foreign Minister in Budapest which referred to the Secretary-General's November 13 message about observers as well as his talk with Horvath and read as follows:

> With reference to your letter of November 13, 1956 [A/3346] and to the conversation between you and the Hungarian Minister for Foreign Affairs, I have the honour to inform you that the representatives of the Government of the Hungarian People's Republic would be glad to meet you in Rome at a time convenient to you and negotiate about the aid offered by the United Nations as well as to exchange views about the position taken by the Hungarian Government regarding the resolutions of the United Nations.[3]

With acceptance of his offer to go to Budapest thus withheld, Hammarskjöld saw no point in a meeting at Rome, when the Hungarian Foreign

[1] *Ibid.,* Document A/3347, November 14, 1956.
[2] *Ibid.,* Document A/3345 (mimeographed), November 13, 1956.
[3] *Ibid.,* Annexes, agenda item 67, Document A/3358, November 15, 1956.

Minister was already in New York. The text of his reply from Cairo on November 16 follows.

---

6. Cablegram to the Acting Minister and Deputy Minister of Foreign Affairs of Hungary

CAIRO, EGYPT   NOVEMBER 16, 1956

I have the honour to acknowledge receipt of your message of yesterday (A/3358) in reply to my communication of November 13, and the offer I made orally to the Foreign Minister to go to Budapest for a discussion of the basis for humanitarian activities by the United Nations in Hungary. I note that you suggest that the meeting I have offered take place in Rome. I made my offer to discuss in Budapest in view of the value of a broader personal contact with those who would be directly concerned with the matter on your side. Under the circumstances, I propose to discuss the matters mentioned in your latest message with the Foreign Minister on my return to New York which, for other reasons as well as this one, should take place as early as possible—DAG HAMMAR-SKJÖLD, *Secretary-General, United Nations.*

ALSO ON November 16 the Secretary-General formally notified the Assembly that he had formed a group of three distinguished personalities to assist him in meeting the request included in the November 4 resolution for him to investigate the situation caused by foreign intervention in Hungary. They were Judge Oscar Gundersen of Norway, Arthur Lall, India's Permanent Representative to the United Nations, and Alberto Lleras of Colombia, former Secretary-General of the Organization of American States and former President of Colombia. They were requested to prepare a report to Hammarskjöld on the matter.[1]

General Assembly Official Records, Eleventh Session, Annexes, agenda item 67, Document A/3362, November 16, 1956.

[1] *Ibid.,* Document A/3359, November 16, 1956.

7. *Interim Report on Refugees from Hungary, Transmitting a Report Submitted by the Office of the UN High Commissioner for Refugees*

UN HEADQUARTERS, NEW YORK   NOVEMBER 19, 1956

THE GENERAL ASSEMBLY resumed plenary discussion of the situation in Hungary on November 19. On the same day the Secretary-General submitted an interim report on the discharge of his responsibilities in organizing and promoting assistance for refugees from Hungary. He gave a brief accounting of his own actions since November 4 and then appended a longer report received by him that day from the Office of the United Nations High Commissioner for Refugees. The Secretary-General's own account is given in the text below. The principal points in the High Commissioner's report were as follows.

By November 18, 34,000 refugees had entered Austria from Hungary and the flow was continuing at a rate of 2,000 a day. In an addendum dated November 21, the Deputy High Commissioner reported that a drastic increase had just occurred in the daily flow of refugees across the border. This had raised the total now in Austria to over 50,000 in three days. The preliminary estimate of $6,530,000 in relief assistance over the next six months would now have to be revised sharply upward. Besides financial assistance in the provision of relief to the refugees, Austria needed urgent help from other states that could give asylum as quickly as possible to as many refugees as possible. The Deputy High Commissioner had addressed such an appeal to many governments and reported that the response was "a remarkable one." The annexed tabulation showed, for example, that the French government would accept an unlimited number, the Dominican Republic 20,000, Colombia 10,000, West Germany and the United States 5,000, Belgium 4,300, Switzerland 4,000, the United Kingdom 2,500.

1. The General Assembly, at its second emergency special session, adopted resolutions 1004 (ES-II), 1006 (ES-II), and 1007 (ES-II) con-

General Assembly Official Records, Eleventh Session, Annexes, agenda item 67, Documents A/3371, November 19, 1956, and A/3371/Add. 1, November 21, 1956.

cerning in part the refugees who have left and are leaving Hungary as a result of recent events in that country. The following is a brief interim report describing the steps taken by the Secretary-General in implementation of the relief provisions of the above resolutions in so far as they concern refugees, by way of introduction to a report by the Office of the United Nations High Commissioner for Refugees.

2. The text of resolution 1004 (ES-II) was transmitted to Member governments by the Secretary-General by a note of November 4 and the texts of resolutions 1006 (ES-II) and 1007 (ES-II) by a note of November 10.

3. On November 4, the Secretary-General appointed Mr. Philippe de Seynes, Under-Secretary for Economic and Social Affairs, to be responsible for the implementation of the relief provisions of the resolutions referred to in paragraph 1 above.

4. The Secretary-General on the same date asked the Deputy High Commissioner for Refugees to consult with the appropriate international agencies and interested governments with a view to making speedy and effective arrangements for refugees and informed him that special contributions from Member states for this purpose would be made available to him.

5. Since the adoption of the resolutions the Secretary-General has received the sum of $1 million from the United States government. Pledges have also been made by a number of other governments; these are listed in the annex to the attached report of the Office of the United Nations High Commissioner for Refugees. A number of contributions from individuals and private groups have also been received.

6. The Secretary-General presented on November 14 to the Government of the Federal Republic of Austria the sum of $500,000 for refugee relief and on November 19 the sum of $300,000 to the Office of the High Commissioner for Refugees, on receiving from the Deputy High Commissioner a provisional estimate of needs based on the number of refugees in Austria on November 17.

7. The Secretary-General has the honour to present to the General Assembly a report which he has today received from the Deputy High Commissioner for Refugees.

[Text of Deputy High Commissioner's report omitted—EDITORS]

THE GENERAL ASSEMBLY'S renewed debate on the situation in Hungary continued during six meetings on November 19, 20, and 21. There had been widely published reports that Soviet armed forces in Hungary were forcibly deporting large numbers of Hungarians to the Soviet Union and that "a reign of terror" had been instituted in the country. Cuba introduced a draft resolution which, as amended, reiterated the November 4 and 9 calls for the withdrawal of Soviet forces and urged "the Government of the Soviet Union and Hungarian authorities to take immediate steps to cease the deportation of Hungarian citizens and to return promptly to their homes those who have been deported from Hungarian territory." [1]

Argentina, Belgium, Denmark, and the United States introduced a draft resolution noting with appreciation the action taken so far by the Secretary-General and the High Commissioner in behalf of the refugees from Hungary, calling upon governments and nongovernmental organizations for contributions to the care and resettlement of the refugees and requesting the Secretary-General and High Commissioner to make an immediate appeal for funds to meet presently estimated minimum needs.[2]

Both on the Assembly floor and in messages from Budapest the Hungarian government categorically denied that there had been a single deportation of an "arrested person," though declaring that it had become "absolutely necessary to track down Fascist terrorists, antisocial instigators, and armed bandits" and to make arrests in order to restore law and order.[3] These denials were supported by Soviet bloc delegates.

India, Ceylon, and Indonesia introduced an even-handed resolution aimed at giving Assembly support for the Secretary-General's efforts to persuade the Hungarian government to admit UN observers and to arrange a personal visit to Budapest for talks with its leaders on the scene. The resolution, in its finally revised form, read as follows:

The General Assembly,

Noting that certain Member states have affirmed that Hungarian nationals have been forcibly deported from their country,

Noting further that certain other Member states have categorically affirmed that no such deportations have taken place,

Recalling paragraph 5 of its resolution 1004 (ES-II) of November 4, 1956, in which the Government of Hungary is asked to permit observers designated by the Secretary-General to enter the territory of Hungary, to travel freely therein, and to report their findings to the Secretary-General,

Noting that the Secretary-General is pursuing his efforts in this regard with the Hungarian government,

Noting further that the Secretary-General has urged Hungary as a

---

[1] *Ibid.,* Document A/3357/Rev. 2, November 18, 1956.
[2] *Ibid.,* Document A/3374, November 20, 1956.
[3] *Ibid.,* Document A/3373, November 20, 1956.

Member of the United Nations to cooperate with the great majority in
the clarification of the situation,

    1. *Urges Hungary* to accede to the request made by the Secretary-
General without prejudice to its sovereignty;

    2. *Requests* the Secretary-General to report to the General Assembly
without delay.[4]

It was during discussion of this resolution that the Secretary-General
made the statement that follows in response to a request from Krishna
Menon. In the voting that followed the Asian resolution was adopted by 57
to 8 with 14 abstentions. The stronger Cuban resolution was also adopted,
55 to 10 with 14 abstentions. Poland and Yugoslavia, which voted against
the Cuban resolution, abstained on the Asian resolution. The 4-Power resolution on refugees was approved 69 to 2 with 8 abstentions after Hungarian
amendments recommending cooperation in securing the speedy return of the
refugees to Hungary had been defeated. Hungary and Romania then cast the
only "no" votes on the resolution, with the rest of the Soviet bloc abstain-
ing.

---

8. *Statement in the General Assembly*

UN HEADQUARTERS, NEW YORK   NOVEMBER 21, 1956

The representative of India invited me to give my comments on the
views he expressed concerning the present state of relations between me
and the Government of Hungary. I will do so very briefly.

    I communicated at once the resolution of the General Assembly of
November 4 to the Government of Hungary. When, after a few days, I
had had no reaction, I sent a request drawing attention to the wish of
the General Assembly that observers assigned by me be admitted to
Hungary. In reply to that communication I received later, after some
further exchanges, a statement to the effect that the Government of
Hungary felt that the presence of United Nations observers in Hungary
was not warranted. I then replied with an appeal to the Government of
Hungary indicating that I felt that there was reason for reconsideration

  General Assembly Official Records, Eleventh Session, 586th Plenary Meeting,
November 21, 1956.

  [4] General Assembly Resolution 1128 (XI), November 21, 1956.

of that judgment in view of the serious concern felt by members of the General Assembly itself.

At about the same time, I offered to go to Budapest—then, in the first instance, for discussions concerning humanitarian activities. My offer to go to Budapest stands firm. However, in later exchanges with the Government of Hungary, the Government of Hungary proposed Rome—I suppose for practical reasons. At the same time, however, it indicated that it would like the discussions to extend beyond the sphere of humanitarian activities and cover also aspects of the General Assembly resolutions in general.

If it had not been for matters of extreme urgency, known to this Assembly, I would myself already, in the last two days, have taken up that thread and continued the discussions which, as appears from what I have said, I cannot regard as concluded.

It follows from the previous exchange of views that it is natural to take up the thread in personal talks here where we left it. It also follows that there is no refusal from the side of Hungary which makes it impossible for me to say that I wish to maintain my offer to go personally to Budapest and, in that context, to discuss not only humanitarian activities but, likewise, the wider aspects which the Government of Hungary itself brought into the picture.

DURING THE WEEK following November 21 the Secretary-General talked privately with the Hungarian Foreign Minister, Imre Horvath, urging again that his government reconsider its opposition to United Nation observers and maintaining his offer to go to Budapest for face-to-face discussions. He also talked with Soviet delegates concerning these matters and on the charges of deportations that had been made. He received no encouragement from the latter but was told by Horvath that the question of a visit to Budapest was still under consideration by the Hungarian government and it was hinted that a positive reply might be forthcoming. When, after a week, no new word had come from Budapest, Hammarskjöld felt he could delay no longer making an interim report to the General Assembly on the status of compliance with the various resolutions and on his own private efforts. On November 28 he addressed letters to the chairmen of the Hungarian and Soviet delegations requesting written replies on questions which should be taken into account in his report. These letters were not made public. When he circulated his report of November 30 (next following text) no reply had come in from Budapest. The response of the chairman of the Soviet delegation, V. V. Kuznetsov, which was appended to the Secretary-General's report, briefly reaffirmed the general Soviet position on the question of Hungary and rejected the charge of deportations as "based on slanderous rumors."

In his talks with Horvath on a visit to Budapest Hammarskjöld had revived the formula he had used successfully in arranging his 1954 talks in Peking with Chou En-lai in the case of the imprisoned American fliers.[1] While the aims expressed in the Assembly's resolutions would guide his efforts, he did not propose to come to Budapest as the agent of the Assembly majority, with the adversary relationship that would imply. He wished to make the contact on his own initiative because of those responsibilities as Secretary-General in matters of peace and security which derived directly from the Charter, general responsibilities which were separate from and not dependent upon decisions of the representative organs in specific cases. The Secretary-General officially informed the Assembly of this approach in the latter part of paragraph 10 of his November 30 report (following text).

---

9. Report to the General Assembly
on the Situation in Hungary

UN HEADQUARTERS, NEW YORK   NOVEMBER 30, 1956

I

1. In a number of resolutions, the General Assembly has adopted decisions concerning various aspects of the situation in Hungary and requested action on the part of the United Nations referring thereto. The main decisions adopted have covered the withdrawal of troops from Hungarian territory and related questions, including that of deportations; investigations of the situation caused by foreign intervention in Hungary; and humanitarian activities, including assistance to refugees. The Secretary-General has been requested to report to the General Assembly on compliance with its decisions, as well as on the development of such activities as the United Nations has decided upon.

2. By circulation of the messages exchanged, the General Assembly

General Assembly Official Records, Eleventh Session, Annexes, agenda item 67, Document A/3403, November 30, 1956.

[1] See *Public Papers of the Secretaries-General of the United Nations, Volume II; Dag Hammarskjöld, 1953–1956*, Columbia University Press, 1972.

has been kept currently informed of the Secretary-General's efforts to arrange for direct observation in Hungary and of the reactions of the Hungarian government to his *démarches*. Apart from these exchanges, a number of personal contacts concerning the matter have taken place.

3. Through an interim report dated November 19, 1956 (A/3371), the Secretary-General has informed the General Assembly about the development up to that date in the field of assistance to refugees.

4. The document now submitted to the General Assembly is intended to register aspects of the present situation about which the General Assembly may at this stage wish to be informed.

II

5. By letters of November 28, 1956, to the Chairmen of the delegations of Hungary and of the Union of Soviet Socialist Republics, the Secretary-General, drawing the attention of the governments to General Assembly resolutions 1127 (XI), 1128 (XI), and 1129 (XI) on the situation in Hungary, of November 21, 1956, which had been transmitted to the governments immediately after their adoption—addressed requests to the governments for information on points to be taken into account in an interim report on implementation of the various resolutions. In the case of the Hungarian government, special attention was drawn to the question of observers. The requests to the two governments were intended to bring the information in the report as closely up to date as possible.

6. The Secretary-General received on November 29 a reply to his letter of November 28 from the Chairman of the USSR delegation. The reply is annexed to this report.

7. At the time of writing this report the Secretary-General has not yet received a reply from the Government of Hungary. He has, however, been informed that, due to difficulties in transmission, his request of November 28 did not reach Budapest until some time in the course of November 29. The Secretary-General will circulate separately the reply he expects from the Hungarian government as soon as it is received.

8. No information is available to the Secretary-General concerning steps taken in order to establish compliance with the decisions of the General Assembly which refer to a withdrawal of troops or related political matters.

III

9. The efforts of the Secretary-General have been directed primarily to obtaining permission from the Hungarian government for observers, named by the Secretary-General, to enter Hungary for the purposes prescribed. So far no such permission has been given.

10. The Secretary-General has offered to go personally to Budapest for discussions with the government. This offer was confirmed in the course of the debate in the General Assembly on November 21 (586th meeting). The Secretary-General has been informed that this question is under consideration by the government. It is his hope that the reaction will be positive and that he will be invited to make a personal contact in Budapest. If an invitation is received, it would be his intention so to organize the visit as to cover not only the humanitarian activities, to which his offer originally referred, but also in general the position taken by the Government of Hungary regarding the resolutions of the United Nations, as indicated by the government itself in a cablegram dated November 15, 1956, addressed to the Secretary-General (A/3358). While the aims of the United Nations in the case of the situation in Hungary, as set out in the various General Assembly resolutions on the matter, would guide his efforts in Budapest, it seems appropriate that the contact of the Secretary-General with the Hungarian government be considered as based on his position under the Charter of the United Nations, with the wider scope that such a standpoint might give to his approach.

IV

11. The arrangements for direct observations in Hungary, to which reference has been made above, were part of the wider plan adopted by the General Assembly, which requests the Secretary-General to investigate the situation caused by foreign intervention in Hungary, to observe the situation directly through representatives named by him and to report thereon to the General Assembly. In addition to the efforts mentioned above, certain other measures have been taken in implementation, or in preparation of the implementation of the plan.

12. On November 12, the Secretary-General announced that he had taken steps to establish a group to assist him in fulfilling the investiga-

tory duties mentioned in paragraph 4 of resolution 1004 (ES-II) adopted by the General Assembly on November 4, 1956, regarding the situation in Hungary, and on November 16 he informed the General Assembly (A/3359) that this group would consist of Judge O. Gundersen, Mr. A. Lall, and Mr. A. Lleras.

13. This group has been examining some material at present available to the Secretariat. The Secretary-General has been informed, however, that this material does not provide a sufficient basis for a report to him at the present stage and that the group, moreover, deems it essential that its work should be supplemented by and coordinated with such findings as might result from the process of direct observation in Hungary. Since arrangements have not been concluded for effecting observation in Hungary, the stage has not yet been reached where it is possible to present a comprehensive report. Meanwhile, however, the investigating group is continuing to examine available material with reference to certain broad issues. In this connection the Assembly will recall that the Secretary-General stated as his view that the investigation should be based on available and confirmed material. It will be clear that for these criteria to be fulfilled some cooperation of those Member governments mainly concerned will be necessary. At this stage the Secretary-General would only draw the attention of Member governments to this point, which is likely to become one of immediate relevance when the group advances further its consideration of specific issues.

V

14. The situation in the field of humanitarian activities is more advanced. The Secretary-General need not here raise the question of refugees. He can therefore limit himself to the following observations concerning humanitarian assistance in general.

15. As requested by the General Assembly, the Secretary-General issued an appeal on November 15 to governments for contributions in support of relief to Hungary. So far, few governments have made contributions to the United Nations fund. Some have indicated that humanitarian aid is being channelled through national Red Cross societies and the International Committee of the Red Cross. The Secretary-General has been informed that an agreement has been concluded between the International Committee of the Red Cross and the Hungarian Red Cross covering the distribution of relief supplies to Hungary.

16. The Secretary-General has undertaken negotiations with the International Committee of the Red Cross with a view to channelling through that organization contributions for relief in Hungary made to the United Nations.

17. He has consulted with the heads of the specialized agencies who expressed readiness to cooperate in appropriate ways as and when required.

18. He has requested the Hungarian government to indicate the specific requirements of relief needs so as to be in a position to make these needs known to governments and to private humanitarian organizations wishing to offer aid. With the cooperation of the Hungarian government, he hopes, as requested by the General Assembly, to be in a position at all times to assist in the assessment of relief needs and to report to the General Assembly on the results of relief efforts in Hungary.

VI

19. By the means and through the channels available to him, the Secretary-General has used his best endeavours to further compliance with all the various decisions of the General Assembly on the situation in Hungary. The nature of the problem, and insufficient information concerning some of the basic assumptions for his activities, have complicated the task. It has already been mentioned that it seemed natural to him to concentrate first of all on the investigatory activities. This has been so as progress concerning these activities is of key significance for a successful approach to other points raised by the General Assembly.

20. His offer to go personally to Budapest should be seen in this light; it seemed to him that when a satisfactory basis for progress did not prove attainable through an exchange of communications, the initial step had to be the establishment of a direct personal contact. While discussions concerning his visit to Budapest were going on, he found it appropriate to suspend his reporting to the General Assembly. As long as these discussions had not been concluded, he did not consider it likely that considerations based on an interim report would be to the purpose.

21. However, although a reply to his latest request for clarification has not been received from the Government of Hungary, the Secretary-General has not considered it possible to wait any longer before reporting to the General Assembly. If the present report were to be taken up for consideration, he assumes that full account will be taken of the fact

that he is still awaiting a reply from the Hungarian government and that therefore the possibility of a visit by the Secretary-General to Budapest in the near future remains open.

[ANNEXES OMITTED]

ON DECEMBER 3 the Secretary-General received the following cable from Budapest on the questions of UN observers and his own proposed visit to Hungary:

> With reference to the negotiations conducted between Your Excellency and Mr. Imre Horvath, the Minister for Foreign Affairs and Delegate to the United Nations of the Revolutionary Workers' and Peasants' Government of the Hungarian People's Republic, I have the honour to inform you of the following on behalf of the Hungarian government.
>
> 1. The Hungarian government maintains its earlier position that the events which took place in Hungary since October 23, 1956, constitute exclusively the internal affairs of Hungary and do not belong to the competence of any international organization, including the United Nations organization. Consequently, the Hungarian government is, as before, of the opinion that the permission for United Nations observers to enter the territory of Hungary would violate the sovereignty of Hungary and would be contrary to the principles of the United Nations Charter.
>
> 2. In the middle of November 1956, you declared that on the occasion of your trip to Egypt you would like to meet the representatives of the Hungarian government in Rome or Budapest. Led by the desire that you should get satisfactory personal information of the situation in Hungary, the Hungarian government persists in its willingness expressed previously that its representative should negotiate with you in Rome or New York without delay.
>
> In order to make it possible for you to conduct direct negotiations with the Hungarian government, the Revolutionary Workers' and Peasants' Government of the Hungarian People's Republic is ready to welcome you in Budapest at a later date appropriate for both parties. ISTVAN SEBES, Acting Minister for Foreign Affairs of the Hungarian People's Republic.[1]

The General Assembly resumed its consideration of the Hungarian question in a series of six plenary meetings on December 3, 4, and 5. In the course of debate during the afternoon of December 4 on a new resolution

---

[1] *Ibid.,* Document A/3414, December 3, 1956.

on the question of United Nation observers the Hungarian Foreign Minister declared he was ready "at any convenient time" to discuss the date and arrangements for a visit to Budapest by the Secretary-General. Hammarskjöld replied that he would get in touch with the Hungarian representative "immediately." At the beginning of the evening meeting on December 4 he made the statement given in the text that follows. A motion by India that the General Assembly accept the Secretary-General's statement was adopted by 54 to 0 with 23 abstentions.

10. Statement in the General Assembly on Proposed Visit to Budapest

UN HEADQUARTERS, NEW YORK   DECEMBER 4, 1956

Following this afternoon's meeting, I had a conversation with the representative of Hungary concerning the date and other arrangements for my visit to Budapest. I consider it impossible for me personally to be absent from Headquarters for another week. On that basis, I could be in Budapest on December 16. The representative of Hungary has suggested to his government that I arrive in Budapest on that day. I intend to stay in Budapest for December 16, 17, and 18. As to the other practical arrangements, we have had a preliminary exchange of views. We shall resume our discussion of those arrangements tomorrow.

In order to prepare for my visit, I have arranged for Mr. Philippe de Seynes, Under-Secretary in charge of the Department of Economic and Social Affairs, to leave for Budapest as part of my own staff during the next few days. The representative of Hungary will suggest to his government that Mr. de Seynes arrive in Budapest one week in advance of me. He should remain for the duration of my own visit. If this arrangement were not made, I would suggest an earlier date for my own departure.

General Assembly Official Records, Eleventh Session, 608th Plenary Meeting, December 4, 1956.

AT THE CONCLUSION of its night meeting of December 4 the General Assembly had adopted a resolution introduced the day before by the United States and thirteen other Member states calling upon the Soviet Union and Hungary to consent by December 7 to receive United Nation observers and requesting the Secretary-General in the meantime "to arrange for the immediate dispatch to Hungary and other countries as appropriate of observers named by him." [1] The vote was 54 to 10 with 14 absentions. The latter included Finland and thirteen Arab-Asians, while Yugoslavia joined the Soviet bloc in voting "no."

The Secretary-General reported on the discharge of his responsibilities under this resolution in the "Note" to the General Assembly that follows and concluded with a pessimistic reference to the pending proposal for a December 16 visit to Budapest.

The day after Hammarskjöld submitted his "Note" Austria replied that it would admit United Nations observers, but Yugoslavia declined. On December 9 and 10, Czechoslovakia and Romania also refused and the Soviet Union reiterated its objection to the December 4 resolution as contrary to the Charter and international law. On December 12 a *note verbale* from the Permanent Mission of Hungary rejected the proposed date of December 16 for the Secretary-General's visit to Budapest in the following terms:

The Hungarian government refers to its previous statements which express its willingness to conduct negotiations with the Secretary-General. It refers also to the fact that on December 3 it informed the Secretary-General of its willingness to receive him in Budapest at a later date appropriate for both parties. The Hungarian government states also that December 16, which has been designated by the Secretary-General as a date for his visit to Budapest, is not appropriate for the Hungarian government. On the other hand, the Hungarian government will at a later date set forth a proposal through its representatives in New York for the purpose of reaching an agreement on the visit of the Secretary-General.[2]

This reply effectively ended the Secretary-General's hope that a visit to Budapest might be arranged in time to give him some possibility to accomplish anything of value.

---

[1] General Assembly Resolution 1130 (XI) of December 4, 1956.

[2] General Assembly Official Records, Eleventh Session, Annexes, agenda item 67, Document A/3435/Add. 6, December 12, 1956.

11. Note to the General Assembly

UN HEADQUARTERS, NEW YORK   DECEMBER 7, 1956

1. The General Assembly, in its resolution 1130 (XI) adopted on December 4, 1956, reiterated "its call upon the Government of the Union of Soviet Socialist Republics and the Hungarian authorities" to comply with previous resolutions on the situation in Hungary and to permit United Nations observers to enter the territory of Hungary, to travel freely therein and to report their findings to the Secretary-General. In the same resolution, the General Assembly requested that the consent to receive United Nations observers be communicated to the Secretary-General not later than December 7, 1956.

2. Immediately on the adoption of the said resolution, I transmitted the text to the representatives of the two countries directly concerned. I further addressed to them letters drawing attention to the special request mentioned above and to my need to receive their replies at the latest on December 7. At the time of the writing of this report (December 7, 6:00 P.M.), I have not received any replies.

3. In the said resolution of December 4, the General Assembly also recommended that I arrange for the immediate dispatch to Hungary and other countries, as appropriate, of observers named by me pursuant to paragraph 4 of resolution 1004 (ES-II). The General Assembly requested all Member governments to cooperate by extending such assistance and providing such facilities as might be necessary for the effective discharge of the responsibilities of the observers.

4. In pursuance of this recommendation I addressed at once letters to the permanent representatives of Austria, Czechoslovakia, Romania, and Yugoslavia, wherein, with reference to the last two paragraphs in the resolution of December 4, I asked for information whether observers named by me would be permitted to enter the countries in question for the purpose prescribed, in case it were indicated that such a visit would be useful for their work under the terms of reference established

General Assembly Official Records, Eleventh Session, Annexes, agenda item 67, Document A/3435, December 7, 1956.

by resolution 1004 (ES-II). Pending replies to these questions, I have not been able to arrange for the dispatch of any observers to the region.

5. As the Assembly is aware, the Government of Hungary on December 3 stated that it was ready to welcome the Secretary-General in Budapest "at a later date appropriate to both parties." In response, on December 4, I suggested that I could be in Budapest on December 16. I have not received any official reaction to this suggestion. If the visit cannot be made at the time proposed, it may be questioned whether it would be to the purpose.

THE GENERAL ASSEMBLY resumed discussion of the Hungarian question in a series of meetings December 10, 11, and 12. The majority considered that since the Assembly's earlier resolutions on withdrawal and admission of observers had all failed to produce any results the time had come formally to condemn the Soviet Union for violating the United Nations Charter. The United States and nineteen other Members joined in sponsoring the following resolution:

The General Assembly,

Deeply concerned over the tragic events in Hungary,

Recalling those provisions of its resolutions 1004 (ES-II) of November 4, 1956, 1005 (ES-II) of November 9, 1956, 1127 (XI) of November 21, 1956, and 1130 (XI) of December 4, 1956, calling upon the Government of the Union of Soviet Socialist Republics to desist from its intervention in the internal affairs of Hungary, to withdraw its forces from Hungary, and to cease its repression of the Hungarian people,

Recalling also those provisions of its resolutions 1004 (ES-II) and 1027 (XI), calling for permission for United Nations observers to enter the territory of Hungary, to travel freely therein, and to report their findings to the Secretary-General,

Having received the report of the Secretary-General (A/3403) of November 30, 1956, stating that no information is available to the Secretary-General concerning steps taken in order to establish compliance with the decisions of the General Assembly which refer to a withdrawal of troops or related political matters, and the note of the Secretary-General (A/3435) of December 7, 1956,

Noting with grave concern that there has not been a reply to the latest appeal of the General Assembly for the admission of United Nations observers to Hungary as contained in its resolution 1130 (XI),

Considering that recent events have clearly demonstrated the will of the Hungarian people to recover their liberty and independence,

Noting the overwhelming demand of the Hungarian people for the cessation of intervention of foreign armed forces and the withdrawal of foreign troops;

1. *Declares* that, by using its armed force against the Hungarian people, the Government of the Union of Soviet Socialist Republics is violating the political independence of Hungary;

2. *Condemns* the violation of the Charter of the United Nations by the Government of the Union of Soviet Socialist Republics in depriving Hungary of its liberty and independence and the Hungarian people of the exercise of their fundamental rights;

3. *Reiterates* its call upon the Government of the Union of Soviet Socialist Republics to desist forthwith from any form of intervention in the internal affairs of Hungary;

4. *Calls upon* the Government of the Union of Soviet Socialist Republics to make immediate arrangements for the withdrawal, under United Nations observation, of its armed forces from Hungary and to permit the reestablishment of the political independence of Hungary;

5. *Requests* the Secretary-General to take any initiative that he deems helpful in relation to the Hungarian problem in conformity with the principles of the Charter and the resolutions of the General Assembly.[1]

This resolution was adopted by a vote of 55 to 8 with 13 abstentions. Hungary did not vote, its representative having declared its delegation would not participate further in the work of the Assembly because of the continuing attacks upon Hungary's "sovereignty" and "rights" by "the United States—led" majority. The abstainers included Finland and Yugoslavia as well as the Arab-Asian group which had also abstained on most of the earlier resolutions. Led by Krishna Menon, they also called for withdrawal of Soviet forces and the admission of United Nation observers and deplored the resort to force and violence but they considered the Assembly should follow the road of negotiation, not denunciation, in seeking to remedy the situation.

They offered a series of amendments to alter the language of the 20-Power resolution in this direction and India, Burma, Ceylon, and Indonesia sponsored a separate resolution to similar effect. All but one of the amendments were defeated and the 20-Power resolution was adopted. India and its cosponsors then decided not to press their substitute resolution to a vote.

[1] General Assembly Resolution 1131 (XI), December 12, 1956.

12. *Interim Report to the General Assembly on Relief to the Hungarian People*

UN HEADQUARTERS, NEW YORK   DECEMBER 12, 1956

IN THIS REPORT the Secretary-General informed the General Assembly of the latest developments in assistance to refugees from Hungary and also placed on record the agreement he had reached with the International Committee of the Red Cross to act as agent of the United Nations relief program in the distribution inside Hungary of contributed relief supplies.

1. In the resolutions recently adopted by the General Assembly with regard to humanitarian activities to assist the Hungarian people, two distinct types of assistance were envisaged, namely, (*a*) assistance to refugees from Hungary; and (*b*) relief to the Hungarian people in Hungary.

2. The Secretary-General, on November 19, 1956, made an interim report to the General Assembly on refugees from Hungary (A/3371 and Add.1). On November 29, he and the Deputy United Nations High Commissioner for Refugees issued a joint appeal to governments to provide assistance for Hungarian refugees. They stated that, while it was not possible to estimate exactly the dimensions of the problem over the next six months, and taking into account the resources in prospect, not less than a further $10 million would be required for meeting the minimum needs of an estimated 60,000 Hungarian refugees in Austria. Since that date refugees have continued to reach Austria, the total number as at December 12 being 129,555. Of this total 57,413 have been transported to countries of asylum, leaving 72,142 still in Austria. Although the number of refugees there is now somewhat higher than the average figure of 60,000 for whom it was estimated that care and main-

General Assembly Official Records, Eleventh Session, Annexes, agenda item 67, Document A/3443, December 12, 1956.

tenance would be required over a six-month period, it would appear that that figure still represents a reasonable estimate for planning purposes. In this connection it is appropriate to emphasize that, while the generous offers of governments to accept refugees for asylum are most warmly welcomed, such offers do not dispense with the need for the provision of cash contributions for the care of the refugees remaining in Austria and who are proving such a heavy burden on the Austrian economy.

3. With regard to Hungarian refugees entering Yugoslavia, on November 15 the government of Yugoslavia informed the Office of the United Nations High Commissioner for Refugees that the number of such refugees was approximately 300. In acknowledging the offer of the High Commissioner's Office to provide assistance to the refugees in Yugoslavia, the government stated that it would take advantage of the offer should the number of refugees increase. In a note dated December 6, the Permanent Mission of Yugoslavia informed the Secretary-General that an agreement had been reached between the governments of Yugoslavia and of Hungary providing for repatriation to Hungary, on December 7 and 9, of the 141 refugees who had freely expressed their wish to return to that country. The note also stated that the remainder of the refugees, whose number at December 6 exceeded 600, would be treated in conformity with their wishes, *viz.,* refugees wishing to emigrate to other countries would be given the possibility to do so, while those wishing to remain in Yugoslavia would be allowed to remain there. The Secretary-General and the High Commissioner will remain in contact with the Yugoslav government in respect of assistance to these refugees.

4. With regard to relief to the Hungarian people in Hungary the Secretary-General, on November 15, addressed a preliminary appeal to governments inquiring what assistance they would be prepared to give to implement General Assembly resolutions 1004 (ES-II) and 1007 (ES-II), adopted on November 4 and 9. While many governments replied on the action they were taking, or proposed to take, through other channels, few governments offered to make contributions through the United Nations. The Secretary-General already reported this to the General Assembly (A/3403). At the same time he stated that he had undertaken negotiations with the International Committee of the Red Cross with a view to channelling through the Committee contributions for relief in Hungary made to the United Nations. These negotiations

are now completed and have resulted in an agreement which was signed on December 4. The text of the agreement, which was communicated to the Hungarian government on December 4 and which has been brought to the attention of the executive heads of the interested specialized agencies, is annexed to the present report.

5. The International Committee of the Red Cross has informed the Secretary-General, by a letter dated December 7, of the current situation in Hungary, as follows:

Our delegation at Budapest has, with the agreement of the Hungarian authorities, established three different assistance programmes, as follows:

(1) From December 4 or 5, distribution of milk and cod-liver oil to 173,000 children under the age of six.

(2) From December 8, approximately, distribution of one hot meal per day to 50,000 children from six to sixteen years old, in the most badly damaged section of Budapest. The programme for children of this age-category will then be extended progressively so as to supply various foods to 150,000 children.

(3) From the middle of December, the distribution each week of food packages for 100,000 persons in the following categories: shelterless persons, persons without support, the aged, disabled persons, and families with more than four children.

These programmes will require assistance on a considerable scale. Our delegation states that, in order to maintain them until the end of April, the following amounts will be necessary:

Powdered milk	3,437 tons
Cod-liver oil capsules	21,110,000
Fats	545 tons
Meat, fish, cheese	1,375 tons
Cereals	1,850 tons
Sugar	545 tons
Flour	1,900 tons
Soap	90 tons

As a supplement to the programmes listed above, other urgent assistance would be necessary, namely:

Coal for hospitals, asylums, shelters, etc., at Budapest	36,000 tons
Woollen blankets	100,000
Window glass	100 tons
Packages of diapers	10,000

The supplies now available will last only until about January 15. In other words, further aid is urgent and essential.

It should further be pointed out that the action thus undertaken by the Red Cross will constitute only initial emergency assistance to those whose needs are most imperative, but will actually reach only about 4 percent of the Hungarian population.

6. The International Committee of the Red Cross indicated further that it is necessary to consider immediately a very appreciable expansion of the programme of assistance and that it proposed to forward to the Secretary-General within a week or ten days further estimates of relief requirements.

7. The Secretary-General has established administrative and operational arrangements for the speedy and effective utilization of contributions for humanitarian assistance to the Hungarian people within Hungary and to the refugees. Responsibility for coordination of the efforts to aid Hungarian refugees has been placed upon the United Nations High Commissioner for Refugees. As stated above, the Secretary-General has entered into an agreement with the International Committee of the Red Cross for the distribution in Hungary of supplies made available to that Committee through contributions to the United Nations.

8. In the light of these actions and in order to give practical effect to the resolutions of the General Assembly, the Secretary-General now urges governments to make contributions to the United Nations funds which he has established for each of these programmes.

9. The Secretary-General also wishes to draw the attention of the General Assembly to the desirability of maintaining the greatest flexibility in the allocation of funds as between the refugee programme and the programme of relief within Hungary respectively. By contributing through the United Nations, governments will ensure that their contributions for and to the Hungarian people will be allocated in such a way as to reflect sensitively the changing needs of the two programmes.

10. Finally, with regard to contributions by voluntary organizations and the general public for assistance to the Hungarian people, also envisaged by the resolutions of the General Assembly, the Secretary-General would welcome any suggestions which governments may care to make for the coordination of national fund-raising efforts from private sources. Response to appeals for funds from such sources may be more effective when a coordinating body, such as a national committee of leading citizens, organizes the appeal and ensures the widest publicity for it. The Secretary-General would be glad to cooperate in any way

that may be considered useful with such national committees or other bodies participating in this work.

Agreement between the United Nations and the International Committee of the Red Cross Regarding Relief to the Hungarian People

Letter dated December 4, 1956, from the Secretary-General (signed on his behalf by the Deputy Director of the European Office of the United Nations) to the President of the International Red Cross

The General Assembly of the United Nations at its second emergency special session has requested the Secretary-General to take immediately the necessary measures to bring aid to the population of Hungary.

Considering that the International Committee of the Red Cross has been engaged in emergency relief activities in Hungary and has concluded an agreement with the Hungarian Red Cross to this effect, I wish to ask you if the International Committee would accept to cooperate with the United Nations in this humanitarian programme, under the following conditions:

1. The Committee, at the request of the Secretary-General agrees to use any funds as may be transferred to it by the United Nations for the exclusive purpose of providing immediate aid to the population of Hungary, in particular by furnishing medical supplies, foodstuffs, and clothing. The responsibility assumed by the Committee in this respect will commence upon receipt of any such funds and will terminate after the distribution of relief supplies to the Hungarian population or, in the event of cessation of the programme upon return to the United Nations of any unused portion of such funds or of supplies purchased with such funds.

2. The Committee will undertake responsibility for the distribution of such supplies as may be furnished by the United Nations. The Committee may indicate to the United Nations the types of relief goods regarded as most appropriate for the purpose of the programme.

3. In accordance with the principles of the Red Cross and in the spirit of the Geneva Conventions, the Committee will distribute relief

under this programme without discrimination and on the basis of need alone.

4. While making every effort to carry out this programme as rapidly as possible, the Committee will retain sole responsibility for the schedule (French: "cadence") of distribution of relief supplies. In the event of difficulties or obstacles arising in the execution of the programme the Committee will, if necessary, report to the United Nations but it will be solely responsible for taking appropriate measures.

5. The Committee will supply all organizational, supervisory, and technical personnel, services, and equipment required for the operation of the programme.

6. The United Nations will defray such administrative and operational costs of the Committee attributable to the performance of the United Nations relief programme as may be agreed between the United Nations and the Committee.

7. The Committee will be the sole agency to carry out the relief programme on behalf of the United Nations with the contributions made pursuant to resolution 399 (resolution 1007 (ES-II)) adopted by the General Assembly at the second emergency special session on November 9, 1956. This shall not be construed to limit the right of other United Nations agencies to carry out assistance programmes in accordance with their terms of reference and in agreement with the Hungarian authorities.

8. The United Nations recognizes the Committee as an independent and autonomous organization which undertakes to perform the services envisaged in this agreement. The performance of such services will not in any way place the Committee in a subordinate position towards the United Nations, and the Committee will not be required to carry out any task other than those set forth in this agreement.

9. The Committee will submit to the Secretary-General monthly operational reports and financial reports of costs incurred in the performance of its responsibilities under this agreement.

10. The United Nations and the Committee will act in close collaboration in regard to the planning and the implementation of the programme. In particular, the Committee will extend full cooperation to any representative who may be sent to Hungary by the Secretary-General in connection with the programme.

11. Nothing contained in this agreement will affect any of the other activities which the Committee already is carrying out or may carry out in Hungary in the performance of its traditional role.

12. This agreement may be terminated by either party on one week's notice subject, if possible, to prior consultation. The termination of this Agreement will not affect the responsibilities of either party under the Agreement with respect to the completion of the distribution of supplies still outstanding at the date of termination.

I should greatly appreciate receiving your confirmation that the International Committee of the Red Cross accepts the proposals contained in this letter. Following such confirmation, the Secretary-General will inform the Hungarian Government of this agreement.

For and on behalf of the Secretary-General:

GEORGES PALTHEY
Deputy Director, European Office
of the United Nations

*Letter dated December 4, 1956, from the President
of the International Committee of the Red Cross
to the Deputy Director of the European Office
of the United Nations*

The International Committee has received your letter of December 4, 1956, concerning United Nations emergency relief to the Hungarian people and the proposals for cooperation by our organization.

I am happy to inform you that the International Committee, which is already engaged in the dispatch and distribution of Red Cross supplies in Hungary, agrees to undertake the distribution of United Nations aid as well, in accordance with the conditions set forth in your letter, namely:

[For the text of the agreement, see above letter dated December 4, 1956, from the Secretary-General to the President of the International Committee of the Red Cross.]

LEOPOLD BOISSIER
President of the International
Committee of the Red Cross

13. *Further Report to the General Assembly on the Situation in Hungary*

UN HEADQUARTERS, NEW YORK   JANUARY 5, 1957

IN THIS REPORT, for the reasons given in the text below, the Secretary-General suggested that the responsibilities given to him in earlier General Assembly resolutions for investigating the situation in Hungary might now be transferred to a special committee of the Assembly with somewhat broader terms of reference (see also commentary following the text).

1. In a report to the General Assembly (A/3403) of November 30, 1956, the Secretary-General gave an interim account of action taken by him on the basis of various resolutions adopted by the General Assembly concerning the withdrawal of foreign troops from Hungarian territory and related questions, including that of deportations, and concerning investigations of the situation caused by foreign intervention in Hungary. Humanitarian activities, including assistance to refugees, have been dealt with mainly in other reports.

2. In his report of November 30 the Secretary-General drew the attention of the General Assembly specifically to the steps taken for investigation and observation of the developments in Hungary. As announced to the General Assembly on November 16 (A/3359), a group of three had been established by the Secretary-General to assist him in fulfilling the investigatory duties with which he had been charged by the General Assembly. This group consisted of Mr. O. Gundersen, Mr. A. Lall, and Mr. A. Lleras. The Secretary-General wishes to include in the present report an account of the views expressed by this group concerning the nature of and conditions for the investigations with which it was charged.

3. The group presented to the Secretary-General on December 15, 1956 the following note:

General Assembly Official Records, Eleventh Session, Annexes, agenda item 67, Document A/3485, January 5, 1957.

Referring to our conversation with you yesterday when we exchanged views regarding the task of investigation which you asked us to undertake in pursuance of Assembly resolution 1004 (ES-II) dated November 4, 1956, and in accordance with your information to the General Assembly (A/3359) of November 16, 1956, we would like briefly to state our views at the present stage.

Already in the first conversation we had with you we noted that the resolution of the General Assembly of November 4, 1956, appeared to envisage the process of investigation, observation, and reporting as a unified one. Moreover, that resolution, as also subsequent resolutions of the General Assembly, called on the governments concerned to assist in the process of fact-finding and assessment of the Hungarian situation. While we immediately set out to examine the material made available to us in New York we found that it did not contain sufficient evidence for a broad-based investigation of the events that had taken place in Hungary. We found ourselves, as it were, in possession of a fringe of the material which we would have required for the kind of assessment of the situation which we felt that the General Assembly had had in view. In short, what we have looked at is the available and generally known material which does not put us in a position to add anything significant to what is common knowledge about the situation in Hungary. We have also taken note of the fact that as a result of your approaches in pursuance of General Assembly resolution 1130 (XI) dated December 4, 1956, only one country of those requested has found it possible to offer facilities for observation.

Until it is possible to open up further sources of reliable material through observation on the spot in Hungary and by the cooperation of the governments directly concerned, there would be little purpose in our attempting an assessment of the present situation or of recent events. In these circumstances the question arises as to whether it is not best for the process of investigation to be suspended for the present and for the matter to be reexamined at a later stage.

4. Serious consideration should be given to the conclusion of the group that, short of access to reliable material provided through observation on the spot in Hungary and by the cooperation of the governments directly concerned, there would be little purpose in attempting an assessment of the present situation or of recent events.

5. So far there has been no possibility for representatives of the United Nations to make direct observations in Hungary, nor has the cooperation necessary for the investigations been forthcoming from governments directly concerned. Under these circumstances, the only source of new and direct information possibly available might be hearings with refugees from Hungary, conducted, in the first place, in neighbouring countries.

6. The Government of Austria has declared itself prepared to re-

ceive observers for such a purpose. Offers to the United Nations to send observers for hearings with refugees have been received from the United States of America and Italy. Some additional points of significance might be established through hearings with refugees in these countries, but, in order to yield results of value, such hearings must be extensive and organized in a juridically satisfactory form.

7. The Secretary-General continues, on his part, to try to further the aims of the General Assembly, pursuant to paragraph 5 of the last resolution on the Hungarian question (resolution 1131 (XI)). He has, under present circumstances and pending also the result of efforts along other lines, hesitated now to initiate, himself, further investigatory activities, including hearings with refugees.

8. The Secretary-General has felt that this might be the proper time for a reconsideration of the form to be given to the investigatory activities. In view of the active and continued concern of the General Assembly for the development, the Assembly may now wish to establish a special *ad hoc* committee which would take over the activities of the group of investigators established by the Secretary-General and follow them up under somewhat broader terms of reference.

9. Such a committee should obviously serve as an organ of the General Assembly for a continued observation of developments in relation to Hungary in all those respects which may be of relevance to the Assembly. The work of a committee with such a mandate might facilitate for the General Assembly the consideration of matters relating to Hungary beyond what could be achieved through an investigation of the kind with which the Secretary-General has been charged. The committee, if established, should report directly to the General Assembly. It would be entitled to all the assistance and facilities which the Secretariat might provide for it in the fulfillment of its task.

THE GENERAL ASSEMBLY resumed its plenary meetings on Hungary January 9 and 10, 1957. In response to Hammarskjöld's suggestion the United States and twenty-three other Members sponsored a draft resolution to establish a special committee of investigation. The text, as adopted, was as follows:

The General Assembly,

Recalling its previous resolutions on the Hungarian problem,

Reaffirming the objectives contained therein and the continuing concern of the United Nations in this matter,

Having received the report of the Secretary-General of January 5, 1957 (A/3485),

Desiring to ensure that the General Assembly and all Members of the United Nations shall be in possession of the fullest and best available information regarding the situation created by the intervention of the Union of Soviet Socialist Republics, through its use of armed force and other means, in the internal affairs of Hungary, as well as regarding developments relating to the recommendations of the General Assembly on this subject,

1. *Establishes,* for the above-mentioned purposes, a Special Committee composed of representatives of Australia, Ceylon, Denmark, Tunisia, and Uruguay, to investigate, and to establish and maintain direct observation in Hungary and elsewhere, taking testimony, collecting evidence and receiving information, as appropriate, in order to report its findings to the General Assembly at its eleventh session, and thereafter from time to time to prepare additional reports for the information of Member states and of the General Assembly if it is in session;

2. *Calls upon* the Union of Soviet Socialist Republics and Hungary to cooperate in every way with the Committee and, in particular, to permit the Committee and its staff to enter the territory of Hungary and to travel freely therein;

3. *Requests* all Member states to assist the Committee in any way appropriate in its task, making available to it relevant information, including testimony and evidence, which Members may possess, and assisting it in securing such information;

4. *Invites* the Secretary-General to render the Committee all appropriate assistance and facilities;

5. *Calls upon* all Member states promptly to give effect to the present and previous resolutions of the General Assembly on the Hungarian problem;

6. *Reaffirms* its request that the Secretary-General continue to take any initiative that he deems helpful in relation to the Hungarian problem, in conformity with the principles of the Charter of the United Nations and the resolutions of the General Assembly.[1]

In the debate the great majority of delegates spoke in support of the resolution, deeming it necessary that public opinion should have as objective and complete information as possible about the Hungarian revolt and its suppression and that it was the duty of the United Nations to continue to concentrate attention on the question and to demonstrate that the law of the Charter applied to all. The Hungarian government, in a *note verbale* to the Secretary-General, vigorously protested against the resolution as a gross violation of the domestic jurisdiction clause of the Charter and the Soviet delegate during the debate rebuked the Secretary-General for departing from the

---

[1] General Assembly Resolution 1132 (XI), January 10, 1957.

objectivity required of his office by proposing a committee of investigation. The resolution was adopted by a vote of 59 to 8 with 10 abstentions on January 10.

The Special Committee on the Problem of Hungary was organized in New York on January 17, with the following members: Alsing Andersen of Denmark, chairman; K. C. O. Shann of Australia, rapporteur; R. S. S. Gunewardene of Ceylon; Mongi Slim of Tunisia; and Enrique Rodríguez Fabregat of Uruguay. It began its work at once, heard its first witnesses, and submitted a preliminary interim report to the General Assembly on February 20 [2] before proceeding in March to Geneva for further hearings in Europe.

[2] General Assembly Official Records, Eleventh Session, Annexes, agenda item 67, Document A/3546, February 20, 1957.

❧ *1957* ❧

Second Report to the General Assembly
on the Clearing of the Suez Canal

UN HEADQUARTERS, NEW YORK   JANUARY 10, 1957

THE FIRST PART of this report gives a step-by-step account of the preliminary planning and preparation for the United Nations Canal clearance operation from early November 1956 to the start of work in the Canal itself by the United Nations salvage fleet at the end of December. The first annex outlines the plan of operations with a target date of early May for resumed transit by ships of maximum draft. The second annex gives the text of an exchange of letters between Hammarskjöld and Fawzi, dated January 8, which constituted the Canal clearance agreement between the United Nations and Egypt. The third annex gives the text of a letter from the Secretary-General addressed to all Member governments requesting advances totaling at least $10 million for interim financing pending final cost estimates and a decision by the General Assembly on how the costs should be shared. Commentary on the background follows the text.

---

1. In a resolution, November 2, 1956 (997 (ES-I)), the General Assembly urged that, "upon the cease-fire being effective, steps be taken to reopen the Suez Canal."

2. In communications, November 6, from the governments of France and the United Kingdom, concerning the cease-fire and a cessation of military operations (A/3306, A/3307), the governments pointed out "that the clearing of the obstructions in the Suez Canal and its approaches, which is in no sense a military operation, is a matter of great urgency in the interest of world shipping and trade." It was added that the Anglo-French force was equipped to tackle this task and that the

General Assembly Official Records, Eleventh Session, Annexes, Volume II, agenda item 66, Document A/3492, January 10, 1957.

governments therefore proposed that the technicians accompanying the Anglo-French force should begin this work at once.

3. In reply to these letters, November 7 (A/3313, A/3314), the Secretary-General said that he would as soon as possible revert to the offer to assist in the technical operations for reopening the Suez Canal. He was exploring the possibility of having this work carried out under United Nations auspices by agents from countries not involved in the present conflict.

4. On November 8, the Secretary-General made approaches to Netherlands and Danish salvage firms, indicated by the Government of the Netherlands and the Government of Denmark in reply to previous queries from the Secretary-General. These firms, Svitzer and Smit, indicated their agreement to assist as required in the clearing operation.

5. The Secretary-General visited Cairo, November 15 to 17. In the course of his discussions with the Government of Egypt he raised also the question of the Canal clearing operation. The Government of Egypt requested the assistance of the United Nations in the clearing of the obstructions of the Suez Canal, to start immediately on the reestablishment of normal conditions in Port Said and the Canal area, including the withdrawal of non-Egyptian forces. On the basis of the previous relevant decisions of the General Assembly, the Secretary-General declared that the United Nations in principle was willing to assume the task.

6. The Secretary-General submitted a report on the clearing of the Canal to the General Assembly on November 20 (A/3376). In this report the Secretary-General said: "The Secretary-General would propose that the General Assembly, confirming in this respect its previous decisions, should authorize the Secretary-General to proceed with his exploration of existing possibilities and to negotiate agreements with such firms as might speedily and effectively undertake the clearing operations. As indicated above, he would, given the approval of the General Assembly to this proposal, intend to address himself to firms in countries outside the present conflict. In his contacts with the firms approached, he would try to clarify to what extent they, in turn, may need assistance from enterprises not directly approached by the United Nations" (A/3376, paragraph 5). He further stated that, although it was not proposed that the work begin until after the withdrawal of non-Egyptian forces from Port Said and the Canal area, he considered it possible to pursue negotiations and, in agreement with the Government of

Egypt, to arrange for the necessary survey of the conditions in the Canal without delay.

7. The General Assembly, on November 24, adopted a resolution [resolution 1121 (XI)] in which the Assembly noted with approval the progress so far made by the Secretary-General in connection with arrangements for clearing the Suez Canal, as set forth in his report, and authorized him to proceed with the exploration of practical arrangements and the negotiation of agreements, so that the clearing operations might be speedily and effectively undertaken.

8. The same day as the General Assembly adopted the aforementioned resolution, the Svitzer and Smit firms were requested to dispatch to the scene such salvage ships and other equipment as had been earmarked or put in readiness in various ports during the previous two weeks, and to activate arrangements for supplementing their own available craft by contracting for craft from salvage concerns in different countries outside the conflict.

9. In order to assist him in the conduct of the clearing operation, the Secretary-General engaged Lieutenant-General Raymond A. Wheeler. He further agreed with Mr. John J. McCloy to advise him on the financial problems arising in this context. After completion of the necessary planning work at Headquarters, and after the official announcement of the governments of France and the United Kingdom, December 3, of their intention to withdraw their forces, General Wheeler arrived in Egypt on December 8 with a team of salvage surveyors, drawn from the private salvage firms approached and from the Ralph M. Parsons Engineering Company, Los Angeles, the latter to survey damage to workshops. General Wheeler and his staff immediately started a survey of obstructions in the Canal, below El Cap, in cooperation with the Egyptian Suez Canal Authority. This stretch of the Canal, south of the cease-fire line, was for obvious reasons not accessible to the British and French units. A survey of workshop installations was conducted by General Wheeler's group in Port Said.

10. The report on the United Nations clearing operation, approved by the General Assembly, November 24, assumed that the work would be undertaken by private firms from nations outside the conflict which, however, in their turn, should be able to arrange for assistance from enterprises not directly contacted by the United Nations. The technical advisers of the Secretary-General studied what additional assistance might be necessary in order to supplement the arrangements made with the

private salvage firms which had been engaged. On the basis of these studies it was found that the United Nations might need to use resources from the Anglo-French units in Port Said in the following respects:

(*a*) Although the United Nations salvage fleet would alone conduct the operation, it would not be legitimate that specific salvage projects under way on individual vessels should be dropped by Anglo-French salvage crews and the long and complicated salvage work recommenced by the United Nations. Such work should therefore continue and be brought to the speediest possible conclusion under General Wheeler's direction.

(*b*) The United Nations might wish to take over six selected vessels for use south of El Cap with non-British crews, recruited by the United Nations, but with a certain number of British officers in charge, for a few days, of the handing over of the vessels to those responsible on the United Nations side.

These needs were registered in instructions to General Wheeler, December 9. The governments of France and of the United Kingdom were informed about the conclusions. They were communicated also to the Government of Egypt.

11. After discussions in New York and Port Said the United Nations, upon the withdrawal of the Anglo-French forces on December 22, took over responsibility for practically all British and French salvage ships and some supporting ships then in Port Said. The vessels remaining there were intended to follow up work already in hand, with their British and French crews but under United Nations orders. To the extent that certain specified work was completed by each, the ships would be withdrawn. The technical advisers of the United Nations proposed a redisposal of the resources available, using vessels from private firms down the Canal, while reserving the British-French ships, including those present from among the six, to assist in the operations in Port Said harbour.

12. The United Nations salvage operations started at the southern end of the Canal on December 28, and at the northern end of the Canal on December 31, 1956. The operations were based on a plan for the use of available resources, elaborated by General Wheeler and his technical advisers in consultation with representatives of the Secretary-General. The plan was based on an appraisal of technical needs, as estab-

lished in the course of preceding studies. As elaborated by General Wheeler, the plan met with the approval of the Egyptian authorities. Details concerning the resources utilized by the United Nations and regarding the plan, are presented in annex 1 to the present report.

13. After discussions in New York and Cairo, an exchange of letters between the Government of Egypt and the Secretary-General has taken place in order to provide an agreed basis for the cooperation between the United Nations and the Egyptian authorities. The exchange of letters, constituting the necessary agreement, has been approved by the Advisory Committee. It is annexed to the present report (annex 2).

14. The Secretary-General is not yet in a position to submit to the General Assembly complete cost estimates for the clearing operation. Pending the presentation of such estimates, he does not wish to make any definite proposals regarding the way in which the costs should be covered. This question is referred to the Advisory Committee for preliminary consideration.

15. In order to meet immediate needs for funds to cover initial and current costs pending a final decision, the Secretary-General has approached all Member governments suggesting that they might advance to the United Nations the funds required during the first phase. The note addressed to the Member governments is annexed to the present report (annex 3).

16. In response to his approach to the Member governments, the Secretary-General has received firm assurances from a number of governments that assistance by way of interim advances will be forthcoming. Substantial amounts have already been made available, and additional advances will be received at an early date following necessary executive or legislative approval. Some governments, in acknowledging the Secretary-General's communication, have informed him that the matter will be taken up forthwith. The Secretary-General has reason to believe that, as a result of the responses so far received, sufficient funds will be in hand during the month of January for the purpose of financing the initial stages of United Nations operations for the clearance of the Suez Canal.

17. The definite financial proposals, referred to in paragraph 14 above, will provide also for reimbursement of advances made.

Summary of Plan of Work and of Resources for its Execution

1. The plan of operations covers tasks to be completed in three general stages, making possible the resumption of normal traffic in the Canal. Some of the work at each stage will overlap and thus assist the completion of the following stage.

(*a*) The first stage covers tasks which would allow transit by vessels of a 25-foot draught (about 10,000 tons). This includes the clearance of nine obstructions and two bridges. It has been estimated that this phase of the work will be completed by early March.

(*b*) The second stage covers the removal of other obstructions which would make possible the transit of vessels of maximum draught. During this stage, further effective obstructions would be removed from within the main channel and the task is expected to be completed by early May.

(*c*) The work in the final stage will centre on obstructions which, while not hampering transit traffic, would need to be removed from ports, basins, and channels. This stage would also include work in restoration of docks and harbourages to their original condition.

The experience in the salvage operations during the first ten days gives every reason for optimism regarding the meeting of the above schedule.

2. Concurrently with the execution of each stage of the clearance work, the restoration of communications, lighting, and workshop facilities necessary to a safe and effective transit operation will be undertaken.

3. The work will be performed under General Wheeler's direction within the framework of the overall relations established by the agreement on the clearing operations (annex 2). The Egyptian Suez Canal Authority, where appropriate, will cooperate in the execution of the established plans to the extent of the resources available to it.

4. The salvage resources which will be utilized by the United Nations will consist of:

(*a*) A fleet, as of January, of thirty-two salvage vessels including supporting tugs with crews drawn from six countries: Belgium, Denmark, Germany, Italy, the Netherlands, Sweden, and Yugoslavia.

(*b*) Eleven Anglo-French salvage craft and crews (with four Anglo-French support vessels) on a scheduled basis for the completion of certain specified work already in hand by these vessels in Port Said harbour.

5. General management of the salvage operations proper is in the hands of a consortium consisting of Messrs. L. Smit en Co.'s Internationale Sleepdienst of Rotterdam and Messrs. A/S Em. Svitzers Bjergnings Entreprise of Copenhagen. Restoration of the workshops in Port Said will be undertaken by engineers and staff of the Canal Authority with General Wheeler remaining responsible for supervision and the provision of additional specialists as required. Restoration of communication and lighting requirements will be undertaken by General Wheeler in conjunction with the General Electric Company of the United States and the International Telegraph and Telephone Corporation, respectively. Plans for this work will be carried out in collaboration with the Canal Authority to assure the attainment of navigable conditions at each completed stage of the overall plan. Dredging operations necessary to the immediate navigation needs of the cleared channel at stage one and stage two of the operation will likewise be put in hand in collaboration with the Canal Authority by General Wheeler, who is currently in consultation with appropriate contracting companies who have the necessary equipment available in the area.

ANNEX 2

*Agreement between the United Nations and the Government
of Egypt Regarding the Clearance of the Suez Canal*

*Letter dated January 8, 1957, from the Secretary-General,
addressed to the Minister for Foreign Affairs of Egypt*

I have the honour to refer to the request of the Government of Egypt for assistance of the United Nations in arrangements for clearing the Suez Canal.

In accordance with the authority which has been granted to the Secretary-General by the General Assembly, and on the basis of preliminary exploration and negotiation, I am in a position to advise you that the United Nations would be prepared to assist the Government of Egypt by undertaking the operation necessary for the speedy clearance of the Canal. The general plans for this assistance would be elaborated in consultation with the Government of Egypt and, when approved by the government, implemented under the instructions of the Secretary-General. The Secretary-General would be authorized by the Government of Egypt to carry out the task as a matter of priority as effectively and expeditiously as practicable with freedom for him to use the equipment available which he finds necessary for the operation.

It is envisaged that the United Nations would conduct the clearance operation through contractual arrangements with private firms which would have the primary responsibility for the work under the direction and control of the Secretary-General and his special representative. Such subcontractual arrangements as may have to be entered into by the prime contractors in order to expedite the work would be subject to the approval of the Secretary-General.

The undertaking would be regarded as a United Nations enterprise and its personnel would be under obligation to discharge their functions and regulate their conduct solely in the interests of the United Nations. In keeping with the United Nations responsibilities, the vessels would fly the flag of the United Nations in place of their national flags. The property and persons engaged in the clearance operation (including the contractors, subcontractors, and their personnel) would, in view of their United Nations character, be covered by the Convention on the Privileges and Immunities of the United Nations to which Egypt is a party, in so far as it may be applicable *mutatis mutandis*. In the application of the aforesaid Convention the United Nations shall pay due regard to any representations made by the Government of Egypt in so far as it is considered that effect can be given to such representations without detriment to the interests of the United Nations.

As the clearance of the Canal has to be completed with the utmost speed and effectiveness, the United Nations, in consultation with the Egyptian government, will take all measures required in order to avoid unnecessary damage to persons and property. It is understood that the United Nations would not incur responsibility for possible damage to Egyptian ships lying in the Canal from such activities as it considers necessary to speed the clearance of the Canal. It would also be understood that the United Nations would retain the rights of a salvor in respect of vessels or property salvaged in the course of the clearance operations, other than vessels and property of the Government of Egypt.

The United Nations will, of course, keep the Government of Egypt currently and fully informed of the progress of the operations and the

Government will, I am sure, render all such assistance as may be required by the United Nations for this task.

If the points set forth in this letter are acceptable to the Government of Egypt, this letter and the reply of the government will be considered as constituting an agreement between Egypt and the United Nations, effective from the date of the reply.

DAG HAMMARSKJÖLD
Secretary-General

Letter dated January 8, 1957, from the Minister for Foreign Affairs of Egypt, addressed to the Secretary-General

I have the honour to refer to your letter of January 8, 1957, in which you have been so good as to inform me that the United Nations would be prepared to assist the Government of Egypt by undertaking the operation necessary for the speedy clearance of the Suez Canal, and I have the pleasure to advise you in the name of the Government of Egypt of its full agreement on, and acceptance of, the terms of your letter. You may rest assured that the Government of Egypt will give its fullest co-operation and assistance to the operation.

The Government of Egypt agrees, furthermore, that your letter and this reply will be considered as constituting an agreement between Egypt and the United Nations.

MAHMOUD FAWZI
Minister for Foreign Affairs

ANNEX 3

Note Dated December 23, 1956, from the Secretary-General to Member Governments Regarding Interim Advances to the Fund for the Clearance of the Suez Canal

The Secretary-General of the United Nations presents his compliments to the Permanent Representative of . . . and has the honour to call attention to resolution 1121 (XI) adopted by the General Assembly on November 24, 1956, on the subject of the clearance of the Suez

Canal, under which the Secretary-General is authorized to proceed with the exploration of practical arrangements and the negotiation of agreements so that the clearing operations may be speedily and effectively undertaken.

In accordance with the above resolution of the General Assembly, the Secretary-General has entered into obligations with contractors and others. For the financing of these obligations appropriate arrangements need urgently to be made, if the clearance operations are to proceed without interruption or delay. The Secretary-General intends to report to the General Assembly at an early date on a final plan with respect to the total obligation for the clearance of the Canal. Pending a decision on such a plan it is essential that immediate cash needs are adequately provided for on an interim and provisional basis. The Secretary-General would therefore much appreciate any indication which the Permanent Representative is able to give him, if possible, before January 1, 1957, as to the measure of financial assistance it can make available by way of an advance which would be without prejudice to the nature and extent of the government's participation in such overall financial settlement as may eventually be agreed upon.

In order that he may be enabled to discharge the responsibilities entrusted to him in connection with this vital United Nations undertaking, the Secretary-General trusts that Member governments who are able and willing to assist in the manner and on the basis indicated, can urgently provide interim financing to the extent of not less than $10 million.

If, as the Secretary-General hopes, His Excellency's government is able to react favourably to this request, he will be glad to provide, to the extent possible, such further information concerning this matter [as] His Excellency may require.

The Government of Egypt has given its assurance that the United Nations will have the full cooperation of that government in the execution of its part in the Canal clearing operations.

AS INDICATED in paragraph 10 of the Report it was at first thought the United Nations salvage fleet might need the help in work down the Canal of six British vessels selected from the British-French salvage fleet which had been working in Port Said harbor. These would, however, be operated by

non-British crews recruited by the United Nations. This proposal precipi-
tated a row which made headline news, especially in Britain.

From the time of the cease-fire on November 6 the British and French
governments had sought to win agreement to clearing the Canal with their
own salvage fleet. Through the following weeks they had fought a rear-guard
action to that end, hoping they could thus preserve some leverage for themselves in the ultimate Suez settlement. At first they maintained the United
Nations could not possibly do the job without them. The Organization had
no experience and could not find equipment anywhere to equal the Anglo-
French fleet, "the best in the world."

They were bitterly disappointed when Hammarskjöld quickly demonstrated they were wrong, acting with a team composed of Andrew W. Cordier assisted by Alfred G. Katzin from the Secretariat, John J. McCloy,
Chairman of the Chase-Manhattan Bank and former President of the International Bank, who was enlisted as business and financial advisor, and Lieu-
tenant General Raymond A. Wheeler, former Chief of the United States
Army Corps of Engineers, now engineering consultant to the International
Bank on such matters as the Aswan Dam project, who was placed in charge
of the clearance operations.

Nevertheless the sniping had continued. The First Lord of the Admiralty,
Viscount Hailsham, in particular, made a series of highly emotional and
caustic public attacks upon the United Nations salvage plans. When the Assembly approved the Secretary-General's first clearance report on November
24, however, Selwyn Lloyd had offered Britain's help "in any way wanted"
in the task. Now in mid-December the Conservative cabinet responded with
one more reflex from the old imperial days to his request for six ships to
work in the Canal without their crews.

Once again there was an ultimatum, this time directed not to Egypt but
to the Secretary-General. The United Nations must take over the whole Anglo-French salvage fleet, or it could have none of it. No British vessel could
be used without its crew. Security down the Canal for British crews should
be provided by UNEF sentries on the vessels and UNEF patrols along the
Canal bank, thus keeping UNEF in the Canal area, contrary to the plan accepted by the Assembly and Egypt, after the evacuation of Port Said.
Finally Hammarskjöld was told that unless agreement was reached within
seventy-two hours the entire Anglo-French salvage fleet would be ordered to
withdraw from Port Said. This last was an empty threat in the light of Britain's own interest in reopening the Canal to traffic as soon as possible. Her
salvage vessels were currently engaged in clearing Port Said harbor of sunken vessels and much work there remained to be completed. Their departure
now would make it necessary to start all over again and cause many weeks'
delay.

Hammarskjöld avoided public controversy but reacted coolly and firmly
in private. The United Nations could not be forced to accept more of the
Anglo-French salvage fleet than was needed to supplement its own resources, just as, in the beginning, it could not be forced to include the Brit-

ish and French in a United Nations Force. As to British-manned craft working down the Canal, their request for the protection of UNEF guards and patrols showed that they themselves recognized the additional security risks this would involve. Quite aside from the question of using UNEF for such a purpose, the Secretary-General could not possibly take the chance of clashes and incidents which might interrupt and complicate the UN clearance operation. If the ships could not be handed over without their crews, he would therefore have to do without them down the Canal even if that should entail some delay in completing the task.

London did not, of course, carry out its ultimatum and the United Nations plan of operations was revised in such a way that no slow-down in clearing the Canal resulted. Four German salvage craft with heavy lifting equipment under contract with the UN fleet would be sent down the Canal instead of being used in Port Said and the Anglo-French salvage craft with their crews would work instead to complete the clearance tasks already in progress in Port Said and then be phased out.

Hammarskjöld sent Cordier and Katzin to Egypt on Christmas Day to complete working out with General Wheeler the revised plan summarized in paragraph 11 of the Report. This was then discussed and agreed with the Egyptian Canal authorities and with the government. Cordier had a long talk with Nasser on December 30 which cleared away some problems concerning UNEF as well as the Canal clearance. The next day Nasser gave the green light for the salvage work to begin in the Canal proper, just ten days after the evacuation of British and French troops from Port Said.

Paragraph 11 of the Report, it may be noted, states that the United Nations on December 22 "took over responsibility for *practically all* [italics added] British and French salvage ships and some supporting ships then in Port Said." This amounted to eleven salvage and four supporting craft, a far cry from the forty vessels composing the entire fleet, most of which never reached the scene, which the British ultimatum had at first demanded that Hammarskjöld accept.

The basic clearance agreement with Egypt contained in annex 2 of the Report had been originally drawn up in New York during December and the draft cleared with the UNEF Advisory Committee before being forwarded to the Egyptian government for its consideration. It was accepted almost unchanged and initialled in Cairo immediately after Cordier's visit and then sent back to New York for Hammarskjöld's and Fawzi's signatures after final approval by the Advisory Committee. Constantin A. Stavropoulos, the United Nations Legal Counsel, was charged with preparing this and subsidiary legal papers on the Suez Clearance operation as well as the legal agreement on the status of the UN Emergency Force in Egypt, and was in Cairo at the time completing negotiations with the Egyptian government on the latter (see page 500).

As noted in paragraphs 14 to 17 of the Report, sufficient advances (in effect, interest-free loans) from several governments were now either in hand or on the way to provide interim financing for the clearance operation and the question of how the costs should ultimately be shared had been taken up in the UNEF Advisory Committee for preliminary consideration. Realistically the alternatives appeared to lie between United Nations budget assessments and a surcharge on the Canal tolls paid by users, or some combination of the two. Hammarskjöld was not anxious to introduce the question at a time when the manner of financing UNEF was already a source of controversy, but at this time he thought it would be necessary to bring up the issue before the Assembly session adjourned later in the winter, once accurate cost estimates had been completed.

Second Report on Clearing of Suez Canal   485

the question of how the costs should ultimately be shared had been taken up
in the UNEF Advisory Committee for preliminary consideration. Realistic
ments and a surcharge on the Canal tolls paid by users, or some combination of
a time when the manner of financing UNEF was already a source of
controversy, but
the
accurate cost estimates had been completed.

Report to the General Assembly on Compliance
with Resolutions Calling for Withdrawal
of Troops and other Measures

UN HEADQUARTERS, NEW YORK   JANUARY 15, 1957

THE DAY before the Secretary-General issued the following report the Israeli
government had, after repeated prodding, at last committed itself to complete, by January 23, the withdrawal of its forces from the Sinai with the
important exception of "the Sharm el-Sheikh area." This would be the subject of further discussion. The Israeli reply was silent on Gaza. It was apparent that Israel intended to seek concessions in both areas before any further
withdrawal, although its demands were not formally presented to the United
Nations until a week later (see page 472).

In this report the Secretary-General followed the line to which he would
firmly adhere during the following seven weeks. Unconditional withdrawal,
like the cease-fire, was an essential preliminary to "a development through
which a stable basis may be laid for peaceful conditions in the area." After
withdrawal the way forward should lie in renewed efforts to establish, on
both sides, full compliance with all the articles of the Armistice Agreement.
Since both sides had for years violated various articles of the Agreement this
would not be a return to the *status quo ante,* but a development forward to
peaceful conditions under a state of law. The presence of UNEF, as well as
UNTSO, could be of great value in such a development.

Part One

1. A report on compliance with the General Assembly resolutions 997
(ES-I) and 1002 (ES-I) of November 2 and 7, 1956, with particular reference to the withdrawal of forces, was submitted to the General Assembly by the Secretary-General on November 21, 1956, as Document
A/3384. At that time only limited withdrawals had taken place. On
December 22, 1956, however, the withdrawal of the Anglo-French
forces was completed, thus achieving full compliance with one aspect of

General Assembly Official Records, Eleventh Session, Annexes, Volume II,
agenda item 66, Document A/3500 and Add. 1, January 15, 1957.

the requirement defined in the four resolutions of the General Assembly relating to withdrawal of forces (resolution 997 (ES-I) of November 2, 1956, resolution 999 (ES-I) of November 4, 1956, resolution 1002 (ES-I) of November 7, 1956, and resolution 1120 (XI) of November 24, 1956). Thereafter, those aspects of compliance concerning withdrawal of forces have involved only Israel troops.

2. An oral report on the extent of the withdrawal of Israel forces at that time and the further withdrawal in prospect, was presented by the Secretary-General at the 632nd plenary meeting of the General Assembly on December 21, 1956.

3. On the basis of the several relevant resolutions, the Secretary-General has held extensive discussions with representatives of the Government of Israel, aiming at full compliance with the withdrawal requirements by the earliest possible date. In the course of these discussions, which have taken place since the letter of the Permanent Representative of Israel of November 24, 1956, reported the first Israel withdrawal (A/3389 and Add. 1), the Israel representatives have announced further withdrawals of Israel troops, which have occurred in phases as follows:

(*a*) On December 3, 1956, withdrawal from the Suez Canal area, along the length of the Canal, to a distance of some 50 kilometres;

(*b*) On January 7 and 8, 1957, withdrawal to a line roughly following meridian 33 degrees 44 minutes, leaving no Israel forces west of El Arish;

(*c*) On January 15, withdrawal eastward another 25 to 30 kilometres, except in the area of Sharm el-Sheikh. This phase involved the entry into El Arish and St. Catherine's Monastery of United Nations forces, which have closely followed the Israel withdrawals.

4. On January 14, the Representative of Israel, on behalf of his government, conveyed to the Secretary-General the following communication concerning an intended further withdrawal:

By January 22 the Sinai desert will be entirely evacuated by Israel forces with the exception of the Sharm el-Sheikh area, that is, the strip on the western coast of the Gulf of Aqaba which at present ensures freedom of navigation through the Straits of Tiran and in the Gulf.

In connection with the evacuation of this strip the Government of Israel is prepared to enter forthwith into conversations with the Secretary-General.

The Commander of UNEF is to meet with the Commander of the Israel forces to make arrangements for carrying out this latest phase of

the withdrawal. At this meeting, the Israel Commander will be requested to define the precise meaning of "the Sharm el-Sheikh area"
and "the strip on the western coast of the Gulf of Aqaba."

5. The intentions of the Government of Israel concerning compliance
with the resolutions by withdrawal of Israel forces from the Gaza Strip
have not yet been made known to the Secretary-General.

Part Two

, 6. The basic resolution of the General Assembly on the Middle East
crisis (November 2, 1956) urged a prompt withdrawal of the forces of
all parties to the armistice agreements behind the armistice lines and requested the Secretary-General "to observe and report promptly on the
compliance" with the resolution, for such further action as may be
deemed appropriate in accordance with the Charter. The resolution also
covered other points of significance to progress toward improved conditions in the region. Thus, in the same operative paragraph in which the
request was made for a withdrawal of forces behind the armistice lines,
the parties were urged "to desist from raids across the armistice lines
into neighbouring territory and to observe scrupulously the provisions
of the armistice agreements." The three points in this operative paragraph, while existing simultaneously within the terms of the paragraph,
were not linked together conditionally.

7. The request in the resolution of November 2 that the Secretary-
General observe and report on compliance was later added to in resolution 999 (ES-I) of November 4 wherein the Secretary-General, with the
assistance of the Chief of Staff and the members of the United Nations
Truce Supervision Organization, is asked "to obtain compliance of the
withdrawal of all forces behind the armistice lines." The discussions
with representatives of the Government of Israel, the results of which
have been noted above, have been conducted on the basis of this mandate to the Secretary-General for taking action to achieve full implementation of the request for withdrawal. The resolution of November 4,
asking the Secretary-General to undertake specific executive responsibilities, covered also the implementation of the cease-fire and the halting
of the movement of military forces and arms into the area, but was not
extended to the other points in the resolution of November 2.

8. In consequence of the intended withdrawal announced in the latest
communication to the Secretary-General from the Government of Israel
on January 14, 1957, the United Nations Emergency Force on January

22 will reach the armistice demarcation line wherever it follows the northeastern boundary of the Sinai desert. At that stage the last two points in operative paragraph 2 of the resolution of November 2 will assume added importance.

9. One of these points is the request for full observance of the provisions of the armistice agreements. This request makes it clear that the withdrawal of Israel forces must be behind the armistice line as it has been established in the General Armistice Agreement between Egypt and Israel. In this context it is to be noted, therefore, that the Israel communication is silent about withdrawal from the Gaza Strip which, according to this armistice agreement, falls on the Egyptian side of the armistice demarcation line. Further discussions with the representatives of Israel are required on this point. It is assumed that the Government of Israel wishes to make further observations on the question. Thus, when presenting the aforementioned communication on January 14, 1957, the Representative of Israel stated orally that his Government is prepared "at an early stage" to discuss with the Secretary-General "proposals for arrangements for the Gaza Strip."

10. The other point which is mentioned together with the request for withdrawal refers to raids across the armistice demarcation lines into neighbouring territory. Such raids are prohibited also in the armistice agreements. The call for general observance of these agreements reinforces the specific request to the parties to desist from raids. The cease-fire assurances given to the Secretary-General by the parties in April and May 1956 lent further legal solemnity to the relevant articles in the armistice agreements.

11. The United Nations Truce Supervision Organization established under the armistice agreements assists, as one of its main duties, in the prevention of incursions and raids. It is in accord with the call for scrupulous observance of the armistice agreements for the parties to take all appropriate measures to give UNTSO the support necessary to render it fully effective. It is a primary duty of the United Nations Emergency Force to supervise and enforce the cease-fire to which the parties committed themselves in response to the request of the General Assembly in the resolution of November 2. Appropriate liaison should be established between these two United Nations auxiliary organizations. Further consideration may have to be given to the question of the extent to which the Force might assume responsibilities so far carried by the Truce Supervision Organization.

12. The Secretary-General considers that, in view of the serious de-

velopments which have taken place, it would assist the two United Nations organs and facilitate compliance with this specific point in the resolution of November 2, if the parties were formally to reconfirm their undertakings to desist from raids and to take active steps to prevent incursions. When full implementation of the request for withdrawal of forces behind the armistice line is ensured, such reaffirmations should, therefore, in the Secretary-General's view, be solicited from all the parties.

13. The communication of January 14 from the Government of Israel, in making an exception for the Sharm el-Sheikh area as "the strip on the western coast of the Gulf of Aqaba which at present ensures freedom of navigation in the Straits of Tiran and in the Gulf," indicates that the evacuation of the strip is anticipated, although further conversations with the Secretary-General are suggested in connection with this evacuation. The area referred to and the islands opposite Sharm el-Sheikh are Egyptian territory, or territory under Egyptian jurisdiction on the basis of an agreement with Saudi Arabia. Under the terms of the General Assembly resolution, the forces should be withdrawn from these territories. The Israel declaration of November 8 stated that Israel would be willing to "withdraw its forces from Egypt" (A / 3320).

14. The international significance of the Gulf of Aqaba may be considered to justify the right of innocent passage through the Straits of Tiran and the Gulf in accordance with recognized rules of international law. The Secretary-General has not considered that a discussion of the various aspects of this matter, and its possible relation to the action requested in the General Assembly resolutions on the Middle East crisis, falls within the mandate established for him in the resolution of November 4.

15. Like the cease-fire, withdrawal is a preliminary and essential phase in a development through which a stable basis may be laid for peaceful conditions in the area. When the General Assembly, in its various resolutions concerning the recent crisis in the Middle East, gave high priority to the cease-fire and the withdrawal, the position of the Assembly reflected both basic principles of the Charter and essential political considerations.

16. The Assembly, in taking this position, in no way disregarded all the other aims which must be achieved in order to create more satisfactory conditions than those prevailing during the period preceding the crisis. Some of these aims were mentioned by the Assembly. Others are

to be found in previous decisions of the United Nations. All of them call for urgent attention. The basic function of the United Nations Emergency Force, to help maintain quiet, gives the Force great value as a background for efforts toward resolving such pending problems, although it is not in itself a means to that end.

17. It is essential that, through prompt conclusion of the first phases of implementation of the General Assembly resolutions, Member governments should now be enabled to turn to the constructive tasks to which the establishment and the maintenance of the cease-fire, a full withdrawal of forces behind the armistice lines, a desisting from raids, and scrupulous observance of the armistice agreements, should open the way.

AT EGYPT'S request the General Assembly resumed its Middle East discussions on January 17. A resolution was introduced by twenty-five Asian-African countries recalling previous resolutions on Israeli withdrawal, noting the Secretary-General's Report of January 15, noting "with regret and concern" Israel's failure to comply and requesting "the Secretary-General to continue his efforts for securing the complete withdrawal of Israel in pursuance of the above-mentioned resolutions, and to report on such completion to the General Assembly, within five days." [1] Before it was introduced, the language of the resolution had undergone considerable modification to meet Western wishes. In its original version it had called for Israel's withdrawal within five days and for consideration of sanctions if the time limit was not met.

The debate on the Secretary-General's report and the 25-Power resolution extended through five plenary meetings on January 17, 18, and 19.[2] There was nearly unanimous support for the call upon Israel to complete its withdrawal but there were many differences, both in substance and emphasis, on how the United Nations should proceed with the questions of Gaza and the Straits of Tiran.

At one extreme the Australian and New Zealand delegates thought Egypt should not be permitted to resume control of either area and UNEF should stay in both pending a peaceful settlement. Kuznetsov of the USSR was not slow to use this attitude as evidence of a "Western plot" to turn UNEF into an occupation force. Krishna Menon, on the other hand, thought the Secretary-General had been too patient with Israel's delays, "prevarications," and demands for advance guarantees. UNEF was in Egypt to secure complete and unconditional Israeli withdrawal behind the armistice line and any ex-

[1] *Ibid.*, agenda item 66, Document A/3501/Rev. 1, January 17, 1957.
[2] *Ibid.*, 638th–642nd Plenary Meetings, January 17, 18, and 19, 1957.

tension of its mandate thereafter would require new consultations and agreements with all concerned.

Lester Pearson spoke for a middle position supported by several Western Europeans. While it was regrettable that Israel had not yet completed its withdrawal it was also regrettable that more progress had not been made toward ensuring against a return to the old state of affairs. He urged the Secretary-General in his next report to give his views on how UNEF might be used to prevent a return to raids from the Gaza Strip, to support freedom of navigation through the Straits of Tiran and in general to achieve peaceful and stable conditions along the line between Israel and Egypt.

When the debate drew to a close Eban professed to see, both in the Assembly and "throughout the world," endorsement of Israel's insistence on measures to ensure that hostilities could not be renewed. "As the days go by," he said "the consensus of opinion grows in favor of a course of action in the Straits of Tiran and in Gaza which would block the path to avoidable tragedy and disaster." It was regrettable, he said, that none of this "constructive thinking" was reflected in the withdrawal resolution. Fawzi, however, feared a "filibuster" was beginning to gain strength. He hoped that it would be "nipped in the bud" and that the Assembly would fulfill its duty to secure complete withdrawal of "the aggressors" without further delay.

The Assembly then adopted the "five-day" resolution by an overwhelming margin on January 19. The vote was 74 to 2 with 2 abstentions. Only Israel and France voted "no" and only Cuba and Costa Rica abstained.

The Israeli response to the General Assembly's January 19 resolution came on January 23 in the form of an *aide-mémoire* [3] transmitted to the Secretary-General and a speech on the same day by Prime Minister Ben-Gurion in the Knesset.

The *aide-mémoire* stated Israel's position on Sharm el-Sheikh and the Gaza Strip, giving at some length an account of the historical, political, and legal reasons for the position taken. As to withdrawal, the essence of the reply to the Assembly was as follows:

Israel would withdraw from Sharm el-Sheikh if UNEF were stationed there "to see to it that freedom of navigation was maintained and belligerent acts avoided in the Gulf of Aqaba and the Straits of Tiran" and would "maintain its position" there until "a peace settlement was achieved or when secure freedom of navigation was guaranteed by other international instruments to which Israel was a party."

Israeli military forces would be withdrawn from the Gaza Strip, but Israeli civilian administration, including police, would remain. Not only would the Gaza Strip not be returned to Egyptian administration, but UNEF itself would be excluded from the territory.

In his speech to the Knesset, Ben-Gurion rejected in the strongest terms any return to the Armistice Agreement with Egypt. Israel, he said, was pre-

---

[3] *Ibid.*, agenda item 66, Document A/3511, January 24, 1957.

pared to sign "immediately with Egypt an agreement of nonbelligerency and mutual nonaggression, but the Armistice Agreement, violated and broken, is beyond repair." [4]

Israel's attitude toward the Armistice Agreement and its proposal to retain control of the Gaza Strip were wholly unacceptable. Under its terms the Armistice Agreement could not be denounced unilaterally and remained the law no matter what Israel said. Furthermore the Security Council in approving the Agreement in 1949 had reaffirmed its cease-fire order of 1948, which was binding under Chapter VII of the Charter. Throughout the following years the Council had upheld the Agreement, denounced violations when they occurred, and called upon both sides to comply fully with its terms. Since November 1 the General Assembly had reaffirmed the same stance in resolution after resolution calling upon Israel to withdraw behind the armistice line. As to the Gaza Strip, it was left under Egyptian control by the terms of the Armistice Agreement and this could not be altered in Israel's favor except by a settlement agreed between Israel and Egypt.

Israel's demand that UNEF stay at Sharm el-Sheikh until "secure freedom of navigation was guaranteed" through the Straits of Tiran went against a fundamental principle approved when UNEF was established—that it would not be used to tip the balance one way or the other—in the settlement of political or legal issues in dispute. Though there was much sympathy and support for Israel's right to freedom of navigation in these waters, the extent of the right of innocent passage there under international law was a matter of dispute. The stationing of UNEF at Sharm el-Sheikh, as anywhere else on Egyptian territory, also required Egypt's consent. Israel's stand could not have been better calculated to make more difficult reaching a tacit understanding with Egypt to continue a UNEF presence on the Straits after Israeli withdrawal.

Hammarskjöld and the UNEF Advisory Committee, when they met on January 24, agreed that the tone of the Israeli response to the Assembly's January 19 resolution could easily lead to an extremely grave crisis. Unless Israel could somehow be persuaded to draw back promptly from the position it had taken, the question of imposing sanctions to enforce compliance would confront the Members in an acute and dangerous form.

The Secretary-General was required by the January 19 resolution to make a report to the General Assembly on January 24. What he said in that report would determine in large degree whether the threatened showdown on sanctions could be averted in the ensuing debate. Hammarskjöld believed the only way forward lay in carrying further the line of development suggested in his January 15 report. His soundings with members of the Advisory Committee and other delegates indicated wide support for his giving such a lead to the Assembly. But it was an extremely delicate task to strike

---

[4] *Ibid.,* Document A/3527, Annex V, February 11, 1957.

a balance among the various views and interests in such a way as to hold together the always uneasy alliance forming the Assembly majority and to give new momentum to the United Nations peace effort.

How skillfully Hammarskjöld met the challenge is evident in the text that follows. The essence of his message to Israel was this: You cannot exact a price for completing withdrawal which would violate the Armistice Agreement and the resolutions of the Assembly; after you withdraw, however, steps can be taken, if you will cooperate, to strengthen the armistice régime in such ways as to provide the security you seek against a resumption of raids across the armistice line and interference with innocent passage for your shipping in the Gulf of Aqaba and the Straits of Tiran.

In his speech to the Knesset denouncing the Armistice Agreeement as "beyond repair," Ben-Gurion had offered instead to sign "immediately with Egypt an agreement of nonbelligerency and mutual nonaggression." The Secretary-General pointed out in his report that the first article of the Armistice Agreement already constituted what was, in effect, a nonaggression pact. This could be reaffirmed along with other provisions of the agreement restricting deployment of Israeli and Egyptian military forces which had been progressively undermined and violated by one side or the other.

In private discussions with members of the UNEF Advisory Committee and other delegates Hammarskjöld explained the background for the emphasis he placed in section C of his report on gaining full compliance with Articles VII and VIII restricting military deployment on both sides. During his cease-fire mission in April 1956 he had, as he reported to the Security Council at the time, received assurances from both Egypt and Israel of their cooperation in this respect *provided* it was "within the framework of a full return to the state of affairs envisaged in the Armistice Agreement" and that implementation was related "to other steps in fulfillment of the aims" of the Agreement (see page 102).

Thus implementation of Articles VII and VIII had earlier been conditionally accepted and could now become a key factor in making a fresh start toward effective pacification of the borderline area. This also would greatly strengthen the case against exercise by Egypt of any claimed rights of belligerency upon Israeli ships.

Hammarskjöld also suggested that UNEF might be deployed on the Israeli side of the armistice line, as well as on the Egyptian side, at least in the El Auja demilitarized zone long illegally occupied by Israeli troops. Such a deployment would strengthen UNEF's capacity to act as a peaceful buffer along the ADL (armistice demarcation line) and make it possible for UNEF to take over some supervisory duties from UNTSO. This would require, however, a new decision of the General Assembly and the consent of both Israel and Egypt. The latter had all along considered that UNEF should be stationed on both sides of the armistice line and Hammarskjöld was able to include in his report that he had "been informed of the desire of the Government of Egypt that all raids and incursions across the armistice line, in both directions, be brought to an end and that United Nations auxiliary organs afford effective assistance to that effect."

There was virtually no support in the Assembly for Israel's proposal to retain administrative control of the Gaza Strip, but Canada and others in the Western camp were urging instead a United Nations administration of the Gaza Strip to replace Egyptian administration. This was vigorously opposed by the Arab-Asian states. The Secretary-General limited himself to pointing out why Egypt's right to administer the Strip was upheld by international law and that while the Assembly could recommend United Nations administration, Egyptian consent would be required.

Hammarskjöld's report did not, of course, accept Israel's demand that UNEF stay at Sharm el-Sheikh until Egypt accepted Israel's position on its rights in the Straits of Tiran. But he did point out that even partial restoration of the armistice régime would leave any claim by Egypt to the exercise of belligerent rights so much in doubt that *de facto* the claim should not be exercised. Full implementation of the Armistice Agreement, he added, would give the case against all acts of belligerency "full cogency." In the meantime, it might be agreed that UNEF be deployed at Sharm el-Sheikh after Israeli withdrawal in support of peace and quiet and mutual restraint in the area.

Hammarskjöld was careful to present his report and his proposals within a legal framework. He refrained from indicating publicly his views on how the political negotiations to implement them might be phased, because the time was not ripe for that. But he spoke privately in the Advisory Committee of the sequence of steps he hoped for: *first,* withdrawal; *second, de facto* abstention by Egypt from interference with free passage by Israeli ships through the Straits of Tiran; *third,* formal assurances from both sides of complete abstention from raids across the line; *fourth,* simultaneous assurances by Israel of withdrawal from the El Auja demilitarized zone and the defensive zones on its side of the line and, by Egypt, from the defensive zones on the Egyptian side, to be followed by assurances from Egypt on freedom of navigation by Israel; *fifth,* formal reaffirmations by both sides of Article I as a general nonaggression pact.

Report to the General Assembly in Pursuance of General Assembly Resolution 1123 (XI) on Israeli Withdrawal

UN HEADQUARTERS, NEW YORK   JANUARY 24, 1957

Part One

1. In resolution 1123 (XI) adopted on January 19, 1957, the General Assembly, after recalling its resolution of November 2, 4, 7, and 24, 1956, requested the Secretary-General "to continue his efforts for securing the complete withdrawal of Israel in pursuance of the above-mentioned resolutions, and to report on such completion to the General Assembly, within five days."

2. In pursuance of the resolution of January 19, the Secretary-General held further discussions on withdrawal with the representative of the government of Israel on January 20 and 23. On January 23, the Government of Israel presented its views in an *"aide-mémoire* on the Israel position on the Sharm el-Sheikh area and the Gaza Strip." This *aide-mémoire* has been circulated separately with a note by the Secretary-General (A/3511).

3. At the expiration of the time limit set by the resolution for the Secretary-General to report to the General Assembly, Israel has not fully complied with the requests of the General Assembly for withdrawal. The present situation, following the latest phase in the withdrawal of Israel forces on January 22, 1957, is shown on the map in the attached annex. [Annex not reproduced—EDITORS]

4. The views of the Secretary-General on the urgency of the prompt conclusion of the first phases of implementation of the General Assembly resolutions, as expressed in the previous report (A/3500 and Add. 1), remain firm. The further comments he considers it desirable to make are presented in Part Two of the present report.

General Assembly Official Records, Eleventh Session, Annexes, Volume II, agenda item 66, Document A/3512, January 24, 1957.

Part Two

A

5. To help toward solutions of the pending problems in the area, United Nations actions must be governed by principle and must be in accordance with international law and valid international agreements. For his part, the Secretary-General, in carrying out the policies of the United Nations, must act with scrupulous regard for the decisions of the General Assembly, the Security Council, and the other principal organs. It may be useful to note the implications of the foregoing for the actions of the United Nations and of the Secretary-General in the present situation. In this regard, it would seem that the following points are generally recognized as noncontroversial in the determination of the limits within which the activities of the United Nations can be properly developed. Within their scope, positive United Nations measures in the present issue, rendered possible by full compliance with the General Assembly resolutions, can be and have to be developed, which would represent effective progress toward the creation of peaceful conditions in the region.

(*a*) The United Nations cannot condone a change of the *status juris* resulting from military action contrary to the provisions of the Charter. The Organization must, therefore, maintain that the *status juris* existing prior to such military action be reestablished by a withdrawal of troops, and by the relinquishment or nullification of rights asserted in territories covered by the military action and depending upon it.

(*b*) The use of military force by the United Nations other than that under Chapter VII of the Charter requires the consent of the states in which the force is to operate. Moreover, such use must be undertaken and developed in a manner consistent with the principles mentioned under (*a*) above. It must, furthermore, be impartial, in the sense that it does not serve as a means to force settlement, in the interest of one party, of political conflicts or legal issues recognized as controversial.

(*c*) United Nations actions must respect fully the rights of Member states recognized in the Charter, and international agreements not contrary to the aims of the Charter, which are concluded in exercise of those rights.

6. Point 5 (*a*) above, in general terms, is clearly reflected in the var-

ious decisions of the General Assembly on withdrawal of troops behind the armistice lines. Its further consequences with respect to *de facto* situations of a nonmilitary nature in various territories will require consideration in later parts of this report in connection specifically with the bearing of point (*c*) above on the cases at issue.

7. Point (*b*) above finds expression in the second and final report on the United Nations Emergency Force from which the following passages may be quoted. "It follows from its [UNEF's] terms of reference that there is no intent in the establishment of the Force to influence the military balance in the present conflict and thereby the political balance affecting efforts to settle the conflict" (A/3302, paragraph 8). Further, "nor, moreover, should the Force have military functions exceeding those necessary to secure peaceful conditions on the assumption that the parties to the conflict take all necessary steps for compliance with the recommendations of the General Assembly" (A/3302, paragraph 12).

8. Point (*c*) is reflected in General Assembly resolution 997 (ES-I) of November 2, 1956, wherein the parties are urged to observe scrupulously the armistice agreements.

B

9. In considering the situation in Gaza the following should be taken into account.

10. Article V of the General Armistice Agreement between Egypt and Israel of February 24, 1949, provides that the armistice line established in Article VI "is not to be construed in any sense as a political or territorial boundary, and is delineated without prejudice to rights, claims, and positions of either party to the armistice as regards ultimate settlement of the Palestine question." It goes on to say that "The basic purpose of the armistice demarcation line is to delineate the line beyond which the armed forces of the respective parties shall not move. . . ."

11. Although the armistice line thus does not create any new rights for the parties on either side, it resulted in a *de facto* situation by leaving the "control" (see Article VII) of the territory in the hands of the government, the military forces of which were there in accordance with the stipulations of the armistice. Control in this case obviously must be considered as including administration and security.

12. In Article IV it is recognized that rights, claims, or interests of a

nonmilitary character in the area of Palestine covered by the agreement may be asserted by either party and that these, by mutual agreement being excluded from armistice negotiations, shall be, at the discretion of the parties, the subject of later settlement. It follows that the *de facto* administrative situation created under the armistice may be challenged as contrary to the rights, claims, or interests of one of the parties, but that it can be legally changed only through settlement between the parties.

13. The Armistice Agreement was signed by both parties and, according to Article XII, remains in force until a peaceful settlement between them is achieved. It was approved by the Security Council. Whatever arrangements the United Nations may now wish to make in order to further progress toward peaceful conditions, the agreement must be fully respected by it. Thus, the United Nations cannot recognize a change of the *de facto* situation created under Article VI of the agreement unless the change is brought about through settlement between the parties; nor, of course, can it lend its assistance to the maintenance of a *de facto* situation contrary to the one created by the Armistice Agreement. These considerations exclude the United Nations from accepting Israel control over the area, even if it were of a nonmilitary character. They would also exclude the deployment of the United Nations Emergency Force necessary, in the absence of Israel troops, if arrangements such as those proposed by the Government of Israel were to be implemented.

14. Deployment of the Force in Gaza, under the resolutions of the General Assembly, would have to be on the same basis as its deployment along the armistice line in the Sinai peninsula. Any broader function for it in that area, in view of the terms of the Armistice Agreement and a recognized principle of international law, would require the consent of Egypt. A widening of the United Nations administrative responsibilities in the area, beyond its responsibilities for the refugees, would likewise have to be based on agreement with Egypt. It follows, therefore, that although the United Nations General Assembly would be entitled to recommend the establishment of a United Nations administration and to request negotiations in order to implement such an arrangement, it would lack authority in that recommendation, unilaterally, to require compliance.

C

15. In its first article, the Armistice Agreement between Egypt and Israel provides that no aggressive action by the armed forces—land, sea, or air—of either party shall be undertaken, planned, or threatened against the people or the armed forces of the other. The same article establishes the right of each party to its security and freedom from fear of attack by the armed forces of the other. This article assimilates the Armistice Agreement to a nonaggression pact, providing for mutual and full abstention from belligerent acts. A restoration of relations between the parties, more stable than those now prevailing, can therefore be based on a reaffirmation of this article of the Armistice Agreement. It is natural to envisage that such a reaffirmation should extend also to other clauses of the Armistice Agreement, especially to those in which the substance has an immediate bearing on the state of tension prevailing at the outbreak of the crisis. The Secretary-General, in this context, wishes to draw attention specifically to Articles VII and VIII, which provide for restrictions on the deployment of the military forces of the parties along both sides of the armistice demarcation line. The provisions of Articles VII and VIII have been undermined progressively by the developments in recent years, and, at the beginning of the crisis, were not being fulfilled. There is universal recognition that the condition of affairs of which this deterioration formed a part should not be permitted to return. Renewed full implementation of the clauses of the Armistice Agreement obviously presumes such an attitude on the part of the governments concerned, and such supporting measures as would guarantee a return to the state of affairs envisaged in the Armistice Agreement, and avoidance of the state of affairs into which conditions, due to a lack of compliance with the agreement, had progressively deteriorated.

16. Whatever the state of noncompliance with the Armistice Agreement in general before the crisis, it would seem apparent that a by-passing of that agreement now would seriously impede efforts to lay the foundation for progress toward solutions of pending problems. A return to full implementation of Articles VII and VIII would be a valuable step toward reduction of tension and the establishment of peaceful conditions in the region. The provisions in these articles were the result of careful analysis of the military situation, and the objectives defined in

the course of the armistice negotiations should still have validity as steps in the desired direction. If the military clauses of the Armistice Agreement were again to be fully implemented, this would have important positive bearing on other problems in the region.

17. According to Article VII, Egyptian "defensive forces" only may be maintained in the area of the western front under Egyptian control. All other Egyptian forces shall be withdrawn from this area to a point or points no further east than El Arish-Abou Aoueigila. According to the same article, Israel "defensive forces" only, which shall be based on the settlements, may be maintained in the area of the western front under Israel control. All other Israel forces shall be withdrawn from this area to a point or points north of the line delineated in the special memorandum of November 13, 1948, on the implementation of the resolution of the Security Council of November 4, 1948. The definition of "defensive forces" is given in an annex to the agreement.

18. Article VIII of the agreement provides that an area comprising the village of El Auja and vicinity, as defined in the article, shall be demilitarized, and that both Egyptian and Israel armed forces shall be totally excluded therefrom. The article further provides that on the Egyptian side of the frontier, facing the El Auja area, no Egyptian defensive positions shall be closer to El Auja than El Qouseima and Abou Aoueigila. It also states that the road Taba-Qouseima-Auja shall not be employed by any military forces whatsoever "for the purpose of entering Palestine."

19. The agreement provides that the execution of its provisions shall be supervised by the Mixed Armistice Commission, established under it, and that the headquarters of the Commission shall be maintained in El Auja.

20. The United Nations Emergency Force is deployed at the dividing line between the forces of Israel and Egypt. The General Assembly concurred in paragraph 12 of the Secretary-General's second and final report (A/3302) which specifically referred to the deployment of the Force on only one side of the armistice line. On this basis, the Force would have units in the Gaza area as well as opposite El Auja. With demilitarization of the El Auja zone in accordance with the Armistice Agreement, it might be indicated that the Force should have units stationed also on the Israel side of the armistice demarcation line, at least, in that zone. Such deployment, which would require a new decision by the General Assembly, would have the advantage of the Force being in

a position to assume the supervisory duties of the Truce Supervision Organization in all the territory where that Organization now functions under the Armistice Agreement between Egypt and Israel. In both Gaza and El Auja, the functions of the Truce Supervision Organization and the Force would somewhat overlap if such an arrangement were not to be made. As an arrangement of this kind was not foreseen by the Armistice Agreement, it obviously would require the consent of the two parties to that agreement. Such mutual consent might be given to the United Nations directly, especially since the arrangement would be on an *ad hoc* basis.

21. The implementation of Articles VII and VIII of the agreement would at present be facilitated by the fact that there are no Egyptian military positions in the area under consideration and that, therefore, implementation by Israel does not require a simultaneous withdrawal of military units on the Egyptian side. The condition which must be fulfilled in order to establish reciprocity, would be Egyptian assurance that Egyptian forces will not take up positions in the area in contravention of Articles VII and VIII. Up to now Egypt has moved into Sinai only small police units which have been considered necessary in support of the reestablished local civil administrations.

22. As indicated in the previous report (A/3500 and Add. 1), the United Nations Emergency Force and the Truce Supervision Organization, with their respective responsibilities for the cease-fire, should co-operate in the prevention of incursions and raids across the armistice demarcation lines. It was further indicated in the same report that, once the withdrawal is ensured, in implementation of the General Assembly resolution of November 2, 1956, formal assurance should be solicited from the parties to desist from raids and to take active measures to prevent incursions. In the course of the discussions which have taken place since the circulation of his last report, the Secretary-General has been informed of the desire of the Government of Egypt that all raids and incursions across the armistice line, in both directions, be brought to an end, and that United Nations auxiliary organs afford effective assistance to that effect.

D

23. In connection with the question of Israel withdrawal from the Sharm el-Sheikh area, attention has been directed to the situation in the

Gulf of Aqaba and the Straits of Tiran. This matter is of longer duration and not directly related to the present crisis. The concern now evinced in it, however, calls for consideration of the legal aspects of the matter as a problem in its own right. It follows from principles guiding the United Nations that the Israel military action and its consequences should not be elements influencing the solution.

24. As stated in the previous report (A/3500 and Add. 1), the international significance of the Gulf of Aqaba may be considered to justify the right of innocent passage through the Straits of Tiran and the Gulf in accordance with recognized rules of international law. However, in its commentary to article 17 of the articles of the law of the sea (A/3159, page 20), the International Law Commission reserved consideration of the question "what would be the legal position of straits forming part of the territorial sea of one or more states and constituting the sole means of access to the port of another state." This description applies to the Gulf of Aqaba and the Straits of Tiran. A legal controversy exists as to the extent of the right of innocent passage through these waters.

25. Under these circumstances, it is indicated that whatever rights there may be in relation to the Gulf and the Straits, such rights be exercised with restraint on all sides. Any possible claims of belligerent rights should take into account the international interests involved and, therefore, if asserted, should be limited to clearly noncontroversial situations.

26. The Security Council, in its resolution of September 1, 1951, concerning passage of international commercial shipping and goods through the Suez Canal, considered "that since the armistice régime, which has been in existence for nearly two and a half years, is of a permanent character, neither party can reasonably assert that it actively is a belligerent or requires to exercise the right of visit, search and seizure for any legitimate purpose of self defence," a basis on which the Council called upon Egypt to terminate the restrictions on the passage of international commercial shipping and goods through the Suez Canal. This general finding of the Security Council has a direct bearing on the question here under consideration. It remains valid and warrants corresponding conclusions as long as the assumptions defined by the Council remain correct. However, in later years, an ever widening noncompliance with the Armistice Agreement has developed, ending in the Israel military action of October 29, 1956, as a result of which Israel still has

military forces on Egyptian territory contrary to the Armistice Agreement. It may be further noted that Israel, in its communication of January 23, 1957, makes proposals concerning the Gaza Strip which cannot be reconciled with maintaining the validity of the Armistice Agreement.

27. The armistice régime may be considered as operative, at least in part, provided forces are withdrawn behind the armistice lines, even if noncompliance were to continue in relation to other substantive clauses of the Armistice Agreement. It follows from the finding of the Security Council in 1951 that under such circumstances the parties to the Armistice Agreement may be considered as not entitled to claim any belligerent rights. Were the substantive clauses of the Armistice Agreement, especially Articles VII and VIII, again to be implemented, the case against all acts of belligerency, which is based on the existence of the armistice régime, would gain full cogency. With such a broader implementation of the Armistice Agreement, the parties should be asked to give assurances that, on the basis established, they will not assert any belligerent rights (including, of course, such rights in the Gulf of Aqaba and the Straits of Tiran).

28. As a conclusion from paragraphs 24 to 27, it may be held that, in a situation where the armistice régime is partly operative by observance of the provisions of the Armistice Agreement concerning the armistice lines, possible claims to rights of belligerency would be at least so much in doubt that, having regard for the general international interest at stake, no such claim should be exercised in the Gulf of Aqaba and the Straits of Tiran. Such a *de facto* position, if taken, obviously would be a part of efforts to reestablish as complete an armistice régime as possible and, as such, would be detached from the policy of implementation of the unconditional General Assembly request for withdrawal behind the armistice lines. The situation resulting from such a position should be stabilized when the Armistice Agreement is more fully implemented.

29. Israel troops, on their withdrawal from the Sharm el-Sheikh area, would be followed by the United Nations Emergency Force in the same way as in other parts of Sinai. The duties of the Force in respect of the cease-fire and the withdrawal will determine its movements. However, if it is recognized that there is a need for such an arrangement, it may be agreed that units of the Force (or special representatives in the nature of observers) would assist in maintaining quiet in the area beyond what follows from this general principle. In accordance with the general legal principles recognized as decisive for the deploy-

ment of the United Nations Emergency Force, the Force should not be used, so as to prejudge the solution of the controversial questions involved. The Force, thus, is not to be deployed in such a way as to protect any special position on these questions, although, at least transitionally, it may function in support of mutual restraint in accordance with the foregoing.

E

30. In the last report (A/3500 and Add. 1), it was stated as essential that through prompt conclusion of the first phases of implementation of the General Assembly resolutions, Member states should now be enabled to turn to the constructive tasks to which the establishment and the maintenance of the cease-fire, a full withdrawal of forces behind the armistice lines, a desisting from raids, and scrupulous observance of the armistice agreements, should open the way.

31. The report paid special attention to the problem of raids. In the debate following its presentation, concern was expressed about the problems which might arise in connection with the withdrawal of Israel forces from the residual areas held at Gaza and at Sharm el-Sheikh. These latter issues, and the Israel views on the manner in which they might be met, have been the subject of the communication of January 23 from the Government of Israel (A/3511).

32. In the present report to the General Assembly on the situation now prevailing, the Secretary-General has endeavoured to clarify both the limits on United Nations action set by considerations of principle and law, and the directions in which such action might be usefully developed in the case of the two last mentioned problems and related questions. The basis for doing so has been primarily the Armistice Agreement between Egypt and Israel, scrupulous observance of which was requested by the General Assembly in its resolution of November 2, 1956. The Secretary-General believes that the concern expressed in the General Assembly debate in connection with the final withdrawal can be met in a satisfactory manner within the obligation resting on the United Nations to base its action on principle, on international law, and international agreements. A development of United Nations action, as indicated, would represent a significant step in preparation of further constructive measures.

33. Among the further problems which require the attention of the

General Assembly it is natural in this context to draw attention specifically to the refugee question. In this connection, the development of the situation in Gaza may require special attention and may impose added responsibilities on the United Nations.

34. It is essential that forthcoming efforts, aimed at continued progress, should concentrate on concrete issues. They should maintain the momentum gained during the preceding phase, as illustrated by the rapid development both of the United Nations Emergency Force and of the Canal clearing operation. This will require from the parties a willingness to cooperate with the United Nations towards objectives transcending the immediate issues at stake. Practically all of these issues are complicated and delicate. They might develop into serious stumbling blocks if they are not approached in a constructive spirit seeking essentials. Progress will not be possible if temporary complications of narrow scope are permitted to divert attention from solutions of wide significance.

THE GENERAL ASSEMBLY began discussion of the Secretary-General's report on January 28 but no resolution was introduced until February 1. In response to questions at a meeting with the UNEF Advisory Committee on January 26, Hammarskjöld had indicated his belief that a generally worded endorsement of the aims and approach proposed in his report was all that should be attempted now. With Israeli troops still on Egyptian soil, it would be premature to attempt to go further in spelling out specific recommendations for subsequent steps.

The next five days were chiefly occupied in negotiations aimed at wording of a resolution which would command at least a two-thirds majority. It was a difficult undertaking. Israel's stance, supported by a massive public relations campaign, especially in the United States, hardened the resistance of Egypt and the other Arab states to any move that might appear to reward Israel at Egypt's expense. Widespread Western support for Israel's position on free passage for her ships through the Straits of Tiran and for an expanded United Nations role in the Gaza Strip fed Arab-Asian suspicions of a desire to use UNEF as a form of pressure upon Egyptian policy.

U.S. Ambassador Lodge and members of the UNEF Advisory Committee played key roles in the negotiating process. Fortunately they had Hammarskjöld's report as the basis of their work, for its impartiality, careful legality, political judgment and constructive aims drew almost universal expressions of admiration from the delegates. Finally agreement was reached on two resolutions with the same sponsors—Brazil, Colombia, India, Indonesia, Norway, the United States, and Yugoslavia. Four of the sponsors were members of the Advisory Committee and six had contributed contingents to UNEF. Politically the sponsorship embraced the Asian, North Atlantic and Latin American groupings. The first resolution was concerned with Israeli withdrawal, the second with action which should follow withdrawal. They were as follows:

Resolution 1124 (XI) of February 2, 1957

The General Assembly,

Recalling its resolutions 997 (ES-I) of November 2, 1956, 998 (ES-I) and 999 (ES-I) of November 4, 1956, 1002 (ES-I) of November 7, 1956, 1120 (XI) of November 24, 1956, and 1123 (XI) of January 19, 1957,

1. *Deplores* the noncompliance of Israel to complete its withdrawal behind the armistice demarcation line despite the repeated requests of the General Assembly;

2. *Calls upon* Israel to complete its withdrawal behind the armistice demarcation line without further delay.

Resolution 1125 (XI) of February 2, 1957

The General Assembly,

Having received the report of the Secretary-General of January 24, 1957 (A/3512),

Recognizing that withdrawal by Israel must be followed by action which would assure progress towards the creation of peaceful conditions,

1. *Notes with appreciation* the Secretary-General's report and the measures therein to be carried out upon Israel's complete withdrawal;

2. *Calls upon* the governments of Egypt and Israel scrupulously to observe the provisions of the General Armistice Agreement between Egypt and Israel of February 24, 1949;

3. *Considers* that, after full withdrawal of Israel from the Sharm el-Sheikh and Gaza areas, the scrupulous maintenance of the Armistice Agreement requires the placing of the United Nations Emergency Force on the Egyptian-Israel armistice demarcation line and the implementation of other measures as proposed in the Secretary-General's report, with due regard to the considerations set out therein with a view to assist in achieving situations conducive to the maintenance of peaceful conditions in the area;

4. *Requests* the Secretary-General, in consultation with the parties concerned, to take steps to carry out these measures and to report, as appropriate, to the General Assembly.

The wording of the second resolution was a compromise between those such as Canada which wished to be more specific about the functions of

UNEF in Gaza and at Sharm el-Sheikh and those such as India which wished to avoid any suggestion of pressure on Egypt in either area. Paragraph 3 was clear-cut in one new particular—"on" the armistice demarcation line meant that UNEF should be deployed on both sides of the ADL. For the rest, the endorsement of the proposals in the Secretary-General's report was in general terms and, though awkwardly phrased, supported his judgment of the legal and political framework within which he should proceed.

With Israeli troops still in Egypt and Israel proclaiming the Armistice Agreement a dead letter, the Arab states could not be persuaded to support the second resolution. As we shall see, they decided to abstain.

For the United States Lodge took a strong lead in the debate. Israel's withdrawal must take place before any of the measures proposed in the second resolution could be undertaken. The withdrawal must be complete, including Sharm el-Sheikh and civilian administration in Gaza. Withdrawal should take place "forthwith, and by forthwith we mean that the withdrawal should take place in only the few days necessary physically to move the forces behind the armistice demarcation line." Then he added the following: "While I am on the subject of withdrawal, which of course is the sole object of the first draft resolution and which is the governing and overriding consideration of the second draft resolution, let me also say this in all seriousness and solemnity: that I cannot predict the consequences which can ensue if Israel fails to comply with the will of the General Assembly as expressed in the pending draft resolutions." [1]

Israel was already feeling the effects of the suspension of various U.S. government economic and financial aid programs and her economic viability as a nation depended on continuing assistance from U.S. governmental and private sources. These words were a clear warning of the Eisenhower administration's determination to maintain and, if necessary, tighten the pressures of this form of sanction.

Lodge also gave his complete support to the Secretary-General's view and proposals for strengthening the armistice régime. He stressed especially that UNEF should be stationed on both sides of the armistice line and the belief of the United States that it should also be deployed at Sharm el-Sheikh to separate Egyptian and Israeli land and sea forces there.

Lester Pearson and Krishna Menon both spoke in support of the second resolution, but there were sharp differences in emphasis and approach between the two. Pearson had wanted the Assembly to go on record with stronger and more specific affirmative language in support of the measures suggested in Hammarskjöld's report to prevent a return to the conditions prevailing prior to October 29, 1956—for example, the raids across the armistice line and the Egyptian blockade of the Gulf of Tiran. He agreed that Israel's withdrawal must precede such measures but Assembly approval of them now was needed to help persuade Israel to withdraw. Thus the resolu-

---

[1] *Ibid.,* 651st Plenary Meeting, February 2, 1957.

tions were interrelated. He did not regard this as yielding to Israeli conditions since the measures proposed were desirable in their own right. He then proceeded to give his interpretation of the resolution, with all the emphasis on steps that *"must"* be taken and only passing recognition of the fact that most of these required the consent and cooperation of Egypt and Israel and could not be imposed by the Assembly or the Secretary-General.

Menon, on the other hand, put the emphasis on Egypt's sovereign right of consent to the deployment of UNEF anywhere on its territory and on the primacy of UNEF's functions in relation to withdrawal. The Force could not be used as a form of pressure upon Egypt, whether in relation to Gaza or the Straits of Tiran, nor exercise any of the rights of an occupying force. After withdrawal it must be placed on both sides of the armistice line and any deployment at Sharm el-Sheikh or elsewhere on Egyptian territory could only be in agreement with Egypt.

When he spoke for Egypt Mahmoud Fawzi used firm language to present the position of his government on "the question of Israel's withdrawal." Israel should withdraw immediately and UNEF was then "to take positions exclusively on both sides of the armistice demarcation line." The consent of the Egyptian government was "an indispensable prerequisite" to the stationing and deployment of UNEF, which was not in Egypt "to resolve any question or to settle any problems, be that problem in relation to the Suez Canal, to Palestine or to freedom of passage in territorial waters." [2]

This statement appeared to rule out the stationing of UNEF at Sharm el-Sheikh, but the position was not as uncompromising as it seemed. Fawzi had carefully limited the definition of UNEF's functions to its duties in relation to Israeli withdrawal, which were to end up on the armistice line. He left open the question of subsequent steps that might be taken to strengthen the armistice régime under the second resolution. Hammarskjöld's report had already ruled out using UNEF to "resolve" the question of innocent passage through the Straits of Tiran. The Secretary-General had based his case against exercise of any belligerent rights in the Straits mainly on returning to and strengthening the armistice régime and had suggested that it might be agreed in that connection to leave a unit of UNEF at Sharm el-Sheikh "in support of mutual restraint."

Finally there was the flat statement in Hammarskjöld's report "of the desire of the Government of Egypt that all raids and incursions across the armistice line, in both directions, be brought to an end, and that United Nations auxiliary organs afford effective assistance to that effect." Fawzi did not refer to this statement, thus permitting it to stand in the record as a statement to the Assembly of Egypt's position, though made by the Secretary-General.

Speaking for Israel Eban stood firm on the demands made in his government's *aide-mémoire* of January 23. He was critical of the Secretary-General's report and declared the armistice régime lay "in ruins." This was

[2] *Ibid.*

entirely Egypt's fault because of its implacable hostility and belligerency since 1949. Israel thus could not regard the agreement as a basis for future relations with Egypt. Eban was encouraged to note that more delegations had now recognized the need for guarantees against a return to the conditions that had prevailed before October 29. UNEF should be empowered to prevent Egyptian interference with Israeli shipping through the Straits of Tiran, whereas Egypt's attitude, if accepted, would make UNEF no more than an instrument of Egyptian policy. On the question of whether Israel would agree to UNEF's deployment on the Israeli side of the armistice line as well as the Egyptian side Eban had not a word to say.[3]

The votes, which came just after midnight on February 2, were as follows. The withdrawal resolution was adopted 74 to 2 with 2 abstentions. Israel and France were alone in voting "no," and the Netherlands and Luxembourg abstained. The second resolution, on future measures, was adopted 55 to 0 with 22 abstentions. The latter included the Soviet bloc of 8, the 11 Arab states, and Israel, France, and the Netherlands. Except for the Arabs, all the Asian-African States joined the United States, Western Europe (excepting France and the Netherlands), Canada, Australia, New Zealand, and Latin America in voting "yes."

During the debate Sir Percy Spender of Australia had made a long speech which was mainly a learned commentary on the international law aspects of Hammarskjöld's report (Sir Percy was elected the next year to the International Court of Justice). While agreeing with most of Hammarskjöld's positions on the law, he declared himself unable to accept, without "significant modifications" the general proposition that "the use of military force by the United Nations other than that under Chapter VII of the Charter requires the consent of the States in which the force is to operate." The point of his argument was that the right of consent was not unlimited and he cited the "good faith" agreement with Egypt to that effect. Otherwise UNEF would be at the mercy of Egyptian will, a proposition which Eban was quick to pick up. In Sir Percy's view the United Nations already had the right to station UNEF at Sharm el-Sheikh and to act as a buffer at Gaza on the Egyptian side of the line without requiring Egyptian consent in the former case or raising the issue of placing UNEF on the Israeli side of the line as well in the latter case.[4]

Hammarskjöld made an immediate reply in the statement that follows. The Assembly had endorsed the statement in his second report on UNEF on November 7 that the function of UNEF was to follow the Israeli withdrawal to the armistice line. Though he limited himself to terming it "a practical question not yet fully clarified" his own view was that the stationing of UNEF at Sharm el-Sheikh on the terms demanded by Israel certainly would require an additional consent by Egypt, since it would be going beyond the scope of the "general" consent of the "good faith" agreement.

[3] *Ibid.*, 652nd Plenary Meeting, February 2, 1957.
[4] *Ibid.*, 649th Plenary Meeting, February 1, 1957.

Statement in the General Assembly during
Debate on Israeli Withdrawal

UN HEADQUARTERS, NEW YORK   FEBRUARY 1, 1957

In his speech, the representative of Australia raised one point on which he declared himself unable to agree with the proposition I had propounded in my report, and solicited a clarification. The proposition referred to is the one according to which the use of military forces by the United Nations, other than that under Chapter VII of the Charter, requires the consent of the state in which the force is to operate.

I do not believe that this principle can be challenged, as it is only under Chapter VII that the United Nations, in this case the Security Council, can take decisions which may infringe upon the sovereignty of Member Nations. Nor do I believe that the second part of the proposition, which requires complete impartiality in the activities of such a force—a condition fully stated already in the basic report on the Force [A/3302]—can be challenged.

However, I fully agree with the representative of Australia that, if this were the whole story, the situation would be most unsatisfactory. In practice, the consent obviously must be qualified in such a way as to provide a reasonable basis for the operations of the United Nations Force. That is exactly the reason why, in November 1956, an arrangement was agreed upon with the Government of Egypt, according to which the Government of Egypt declared that, when exercising its sovereign rights on any matter concerning the presence and functioning of the United Nations Emergency Force, it would be guided in good faith by its acceptance of the General Assembly resolution [1000 (ES-I)] of November 5, 1956 [A/3375, annex].

The representative of Australia has rightly drawn attention to this, which, in the case under consideration, is the necessary supplement to the basic Charter principle. In these circumstances, obviously, the situation facing the Assembly has to be judged in the light of the general

General Assembly Official Records, Eleventh Session, 649th Plenary Meeting, February 1, 1957.

principle I have stated—and which, in the report, I had no reason to state in anything but the most general terms—and the agreement by which the Government of Egypt has given its consent, qualified so as to provide a basis for the operations of the Force.

This is the legal situation which is consistently reflected in the last report. To the extent that the movements of the United Nations Force are supposed to follow from the duties of the Force in relation to the cease-fire and the withdrawal, the matter, in the report, has been regarded as noncontroversial, as it is covered by Egypt's general consent while, on the other hand, as regards activities of the United Nations Force which would extend beyond what is covered by this consent, an additional consent has been considered as necessary.

I thus do not believe that there is any difference of views as to this legal issue, between the representative of Australia and myself. The question which is not yet fully clarified is how far in the practical cases under consideration the duties of the Force go, and how far, therefore, certain arrangements for the Force are covered or not by the consent given by Egypt as qualified by its assurance of interpretation in good faith of the basic decisions of the General Assembly.

THE ISRAELI GOVERNMENT decided to stand fast on its demand for guarantees in advance of withdrawal, despite the overwhelming votes in the General Assembly on February 2 and Lodge's warning. The debate had indicated much support for free passage of Israeli shipping through the Straits of Tiran and considerable sympathy in the West for some form of United Nations administration in Gaza, or at least a stronger United Nations voice in its affairs. Israel believed it was gaining ground in public opinion and chose a delaying tactic which it sought to use in such a way as to confuse the issue and reinforce the massive public relations and lobbying campaign that had been mounted for its cause, especially in the United States.

When Hammarskjöld asked Eban for Israel's response to the Assembly's resolutions he was met by two counter requests from Israel. If positive replies were given, this, it was said, would influence Israel's attitude. First, Egypt should be requested to make a prior commitment to abstain from all belligerent acts "by land, air, and sea" when Israeli troops withdrew; second, a firm commitment was requested that UNEF stay on at Sharm el-Sheikh until another effective means was agreed to ensure freedom of navigation through the Straits of Tiran.

These demands reversed the order approved by the Assembly in its two resolutions: first, unconditional withdrawal, then steps aimed at creating more peaceful conditions than had prevailed in the past between Israel and Egypt. Furthermore Eban had spoken only of the withdrawal of troops. Hammarskjöld told him he could not consider the two requests until he received assurance that Israel understood the Assembly's first resolution included the withdrawal of Israeli civil and police administration from Gaza, as well as troops. The Secretary-General also wished to know whether Israel would consent to stationing UNEF on its side of the armistice line, just as Egypt's consent would be required to stationing UNEF at Sharm el-Sheikh on the terms asked by Israel.

Eban said his government would not reply on either point until its own requests had been answered. Thus there was a stalemate and Israel attempted to pass the blame to the Secretary-General for the delay because he had not acted on its requests. After several consultations with the UNEF Advisory Committee and one more unsuccessful conversation with Eban, Hammarskjöld submitted the report that follows to the Assembly, accompanied by the texts of the written exchanges with Eban.

Part Two of his report included a discussion of how the steps proposed in the Assembly's second resolution might be progressively negotiated and effected, provided there was cooperation from both Egypt and Israel. In this connection he noted that Egypt had reaffirmed to him its intention "to observe fully the provisions of the Armistice Agreement . . . *on the assumption, of course, that observance will be reciprocal"* [italics added—EDITORS]. Hammarskjöld did not say so, but over the years the Security Council had found Israel guilty of violating various articles of the Armistice Agreement far more frequently than Egypt. Some of these violations, like Israel's military presence in El Auja, were of long standing. Now Israel was calling for a new Egyptian commitment to nonbelligerency such as that already called for in Article 1 of the Agreement and at the same time refusing to return to the armistice régime as a whole. This amounted to a demand that Egypt comply fully with Article 1, while retaining for Israel the advantage gained by its own previous violations of other articles.

Hammarskjöld, on the other hand, pointed out that progress toward full compliance with the Armistice Agreement must include not only the commitment to nonbelligerency of Article 1, but the other articles as well, and that the process must involve parallel and reciprocal steps by both sides who must "time and again show willingness to accept some risks as a condition for progress." Failure to give the necessary cooperation, he warned, could lead to collective measures under the Uniting-for-Peace resolution and these, in turn, might introduce "new elements of conflict."

Report to the General Assembly in Pursuance of General Assembly Resolutions 1124 (XI) and 1125 (XI) on Israeli Withdrawal

UN HEADQUARTERS, NEW YORK   FEBRUARY 11, 1957

Part One

1. The General Assembly on February 2, 1957, adopted resolutions 1124 (XI) and 1125 (XI) concerning the Middle Eastern question. In resolution 1124 (XI) the General Assembly, deploring "the noncompliance of Israel to complete its withdrawal behind the armistice demarcation line," called upon Israel to complete this withdrawal without further delay. In resolution 1125 (XI) the General Assembly, recognizing that withdrawal by Israel must be followed by action which would assure progress towards the creation of peaceful conditions, noted with appreciation the Secretary-General's report and the measures therein "to be carried out upon Israel's complete withdrawal," called upon the governments concerned scrupulously to observe the Armistice Agreement, and stated that it considered that, after full withdrawal of Israel from the Sharm el-Sheikh and Gaza areas, various measures, as proposed in the Secretary-General's report, would be required for the scrupulous maintenance of the Armistice Agreement. The General Assembly requested the Secretary-General in consultation with the parties concerned, to take steps to carry out the measures envisaged and to report, as appropriate, to the General Assembly.

2. The Secretary-General on February 3 transmitted the two resolutions to the representatives of Egypt and Israel. He asked the representative of Israel to meet with him on February 4, at which time he hoped to learn the position of the Government of Israel, particularly, as a matter of special urgency, on resolution 1124 (XI) concerning withdrawal. On February 4 the representative of Israel, in reply to this request, presented an *aide-mémoire,* which is annexed to this report (annex I).

General Assembly Official Records, Eleventh Session, Annexes, Volume II, agenda item 66, Document A/3527, February 11, 1957.

3. In the *aide-mémoire* the Government of Israel requests the Secretary-General "to ask the Government of Egypt whether Egypt agrees to the mutual and full abstention from belligerent acts, by land, air, and sea, on withdrawal of Israel troops." In another point in the *aide-mémoire* clarification is sought by Israel as to whether, "immediately on the withdrawal of Israel forces from the Sharm el-Sheikh area, units of the United Nations Emergency Force will be stationed along the western shore of the Gulf of Aqaba in order to act as a restraint against hostile acts; and will remain so deployed until another effective means is agreed upon between the parties concerned for ensuring permanent freedom of navigation and the absence of belligerent acts in the Straits of Tiran and the Gulf of Aqaba."

4. The first of these two points in the Israel *aide-mémoire* must be understood as a request for action in implementation of resolution 1125 (XI), while the wording of the request leaves open the question whether it involves a willingness to comply with the demand for withdrawal in resolution 1124 (XI), even given a positive response by Egypt. The Secretary-General, at the meeting with the representative of Israel, asked whether, with regard to Gaza, it is understood by the Government of Israel that the withdrawal must cover elements of administration as well as military troops, forces, and units. A clarification on this point appeared to be a prerequisite to further consideration of the Israel *aide-mémoire*. This point and the following one are related, as there is an unavoidable connection between Israel's willingness to comply fully with resolution 1124 (XI) as concerns the Gaza Strip and what may be done toward maintaining quiet in the Sharm el-Sheikh area. It is unrealistic to assume that the latter question could be solved while Israel remains in Gaza.

5. The second of the points in the Israel *aide-mémoire* requests a "clarification" which, in view of the position of the General Assembly, could go beyond what was stated in the last report only after negotiation with Egypt. This follows from the statements in the debate in the General Assembly, and the report on which it was based, which made it clear that the stationing of the Force at Sharm el-Sheikh, under such terms as those mentioned in the question posed by Israel, would require Egyptian consent. In the light of this implication of Israel's question, the Secretary-General considered it important, as a basis for his consideration of the *aide-mémoire,* to learn whether Israel itself, in principle, consents to a stationing of UNEF units on its territory in implementa-

tion of the functions established for the Force in the basic decisions and noted in resolution 1125 (XI) where it was indicated that the Force should be placed "on the Egyptian-Israel armistice demarcation line."

6. Concerning his two questions, the Secretary-General received on February 5 a letter from the Permanent Representative of Israel. The letter is annexed to this report (annex II). The answer of the Secretary-General to this communication was transmitted by his letter of February 6 (annex III).

7. A further meeting with the representative of Israel was held, on the invitation of the Secretary-General, on February 10. Following the meeting, the representative of Israel sent the Secretary-General an additional letter, received on February 11. This letter is likewise annexed to the report (annex IV).

8. This latest communication received from the representative of Israel does not add any new information. Thus it is still an open question whether Israel, under any circumstances, accepts full implementation of resolution 1124 (XI), which, as pointed out above, requires withdrawal from the Gaza Strip of Israel's civil administration and police as well as of its armed forces. Further, it is still an open question whether Israel accepts the stationing of units of the United Nations Emergency Force on its side of the armistice demarcation line under resolution 1125 (XI), concerning which, in a similar respect, Israel has raised a question which requires clarification of the Egyptian stand. In case Israel were to receive the assurance from Egypt, which it has requested the Secretary-General to ask for as an action in implementation of resolution 1125 (XI), the representative of Israel in his latest communication has stated only that his government "would formulate its position on all outstanding questions in the light of Egypt's response."

9. The fact that the Government of Israel has not found it possible to clarify elements decisive for the consideration of its requests, has complicated the efforts to achieve implementation of the resolutions of the General Assembly. If this development has "adversely affected the time schedule for the withdrawal" of Israel forces, about which the Secretary-General had not been informed, an ultimate reason is that Israel's request for an assurance from Egypt concerning the cessation of all belligerent acts has been put forward while Israel itself, by continued occupation, maintains a state of belligerency which, in the case of Gaza, it has not indicated its intention fully to liquidate.

10. The Secretary-General shares the view of the Government of Is-

rael that his offices may serve as a means for an interchange between Member states of "proposals and ideas," but wishes to draw attention to the fact that the action which the Government of Israel has requested cannot be regarded as properly described in such terms, as it would be an action within the scope of resolution 1125 (XI) and in implementation of this resolution which, although closely related to resolution 1124 (XI), has, at least, full and unconditional acceptance of the demand in that resolution as its prerequisite.

11. The Secretary-General does not consider it necessary here to discuss other points in the latest Israel communication, to which he will have to revert in forthcoming discussions with the representative of Israel.

Part Two

12. The General Assembly, in adopting resolutions 1124 (XI) and 1125 (XI), was guided by the need to "assure progress towards the creation of peaceful conditions" in the area. It was recognized that this objective—which was also the theme of the Secretary-General's report (A/3512) on which the debate in the General Assembly was based— required, as an initial step, withdrawal of Israel behind the armistice demarcation line, to be followed by various measures within the framework of the Armistice Agreement. These measures aimed at "a return to the state of affairs envisaged in the Armistice Agreement, and avoidance of the state of affairs into which conditions, due to a lack of compliance with the agreement, had progressively deteriorated" (A/3512, paragraph 15). With this in view, resolution 1125 (XI) in its operative paragraph 2 called for scrupulous observance of the Armistice Agreement, which, in its first article, establishes the right of each party to "its security and freedom from fear of attack by the armed forces of the other."

13. The position of the Secretary-General, in his efforts to secure implementation of the two resolutions, has been based on the following considerations. First, agreement was widespread in the General Assembly, as reflected in the sequence of the two resolutions, that like the cease-fire, withdrawal is a preliminary and essential phase in a development through which a stable basis may be laid for peaceful conditions in the area. Second, the principle which must guide the United Nations after a change in the *status juris* through military action contrary to the

Charter, as stated in the last report of the Secretary-General (A/3512, paragraph 5 (*a*)), is recognized as expressing a basic rule of the Charter, thus giving a high priority to requests based on that principle. The key significance of resolution 1124 (XI), as indicated by these two considerations, is confirmed by the fact that resolution 1125 (XI) explicitly states that the measures to which it refers are to be carried out "after full withdrawal of Israel" behind the armistice demarcation line.

14. The Secretary-General has understood the General Assembly to see in resolution 1125 (XI) a formal undertaking with respect to measures to be effected upon withdrawal, in the light of which resolution 1124 (XI) should be implemented without delay. This is particularly so, since the United Nations Emergency Force is deployed in the region with an assurance from the Government of Egypt that the Government, when exercising its sovereign rights on any matter concerning the presence and functioning of the Force, will be guided in good faith by its acceptance of the basic General Assembly resolution of November 5, 1956, concerning the Force and its functions [resolution 1000 (ES-I)].

15. Beginning with its initial resolution of November 2, 1956 [resolution 997 (ES-I)], concerning this question, and culminating in its resolution 1125 (XI) of February 2, 1957, the General Assembly has stressed the key importance it attaches to scrupulous observance by both parties of the terms of the Armistice Agreement between Egypt and Israel. In this regard, the Secretary-General is able to report that the Government of Egypt reaffirms its intent to observe fully the provisions of the Armistice Agreement to which it is a party, as indicated earlier in its acceptance (A/3266) of resolution 997 (ES-I) of November 2, 1956, on the assumption, of course, that observance will be reciprocal. Attention should be drawn, in this context, to the statement in paragraph 22 of the last report of the Secretary-General (A/3512) reporting the desire of the Government of Egypt to see an end to all raids and incursions across the armistice line, in both directions, with effective assistance from United Nations auxiliary organs to that effect.

16. The position of the Government of Israel on the Armistice Agreement, as reaffirmed by the representative of Israel in response to a question on the matter during his meeting with the Secretary-General on February 10, was set forth in the letter of January 25, 1957, from the representative of Israel to the Secretary-General (annex V).

17. The relationship between the two resolutions on withdrawal and on measures to be carried out after withdrawal, affords the possibility

of informal explorations of the whole field covered by the resolutions, preparatory to negotiations. Later, the results of such explorations may be used in negotiations through a constructive combination of measures, representing for the two countries concerned parallel progress toward the peaceful conditions sought. However, such explorations cannot be permitted to invert the sequence between withdrawal and other measures, nor to disrupt the evolution of negotiations toward their goal. Progress toward peaceful conditions, following the general policy suggested in the last report to the General Assembly, on which its resolution 1125 (XI) is based, has to be achieved gradually. To disregard this would render the process more difficult and might seriously jeopardize the possibility of achieving desired results. In explorations and negotiations, which in this sense necessarily have to proceed step by step, the parties involved must time and again show willingness to accept some risks as a condition for progress.

18. Peaceful conditions in the Middle East must be created in the interest of all countries in the region and of the world community. The basic principles of the Charter must be asserted and respected, in the very same interest. Neither one of these imperative demands can be met at the expense of the other. The fulfillment of one will make it easier to meet the other, but to have peace with justice, adherence to principle and law must be given priority and canot be conditional. In the present case, efforts to meet the two requirements just stated have so far been frustrated. The United Nations must maintain its position on these requirements and, in doing so, should be entitled to count on the assistance, in the complex process of gradual and sensitive approach to the objectives, in particular of the two Member states directly concerned. If such assistance is not forthcoming, the efforts of the United Nations will be caused to fail, to the detriment of all. In an organization based on voluntary cooperation and respect for the general opinion to which the organization gives expression, the responsibility for such a failure would fall, not on the organization, but on those who had denied it the necessary cooperation. This responsibility extends beyond the immediate issue. It may also, in this case, well have to cover difficulties flowing from possible failure of the United Nations to fulfill its vital functions under the armistice agreements and of the parties to come to grips with the wider problems which call for such urgent attention.

19. The Charter has given to the Security Council means of enforcement and the right to take decisions with mandatory effect. No such au-

thority is given to the General Assembly, which can only recommend action to Member governments, which, in turn, may follow the recommendations or disregard them. This is also true of recommendations adopted by the General Assembly within the framework of the Uniting-for-Peace resolution [resolution 377 (V)]. However, under that resolution the General Assembly has certain rights otherwise reserved to the Security Council. Thus, it can, under that resolution, recommend collective measures. In this case, also, the recommendation has not compulsory force.

20. It seems, in this context, appropriate to distinguish between recommendations which implement a Charter principle, which in itself is binding on Member states, and recommendations, which, although adopted under the Charter, do not implement any such basic provision. A recommendation of the first kind would have behind it the force of the Charter, to which collective measures recommended by the General Assembly could add emphasis, without, however, changing the legal character of the recommendation. A decision on collective measures referring to a recommendation of the second kind, although likewise formally retaining its legal character, would mean that the recommendation is recognized by the General Assembly as being of such significance to the efforts of the United Nations as to assimilate it to a recommendation expressing an obligation established by the Charter. If, in some case, collective measures under the Uniting-for-Peace resolution were to be considered, these and other important questions of principle would require attention; this may also be said of the effect of such steps which, while supporting efforts to achieve peaceful solutions, may perhaps, on the other hand, be introducing new elements of conflict.

21. In the situation now facing the United Nations the General Assembly, as a matter of priority, may wish to indicate how it desires the Secretary-General to proceed with further steps to carry out the relevant decisions of the General Assembly.

[ANNEXES OMITTED]

WHEN THE General Assembly returned to the Middle East question on February 22, its first act was to approve Hammarskjöld's report on the agreement negotiated with Egypt on the legal privileges and status of UNEF on Egyptian territory.[1] Egypt had agreed to grant privileges and immunities to

[1] *Ibid.,* Document A/3526, February 8, 1957.

UNEF going further than the usual such agreement on the stationing of foreign troops. A resolution approving the report was introduced by all ten nations then participating in UNEF and was promptly adopted by a vote of 67 to 0 with 7 abstentions. By this time the arrival of Indonesian and Brazilian contingents had brought UNEF to virtually its full strength of 6,000 men from ten Member states.

The debate then turned to the still unbroken stalemate with Israel over its withdrawal from Gaza and the Sharm el-Sheikh area. A draft resolution calling for the first time for sanctions against Israel was sponsored by Afghanistan, Indonesia, Iraq, Lebanon, Pakistan, and Sudan. It read as follows:

The General Assembly,

Recalling its resolutions 997 (ES-I) of November 2, 1956, 998 (ES-I) and 999 (ES-I) of November 4, 1956, 1002 (ES-I) of November 7, 1956, 1120 (XI) of November 24, 1956, 1123 (XI) of January 19, 1957, and 1124 (XI) of February 2, 1957,

Noting the report of the Secretary-General dated February 11, 1957 (A/3527),

Viewing with grave concern the failure of Israel to comply with the terms of the above-mentioned resolutions,

1. *Condemns* Israel for its noncompliance with the said resolutions;

2. *Calls upon* all states to deny all military, economic or financial assistance and facilities to Israel in view of its continued defiance of the aforementioned resolutions;

3. *Requests* all states to provide the Secretary-General with information on their implementation of the present resolution;

4. *Requests* the Secretary-General to report again on the implementation of the present and previous resolutions of the General Assembly.[2]

Just before Charles Malik of Lebanon formally introduced this resolution the Secretary-General made the oral statement reproduced in the first following text. The "outside" discussions to which he referred in appreciative terms had consisted of renewed efforts by the Eisenhower administration to persuade the Israeli government to comply with the Assembly's withdrawal resolutions.

On February 11 Dulles had handed Eban a statement of the United States position on the Gaza Strip and the Straits of Tiran which he hoped would be sufficient to relieve Israel's fears of a return to belligerency in either area. On Gaza the *aide-mémoire* did not go beyond the terms of the Secretary-General's January 24 report and the General Assembly's second resolution of February 2, but it promised vigorous American support for the use of UNEF and other measures against any revival of raids across the armistice line from Gaza or elsewhere.

On the Straits of Tiran, the *aide-mémoire* offered American support for freedom of Israeli shipping going a step further than before. Not only did

[2] *Ibid.,* Document A/3557, February 22, 1957.

the United States believe that UNEF should stay at Sharm el-Sheikh until it was clear that no claim to belligerent rights would be exercised by Egypt, as Lodge had already stated in the Assembly, but "in the absence of some overriding decision to the contrary, as by the International Court of Justice, the United States, on behalf of vessels of United States registry, is prepared to exercise the right of free and innocent passage *and to join with others to secure general recognition of this right*" [italics added].

The *aide-mémoire* reaffirmed unequivocal United States support for the Assembly's position that full and unconditional withdrawal must precede the "other measures" mentioned in the second February 2 resolution but concluded with the following:

> The United States is prepared publicly to declare that it will use its influence, in concert with other United Nations Members, to the end that, following Israel's withdrawal, these other measures will be implemented. We believe that our views and purposes in this respect are shared by many other nations and that a tranquil future for Israel is best assured by reliance upon that fact, rather than by an occupation in defiance of the overwhelming judgment of the world community.[3]

The *aide-mémoire* was accompanied by oral warnings that the United States could go no further toward meeting the Israeli position and of the serious consequences of further delay in completing the withdrawal. Nevertheless the Ben-Gurion government decided to hold out for firmer guarantees, especially in the Gaza Strip. There it continued to insist that the territory should not under any circumstances return to Egyptian administration. This reply was accompanied by a stepped-up campaign in Congress and the public media to depict the Eisenhower administration's attitude toward Israel as unjust and rigid. The President and Dulles responded on February 17 by publishing the full text of the February 11 *aide-mémoire*, with an accompanying statement which included the following comment:

> Israel would prefer to have the future status of the Gulf of Aqaba and the Gaza Strip definitely settled to its satisfaction prior to its withdrawal, and as a condition thereto. But all Members of the United Nations are solemnly bound by the Charter to settle their international disputes by peaceful means and in their international relations to refrain from the threat or use of force against the territorial integrity of any state. These undertakings seem to preclude using the forcible seizure and occupation of other lands as bargaining power in the settlement of international disputes.

The statement pointed out that the United Kingdom and France had withdrawn their forces "promptly and unconditionally" long ago and the United States believed "Israel should do likewise." [4]

---

[3] *United States Policy in the Middle East, September 1956–June 1957, Documents,* Department of State Publication No. 6505, Government Printing Office, August 1957, pp. 291–292.

[4] *Ibid.,* p. 292.

Eisenhower was visiting Secretary of the Treasury George Humphrey at his place in Thomasville, Georgia, when Israel's negative reply to the February 11 offer was received. He discussed privately with Dulles, Humphrey, and Lodge the question of sanctions if Israel could not be persuaded to change its stand. In his memoirs he recalls getting U.S. Treasury estimates that Israel bond sales and private gifts in the United States amounted to about $100 million a year and expressing his own preference for "a resolution which would call on all United Nations members to suspend not just government but private assistance to Israel," adding "Such a move would be no hollow gesture." [5]

Eban hurried back to Israel for consultations on the crisis and Eisenhower cut short his Georgia vacation to return to Washington to deal with the rising tide of domestic support for Israel's stand. Senator Knowland, the Republican majority leader, had already been persuaded to declare that sanctions against Israel would be both "immoral and insupportable" when no sanctions had been imposed on the Soviet Union for its intervention in Hungary. Now Lyndon B. Johnson, the leader of the Senate Democrats, took up the theme in a letter to Dulles declaring that "the UN cannot apply one rule for the strong and another for the weak; it cannot organize its economic weight against the little state when it has not previously made even a pretence of doing so against the large states." On February 19 the Senate Democratic Policy Committee unanimously endorsed the Johnson letter and called on the President to resist any attempt in the United Nations to impose sanctions. [6]

The next day Eisenhower, Dulles, and Lodge had a long meeting with 26 Congressional leaders of both parties during which they vigorously defended and explained the administration's position but were unable to achieve a consensus. That night the President took his case to the nation on television and radio. He reviewed the many steps the United States had taken to meet Israel's concerns and the commitments to future action in support of the second February 2 resolution but on the central issue he was absolutely firm. Israel had attacked and invaded Egypt and was demanding a price for withdrawal.

"If the United Nations once admits that international disputes can be settled by using force," he said, "then we will have destroyed the very foundation of the organization and our best hope of establishing a world order. That would be a disaster for us all. I would, I feel, be untrue to the standards of the high office to which you have chosen me if I were to lend the influence of the United States to the proposition that a nation which invades another should be permitted to exact conditions for withdrawal."

He dismissed the argument that "Israel's default should be ignored" because the Soviet Union had successfully defied United Nations resolutions on Hungary. Because of the Soviet Union's size and power it was "relatively impervious" to sanctions other than moral pressure and this had been and

[5] Eisenhower, *Waging Peace*, pp. 185–186.
[6] *New York Times*, February 20, 1957.

continued to be vigorously applied. He also rejected the argument that Israel should not be pressed to unconditional withdrawal because Egypt had in the past violated the Armistice Agreement and international law. Both sides had been guilty of such violations, he said, and those charged to Egypt "constitute no justification for the armed invasion of Egypt by Israel which the United Nations is now seeking to undo."

Finally, he indicated United States support for sanctions if Israel did not promptly change its mind with the words "I believe that—in the interests of peace—the United Nations has no choice but to exert pressure upon Israel to comply." [7] In a private cable sent the same day to Ben-Gurion he made this more explicit: "I would greatly deplore the necessity of the United States' taking positions in the United Nations, and of the United Nations itself having to adopt measures which might have far-reaching effects upon Israel's relations throughout the world." [8]

At a decisive moment, Eisenhower thus put the full weight of his office and his great personal prestige behind the line followed by Hammarskjöld and steadfastly supported by Lodge. His stand blunted the effects of pro-Israeli opposition at home and stemmed the tendency toward disintegration of the shaky Western-Asian alliance at the United Nations. In Israel too it had a strong impact. Though Eban would make one final effort to extract some further promises when he returned three days later to the United States, the clear message of Eisenhower's public speech and private cable—that the game of delay to win guarantees must finally come to an end—sank home during the course of the week that followed.

The Assembly had postponed consideration of the Secretary-General's February 11 report while these steps by the United States government were under way. For his part Hammarskjöld had been able to persuade Fawzi to agree to his making a statement of Egyptian intentions to cooperate in giving the United Nations a stronger role in the Gaza Strip. The statement, it will be noted, did not commit Egypt to hand over administration of the Gaza Strip to the United Nations as Pearson and some others in the Western camp were advocating. Only "in the first instance" would the take-over "be exclusively by UNEF," as had happened at Port Said. Thereafter the commitment was to Egyptian cooperation in making special and helpful arrangements with UNEF and other United Nations bodies along the armistice line and within the Strip, aimed at ending raids and securing peaceful conditions.

After the Secretary-General had read his statement and Malik had introduced the sanctions resolution the Assembly adjourned without further debate and did not meet again until February 26.

[7] *United States Policy in the Middle East*, pp. 301–307.
[8] Eisenhower, *Waging Peace*, p. 187.

Statement on Gaza in the General Assembly
during Debate on Israeli Withdrawal

UN HEADQUARTERS, NEW YORK   FEBRUARY 22, 1957

On February 11 I submitted the report [A/3527], in pursuance of the resolution [1125 (XI)] of the General Assembly of February 2. Events since then have not called for a further report and I have presented none. It is well known, however, that discussions have been carried on outside this house in the continuing resolve to attain the goals defined in the several resolutions of the General Assembly. I have maintained close contact with these activities and have been kept well informed on them. These serious efforts to break through the unfortunate impasse and to unlock the door to constructive endeavour are deserving of warm appreciation.

Insofar as United Nations activities and positions are concerned, developments in the interim have given no reason to revise any of the substance of the previous report. However, in the light of some subsequent discussions in which I have engaged, I may make the following statement in the nature of a supplement to that report.

The Secretary-General states with confidence that it is the desire of the Government of Egypt that the take-over of Gaza from the military and civilian control of Israel—which, as has been the case, in the first instance would be exclusively by UNEF—will be orderly and safe, as it has been elsewhere.

It may be added with equal confidence that the Government of Egypt, recognizing the present special problems and complexities of the Gaza area and the long-standing major responsibility of the United Nations there for the assistance of the Arab refugees, and having in mind also the objectives and obligations of the Armistice Agreement, has the willingness and readiness to make special and helpful arrangements with the United Nations and some of its auxiliary bodies, such as UNRWA and UNEF. For example, the arrangement for the use of UNEF in the area should ensure its deployment on the armistice line at the Gaza Strip and the effective interposition of the Force between the armed forces of Egypt and Israel.

General Assembly Official Records, Eleventh Session, 659th Plenary Meeting, February 22, 1957.

Similarly, the assistance of the United Nations and its appropriate auxiliary bodies would be enrolled toward putting a definite end to all incursions and raids across the border from either side.

Furthermore, with reference to the period of transition, such other arrangements with the United Nations may be made as will contribute towards safeguarding life and property in the area by providing efficient and effective police protection; as will guarantee good civilian administration; as will assure maximum assistance to the United Nations refugee programme; and as will protect and foster the economic development of the territory and its people.

WHEN EBAN returned from Israel he went first to Washington for talks with Dulles on February 24 and then to New York for talks with Hammarskjöld the next day. He had new instructions.

On the Straits of Tiran Israel was now willing to drop its demand for an advance guarantee that UNEF remain at Sharm el-Sheikh until freedom of navigation was formally confirmed by agreement with Egypt. Israeli troops would withdraw from the Gulf of Aqaba, given assurance that the United States and others would exercise the right of freedom of passage, that UNEF's function, when it moved into Sharm el-Sheikh would be to prevent acts of belligerency and that the Assembly would be informed before a withdrawal of UNEF from the area. Israel also raised the question of adding a naval patrol to UNEF to ensure freedom of passage through the Straits.

The Israeli government remained as strongly opposed as ever to the return to the Gaza Strip of Egyptian military or civilian administration in any form, but it was now prepared to recede from its previous insistence that Israel should retain exclusive civil and police administration in Gaza and that UNEF be given no role there in these respects. Eban was instructed to explore the possibilities for building on the widespread Western support for a stronger UN role in Gaza in a way that would lead to excluding the return of Egypt.

In Washington Eban was reassured on the Straits of Tiran but not on Gaza. He then returned to New York for talks with Hammarskjöld and with delegates who had shown sympathy for Israel's concerns. His aim was to find an acceptable formula under which the issue of Israeli withdrawal from Sharm el-Sheikh could be settled separately from the issue of withdrawal from the Gaza Strip.

The Secretary-General reported to the Assembly on his conversations with Eban in the text that follows. With respect to the Straits of Tiran it will be noted that he gave essentially affirmative replies to Eban's questions on the function of UNEF at Sharm el-Sheikh and on advance notice before any withdrawal. His negative reply on the proposed UNEF naval patrol was based on the fact that the function of such a patrol would obviously be to lend support to one side against the other on an issue not yet settled under international law—that is, the extent of rights of innocent passage in territorial waters of this description.

In reply to the questions concerning Gaza the Secretary-General was firm on Egypt's legal rights in Gaza under the Armistice Agreement but declined to express an opinion on possible *de facto* developments after Israeli withdrawal beyond stating his belief that the cooperative arrangements with Egypt envisaged in his February 22 statement would meet the wishes of the Assembly.

Eban's questions and his statements of Israel's position indicated that Israel sought to postpone the withdrawal from Gaza of its civil administration and police pending the creation of an Assembly "fact-finding mission" to go to the area and make recommendations for Gaza's future. This was confirmed in unmistakable terms by Ben-Gurion in a speech to the Knesset. This attitude prompted the Secretary-General's observation in the text below that "in the light of Israel's stand on Gaza it may be seriously doubted that the question of Aqaba can be solved separately, as intended by Israel's approach"—a polite reminder that Israel would be in a poor position to claim the rights of nonbelligerency in the Straits of Tiran while retaining the fruits of belligerency in the conquered territory of Gaza. Israel's stand also did not conform with the Assembly's withdrawal resolution of February 2 which called for complete and unconditional withdrawal from Gaza, administrative as well as military, "without further delay."

On the question of UNEF deployment on both sides of the armistice line, as recommended in the Assembly's second resolution of February 2, Israel maintained its unresponsive silence. Eban's reply to the Secretary-General's question on this point (Part III, paragraph A, of the following text) turned a blind eye toward the obviously central significance of an affirmative response upon Israel's own security. Deployment on both sides of the line would put UNEF in a much stronger position to maintain peace and quiet than if it remained only on the Egyptian side. It would also be more equitable and thus improve prospects for winning consent from both sides to the reciprocal steps through which Hammarskjöld hoped to move toward a fully effective armistice régime in Gaza and elsewhere.

Note on Exchange of Views with Israel on Gaza and the Gulf of Aqaba

UN HEADQUARTERS, NEW YORK   FEBRUARY 26, 1957

---

1. On February 22, 1957, the Secretary-General made an oral statement to the General Assembly in the nature of a supplement to the report of February 11 (A/3527) regarding United Nations responsibilities in the Gaza area. In his statement, the Secretary-General referred to discussions carried on outside of the United Nations and expressed the opinion that these efforts to break through the unfortunate impasse and unlock the door to constructive endeavour were deserving of warm appreciation.

2. Following the discussions outside the United Nations, the Secretary-General had two meetings with the Permanent Representative of Israel, Mr. Eban, on the latter's initiative, on February 25.

3. A memorandum containing a summary of the exchange of views in the first of these two meetings, as confirmed by both parties, is presented for the information of the General Assembly as an annex to this note.

4. At the second meeting, the discussion mainly centred around the special memorandum also attached in the annex, with specific reference to the question which is to be found in II, A, 3, of the summary of the exchange of views. The Secretary-General, in commenting on the second paragraph of this special memorandum, made it clear that, while explaining the framework which determined its interpretation, he had not expressed an opinion on the possible *de facto* development. A judgment on this *de facto* development would be premature, since it depends on decisions to be taken after the withdrawal of Israel from the Gaza area. Thus, the paragraph did not deal with the question with which the Government of Israel was concerned in its assumptions for the discussion of withdrawal. According to the decisions of the General Assembly, the withdrawal would have to be unconditional. The Secretary-Gen-

eral felt that the development envisaged in his statement of February 22 would meet the wishes of the General Assembly concerning the situation that should be envisaged in Gaza after Israel's withdrawal.

ANNEXES

Memorandum of Important Points in the Discussion Between the Representative of Israel and the Secretary-General on February 25, 1957

1. Gulf of Aqaba and Straits of Tiran

A. The representative of Israel, stating that his government's primary concern in this area was in measures designed to reduce the risk of reoccurrence of acts of belligerency after the withdrawal of Israel, raised the following three questions:

1. Following the withdrawal of Israel's forces, would the function of the Emergency Force be as described in the Secretary-General's memorandum of January 5 in response to Mr. Eban's questions, namely, the prevention of possible acts of belligerency?

2. In connection with the duration of UNEF's deployment in the Sharm el-Sheikh area, would the Secretary-General give notice to the General Assembly of the United Nations before UNEF would be withdrawn from the area, with or without Egyptian insistence, or before the Secretary-General would agree to its withdrawal?

3. The question of adding a naval unit to UNEF for purposes of instituting a United Nations naval patrol in the Gulf of Aqaba and Straits of Tiran to ensure free and innocent passage.

B. The responses of the Secretary-General to these questions are summarized as follows:

1. With regard to the function of UNEF in the prevention of belligerency, the answer is affirmative, subject to the qualification that UNEF is never to be used in such a way as to force a solution of any controversial political or legal problem.

2. On the question of notification to the General Assembly, the Secretary-General wanted to state his view at a later meeting. An indicated procedure would be for the Secretary-General to inform the Advisory Committee on the United Nations Emergency Force, which would determine whether the matter should be brought to the attention of the Assembly.

3. The question of the naval unit, in that it implies a function which would go beyond the prevention of belligerent acts as envisaged in the basic General Assembly resolutions, would be beyond the competence of the Secretary-General on the basis of those resolutions.

II. Gaza

A. The representative of Israel defined the policy of his government with regard to Gaza as follows:

1. The policy of Israel is overridingly one of opposition to Egyptian civilian administration or military control in Gaza; Israel cannot compromise on the direct or indirect return of Egypt to Gaza.

2. Egypt has violated continuously the Armistice Agreement and is in a state of belligerency against Israel which is incompatible with the Armistice Agreement. That agreement, therefore, cannot be invoked to bring Egypt back to Gaza.

3. The question was raised whether a *de facto* United Nations administration in Gaza as outlined in the recent statement of the Secretary-General would exclude Egypt's return to the area.

4. It was suggested that after the withdrawal of Israel's armed forces, the General Assembly should send a "fact-finding Commission" to Gaza to investigate the situation and to make recommendations to the General Assembly for the achievement of its objectives.

B. The Secretary-General responded as follows:

1. Egypt is given the right to control the Gaza Strip by the Armistice Agreement. This being binding on the Secretariat, the Secretary-General's concentration has been on arrangements to secure peace and quiet in the area—always on the assumption of the Egyptian legal position.

2. Question 3 is dealt with in a special memorandum annexed hereto.

3. In the light of Israel's stand on Gaza it may be seriously doubted that the question of Aqaba can be solved separately, as intended by Israel's approach.

III. Deployment of the United Nations Emergency Force

A. With regard to the question of stationing of UNEF on both sides of the armistice line and in the El Auja area, the representative of Israel stated that he has not considered this question as related to the problems of Gaza and Aqaba, which in his view were the urgent problems because it was from there that the withdrawal of forces was envisaged.

Special Memorandum

In the discussion between the Permanent Representative of Israel and the Secretary-General, the former asked the Secretary-General whether his statement in the General Assembly, Friday, February 22, meant that after the take-over, the United Nations would have "exclusive administration" of the Gaza area. The question was motivated by the fact that the Government of Israel could not accept the return of Egyptian civilian or military administration, directly or indirectly, to the area. Withdrawal from the area was discussed by the Israel government on the assumption that no such return would take place.

The Secretary-General in reply pointed out that his statement obviously was made within the framework of the legal situation established by international agreement. He could neither detract from, nor annul, any rights existing under the Armistice Agreement. His statement indicated practical arrangements, envisaged within the framework of Egyptian control of the territory as established by the agreement, and could, therefore, not be understood as limiting Egyptian rights within the area under the terms of the agreement.

LESTER PEARSON made a speech in the General Assembly on February 26 which went far toward meeting Israel's position. He urged Assembly action to provide "an agreed basis" for withdrawal by first adopting detailed recommendations on the arrangements that would follow withdrawal.

In the Gaza Strip he supported recommending United Nations responsibility for civil administration to "the maximum possible extent" by agreement with Egypt. Israel would not be required to withdraw its administrative personnel immediately since time would have to be allowed for a smooth transition to the United Nations. To this end he suggested the Secretary-General might appoint a UN Commissioner for Gaza to make the necessary arrangements in cooperation with both Israeli and Egyptian representatives.

On the Gulf of Aqaba issue Pearson believed the Assembly should assert "that there should be no interference with innocent passage through or any assertion of belligerent rights in the Straits of Tiran." On the deployment of UNEF, on the other hand, Pearson firmly maintained Canada's position in favor of its stationing on both sides of the armistice line and for the withdrawal of Israeli armed forces from the El Auja demilitarized zone.[1]

Pearson's advocacy of assurances to Israel in advance of withdrawal did not have majority support in the Assembly, which had repeatedly called for unconditional withdrawal as the first step, and he did not submit any resolution embodying his proposals. The Assembly again adjourned its debate after three other speakers, Rifai of Jordan, Zeineddine of Syria, and Sobolev of the USSR had all spoken in support of the sanctions resolution.

Eban meanwhile had returned to Washington in pursuit of his efforts to find some formula for the assurances Israel was still demanding. Premier Guy Mollet and Foreign Minister Christian Pineau of France had arrived there for a meeting of reconciliation with Eisenhower and Dulles after the split over their Suez adventure. It was evident that the Assembly would not vote for any concessions to Israel going beyond the second February 2 resolution and these two old partners in the attack on Egypt now helped to persuade Israel to agree to a procedure for withdrawal that would be acceptable to both Israel and the United States.

Israel would announce to the Assembly its decision to withdraw from both Gaza and Sharm el-Sheikh without setting conditions but on the basis of certain expectations and assumptions. The United States would then respond affirmatively, followed by Great Britain, France, Canada, and other Western states. On United States insistence that the withdrawal from Gaza be immediate and include both civil and military elements Israel reluctantly abandoned its attempts to postpone withdrawal of its administration pending the results of a United Nations fact-finding mission or the appointment of a United Nations Commissioner as Pearson had suggested.

By February 28, when the Assembly resumed discussion of the Middle East, arrangements were sufficiently advanced to enable Mordecai K. Kidron, an alternate Israeli delegate, to announce that a statement on Israel's plans for withdrawal would be ready by the following afternoon.

The news reports from Washington during the past two days, with their emphasis on the presence and opinions of Mollet and Pineau, provoked the usually cool and courteous Mahmoud Fawzi to an angry and emotional speech. He denounced "world political Zionism" for making a mockery of the United Nations and complained of seven adjournments of previously scheduled Assembly meetings due to "Israel's playing for time." Though he thanked the United States for its efforts to persuade Israel, he thought Egypt and the United Nations had been ignored while "those who are consulted . . . those who are allowed into the holy of holies . . . are none other than the group of conspirators and aggressors who, during these days, are most conspicuously and blatantly represented in Washington." [2]

Rifai of Jordan followed with a speech attacking Pearson's proposals and the next morning, March 1, Krishna Menon chimed in with a long speech

[1] *Ibid.*, 660th Plenary Meeting, February 26, 1957.
[2] *Ibid.*, 664th Plenary Meeting, February 28, 1957.

reaffirming India's position. There were a few other Arab-Asian or Soviet bloc interventions, but most delegates were waiting for the Israeli statement.

Mrs. Golda Meir was the first speaker at the afternoon session on March 1, followed immediately by Ambassador Lodge. Their statements had been mainly drafted in Washington over the preceding two days and the formulations of each side's commitments compared and cross-checked. Nevertheless, they did not hang together well.

Mrs. Meir began by announcing Israel's "plans for full and prompt withdrawal from the Sharm el-Sheikh area and the Gaza Strip, in compliance with General Assembly resolution 1124 (XI) of February 2, 1957," thus implicitly making withdrawal unconditional, and then followed with Israel's "expectations" and "assumptions" on what would follow.[3]

On the question of UNEF's deployment at Sharm el-Sheikh she quoted Lodge's earlier support for continuing the presence of UNEF there until it was clear that peaceful conditions in the Straits of Tiran had been in practice established. She also noted the Secretary-General's February 26 assurance about giving advance notice to the UNEF Advisory Committee of any proposal for the withdrawal of UNEF, adding that Israel had reason to believe "many Members of the United Nations would be guided by the view expressed by Mr. Lodge."

On the question of right to freedom of passage through the Gulf of Aqaba and the Straits of Tiran she referred to the declaration in Dulles' February 11 memorandum of United States readiness to exercise this right on its own behalf "and to join with others to secure general recognition of this right." Since then, she said, Israel had been informed that "other leading maritime powers" intended to join the United States in such a stand.

Mrs. Meir also quoted President Eisenhower's statement in his February 20 television speech that "we should not assume that, if Israel withdraws, Egypt will prevent Israel shipping from using the Suez Canal or the Gulf of Aqaba" and said "this declaration has weighed heavily with my government in determining its action today."

Thus far the positions of Israel and the United States on the Gulf of Aqaba question were in correspondence. But Mrs. Meir went further in the following declaration: "Interference by armed force, with ships of Israel flag exercising free and innocent passage in the Gulf of Aqaba and through the Straits of Tiran, will be regarded by Israel as an attack entitling it to exercise its inherent right of self-defense under Article 51 of the United Nations Charter *and to take all such measures as are necessary to ensure the free and innocent passage of its ships in the Gulf and in the Straits*" [italics added]. As worded this was an assertion of the right to go to war, if necessary, to keep the Straits open and it went far beyond United States intentions on the manner in which recognition of the right to innocent passage should be asserted.

---

[3] See *ibid.*, 667th Plenary Meeting, March 1, 1957, for the full texts of the Israeli and United States statements.

When Ambassador Lodge in his own speech took note of the various declarations made by Mrs. Meir on behalf of Israel he characterized them as *"For the most part* [italics added—EDITORS] . . . restatements of what has already been said by the Assembly or by the Secretary-General in his reports, or hopes and expectations which seem to us not unreasonable in the light of the prior actions of the Assembly." He made no mention of the declaration about Article 51 but when he quoted the relevant paragraphs of the February 11 memorandum on the United States position in support of freedom of passage he added that "these views are to be understood in the sense of the relevant portions on the law of the sea of the report of the International Law Commission covering the work of its eighth session, from April 23 to July 4, 1956." This was the same report which had prompted the Secretary-General's comment in his January 24 report to the General Assembly (see page 483): "A legal controversy exists as to the extent of the right of innocent passage through these waters. Under these circumstances it is indicated that whatever rights there may be in relation to the Gulf and the Straits, such rights be exercised with restraint on all sides."

On the question of Gaza's future there was a wide divergence between Israel's assumptions as defined in Mrs. Meir's speech on the one hand and, on the other, the previous statements of Hammarskjöld to which she referred and what Lodge said in the speech that followed.

First of all, she said, Israel assumed "that the take-over of Gaza from the military and civilian control of Israel will be exclusively by the United Nations Emergency Force." This formulation omitted entirely the qualifying words in the Secretary-General's February 22 statement that the take-over *"as has been the case* [e.g., Port Said] *in the first instance* [italics added —EDITORS] would be exclusively by the United Nations Emergency Force."

Mrs. Meir then proceeded as follows:

(*b*) It is, further, Israel's expectation that the United Nations will be *the* [italics added—EDITORS] agency to be utilized for carrying out the functions enumerated by the Secretary-General, namely . . . safeguarding life and property in the area by providing efficient and effective police protection; as will guarantee good civilian administration; as will assure maximum assistance to the United Nations refugee programme; and as will protect and foster the economic development of the territory and its people.

(*c*) It is, further, Israel's expectation that the aforementioned responsibility of the United Nations in the administration of Gaza will be maintained for a transitory period from the take-over until there is a peace settlement, to be sought as rapidly as possible, or a definitive agreement on the future of the Gaza Strip.

The quotation from Hammarskjöld's February 22 statement was torn from its context in a way to suggest that the Egyptians would be replaced by a United Nations administration of Gaza, as Israel desired. What the Secretary-General had said in that statement and in his note of February 26 referred to Egypt's willingness to make special arrangements to strengthen the UN position in Gaza within the framework of continued Egyptian control of the territory as provided in the Armistice Agreement. Furthermore the period of transition of which he had spoken plainly referred to the transition from the initial take-over by UNEF to arrangements agreed with Egypt. There had not been the slightest suggestion that the transition period would continue until a peace settlement.

Mrs. Meir concluded her list of "expectations" on Gaza with the statement that "if conditions are created in the Gaza Strip which indicate a return to the conditions of deterioration which existed previously, Israel would reserve its freedom to defend its rights." The reservation seemed to suggest, and certainly did not exclude, an intention to resort again to military action if matters in Gaza did not proceed as Israel desired.

Nowhere in the Israeli statement was there any reference to the General Assembly's second resolution of February 2 which called upon both Israel and Egypt to abide scrupulously by the Armistice Agreement and urged deployment of UNEF on both sides of the armistice line and the other measures proposed in the Secretary-General's January 24 report.

In his statement of the United States' position on Gaza Ambassador Lodge took pains to quote in full Hammarskjöld's February 22 statement, thus restoring the part Mrs. Meir had used to its context of cooperative arrangements with Egypt. The United States, he said, endorsed the Secretary-General's view that the future of the Gaza Strip must, from the juridical standpoint "be worked out within the framework" of the Armistice Agreement. He than added, "the United States can, I think, properly entertain the hope that such a useful role for the United Nations and its subsidiary bodies as the Secretary-General has described could usefully continue until there is a definitive settlement respecting the Gaza Strip or some final general agreement between the parties."

Lodge's statement put primary emphasis on making the armistice régime effective as an essential first step toward peace. Among his points were the following:

> . . . the vital necessity for full and strict compliance by Israel and Egypt with their international obligations, including the Armistice Agreement. Governed by their obligations under the Charter, Israel and Egypt should base their relations on full observance of the armistice.
>
> Once Israel has completed its withdrawal in accordance with the resolutions of the General Assembly, and in view of the measures taken by the United Nations to deal with the situation, there is no basis for either party to the Armistice Agreement to assert or exercise any belligerent rights. . . .

Lodge defined the United States commitment to future action as follows: "If . . . there should be any recurrence of hostilities or any violation by either party of its international obligations, including those of the Armistice

Agreement, then this would create a situation for United Nations consideration. The United States would consult with other Members of the United Nations to consider appropriate action which they or the United Nations might take. . . ."

Finally, he recalled the obligation placed on all Members under Article 2 of the Charter "of settling their international disputes by peaceful means and refraining from the use of force against the territorial integrity of any state."

In sum: On the Straits of Tiran the United States agreed with Israel on freedom of passage but differed on the manner in which the right should be asserted; on the administration of Gaza there was a wide divergence between Israel's "expectation" of a United Nations administration and no Egyptian return on the one hand and the United States' recognition of Egypt's juridical rights there, its support for arrangements with Egypt such as those suggested in the Secretary-General's statements and its "hope" that such arrangements might continue until a peace settlement; on the Armistice Agreement there was no meeting of minds at all, with the United States maintaining full support for the position taken by the Assembly majority and the Secretary-General and Israel's silence indicating that it continued to regard the Armistice Agreement as dead.

At the close of the Assembly's meeting on March 1 the Secretary-General had made the following announcement:

> I should like to inform the General Assembly of the following. Noting the plans of the Government of Israel, as announced today, for full and prompt withdrawal from the Sharm el-Sheikh area and the Gaza Strip in compliance with resolution 1124 of February 2, 1957, and noting further that the Government of Israel proposes that a meeting be held immediately between the Chief of Staff of Israel's Defence Army and the Commander of the United Nations Emergency Force in order to arrange for the United Nations to take over its responsibilities in the Sharm el-Sheikh and Gaza areas, I have this afternoon instructed the Commander of the United Nations Emergency Force, as a matter of the utmost urgency, to arrange for a meeting with the Israel Chief of Staff tomorrow, March 2, if at all possible, or, if not, as soon as possible thereafter.[4]

However, there was a forty-eight—hour delay caused by a political storm in Israel over Lodge's statement. Expectations had been built up of a United States commitment much closer to the Israeli concept of a United Nations administration in Gaza in place of the Egyptians rather than the cooperative arrangements with Egypt suggested in Hammarskjöld's February 22 statement.

Israel and the United States both contributed to confusion over the extent and exact meaning of the United States commitment on the future of Gaza.

[4] *Ibid.*, 666th Plenary Meeting, March 1, 1957.

As we have seen, Israel began it in Mrs. Meir's speech by using a quotation taken from its context in Hammarskjöld's February 22 statement in such a way as to express Israel's expectation of a United Nations administration and no return of Egypt. Lodge's reply quoted the February 22 statement in full and carefully endorsed the Secretary-General's position on future arrangements for Gaza, which was quite different from Israel's. However the difference was not explicitly spelled out and the reply included the general statement, qualified by the words "for the most part," that Israel's "hopes and expectations . . . seem to us not unreasonable." Lodge's reply was also ambiguously phrased in its reference to the United States "hope" that the United Nations role in Gaza "which the Secretary-General has described could usefully continue until there is a definite settlement." The Secretary-General's February 22 statement had differentiated between two groups of special arrangements with Egypt to strengthen the United Nations role in Gaza—the first group of indefinite duration, the second applicable to the temporary "period of transition" between the United Nations take-over and the return of Egyptian administration. Did the United States accept the difference or did its "hope" include continuing the transitional measures as well? The language was unclear although the general thrust of Lodge's statement was to endorse the Secretary-General's position whenever it differed from Israel's.

Earlier in the day on March 1 Secretary of State Dulles had met with representatives of the Arab states in Washington and afterward issued a press release stating that he told them the "Israeli withdrawal would involve no promises or concessions whatsoever to Israel by the United States, but would be predicated wholly upon the prior decisions of the United Nations General Assembly and the reports of the Secretary-General and the public position of the United States, notably the position expounded by President Eisenhower in his address of February 20." [5] None of the above gave the slightest support for excluding a return of Egypt to Gaza.

When word reached Washington that the Israeli government was hesitating, after Lodge's speech, to proceed with the withdrawal commitment it had just made, Eisenhower hastened on March 2 to send a cable to Ben-Gurion which was made public. After welcoming the decision to withdraw and expressing the hope that the withdrawals "will go forward with the utmost speed" the President's cable included the following passage:

> It has always been the view of this government that after the withdrawal there should be a united effort by all of the nations to bring about conditions in the area more stable, more tranquil, and more conducive to the general welfare than those which existed heretofore. Already the United Nations General Assembly has adopted resolutions

[5] *United States Policy in the Middle East, September 1956–June 1957, Documents,* Department of State Publication No. 6505, Government Printing Office, August 1957, pp. 327–328.

which presage such a better future. Hopes and expectations based thereon were voiced by your Foreign Minister and others. I believe that it is reasonable to entertain *such hopes and expectations* [italics added—EDITORS] and I want you to know that the United States, as a friend of all of the countries of the area and as a loyal member of the United Nations, will seek that such hopes prove not to be vain.[6]

The cable omitted the qualifying words "for the most part" which Lodge had applied to the Israeli hopes and expectations. This, and its generally more positive tone, provided sufficient reassurance to overcome dissension in Ben-Gurion's coalition cabinet and enable the government to proceed.

General Dayan was instructed to meet at once with General Burns on plans for the withdrawal and Mrs. Meir announced at the beginning of the Assembly session the afternoon of March 4 that the two had already met earlier that day and reached full agreement on the technical details. Later in the meeting the Secretary-General confirmed this news on the basis of a report to him from General Burns (first following text). Since Mrs. Meir had linked her announcement with her own March 1 withdrawal statement, Hammarskjöld, it may be noted, was at pains to put on the record that General Burns was acting under instructions "to arrange for full and *unconditional* withdrawal of Israel's military and civilian units with *initial* [italics added—EDITORS] take-over exclusively by UNEF."

In Washington Dulles now proceeded to throw cold water on assertions that the United States supported Israel's position against any return by Egypt to Gaza. At his press conference in Washington on March 5 the following exchanges occurred:

Q: Mr. Secretary, is it the U.S. position that UNEF should stay in Gaza until there is some definitive agreement on that area, and that Egyptian authorities should not revert there? Is that not a correct statement of the U.S. position?

A: I am going to have to ask you to read Ambassador Lodge's speech, which expressed our position on that point. And if I should attempt to restate it by memory I might inadvertently put it slightly differently. What I want to do is to stick exactly to what Ambassador Lodge said, because that was a very carefully considered statement.

. . . .

Q: Mr. Secretary, in the President's letter to Ben-Gurion the President says he hopes that the expectations raised by the Israeli Prime Minister will not be proven in vain—more or less like that. Would you say that this includes that part of Mrs. Meir's speech where she expressed the hope that the Egyptian troops would not return to Gaza?

A: I do not think that the President's letter should be read as endorsing every detail of everything that was said. The President's letter referred to the fact that statements were made by the Foreign Minister of

6 *Ibid.*, pp. 332–333.

Israel and by others with relation to their hopes and expectations. The others included, of course, the statement made by Ambassador Lodge as well as the statement by Mrs. Meir, and there were other statements made there. The President's letter, I think, referred generally to the hopes and expectations for a better future for the area, and should not be interpreted as necessarily an endorsement of every detail of everything that everybody said because, indeed, some of those statements were in conflict with each other.[7]

During the conference Dulles also flatly denied that Israel had been given any private assurances "which go beyond or which are different from" the public statements in which the U.S. position had been "fully and totally set forth."

The discussion in the Assembly of Israel's statement of expectations and the United States response extended through three plenary meetings on March 1, 4, and 8.[8] The record that emerged was fairly clear on the Straits of Tiran and very confused on the future of Gaza. On both issues there were many statements "in conflict with each other," as Dulles had put it.

Israel had reason to be satisfied with the line-up of Western maritime powers speaking in support of the right to freedom of navigation through the Straits of Tiran. The Western Europeans, Canada, Australia, and New Zealand gave solid backing to the United States position on this issue. Spokesmen for the Asian and Arab states and the Soviet bloc, on the other hand, generally defended the view that the Straits were Egyptian territorial waters and upheld Egypt's corresponding rights under international law. Most of the Latin Americans were silent on the question but Urrutia of Colombia saw a conflict of legal rights between Egypt and the maritime powers which should be treated as a question of law, not politics.

The delegates were generally and notably silent on Israel's assertion of its right under Article 51 to use force to keep the Straits open to her shipping. Of the four who referred to it, Lall described the claim as "totally untenable" and Urrutia said Article 51 was not applicable in his opinion. Walker of Australia said his government understood that the exercise of this right would be subject to making "full use of existing UN organs and machinery in seeking redress against any act of belligerency" and Georges-Picot of France saw "a possible resort" to Article 51 as an acceptable position.

In the discussion on the Gaza Strip the statements of those most sympathetic to Israel's concerns varied widely in their formulations of policy. France and the Netherlands seemed to accept Israel's expectations as stated by Mrs. Meir; the United Kingdom backed the Canadian position; Australia, New Zealand, Italy, and Portugal associated themselves with the United States; Norway, Sweden, and Denmark supported a stronger role for

[7] *Ibid.*, pp. 335–336.
[8] General Assembly Official Records, Eleventh Session, 666th–668th Plenary Meetings.

the United Nations in Gaza within the framework of the February 2 resolution and the Secretary-General's February 22 statement.

There was a tendency to fudge or ignore the quite fundamental difference already pointed out (pages 514–16) between the position of Israel on the one hand and those of the United States, the Secretary-General and the majority of the Assembly on the other. Canada went further than the United States in its support for an international administration of Gaza but, like the United States, it also recognized Egypt's juridical rights under the Armistice Agreement to administer the territory. Thus Egypt's agreement would be required to realize either the Canadian plan or the American "hope" that the special arrangements mentioned in the February 22 statement might continue until a peace settlement.

In his speech on March 4 Pearson gave a somewhat disingenuous explanation of his failure to introduce a resolution by which the Assembly would recommend an international administration such as he had proposed. He had wanted to do it, he said, but had been persuaded that the Secretary-General already had the necessary authority under earlier resolutions. Actually such a resolution would have fallen well short of a majority and encountered the opposition not only of Egypt but of the Afro-Asians, the Arabs, and the Soviet bloc, and the United States had strongly advised against the attempt.

Three members of the UNEF Advisory Committee reminded the Assembly of the realities of applicable law and the limitations on UNEF's authority previously endorsed in a whole series of resolutions.

Gunewardene of Ceylon declared that free navigation in the Straits, the future of the Gaza Strip and the overall Palestine question were all questions of negotiation. The United Nations could not impose its will on the parties, it could only render its good offices.

Urrutia of Colombia stressed that the administration of Gaza belonged to Egypt under the Armistice Agreement and it was necessary within that framework to negotiate with both sides cooperative arrangements to prevent resumption of raids and acts of reprisal in either direction. UNEF could not remain in Egypt "a single day" without the latter's consent. If that consent should be withdrawn he would propose in the Advisory Committee that the matter be brought immediately to the General Assembly or Security Council.

Lall of India pointed out that the meaning of the Secretary-General's February 22 statement had been misrepresented in assertions on the future of the Gaza Strip made by Israel and some others. In general he was in substantial agreement with Urrutia. UNEF could not be used to replace the invaders, it could not be an occupying force, it could not stay without Egypt's consent. As to the Straits of Tiran and the Gulf of Aqaba assertions of the right of freedom of passage were mere assertions and could not settle the legal issue. Yugoslavia and Indonesia, both with units serving in UNEF, also strongly endorsed these positions.

For Egypt Fawzi declared that "nothing said by anyone here or elsewhere" could detract from the Assembly's position that Israel's withdrawal should be "immediate and unconditional" nor "affect the fullness and law-fulness of Egypt's rights and those of the Arab people of the Gaza Strip." He hailed "the plane of legality and adherence to the Charter on which the Assembly has maintained and is still maintaining its approach" and observed that no Member, not even Israel, "has come here and openly stated that the United Nations should put a premium on aggression or subscribe to the so-lution of problems or the settlement of disputes being accomplished by force of arms, or by unilateral statements of policy, of intentions, or of hopes and expectations, or by any means or through any processes which would negate and go counter to the means and processes already outlined and stipulated by the Charter of the United Nations." [9]

As the debate drew to its end Eban spoke of "the wave of sympathy that has flooded towards" the people of Israel "in its just and righteous cause from the public opinion of a great part of the world," reaffirmed Israel's "reasonable expectation" of the replacement of Egyptian control in Gaza by a United Nations administration until a definitive peace settlement and asked the rhetorical question: "Will Israel's faith be rewarded so that others may have faith in the integrity of international processes?" [10]

Ben-Gurion gave a more realistic assessment in a speech to the Israeli Knesset when reporting on the withdrawal. In spite of all the declarations, he said, there was no absolute certainty that the Egyptians would not return or be brought back to the Strip, either as a civilian administration or as a military occupation force, on the pretext of the Armistice Agreement.[11]

Except for reporting on the progress of withdrawal arrangements Ham-marskjöld took no part in the Assembly discussion that followed Israel's March 1 statement. His own position on Gaza had been clearly established in his January 24 report, his statement of February 22, and his note of February 26. Juridically administration of the Gaza Strip belonged to Egypt. *De facto* he had sought and secured assurances of Egypt's willingness to cooperate after the initial take-over in arrangements for a stronger role for the United Nations in Gaza than before and in the prevention of raids from either side. He was, however, disturbed by the ambiguities and confu-sion which characterized the debate, including in some cases a stretching and twisting of his February 22 statement quite out of shape.

The fundamental contradiction between the positions of the United Na-tions and Israel on the future of Gaza remained, despite the tendency of the Lodge and Meir statements on March 1 and of many of the subsequent speeches to obscure or to skirt it. Outside the Assembly hall, in a speech to the UN Correspondents Association on March 5, Mrs. Meir reverted to the more extreme formulation of Israel's attitude as earlier reported in Hammar-

---

[9] *Ibid.*, 667th Plenary Meeting.   [10] *Ibid.*, 668th Plenary Meeting.
[11] From speech in the Knesset March 5, 1957, as summarized in David Ben-Gurion's *Israel's Security and Her International Position, Before and After the Sinai Campaign*, reprint from the Israel Government Year Book, 1959–1960.

skjöld's February 26 note to the Assembly. Israel, she said, would not toler-
ate the return of Egypt to Gaza in any form until its future status had been
settled. This was the same day on which Dulles made the press conference
comments in a quite different vein which were quoted earlier and her
speech deepened the Secretary-General's concern. He consulted with members of the UNEF Advisory Committee and other delegates in a series of
meetings on March 5, 6, and 7. There was general recognition of the difficulties and dangers ahead which were posed by the continuing contradiction, but a solid consensus that he should proceed anyway and try to maneuver things in such a way as to avoid a new confrontation.

On March 8 the Secretary-General reported to the Assembly (second
following text) the completion of Israeli withdrawal and informed it that he
would now proceed with his mandate under the second resolution of February 2. It will be noted that he refrained from any direct discussion of next
steps in Gaza after the initial take-over period but he made quite explicit
the line he would follow in the statement that "the stand of the General Assembly is to be interpreted in the light of the report of the Secretary-General of January 24 (A/3512), which the Assembly noted 'with
appreciation.' " He also used the occasion to remind the Assembly of the
call in that resolution for placing UNEF on both sides of the armistice line,
something that had been rarely mentioned in the last debate, and he placed
on record his understanding of how the Assembly wished him to proceed
with "the other measures" proposed in the January 24 report. These included the extent of UN responsibilities in Gaza.

Hammarskjöld supplemented his report by an oral statement during the
Assembly's final meeting on March 8 (third following text). This was mainly
devoted to an appeal for additional funds for UNRWA to help it to meet its
additional responsibilities in the Gaza Strip after the take-over.

Withdrawal Statement in the General Assembly

UN HEADQUARTERS, NEW YORK   MARCH 4, 1957

I have now received a report from the Commander of the United Nations Emergency Force on his talks earlier today with Israel's Commander-in-Chief. There is agreement on the technical arrangements for the withdrawal and for the movement of the United Nations Emergency Force into the Gaza Strip and the Sharm el-Sheikh area. I do not feel that I should give here any details regarding these technical arrangements. The instructions to General Burns were to arrange for full and unconditional withdrawal of Israel's military and civilian units with initial take-over exclusively by the United Nations Emergency Force.

I noted the suggestion by the distinguished delegate of Canada that I report to the General Assembly on completion of withdrawal. It is my intention to inform the General Assembly about relevant developments and, of course, especially of the withdrawal.

Important and difficult administrative problems arise in the present phase of the United Nations efforts. If they can be fully resolved on the basis of the authority already granted the Secretary-General will, as has been pointed out in the debate, depend partly on the willingness of the parties and of the Assembly itself to give its previous decisions a practical interpretation. However, I have to reserve my right to report to the General Assembly on this matter and on the financial consequences of present efforts when, as already indicated, I report on withdrawal developments.

General Assembly Official Records, Eleventh Session, 667th Plenary Meeting, March 4, 1957.

Second Report to General Assembly in Pursuance of the General Assembly Resolutions 1124 (XI) and 1125 (XI) on Israeli Withdrawal

UN HEADQUARTERS, NEW YORK   MARCH 8, 1957

I

1. The General Assembly, on February 2, 1957, adopted resolution 1124 (XI) in which, after recalling its previous resolutions on the same subject, the Assembly called upon Israel to complete its withdrawal behind the armistice demarcation line without further delay.

2. The Foreign Minister of Israel, on March 1, announced in the General Assembly the decision of the Government of Israel to act in compliance with the request in this resolution. The same day the Secretary-General instructed the Commander of the United Nations Emergency Force, as a matter of the utmost urgency, to arrange for a meeting with the Israel Commander-in-Chief, in order to agree with him on arrangements for the complete and unconditional withdrawal of Israel in accordance with the decision of the General Assembly.

3. On March 4, the Foreign Minister of Israel confirmed to the General Assembly the Government of Israel's declaration of March 1. The same day the Commander of the United Nations Emergency Force met at Lydda with the Israel Commander-in-Chief. Technical arrangements were agreed upon for the withdrawal of Israel and the entry of the United Nations Emergency Force in the Gaza Strip during the hours of curfew on the night of March 6/7. Arrangements were made for a similar take-over of the Sharm el-Sheikh area on March 8.

4. On March 6, General Burns reported that the "United Nations Emergency Force troops are now in position in all camps and centres of population in the Gaza Strip." At that stage the operation had been carried out according to plan and without incidents. At 04.00 hours GMT

General Assembly Official Records, Eleventh Session, Annexes, Volume II, agenda item 66, Document A/3568, March 8, 1957.

March 7 all Israelis had withdrawn from the Gaza Strip with the exception of an Israel troop unit at Rafah camp. By agreement, the last Israel element was to be withdrawn by 16.00 hours GMT March 8. Full withdrawal from the Sharm el-Sheikh area would be effected by the same time.

5. On March 7, the Commander of the United Nations Emergency Force notified the population of Gaza that

. . . the United Nations Emergency Force, acting in fulfillment of its functions as determined by the General Assembly of the United Nations with the consent of the Government of Egypt, is being deployed in this area for the purpose of maintaining quiet during and after the withdrawal of the Israel defence forces. Until further arrangements are made, the United Nations Emergency Force has assumed responsibility for civil affairs in the Gaza Strip. . . . The United Nations Relief and Works Agency for Palestine Refugees in the Near East (UNRWA) will continue to carry out its responsibility and will continue to provide food and other services as in the past. UNEF and UNRWA will do their best to relieve pressing needs which may arise from the present situation.

6. The Secretary-General, thus, is now in a position to report full compliance with General Assembly resolution I of February 2, 1957 [1124(XI)].

II

7. On February 2, the General Assembly adopted a second resolution [1125 (XI)] "recognizing that withdrawal by Israel must be followed by action which would assure progress towards the creation of peaceful conditions" in the area. Under the terms of this resolution, the completion of withdrawal puts its operative paragraphs into full effect.

8. In the resolution on action to follow a withdrawal, the General Assembly requested the Secretary-General, in consultation with the parties concerned, to carry out measures referred to in the resolution and to report as appropriate to the General Assembly. The Secretary-General will now devote his attention to this task. The stand of the General Assembly in the resolution is to be interpreted in the light of the report of the Secretary-General of January 24 (A/3512), which the Assembly noted "with appreciation."

9. Specifically, the General Assembly called upon the governments of Egypt and Israel scrupulously to observe the provisions of the General Armistice Agreement between Egypt and Israel of February 24,

1949, and stated that it considered that, after full withdrawal of Israel from the Sharm el-Sheikh and Gaza areas, the scrupulous maintenance of the Armistice Agreement "requires a placing of the United Nations Emergency Force on the Egypt-Israel armistice demarcation line."

10. The Assembly further stated that it considered that the maintenance of the Armistice Agreement requires the implementation of "other measures as proposed in the Secretary-General's report," with due regard to the considerations set out therein, with a view to assist in achieving situations conducive to the maintenance of peaceful conditions in the area. This statement, as it was formulated, read together with the request to the Secretary-General to consult with the parties, indicates that the General Assembly wished to leave the choice of these "other measures" to be decided in the light of further study and consultations.

III

11. Arrangements made by the Commander of the United Nations Emergency Force provided for an initial take-over in Gaza by the Force. This was in accordance with the statement of the Secretary-General to the General Assembly on February 22, that "the take-over of Gaza from the military and civilian control of Israel . . . in the first instance would be exclusively by UNEF." Instructions from the Secretary-General to the Commander of the United Nations Emergency Force reflected the position thus reported to the General Assembly. The notification by the Commander quoted in Section I above indicates the basis for this initial take-over as well as its extent. The same statement indicates the importance of the role that UNRWA can play in the initial takeover.

12. In accordance with decisions of the General Assembly, UNRWA has important functions in relation to the refugees in Gaza, which constitute the major part of the population of the area. Because of these normal functions and of the additional contributions which that agency can make in aiding the nonrefugee population, UNRWA is of essential assistance to the United Nations Emergency Force in its present operation. Therefore, and on the assumption that this course is in accordance with the General Assembly's wishes, the Director of UNRWA has agreed with the Secretary-General in this phase of the development to extend its immediate assistance beyond its normal functions. This

would be done in fields which are related to those functions and in which a sharing of responsibilities devolving on the United Nations Emergency Force at the initial take-over seems indicated. The Secretary-General wishes to express his appreciation for this assistance, of which he feels he can avail himself within the terms established for the United Nations Emergency Force as they have to be applied in the present phase of its activities. To the extent that UNRWA in this context is incurring additional costs, the reason for which is within the sphere of the responsibilities of the United Nations Emergency Force, a question of compensation will arise for later consideration.

13. The United Nations may also incur other additional costs than those caused by the assistance rendered by UNRWA. The Emergency Force may be in need of expert advice that can properly be provided by the Secretariat. If members of the Secretariat are taken over by the United Nations Emergency Force on a secondment basis, the cost obviously will be finally provided for as UNEF expenditures under the relevent resolutions of the General Assembly. In other cases costs should be carried by the Secretariat in the normal way.

14. The Secretary-General finally wishes to inform the General Assembly that arrangements will be made through which, without any change of the legal structure or status of the United Nations Truce Supervision Organization, functions of UNTSO in the Gaza area will be placed under the operational control of the Force. A close cooperation between UNTSO and UNEF will be maintained.

Statement in the General Assembly
Supplementing March 8 Report
on Israeli Withdrawal

UN HEADQUARTERS, NEW YORK   MARCH 8, 1957

The General Assembly has before it a report on the Israel withdrawal. I would like to supplement the report with the latest available information.

The last Israel troops cleared Rafah Camp at 16.45 hours GMT yesterday, March 7. Thereafter, there were no Israel troops in the Gaza Strip.

United Nations Emergency Force troops entered Sharm el-Sheikh at 16.00 hours GMT today, March 8. The Israel withdrawal by sea is proceeding as planned. By now no Israel forces remain in Sharm el-Sheikh, or on Tiran Island. However, a number of inoperable Israel vehicles, with a small party of mechanics and dock personnel, will remain in Sharm el-Sheikh until they can be evacuated by sea, on March 12.

Having taken the floor for this addition to my report on the withdrawal, I would ask the President's permission to elaborate on another point mentioned in the report to which I feel entitled to direct special attention for reasons which I hope will be fully appreciated by the Members.

In the report I have referred to the important role which will be played by the United Nations Relief and Works Agency for Palestine Refugees in the Near East in assisting the Force in its immediate task in the present phase of its operation. For the past several years, UNRWA has been charged by the General Assembly with the task of aiding the Palestine refugees in four different areas. In Gaza, the refugees number about 220,000, some two-thirds of the total population. UNRWA has fed them, provided shelter for those who needed it and, in cooperation with the civilian organization, provided or paid for their medical care and welfare. Of the remainder of the population of about

General Assembly Official Records, Eleventh Session, 668th Plenary Meeting, March 8, 1957.

100,000 people, about 60 percent have required assistance, and this has normally been provided by the civilian administration. In this initial period, UNRWA will now necessarily be called upon to extend its services to include the distribution of rations to the needy nonrefugees in Gaza. I envisage a similar extension of its activities in respect of the operation of hospitals, schools, and welfare activities for all of the population.

Although these extended responsibilities go beyond UNRWA's terms of reference, which apply only to services to Palestine refugees, the Director of UNRWA, as indicated in the report, has agreed to assume these tasks within the limits of practical possibilities and within the framework set by the present obligations of the Force.

The Assembly certainly shares my view that UNRWA at this moment plays a role which is more important than ever. Without UNRWA's contribution, the task of the Force in this initial phase would have presented insuperable difficulties. Its position is considerably strengthened by the stocks, facilities, and trained personnel that UNRWA has on the spot.

In the circumstances to which I referred, I feel entitled to draw the attention of the Assembly to the very grave and urgent problem of UNRWA's finances. The Director has already stressed and explained this situation in his annual report and his special report and in his statements to the Special Political Committee. I have not gone into the financial problems arising at this stage of our work, but it should be obvious, in the light of what I have said and of the explanations given by the Director, that substantial payments are required immediately in support of UNRWA's activities. The Members of the Assembly will certainly appreciate that the United Nations cannot contemplate curtailing its operation for the Palestine refugees elsewhere while continuing or expanding its services in Gaza. If UNRWA's budgets were fully subscribed, this would provide, at least temporarily, reserves urgently needed for the increasing responsibilities in Gaza. It is, therefore, imperative that outstanding pledges be paid immediately and that pledges and payments be increased to the full extent of the capacity of Member governments.

EGYPT had agreed that the initial take-over in Gaza should be exclusively by UNEF but the duration of the initial period had been left completely open except for the phrase "as has been the case" in the Secretary-General's February 22 statement. In Port Said a strong body of Egyptian troops had arrived the day after the British and French completed their evacuation. In the Sinai, however, Cairo had sent forward only civil police and units of the frontier force in accordance with an earlier understanding with the Secretary-General. Now Hammarskjöld thought the period of exclusive UNEF responsibility in Gaza could be extended for at least two weeks. This would provide time for negotiating the arrangements with Egypt for a stronger United Nations role in Gaza as envisaged in the February 22 statement. In talks with Fawzi he had stressed the need for such a breathing spell, especially in view of the sharp contradiction between Israel's "expectation" and the United Nations stand on Egypt's rights under the Armistice Agreement. He thought that Fawzi, while making no commitment, understood the point very well.

On instructions from Hammarskjöld, General Burns' proclamation on March 8 to the population of Gaza declared simply that "until further notice the UNEF has assumed responsibility for civil affairs in the Gaza Strip," thus leaving open the duration of the initial period and making no mention of a return of Egyptian administration. The next day Hammarskjöld dispatched Ralph Bunche to join General Burns in working out preliminary arrangements for Gaza in agreement with Egypt pending the Secretary-General's own arrival a few days later.

The wording of the Gaza proclamation was tailored to avoid arousing Israel at a critical moment. It was, however, quite out of tune with the mood of the Palestinian Arab population crowded into the Strip. They had just been freed after four months of occupation by the Israelis. Few understood UNEF's mission and to many it seemed that another foreign, non-Arab army was taking over. Extremist agitators spoke to this mood and the streets were quickly filled with crowds calling for the return of Egypt. Furthermore General Burns and his unit commanders met a very reserved response from local officials and notables to their requests for cooperation.

In Cairo the nationalist sensitivities and suspicions always present in Nasser's inner circle had been sharpened by the ambiguities of the Washington deal with Israel, the advocacy in the Assembly by Pearson and others of an international Gaza administration, and the reiterated assertions from Israel that Egypt should not be permitted to return to Gaza in any form. Fawzi had not yet returned from New York to provide a balanced firsthand appraisal of UN intentions as a counterweight to the suspicions of such men as Aly Sabry in the inner circle.

Before Bunche arrived, Brigadier Helmy, the Egyptian liaison officer assigned to UNEF, had approached General Burns about establishing a liaison office in Gaza in the next day or two with several Egyptian officers and men on his staff. Except for the timing, the proposal was natural enough, but Helmy agreed to wait until Burns received instructions from UN Headquarters. Then on March 10 UNEF guards at the police station in Gaza fired in the air while dispersing a riotous crowd and a ricochet bullet fatally wounded an Arab youth. This incident was reported in inflammatory and exaggerated fashion in the Egyptian press and radio.

The next day, without prior warning and before Bunche had met with government officials, it was announced to the press in Cairo that the Egyptian government had appointed General Hassan Abdul Latif as Administrative Governor of Gaza and had decided that the Egyptian Administration should take over its duties in the Gaza Strip immediately. The communiqué went on to accuse UNEF of overstepping its functions and firing on the Gaza population; Egypt had agreed to the stay of UNEF only within limits fixed by the United Nations—that is, to enforce the cease-fire and follow withdrawal of enemy forces to the Armistice Line; Egypt did not agree that UNEF should perform other functions.

The announcement caught the Secretary-General by surprise. Egypt's legal right to administer the Strip was not at issue, but Hammarskjöld thought the Egyptian government understood the need to refrain from overt moves such as this pending discussion and agreement on cooperative arrangements in Gaza. He immediately consulted the Advisory Committee and met almost daily with them for the next eight days.

Bunche met with Nasser on March 13. He did not succeed in persuading the Egyptian president to postpone the departure of General Latif and his administrative staff for Gaza, but Nasser did agree to wait for discussions with the Secretary-General on the problems covered in the February 22 statement. Nasser also said that no Egyptian troops would be sent into the Strip and that a renewal of fedayeen activities would not be countenanced. The next day an Egyptian government communiqué adopted a tone different from that issued on March 11. It declared "that full cooperation marked relations between Egyptian authorities and UNEF and that Egypt does what she can to help UNEF to carry out the duties placed upon their shoulders by the UN resolutions . . . the inhabitants of the Gaza sector look upon UNEF as friendly forces and cooperate with them for the sake of peace and in order that the mission entrusted to them by the UN may be realized." [1] General Latif followed the same line in his first speech to the inhabitants after entering Gaza on March 14. Thereafter the situation in Gaza much improved and Bunche was able to report on March 19, just before Hammarskjöld left for Cairo, that Gaza was completely peaceful, with UNEF in full evidence all over the Strip, no demonstrations, no Egyptian troops, and no inciting against Israel of which UNEF was aware.

There was, of course, a strong and angry Israeli reaction to the return of Egyptian administration to Gaza but it was confined to polemics and diplomatic protest and the threat of a military response which was not carried out. In the Knesset, Ben-Gurion reserved Israel's freedom of action, adding, "If the time comes when that action is appropriate and necessary, the Government of Israel will not, of course, give prior notice of its intention." [2]

[1] The text of this communiqué, as of the preceding one, was cabled to UN Headquarters from Cairo.
[2] *New York Times,* March 14, 1957.

Mrs. Meir flew back to the United States to protest in person, on March 18, first to U.S. Secretary of State Dulles and then to Hammarskjöld. She complained to Dulles that what had happened was quite contrary to Israel's expectations and implied that the United States had not lived up to assurances Israel thought it had been given. She told Hammarskjöld he should have spoken up in the Assembly if he had reservations about the formulation of Israel's position in her March 1 statement, adding the extraordinary assertion that everyone who had not dissented at the time shared responsibility for its correctness. As we have seen the record gave little support to her complaints. It was impossible for the Israeli government not to have been aware right along that differences on Gaza between itself and the United States and United Nations had only been thinly papered over and not resolved by the procedure staged on March 1 with its agreement.

Concern over the premature Egyptian move and its possible consequences for negotiating satisfactory arrangements in fulfillment of the February 22 commitments was another matter. After completing thorough consultations with the Advisory Committee, Hammarskjöld flew off to Cairo on March 19 for his talks with Nasser and Fawzi.

In his talks at Cairo on arrangements for Gaza the Secretary-General chose a straightforward, pragmatic approach to the problem. At Hammarskjöld's request General Burns set down on paper the points on which he, as UNEF's commander, considered Egyptian cooperation to be necessary to the effective performance of the Force's peace-keeping functions at the armistice line. These were then discussed with the Egyptian government in the context of that part of the February 22 statement concerning "special and helpful arrangements" with Egypt after the period of initial take-over.

General Burns asked that the Egyptian government make effectively known to the Gaza population its policy to prevent infiltration, including the reinstitution of regulations and penalties and recognition of the right of UNEF to assist in enforcing the regulations in cooperation with the Palestinian police. UNEF would have the right to arrest infiltrators in a zone up to 500 metres deep on the Gaza side of the demarcation line, who would then be handed over to the police authorities. UNEF's right to fire in self-defense would also be made known to the population and its rights to full freedom of movement, in accordance with the February 8, 1957, agreement, would be reaffirmed for the Gaza Strip, and in the Sinai between its base at Rafah, the airport at El Arish, the headquarters in Gaza, and units of UNEF along the Egyptian side of the armistice line and international frontier. In addition the airstrip at Gaza would be manned by UNEF; UNEF aircraft would continue to have the right to fly freely over the Sinai and Gaza could be used as a port of entry for UNEF supplies.

The Egyptian government accepted all these stipulations. In addition it agreed that UNEF should have the right to fire on infiltrators coming at night from either direction who refused to halt, provided that Israel on its side also accorded this right. With the exception of the last point the Egyptian commitments to UNEF were not conditioned to reciprocal action by

Israel of acceptance of UNEF on the Israeli side of the line. In his negotiations Hammarskjöld sought, and largely succeeded in obtaining, agreement to arrangements on the Egyptian side that would make it possible for UNEF to function effectively even if Israel could not be persuaded to accept the Assembly's call for UNEF's deployment on the Israeli side as well.

The understanding on these arrangements was not formalized nor were the detailed terms made public immediately. Hammarskjöld had negotiated them subject to the approval of the UNEF Advisory Committee and the consent of governments contributing units to the Force. Upon his return from Cairo the Secretary-General met with the Committee to review the proposed arrangements and his impressions of Egypt's attitude. Hammarskjöld returned to New York convinced that Egypt wished UNEF to continue. The sudden move to restore Egyptian administration to Gaza reflected sensitivity over the maintenance of its sovereign rights, not a wish to shorten UNEF's stay contrary to the decisions of the General Assembly. Egypt had now accepted the practical arrangements General Burns had requested in the Gaza area. Hammarskjöld was also able to report that there was no present disposition to disturb the continued deployment of UNEF at Sharm el-Sheikh and Egypt had affirmed the commitment that the Advisory Committee be given prior notice of any change of policy in this respect.

Egypt had effectively closed the door on the hoped-for administrative role in Gaza for the United Nations before the talks with Hammarskjöld even began but he and the Advisory Committee agreed that the prospects were good for a degree of cooperation sufficient to UNEF's central peace-keeping function at the armistice line. The Advisory Committee's conditional but generally positive response in the text that follows was basically Hammarskjöld's draft and approved unanimously. It was put on public record as a United Nations press release soon after its receipt in Cairo.

Statement on Arrangements with Egypt
for the United Nations Emergency Force

It will have been noted from the communiqué on the UNEF Advisory Committee meeting of March 28 that the Committee reviewed the practical arrangements for the functioning of the UNEF with regard to Gaza that had been studied with the Egyptian Government and with the Commander of UNEF during the Secretary-General's visit to Cairo. The communiqué also stated that the Advisory Committee "noted with satisfaction the progress so far made."

At its next meeting, March 29, 1957, the Advisory Committee agreed that the Secretary-General should transmit the following statement to the Government of Egypt:

The Advisory Committee notes with appreciation the Secretary-General's statement on the understanding reached with the Government of Egypt concerning the arrangements under which the United Nations Emergency Force would operate and which are established in accordance with the requirements of the Force as presented by the Commander. If, in practice, these arrangements were to prove insufficient or unsatisfactory, the Committee would have to revert to the issue and consider with the Secretary-General such further proposals as he might make or wish to make to the Government of Egypt in order to provide for satisfactory conditions for the functioning of the Force.

However, the Committee hopes that the arrangements at present envisaged with Egypt, as they may by agreement be elaborated in practice, will prove satisfactory in the context of the continuance of the agreed stationing of the Force at the armistice demarcation line as a deterrent to incursions and other disturbances. It was agreed that decisive significance attaches to the effective clarification to the population of Egypt's policy to prevent infiltration across the demarcation line, and it was noted that measures for the enforcement of this policy will be taken by the Government of Egypt and that the United Nations Emergency Force will, as a matter of right, have the duty to assist in the enforcement.

It should be mentioned that the Government of Egypt has advised the Secretary-General that:

UN Press Release SG/583, April 1, 1957.

1. Egypt is making known effectively to the refugees and other inhabitants of the Strip that it is Egyptian policy to prevent infiltration across the demarcation line, and this will be reemphasized from time to time, as necessary.

2. The Egyptian regulations against infiltration, which include penalties, are being again put into force. The role of UNEF in assisting in the prevention of infiltration will be made clearly known to the population of the Gaza Strip by the appropriate authorities.

BEFORE Hammarskjöld left for Cairo Israel had renewed its request that he put to the Egyptian government the question whether it agreed to full abstention from all belligerent acts by land, air, or sea. When this request had been made in early February Israel was itself actively exercising belligerency by its continued occupation of Gaza and Sharm el-Sheikh and Hammarskjöld had refused to act (page 492). With the Israeli withdrawal complete the Secretary-General now agreed to put Israel's question and he did so. As he informed the Advisory Committee on his return to New York, however, he also put three questions of his own. These were aimed at a reaffirmation of Article I of the Armistice Agreement, which he had characterized in his January 24 report to the Assembly as, in effect, a nonaggression pact (page 480). The questions were so formulated that they could be put in identical terms to both Egypt and Israel as a step toward implementation of the Assembly's resolution 1125 (XI) of February 2, which began with a call on both governments for scrupulous observance of the Armistice Agreement.

The questions were as follows:

1. Is the Government of Egypt (Israel) willing "with a view to promoting the return to permanent peace in Palestine and in recognition of the importance in this regard of mutual assurances concerning the future military operations of the parties" (a direct quote from the Armistice Agreement) to reaffirm its adherence to the principles enunciated in points 1 to 4 of the Egyptian-Israeli Armistice Agreement?

2. In reaffirming its adherence to the principles of Article I, does the Government of Egypt (Israel) accept an interpretation of that article in line with what was stated in the January 24 report, as supported by the resolution of the Security Council of September 1, 1951, or does the government refer solely to action directly mentioned in the four principles?

3. Will the Government of Egypt (Israel), on the basis of a mutual reaffirmation of Article I and on conditions of reciprocity, take the steps necessary in order to establish full implementation of the Armistice Agreement so as to provide for "a return to the state of affairs envisaged in the Armistice Agreement and avoidance of the state of affairs into which conditions, due to lack of compliance with the Armistice Agreement, had progressively de-

teriorated" [quotation from his January 24 report—EDITORS] prior to Israeli military intervention on October 29, 1956?

Hammarskjöld communicated the texts of these questions privately to the Advisory Committee. They were not made public but the Secretary-General did say at his next press conference on April 4 (page 538) that he had approached both Israel and Egypt "concerning Article I," without giving any particulars. Despite difficulties for both Israel and Egypt, Hammarskjöld hoped for replies of a kind that would at least provide room for maneuver in the directions spelled out in his January 24 report and endorsed by the Assembly. Though Israel had so far maintained its insistence that the Armistice Agreement had been wrecked beyond repair, it was simultaneously calling for a nonaggression pact with Egypt. On the other side, Egypt had already reaffirmed support for the Armistice Agreement but it had also always maintained its right under international law to restrict Israeli shipping through the Suez Canal despite the Security Council's 1951 resolution to the contrary.

In addition to the questions on Article I of the Armistice Agreement the Secretary-General decided that the time had come to address a formal request to the Government of Israel for its consent to the deployment of UNEF on the Israeli side of the armistice line as well as on the Egyptian side. He discussed the draft of his letter to Mrs. Meir on this matter with the Advisory Committee on March 29 and received its full endorsement. Unlike the message to Egypt on the arrangements for Gaza this letter was not made public but its dispatch to the Israeli Foreign Minister was timed to coincide with the Advisory Committee's public conditional approval of the arrangements made with Egypt on the Gaza side of the armistice line.

From Transcript of Press Conference

UN HEADQUARTERS, NEW YORK APRIL 4, 1957

THIS WAS the Secretary-General's first general press conference since the autumn of 1956 and the correspondents' questions naturally concentrated on the talks with Nasser, on UNEF, Gaza, the Suez Canal, and related matters. Among Hammarskjöld's responses his reaction to a suggestion that UNEF be made permanent and his discussion of the negotiating strengths and weaknesses of the Secretary-General as compared to a government are of special interest. There were several questions concerning the efforts currently being made to persuade Egypt to a negotiated settlement of the Suez Canal dispute and the role of the Secretary-General in this regard about which a few words of background are in order.

During the winter Hammarskjöld had engaged in quiet, behind-the-scenes efforts to lay the basis for a renewal of negotiations between Egypt and the users. The British and French governments had earlier belittled the value of the progress registered in the Secretary-General's letter to Fawzi of October 24, 1956, and had sabotaged plans for further talks with Egypt in favor of armed invasion. Now they pressed the Secretary-General to persuade Egypt to resume the foreign ministers' talks on the basis of the Six Principles and his correspondence with Fawzi. The Egyptian government, on the other hand, was not willing, at least not yet, to negotiate directly with representatives of nations that had so recently seized Port Said, though it was quite willing to talk to Hammarskjöld about the matter.

The Secretary-General thus undertook the role of go-between for the users on the one hand and Egypt on the other. On February 19 he passed along to Fawzi a proposal for an interim arrangement pending a final settlement that had been agreed upon among the United States, Britain, France, and Norway. It was proposed that Egypt designate either the International Bank or the United Nations itself to collect all the Canal tolls, returning 50 per cent to Egypt to cover operating costs and retaining the other half until a final settlement. This proposal was flatly rejected early in March by President Nasser's government which declared that all tolls should be paid to the Suez Canal Authority, but made no counterproposal of its own.

On March 18, with the Canal about to reopen for traffic and just before Hammarskjöld flew to Cairo for his talks with Nasser, the Egyptian government issued a memorandum declaring:

1. That Egypt is still determined to respect in letter and in spirit the Constantinople Convention concluded in 1888.

UN Note to Correspondents No. 1571, April 4, 1957.

2. The system of levying of Canal tolls will remain as it used to be, according to the last agreement concluded between the Egyptian government and the nationalized Suez Canal Company.

3. The question of compensation and claims resulting from nationalization would be settled by either direct agreement or by arbitration.

4. Canal tolls are to be paid in advance to the Suez Canal Authority either in Egypt or to its nominees.

5. The Suez Canal Authority shall create a special fund for improvement programs or any other programs destined to meet the increase of traffic in the Canal, said fund to be fed by allotting to it a certain proportion of the dues, which shall not be less than the average proportion allotted by the former Suez Canal Company to such programs.[1]

Issuance of this memorandum reflected the determination reached by President Nasser to oppose negotiation of any new multilateral agreement on the operation of the Canal and to proceed on a unilateral basis. During his stay in Cairo Hammarskjöld spent many hours in efforts to persuade Nasser to change his mind, but he was not successful. The United States government, acting mainly through Ambassador Hare in Cairo, then tried its hand, with Hammarskjöld standing aside as a negotiator but continuing to serve as a consultant to each side. This was the situation when the Secretary-General met the press on April 4.

. . . QUESTION: In one of your reports during the debates last year and early this year, you referred to one of the clauses in the Armistice Agreement between Israel and Egypt and you stated, I believe, something to the effect that it assimilates into a nonaggression pact. I was wondering what progress you made along those lines during your recent discussion in Cairo with President Nasser.

THE SECRETARY-GENERAL: This is a point on which I can give you some hard news in the sense that on this, as on other points, I have tried to follow up the plans I presented in my reports; that is to say, in the effort to get back toward an implementation of the armistice agreements as they were intended to function, not as they turned out to function, after years of deterioration, I have approached the Government of Egypt and the Government of Israel in particular concerning Article I, the one to which you refer. So far, I have no replies, but it happened a

---

[1] Distributed to foreign diplomatic missions in Cairo and issued as a press release by the Egyptian delegation to the United Nations but not as a United Nations document or press release.

short while ago, and it is for that reason no source of surprise that so far there is nothing on the table.

QUESTION: Mr. Secretary-General, what at present is the precise role and, I might say, the situation of UNEF and of the United Nations as a whole in Gaza and in Sharm el-Sheikh?

THE SECRETARY-GENERAL: As you know, the UNEF is in Sharm el-Sheikh under the very rules and under the principles which were spelled out concerning that specific point in the report, I believe, of January 24. I have nothing to add to what I said in that report on that score.

As regards Gaza, that is the point of concentration of the UNEF troops. The UNEF functions in Gaza for those purposes which were laid down by the General Assembly. There is a definition of the functions of UNEF, and that definition has not been changed; that definition applies in Gaza as elsewhere. That means that the UNEF has as a predominant function to safeguard peace between the two countries which recently have been in open conflict.

QUESTION: I have two questions. According to the Israel press, you intend again to go next week to the Middle East, this time including Israel in your visit. Is that correct?

Some days ago the American press told a story about the plan suggested by the United Nations to build a mined fence along the border of the Gaza Strip. This morning we learned that Israel intends to build such a fence on its own territory along the Gaza border. What have you to say on this project? Has it been suggested by the United Nations? What is the attitude of Egypt to this plan? Is it at all realistic?

THE SECRETARY-GENERAL: You have asked two rather different questions, and I may reply to them separately, as I hope you intend me to do.

On the first one, I just have nothing to say because I have not laid down any plans for a return or any plans excluding a return. The situation is just simply that my suitcases are, so to say, always packed in a situation like the present one. If it would serve a useful purpose, I would be happy to go, and go at once, to Egypt or Israel, whatever is called for. As you raised the point, I may mention that in these cases I must generally be guided by the immediate need. I have just returned here last week straight from Cairo. I do not think that there is any need for much imagination to see that there were some rather urgent matters for me to attend to, referring also to the Canal talks, and perhaps especially the Canal talks, of which you are well informed. Therefore, the information you quote from the Israel papers is premature and not based on anything said from here or on any plans laid here. But, on the other hand, quite frankly, if the situation develops so that it calls for such a direct contact I would be happy to take it.

The second question, concerning the fence, is, as you know, a question of very long date. It arose in the discussions last year. It has arisen again. There have been discussions between the Commander and his representatives on the one side and the authorities on the other side. I am not fully informed about how far those plans or those discussions have advanced as of the present. Personally, I believe that the fence idea has advantages but that it should, like all such ideas, be applied with some common sense. We do not solve the problems of that area by building up a fence all along the armistice demarcation line, all around Gaza, but there are sensitive spots which in our experience present special difficulties for shepherds, marauders, and whatnot, and where the policing activities at the armistice demarcation line by the UNEF would be facilitated by the erection of such a fence. But frankly, that seems to me to be, on the whole, a technical detail which I leave, with the greatest confidence, to the Commander.

QUESTION: Mr. Hammarskjöld, I should like to ask a little more basic question. You had many long talks with Prime Minister Nasser. What can you say now, at the end of those talks, as to your impression of his willingness to cooperate with the aims and purposes of the United Nations General Assembly?

THE SECRETARY-GENERAL: I think I can speak with confidence built on what, so to say, has emerged in practice. I should say—speaking more about what you have in your hands than about this and that for the future—that as to the proposals we made, the Commander of the UNEF and myself in Cairo, we got full cooperation and you can draw your own conclusions from that.

QUESTION: Mr. Secretary-General, may I ask whether the Canal talks that are now going on are, in your estimation, in line with your proposals of October 24, including your proposals for policing and arbitration?

THE SECRETARY-GENERAL: The Egyptian proposals, as they were published, do not run counter to the October 24 letter but cover only part of the ground. There are points in that letter which have been, if not left aside, at least not elaborated. For that reason my reply to your first basic question must be that there is no conflict between the proposals now put forward and the proposals of October 24, although they do not fully correspond, as the Egyptian proposals do not cover the whole distance of the October 24 proposals.

As to the special question of arbitration, I think that the Egyptian government goes practically the whole way on the October 24 paper.

QUESTION: In following that up, may I ask whether it is your intention to promote your October 24 proposals in more detail and more fully?

THE SECRETARY-GENERAL: I have never abandoned that basis for my activities. That is the direction in which I try to influence the development to the best of my ability and with the somewhat meagre equipment which I necessarily have. As you know, the Secretary-General in such conditions is in a situation rather different from the situation of a Government.

QUESTION: May I ask a more general question. As Secretary-General, do you think it a propitious and wholesome development that the actual responsibility for dealing with world tensions has shifted and is shifting from the Security Council to the General Assembly?

THE SECRETARY-GENERAL: This is a difficult value judgment. I think we should see a little more what comes out of actual developments in the next Assembly or in the next couple of years. I must say that the constitutional development which has taken place is one which I personally feel requires very, very careful attention. The increased responsibility of the General Assembly itself I do not think is anything which should give anybody cause for concern. But it is, of course, something which at the same time calls for some serious thinking so that we do not somehow unwittingly and unwillingly get off the rails. That is to say, for me it is a development about which it is impossible to say whether it is, in your words, sound or not. It will depend on the wisdom with which we are able to fill out the framework which has been created by the shift of balance constitutionally.

In summing up, I want to say that to me it does represent a serious problem to which we must give all attention.

QUESTION: Mr. Hammarskjöld, reporters in the Gaza Strip have recently reported that fedayeen groups have begun to reorganize in the Strip and that civilians in the Strip are carrying arms—revolvers and submachine guns. Has that information come to your attention? What is being done about it? May I conclude with the more general question: Who actually is in charge of the internal policing of the Gaza Strip?

THE SECRETARY-GENERAL: There is no report confirming the newspaper stories in this respect. The Commander has not found it necessary to draw my attention to any such developments so far.

As to the responsibility, the UNEF has a position and works under such arrangements that it should be able to see to it that in this way there is no development behind them which contradicts the purposes they are serving at the armistice demarcation line.

QUESTION: In a report made in the past on the Middle East, you happened to point out one of the difficulties in implementing the armistice agreements between the parties as being the different interpretations they had of these agreements. At that time, as I understood it, there was no specific machinery in mind to bridge this difficulty. Now that you have said today that you intended to go back to the implementation of the armistice agreements as they were intended to be implemented, I wonder whether you have any specific machinery to bridge this difficulty which you mentioned in an earlier report with regard to the interpretation of armistice agreements?

THE SECRETARY-GENERAL: You are right in referring to that problem because it is a very crucial one in the whole question of implementation. At that stage, I well remember that I said that I had drawn the attention of the governments to certain weaknesses in the machinery. You know that quite a few things have happened since then. For that reason, they have been more engaged with other problems which seemed to them to be perhaps less academic.

I myself feel the way I felt then. I would like to bring their attention again to this problem because I believe that that is one of the directions in which we could, so to say, bolster the machinery so as to facilitate a less unharmonious development than we have seen.

QUESTION: Assuming Mr. Jarring succeeds in finding common ground for settlement of the Kashmir question, it would seem that there would be some reason for India to be worried about the validity of any agreement with the present Government of Pakistan which has never faced a popular election. Any settlement reached could be refuted by a future elected government. Therefore, do you think that any settlement reached in this situation will be a lasting solution to this problem?

THE SECRETARY-GENERAL: Would you permit me on this point to wait until we have the Jarring report and to see if and when the question does arise in the form you put it now? As matters now stand, it is obviously a hypothetical question and I think it is wise for me not to engage in a discussion of it.

QUESTION: May I ask a general question? Would you give us your opinion on whether it is consistent with the Charter of the United Nations for one Member state to proclaim itself to be in a state of war with another Member state?

THE SECRETARY-GENERAL: Let us leave aside the Charter for a moment and look at the legal facts. Let us also forget about the term "belligerency" and all that.

After all, there are quite a few situations where you know there is not a peace settlement. What word you use is mainly a question of taste in order to characterize a situation where there is no peace settlement. The fact that there is no peace settlement is obviously highly regrettable, but in itself, legally and technically speaking, it is not against any Charter provision. From that you should not conclude that I either endorse or reject any specific terminology which this or that government uses in its political debate. What I want to point out is that the state of no peace in the technical and legal sense is something with which we regrettably have to live. For that reason, it is not something about which we need to raise the question of Charter principles.

QUESTION: I would like to ask two questions. You said before that the position of Secretary-General does not correspond to that of a government. I wonder whether, on your visits to various capitals, you found that it was difficult for you to negotiate since you had no point to refer back to? Have you given any thought to setting up a political department so that they can refer back to you?

My second question is: Can you comment on the Hungarian situation now?

THE SECRETARY-GENERAL: To my mind, the first question you raised is a rather interesting one. It is partly insufficiently understood and partly insufficiently explored. I would say this: that the Secretary-General does not suffer from the fact that he has nobody to refer back to provided that the main organs of the United Nations, the Security Council or the General Assembly, have taken clear decisions on general terms of reference, short of which, of course, the Secretary-General is forced to undertake a kind of policy-making which from the point of view of Member governments I feel may be considered unsound, or at least not in line with the kind of procedures we should have here.

On the other hand he finds himself in a situation where he lacks not means of pressure, but the kind of weight which every government necessarily has because it is part of the world picture, part of the whole pattern of trade, policy-making, and so on and so forth. That is partly compensated for by one fact. Because he has no pressure group behind him, no territory, and no parliament in the ordinary sense of the word, he can talk with much greater freedom, much greater frankness, and much greater simplicity in approaching governments than any government representative can do. In summing up, I would say that the lack of a superior body to which to refer does not matter if there is a clear-cut policy line laid down by the main bodies here. The lack of means of "pressure"—if the word is not misunderstood—is in a certain sense a weakness which, however, is compensated for, and in some respects perhaps more than compensated for, by the freedom of action, the freedom of expression, which the Secretary-General can grant himself and which, I am happy to note, governments do grant him.

You talk about the possibility of some kind of policy-making body, a political division. I do not remember exactly what you called it. In a sense, you have it, in the Middle Eastern question at present as regards the UNEF, in the Advisory Committee. The Advisory Committee has proved to be an extremely useful body to which I owe a great debt of gratitude for the assistance they have given me in a free exchange of views which has clarified both the reactions of the General Assembly and my own thinking and for the support they have given to me in practice—also in other respects. It may be that such an Advisory Committee system in particularly crucial questions may prove an avenue towards a more balanced cooperation in fields like this one between the Secretary-General and the policy-making bodies, in the first place, of course, the General Assembly.

I replied so fully to this question that I have forgotten your second question. What was it?

QUESTION: I wondered whether you had anything to report on the Hungarian situation?

THE SECRETARY-GENERAL: No, there is nothing today.

QUESTION: With regard to the Suez Canal problem, do you think it would help if the question was discussed in the Security Council? Or would you favour private negotiations bilaterally or multilaterally?

THE SECRETARY-GENERAL: In fact, various governments have already embarked on the second road. I do not think it is a good idea to jump from one form to the other unless and until the possibilities offered by the form already chosen have been exhausted. Whether or not this is the case can best be decided by those negotiating.

QUESTION: When you were in Cairo, did you take up in your talks with President Nasser the crucial question of free passage for Israeli ships through the Suez Canal?

THE SECRETARY-GENERAL: There was not a single part of the Middle Eastern problem in which Egypt is a partner, or to which it is a party, which I did not cover in my talks in Cairo.

QUESTION: Did he promise anything or say anything on that question?

THE SECRETARY-GENERAL: I think that I must stick to my general rule not to inform the press first about what may happen in talks of that nature. I refer to what I said a moment ago. I have considerable freedom of expression in such discussions. On the other hand, obviously I am bound to observe some simple rules of discretion.

QUESTION: Assuming that a final peace settlement in the Middle East is still a long way off, do you feel that it is in the interests of both sides for UNEF to stay indefinitely in the Gaza Strip and in Sharm el-Sheikh? Are you making plans for a long stay?

THE SECRETARY-GENERAL: I would put my reply in this way: I would be unhappy to see the breakup of the UNEF arrangement until we had such a background change of the situation as would to my mind render the UNEF unnecessary in its present form. We are not there yet. In fact, what I say corresponds very closely to the stand which I understand to be the stand of the General Assembly—that is to say, that as long as UNEF has the functions which were determined and decided upon by the General Assembly it should of course remain in order to fulfill those functions. That is, short of such a change in the situation as would provide us with some better means for the purpose; I have nothing special in mind. I just make that reservation as a matter of course.

. . . QUESTION: Do you feel that Egypt will permit the UNEF to stay in Gaza and at Sharm el-Sheikh indefinitely if it is not stationed also on the Israeli side? And secondly, is there any way of avoiding a possible crisis if Israel attempts to send a ship through the Suez Canal?

THE SECRETARY-GENERAL: On the first point, I think that we have seen, in the last five months, so many changes in the situation, so many new elements brought in, that you will understand if I consider it a little bit futile to crystal-gaze. All I can say is that there is at present full understanding between the Government of Egypt and ourselves as to deployment of the UNEF on the Egyptian side. The further developments are things which I would rather leave aside in this discussion. I think that the situation as it now stands, and as far as it goes, should be considered satisfactory, a view which, as you know, was expressed not only by the Advisory Committee, but most recently echoed by Mr. Dulles in his press conference.

Your second question referred to the situation in the Suez and the possibility of avoiding a clash there. On that point I can only refer to what has been said in public from the two sides. They speak for themselves; I do not speak for them. What the situation might be if and when we were to run into trouble because of this or that stand is something which I would rather leave aside for the moment and not comment on.

QUESTION: May I ask why you have kept the terms of the UNEF agreement with Egypt, as it relates to Gaza, in a state of secrecy, and why an operative agreement of that type as a public matter should have been secret?

THE SECRETARY-GENERAL: Because it is a stage in a process where I think the right moment for full publicity will be at a somewhat later time when things have been more fully developed in practice and the situation has become more settled. There is nothing more remarkable to it than that. You know very well from negotiations conducted by, for example, the United States that, not as any matter of secrecy or quiet or whatnot, but just as a part of sound procedure, one does not, so to say, bring everything out when one is still in the run. We have reached a certain stage in the developments that is a basis for further developments. I would rather reserve, as I said, any statement on these various matters until a stage when the situation is clarified more in detail and more definitely.

QUESTION: Would you suggest that the UNEF be a permanent element in United Nations operations for future emergencies? A kind of permanent force?

THE SECRETARY-GENERAL: We have to see a little bit what the UNEF is and how it came into being. You know well that, under the Charter, a United Nations force was envisaged in quite different terms. It was envisaged under the terms of Chapter VII—that is to say, to be used after a decision of the Security Council, a decision which was mandatory and compulsory. The whole operation this time was an operation under the Uniting-for-Peace resolution—that is to say, in the General Assembly.

The Assembly has not got the rights of the Security Council, and a force set up by the Assembly is, for that reason, tied by the Charter rules in other Chapters and other parts of the Charter than Chapter VII. It is not anything that, so to say, can be used as a means of enforcement of a specific policy. That is the great difference between the UNEF and a force as envisaged in the Charter itself. I do believe that this specific form, although useful under the circumstances, valuable as to the experience it yields, is too much tied to a specific case and a specific set of circumstances to be able to serve directly as a basis for further development.

On the other hand, I think that the experiences are such and the lessons we have learned are such that it will render much easier the buildup of a kind of United Nations force, perhaps also outside Chapter VII, or within Chapter VII, which should be a lasting element in the United Nations equipment.

To sum up, I would thus say that I scarcely see the possibility of just letting the UNEF, as it was formed and developed last fall, become the basis for a continuous organic development. I would rather see it as a kind of experimental prototype from which we learn a great deal and which, I hope, will make it easier at a later stage to renew the discussion and reach results concerning a United Nations force as a formal part of our equipment.

QUESTION: I hope you will pardon me if I repeat a question which may have been asked before; I have not heard all of them. Would you care to comment on the present status of Israel's request made to you repeatedly for a "yes" or "no" answer from Egypt as to whether it considered itself in a state of belligerency?

THE SECRETARY-GENERAL: The question has not been asked before. The present status is that the question which the Government of Israel asked me to transmit to Egypt was formally transmitted to Egypt in the course of my visit to Cairo. At my departure from Cairo I had so far not received a reply. As you know, I have not been home many days and quite a few things have happened. In those days I have not heard anything about it.

QUESTION: President Eisenhower said again yesterday that it should not be assumed that Egypt will bar the ships of any country when the Canal is reopened. How do you feel about that assumption?

THE SECRETARY-GENERAL: I have no reason to comment on the statement made by the President. I think it is a wise assumption.

QUESTION: You said before that you have not so far received any reply from Egypt with regard to nonbelligerency. You said also that a short time only had elapsed. What time would you consider long enough in which to expect such a reply or to say a reply was overdue?

THE SECRETARY-GENERAL: Does that not somehow depend on the circumstances? Is it possible to state a general rule when, from your point of view, it is appropriate to reply to a friend of yours, or to a foe of yours? After all, it has to be seen in the total setting. Mind you, I did not say what I said concerning the timetable in justification or defence of anything. I wanted to point out that the timetable having been what it is, there is no reason for comments in either direction on the fact that, so far, there has been no reply.

QUESTION: Although the Egyptian memorandum on the Suez Canal does not make any reference to the Six Principles of the Security Council, do you feel that all these six principles are mentioned in that memorandum in some way? Is there any one that is not mentioned in it?

THE SECRETARY-GENERAL: That depends largely on the interpretation of the memorandum. The principles, as you remember, were not called principles by the Security Council, but were called requirements. That is to say, they were requirements which should be met by any arrangement established for the Canal. Whether or not the Egyptian proposals do meet those requirements is a question of interpretation of the text, on the one side, and of the requirements, on the other hand. You know that the requirements have been interpreted in different ways. I should like, however, in this context to draw your attention again to my proposals of October 24 to Egypt because they are of interest just as an illustration to your question. Those proposals were said in the very letter, if satisfactorily handled, to meet my understanding of the requirements. What I feel or do not feel may not be too important or interesting in this context, but what is more important and interesting is that, later, in various capitals when this matter has been discussed publicly—for example, in parliaments—it has been obvious that the view was accepted that a plan developed on the lines of the October 24 letter would meet the requirements. That is a guidance at least in the interpretation of the six requirements as it has developed in the past few months. But I would leave it to others to say whether or not this proposal meets all the requirements—if all the requirements are, so to say, covered. I have already said that the proposals elaborate only part of what was said in the October 24 letter, leaving other matters more or less aside. That does not mean that those matters necessarily are brushed aside; it may mean that they are left to the development in practice and, for that reason, it may be wise to add that the full reply to your question necessarily will depend also upon how various points in the Egyptian proposal are put into effect.

QUESTION: May I come back for a moment to the Hungarian question? You said that there were no new developments; but do you not envisage an Assembly meeting? Before the last session of the Assembly adjourned there were some representatives who even wanted a debate on the interim report. Then we learned that the debate would take place only if and when the final report was available. What is the situation now?

THE SECRETARY-GENERAL: I have no information concerning the reactions of the delegations. I guess that the full report of the Committee will be forthcoming fairly soon. It may be that some of you know the timetable regarding the report of the Hungarian Committee. It will be the last half of the month, Mr. Cordier says. My guess would be that delegations would like to have a look at that report and decide in the light of their impressions of it.

QUESTION: Returning to the question, when is a reply overdue, would you repeat your question to the Egyptian government, say, within a month, or at the end of a month, if a reply is not forthcoming?

THE SECRETARY-GENERAL: You are formalizing the issue far too much. A question raised by me is never abandoned by me; it is kept alive.

QUESTION: On the matter of the financing of the UNEF and the Canal clearance, do you think that is a matter for the Assembly to deal with fairly soon?

THE SECRETARY-GENERAL: I think none of those questions necessarily calls for a meeting of the Assembly soon. As to the Canal, you know there are a limited number of countries which have put up advances, and we can manage what is our responsibility—or rather the responsibility we have undertaken on the basis of those advances. If the governments are not pressing too hard for a very quick decision or very early repayment, I think the sound approach would be that the matter will be settled as early as possible during the twelfth session. But it depends on their view of it. I must say that, so far, they have not shown any impatience. They understand that the issue, although important, is not one in the front line, but that we should take it up in due time and in good order. I certainly feel that none of the Governments which have provided advances would consider the question of such significance as to warrant the reconvening of the eleventh session for special meetings.

As to the UNEF, that question, you know, is a different one. The General Assembly has given sufficient financial authority to keep the UNEF operation going well into the time of the twelfth session. However, there are some—I would not exactly call them legal—but some questions of principle involved which are at present being discussed. I hope that, again, those who are the most interested parties in this case —the contributing governments—will see their way to a solution of those questions of principle which will not render it necessary to have a meeting of the General Assembly again. Again, I would say that it is my strong impression that those governments have a very keen sense of proportion and would not like to create any unnecessary fuss or difficulties which would force all delegations to get together again on what is not an immediately urgent matter.

QUESTION: Could you comment on the story which appeared during Mr. McCloy's visit to Cairo to the effect that the Egyptian government had requested a loan from the United Nations or the International Bank in connection with the equipment of the Canal?

THE SECRETARY-GENERAL: There has been no such request, either directly to me or via Mr. McCloy.

QUESTION: I wonder if you would mind clearing up what may seem to be a very petty point. There were certain mumblings, apparently among some of your aides in Cairo—mumblings which were heard back here —to the effect that Israel had "snubbed" you by not specifically inviting you to come there. Would you care to comment on how you feel about your relationships at this point with the Government of Israel, in view of the fact that they had said that you would be welcome there?

THE SECRETARY-GENERAL: People really are too sensitive on my behalf. I have never considered myself "snubbed." I think that this was a good, sound business relationship, where they very kindly said that I was welcome and where I said that, as matters had developed, I really felt that my most immediate and urgent need was to take up certain talks here. That is the whole story, and those who read into it either a snub by me or a snub by Israel are just too sensitive.

QUESTION: I think that you have said that you are unaware of any revival of the fedayeen organization in the Gaza Strip. Could you tell us whether it would be possible for the UNEF, under the present arrangements, to detect such a development and perhaps act against it?

THE SECRETARY-GENERAL: My reply would be: Yes, under present arrangements. That does not, of course, mean that we can have a watchful eye in every corner. In general terms, however, my reply is: Yes.

QUESTION: In this question, I am trying to establish the trend and direction of the negotiations with regard to the Suez Canal issue. At the present time, the major negotiation seems to be by way of direct talks, through the embassies and otherwise, between Washington and Cairo. I wonder where the Washington talks and Washington's responsibilities for these negotiations begin and whether in the present talks, so far as you know, the United States also speaks for the major users.

THE SECRETARY-GENERAL: My reply to the first question would be this: As matters now stand, the discussion is going on between certain embassies and the government in Cairo. I am kept fully informed; there is no need for me, so to speak, to squeeze myself in between. To the extent that this or that government wants to have my reaction, it gets that reaction—and that is all. That is to say, I am, so to speak, part of the picture but am not engaged in any direct talks or negotiations.

As regards the second point, it is of course for the United States to reply. I think, however, that if you have put the question you should not find it difficult, with your knowledge of the whole development, to see what the reply is likely to be.

QUESTION: I have raised this point only because, as you may be aware, a number of friends of the United Nations of long standing have privately expressed some concern—justifiably or not—over the possibility that in such a complicated arrangement of consultations it is possible for some governments to fail in their negotiations, to blunder, and then to permit the United Nations to "hold the bag" and take the responsibility for their failures. I am not worried about this so long as you are in office, but I am wondering whether you are worried about it.

THE SECRETARY-GENERAL: No, I am not worried about it, although I cannot deny the theoretical possibility. But, you know, there are so many theoretical possibilities in the world that we just cannot afford to go around being worried about them.

QUESTION: Could you give us any report on the progress of the negotiations concerning cooperation between the United Nations Relief and Works Agency and technical assistance agencies, on the one hand, and Egypt, on the other hand, in caring for the people in Gaza?

THE SECRETARY-GENERAL: This is one of the matters which I had no time to cover myself and which was, therefore, left open for further discussion between the Egyptian authorities and Mr. Labouisse as Director of UNRWA and Mr. Bunche as, let us say, personal representative of the Secretary-General. I have no recent reports on developments, but this question—which, as you know, belongs to the last phrase in the much-discussed statement of February 22—is under study.

QUESTION: You helped to work out the six requirements concerning the Suez Canal. One of those requirements was that the Canal should be open to shipping of all nations, without discrimination—overt or covert. Do you consider that this means all nations, regardless of whether Egypt may fail to recognize one of those nations?

THE SECRETARY-GENERAL: I regard that as a direct translation into a Security Council text of the basic principle of the Constantinople Convention. The reply to your question depends upon what is the correct interpretation of the Constantinople Convention.

QUESTION: It is not always easy to tell, from your reports, whether you now enjoy your job. Can you tell us whether you do enjoy your job?

THE SECRETARY-GENERAL: Well, it seems incredible but I do—and I have also enjoyed this press conference. Thank you.

Address on Human Rights and the Work for Peace at the Fiftieth Anniversary Dinner of the American Jewish Committee

NEW YORK   APRIL 10, 1957

THE INVITATION to speak at the fiftieth anniversary dinner of the American Jewish Committee, which was also Hammarskjöld's fourth anniversary as Secretary-General, came at a time when he had been subject to widespread and often sharp criticism both in Israel and among the Jewish community in the United States because of his unequivocal stand against the Suez invasion. His response was to write for the occasion the revealing statement of his personal philosophy in the work for peace and human rights that follows.

Nine days later Hammarskjöld wrote a private letter to Ben-Gurion suggesting a renewal of their direct personal contact after a "long time of silence" and "grave disappointments on both sides." He concluded the letter with these words: "I hope that your Mission in New York has sent you a copy of an address I made about a week ago in the American Jewish Committee. I asked them to do so because, when writing it, I thought of you as my main audience." (See also page 577.)

Early during my time of service at the United Nations I had the privilege of meeting with this Committee for a discussion of human rights. May I say how highly I appreciate your invitation today and your wish to have me take part in this fiftieth anniversary observance, where again you are devoting attention to the development of human rights.

We in the United Nations know well the significant contribution that the American Jewish Committee, through the Consultative Council of Jewish Organizations, has made since 1946 to the work carried on through the United Nations for the advancement and protection of human rights and we pay honor to the spirit of dedication to universal principles which you have shown on so many occasions.

This is an anniversary observance for you. It happens also to be an

UN Press Release SG/585, April 10, 1957.

anniversary for me. And so I hope you will forgive my sharing with you some personal thoughts which also have relevance to the broader issues with which we are all of us concerned.

Four years ago today, I was inducted into my present office, to which I had been catapulted without previous soundings, indeed, without any prewarning. I felt that it was my duty to accept it, not because of any feeling of confidence in my personal capacity to overcome the difficulties which might arise, but because, under the conditions then prevailing, the one to whom the call had come seemed to me in duty bound to respond.

The situation that faced me at the very outset has proved not to be unique. It has been repeated several times in the past few years, most recently in relation to problems of the Middle East. The other day, returning from the latest visit to that area on a UN mission, I read a book by Arthur Waley—certainly well known to many of you as one of the great interpreters of Chinese thought and literature and as one of those great Jewish students of humane letters who have so splendidly enriched our cultural tradition. In his work Waley quotes what an early Chinese historian had to say about the philosopher Sung Tzu and his followers, some 350 years B.C. To one who works in the United Nations, the quotation strikes a familiar note. It runs as follows:

Constantly rebuffed but never discouraged, they went round from state to state helping people to settle their differences, arguing against wanton attack and pleading for the suppression of arms, that the age in which they lived might be saved from its state of continual war. To this end they interviewed princes and lectured the common people, nowhere meeting with any great success, but obstinately persisting in their task, till kings and commoners alike grew weary of listening to them. Yet undeterred they continued to force themselves on people's attention.[1]

Is this a description of a quixotic group, whose efforts are doomed to failure? The wording, with its tone of frustration, may lead us to think so. However, I believe that this interpretation would be wrong. The historian tells us about a group engaged in a struggle he considers very much worth while and one which will have to go on until success is achieved.

The half-ironical, half-sad note which he strikes indicates only his knowledge of the difficulties which human nature puts in the way of

[1] Arthur Waley, *The Way and Its Power*, George Allen and Unwin Ltd., 1934, p. 90.

such work for peace. His pessimism is tempered by the mild sense of humor and the strong sense of proportion of a man seeing his own time in the long perspective of history. We can learn from his attitude, both in our efforts to move towards peace and in our work for universal recognition of human rights.

We know that the question of peace and the question of human rights are closely related. Without recognition of human rights we shall never have peace, and it is only within the framework of peace that human rights can be fully developed.

In fact, the work for peace is basically a work for the most elementary of human rights: the right of everyone to security and to freedom from fear. We, therefore, recognize it as one of the first duties of a government to take measures in order to safeguard for its citizens this very right. But we also recognize it as an obligation for the emerging world community to assist governments in safeguarding this elementary human right without having to lock themselves in behind the walls of arms.

The dilemma of our age, with its infinite possibilities of self-destruction, is how to grow out of the world of armaments into a world of international security, based on law. We are only at the very beginning of such a change. The natural distrust in the possibility of progress is nourished by unavoidable setbacks and, when distrust is thus strengthened, this in turn increases our difficulties.

The effort may seem hopeless. It will prove hopeless unless we, all of us, show the persistence of Sung Tzu and his followers, and unless peoples and governments alike are willing to take smaller immediate risks in order to have a better chance to avoid the final disaster threatening us if we do not manage to turn the course of developments in a new direction.

The United Nations finds itself in a difficult stage of its development. It is still too weak to provide the security desired by all, while being strong enough and alive enough effectively to point out the direction in which the solution must be sought. In its present phase the Organization may look to many like a preacher who cannot impose the law he states or realize the gospel he interprets. It is understandable if those who have this impression turn away in distrust or with cynical criticism, forgetting that setbacks in efforts to implement an ideal do not prove that the ideal is wrong, and overlooking also that at the beginning of great changes in human society there must always be a stage of such frailty or seeming inconsistency.

It is easy to say that it is pointless to state the law if it cannot be enforced. However, to do so is to forget that if the law is the inescapable law of the future, it would be treason to the future not to state the law simply because of the difficulties of the present. Indeed, how could it ever become a living reality if those who are responsible for its development were to succumb to the immediate difficulties arising when it is still a revolutionary element in the life of society? The history of the Jewish people offers some of the most magnificent examples of how ideals and law may be brought to victory through courageous assertion of new universal principles which the wise call folly when they are first introduced in a society shaped on a different pattern.

The thoughts I have tried to express apply to practically the whole field of United Nations activities, but in particular to the work of the Organization for the implementation of the principles of the Charter in the fields of international security and disarmament and in the field of fundamental human rights. They apply likewise to the United Nations itself as an experiment in international organization.

But is not an experiment something tentative and passing? And should not the United Nations be regarded as something definite and lasting? I think it is important to be clear on this point. Certainly the experiences and achievements of the United Nations as it is today are helping us to build the future. The United Nations is something definite also in the sense that the concepts and ideals it represents, like the needs it tries to meet, will remain an ineluctable element of the world picture. However, that does not mean that the present embodiment of the groping efforts of mankind towards an organized world community represents a definite shape for all time. The United Nations is, and should be, a living, evolving, experimental institution. If it should ever cease to be so it should be revolutionized or swept aside for a new approach.

The growth of social institutions is always one where, step by step, the form which adequately meets the need is shaped through selection, or out of experience. Thus an effort that has not yielded all the results hoped for has not failed if it has provided positive experience on which a new approach can be based. An attempt which has proved the possibility of progress has served the cause of progress even if it has had to be renewed again and again, and in new forms or setting in order to yield full success.

When we look back over the experiences in the United Nations over the past few months, we may differ amongst ourselves as to the wisdom of this or that particular stand and we may have doubts about the end result of this or that step. But I think we all can agree on the value and historical importance of certain developments.

First of all, it proved possible in an emergency to create for the first time a truly international force. This force, although modest in size and, for constitutional reasons, also modest in aim, broke new ground which inevitably will count in future efforts to preserve peace and promote justice.

I think we can likewise agree that the fact that the United Nations could undertake and carry through a major field operation like the clearance of the Suez Canal, where no government was in a position to accomplish the task, indicated possibilities for international organization which, once proven, cannot in the future be disregarded.

Finally, deeply regrettable though the conflicts of views and interests were, it should not be forgotten that those who now feel they had to sacrifice for the maintenance of a principle, in a different situation may be the first to profit from the fact that the principle was maintained. As individuals we know that the law which restrains us likewise protects us. The same holds true in international life.

Some moments ago I referred to the fact that lasting peace is not possible without recognition of fundamental human rights and that human rights cannot reach their full development unless there is peace. The United Nations cannot lay down the law for the life within any national community. Those laws have to be established in accordance with the will of the people as expressed in the forms indicated by their chosen constitution. But just as the United Nations can promote peace, so it can, in joint deliberations, define the goals of human rights which should be the laws of the future in each nation. Whatever the distance between these goals and the everyday reality we meet all around the world, it is not vain thus to set the targets as they present themselves to the most mature political thinking of our age.

The Universal Declaration of Human Rights, adopted by the General Assembly nine years ago, is not, of course, a treaty and has in itself no force of law, but as "a common standard of achievement for all peoples and all nations" it crystallizes the political thought of our times on these matters in a way influencing the thinking of legislators all over the world. The relationship of man to society is a relationship for which every generation must seek to find a proper form. In a world where the memory is still fresh of some of the worst infringements on human rights ever experienced in history, the Declaration should give direction to those who now carry the responsibility for a sound development of society.

You well know that the United Nations has for years struggled with the problem how to translate the Declaration of Human Rights into the text of an international convention or conventions. It is not surprising that in a world with very different cultural traditions, and among countries showing very different degrees of advancement of social institutions, such a translation has proved difficult. But the failure so far to reach agreement over the whole field should not lead us to believe that the work to realize the fundamental human rights has come to a standstill. The decisive fact in the end will not be the translation of principles into the text of an international convention, but the transformation of society through growing recognition of the principles in the life of the peoples.

You have put "the pursuit of equality at home and abroad" as a motto of your anniversary. Interpreted in a broad sense these words reflect a basic human right, equal in significance to the right to security and freedom from fear.

I had, last year, the privilege of visiting a couple of kibbutzim in Israel and of talking to people coming from many lands, who were devoting their lives to these courageous experiments in practical and total democracy. I looked upon them as fellow workers in an "experiment in progress." Through such experiments alone can progress be achieved.

I also remember experiences of experiments in community development in India. There I met the same enthusiasm, the same devotion, the same idealism as in the kibbutzim. Yet, how different a situation it was! In one case there were people, stepping out of their Western societies of highly organized and specialized industrial life in order to create new collectives, pioneering in the building up of a strong economic life on a barren soil. In the other case, communities which, although living in a rich land, so far had remained poor for the lack of the revolutionary development carried to fruition by Western individualism, but the members of which now devoted all their energy toward taking the giant step into the economic and social world of today.

In both cases we meet a realization in practice of basic human rights. The difference, however, indicates the diversity of the problem and this calls for great flexibility in our approach and in the choice of the ways in which the various societies may become integrated into a world community.

The underlying problems now making the Middle East such a troubled area, should be understood partly in the terms of which these two experiments in community development may serve as illustrations. They lend special weight to the undertaking of the Member Nations in the Charter "to practice tolerance."

The words just quoted from the Charter are among those which link its text to a great ethical tradition. They are often overlooked, sometimes brushed aside as empty ornaments without political significance, sometimes honored by lip service. However, they represent an element without which the Charter and the system it creates would disintegrate. Both the work for peace and the work for human rights must be anchored in and inspired by a general approach which gives balance and substance to the results. Peace cannot be enforced for selfish reasons, equality cannot be imposed as an abstract concept. In fact, attempts to do so account for some of the darkest episodes in history.

The work for peace must be animated by tolerance and the work for human rights by respect for the individual. A student of the growth of human rights through the ages will recognize its close relationship to the development of tolerance inspired by intellectual liberalism or, perhaps more often, by ethical concepts of religious origin. Attempts are made to link the development of human rights exclusively to the liberal ideas which broke through to predominance in the age of enlightenment. However, to do so means to me to overlook the historical background of those ideas. It means also cutting our ties to a source of strength that we need in order to carry the work for human rights to fruition and to give to those rights, when established, their fitting spiritual content.

To some, the word "tolerance" may sound strange in a time of "cold war" and of negotiations "from positions of strength"; it may have an overtone of meekness or appeasement. And yet, have we reason to believe that what was true in the past is no longer true? It is not the weak but the strong who practice tolerance, and the strong do not weaken their position in showing tolerance. On the contrary, only through tolerance can they justify their strength in the face of those counteracting forces that their own strength automatically sets in motion.

I am sure that this holds true of all those in the present world situation who may be, or may consider themselves to be "strong," be it the industrialized West in relation to the underdeveloped countries, be it the powers whose military resources give them key positions, be it those who have achieved a state of democracy and of recognition of human rights toward which others are still groping.

I remember in this context words from another translation by Arthur Waley—this time from Tao Te Ching. Its paradoxical form and mystical background should not lead us to overlook its realism: "Heaven arms with pity those whom it would not see destroyed."

Over the ages and over the continents, these words join with those of the psalmist: "There is mercy with Thee; therefore shalt Thou be feared."

FROM TRANSCRIPTS OF
PRESS CONFERENCES

APRIL–JUNE 1957

DURING THE three weeks that had elapsed since the Secretary-General's last press conference the United States was no more successful than Hammarskjöld had been in persuading the Egyptian government to reopen negotiations toward a new international agreement on the operation of the Suez Canal. President Nasser remained determined on the unilateral course foreshadowed in the March 18 Memorandum. Acting in his capacity as trusted consultant behind the scenes to both Egypt and the users, the Secretary-General then tried his influence in behalf of language in the forthcoming Egyptian Declaration which would make it more nearly acceptable as an international instrument to the Western powers and, as he frankly told Foreign Minister Fawzi, to himself as well. He had some success, especially in strengthening the Egyptian commitment to binding arbitration and in reaffirming Egypt's earlier endorsement of the Six Requirements of the Security Council's resolution of October 13, 1956. However, he was not able to persuade Egypt to indicate that the Declaration was intended as an interim document, pending later negotiation of a multilateral instrument. Nor did he succeed in an effort to make of the Declaration a more two-sided affair through a procedure by which the General Assembly, on behalf of the United Nations, would later formally take note of the Egyptian commitment.

The texts of the Declaration, Fawzi's covering letter and Hammarskjöld's response were as follows.[1]

Letter from the Minister for Foreign Affairs of Egypt
to the Secretary-General, Transmitting the Declaration of
the Egyptian Government, Dated April 24, 1957, Concerning
the Suez Canal and the Arrangements for its Operation

April 24, 1957

The Government of Egypt are pleased to announce that the Suez Canal is now open for normal traffic and will thus once again serve as a link between the nations of the world in the cause of peace and prosperity.

The Government of Egypt wish to acknowledge with appreciation and gratitude the efforts of the states and peoples of the world who

[1] Security Council Official Records, Twelfth Year, Supplement for April-May-June 1957, Documents S/3818, April 24, 1957, and S/3819, April 25, 1957.

contributed to the restoration of the Canal for normal traffic, and of the United Nations whose exertions made it possible that the clearance of the Canal be accomplished peacefully and in a short time.

On March 18, 1957, the Government of Egypt set forth in a memorandum basic principles relating to the Suez Canal and the arrangements for its operation. The memorandum contemplated a further detailed statement on the subject. In pursuance of the above, I have the honour to enclose a copy of the Declaration made today by the Government of Egypt in fulfillment of their participation in the Constantinople Convention of 1888, noting their understanding of the Security Council resolution of October 13, 1956, and in line with their statements relating to it before the Council.

I have the honour to invite Your Excellency's attention to the last paragraph of the Declaration which provides that it will be deposited and registered with the Secretariat of the United Nations. The Declaration, with the obligations therein, constitutes an international instrument and the Government of Egypt request that you kindly receive and register it accordingly.

MAHMOUD FAWZI
Minister for Foreign
Affairs of Egypt

Declaration

In elaboration of the principles set forth in their memorandum dated March 18, 1957, the Government of the Republic of Egypt, in accord with the Constantinople Convention of 1888 and the Charter of the United Nations, make hereby the following Declaration on the Suez Canal and the arrangements for its operation.

1. *Reaffirmation of the Convention*

It remains the unaltered policy and firm purpose of the Government of Egypt to respect the terms and the spirit of the Constantinople Convention of 1888 and the rights and obligations arising therefrom. The Government of Egypt will continue to respect, observe, and implement them.

2. *Observance of the Convention and of the Charter of the United Nations*

While reaffirming their determination to respect the terms and the spirit of the Constantinople Convention of 1888 and to abide by the Charter and the principles and purposes of the United Nations, the

Government of Egypt are confident that the other signatories of the said Convention and all others concerned will be guided by the same resolve.

3. *Freedom of navigation, tolls, and development of the Canal*

The Government of Egypt are more particularly determined:

(*a*) To afford and maintain free and uninterrupted navigation for all nations within the limits of and in accordance with the provisions of the Constantinople Convention of 1888;

(*b*) That tolls shall continue to be levied in accordance with the last agreement, concluded on April 28, 1936, between the Government of Egypt and the Suez Canal Maritime Company, and that any increase in the current rate of tolls within any twelve months, if it takes place, shall be limited to 1 percent, any increase beyond that level to be the result of negotiations, and, failing agreement, be settled by arbitration according to the procedure set forth in paragraph 7 (*b*);

(*c*) That the Canal is maintained and developed in accordance with the progressive requirements of modern navigation and that such maintenance and development shall include the eighth and ninth programmes of the Suez Canal Maritime Company with such improvements to them as are considered necessary.

4. *Operation and Management*

The Canal will be operated and managed by the autonomous Suez Canal Authority established by the Government of Egypt on July 26, 1956. The Government of Egypt are looking forward with confidence to continued cooperation with the nations of the world in advancing the usefulness of the Canal. To that end the Government of Egypt would welcome and encourage cooperation between the Suez Canal Authority and representatives of shipping and trade.

5. *Financial arrangements*

(*a*) Tolls shall be payable in advance to the account of the Suez Canal Authority at any bank as may be authorized by it. In pursuance of this, the Suez Canal Authority has authorized the National Bank of Egypt and is negotiating with the Bank of International Settlement to accept on its behalf payment of the Canal tolls.

(*b*) The Suez Canal Authority shall pay to the Government of Egypt 5 percent of all the gross receipts as royalty.

(*c*) The Suez Canal Authority will establish a Suez Canal Capital and Development Fund into which shall be paid 25 percent of all gross receipts. This Fund will assure that there shall be available to the Suez Canal Authority adequate resources to meet the needs of development and capital expenditure for the fulfillment of the responsibilities they have assumed and are fully determined to discharge.

6. *Canal Code*

The regulations governing the Canal, including the details of its operation, are embodied in the Canal Code which is the law of the Canal. Due notice will be given of any alteration in the Code, and any such alteration, if it affects the principles and commitments in this Declaration and is challenged or complained against for that reason, shall be dealt with in accordance with the procedure set forth in paragraph 7(*b*).

7. *Discrimination and complaints relating to the Canal Code*

(*a*) In pursuance of the principles laid down in the Constantinople Convention of 1888, the Suez Canal Authority, by the terms of its Charter, can in no case grant any vessel, company, or other party any advantage or favour not accorded to other vessels, companies, or parties on the same conditions.

(*b*) Complaints of discrimination or violation of the Canal Code shall be sought to be resolved by the complaining party by reference to the Suez Canal Authority. In the event that such a reference does not resolve the complaint, the matter may be referred, at the option of the complaining party or the Authority, to an arbitration tribunal composed of one nominee of the complaining party, one of the Authority, and a third to be chosen by both. In case of disagreement, such third member will be chosen by the President of the International Court of Justice upon the application of either party.

(*c*) The decisions of the arbitration tribunal shall be made by a majority of its members. The decisions shall be binding upon the parties when they are rendered and they must be carried out in good faith.

(*d*) The Government of Egypt will study further appropriate arrangements that could be made for fact-finding, consultation, and arbitration on complaints relating to the Canal Code.

8. *Compensation and claims*

The question of compensation and claims in connection with the nationalization of the Suez Canal Maritime Company shall, unless agreed between the parties concerned, be referred to arbitration in accordance with the established international practice.

9. *Disputes, disagreements or differences arising out of the Convention and this Declaration*

(*a*) Disputes or disagreements arising in respect of the Constantinople Convention of 1888 or this Declaration shall be settled in accordance with the Charter of the United Nations.

(*b*) Differences arising between the parties to the said Convention in respect of the interpretation or the applicability of its provisions, if not otherwise resolved, will be referred to the International Court of Justice. The Government of Egypt would take the necessary steps in order to accept the compulsory jurisdiction of the International Court of Justice in conformity with the provisions of article 36 of its Statute.

10. *Status of this Declaration*

The Government of Egypt make this Declaration, which reaffirms and is in full accord with the terms and spirit of the Constantinople Convention of 1888, as an expression of their desire and determination to enable the Suez Canal to be an efficient and adequate waterway linking the nations of the world and serving the cause of peace and prosperity.

This Declaration, with the obligations therein, constitutes an international instrument and will be deposited and registered with the Secretariat of the United Nations.

Letter from the Secretary-General to the Minister for Foreign Affairs of Egypt

April 24, 1957

I have the honour to acknowledge the receipt of your letter of April 24, 1957, transmitting for deposit the original of a Declaration dated April 24, 1957, on the Suez Canal and the arrangements for its operation.

Pursuant to your request, the original of the Declaration has been deposited in the archives of the United Nations.

I have noted that the Declaration has also been transmitted for the purpose of registration. I understand that the Government of Egypt consider that the Declaration constitutes an engagement of an international character coming within the scope of Article 102 of the Charter, and therefore registration has been effected in accordance with Article 1 of the regulations to give effect to that article. The certificate of registration will be forwarded to you in due course.

Your letter, together with the Declaration, will be circulated as a document of the General Assembly and the Security Council.

DAG HAMMARSKJÖLD
Secretary-General

There was no reference in these communications to the use of the Canal by Israeli shipping, but the Egyptian government had indicated quite clearly in recent days its intention to continue its restrictions, relying as before on the ambiguous exception for security reasons included in the Constantinople Convention. When the Secretary-General met the press on April 25 there were more questions on this particular aspect than on the general issue between Egypt and the Western users of the Canal.

Correspondents whose questions reflected the Israeli point of view were always well represented at the United Nations. On this occasion it may be noted that some questions were so orchestrated as to prompt the Secretary-General to remark that his press conference was "developing into a parliament with consecutive questions." He quickly added that he did not mind at all and proceeded to a firm rejection of charges of a dual standard and a clarifying discussion of the effect of the Security Council's 1951 decision in relation to the armistice régime and the role of the International Court in relation to the Constantinople Convention.

---

1. From Transcript of Press Conference

UN HEADQUARTERS, NEW YORK   APRIL 25, 1957

. . . . QUESTION: Mr. Secretary-General, in view of the request yesterday by the Government of Egypt to register the declaration and the arrangements on the Suez Canal as an international instrument, I wonder if you can tell us just what an international instrument is. What makes an instrument international?

THE SECRETARY-GENERAL: That is really a question for lawyers. But I think I can give you some background in order to help you understand better what the situation is.

First of all I can tell you that it was registered and this was done in line with United Nations legislation. There was nothing new or remarkable in that. Article 102 of the Charter provides for registration of international treaties and agreements as a must. However, in order to understand the article, you have to go back into its history. It goes back, of course, to the San Francisco Conference where they discussed to what extent there should be such registration. Their report made it per-

UN Note to Correspondents No. 1590, April 25, 1957.

fectly clear that the Committee which proposed this text had also in mind what it called "unilateral engagements of an international character." I think that expression is a good one because it does mean that if some country wants to tie its hands by declaring that it intends to act in a certain way in relation to the world community and other nations, it can go on record with that as a unilateral engagement of an international character.

The matter was also considered later in committees here at the General Assembly, and then it has been made perfectly clear that in this respect agreement should be read in the very wide sense of including also unilateral declarations. In fact various types of unilateral declarations have been registered in the past.

There is another point, however, which I think you may have observed or which at all events should be observed in this context. We publish a monthly statement on agreements under Article 102 which are registered by the United Nations. That monthly statement is prefaced by a note by the Secretariat which explains the character of registration. What is said in that text is of course decisive for the interpretation of the present situation and for the effect of the registration of the Egyptian Declaration. It did not require very much imagination on my side to anticipate this question from you or from one of your colleagues so I brought the text of this standing introduction, which I would like to read to you because I think it is the best explanation I can give. This, I repeat, is the explanation given in every single monthly statement:

However, since the terms "treaty" and "international agreement" have not been defined either in the Charter or in the regulations, the Secretariat under the Charter and the regulations follows the principle that it acts in accordance with the position of the Member state submitting an instrument for registration, and that so far as that party is concerned the instrument is a treaty or an international agreement within the meaning of Article 102.

There is also a statement in the introductory note to the effect that registration as such does in no way change the legal character of a document. The status such a document has it has independently of registration.

Then you may well ask: What does it mean that we register it? In a case like this one, my interpretation is that it does mean that it is put on official United Nations record that the government—in this case the Government of Egypt—which submits the unilateral engagement, unilateral declaration, itself regards that declaration as an international engagement in relation to those who are the interested parties in the story; that is to say, this does not define the nature of the document from the point of view of the other nations, but it does put on record the character of the document as interpreted by the country submitting it for registration.

You can very well see that what is said here in the introductory note is more or less a matter of course. If a country comes to us and says, "We regard ourselves as bound by this Declaration," who are we to say, "You are not"?

I think that is a fairly complete reply. Mr. Stavropoulos is here, and if his professional expertise disagrees with me he might perhaps correct me.

MR. STAVROPOULOS: You could not have made a better exposé, sir. If I may, I should like to add something with regard to the question asked before: What is an international instrument? Of course, it is difficult to make a definition, but it is an instrument which has an international effect, and that is what the present international instrument is.

QUESTION: Could I ask a rather abstract question about the claim of belligerency and its relation to the Charter? I should like to ask you today about the specific case of Egypt, which not only holds a position of no peace but asserts and exercises active rights of belligerency, although these rights were explicitly ruled out by the Security Council resolution of September 1951. Do you think that this type of belligerency is consistent with Charter obligations? Secondly, last time you indicated that the requirement laid down by the Security Council for keeping the Canal open to all nations without discrimination should be read in the light of the correct interpretation of the corresponding articles of the Constantinople Convention. Who in your view would be qualified to give this correct interpretation? Don't you believe that the Security Council resolution of 1951 prohibiting the blocking of the Canal to Israeli shipping has a standing of its own quite independent of any interpretation of the Convention?

THE SECRETARY-GENERAL: I note with very great interest that this gathering is developing into a parliament with consecutive questions. Why not? As we have no other parliament in which I am, so to say, responsible in this peculiar way, I do not mind it in any sense.

On the first point, I think the reply is a very simple one. A ruling by the Security Council is the law, at least for the Secretary-General. That is irrespective of any article of the Charter. I think that is a fairly complete reply to the factual question you asked this time as a follow-up to the very general question you asked last time.

As to authority to interpret the Convention, I think that you have a reply in a sense in the very Declaration which Egypt tabled yesterday where they referred to the International Court at The Hague. It is certainly a case where a legal conflict, or a difference concerning the legal issues, can properly be brought before the International Court.

QUESTION: Could I follow that question for just a second by asking you what the Secretary-General is doing or plans to do to get compliance from Egypt on the 1951 resolution, which you say you regard as the law for you?

THE SECRETARY-GENERAL: I think I have done everything I can do as an officer of the law with the authority the Secretary-General has under the Charter, which, as you know, is in various respects limited. I am not a policeman with a gun, or anything like that. I can use what the Secretary-General is supposed to use: the diplomatic means available to any diplomatic representative. If you want to call it persuasion, that is one possible term. Anyway I have done what I can in order to implement those decisions.

QUESTION: Would you care to tell us a little more specifically what those things are?

THE SECRETARY-GENERAL: Don't you think that is going a little beyond what is normal?

QUESTION: Not in a parliament, sir.

QUESTION: In this question of belligerency, it seems that a double standard has been raised in that Egypt is exercising belligerent rights, their refusal to allow Israeli shipping through the Canal being such an exercise. But Israel, when it exercises belligerent rights under provocation, is condemned. Is there not a double standard being set up here, and do you not have the way written into the Charter for you as the Secretary-General to bring this to the notice of the Security Council when there is such a danger to peace being created?

THE SECRETARY-GENERAL: In fact, your question brings us very deeply into the whole problem of the Middle East. I think, although this is perhaps not the best forum for a discussion of such rather complicated issues, it might be necessary to go back to some basic notions here. I think that everybody agrees that as long as there is no peace agreement, or peace settlement, the situation is ruled by the Armistice Agreement as such—that is the only legal document there—plus, of course, the Charter.

Rights exercised cannot be rights contrary to the Armistice Agreement, with this or that kind of interpretation of the Armistice Agreement. When the Security Council said that Egypt could not interfere with shipping, it based that in the first instance on an interpretation of the armistice régime as established by the Armistice Agreement. Of course, the finding made by the Security Council has an independent value. It is a high organ of the United Nations, and its findings are definitely independent facts. But this was the content of what was said: such interference was contrary to an armistice régime. That is to say, in that respect, to use the terminology you use now, they felt that, if there were any rights which could be called belligerent rights, they did not include, according to their interpretation of the armistice régime, this right to interfere with the shipping.

You are fully aware of the fact that this is not in any sense the only point on which the parties are in a state of noncompliance with the armistice régime or with the Armistice Agreement. I say "the parties" because there is no difference in that respect between the parties. There are various forms, various degrees, of noncompliance, but noncompliance is widespread. If you mean by "acts of belligerency" acts which are not only acts excused by the fact that there is no peace settlement but acts contrary to the legal state of affairs in the region, I think that you should under such acts include acts of noncompliance. Going back to your basic question, I, for that reason, do not feel it is justified in the way you did to talk about a dual standard. I think that the standard maintained by the United Nations is one where, with the means available, we try to get a compliance with the Armistice Agreement and the armistice régime all around. We do it, I think, with the highest degree of impartiality that we find possible. That is at least the spirit in which we work, and I hope it is properly understood and interpreted in that spirit.

QUESTION: Mr. Secretary-General, since the Egyptian Declaration has been registered officially with the United Nations, which makes it a binding instrument as far as Egypt is concerned, does that not mean that this cannot be changed by Egypt, that this is Egypt's final terms and that, therefore, no further negotiation is possible? Secondly, in your view, does this instrument conform entirely with the Six Principles laid down by the Security Council last October?

THE SECRETARY-GENERAL: As to the last question, I think you will excuse me for not going into a discussion, as the matter is going to be debated tomorrow in the Security Council. As undoubtedly this point will be raised there, I think it would not be proper for me to discuss it here in anticipation.

As to the first point, my understanding of the legal situation is that the registration as such does not make the document irrevocable, because it is, as you said yourself, binding upon the party submitting it, with the character they have given to the document itself. That is to say, in that sense, it can be superseded either by another declaration or by an agreement.

. . . . QUESTION: If I may refer to the Constantinople Convention, Article IV opens with this statement: "The maritime canal remaining open in time of war as a free passage even to the ships of war of belligerents, according to the terms of Article I. . . ." My question is: Am I to understand that to mean that, on the basis of Article I, even ships of belligerent nations may use the Canal?

THE SECRETARY-GENERAL: That is a matter of international debate, because there is in the same Convention a reference to security. How those who once drafted the Convention put these various aspects together and made them a logical whole, I cannot tell. It is exactly the kind of question on which the International Court would be competent to judge.

QUESTION: You said that yesterday's declaration by Egypt can be superseded by another declaration. Does this, in connection with what you said about international instruments, imply that Egypt can change this declaration unilaterally?

THE SECRETARY-GENERAL: Not short of observing the same procedure. If a country makes a unilateral declaration and gets it registered here, the registration has the effect that the declaration can be invoked by other Member countries as a valid international document. That is to say, it remains valid until and unless it is formally revoked in the same form.

QUESTION: By the same government?

THE SECRETARY-GENERAL: By the same government. That is to say, as long as it stands registered here, it is a binding international instrument.

QUESTION: But Egypt can revoke it any day?

THE SECRETARY-GENERAL: Egypt is entitled to revoke it as long as it remains a purely unilateral instrument.

. . . . QUESTION: You were credited with playing a major role in having broken the deadlock which at one point showed during the Suez negotiations between Egypt and the United States. Since your last press conference the role you have played seems to have changed to a very large extent in the Suez talks. Would you care to comment about your efforts in this field, particularly to what extent the views you communicated to the Egyptian government were reflected in the latest declaration made yesterday?

THE SECRETARY-GENERAL: I would not like to go into any detail as I do not think that that would in any way be proper. There has in fact not been any change in my role. I have not been a negotiating party. I have, on the other hand, been in a relationship of close contact on the basis of mutual confidence with both Egypt and the United States; that is to say, I have had the useful position of being able to comment on both sides, to make suggestions, to give advice, if it is of any value. To what extent it has been of value is for others to judge. I would not like to go into the matter.

QUESTION: I should like to follow up the previous question. The question spoke of a deadlock being broken which implies an agreement having been arrived at. Do you see a deadlock as having been broken and do you see an agreement as having been arrived at?

THE SECRETARY-GENERAL: May I, on this point, embark on a very dangerous role and criticize the press. You use such rather drastic language and my own language as you know, is rather flat. I would never have used the word "deadlock." I would not use the other word either.

QUESTION: Mr. Secretary-General, can you tell us of any prospects which may exist for changing the revocable character of Egypt's Declaration and giving all the parts of it a multilateral character which might be less revocable?

THE SECRETARY-GENERAL: Well, the obvious way to get out of a unilateral agreement into something irrevocable, or irrevocable short of agreement, is of course to change it to a multilateral agreement. In order to get into a multilateral agreement, you will have to have other parties which agree to the text. That is to say, the natural process is one where the declaration, with or without changes, after further consultations or after negotiations, is, so to say, mutually approved in an international context, thus changing it into an agreement in the regular sense of the word. Then of course it is irrevocable unless the other parties agree to revoke it.

. . . . QUESTION: Mr. Secretary-General, inasmuch as this Declaration accepts arbitration procedures and a compulsory jurisdiction of the World Court, do you foresee the possibility that the question of Israel's use of the Suez Canal might be referred to these procedures?

THE SECRETARY-GENERAL: My reply would be "yes," but I am no authority on it because there are higher bodies which can decide on that issue. There are the governments concerned which can decide on it. But as a reasonably well-informed observer, my reply would be "yes."

QUESTION: Your brief announcements of the recent meetings of the Advisory Committee on the UNEF have mentioned—that is the only topic they have mentioned—the financing of the Force, from which some of us assume there must be a problem. What is the problem in connection with the financing of the Emergency Force?

THE SECRETARY-GENERAL: In general terms, this one: When we got started everything was, as you know, improvised and had to be improvised because we had to get going in a very few days. Then I introduced a very general formula that the contributing countries should carry the burden or pay the costs for equipment and salaries. Nobody knew the time this operation might last, and for that reason nobody could say exactly what this burden meant in economic terms.

Now we have had it going for half a year and that of course makes it necessary to look at the system we applied. And it may be felt that such costs are quite considerable for those governments which contribute and that it is unreasonable that they should just continue to agree to pay all those costs which we had in mind at the very beginning. It would mean they would make contributions voluntarily to this specific branch of United Nations activities which exceed by far their contributions to the Organization as such. I think everybody can recognize that, at a certain point, that becomes unreasonable.

Now we have a kind of half-year turnover of the troops and for this reason after half a year it is reasonable to look at the problem of finance. That is the problem which has been discussed with the contributing governments and the Advisory Committee. It is no new headache; it is just something which necessarily comes up as the operation extends in time. Why should those eight or ten governments carry this burden without wider distribution of financial responsibility, at least when we come to the stage where their initial promises must be considered as exhausted, so to speak, when we have come to the point which goes beyond what they had any firm reason to anticipate when they first decided on their contributions? That is the whole story.

. . . . QUESTION: I would like to go back to the Gaza question for a moment. As you know, Israel has sent in at least two letters recently expressing concern over incursions and incidents along the border. I should like to ask first, has the Advisory Committee considered possible measures to stop this? Secondly, do you think it would be useful for the Advisory Committee to send a subcommittee or some smaller group there to look into this question?

THE SECRETARY-GENERAL: The Advisory Committee is fully seized of all the information we have from this or other sources and from our own people out in the field and has of course considered it and evaluated it. I may get back to the question of substance in a moment.

First I would like to reply to the second part of your question. As I share the responsibility for this administration with the Advisory Committee, I would consider it personally most helpful to have some kind of visit of members or a group from the Advisory Committee to the region. That is a personal opinion, it is obviously for the Committee to decide, but I repeat it: personally I would welcome it because this is a shared responsibility, it is a fruitful cooperation and if they felt that first-hand impressions and first-hand discussion would help them in that cooperation, I would be the first one to encourage them to go.

But I would like to add one word concerning these various incursions. I hope that when you read the information which is available you give some thought to the character of the incursions. I think it is highly illuminating if you study it. Sometimes—and I quite understand that it is easy to have slips of the pen—they are called, in headlines or in other texts, raids. I think that if you look at what has really happened according to these various reports, you cannot under any circumstances use the name raids for them. Incursions is a technical and dull term but I think it properly describes what is happening. I think it is essential to keep that in mind because it certainly does not help either the United Nations in its effort to establish orderly conditions and maintain peaceful relations in the area, or any of the parties, when the significance of these various things is, so to speak, exaggerated by descriptions which lead the thought in different and much more dangerous directions.

QUESTION: In a speech made during the past week, Mr. Dulles laid great emphasis upon the United Nations. In recently published letters, Premier Bulganin of the Soviet Union has had much to say, in the way of sermons, lectures, and other declarations, on the importance of the United Nations. In view of the fact that these two powers represent the ultimate polarity of power in the world today and that they probably—in fact, certainly—did not get together and agree upon these avowals of love, what long-range significance do you think that there is in the placing of so much emphasis by these two powers on the United Nations? What long-range importance has that for the world organization?

THE SECRETARY-GENERAL: I might perhaps say—and I do not think I would be exaggerating in any way in saying this—that, from our point of view, the importance of these various statements is that they should drive home to the man-in-the-street and to other governments that these very powerful governments consider the added element of multilateral diplomacy, the added techniques which are provided by the United Nations, as an essential tool in the effort to make some kind of progress. You see that I avoid talking about the United Nations as an organization: I talk about the facilities provided by the United Nations, even to these very powerful governments. It is food for thought that they regard these methods as useful, and indeed necessary.

. . . .

THE SECURITY COUNCIL met twice on April 26 at the request of the United States for a preliminary discussion of the Egyptian Declaration. A majority of the members considered that it did not fully meet the six requirements of the October 13, 1956, resolution. The principal criticisms concerned the failure to provide for an organized system of cooperation between Egypt and the users of the Canal and the unilateral nature of the Declaration. Georges-Picot of France and Sir Pierson Dixon of Great Britain, in particular, asserted that an international undertaking of this unilateral character could be unilaterally amended or withdrawn at will and renewed their call for a negotiated multilateral agreement. Ambassador Urrutia of Colombia and General Romulo of the Philippines, on the other hand, thought that the articles on arbitration, the Constantinople Convention and the jurisdiction of the International Court constituted irrevocable undertakings binding on Egypt and that other provisions pointed to further negotiations. They considered the Declaration a step forward in the right direction. For the United States Ambassador Lodge agreed that the Declaration did not fully meet the six requirements but much would depend on how the Declaration was implemented; the Council should remain seized of the question, he said, while the Declaration was given a trial. The Secretary-General was silent at the meeting, no resolution was offered, and the Council did not meet again on the question until May 20.

Early in May a meeting of the Suez Canal Users Association resulted in criticism, but not rejection of the Declaration and a decision to leave up to individual member nations of SCUA, the question of resuming use of the Canal under the Egyptian regulations. By the middle of the month, when the Macmillan government decided to permit British ships to use the Canal, France was left alone in maintaining a boycott. The government of Mollet and Pineau was most unhappy and so was the die-hard wing of the Conservative party in Britain.

In the meantime Hammarskjöld had received a private appeal from Selwyn Lloyd for help in persuading Egypt to further clarify its position on the question of amending or withdrawing its Declaration. The Secretary-General sent a private letter to Fawzi in which he said it was his own impression that Egypt intended the Declaration to be of a sanctity similar to the Constantinople Convention or a multilateral agreement. If so, he considered that unilateral amendment or withdrawal would be incompatible with the spirit in which the Declaration had been submitted and he urged the value of a clarifying public statement to this effect as soon as possible.

Fawzi had not responded to this suggestion nor had he sent the required letter accepting the compulsory jurisdiction of the International Court in fulfillment of paragraph 9(*b*) of the Declaration when the Security Council reopened its discussion in two meetings May 20 and 21 at the request of France.

Pineau was the only foreign minister to travel to New York for the sessions. France had wanted a new resolution reaffirming the six requirements and calling for a resumption of negotiations but the United States opposed this course. Pineau was persuaded not to introduce any resolution and to accept instead a procedure under which the Council would remain seized of the question and the President, who was Ambassador Lodge for the month of May, would place on record the opinion of a majority of members that the six requirements had not yet been fully met and that there were various doubts and uncertainties which required further action or clarification by the Egyptian government.

Speaking for Egypt, Ambassador Loutfi maintained that the Egyptian Declaration either fulfilled or was "in accord with" each of the six requirements. In somewhat roundabout fashion he also went part way toward accepting Hammarskjöld's private advice that Egypt make clear it considered its Declaration just as binding as if it were a multilateral agreement. Loutfi did this by using a quotation from a speech by Fawzi in the Council in October 1956 concerning the third principle (insulation of the operation of the Canal from the politics of any country). Fawzi had said "We believe that the real insulation of the Canal from politics would best be guaranteed by a solemn and *internationally binding commitment* [italics added—EDITORS] in the form of a reaffirmation or a renewal of the 1888 Convention." Loutfi then continued: "Egypt has chosen. It has reaffirmed the Convention of 1888. I do not think that the guarantees, especially the legal guarantees, contained in the Declaration existed when the Canal was being operated by the former Suez Canal Company."[1]

The Security Council did not meet again on the question. In July Egypt filed its formal acceptance of the compulsory jurisdiction of the International Court. Except for the continued ban on Israeli shipping the operation of the Canal under the new régime proved to be satisfactory. With the assistance of the good offices of Hammarskjöld and Eugene Black of the International Bank, an agreement on compensation to the old Suez Canal Company was reached a year later, without having to resort to arbitration (see Volume IV).

---

2. From Transcript of Press Conference

UN HEADQUARTERS, NEW YORK   MAY 16, 1957

MENTION WAS MADE earlier (page 553) of a private letter written by Hammarskjöld on April 19 to David Ben-Gurion about a renewal of their direct personal contact. The Secretary-General wrote that he would be happy to come to Jerusalem early in May if Ben-Gurion thought talks might be worthwhile. There was the special question of the Assembly's call for full implementation of the Armistice Agreement and the deployment of UNEF on both sides of the armistice line. There was also a broader question—how to get over the "dead point" between them in efforts to get nearer to "the target we have in common—in your case peace for Israel, in my case perhaps just simply peace." For neither side would renewal of the talks from their last meeting in July 1956 "be an easy step, but if we have any faith in the possibility of progress, we cannot afford not to take our chance," Hammarskjöld had written.

Ben-Gurion's reply did not come until after Hammarskjöld had left for Europe where, after talks with Pope Pius XII and leaders of the Italian government in Rome, his principal concern was a planning session in Geneva of the Atomic Advisory Committee for a second Geneva Conference on the Peaceful Uses of Atomic Energy in 1958. The Israeli Prime Minister flatly refused to discuss either the Armistice Agreement or UNEF deployment issues unless and until Egypt agreed to renounce all claims to belligerency as

UN Note to Correspondents No. 1601, May 16, 1957.

[1] Security Council Official Records, Twelfth Year, 778th Meeting, May 20, 1957.

demanded by Israel. Nevertheless he hoped Hammarskjöld would come, for he was certain each had things to tell the other on the chances for peace in the area. After a further exchange during which the Secretary-General made sure that Israel's refusal to talk now on the Assembly resolution was not to be read as implying a decision formally to reject the resolution, he decided to go ahead with the visit. He was in Jerusalem May 9 to 11, was given a friendly reception by both Ben-Gurion and Mrs. Golda Meir, and engaged in private talks totaling about ten hours.

When he met the press on May 16 soon after his return to Headquarters (following text) the Secretary-General began with an enthusiastic account of the results of the Atomic Advisory Committee meeting in Geneva, but the correspondents were more interested in his Jerusalem talks and other Middle East developments. Hammarskjöld refused to give any details but his explanation of why he considered the visit "useful," with its emphasis on "mutual confidence" and on understanding the problems of "the other side," was also useful to perceptive correspondents. In the privacy of a UNEF Advisory Committee meeting the day before he had spoken of reestablishing "an atmosphere of, I would even say, mutual trust on the top level in spite of the basic and sharp differences of views on quite a few issues," adding, "For that reason, while all the wounds remain they are no longer infected."

Hammarskjöld had also told the UNEF Advisory Committee that he was now having second thoughts about the utility or necessity of publishing the correspondence with Israel about belligerency, the Armistice Agreement and UNEF deployment and he found that the committee members agreed with him. During his press conference, it should be noted, he passed up two opportunities to renew public pressure on Israel on the deployment issue.

THE SECRETARY-GENERAL: Ladies and gentlemen, since we met last time I have been away, as you know, for a fortnight and there is one part of the picture, one part of the experience, to which I would like to draw your attention.

I would like to do so not only because it seems to me to have been overlooked, but because I think it is a very significant piece of news which, in my judgment, should be considered newsworthy. You know that during my stay in Geneva we had a meeting of the Advisory Committee with regard to the second Atom Conference. A decision was reached, as you have seen, on holding the Conference in 1958 and on holding it in Geneva early in September. That in itself, of course, is news, but that perhaps would not justify my mentioning it here. What I want to point out is that work which normally could have taken a week or ten days, or something like that, was easily completed in three days. I am not stressing the time element as such, but the fact that this time, in 1957, those very difficult and controversial questions could be discussed in an international committee of experts so effectively and in such a favorable atmosphere that such a favorable result was possible. I can testify that indeed we had in that committee a splendid spirit of cooperation and very favorable results.

I myself, of course, cannot have any judgment on the significance of the new Conference or the program elaborated for that Conference, but I can quote those very qualified experts who said that the program on which agreement was reached so quickly is a program which is more significant, more interesting, than the program of the first Conference. I think that is news indeed and news which deserves all our attention.

Apart from that, I do not think there is anything I need to say about this visit to Europe. I am sure that other aspects may come up in the course of the questioning. But again I would like to say that no experience could be more satisfactory, more encouraging, than the speedy and constructive approach to the next Conference on Atomic Energy. Now the floor is yours.

. . . . QUESTION: Mr. Hammarskjöld, we have had some very meagre reports on your conferences with Prime Minister Ben-Gurion in Jerusalem. I wonder if you would care to tell us a little more about the meetings with him?

THE SECRETARY-GENERAL: On this occasion I am not alone in my responsibility for what may seem an unduly silent attitude. You may have observed that Mr. Ben-Gurion has been just as silent as I have, and I do not think that I should in any way depart from the good example he has set.

QUESTION: *Davar* of Tel Aviv reported that in your conversations in Jerusalem you recognized that Egypt's refusal to allow Israel's ships to pass through the Suez Canal is illegal from the standpoint of the United Nations Charter. At the same time some French papers carried reports that you sought to persuade the Israel government to avoid testing her rights to use the Canal by sending a ship through it. What did you suggest, an appeal to The Hague?

THE SECRETARY-GENERAL: Mr. Steinbeck calls his last novel a fabrication. That is a new word in my vocabulary, but I have found plenty of use for it. I find use for it also in this specific case. As to my stand on passage of Israeli ships through the Canal, I have already made it perfectly clear that a decision by the Security Council is the law for the Secretary-General as the Executive.

QUESTION: Mr. Hammarskjöld, could you say whether your hopes have dimmed or brightened regarding the placing of UNEF troops on the Israeli side of the armistice line?

THE SECRETARY-GENERAL: There are no further comments to make on that question today.

QUESTION: Mr. Secretary-General, could you tell us a little about the relationship in your mind between UNEF and UNTSO, particularly as to El Auja and the Gaza Strip?

THE SECRETARY-GENERAL: I think we can leave aside those details you referred to last, that is to say, the responsibilities in relation to specific areas, and look at the general problem. I think I have said in one report to the General Assembly that in a certain sense and to a certain extent the functions of UNTSO and UNEF are overlapping. We have, of course, made arrangements to avoid either a collision of duties or such an overlapping of functions, and the present arrangement is such that, without in any way shelving UNTSO and UNTSO responsibilities, for example, in Gaza, they are partly taken over by UNEF. In fact, General Burns, operating in Gaza, wears two hats. He is Commander of the UNEF. However, as you know, he is Chief of Staff of UNTSO, and although he is free from his obligations in areas where he has no operative functions, he wears that second hat also in those areas where he acts as Commander of UNEF; that is to say, there is a kind of union in the person of Burns which, of course, facilitates considerably the proper kind of cooperation.

What I want to stress is that for all practical purposes we have simplified operations so that, of course, only one organ functions for one purpose in one spot, while, on the other hand, we have not in any way reduced or changed or modified the position in principle and the responsibilities in principle of UNTSO in Gaza or any other area.

QUESTION: Could I follow it with this question. How many personnel from UNTSO have now been absorbed into UNEF?

THE SECRETARY-GENERAL: There is a very small number at present, ten.

QUESTION: Going back to Geneva, Mr. Secretary-General, there are more than rumors, apprehensions, that Mr. Myrdal's departure from ECE may be another forceful step in abandoning the philosophy of economic planning in the basic thinking of the United Nations Secretariat, and those people say that the Secretary-General, as one of the few surviving Keynesians, would not be able to stem the tide of economic liberalism of the old classical theory. Is there any change in the basic economic thinking of the Secretariat?

THE SECRETARY-GENERAL: No. This is a dramatic presentation of a very simple fact. I am happy to note that no single personality, not even the Secretary-General, puts such a heavy stamp on the teamwork which is going on in Geneva and here as to, so to say, infuse it with any special economic doctrine. I think we would be very much amiss if we were to push this or that kind of approach of a more doctrinaire character. That has not happened here; it has not happened in Geneva. I think that our duty is collectively to reflect as well as we can not this or that trend in political thinking in economics, but certainly the development of economic thinking at its best. It is eclectic; it is pragmatic, if you want. From that point of view the scientist may sometimes feel a little unhappy because everyone who has this kind of academic background, whether it is Mr. Myrdal or Mr. Hammarskjöld, of course likes to think in his own way. But I think we are all solidly and well coordinated and subordinated to the major responsibility. The reply, therefore, is just simply that there will be no change of policy. I do not think Mr. Myrdal has felt isolated in a world with certain liberal trends. And the Secretary-General certainly does not.

QUESTION: Since the position of the Secretary-General is based on the decision of the Security Council regarding passage through the Suez Canal, could you please tell us how you feel about the threat of the use of force in implementing this decision, and what do you think the United Nations can do in this regard?

THE SECRETARY-GENERAL: I do not know of any specific threat of the use of force. Rather, there are very many threats of the use of force from all sorts of quarters. I deplore them all. They add to a bad atmosphere. They are certainly against the philosophy of the Charter. I hope that they will remain just words, no matter from what quarter they come.

QUESTION: Mr. Secretary-General, there still seems to be one flaw in the deployment of UNEF forces as far as carrying out all the terms of the November 2 resolution are concerned, particularly in regard to raids and incursions along the line. The UNEF has been described as being only one-half on the line rather than on the line. My question is: Is this really a matter of stationing of troops, the UNEF forces, in the physical sense or is it more a matter of authority for UNEF to carry out its function?

THE SECRETARY-GENERAL: I am not quite clear on the sense of your question, but you will correct me if I misunderstood you in any way. Some parts of the implementation of the plans for the UNEF have not made as much progress as I would like to have seen made. However, I do feel, on the other hand, that it has not seriously impaired the efficiency of the UNEF so far. We have this and that kind of straying across the armistice demarcation line, but the total impression is one of reasonable quiet for which certainly the presence of the UNEF is one of the main explanations. That is really understating the case, as I look at it myself. I think the UNEF has proved efficient for its purpose although we have not done everything we originally had in mind when we were setting up the UNEF as frontier guards, to put it that way.

QUESTION: One of the reports emanating from the Near East while you were in Jerusalem quoted you as saying that while the maintenance of a state of war by Egypt *per se* is no violation of the Charter, yet any hostile act by Egypt under that state of war would be considered a violation of the Charter. The question is: the maintenance by Egypt of a blockade in the Suez Canal or in the Straits of Tiran and attacks by fedayeen or for that matter the economic boycott. Would that be considered a hostile act that is in violation of the Charter?

THE SECRETARY-GENERAL: You referred to a distinction which has been already made in a previous press conference and which has been discussed at great length, I think, in other contexts, the distinction between acts which are possible because there is so far no peace settlement and acts which are contrary to the Armistice Agreement. The present state of affairs is ruled by the Armistice Agreement and by the Charter, as I pointed out in a previous press conference. Acts found contrary to the Armistice Agreement, therefore, are ruled out, whatever we call the situation and whatever words we use for the action. On the other hand, there is a limbo, so to say, between what is permissible under the Armistice Agreement and what would not be permissible in the case of a full peace treaty. You see the distinction.

The Security Council, in a famous decision in 1951, ruled that the armistice régime, as established by the Armistice Agreement, excluded the exercise of belligerent rights or rather it said that belligerent rights could not reasonably be exercised. There they gave an interpretation to the Armistice which ruled out acts of the type you mentioned here. Some of them, like raids across the border from one side or the other, are of course ruled out by the very letter of the Armistice Agreement. I repeat it again, whatever the words are which we use in order to describe the situation, the fact is just simply that we should ask ourselves whether or not such and such an act is permissible under the régime established by the Armistice Agreement. If it is not, then it is not excused by any general terminology. If it is that is another matter and we can look at it more as a political issue than as an issue under the Charter.

As to the specific types of action to which you referred, I have no reason to go into recent history, but I think if you check your notes of the events of the last couple of months, you will find that no such concrete acts have taken place. For that reason the concrete issue you raised has not arisen in practice.

QUESTION: You said after your interview that you found that your meeting with Mr. Ben-Gurion was very useful. Can you give us any idea in what sense you considered it highly useful or useful?

THE SECRETARY-GENERAL: Is it not always useful after a long separation, when all sorts of questions of a delicate and sometimes difficult nature have arisen, to get together, sit down, talk frankly and with mutual confidence, and in that way to map out the ground we have to cross, each one on the basis of his specific duties or responsibilities, but always of course keeping in mind what the problems are on the other side? That is, I think, what from my point of view was not only the purpose of this visit but also the end achieved.

. . . . QUESTION: Again this is a question on the banning of nuclear explosions. I wonder whether you have ever considered the possibility of issuing an open appeal to the great powers concerned. Many people consider that such an appeal would add weight to similar appeals by important personalities and organizations throughout the world and would help create public opinion in those countries which could influence the policies of their governments in this respect. As you know, during the last two days the President and the Prime Minister of India and the Prime Minister of Japan made much stronger appeals in this direction than they have ever done before.

THE SECRETARY-GENERAL: I would not consider an appeal from the Secretary-General as useful or even appropriate. My means of action in relation to governments are of a different type. An appeal from the Secretary-General would in fact be an appeal not to governments but over the heads of governments to public opinion. And the Secretary-General, although he holds in some respects a rather independent position, is also always the spokesman and servant of governments.

QUESTION: Your joint communiqué with Mr. Ben-Gurion said that both of you had welcomed clarification, I believe, on various issues. As we understand it, one of the issues may have been a divergence of opinion between yourself and Mr. Ben-Gurion as to whether the armistice régime, as such, is still a valid one. Would you mind commenting on that point, please?

THE SECRETARY-GENERAL: First of all I exclude, as I have already done, any specific comments on my conversations in Jerusalem. As to the specific issue you raise, I think I have made my view perfectly clear and in considered language to the General Assembly and I would not like to improvise on that legal issue. From the point of view of the United Nations, which is in a certain sense a party to the Armistice Agreement, as the Security Council has taken note of it in its decisions —sanctioned it, in a certain sense—it seems obvious that it remains for the Organization a valid document.

. . . . QUESTION: We know so tantalizingly little about what transpired in Israel. Could you, without violating any confidence, tell us even the scope of your conversations in that country?

THE SECRETARY-GENERAL: It was just as broad as you can imagine.

QUESTION: Perhaps you cannot comment on this, but I understand that following your conversation with the Pope, the *Osservatore Romano* said that the Middle East had been discussed. Can you foresee any possibility of the Vatican's playing any kind of role in bringing the disputing parties in the area any closer to agreement or to negotiation?

THE SECRETARY-GENERAL: It is not for me to speak either about the influence or the possible actions of the Vatican. I think that we all highly respect the moral influence of the Vatican and especially of the Pope and I think this moral influence for peace is an asset which can make itself extremely valuable all over the world in the present discussions concerning both problems of detail and general problems.

. . . . QUESTION: At the last press conference, in reply to a question on the Constantinople Convention, you pointed out that there were certain inconsistencies or contradictions and it might be well to get a Court ruling on that. According to reports from Jerusalem, the Government of Israel does not intend to go to the World Court, because under the Charter, they say, the Security Council is superior to the World Court, and they have already made a decision. Is that your understanding of the Charter, sir?

THE SECRETARY-GENERAL: I do not know whom you quote, but it is impossible to talk about superiority for any one of the organs. Each one is superior in its own field of competence. In questions of law it is the International Court of Justice that is the highest international organ.

The Security Council was never set up to be a court of law and has not functioned or made any attempts to function as a court of law.

QUESTION: In this field, sir, which do you think is the competent one, the Security Council or the World Court?

THE SECRETARY-GENERAL: It depends on the angle from which we raise the question. This is a complex question, as you know. Just as in national life you can raise such a problem before different fora and use different channels in order to get results, so you can do in this case. It was once raised, as you remember, in the Security Council. The Security Council found the appeal to be in order and passed a resolution on it, which, however, did not go into an interpretation of the Constantinople Convention. It interpreted the general armistice régime and its consequences. On the other hand, I think that, if the matter is raised as one of interpretation of the Constantinople Convention, most experts and most governments would find that that belongs to the competence and authority of the International Court.

AT HIS PRESS CONFERENCE on June 6 and in remarks at a luncheon of the UN Correspondents Association on June 19 the Secretary-General made clear his belief that this was a time of "convalescence" in the Middle East during which it was wise to avoid renewing old arguments and to keep the temperature as low as possible. When Israeli statements exaggerated the significance of border incidents and professed fears of a revival of the fedayeen he put the situation in perspective for the reporters. He made an oblique reference to the fact that Israel's attitude was preventing deployment of UNEF on both sides of the armistice line but said the situation was not one in which he felt he should raise the issue again in public.

Hammarskjöld did confirm that the question of a fence was under "active consideration." Behind the scenes he suggested to both parties a double fence, one on the Israeli side and one on the Gaza side. He also asked for and received active cooperation from the Egyptians in Gaza in better enforcement of measures to keep the restless Palestinian refugees away from the armistice line. These measures proved to be quite effective and the number of incidents of even a minor nature declined sharply in succeeding months. The fence, however, was never built. Israel had actively supported building one on the Egyptian side, but lost interest when asked to agree to one on their side, too.

At this time Hammarskjöld was still hoping for an Egyptian reply to the three questions on Article I of the Armistice Agreement which he had addressed at the end of March. Even if Egypt refused a direct reply to Israel's query a reply to his own questions would have given him an opportunity to reopen a dialogue with Israel on reciprocal commitments to nonbelligerency under Article I. But, as he remarked sadly on June 19, his "correspondence with various capitals in the Middle East recently has been a little bit on the one-sided side." Even Egypt's formal acceptance of the compulsory jurisdiction of the International Court on the Suez Canal question which had been promised in the Declaration of April 24 was not forwarded to the Secretary-General until July 18.

---

3. From Transcript of Press Conference
UN HEADQUARTERS, NEW YORK   JUNE 6, 1957

BEGINNING WITH Hammarskjöld's press conference of June 6 it was arranged that the verbatim transcripts identify the correspondents asking questions. Thereafter this practice was followed a good deal of the time, but was not consistently maintained.

. . . . MR. HOROWITZ (*World Union Press*): During the past few weeks there have been reports of breakthroughs in the UNEF lines at the Gaza frontier. There have also been reports of the planting of mines. I have been wondering whether there has been, in some form, a lack of proper security measures on the part of the United Nations Force on the border which have permitted such incidents to take place. This also brings up the question of a fence. I wonder whether you have given that question any consideration.

THE SECRETARY-GENERAL: I think that a few observations are necessary on the first point. First of all, you have referred to the "past few weeks"; in fact, you are referring to two mining incidents last week. One of these mining incidents took place two and one-half kilometres from the demarcation line; the other one took place practically on the demarcation line—only twenty metres from it, according to the information I have. If they could be properly characterized as "breakthroughs"—which is the term you have used—they certainly

UN Note to Correspondents No. 1610, June 6, 1957.

would give a reason for even more concern than I naturally feel about every such incident.

I think, however, one must recognize that that part of the world is not such that, behind a story of this kind, there need be any breakthrough. One, or possibly two men can sneak through any kind of military line. That happens even with a cordon of the most effective kind, and, unhappily, mines are still lying around in the ground in Gaza and have been picked up, and can be picked up, by anyone. That is to say, it certainly indicates that the present—so to speak—human fence is not watertight; but it does not, on the other hand, indicate that it is so loose as to make possible a breakthrough, to use your term again.

I feel, generally speaking, that I am on solid ground in warning against too far-reaching conclusions from incidents of this type, either as to the intentions back of the incidents or as to the effectiveness of UNEF.

If you will permit me to turn to the effectiveness of UNEF and the effectiveness of our arrangements generally, you know that we have not been able to follow through the program which was established by the General Assembly. I, for one, would be happy to see further developments in the direction thus indicated. But, on the other hand, I do not feel that this is either a time or a situation in which I should go into that aspect of the matter or raise that issue again. That leaves us partly with the question of the type which you indicated—the question of a fence, which is under what, in professional language, is called active consideration. I guess that this additional word "active" is to indicate that the consideration really is serious and not just a nice way of turning aside a question. The issue is in no way dead. We have not reached solutions or formulae which satisfy us or others, but we are pursuing the matter, and I think that if it is really considered to be an additional safeguard of significance, we shall certainly end by finding some way of getting it.

MR. SWET (*Maariv*): You certainly have heard about the decision of the Arab League to tighten the boycott and blockade against Israel and to extend the boycott to all foreign concerns which do business with Israel. What is your attitude to that? Do you not consider that it is a flagrant violation of the United Nations Charter? Does the United Nations intend to take any measures to stop this action of the United Nations Member group against another Member of the United Nations?

I have another question. According to Reuters, the Norwegian tanker

Westward was refused permission to pass through the Suez Canal while on her way from Tel Aviv to the Persian Gulf. The CBC and many other sources said yesterday that the tanker had passed through the Canal without any interference. What does the United Nations know about it?

THE SECRETARY-GENERAL: As to the second question, I do not know any more than what you have read. I read the same dispatches. But there is one indication which supports the later series of dispatches or cables, and that is that we certainly would have heard about it in another way if it had really been stopped. Therefore, I not only prefer to believe the later reports, but I think there is a reason to believe that they are right.

Regarding the boycott, it is, as you know, a move in line with the repeatedly declared policy of that group of countries. I think that the evaluation of that policy has been given by the proper United Nations organs already, and what they have said on other similar occasions necessarily applies also in this case. I would go this far and say again what I have said before that, as a matter of course, I endorse those previous decisions and the principle endorsed in those decisions as my own. I have to do it professionally, and I do it also personally.

MR. MEZERIK (*International Review Service*): I want to take up the question of the infiltrations in the Gaza Strip which were reported as being the subject of a special statement from Israel on June 2, in which it is said that there were more than fifty instances of theft and border incursions on the Gaza Strip since the Israelis withdrew. I should like to ask you, in connection with this, whether, in conformity with the statement made by you on April 1, in which you said that the Government of Egypt had advised you that Egypt was making known effectively to the refugees and other inhabitants of the Strip that it was Egyptian policy to prevent infiltration across the demarcation line, and also that Egyptian regulations against infiltration, which included penalties, were being put into force, these things have been done; and what is the role of UNEF in preventing infiltration, which was also mentioned here?

THE SECRETARY-GENERAL: The infiltrations to which you refer, with the high number of fifty, are, I think, difficult to evaluate without looking at the things which really have happened. I think that this is a typical case where statistics and the generalization implied in statistics are definitely rather dangerous. I would, for that reason, advise you, when you ponder on this problem, to go back into the story and to see a little bit what these incursions, which now are lumped together as fifty, have meant. I would also invite you to look at the incursions in the opposite direction, with the same proviso: be cautious with statistics. The UNEF has difficulty in this case because it is not fully, and never immediately, informed and has no possibility, such as UNTSO once had, of following through with investigations of its own. That, of course, does not mean that it is not interfering and doing what is its duty under its terms of reference in every case which comes to its attention and which is within the orbit of its judgment and action. As to the Egyptian attitude on these matters, I am not now aware of any very recent developments where this has been, so to speak, highlighted as a specific problem; but I know, on the other hand, that what was once promised has been done. I would, however, like to refer to Mr. Bunche, who may be more up to date if there have been recent developments on this special point.

MR. BUNCHE: There have been no recent developments. It is only necessary to add that in most of these incidents—if it is fifty—we have had no reports at all and are not informed, therefore, about the details. But we do know from sketchy information that many of them are inconsequential. Others are thefts—I was going to say normal thefts—in that area, of irrigation pipe, animals, and other incidents of animals straying across the line. There have been casualties only in the two mine incidents reported last week.

. . . . MR. LESUEUR (*Columbia Broadcasting System*): I would like to ask whether you consider the status now existing in the Middle East approaches that of the status before the Armistice, and if so whether a state of belligerency still exists in the Middle East?

THE SECRETARY-GENERAL: A comparison backwards is very difficult, and what I say can be nothing more than a very personal impression. I cannot speak with any specific authority. I would say that on the basic things which interest you most it is most definitely not a return to the situation we had before. There are fundamental changes in it, and I for one believe that those changes are for the better. There is a continuous development which has been going on, as I once expressed it, behind the smoke screen of continued difficulties; and one day, if we manage to lift the smoke screen, I think we may have the pleasant surprise of seeing some solid progress. It is rather intangible, you know, as regards these matters, because progress necessarily is up to 50 percent psychological. For that reason it is difficult to put your finger on it and describe it. I refer again to what I said in the beginning. I can talk only as somebody who follows it closely and gives expression to personal impressions. We have discussed several times the question of belligerency and the use of the term, what it means, what it does not mean, what it justifies, and what it does not justify. If I have to add anything to what has been said before, it might perhaps be that belligerency, as the word is now understood in common usage—that is to say, a kind of active or quasi-active state of war—cannot be admitted as existing in the area, and I do not think that the deplorable and regrettable incidents to which reference has been made in any way contradict my judgment if I say that it does not exist.

. . . . MRS. GRAY (*Greenwich Time*): Mr. Secretary-General, when the Security Council recently considered the Syrian complaint about building a bridge in the demilitarized zone there, the members of the Council strongly upheld the Armistice Agreement as the law for the zone and the UNTSO Chief of Staff as the authority for implementing the provisions of the agreement, as well as freedom of movement for observers. My question is: Is this applicable to each demilitarized zone under the separate Armistice Agreements, including El Auja?

THE SECRETARY-GENERAL: There is, legally speaking, and from the point of view of the Security Council, as I understand its decisions, no difference between the various areas covered by different armistice agreements. It is exactly the same position. Politically for the moment we are of course in difficulty because, as you know, from the Israel government expression has been given to the view that, without being canceled or annulled, somehow the Egypt-Israel Armistice Agreement is, let us say, put in such serious jeopardy as not to function at all. I do not know exactly how to describe this somewhat ambiguous legal situation. From that point of view one of the governments concerned makes a difference between the various armistice agreements, and that of course has a bearing on the developments in the field and on the discussion. But I repeat what I said in the beginning. The reply to your question is definitely, on the basis of the Security Council's jurisprudence, that the various armistice agreements and the areas covered by the various armistice agreements are legally in the same position.

MISS FREDERICK (*National Broadcasting Company*): Mr. Secretary-General, you said a moment ago that the situation in the Middle East had not returned to what it was before the war. Would you be more specific and tell us exactly how it has not returned to the situation it was before the war?

THE SECRETARY-GENERAL: When I referred, as you may remember, to what I felt to be the basic situation, I added concerning that, that it was very difficult for me to be specific because it is a question of psychology, of attitudes, actions, and anticipation of the future, and so on and so forth. Political thinking in governments and among peoples does develop, and I think there has been such a development going on. If, on the other hand—I forgot to give that reply, and I should perhaps have given it—you look at the practical aspects, I think that everybody can see for himself that the situation is a different one in the sense that the very presence of the UNEF with its functions has introduced a most important new element in the picture, which at least gives you a period during which various matters can be discussed on new assumptions.

MISS FREDERICK (*National Broadcasting Company*): May I follow that up, Mr. Secretary-General? When you say there is a psychological change there, does that mean that the parties are any closer to some kind of negotiation of their differences than they were before the war?

THE SECRETARY-GENERAL: You put the question in such a concrete form that you really called, not a bluff but, so to speak, the vagueness of my general impression. I think that this attitude to which I referred is far from articulate and probably could not be expressed in the words you used, but is an improvement of the psychological situation which, if maintained and strengthened, may provide us with a basis on which I could reply to your question with a "yes"; I would feel rather rash if I did that today.

MR. EDINGER (*Agence France-Presse*): During the last debate in the Security Council on Suez, several members of the Council asked you to continue your talks with the Egyptian government or representative in order to find out some new particulars about the Suez régime and the Declaration of Egypt of April 26. May I ask you if you have spoken to the Egyptian representative about Suez and if the talks are continuing between you and the Egyptian government?

THE SECRETARY-GENERAL: What members of the Security Council did was perhaps rather to ask me to continue the contact which was already functioning, to continue the contact with of course the expectation of a step-by-step clarification of stands in order to get the necessary supplements on such points, where it was felt that such supplements were needed in order to give a firmer basis.

I have, as a matter of course, continued those talks and I remain in very active contact indeed both with the representative of Egypt and, through him, with his government.

MR. BEER (*Neue Zürcher Zeitung*): I had wanted to ask the same question as Mr. Edinger, but with your permission I will ask this other question. Since these contacts are going on, is it not rather disappointing, from the general point of view, that the first step which might be expected has not been taken from the Egyptian side: that is, the adherence to the compulsory jurisdiction of the International Court?

THE SECRETARY-GENERAL: This should naturally be a very early step. Of course I can in no way explain why there has been a delay; I hope it will not continue very much longer.

MR. HOROWITZ (*World Union Press*): In regard to your reply to Mr. Lesueur and Miss Frederick, may I ask you whether you consider full acceptance of the armistice agreements as the first step toward a peace settlement? The reason I am asking this is because lately there have been pronouncements from Arab leaders that they view the 1947 resolutions as the only step toward some kind of settlement between Israel and the Arab states.

THE SECRETARY-GENERAL: I think I made my stand on the armistice agreements very clear in reports; but to try to sum up my reaction I would say this: if we do not give their proper weight to the armistice agreements we shall have rather an anarchic state of affairs because they are the legal documents by which we have to work. For this reason I would be sorry if they were to be thrown out of the window and I consider it a very natural duty for me to give them all the weight and the sanctity they can have. That does not mean that every single clause is still alive. They were drafted a very long time ago, and as a matter of course there are clauses which are vital and those which are less vital than they were at the beginning. I feel specifically that the first and the second articles of those armistice agreements, which refer to the general state of affairs and to the cease-fire, are "musts." If they are not upheld, if they are not respected, we just do not have the springboard from which we have to jump.

How far, on that basis, we can or should go in practical politics, in the detailed implementation, is a question which I would leave myself for a somewhat later stage, while maintaining the principle that the armistice agreements, being the key legal documents in the area, are to be respected.

MR. GABRIEL (*Transradio News Agency*): I wish to ask two questions pertaining to certain constitutional aspects of the United Nations which I think involve the spirit and the prestige of the Organization.

First is the recent tendency on the part of a number of delegations in voting not to vote at all. I do not know what the constitutional aspect of this is. I know that many of them knocked at the door of the United Nations very frantically and are now playing hookey and in many conferences their seats are empty. The constitution talks about being "able and willing to carry out these obligations." My question: What is the constitutional status of a vote other than yes, no, or abstention—that is to say, a truant vote?

My second question is: What is the obligation of Member states in respect of the question of underhand slander either of the United Nations directly or through the Secretariat? I notice lately a tendency toward an underhand slander campaign against the Secretary-General. My question is: What is the constitutional or ethical obligation of Member states in respect of poison propaganda tactics and also, how do you personally react to them?

THE SECRETARY-GENERAL: On the first question, if we try to rationalize it and find some kind of word covering the situation you have in mind, I think that the word "absent," physically or in some other way, would be adequate. We would have: yes, no, abstention, absent.

On the second point, I do not know that any other laws—ethical or otherwise—apply to Member states than to you, ladies and gentlemen, and to myself. There are some simple rules of human intercourse and human living together which certainly should be observed by everybody. I am not aware of the background of what you say and therefore it does not strike me as very necessary to express a personal opinion concerning what may or may not be said concerning myself. But if I am to give a hypothetical reply to what is, I hope, a hypothetical question, I would say I do not care a bit.

MR. OATIS (*Associated Press*): The British government has announced that it will start shipping more goods to Communist China. How does this affect the United Nations embargo on strategic shipments to Communist China adopted in 1951? How does it affect the possibility of Communist China eventually sitting here in this building?

THE SECRETARY-GENERAL: This is certainly a rather relevant question, but you will excuse me if, in the stage where we find that question just now, I prefer to say "no comment."

. . . . MR. LEICHTER (*Austrian News Agency*): Mr. Secretary-General, the last two debates in the Security Council ended without anybody introducing a resolution and with the President of the Council summing up the debates. Do you think this may grow into a method of avoiding the veto and of relying rather on the moral power of public opinion as summed up by the President of the Council than on the sanction power or the powers of resolutions which, in many cases, practically do not exist?

THE SECRETARY-GENERAL: I would not like to generalize in that way at all and I would not like to guess about future tendencies. There are situations where this procedure seems to be very appropriate, and I believe that this one is a case in point. It is very appropriate because there is no need to try to hammer out, so to say, a text which may take a very long time without really adding anything to what comes out of it. The discussion as such gave sufficient guidance to the Chief of Staff and to me. We are in a position, when the matter is of this nature, to draw conclusions. There is no specific need to spell these matters out.

In other cases when it is a question of, let us say, Security Council jurisdiction, the method of course is not appropriate because a vote must be taken. For that reason, I think we can register that there is recognition of the fact that in some situations the most practical procedure is the one resorted to, without believing that there will be a tendency to abuse that method.

. . . . MR. CARPENTER (*Associated Press*): Could you bring us up to date on the developments in the case of the American flyers in Red China. We have not heard anything about that in some time. Are there not still some in prison? What is being done in this connection?

THE SECRETARY-GENERAL: There are definitely no American flyers in prison because that story, to the extent that I am aware of it, was settled by 1955. There are still Americans in prison in China. My only knowledge is indirect. I think that that question should be directed to the American authorities as they are negotiating the issue.

. . . .

From Transcript of Remarks at Luncheon of the
United Nations Correspondents Association

NEW YORK JUNE 19, 1957

The Secretary-General was introduced by Bruce Munn (*United Press*), President of the United Nations Correspondents Association.

In the course of his introduction Mr. Munn used a quotation from *Macbeth,* "We have him not and yet we see him still," in commenting that the correspondents had met the Secretary-General infrequently in the past year "because of the tremendous load that must be carried" by his office.

THE SECRETARY-GENERAL: It is pleasant indeed to be here again. It is partly a sign of the times, because, as you know, between the last time that I was here and this occasion we have been passing through a period which really does invite another quotation from *Macbeth,* a quotation just as well known as the one referred to by Mr. Munn—that is, "a tale told by an idiot, full of sound and fury." I would not necessarily accept the first part of the quotation, but I think that we are in perfect agreement about the sound and fury. And those who, in all modesty, have tried to go against the remaining part of that quotation—the part which says "signifying nothing"—and have tried to have it all make sense have really had a somewhat busy time.

We have, of course, met a few times during this period at press conferences. I, for one, have been very happy that it has been possible to take up that good tradition again. I certainly want us to continue it. But I think that these press conferences have shown one thing—namely, that in a period of the present type, there are some difficulties involved in having the conference operate in the way we on both sides would like. What I think we want is an exchange, not only of information, but also of views; a give-and-take over the table. I think that in the United Nations Headquarters—in that glass building—you the representatives of the press, and we on the Secretariat side, are living together in a way which should make these kinds of contacts not a one-sided but a two-

UN Note to Correspondents No. 1616, June 19, 1957.

sided affair. I have indeed, through the years, learned a lot from these press conferences; therefore, in my own experience it has been a question of give and take, and I should like the process to develop further in that direction.

Now, to say that I should like the process to develop further in that direction and at the same time to have sometimes so little to give myself is rather embarrassing. That is really what I had in mind when I referred to the recent press conferences. They have somehow been on the somewhat meagre side. The fact is not that I still suffer from that unpleasant diplomatic ailment to which Mr. Munn referred—although, for obvious reasons, I shall never be quite free from it—but that the present period is a curious one which does not lend itself to very much public debate. I think that that is the keynote which I should like to strike on this occasion, where it is in fact possible to speak a somewhat different language from that which is unavoidable in the cold light of Conference Room No. 4.

The present period is, of course, in a certain sense the lull after the sound and the fury. It is, for that reason, a period of convalescence, when it is not a very good idea to stir things up, to make too much noise about lingering symptoms of the illness. It is a period when the temperature should be kept as low as possible, but when, on the other hand, it is all right to have as much fresh air as possible around the bed. From my point of view, that means that I have to—not exactly lie low—but exert more than ever whatever efforts I can make in the direction of keeping alive a sense of perspective; of keeping alive the feeling that, although we have certainly passed through an illness—and a bad one—there are strong and solid chances that the patient will convalesce and get out of bed, provided that we respect some very simple laws of nature.

For that reason, you have found me—as some people say—minimizing what is happening. I do not think that I am doing that. I am just trying to keep a sense of perspective. On the other hand, I am rather reluctant to talk about things—not because I am, so to speak, barred from talking about them, but for another and simpler reason. I do not want in any way to provoke new discussions and comments, a relapse into old arguments, and so forth. Therefore, if you find me a little bit on the dumb side, even on this occasion, it is not because of any undue personal prudence; it is just an expression of the very situation in which we find ourselves. I think that one of the essential things in any attempt on your side to interpret what is going on is to remember that we are in this period where we are trying to heal wounds and to keep the temperature low in order to help the body to restore itself.

In fact, efforts in that direction recently have been successful. I would say that, if you look around at present, you will find that there is a rather universal tendency to strike as low a note as possible, to keep as much of a sense of perspective as possible. I think that this universal tendency to play it that way is really one of the good signs, because, in itself, it does prove that we are on the way to recovery; it does prove that people are animated by the same feelings as those to which I have tried to give expression.

On the other hand, we are necessarily always impatient. It is all right to help the recovery; it is all right to keep things as quiet as possible in order to help the constructive forces—but, on the other hand, we are certainly looking around, and looking eagerly around, for positive expressions of the influence of those constructive forces. If we had such positive expressions, I feel that we certainly would have news—and news of a more solid kind than a mere slow and silent recovery. I would not be frank with you if I did not say that on that point I am, as I have said, a little bit impatient. I see—and I think that my friends in the Secretariat do see—signs of recovery, signs of an attitude which helps the recovery; but we do not yet see the return of the vigor which could bring us out of the sickroom and into the open air.

For that reason, as I evaluate the situation in which we now find ourselves, I do not think that it gives any reason for concern. That is one reason why you have less news than usual. On the other hand, the situation does not in any way justify elation, because too little on the positive side is happening. That is another reason why you do not get very much news just at present. We are, so to speak, in between—in between the period of sound and fury and the period, for which we are hoping, of real and active reconstruction and rebuilding. I think that that estimate is reasonably realistic.

I hope, of course, that if we meet, let us say, before the General Assembly or at the end of the summer, I shall be able to shift the emphasis—being just as convinced concerning the recovery part as I have been here, but striking a happier note concerning the other part. Mind you, I am not at all thinking only of the area to which I have somehow got married in your minds—the Middle East; I am thinking in much broader terms than that.

Those comments were made partly as an explanation for a certain reticence on my part, but also partly as a kind of summing up of my own impression of this latter half of June 1957. I think that what I have said is something which I can justifiably say on this occasion; I should have hesitated to say it at the beginning of a press conference. This does show that the move from the Headquarters building to this "hideaway" [1] does after all loosen my tongue a little bit.

For that reason, in thanking you for this kind invitation, which is very much appreciated both by me and by all my colleagues, I hope that you will find some encouragement for a renewal of the invitation. To the extent that there is any physical possibility for me to respond to such an invitation, I can assure you that I shall be happy to do so. It would be a sign of many pleasant things—among others, that the pressure at Headquarters was a little bit less than it has been, and also perhaps that I felt that I had a little bit more to say than I am likely to say today.

MR. DAVID HOROWITZ (*World Union Press, American Association of English-Jewish Newspapers*): Mr. Hammarskjöld, I do not know whether in the past you have always favored a United Nations police force in any area of the world. May I ask whether, in the light of the UNEF experiment in the Middle East, you see any permanence for such a force in connection with the future of United Nations activities?

THE SECRETARY-GENERAL: I do, indeed. One of the things which came out of this sound and fury was, of course, that we ventured into new areas. San Francisco thought of the police force only in terms of the famous Chapter VII—which is a rather serious chapter. We were forced by circumstances into another field and had to improvise a police force which, in certain respects, may look more modest but which may make contributions that are just as constructive and just as essential. When, in this way, we have discovered—certainly not a new continent —but at least a little island with some pleasant features, I think it is our duty to explore it. For my own part, I have been turning around in my mind the possibility of converting the experience gathered into something solid and fruitful—not by way of the creation of something permanent at present, but by way of, so to speak, such a summary of conclusions from this experience as would make this instrument a part

[1] A reference to the name of the restaurant, "Danny's Hideaway," where the luncheon took place.

of the natural arsenal of which we would all think when the need arose. That is to say, if a situation were to arise where a similar force were again needed and if the application of Chapter VII were still not open, we should not need then to improvise, but should be able to go straight and solidly toward something about which we knew.

MR. ALEXANDER GABRIEL (*Transradio News Agency*): Mr. Hammarskjöld, do you consider that a crucial and important step in the transition from what you call convalescence to elation must necessarily be at least a minimum agreement arising out of the disarmament discussions in London?

THE SECRETARY-GENERAL: I would say, Mr. Gabriel, that such a minimum agreement definitely would be a solid and rather important contribution to the kind of positive development which I have in mind.

MR. ALEXANDER GABRIEL (*Transradio News Agency*): Would you go so far as to say that without it it would be very difficult to get off the ground at all from convalescence?

THE SECRETARY-GENERAL: No, I would not go that far. You certainly could not get that special plane off the runway, but there are other and perhaps less conspicuous planes which you could start flying.

MR. SIMON MALLEY (*Al Gomhouria; Le Progrès Egyptien*): In the light of the *démarche* which the Afro-Asian group at the United Nations made to you the other day concerning the situation in Algeria, I would like to ask you two questions: first, whether you communicated these viewpoints which were expressed to you by Ambassador Ben-Aboud to the French government; and secondly, whether you could tell us something about how you or the United Nations would envisage an international impartial investigation of these incidents?

THE SECRETARY-GENERAL: On the first point, I can refer you to what you know is an established practice. No delegation or group of delegations can bring anything up with me concerning another delegation without its being, from my point of view, a duty at least to inform the latter delegation about the *démarche*. That has, of course, been done. For the rest, I would say that the situation is one which will require further study, further consideration, before I should like to say anything precise about it. That brings us to the more theoretical aspect of the problem, to which you referred in the second place. You know that even for the main organs, the Security Council and the General Assembly, there are very strict limits to the demands of that type that can be put to a Member Nation. The Secretary-General has no such rights. He can, for that reason, act only on the basis of some kind of good offices idea. In doing that, of course, he is himself at least limited to the same extent as the main organs of the United Nations. That is to say, I think that a good offices operation, which would, so to say, potentially infringe upon—or mean that he assumed authority in a way which would infringe upon—safeguards established in the Charter, which have to be respected by the main organs, is out of the question. In other words, in cases of this type—and I do not refer specifically to the case in point but to the several cases of good offices which have arisen in the last few years—the initiative in the final analysis must be an initiative of the government directly concerned. It must be an initiative which is their own in the light of the consideration they wish to give to feelings expressed, but not in response to any specific demand, the legal justification of which we should not bring out for discussion.

The reply to your specific question is that the United Nations cannot in itself envisage an investigation of this or that type. It has first of all to observe the rules of the Charter. From that it does follow that in a case of this type the decision as well as the basic initiative is a question of national and not United Nations concern. I think that is the reply to your question. Under such circumstances, it is obvious that there is no good reason for us here to speculate on how the thing can be done, because it is not for the United Nations to decide.

MR. MAX HARRELSON (*Associated Press*): Mr. Hammarskjöld, you spoke a minute ago about the possibility of using United Nations forces in other situations. I would like to ask about the future of the UNEF units. It has been over six months since UNEF was sent to the Middle East as an emergency measure. Can you tell us something about the possible duration of their stay there or possible measures to relieve the troops which have been contributed?

THE SECRETARY-GENERAL: Or to relieve the countries which are contributing the troops?

MR. MAX HARRELSON (*Associated Press*): The countries, yes.

THE SECRETARY-GENERAL: Three stages, so to say. As to the first point, of course, the decisive factor is the extent of the need; and the extent of the need depends partly on the development of that process of recovery to which I referred.

On the second point you know there is a rotation because it is not a very sound idea morale-wise to keep troops under such peculiar conditions as we have to do here for an undue length of time. Six months seems to be a very reasonable time to turn over, and that is the basis on which we work.

The final point is that, quite apart from all financial considerations, it is always a question of the generosity of governments, to what extent and during which time they are willing to send these battalions out for international service. The generosity has been considerable. I have not seen any weakening in it. On the other hand, personally I do know that in quite a few cases this does in the long run represent a certain strain on the military organization of these various countries with their standing arrangements. For that reason, there must be a feeling for the real usefulness and need of it in order to counteract the obvious disadvantages from which all these contributing countries have to suffer. It is my own conviction that these countries take a very responsible look at the matter. Therefore, I have no reason at all for the moment to worry about the problem. What the future may bring—I think it is a little premature to look into that.

. . . . MR. MORRIS RIVLIN (*The Day-Jewish Journal*): A while ago, Mr. Hammarskjöld, you told us that you had forwarded to Cairo an Israeli request that Egypt give up its rights of belligerency. Did you ever get an answer to that request? If not, is there anything that you should or could do to get an answer?

THE SECRETARY-GENERAL: I must say that my correspondence with various capitals in the Middle East recently has been a little bit on the one-sided side. That is also true about the specific case to which you now refer.

. . . . MR. MAX BEER (*Neue Zürcher Zeitung,* Zurich): Mr. Hammarskjöld, up to now nobody has spoken about the report on Hungary. I think I should ask you whether you have any official opinion, semiofficial opinion, private opinion, or confidential opinion about the way in which this report should be handled by the General Assembly?

THE SECRETARY-GENERAL: I have most definitely, Dr. Beer, even a very strong personal opinion, but I shall not tell you.

MR. MAX BEER (*Neue Zürcher Zeitung,* Zurich): Will you tell me afterwards?

THE SECRETARY-GENERAL: Strictly in your unprofessional discretion, I will.

. . . .

An International Administrative Service—
Memorandum for the Economic and Social Council

PALAIS DES NATIONS, GENEVA   JUNE 10, 1957

THE MEMORANDUM that follows on the Secretary-General's proposal for an international administrative service was discussed by the Economic and Social Council during its regular summer session in July at Geneva. As had happened the year before (page 184) the idea again met with a considerable measure of skepticism. In the end the Council decided to request the Secretary-General to transmit the memorandum to Member states and the specialized agencies for their comments and to report again next year in the light of the reactions received.

As usual Hammarskjöld took a leading part in the discussions of the Council on economic and social issues and problems of coordination and development. In general what he had to say during the session in these respects is adequately reflected in the Introduction to his Annual Report (page 629), and did not break any new ground.

I. Introduction

1. At the Council's twenty-third session (964th meeting) the representative of Indonesia asked whether "the Secretary-General could prepare a paper for the Council at the twenty-fourth session setting out his proposal for an international civil service in more concrete terms, taking into account the possibility of the simultaneous establishment of an international training centre, and having regard to the legal and practical aspects that must be considered." The representative of the Secretary-General, having indicated that such a paper could be prepared, the Council endorsed the Indonesian representative's request.

2. The Secretary-General's proposal for an international administrative service was summarized in documents which he submitted to the twenty-second session of the Council [see pages 210–13, this volume] and the eleventh regular session of the General Assembly [see pages

Economic and Social Council Official Records, Twenty-fourth Session, Annexes, agenda item 4, Document E/3017, June 10, 1957.

279–80, this volume]. It was first advanced, however, in an address before the Canadian branch of the International Law Association in Montreal in May 1956. The Secretary-General there dwelt on the close interrelationship of two major revolutionary developments of our time—that aimed at realizing the principle of self-determination and that aimed at improving the economic and social life of the vast majority of mankind which, so far, has had little share in the benefits of modern technology. He pointed to a factor which—as proved by the experience of the United Nations and the specialized agencies in recent years—has constituted a major obstacle to the full realization of these objectives. "The capacity of a country to absorb large-scale economic assistance," he said, "or to make the best use of its domestic resources, is in no small measure determined by its administrative arrangements. It is significant, for example, that in every one of the reports of the economic survey missions sent out by the United Nations and the International Bank, some reference has been made to the handicap imposed by poorly developed public administration and the shortage of competent officials." The shortage of competent officials therefore represented, in his view, a critical problem towards the solution of which the United Nations should be able to make a useful contribution. This would entail the adoption of an approach somewhat different from those hitherto followed. He referred to the suggestion which had been made shortly before by the Canadian Secretary of State for External Affairs, Mr. Lester Pearson, for the establishment of "an international professional and technical civil service of the United Nations with experts especially trained for work in the underdeveloped areas." The Secretary-General envisaged a career service under international responsibility for qualified men and women of any nationality "who are prepared to . . . work in the less-developed countries of the world as public officials integrated in the national administrations of these countries while maintaining their international status."

II. Existing International Programmes
Regarding Public Administration

3. In recent years there has been no lack of awareness in the United Nations and the specialized agencies of the importance of strengthening and developing public administration in many of the less-developed countries. This objective has been underlined time and again in the de-

bates on economic development in the General Assembly and the Economic and Social Council of the United Nations; as early as 1950 the Administrative Committee on Coordination (ACC) had "become increasingly aware of the degree to which the realization of the economic and social objectives of the Charter and the efficacy of international effort toward achieving those objectives presuppose the strengthening and development of national administrations responsible for economic and social matters" (E/1865, paragraph 6). This same preoccupation may be noted in the Technical Assistance Board's report entitled A Forward Look (E/2885, paragraph 91).

4. Many governments have called upon the expanded and the regular programme of technical assistance of the United Nations and the specialized agencies for help in improving their public administration. The specialized agencies have concerned themselves with advisory and other assistance in building up particular departments and services— especially those dealing with labour problems, agriculture, education, and public health. The United Nations has likewise given assistance in the strengthening of certain ministries, particularly ministries of national economy, industry and commerce, social affairs, and housing. It has also provided advisers in general public service organizations and personnel administration; advisers in specific areas of administration, especially in the budgetary and fiscal fields; aid in the development of public administration training schemes, both within the framework of the public service and in collaboration with universities; the organization of seminars and discussion groups on personnel administration and budget management; and the provision of fellowships for the study abroad of various aspects of administration. Most of these services have been within specific administrative fields and advisory in character. Only in a few cases has the United Nations assigned technical assistance personnel to undertake actual administration or management of government activities.

III. The Need for a New Approach

5. It is of crucial importance that international assistance in the building up and strengthening of public administration should be given greater emphasis. There is ample justification for extending each of the various types of existing programmes, particularly the training programmes, which were dealt with at length by the Technical Assistance

Board in A Forward Look (paragraphs 26 and 27) and are further considered in Sections VIII and IX below. But something of a new departure is also necessary. However productive formal training schemes may be and however essential to achieving the long-range objective of building up efficient national administrations, they do not provide an immediate solution to the urgent problem of the lack of trained administrators. Nor do foreign expert advisers, however resourceful and adaptable they may be. In the course of a tour of duty this spring covering some twenty countries that are receiving technical assistance from the United Nations, the Director-General of the United Nations Technical Assistance Administration (TAA) found that the most significant new emphasis in his discussions was the repeatedly expressed desire of the governments to obtain executive, administrative, or managerial assistance. Many of these governments appeared to feel that, at the present stage, such assistance was necessary if they were to overcome some of the more serious handicaps to their countries' economic development without almost intolerable delays.

6. It is to this immediate problem of the shortage of experienced administrative officials that the Secretary-General's proposal for an international administrative service is directed. The members of such a service (hereafter referred to as "the administrators") should not be limited to the organizational and technical aspects of public administration. They should be made available in response to governments' requests to meet the practical needs for managerial and executive assistance throughout the entire range of public services, particularly those concerned with economic and social development. They should function in the same way as national public servants in the employ of the government, rather than as advisers. It may be anticipated that in some cases they would be assigned through the central government to autonomous public agencies or other organizations.

7. Many of the so-called underdeveloped countries, it is well realized, would not feel the need of such an international administrative service. But the Secretary-General believes that for a number of such countries, and especially those which have not yet had the time to build up administrative traditions and an administrative cadre of their own, it should offer considerable advantages. The United Nations is in a unique position to resolve many of the difficulties—the magnitude of which should not be underestimated—involved in locating officials of the qualifications and standing required, and in negotiating the necessary

arrangements with them. It could obviate or help to meet a number of other difficulties normally encountered by governments in trying to make their own arrangements for such purposes—difficulties relating, for example, to payments in currency unavailable to the government concerned; to arrangements for home leave and family travel and education; and to termination of the arrangement with a minimum of embarrassment if it is not proving to be satisfactory. Since the administrative support would come through the United Nations but within the framework of the national services concerned, overtones of dependence on another country or risks of divided loyalty on the part of the officials concerned should not arise.

IV. Characteristics and Scope of the Proposed Service

8. It follows from the character of the proposed service that, in the performance of their duties, the administrators should be responsible solely to the governments to which they are assigned. They would not report to or take instructions from the United Nations; nor should they take the oath normally required of technical assistance experts that, in the words of Article 100 of the Charter, they would accept instructions from no authority external to the United Nations Organization. That they should have the sense of an international mission is, however, equally important. The administrators would be serving the cause of the United Nations; they should accept the rigorous standards of conduct and competence required of international servants, possess an adequate understanding of the principles of the United Nations, and feel that they can draw upon its resources in the discharge of their duties. For this purpose, an administrator drawn from a national service should normally have a period of orientation at United Nations Headquarters before taking up his first assignment.

9. The service would aim at providing not "experts" in any narrow sense of that term, but experienced administrators versatile enough to occupy with distinction positions of responsibility of many different types and in many different areas of civil administration. The determining factor as to the actual assignments given them should be the needs expressed by the governments concerned. It may be assumed that most requests would be for administrators at relatively senior levels; but it is often important that senior officials be adequately supported at the in-

termediate grades, and some appointments at this level should therefore be contemplated. It would be important to ensure that national officials are not displaced or otherwise penalized; since there would normally be a dearth of such officials, this problem should not often arise, but where it does, a device such as the creation of temporary posts *hors cadre* for international administrators might be useful.

V. Recruitment and Conditions of Service

10. The highest standard would rightly be demanded of the members of the proposed service, with emphasis no less on quality of character and social outlook than on intellectual background and professional competence. Efforts would also be made to draw candidates from many countries. One source would be experts who have served with distinction under the technical assistance programme; another would be regular staff members of the United Nations and the specialized agencies with the requisite experience. Again another important source would be high-ranking officials or former officials from national services. Recruitment for the service should be undertaken through the world-wide facilities that are now at the United Nations' disposal.

11. The administrators should receive from the United Nations approximately the same total remuneration as international officials of comparable standing in the area, including international travel costs. Of this amount, the government should contribute at least the equivalent of the salary of national officials of comparable rank, which would be payable in local currency to the United Nations and used as part of the administrator's emoluments. The government would furthermore be requested to assist in making arrangements for housing, local transportation, and medical and hospital expenses. These amounts should be payable in local currency to the United Nations. Other conditions of service—leave rights, education grants, superannuation payments, etc.—should be based, as far as possible, on those applying to staff members of the United Nations and the specialized agencies.

12. The assignments of administrators would have to be for longer terms than is customary in the case of consultants, if an effective job is to be done. It would be hoped, moreover, that in most cases the administrators could move from one assignment to another with reasonable transitional periods—including periods for briefing and actual service at

Headquarters as appropriate. In this way, a small expert corps of career administrators would gradually be built up.

13. The Secretary-General, acting on behalf of the United Nations, would conclude agreements with the individual administrators as well as with each government to which an administrator would be furnished. In addition, a relationship would be established between the administrator and the government which could be formalized as a contract if required. There would, therefore, exist a three-way legal relationship, which would provide the necessary guarantees both to the governments and to the individual administrators concerned. Each of these relationships is further discussed in the appendix on "Legal Arrangements."

VI. Organization and Method of Operation

14. The most convenient initial arrangement would be for the service to be administered, under the Secretary-General's responsibility, by TAA, as a separate item of United Nations activity. Under such an arrangement, requests would be processed by the Secretariat in consultation with the government concerned in the same manner and with the same machinery as those received under the programmes relating to the development of public administration, social welfare advisory services, and advisory services in human rights already established by the General Assembly.

15. As stated above, the administrators should be able to draw freely on the resources of the United Nations; this would include more particularly the substantive advice of the Department of Economic and Social Affairs and the Public Administration Division of TAA. Such outside assistance as that of universities and professional organizations, whose cooperation is already being afforded to the United Nations, should also be made available to them as required.

16. While the proposed service would seem especially appropriate in certain areas of administration with which the United Nations itself is particularly concerned, the full cooperation of the specialized agencies would be necessary to meet requests for administrators to work in technical ministries and services within their fields. The operation as a whole should be kept under review by ACC with a view to ensuring the fullest use of the resources of the various organizations within the United Nations system.

17. The Secretary-General should report annually on the programme

to the Economic and Social Council, which would exercise general supervision and control.

VII. Initial Arrangements

18. If the scheme outlined above commends itself in principle to the Council, the Council may wish to authorize the Secretary-General to proceed with the establishment of the service on an experimental basis and on a modest scale. As a method of assisting governments under paragraph 2 of Article 66 of the Charter, the experiment could be initiated by a resolution of the Council authorizing the Secretary-General to take preliminary steps on the lines of this report subject to the approval of the General Assembly. Alternatively, the proposal could be referred by the Council to the General Assembly for its consideration and the necessary authorization.

19. To enable the Secretary-General to make a first response to requests that may be received, an appropriation within the 1958 budget estimates of the United Nations would be needed. Since the headquarters functions of recruitment, placement, control, and consultation with governments could initially be handled by the existing machinery of the United Nations Secretariat, costs on this account would be very small and the bulk of such funds as are made available could be used for operations.

20. The Secretary-General would submit his first report to the Council at its twenty-sixth session in the summer of 1958. In the light of this report, which would indicate the degree and scope of the interest displayed by the governments of underdeveloped countries and provide an estimate of the probable costs, the Council could decide whether to establish the service on a more permanent basis. If the decision were positive, definite arrangements for the service, covering *inter alia* finance, could then be made.

21. During the experimental period the Secretary-General would remain in consultation with the executive heads of the specialized agencies through ACC, but, without their specific agreement, he would not provide for services within the substantive competence of their respective agencies.

* * *

*VIII. Training Schemes and the
International Administrative Service*

22. There is a close link between this proposal for an international administrative service and existing or proposed training schemes. The administrator could be of great help in stimulating training within the country and thus increasing the supply of personnel available for promotion to posts of increased responsibility. A good deal of on-the-job training would, moreover, be done by the international administrator himself in the normal course of his duties. One of his principal tasks would be to identify and to train able local officials in such a way that they would be ready to take over on his departure.

23. Experience suggests that training for public service is most effective when it is closely related to the actual tasks and the day-to-day problems of administration. The practical experience gained on the job is often supplemented by in-service training closely associated with the work of departments or, at the higher levels, by a training institute or a staff college associated with the public service. The international administrator could give considerable impetus to in-service training by assisting in the establishment and advising on the programmes of such institutes or colleges.

24. The international administrator could also play a useful role in negotiating arrangements for the training of suitable candidates abroad. This type of training has been successfully accomplished through fellowship programmes, arranged under the auspices of the United Nations, the Colombo Plan, and other regional agencies, or through bilateral technical assistance programmes and other facilities offered by the countries which are administratively more advanced to students from other countries. The programme of fellowship awards forming part of the technical assistance programme, referred to in paragraph 4 above, can be used to supplement local and national resources.

IX. National, Regional, and International Training Projects

25. Training for a particular public service must primarily be provided within the administrative framework of the country concerned; for, whilst certain general principles may be common to all administra-

tions, the more specific requirements of particular governments are conditioned by such factors as the political and economic structure and the administrative practices of the country concerned. Those responsible for the United Nations technical assistance programme have therefore devoted special attention to national training programmes, usually with considerable success. Through this programme, for example, the development of institutes for the teaching of public administration has been stimulated in Egypt, Ethiopia, and Libya, and civil service training schemes have been established in Burma and Israel.

26. Similar projects of a regional character have succeeded in some cases where the circumstances were especially favourable, the most outstanding example being the Advanced School of Public Administration in Central America, located in San José in Costa Rica and serving the republics of Costa Rica, El Salvador, Guatemala, Honduras, and Nicaragua. Other significant similar projects, which include a programme for foreign students, have been developed with United Nations assistance in Brazil and Turkey.

27. Whilst the establishment of an international centre for training in public administration was decided upon by the General Assembly in 1948 (resolution 246 (III)), the time has not yet seemed ripe for the realization of this proposal. There are, however, signs of a return to a more general approach in specific specialized fields of administration. The Economic Development Institute organized by the International Bank for Reconstruction and Development in Washington to assist selected senior officials of underdeveloped countries has made an encouraging start. So have the tax administration programmes organized by Harvard University Law School and by the Inland Revenue Department of the United Kingdom and attended by a number of United Nations fellowship holders. Other programmes of training, specifically designed for fellowship holders from particular areas or in particular subjects, are now under consideration within the United Nations.

28. The TAA has this year undertaken an extensive analysis and evaluation of its public administration training projects. The Secretary-General may have some practical suggestions for the extension of training programmes to put forward after the completion of this inquiry.

APPENDIX

*Legal Arrangements Relating to the Service
and the Administrators*

Relation of the administrator to the United Nations

The administrators would not, of course, be members of the Secretariat since it would not be legally possible, in view of Articles 100 and 101 of the Charter, to give them the status of staff members and, at the same time, make them responsible to governments to the degree envisaged in the proposal. It would, however, be necessary for the United Nations to enter into a contractual relationship with these officials in order to specify the payments and benefits which they would receive from the United Nations. Thus personal benefits for each administrator would be specified in the contract itself and might cover salary, posts, the period of assignment, and entitlement to home leave and repatriation. The contract would also lay down the standards of integrity and conduct governing the administrators, though this could be done alternatively by incorporating by reference the relevant rules laid down by the Secretary-General.

Relation between the United Nations and the employing government

In addition to entering into a contract with the administrator, the United Nations would also conclude an agreement with the government to which he would be assigned covering the conditions of the assignment. These agreements would contain the basic conditions governing the programme and would in addition include specific provision for the protection of the rights and certain immunities of the administrators.

Following the practice in respect of technical assistance agreements, the United Nations and the government would conclude only one agreement which would cover the service of any administrator who might be assigned to the government, thus eliminating the necessity of drawing up separate agreements for each administrator. Whenever possible, a standard text would be used for agreements with all governments, and its terms would be coordinated with those of the contract between the United Nations and the administrator.

Relation of the administrator to the employing government

The conditions of service of the administrator would largely be set by the government, in its general regulations or in the terms of appointment issued by it to the administrator, or in both. It might be necessary in some cases for the administrator and the government to enter into a contract between themselves, notwithstanding the conclusion of an agreement between the administrator and the United Nations and between the latter and the government. Depending upon their administrative provisions or practices, other governments might wish to grant the administrator an appointment to the post he is to fill, in the same manner as any other official of that government. It does not appear that the United Nations could or should insist upon one alternative or the other, but in either case the relationship between the government and the administrator would be made subject to the agreement between the United Nations and the government.

Assignment of the administrator to agencies, corporations, etc.,
below national government level

The United Nations may agree in appropriate circumstances to the assignment of an administrator outside the central or national government itself. In such a case, the contract or appointment mentioned in the preceding paragraph, which would normally have been entered into by the central government and the administrator, would be between the employing organization and the administrator. However, the United Nations would conclude the same agreement with the central government covering the service of the administrator that it would conclude in any other case. This agreement would provide that responsibility for compliance with the usual obligations of employing governments would remain with the central government, notwithstanding the fact that the actual employing agency may be some other organization; and that the contract or appointment made by the employing organization and the administrator would be subject to the agreement between the United Nations and the central government.

Relation between the United Nations or the administrator,
on the one hand, and the government of the country of which
the administrator is a national on the other.

There appears to be no necessity for establishing a special formal legal relationship between the United Nations or the administrator, on the one hand, and the government of the country of which he is a national, on the other, for the purpose of the programme under discussion. Special arrangements might be made by governments covering their nationals employed by the service to ensure that the administrators and their families do not suffer in any way. For example, when the administrator is recruited from the ranks of the government and with its concurrence, the government might agree to reinstate him after a period of detachment as a member of the service, without prejudice to his promotion prospects and without loss of pension and other rights for the time of his detachment. It is expected that matters such as the foregoing would be settled by the administrator and his government directly between themselves, without the intervention of the United Nations.

From Transcript of Press Conference

AT THIS press conference, besides the usual questions on Middle East developments, reference was made to the report of the Assembly's Special Committee on the Problem of Hungary and to Chapter I of the Secretary-General's Annual Report.

The Committee's second and final report on its investigation of the circumstances of the Soviet intervention in Hungary had been issued in June and its carefully documented conclusions presented a powerful indictment of the Soviet course.

Chapter I of the Secretary-General's Annual Report (the Introduction as usual was issued later as a separate document; see page 629) was a straightforward chronological account, without value judgments, of all United Nations action on Middle East questions during the past year, beginning with the Secretary-General's "cease fire" mission in the spring of 1956. In his response to a question Hammarskjöld hoped it would prove useful as "a kind of index" to the record. However, he took pains to disabuse his questioner of any notion that he favored discussion of the problems at the forthcoming Assembly session "in this larger context." On the contrary, as his reply indicated, he was working to avoid a rerun of the bitter debates of last winter and would, for his part, only ask the Assembly for such action as was required on limited and concrete issues. In fact, as will be seen, the Assembly acted only on the questions of financing for UNEF, the clearance of the Suez Canal, and the Palestine refugee program.

During the press conference Hammarskjöld engaged in an extraordinary exchange with the noted Danish writer and explorer, Peter Freuchen, on an unconventional question concerning moral responsibility. After the press conference he carried his response further in remarks at a luncheon that day for visiting members of the World Council of Churches (second following text). A few weeks later Freuchen unexpectedly passed away and Hammarskjöld spoke of him as a friend at the beginning of his press conference on September 5 (page 648).

THE SECRETARY-GENERAL: Ladies and gentlemen, this is a rather quiet time of the year, and we should be grateful for that. Under such circumstances it is, of course, a little doubtful whether there is very much

UN Note to Correspondents No. 1633, August 8, 1957.

sense in a press conference. Events have not been very frequent on the United Nations side recently, and there are no major developments which require background information or discussion. When, all the same, I invited you to this press conference, it was simply because in doing so I wanted to demonstrate that I wish to keep up what I think we agree is a good tradition. If nothing very much comes out of it, at least we have been in touch and we have, so to say, kept alive this contact, which certainly very soon will have to be intensified.

With those introductory words of explanation, I think I have given you the setting, as I see it, for this press conference. Since we met last time, I and my friends in the Secretariat have got a new colleague, Mr. Dobrynin of the USSR [Anatoly F. Dobrynin, UN Under-Secretary 1957–1960, later Ambassador to the United States]. He is present here, and I should like to take this opportunity, now that he has taken up his functions in the Secretariat, to introduce him to you.

MR. DOBRYNIN: I am glad to be coming to the United Nations as Under-Secretary under Mr. Hammarskjöld.

THE SECRETARY-GENERAL: Thank you. I am certain that you will run into each other quite a lot, and for that reason I wanted to take this opportunity just to make you shake hands in this way. That is all from my side at this moment, and now it is up to you to give us something to do.

. . . . MR. CHAIM ISAAK (*Davar,* Tel Aviv): Colonel Leary last week rejected an Israel request for an investigation of Syria's attitude. The request was based on Article I of the Armistice Agreement. Now, if I remember correctly, in your report of April 1956 to the Security Council, you mentioned the need of devising certain procedures to deal with complaints arising out of Article I. Has anything been done in the meantime? What kind of procedures have you in mind?

THE SECRETARY-GENERAL: To my regret, that proposal of mine did not meet with very much response from the governments concerned. What I had in mind, really, was a kind of accepted and regularized Secretariat good offices system—a system where it would be, so to speak, accepted by the parties that where, let us say, the Mixed Armistice Commission's competence was at least in doubt, the Secretariat would be the proper organ to take up certain issues which, under all normal circumstances, would be handled by regular diplomatic channels, channels that, as you know, do not exist in this case.

Now, the fact that no such agreement was reached, adding to the Armistice Agreement, in a somewhat informal way, a new instrument, does not of course in any way bar the Secretariat from functioning in accordance with its competence under the Charter. That is to say, the fact that there is neither access to normal diplomatic means nor, according to the interpretation of the Chief of Staff, the necessary competence for the MAC does not mean that there are not ways in which the matter can be dealt with within the United Nations system.

. . . . MISS PAULINE FREDERICK (*National Broadcasting Company*): Mr. Secretary-General, some time ago you indicated that psychological changes were taking place in the Middle East which, if maintained and strengthened, might eventually lead to some kind of negotiations. Could you say whether those psychological changes are continuing, whether they have been strengthened, and what progress has been made?

THE SECRETARY-GENERAL: Questions of degree are always very difficult. To take the first part of your question: if the tendency is continued, I would say, in my opinion, yes. As you know, and I may use this opportunity to stress it, the last few weeks on the southern border of Israel with Egypt has been a period of very great quiet.

MR. PETER FREUCHEN (*Politiken,* Denmark): Mr. Secretary-General, talking about psychology, haven't you noticed that while you and other great statesmen are working with the great problems, the spirit of unanimity is deteriorating and rotting away inside. For example, take your own country and mine. Canada is copying our furniture; Japan is stealing our things—you know, making silverware; Spain is copying our glassware, and so on. We can see all over that inside there is developing more and more dissatisfaction between neighbors and other countries. Should not the United Nations make some sort of propaganda to try to keep alive the spirit of friendship and brotherhood among nations? It may be that however much you keep people from shooting at each other, inside they still might do much to break down all those things which the United Nations should stand for.

THE SECRETARY-GENERAL: I cannot help feeling that it is for you and for those who feel like you to speak out and to work for that spirit which you have in mind. There are many who do it, as you know. It falls a little bit outside of the professional field of this Organization, which, in a certain sense, is much more modest. We work with human beings as they happen to be, and we have very little hope that we may change human beings. It is enough of a job for us at the present stage to try to get somewhere on the basis of a recognition of weaknesses which we all share.

MR. PETER FREUCHEN (*Politiken,* Denmark): How can you, if you don't think that you can change the minds of people? People have been fighting all the time. I don't understand, but I think you are—pardon me, I should not, of course, say to you that you are wrong—but, ——— ——— ———, you are wrong when you say that it is outside the United Nations task to try to persuade people to help each other and to keep friendship. I think those are the small things which do more harm than the big headlines in the newspapers. Don't you think so too?

THE SECRETARY-GENERAL: I don't think that we can go deeply into a discussion of this question, but let me make it quite clear that I may not be so wrong as you say.

MR. PETER FREUCHEN (*Politiken,* Denmark): I did not mean to say . . .

THE SECRETARY-GENERAL: Let me for one second—as we are likely to have some time for this kind of philosophical discussion as other matters don't seem too pressing—try to explain what I mean. In my case, on one side I wear the hat of the Secretary-General, and on the other hand I am a human being like anybody else. In the first capacity I do not feel like moralizing. In the second capacity I may try to convert my fellowmen. You see that I keep the two functions apart. The second element, the human element, is the one which I think can reconcile you to my general statement that the Secretary-General should not try to be a moral prophet.

MR. LEVON KESHISHIAN (*Al Ahram,* Cairo): Has the Secretary-General played any role as a mediator or intermediary between the old Suez Canal Company and the Egyptian government?

THE SECRETARY-GENERAL: In a very modest sense, because I have it as a kind of informal obligation to follow up the discussions which last took place here in the United Nations in early May and which left various questions pending. All those questions are questions which are under constant consideration and discussion between me and the various parties concerned. For that reason it is true that I have contact on this matter, as a part of the general picture, with Cairo. It is also true that I have had, as I had during the winter, contact with the Canal Company. But the information which has been given concerning my transmitting this and that kind of proposal is unfounded.

MR. LEVON KESHISHIAN (*Al Ahram,* Cairo): May I follow that question? Have these discussions concerned the question of the payment of compensation to the old Company?

THE SECRETARY-GENERAL: If you go back to the general declaration of the Egyptian government on the Canal administration, you will remember that there were certain follow-up actions anticipated in that very document. One was the declaration concerning article 36; another was an agreement on compensation; there was a third and a fourth, and so on. My previous reply just meant to indicate that all those questions which are of UN interest are followed up by me not as a kind of agent for the UN but in the same way in which I have been very closely in touch with this question all the time. The reply to your precise question is obvious. As the question of settlement with the Canal Company is one of the problems left open for further action in the declaration, it is one of the questions which come within the orbit of my activities, as I interpret them.

MR. MORRIS RIVLIN (*The Day-Jewish Journal*): Mr. Secretary-General, speaking about the psychological improvement of the Middle East, don't you think it is very much impaired by the continued and increasing Arab Committee boycott against Israel, and, secondly, is there anything in your opinion that the United Nations can do to end this boycott which certainly is not helping the psychological improvement or any other improvement of conditions in the Middle East?

THE SECRETARY-GENERAL: The matter to which you refer is one of the matters which are a deadweight on our efforts. Our own stand on it is perfectly clear. I think it has been clear all the time. What the United Nations, in this case represented by the Secretary-General, can do is just to keep the line straight in relation to the governments as to the burden he considers these various matters to be on the United Nations effort.

. . . . MISS PAULINE FREDERICK (*National Broadcasting Company*): Have you any indication that the worldwide publication of the Hungarian report has had a beneficial impact on the situation itself? Or, as far as you know, is the situation in Hungary much as it was when the Committee reported?

THE SECRETARY-GENERAL: I am not in a position to judge about the present situation in Hungary. As to the impact of the report I do not think I can add very much to your knowledge. You have certainly seen how it has been received by the world press in general and in various countries. I think it is one of those reports which have been noted more than most documents published by the United Nations. That, in itself, is a kind of reply to your question.

MRS. KAY GRAY (*Greenwich* [*Conn.*] *Time*): In your report on the work of the Organization, all the questions relating to the Middle East were lumped together in Chapter I, giving a picture of all United Nations responsibilities in the region. I wonder if you thought the General Assembly discussion might approach the separate problems in this larger context?

THE SECRETARY-GENERAL: First may I say a word about the presentation in the beginning of this report. It is, as you say, one where we have put all the various elements together. The guiding principle, as you have seen, is strictly one of chronology, and I think that is the best way of approaching the matter.

Speaking to you as representatives of the press I would say that one of the things I do hope for is that this chapter will prove useful as a kind of index to the very, very great bulk of material which you undoubtedly will have to handle not only this fall but in the future.

As to the specific question you now raise, I feel that we may have reached a stage where the most fruitful approach will be one which goes straight for this and that kind of concrete issue. To dig out all the big problems in public debate again and perhaps to run over the ground covered again and again last winter does not seem to me to be a good approach. I for one, therefore, in our activities in the Secretariat, would try to present the General Assembly with reports and statements on limited and concrete issues, all of them belonging to the same family, but not lumped together under some kind of sweeping consideration of the whole problem.

. . . .

Remarks at Luncheon of World Council of Churches

UN HEADQUARTERS, NEW YORK   AUGUST 8, 1957

First of all let me tell you how happy we are in this house that you have chosen this building and this little international territory as the place where you meet when you are here in New York. This is a piece of land, and a house, outside the regular type of political battles, that is, those with a strong national accent. Here, of course, we have our own type of battles, but they are of a different kind and they raise problems about which you yourselves know a good deal: the problems always arising when there is a question of finding the ways and means of bringing peoples together—in spite of differences in background, differences in aims, and differences in philosophy.

It is difficult for me really to describe how this Organization functions. You know a good deal about it, but I should have liked to give you a little of the inside story and inside philosophy.

One thing is obvious: it is outside all national territories, as you have underlined and as I mentioned. It is established on a basis which is common to all.

This is a political organization, an organization which first of all aims at presenting to governments and people a new instrument in their diplomacy, a new means in their efforts to establish the proper kind of international relationship. It has been called a town meeting of the world. I do not think that that exhausts the basic meaning of the United Nations. That is too placid a role. We do not just provide a platform for the national politicians in their discussions about mutual problems. We should be something more and certainly we are something more.

As I said before, we are a new instrument added to the arsenal of the politicians. That is the active role and the role I should like to stress. When you do not hear about debates in the United Nations, that does not mean that not very much is going on. I would say that more is going on when you hear the least about it, because that is often the time when the instrument can be put to its fullest use.

Unnumbered typescript.

If it were just a town meeting on international territory, the question of the ideological background, of the spirit animating the servants of the Organization, would arise only in its most modest sense. Then it would be only a question of parliamentary technicalities, where everybody could live his own life and develop his own ideas, and they would account for very little in the general operation.

Once, however, you recognize that this is much more than a parliament, that it is an active instrument, a tool in the hands of the people and the governments, then the personality, the philosophy, the spirit of the Organization, becomes a very important issue. It is not, and cannot be a dead instrument; it must be a live instrument animated by human aspirations and ideas. For that reason the usefulness of the United Nations in the hands of the peoples and governments will to a large extent depend upon the spirit in which the work is pursued.

There we come to the point where your efforts and our efforts meet, because I can say, about the Organization as such and about its Secretariat, that your aims are its aim. This is the simplest way for me, in this gathering, to define the philosophy which does animate and must animate its operation.

At a press conference this morning I was asked—by the way, by a very famous journalist—a question which, frankly, was outside the framework of a press conference (pages 617–18). He asked me what we would do about the underlying differences in the hearts and in the souls of men. He said, "It is all right what you are doing in the political field, but what does it matter if back of it all there is deterioration of this type?" My reply was the only possible one. It was that I felt that he should, as far as the Secretary-General was concerned, make a distinction between the officer of the Organization and the man. The officer of the Organization should not and could not be a preacher of moralism. The man had the duty of every man to fight against those very tendencies the journalist had in mind, but in doing so, he did it as a man and not as a functionary of the Organization.

This reply may have been complete as far as it went but, of course, in one sense it is not complete. There must be a symbiosis between the officer and the man; the officer, like everybody in the house, must work inspired by the aims of the man. I hope that the developments will be such that it may be said that the ideas of the man are reflected, if not in this or that professional act, at least in the whole spirit of our professional actions.

I mentioned this little story from the press conference for the reason that it brings out the limitations in what we can do. What I ascribed to the *man* in his duty in the situation, as described by the journalist is, I take it, one of those duties which are carried by the churches, by the spiritual leaders, and by every individual who has, so to say, put himself under the law which you all serve and which we wish to serve.

What we can do, inspired by the highest ideals as professionals, is of little avail unless the efforts of our Organization get the support from outside which can be provided only by the spiritual leaders and by those who have the courage to follow them. There your role for the success of the effort in which we on the political level are engaged is obvious. It is so obvious that it would be true to say that the world might do without the special embodiment of political efforts that you find in the United Nations, and survive, but that it could not do without the efforts of which you are representatives.

I hope our efforts will combine and that, in that way, you in your efforts toward richer and deeper spiritual life, in unity, will find yourselves supported by what we can do in the political field, just as I can assure you that we feel, directly and indirectly, the immense value that your efforts have for what we are trying to do.

I think that I could not sum up what I wished to say here in a better way than by voicing the prayer that God may bless your efforts and help us in ours.

From Transcript of Press Conference

UN HEADQUARTERS, NEW YORK   AUGUST 22, 1957

THE SECRETARY-GENERAL'S press conferences on August 22 and September 5 were the last before the beginning of the General Assembly session, when it was his custom to suspend formal sessions with the correspondents. One question on the Assembly's agenda was the election of the Secretary-General, since Hammarskjöld's five-year term would expire in April 1958. Hammarskjöld refused to discuss the subject but his reappointment was by now generally considered a certainty. Most of the questions at his September 5 press conference were prompted by the Introduction to his Annual Report, which had just been distributed.

THE SECRETARY-GENERAL: The words of introduction which I used last time we met could certainly be repeated today—and perhaps with even increased emphasis. I must say that, in thinking over this press conference in advance, I felt that there was so little that could usefully be discussed that it might be a good idea to postpone the conference. I think, however, that you share my view that it is wise to try and maintain a pattern so that all of us may know what the plans are. For that reason, here we are—and it is up to you to give to this little meeting the content which you find possible.

MR. JOVAN SCEKIC (*Radio Belgrade*): First, do your personal plans for the future exclude the possibility of giving us the pleasure of meeting you at press conferences in the next few years? Secondly, what has been your greatest experience so far as Secretary-General?

THE SECRETARY-GENERAL: As to your first question, I do not think that your ambition should be aimed so high; I think it will be quite enough—and a pleasure—to be able to meet with you during this winter.

Your second question is indeed a large one. I do not know whether I would be prepared here and now to try and formulate something which would bring out what I really should like to say in reply to that most

UN Note to Correspondents No. 1636, August 22, 1957.

relevant question. Actually, this is a great total experience in which I would hesitate to emphasize this or that element. It is an experience of extremely encouraging cooperation with governments and their representatives, of unusually fine teamwork—and all of it for aims which I think all of you in this room would agree with me are eminently worthwhile. To break out of that picture any special element may be possible, but I should not like to improvise.

MR. DAVID HOROWITZ (*World Union Press, American Association of English-Jewish Newspapers*): In connection with the question just asked by Mr. Scekic, may I ask whether you feel at this time, in view of the fact that so much unfinished work lies ahead—work into which you have thrown yourself—that the greater possibility is that we shall have the pleasure of having you with us during future press conferences?

THE SECRETARY-GENERAL: I really would not like to pursue this discussion at all. You know just as well as I do that there is not a man in the world who is not expendable.

MISS PAULINE FREDERICK (*National Broadcasting Company*): I believe that Premier Kádár has said that the invitation for you to come to Hungary is still open. Would any useful purpose be served by your going to Hungary to look over the situation?

THE SECRETARY-GENERAL: For me, the question remains open. The problem whether or not a useful purpose would be served is, I think, raised a little bit too early. Let us first see what comes out of the debate in the General Assembly.

MISS FREDERICK: Do you feel that both sides will be adequately presented in the coming session on Hungary?

THE SECRETARY-GENERAL: I hope so.

MR. CHAIM ISAAK (*Davar,* Tel Aviv): In view of the vast quantities of arms which the Soviet Union is supplying to various countries in the Middle East, Senator Humphrey suggested the other day that at its next session the United Nations General Assembly should discuss an agreement to limit the supply of arms to that area. What do you think of such a plan? Do you think that that would be feasible?

THE SECRETARY-GENERAL: I should not like to go into the last part of that question; it brings us a little bit into territory that is too adventurous. I think that the problem which has been raised is primarily a problem for those few countries which are in a position to supply arms. If those countries can agree on a policy on the lines you indicate, that is one thing. It is a different thing for the United Nations with all the countries represented in it, to sit down and make statements about what should be done. I think that this is first of all a case for diplomacy of the classical type, and only in the second instance a question for the United Nations as such.

MR. PASUPULETI G. KRISHNAYYA (*P. G. Krishnayya's News Service and Publications,* Madras and Benares): Could you comment on the report that you are considering a proposal to levy a surcharge on Suez Canal tolls to pay for the cost of clearance? There have been reports that shipping companies are being penalized for actions for which they are not responsible. Are you considering any alternative proposals?

THE SECRETARY-GENERAL: The matter is still under consideration and is still being discussed by governments and by me with governments. I am not yet in a position to say what line is the most practical one, the most generally acceptable one. One can take as a basis very different judgments here. One can work on the basis of interest; one can work on the basis of responsibility; one can work on the basis of, so to speak, engagement in the United Nations decision. On the basis of those different judgments, one can arrive at very different results. The justification for the surtax proposal to which you have referred is, of course, that the clearance of the Canal was in the interest of all world shipping using the Canal.

MISS PAULINE FREDERICK (*National Broadcasting Company*): Mr. Secretary-General, have you any indication that the developments inside Syria have in any way affected the border situation between Syria and Israel? I mean, is the situation more tense or has it changed in any way?

THE SECRETARY-GENERAL: I can only base myself on the facts. After the most regrettable incidents which we had in early July, the situation on that border has been quiet. How that should be linked with the developments within the various countries is very difficult to say. What part in the explanation should be given to the United Nations Observers is also very difficult to say. As to the future, that is, the question of what we may have to look forward to, I would not want to indulge in anything which could not be more than sheer speculation.

MRS. KAY GRAY (*Greenwich Time*): It is obviously too early to ask you to produce any detailed blueprint for peace in the Middle East. However, I wonder whether you would care to indicate what you expect the next move in that direction to be?

THE SECRETARY-GENERAL: I would not like to indicate it, because we are groping—not in the dark—but we are groping for the best road, with a very open mind. It is too early to try to lay down what might come out of that effort. Continued speculation would not be either useful or very interesting. I think it is much better to leave it to this rather pragmatic effort in which we are at present engaged. One thing is obvious, and that is that the quiet in the field which has been maintained now to an astonishing degree for quite a while is the natural first step. If we can get from there to a second stage where this quiet will be regarded not as something more or less remarkable and unexpected but as something which is the only natural thing, we will have come closer to an atmosphere in which this or that practical step can be considered. But as I said, at the present stage it is natural that we, with a completely open mind, try to see where there seems to be a road between the trees in the wood and to take the best road, which we can find, when we reach the stage where we can count on further progress.

. . . . MR. LEVON KESHISHIAN (*Al Ahram,* Cairo): I understand that you are trying to settle a dispute between Jordan and Israel on the Jebel El Mukhabar. Jordan was going to present this to the Security Council, and I understand that you are trying to settle it outside. Is that correct?

THE SECRETARY-GENERAL: As you know, there are certain procedures which we always follow here and which I think are justified by practical experience. One of them is that before bringing matters up for public debate in the United Nations we try whatever means the United Nations may have to reach a solution in other forms. It is natural that very often those simpler and more direct methods lead more quickly to results, if they are available, and my own feeling is that perhaps the means which we have at our disposal in order to settle this conflict have not been fully used and fully exhausted. That is to say that it is a question of the natural stages in a procedure aiming at a solution of the problem where necessarily the open debate in the United Nations comes not at an early stage but somewhat later.

. . . . MR. JOHN D. MOLLESON (*New York Herald Tribune*): Mr. Hammarskjöld, in your report last year it seemed to me that you suggested that your job might be broken down into two parts: one for administration and the other for negotiation and mediation. Was this idea accepted that two men might be chosen to fill those two jobs? What are your thoughts about that now?

THE SECRETARY-GENERAL: You will see later in the course of the Assembly what proposals I will put forward in order to follow up what was said the last time. I think that you gave a somewhat too sharp-edged interpretation to what was said last year. It is quite true that this job has at least two very different aspects. I do not believe, on the other hand, that it is possible in practice to separate them fully. Administration cuts very deeply into politics and vice versa. For that reason, I think that it is necessary to follow what was the idea in the Charter to have centralized "leadership"—excuse the word; I use it within quotes —so as to get the necessary integration. However, that means that the work load of the Secretary-General is such that he always runs the risk of developing into a kind of bottleneck. Procedures should be, and I think can be, devised by which that is avoided without breaking up the fundamental unity of the Secretariat and the office of the Secretary-General.

As I said at the beginning, I think that in the course of the fall you will get a report which spells this out in detail and shows what practical suggestions we arrive at as a possible way to solve the problem.

.   .   .   .

Introduction to the Twelfth Annual Report

AUGUST 22, 1957

ALTHOUGH the Introduction to his Annual Report was dated August 22, distribution of the printed document to governments and release to the press as usual did not take place until somewhat later. In this case the date of publication was September 4. The events of the past year and the Secretary-General's personal part in them gave to his annual policy statement a special significance and interest.

As in 1956, the review of the role of the United Nations in world affairs, formerly included as an introduction to the annual report of the Secretary-General, is transmitted herewith to the Member governments as an addendum at a date closer to the opening of the annual session of the General Assembly.

* * *

During the past year, the United Nations was confronted with some of the most difficult situations it has been called upon to meet since 1945.

In the establishment of the United Nations Emergency Force and the clearance of the Suez Canal, the United Nations also assumed responsibilities previously untried by world organization. On another level and in another direction the investigation made by the special committee on the problem of Hungary was a new departure.

The chapters on "Questions concerning the Middle East" and "The Hungarian question" in the twelfth annual report which I submitted last month give an historical account of these important developments up to June 15, 1957. It may now be useful to offer certain observations arising from the experiences of the past year that bear upon the present situation and possible future courses of development.

General Assembly Official Records, Twelfth Session, Supplement 1A (A/3594, Add. 1), September 4, 1957.

The Palestine Question

As this is written the United Nations Emergency Force is completing its sixth month of deployment on the Egyptian side of the armistice demarcation line with Israel. It has, I believe, been a precondition for the maintenance of general quiet in the area of its deployment, just as in earlier months it played an essential part during the withdrawal of foreign troops from Egyptian territory. Indeed, the Commander and members of the Force have fully earned the admiration and gratitude of the United Nations for the manner in which they have served and continue to serve the cause of peace in the Middle East in a pioneering role accompanied by many difficulties and endowed with limited authority. Equally, thanks should be expressed to the states which have supplied the units composing the Force and given it logistical support.

The present situation in the area is, of course, based on the interplay of many influences. The presence of UNEF, incomplete though its present deployment and other arrangements may be, is an important element. However, the policies of governments and the atmosphere of opinion promoted by governments underlie and influence most decisively the course of development. In this respect the comparative quiet that has prevailed is a welcome symptom. At the same time there have been few, if any, signs of further progress.

The quiet maintained in recent months helps towards creating a favourable setting for future progress towards those basic solutions which are so necessary to the security and well-being of all the nations of the area. Now, as always, progress towards such solutions depends primarily upon attitudes and initiatives of the governments themselves. The United Nations can help by lending its influence, its presence, and the processes of diplomacy which are available to world organization. It can also help by providing an objective judgment of the rights and interests involved.

In the Palestine question the United Nations has two special responsibilities. One of these is in regard to the armistice agreements endorsed by the Security Council. The other is the humanitarian responsibility for the Palestine refugees, who have been under United Nations care for nine years now as homeless victims of events outside their control, while the problems of repatriation or resettlement have remained unsolved by the governments upon whom rests their hope for a life more consonant with human dignity.

To work towards a restoration of the armistice agreements, primarily in their spirit but, in consequence, also in their letter, and to give constructive help to the refugees, are obligations of first priority resting upon the Organization and its Member governments.

There continues to exist, I am convinced, a basic will to peace in the area despite whatever signs there may have been to the contrary. I would be the last to minimize the very great difficulties that lie in the way of steps by governments which are necessary in order to translate this will to peace into concrete progress toward peaceful solutions. These difficulties must nevertheless be surmounted. The United Nations cannot, and of course should not, attempt to do this alone. The governments concerned, with whom the power of decision rests, may not be able to do it alone. But the governments, strengthened by the help available from and within the United Nations, can, and I hope will, decide to lead their peoples step by step upon this road toward a more secure and promising future for them all.

The United Nations Emergency Force

The United Nations Emergency Force is the first of its kind. It was created in a few days under emergency conditions without benefit of precedents. It is a temporary force with a limited mandate and designed to meet a special situation. But the value of such a force in situations like that in the Middle East has, I believe, been fully demonstrated and this value should be preserved for the future.

There is need for careful analysis and study of the UNEF experience in all its aspects in order to give the United Nations a sound foundation, should the Organization wish to build an agreed standby plan for a United Nations peace force that could be activated on short notice in future emergencies to serve in similar ways. Steps have been taken for such a study to be undertaken in the Secretariat.

The indispensable services performed by the UNEF Advisory Committee established by the General Assembly should be noted. In the execution of future mandates of this kind that may be entrusted to the Secretary-General or some other agent of the United Nations I believe that the appointment of such "select committees" composed of representatives of Member states would often be of value and would represent a desirable development in the practices of the Organization.

The Suez Canal

During the past year the United Nations has been concerned with the Suez Canal in two respects. There were the differences over the régime of the Canal which arose after Egypt's nationalization of the Universal Suez Canal Company, some of which are still pending. There was also the responsibility assumed by the United Nations, at the request of the General Assembly and on the invitation of the Government of Egypt, to assist in reopening the Canal after it had been blocked early last November.

Like UNEF, the international clearance operation under the United Nations flag was the first undertaking of its kind attempted by world organization. The vital importance of the Suez Canal to the economies of many nations made this a grave responsibility.

The Canal was reopened to full traffic a little more than three months after the United Nations salvage fleet began its work. This was well ahead of schedule. The cost is estimated at about $8,600,000.

An account of the operation is given in the chapter on the Middle East in the annual report of the Secretary-General. A special report will be presented to the General Assembly later. I am sure that the Member governments would wish to join me in paying tribute to all those who collaborated in carrying this task to a successful and speedy conclusion.

Since April, Suez Canal traffic has returned to the normal flow of recent years. However, various questions regarding the régime of the Canal, following nationalization, have still not found solutions which are generally accepted. It should also be noted that the six-year-old question of Israeli shipping remains in dispute.

Members will recall that a number of such questions and doubts concerning the Declaration registered by Egypt with the United Nations as an international instrument were left pending at the conclusion of the Security Council's meetings last spring. The President of the Council then stated that most members had qualified their acquiescence in the Egyptian Declaration as provisional and that, pending concrete steps, the Egyptian government might wish to take to remove the doubts that had arisen, the Council would remain seized of the question.

Since then, in accordance with the intention expressed in its Declaration, the Government of Egypt has deposited its acceptance of the compulsory jurisdiction of the International Court of Justice in legal disputes arising between the parties to the Constantinople Convention of 1888 in respect of the interpretation or applicability of its provisions. On other questions which arose at the Security Council meetings the Secretary-General has continued his efforts through informal contacts with the parties without as yet being in a position to report further progress.

The Hungarian Question

The Hungarian question will come once more before the General Assembly when the Assembly takes up the report of the investigation made by its Special Committee a few days after this communication reaches the hands of the Member governments. A full account of the United Nations' concern since last October with the Hungarian problem, as well as with relief to the people in Hungary and assistance to Hungarian refugees, has already been transmitted to the Members in my annual report and the detailed findings of the Special Committee on the Problem of Hungary were circulated in its report last June.

In view of the wide interest taken in the constitutional issues that were involved for the United Nations in both the Hungarian and Middle Eastern situations, and the discussions to which they have given rise, it may be useful to review here the manner in which the General Assembly met these constitutional issues.

There was, first, the matter of pronouncing judgment as to the facts and recommending remedial action. In the case of Hungary, just as in the Middle East crisis, there was a difference of opinion between a majority and a minority. In each case, the majority acted in a manner consistent with its interpretation of the applicability of the provisions of the Charter and of the powers granted to the General Assembly by the Charter. In both cases, it should be noted, the majorities were very large.

There was, second, the matter of compliance by the Member states towards whom the Assembly's resolutions were directed. There were varying degrees of compliance at first in the withdrawal of troops from Egyptian territory and eventually full compliance as to withdrawal, though not with respect to some of the other recommendations of the Assembly. In the case of Hungary there was no compliance with the

Assembly's political recommendations, a position based from the constitutional side on the minority's view of the applicability of the domestic jurisdiction clause of the Charter. In these circumstances, the question arose as to the means which the General Assembly might use to
secure compliance.

The Assembly may recommend, it may investigate, it may pronounce
judgment, but it does not have the power to compel compliance with its
decisions. Under the Charter, only the Security Council has the power
to order the use of force, and then only to maintain or restore international peace and security. In the Uniting-for-Peace resolution, the General Assembly adopted a plan under which it might make appropriate
recommendations to Member states "for collective measures, including
in the case of a breach of the peace or act of aggression the use of
armed force when necessary to maintain or restore international peace
and security." Thus, the General Assembly may recommend that Member states give aid, including economic sanctions and military aid, to the
victim of an armed attack in the circumstances envisaged under Article
51 of the Charter. In such a case the power of decision on action implementing the recommendations would rest, as it constitutionally must
under the Charter, with the respective Member governments.

At one stage, when there was delay in compliance with the General
Assembly's resolutions calling for withdrawal of foreign troops from
Egypt, the possibility of recommending sanctions arose but no formal
proposal to that effect was presented in the Assembly. Likewise, in the
case of Hungary, when compliance was refused, no delegation formally
proposed a recommendation by the General Assembly to the Member
states that they apply sanctions or use force to secure the withdrawal of
foreign troops. The judgment of the majority of Member states as to the
course to pursue in this latter case was, instead, reflected in the General
Assembly's resolution of condemnation and decision to order an investigation. Both of these measures were appropriate to the General Assembly's own constitutional authority.

Role of the United Nations

The events of the past year have, I believe, cast a clearer light upon
the role of the United Nations in these times. The Charter, read as a
whole, does not endow the United Nations with any of the attributes of
a superstate or of a body active outside the framework of decisions of

Member governments. The United Nations is, rather, an instrument for negotiation among, and to some extent for, governments. It is also an instrument added to the time-honoured means of diplomacy for concerting action by Governments in support of the goals of the Charter. This is the role the Organization has played, sometimes successfully, sometimes with disappointing setbacks, throughout its life.

From time to time complaints are heard about the limitations upon the Organization's power. It has even been suggested that, unless these limitations are corrected, the usefulness of the United Nations is so questionable that the main effort of the governments in the search for peace should be concentrated in other directions.

This view does less than justice to the contributions of the United Nations in its short life. Especially, it fails to take into account that the real limitations upon action by the Organization do not derive from the provisions of the Charter. They result from facts of international life in our age which are not likely to be bypassed by a different approach or surmounted by attempts at merely constitutional reform.

To turn aside from the United Nations now because it cannot be transformed into a world authority enforcing the law upon the nations would be to erase all the steady, though slow and painful, advances that have been made and to close the door to hopes for the future of world society, towards which present efforts and experiences should be at least a modest stepping-stone.

We should, rather, recognize the United Nations for what it is—an admittedly imperfect but indispensable instrument of nations in working for a peaceful evolution toward a more just and secure world order. The dynamic forces at work in this stage of human history have made world organization necessary. The balance of these forces has also set the limits within which the power of world organization can develop at each step and beyond which progress, when the balance of forces so permits, will be possible only by processes of organic growth in the system of custom and law prevailing in the society of nations.

These processes of adjustment take time. Systems of alliance, maintained side by side with the United Nations in recognition of the prevailing balance of forces may serve a useful purpose during the period through which we are passing. However, most of us agree that such systems of alliance, like other traditional means of diplomacy and defence of the national interest, are limited in their value as safeguards of the present and future security and welfare of our countries. Nations and groups of nations will never again be able to live and to arrogate judgment unto themselves in international affairs in ways which once were a matter of course.

The greatest need today is to blunt the edges of conflict among the nations, not to sharpen them. If properly used, the United Nations can serve a diplomacy of reconciliation better than other instruments available to the Member states. All the varied interests and aspirations of the world meet in its precincts upon the common ground of the Charter. Conflicts may persist for long periods without an agreed solution and groups of states may actively defend special and regional interests. Nevertheless, and in spite of temporary developments in the opposite direction under the influence of acute tension, the tendency in the United Nations is to wear away, or break down, differences, thus helping toward solutions which approach the common interest and application of the principles of the Charter.

I believe that the criticism of the system of one vote for one nation, irrespective of size or strength, as constituting an obstacle to arriving at just and representative solutions tends to exaggerate the problem. The General Assembly is not a parliament of elected individual members; it is a diplomatic meeting in which the delegates of Member states represent governmental policies, and these policies are subject to all the influences that would prevail in international life in any case. Smaller nations are not in the habit of banding together against the larger nations whose power to affect international security and well-being is so much greater than their own. Nor do I see justification for talk about the responsible and the irresponsible among the nations. Finally, the two-thirds rule applied to all major decisions in the General Assembly should serve as a reasonable assurance to those who may not fully share the views that have been here expressed.

In this connection, it is worth recalling that the Uniting-for-Peace resolution, in establishing a procedure intended to safeguard the application of the relevant provisions of the Charter—Articles 10, 11, 12, and 51—in support of the maintenance of peace, did not constitutionally transfer to the General Assembly any of the enforcement powers reserved to the Security Council by the Charter. Enforcement action by the United Nations under Chapter VII continues to be reserved to the Security Council. The relative role and significance of the Assembly and the Council, in practice, reflect general political conditions playing within the constitutional framework which, thus, was maintained in line with the basic concepts of the Charter.

With its increase in membership, the United Nations more fully mirrors the realities of the present world situation than ever before, although necessarily the picture given in the debates and votes in the United Nations can be truly evaluated only after a careful analysis. The United Nations reflects, but is in no sense a cause of, the renaissance of Asia. The awakening of Africa, and the other great changes that are under way in the balance of power and relationships of the peoples are likewise part of the dynamics of history itself. As always, they bring with them many grave problems of adjustment. These all too easily may become the occasion for arousing passion, fear, and hatred, and lead in turn to violent upheavals and to the ultimate disaster of war in this atomic age.

The functions of debate and vote are an essential part of the processes by which the United Nations can assist the governments in avoiding these dangers and in guiding the development in constructive and peaceful directions. But if it is accepted that the primary value of the United Nations is to serve as an instrument for negotiation among governments and for concerting action by governments in support of the goals of the Charter, it is also necessary, I believe, to use the legislative procedures of the United Nations consistently in ways which will promote these ends. In an organization of sovereign states, voting victories are likely to be illusory unless they are steps in the direction of winning lasting consent to a peaceful and just settlement of the questions at issue.

Full weight should also be given to the fact that the processes of adjustment and negotiation which the institutions of the United Nations make available to the Member governments embrace much more than the public proceedings of its Councils and Assembly. In the diplomacy of world organization the quiet work of preparing the ground, of accommodation of interest and viewpoint, of conciliation and mediation, all that goes into the winning of consent to agreed solutions and common programmes, this forms a basis upon which the United Nations can become an increasingly influential and effective force to aid the governments in pursuit of the goals of the Charter.

There are, I believe, promising and practical opportunities for improving the practices and strengthening the institutions of the United Nations in this area of multilateral diplomacy. Especially in the past two years we have begun to explore these opportunities in a number of ways with generally positive results. I hope this evolution of emphasis and practice will be pursued and broadened in the future. This seems to be a more urgent task than to attempt formal constitutional changes, the consideration of which the Committee of the whole Assembly, charged with studying the problem of time and place for a Charter review conference, at all events unanimously wished to postpone until a later stage.

Disarmament

This year has witnessed the most sustained and intensive efforts by the members of the Disarmament Sub-Committee to find common ground since the Sub-Committee was established three and a half years ago. As this is written, the Sub-Committee is continuing its work. In the meantime, it has submitted an interim report to the Disarmament Commission. This, of course, would not be the time for me to comment on the substance of the various proposals presented, or to offer an opinion on the degree of progress toward agreement that may have been made. The serious and extensive nature of the negotiations should in itself, however, be a source of encouragement. It reflects the ever increasing weight attached to the problem of disarmament by the peoples, a concern to which governments are fully responding.

Atomic Energy

Important steps have been taken during the past year towards strengthening organized international cooperation in the use of atomic energy for peaceful purposes. The statute of the International Atomic Energy Agency was unanimously approved last October and, by August, the requisite ratifications had been deposited to bring the Agency into existence. In October, it will hold its first session in Vienna. In the meantime, a draft agreement on the relationship of the new Agency with the United Nations has been negotiated with the Agency's Preparatory Commission by the Advisory Committee on Atomic Energy established by the General Assembly. This will be submitted for approval at the forthcoming sessions of the Assembly and of the Agency. Thus, the new institutional framework through which the governments can work together towards the goal of using atomic energy for man's benefit instead of his destruction is taking shape.

The second scientific conference on the peaceful uses of atomic energy to be convened by the United Nations will take place next summer. The Advisory Committee on Atomic Energy has agreed upon an agenda for the conference which promises to result in a worldwide pooling of further advances in knowledge comparable in significance to what took place at the 1955 scientific conference. In the meantime the General Assembly's Radiation Committee has made progress in its series of fact-finding surveys on the effects of radiation on health, which are being conducted in cooperation with governments, agencies, and scientists. When the Committee's report is made next year, we are likely to have a fuller and more accurate picture than before of the effects and dangers of radiation, and also of possible methods of combating them.

All these steps in international cooperation have received, I believe, inadequate public notice. Viewed in a longer perspective, however, they are opening doors to a future course of development of great and lasting significance. Especially, if they were to be combined with a first constructive advance in the field of disarmament, to which they bear a close relationship, their impact on the trend of events might prove to be of decisive importance.

Ghana and the Charter

In admitting Ghana as its eighty-first Member last March, the United Nations welcomed yet another state which has freely attained independent statehood. This event had a particular significance for the Organization, in the light of its responsibilities under Chapters XI and XII of the Charter. Ghana is not only a formerly dependent territory but includes a former United Nations Trust Territory, British Togoland, which had voted in a free plebiscite held under United Nations supervision to become part of the new state. Thus, British Togoland became the first Trust Territory to attain the status of full self-government or independence, declared in the Charter as a primary objective of the International Trusteeship System. Both the emergence of the new state and the manner in which it has attained its independence are indicative of possibilities inherent in those processes of peaceful change envisaged in the Charter, processes which can contribute materially to realizing its goals. These events mark a new step in the development of the role of the Organization in Africa.

The International Court of Justice

In my annual report two years ago, I expressed the hope that the states which had not accepted the compulsory jurisdiction of the International

Court of Justice might give favourable consideration to so doing in the
near future. I can only express regret that in the intervening period the
number of acceptances of compulsory jurisdiction has declined. Now
only thirty-two states, out of the eighty-four parties to the Statute of the
Court, have accepted that jurisdiction. This is contrary to the hopes,
and indeed the expectations, of those who drafted the Charter at San
Francisco. The Court was then rightly envisaged as having a major part
to play in securing peace.

Even more discouraging today, perhaps, than the decline in the acceptance of compulsory jurisdiction, is the fact that certain states have
replaced or renewed their acceptances by declarations containing new
and far-reaching reservations. The Court has been itself faced with the
problem of late, and I cannot fail to express my own concern over the possibility that the present trend, if not soon halted, may render the whole
system of compulsory jurisdiction virtually illusory.

The Court, like its predecessor under the League, has shown that it
merits universal confidence. I am sure all those interested in the maintenance of peace through the establishment of a just international order,
where strength alone is not the answer, would freely admit that the ultimate aim must lie in the universal acceptance of international law impartially administered by judicial tribunals. Even in the present state of
international society there are many disputes which would be closer to
settlement if the legal issues involved had been the subject of judicial
determination.

I can, therefore, only renew my appeal to states which have not accepted the compulsory jurisdiction of the Court to reconsider their position, and to those which have accepted to give earnest consideration to
any reservations which may seriously weaken the jurisdiction of the
Court.

In any event, more frequent recourse to the Court, whether by way of
compulsory jurisdiction, or by specific agreement in each case, would be
desirable. Every recourse to the Court will be a contribution to the establishment of the international society for which we are working.

Balanced Economic and Social Growth

The *World Economic Survey* and the *Report on the World Social Situation* have shown, on the broad canvas at least, a picture of improving
economic and social conditions throughout much of the world. The

postwar period as a whole has been marked by high levels of economic activity and considerable economic growth. Gains have been registered in the field of health, and improvements are also apparent in some other important aspects of the social situation, including food consumption and education, so far as they can be measured by the statistical yardsticks on which we must depend. But these economic and social gains are small when compared with the needs.

The uneven rates of development in different parts of the world remain a source of concern. While production may be expanding and the level of living in general may be rising, the gains in *per capita* income are greatest in areas that are already economically advanced. The need for more rapid economic growth and social advancement in the less-developed regions of the world is a major challenge. It will be necessary to redouble the efforts of all concerned if we are to achieve these goals.

The *World Economic Survey, 1956,* again focussed discussion on certain significant problems with which governments are grappling at both the national and international levels. While in the years just after the war the level of employment was considered in most countries to be the factor of critical importance, more recently concern has been switched increasingly to questions of expansion and growth.

Among the problems which we face is that of inflation. Where serious inflationary pressures exist, countries have had to steer a difficult course of wage-price policy between the dangers of either contributing to further inflationary pressures or of reversing the process of economic growth. The effect of a lack of balance in the domestic economy, whether due to inflation or to deflation, on external economic relations, renders international coordination of national economic policies essential to their success.

This is but one instance in which consultation among various Governments might usefully be developed, and I welcome the recent action of the Economic and Social Council in requesting the Secretary-General to take the initiative, with appropriate advice, in promoting intergovernmental consultations. Such consultations may prove of particular significance in the field of international trade.

In pursuit of the goal of accelerated economic growth, the development and better utilization of resources are of basic importance. Problems of the development of water and energy resources should receive high priority. A report on integrated river basin development now being prepared by a panel of experts working in collaboration with the

Secretariat is expected to be of assistance in many parts of the world and should result in a clearer definition of some of the more urgent tasks which call for further international cooperation. A practical example of such collaboration, in which the United Nations has a special role to play, is provided by the recent decision of the Economic Commission for Asia and the Far East to support joint action by four riparian countries in the development of the lower Mekong basin.

Continued economic development in the world as a whole depends in large measure upon the possibilities of increasing the supply of energy. As rapid a development of atomic energy as possible is essential. Although atomic energy and possibly other nonconventional sources will come increasingly into use, the demands on conventional sources will go on expanding and they may be expected to continue to supply the greater part of the world's energy needs for some time to come. The Economic and Social Council at its twenty-fourth session underscored the importance of international collaboration in the survey and development of energy resources. This is another matter to which I feel the United Nations should devote increasing attention.

In seeking to achieve more rapid economic growth it is essential to safeguard against social and economic imbalance. Rapid economic growth, when not accompanied by proportionate gains in the social field, or vice versa, may not only hinder advancement in the other field but may slow down social and economic progress in general. Moreover, lack of balance may exist, for example, between agricultural and industrial development, between urban and rural sectors, and between investment in facilities for economic production and in health, education, and other social services. These problems were in the forefront of the Economic and Social Council's debate on the *Report on the World Social Situation*. The Secretariat will pursue the study of this question with a view to better definition of the concept and goals of balanced growth and better understanding of the means of achieving it.

Much of the work now being done within the general programme of industrialization, recently endorsed by the Economic and Social Council and the General Assembly, is concerned with these twin aims of accelerated development and maintenance of economic and social balance. The regional economic commissions, and in particular the Commissions for Latin America and Asia and the Far East, are giving increasing attention to these aims. The development of our work in the Middle East and Africa is also important in this connection. Modest as they are, the recent increases in Secretariat resources dealing with the economic and social problems of these regions are beginning to bear fruit. The in-service training scheme for African economists should make a contribution to the solution of a problem that is especially acute in many areas in that region. A parallel development of work in the social field in Africa is also needed.

The need to accelerate both economic and social development of the less-developed countries is the more evident in view of the rapid growth of their population, which in many cases is now proceeding at an unprecedented pace as a result of recent improvements in health conditions and reduction of death rates. Rates of growth that would double the population in thirty years or less are now not uncommon in the economically less advanced regions of the world; the implications of growth at such a pace cannot be ignored.

In this, as in other fields, the more closely the United Nations programme can be linked with the work of the governments, the more effective its contribution can be. I welcome the recommendations of the Economic and Social Council and the Population Commission for extension of the work on population problems at the regional level, and for direct cooperation, on an increasing scale, between the Secretariat and individual governments in carrying out pilot studies on population questions in various underdeveloped countries. I hope that this approach can also be followed in the future in other fields.

Rising rates of population growth have been accompanied by a massive and increasing flow of migrants from rural areas to the cities, often far in excess of the present opportunities for productive employment in the urban centres, outrunning the capacities for expansion of urban industries and social services, and creating complex problems of social and psychological adjustment to urban ways of living. The Economic and Social Council has urged the development of integrated policies to deal with the problems of urbanization. Such policies will take into account the lagging rhythm of rural development and the increasing pressures of population on the land, as well as the problems that appear in the cities themselves. The Secretariat will devote continuing attention to this important aspect of the problem of balanced development in close cooperation with the specialized agencies.

Technical Assistance

The level of technical assistance has exceeded that of any preceding period. This is attributable in part to the improvement in techniques both of the United Nations and the specialized agencies participating in the Expanded Programme and of the recipient governments in preparing and carrying out technical assistance projects. Despite this favourable development, however, the programme as a whole continues to lack resources adequate to meet the expressed needs of Governments.

By a careful control and redistribution of available resources it has been possible to extend operations in Africa to countries which have recently acquired independent status and to some still dependent territories.

In 1956, the General Assembly acted favourably on my request for an increase in the funds for public administration, in order to enable the Technical Assistance Administration to carry out the substantive responsibilities with which it is charged. Progress has been made on an analytical study of technical assistance in this field, based on the operational experience of the last five years.

More than ever the interest of governments in industrial development has been manifest. Associated with industrialization is the increasing demand for assistance in small-scale industries, economic planning, and surveys of national resources. To this must also be linked the endeavours of technical assistance experts to provide a solution to the accompanying problems of social welfare, housing, and community development in an expanding economy.

A new phase in the administration of the programme has been the experimental posting of certain Headquarters staff to Latin America. This has promising indications and has been endorsed by the countries of the region. I propose further study of this experiment in order to determine the most satisfactory pattern for its continuation.

An International Administrative Service

Last year I suggested the possibility of creating an international administrative service. As requested by the Economic and Social Council at its twenty-third session, I submitted at the Council's summer session this year a proposal for an experimental programme whereby the less-developed countries would be provided, at their request, with experienced administrators to work in their civil service and provide managerial and executive assistance where most needed throughout the public services, particularly those concerned with economic and social development. While the status of the internationally recruited administrator would be regulated under agreement between the United Nations and the government concerned, he would be responsible only to that government in the discharge of his duties.

In accordance with the decision taken by the Council at the recent summer session, I am transmitting my memorandum to Members for comments. A report will be submitted by the Secretary-General to the Council next summer in the light of the views expressed. This report will cover also requests received from interested governments for assistance of this type, and the action it has been possible to take to meet these requests.

Human Rights

Hitherto, the human rights programme has been concerned primarily with the establishment of general standards and broad definitions, such as those proclaimed in the Universal Declaration of Human Rights or set forth in the draft International Covenants on Human Rights.

In the course of the year, the United Nations has directed its attention towards the application of the standards, towards the making of inquiries into the principles and practices in respect to specific rights, and towards the development of the means for nations and peoples to enter into a free exchange of experience in the protection of human rights. This "action programme" calls upon governments to submit reports on human rights every three years, directs the Commission on Human Rights to make intensive studies of specific rights (the first subject being "freedom from arbitrary arrest, detention, and exile"), and authorizes the Secretary-General to organize seminars on human rights, preferably on a regional basis.

The positive objective of this programme, which is still in an experimental stage, is to enable nations and peoples to learn from one another of the results obtained and the difficulties encountered in the promotion of human rights and to benefit thereby. It seems likely that by such means gains will be consolidated and new progress rendered possible.

Coordination

Last year, I stressed the importance of continuous efforts to achieve a greater measure of concentration upon major tasks in the economic, social, and human rights fields. To this end, I presented at the recent summer session of the Economic and Social Council a series of proposals for the "streamlining" of work. These proposals had previously been submitted to the regional economic commissions and to such of the functional commissions as met during the year. The proposals and the guiding principles on which they were based were approved by the Council, and the Secretary-General has been requested to pursue the task for the coming year. The specialized agencies were invited to consider the extent to which they might apply these general guiding principles to their own work.

A general appraisal of the scope, trend, and cost of the programmes of the United Nations and specialized agencies in the economic, social, and human rights fields during the next five years was also called for by the Council. The Administrative Committee on Coordination is to consider and advise further on the procedures for this appraisal and for bringing about the greatest possible interagency cooperation on broad programmes of coordination and development of international action in these fields.

One of the conditions of success in bringing about concerted action and fruitful coordination in general is, clearly, cooperation at the Secretariat level. The tasks mentioned here present the Administrative Committee on Coordination with a serious challenge, testing that spirit of unity, with freedom, which should guide the work of the United Nations family of organizations. However, the success of the coordination that the Committee may achieve will ultimately depend on the attitudes maintained by the Member governments of these various organizations.

Refugees

The influx of over one hundred and seventy thousand Hungarian refugees into Austria and some twenty thousand into Yugoslavia has made new demands on the countries receiving the refugees as well as on the services of the United Nations High Commissioner for Refugees. The response to the appeal of the Secretary-General and the High Commissioner for aid to these refugees was widespread and generous. It showed how much can be accomplished through cooperation among governments and international and voluntary organizations and members of the general public who contributed freely not only funds and materials but also services.

There remains, however, the task of meeting the long-term needs of

Hungarian refugees, particularly young people, awaiting emigration, and assisting the integration of those who wish to remain in their country of asylum. Further, the generous response to the needs of the Hungarian refugees may, perhaps, have tended to obscure the continuing responsibility of the international community for those other refugees within the mandate of the High Commissioner, many of whom have now been refugees for eleven years.

It will be recalled that the Assembly has now to consider whether the Office of the High Commissioner should be continued beyond December 31, 1958. I hope that the recommendation of the Economic and Social Council that the Office be maintained will be accepted so that the High Commissioner may continue to render international protection to the refugees.

At the same time, an urgent effort is required to achieve permanent solutions for the refugees and particularly for those remaining in the camps. A comparatively smaller number of men, women, and children is now involved. More could be done for them if countries were to extend the practice of admitting families as units even when they include admittedly "difficult" cases. Surely it should also be possible to provide the comparatively small sums involved and to take those other measures necessary to bring us beyond the stage of temporary expedients and to lasting solutions.

The United Nations Children's Fund

The important humanitarian work of the United Nations Children's Fund is widely known and requires no comments in this context. Special attention may, however, be drawn to the significant role of UNICEF aid as a catalyst for action of a permanent nature in behalf of children, and as an essential element in the whole scheme of international economic and social aid for underdeveloped countries. As these values become better understood I believe that governments will wish to give increasing support to the work of UNICEF.

DAG HAMMARSKJÖLD
Secretary-General

August 22, 1957

From Transcript of Press Conference

THE SECRETARY-GENERAL: Ladies and gentlemen: before we engage in today's exchange of views, I think that I speak for all of us in renewing here the expressions of regret at the passing of one of our colleagues and good friends, Peter Freuchen. It is quite unnecessary for me to characterize him to you. I am sure that you were happy to count him, as I was, as one of our friends.

You have had before you since yesterday the Introduction to the Annual Report, which, as you know, is the paper in which I try to spell out what I feel I can and should say concerning the major problems facing the United Nations. I have nothing to add; I hope it is clear enough. However, I feel that it might be useful for the emphasis at this press conference to be on whatever explanations and clarifications you might like to have on various statements in that Introduction. Far be it from me, however, to try to direct your questions. This is just an expression of my own reaction in thinking of the possible scope of our discussion today.

MR. GERSHON SWET (*Maariv,* Tel Aviv, Israel): On page 1 you state: "The presence of UNEF, incomplete though its present deployment. . . ." Could you tell us what "incomplete" means?

THE SECRETARY-GENERAL: As you know, the resolution of February 2 asked for deployment on the demarcation line, that is to say, the same on both sides. You know that until now we have had it deployed only on the Egyptian side of the demarcation line. As to the other arrangements, we started out developing this and that kind of detail as to their functions. The discussions have never been followed up to the very end, so to say, because, as conditions improved and the authority of UNEF seemed to be quite sufficient, there was no reason to carry on discussions which, in such a situation, would develop a mildly academic flavor.

MR. ALEXANDER GABRIEL (*Transradio News Agency*): Mr. Hammarskjöld, I direct myself, as you suggest, to your report and particularly

UN Note to Correspondents No. 1641, September 5, 1957.

to the Middle East aspect of it, and I am genuinely seeking enlightenment here in respect to what appears to me a rather difficult point. I get the impression in your successful operations within your own scope, within the jurisdiction of the UN, that you are operating slightly under the handicap of a man who has control of his own floor in a building that is on fire and all the other floors are seemingly about to be subject to great conflagration. I know that you know too that you cannot separate one problem crisis in the Middle East from the other. I want to ask you, sir, if you think you would bring this report up to date if you rewrote it today in the light of recent reports of the last seven days; and, secondly, whether you think that, if this whole thing presents an interrelated series of problems, the unanimity of the big powers might not be a great master key solution to the whole thing?

THE SECRETARY-GENERAL: On the first point, I would like to say that I doubt whether the developments that you have in mind are ripe for any comments in the form which you find in this report. On the second point, I excuse myself for finding that the reply is implied in your question. Of course everything in international politics is much easier when the big powers are agreed, especially if their views are supported by the great majority of the small powers.

MR. SAUL CARSON (*Jewish Telegraphic Agency*): I hope you will forgive me if I bring up something which is not strictly mentioned in your report, but it is a collateral problem. I wonder whether you have heard from any of the Middle East Member states about their stand on aggression. There were requests by Israel last winter and fall for Egypt to declare itself on that particular point. It is certainly, in the minds of some of us, tied up with your request for UNEF to be on both sides of the line. It is tied up with your reiteration of your feeling that there is a will to peace, and some of us feel that possibly a will to peace might be demonstrated by a renunciation of aims of aggression.

THE SECRETARY-GENERAL: The exact situation is this one: I have transmitted questions to the effect you mentioned from the Israel government to the Government of Egypt and to the Government of Syria. I have also myself—it was in April—addressed letters to the Government of Egypt and the Government of Israel concerning their stand on Article I of the armistice agreements. There has so far been no reply to any of these four communications.

MISS MARY FRANCES HARVEY (*Quincy Patriot Ledger*): My question is related to clarification of two points in the report which seemed to be related, at least broadly in theory. On page 1, you say that the United Nations can "also help by providing an objective judgment of the rights and interests involved." You do not further elaborate as to say whether this objective judgment comes from the Legal Department of the United Nations as regards treaties such as the armistice agreements or from a majority vote of the General Assembly or from decisions by fact-finding units such as the MAC.

I wonder what you meant in that case; and then, given the fact that there is such a thing as an objective judgment rendered by or through the United Nations, I wonder then about a statement made on page 3 which says: "Nor do I see justification for talk about the responsible and the irresponsible among the nations." If there is such a thing as an objective judgment, cannot the responsibility or irresponsibility of a nation be validly related to what degree this nation takes into consideration such a judgment of the international community?

THE SECRETARY-GENERAL: On the first point, I think that you covered fairly well the field I had in mind. If you put up a truce observation organization supported by both sides and by the United Nations as such, it is of course, just as with a court of law, a foregone conclusion that what they put on paper must be considered objective, and I do not think that any of the parties have challenged the objectivity of the United Nations representatives. Of course, they have always challenged the objectivity of the other side. But in what lawsuit don't you do that?

As to the Secretariat, of course the same requests and the same conditions apply. The Secretariat has a role to fulfill if it does act objectively. And again, if we are not objective and not considered to be objective, I would say that the parties should criticize us, and publicly, and we would have to defend our stand as best we can. I am happy to note, therefore, that on the whole I think it is recognized that at least there is an unfailing will to objectivity in the Secretariat.

When you come to the Security Council, which has functions similar to, although in no sense identical with, that of a court of law, we know that all sorts of interests conflict in the Council. But I think that if you go to the fact-finding and the basic interpretation of law, the same idea prevails; it should be an objective judgment; that is to say, it should not be an *ex parte* judgment. You can continue in that way through the various United Nations organs. That is what I mean the United Nations can provide. It is just the same as having a mediator or a judge in regular life. At a certain point it is valuable to get somebody who has nothing at stake, and who has some training in studying both facts and law, to say: well, this seems to be the situation. It helps toward a solution. That is really what is meant.

As regards your other question about "responsible" or "irresponsible," I would like to be what you sometimes love to call in the press "philosophical." I think that we are all momentarily irresponsible in our actions and reactions, especially if we are engaged heavily, with our interests, in an issue. But that does not mean that we are irresponsible in a general sense. What I react against is the idea that there is a kind of class distinction between members who cannot be expected to react responsibly and members who are supposed to react responsibly. But that does in no way exclude—and I include myself in the judgment, of course—that we, all of us, momentarily can act under such and such pressures in a way which is, in that specific case, perhaps, somewhat short of responsibility. That is an entirely different issue.

MISS HARVEY: In other words, nations may or may not be responsible within a certain context, and yet you would not divide nations into classes?

THE SECRETARY-GENERAL: I do not think we should go too deep into it. The distinction I make, and which I think should be obvious from the text, is between the sweeping judgment that somebody is irresponsible, and a much more narrow one, that we personally, individually, may feel that in such and such specific situation a reaction falls short of that standard. In that nobody, I think, can exclude himself from the risk of running into that kind of judgment.

MR. JOSEPH P. LASH (*New York Post*): Sir, your report deals with the Middle East primarily in terms of the Arab-Israeli situation, understandably so. But in recent weeks that conflict has been dwarfed by the conflict between the United States and the Soviet Union in the area. Do you see any way in which the United Nations can do something useful about this latter problem?

THE SECRETARY-GENERAL: In a sense I have already replied to your question when I said that I felt that these problems—which obviously Mr. Gabriel had in mind—were raised a little bit too early for me to be in a position to say very much about them. I would like to have the water a little bit more clear before having views on how to fish.

MR. PASUPULETI G. KRISHNAYYA (*P. G. Krishnayya's News Service and Publications,* Madras and Benares): In your Introduction, I think justifiably, you are proud of the work done by the United Nations police force in the Middle East and you indicate that the United Nations would be given more sound foundation should such a force become permanent, at least on a standby basis. Can you give us more information on the steps taken in the Secretariat for a study of the "standby plan for a United Nations peace force that could be activated on short notice in future emergencies"?

THE SECRETARY-GENERAL: As to the steps taken, we have had under discussion for some time the best way to handle it procedurally in the Secretariat, and it is quite likely that one of these days I will make public the composition of a special Secretariat committee which is, so to say, digesting all the details of our experience with UNEF. We have not so far formalized this. In fact it is started and the time is soon ripe for a formalization of this study. I may perhaps, in order to avoid misunderstandings, clarify what is said in the report. When I say on a "standby" basis, I do not mean that such and such forces are reserved in such and such a country. What I mean is really that we have the full set of, so to say, master agreements, master legal texts, master plans for transportation arrangements, and so on and so forth, which are completely flexible. That would mean that we would not have any current costs for this standby arrangement, but we would have a booklet where everything is set out in black and white. So that if we were to run into a situation like the one we had last year, we need not create from day to day; we need not approach governments with a lack of clarity as to the conditions under which they will make contributions. We could just press the button and say: With this set of documents—once approved, I hope, by the General Assembly—and all the legal texts, and so on and so forth, would you be willing to do this or that. That is the modest standby idea which is covered by the phrase in the report.

. . . . MISS PAULINE FREDERICK (*NBC*): In connection with your experience with UNEF, if this organization is put on a more permanent basis, would you say that it should have a stronger military character or a less strong military character? In other words, should it be more heavily armed than UNEF? Should it be able to meet military situations as well as police situations?

THE SECRETARY-GENERAL: I think one should start out from the concrete experience we have had; that is to say, trim it for police functions. That does not, of course, in any way exclude the possibility of further study which looks at additional problems which would arise if such a force were given wider functions. But you see, here again it is a question which is raised fairly early. I go on record with the General Assembly with the fact that we digest in the Secretariat the experience we have had so as to prepare, let me call it, the master texts necessary, and then, of course, we frame them on this specific experience. Whether or not this is considered to be a good idea to be followed up by the General Assembly, it is for the General Assembly to decide, and then the General Assembly may give terms of reference for a follow-up study, after we have ended our part of the job, which may very well bring up the broader aspects which you have in mind. But we start out from the hard facts, and that, of course, will give us quite enough to do, even with the very modest frame which UNEF has got constitutionally.

MISS PAULINE FREDERICK: You usually make recommendations; I wondered if you might recommend to the General Assembly that UNEF should have a stronger military character.

THE SECRETARY-GENERAL: UNEF as such—no. What a standby organization should be, I have not gone very deeply into. My own feeling would be that a standby organization—so to speak in a printed booklet, as I expressed it—should be as flexible as possible, should cover as many alternatives as possible. That is to say, it might cover also the case where a more definite military character is given to the force.

. . . . MR. JOVAN SCEKIC (*Radio Belgrade*): Do you think, or do you hope, that it will be possible during the next two General Assembly sessions, to do something in order "to blunt the edges of conflict among the nations, not to sharpen them"?

THE SECRETARY-GENERAL: Most definitely I think that has been done also, paradoxically enough, in the last two General Assembly sessions. It is something which goes on all the time. The very fact of what goes on, for example, in this room during the General Assembly has that effect. Comparison of notes at a table and in the corridors necessarily influences the thinking and blunts the edges.

MR. JOVAN SCEKIC: Do you think it will apply to the special session of the Assembly?

THE SECRETARY-GENERAL: I hope so.

MR. SAUL CARSON (*Jewish Telegraphic Agency*): The annotated agenda for the twelfth session of the General Assembly carries an item pointing out that the Secretary-General's term expires next April. Would the present Secretary-General accept reappointment to his post?

THE SECRETARY-GENERAL: When the Security Council puts that question to me I shall have to reply.

MISS MARY FRANCES HARVEY (*Quincy Patriot Ledger*): The Introduction to the Report states that there are some questions still pending regarding nationalization of the Suez Canal. I recall that, in the body of the Report, there seems to be an inference that negotiations or some kind of mediation are still continuing regarding the point of insulating the Canal from domestic politics. That seemed to be implied in the language of the body of the Report itself. Does this statement in the Introduction, referring to differences—some of which are still pending— refer to that particular point of insulation of the Canal from domestic politics, and are there negotiations or mediation under way in your office regarding this particular problem?

THE SECRETARY-GENERAL: The whole field of differences of opinion which became clear in the Security Council in May is, so to speak, under continual debate. You know that some governments gave their acceptance provisionally. Some of those problems were such that they could be tackled directly; others are more far-reaching, raising questions of principle. What is said here is, first of all, of course, that there is this lack of general acceptance of the régime as established by the general declaration—it is a well-known fact—and, secondly, that problems which are left pending in this context are subject to continued negotiations—informal negotiations. I would not say that all the controversial points which emerged in the Security Council are handled in that way. I felt that it should be first things first. There are some practical issues which should be brought out of the picture as soon as possible, and for that reason I would not say that my own activities cover the whole field. They have been concentrated at one or two points which seem to me to be of special urgency.

MISS MARY FRANCES HARVEY: Would you be prepared to say what those points are?

THE SECRETARY-GENERAL: One point where the basic approach is clear, but where some things remain to be done, is the one of settlement between the shareholders of the old Company, or the old Company, and the Government of Egypt—the settlement made necessary by nationalization. You know the point is covered in the general declaration, and considerable attention was given to it in the Security Council.

That is a practical issue of immediate significance to quite a lot of people and, for that reason, something where I, usefully, can try to follow up as quickly as possible.

. . . . MRS. KAY GRAY (*Greenwich* [*Conn.*] *Time*): In connection with your report on the International Court, you mentioned, in your appeal to Member governments to accede to compulsory jurisdiction of the Court, that there were many disputes that would be further along toward solution if the legal aspects had been the subject of judicial determination. I wonder whether you would be a little more specific on whether or not you would include the six-year-old question of Israeli shipping in the Suez Canal among those matters.

THE SECRETARY-GENERAL: Well, that may be included. Generally speaking, the recent tendency—the tendency after the Second World War—to treat every international conflict primarily as a political one is, I think, unfortunate. There was an old tradition which was in the opposite direction: to treat it primarily as a legal matter, and then to resolve the remaining political issue in political terms. I believe we would gain by a switch back to the older tradition. One consequence, of course, would be that, when there is a legal element in a conflict, like this Suez matter, there is quite a lot to be said for bringing it to the Court if the general tendency is in that direction. On the other hand, the general tendency is now in the opposite direction, and thus a recommendation that it be taken to the International Court is, in a certain sense, a departure from present trends. If I therefore reply to your question in the affirmative: it is the type of question which could have been treated, first of all, in legal terms, and, secondly, in political terms —it does not for that reason mean that I would sit here now and say that it should be taken to the Court. Do not give it that interpretation.

. . . . MISS PHYLLIS GREENE (*International Review Service*): The 1954 resolution which sent you to Peking in connection with prisoners in China requested you, "in the name of the United Nations, to seek the release, in accordance with the Korean Armistice Agreement, of these eleven United Nations Command personnel, and all other captured personnel of the United Nations Command still detained." Do you consider that your mandate in that respect is still open and, if not, when did it close—and, in any case, when is the last time you communicated with Peking, or Peking with you?

THE SECRETARY-GENERAL: The history of the case is as follows: Absolute priority within the mandate was given, as you know, to the fifteen American flyers, who subsequently were released in 1955. At about that time, the United States government started discussions in Geneva with representatives of the People's Republic of China, discussions which covered part of the ground which could be read into my mandate.

It was not a good idea to cross wires and have discussions going on in two different forms or in two different directions. There was therefore a very clear indication that, as long as these discussions continued, initiatives on my side should be left pending. There was no reason for me to butt into a discussion that was going on. That means that the decision, to the extent that there is not, so to speak, full compliance with it on my side, remains alive, of course, like all such decisions of the General Assembly. But, on the other hand, the situation has been and remains such that no immediate action on my side would be indicated.

MISS GREENE: What about the second part of my question, concerning your communications with Peking? When was the last time that you . . .

THE SECRETARY-GENERAL: Sometime early last year.

. . . . MR. ALEXANDER GABRIEL (*Transradio News Agency*): Is there any reason in your mind why you would feel that you should reject an offer to continue to serve as Secretary-General if you are invited?

THE SECRETARY-GENERAL: Mr. Gabriel, I think my previous reply clearly indicated that I do not like to discuss the issue at all.

. . . .

"The Promise of the UN—
Hammarskjöld Answers Ten Questions"
Article in New York Times Sunday Magazine

SEPTEMBER 15, 1957

1. There are those who say that the UN dream has not been realized. Do you agree?

I am not sure what you mean by "the UN dream." The United Nations is not an end in itself but an instrument created to help the nations in efforts to make progress toward the aspirations declared in the Charter. Of course we remain a very long way from a world order worthy of man's highest dreams. But I believe the United Nations has already added indispensable strength on many occasions to the efforts of those who seek this goal and that it can add much more in the future if its role is clearly understood and loyally supported.

2. Critics of the UN say that the UN cannot keep the peace: that whenever there is a crisis, it must be resolved elsewhere. Do you agree?

Let us first be clear what the United Nations is. The United Nations is not in any respect a superstate, able to act outside the framework of decisions by its Member governments. It is an instrument for negotiation among, and to some extent for, governments. It is also an instrument for concerting action by governments in support of the Charter. Thus the United Nations can serve, but not substitute itself for, the efforts of its Member governments to stop wars, and to prevent them. Understood in this way, I believe a review of the record will show that the United Nations has played a major role in most—though by no means all—of the efforts to keep the peace and resolve the crises that have occurred in international life since it was established. It is only necessary to recall such examples from earlier years as the United Nations' part in ending the fighting that preceded Indonesia's independence, in stopping the fighting in Kashmir between India and Pakistan, in ending the Palestine War, in concluding and helping to maintain the armistice agreements that followed, and in the Korean action and the Korean Armistice. More recently there was the resolution of the Middle Eastern crisis last winter. In general, I believe that the United Nations, if properly used, has proved itself to be the best instrument available to the Member governments for the peaceful resolution of those international conflicts which are not readily soluble by more traditional means of diplomacy.

3. Are you hopeful that world peace will be eventually achieved?

I believe it is possible to develop a peaceful world order in which war is effectively outlawed. The United Nations as it is today represents the beginning of such a development. Of course, there is the ever-present danger of slipping backward again. And even if we succeed in building well during the next decades on the modest advances so far made in the institutions, laws, and customs needed to maintain world peace, each succeeding generation will doubtless be called upon to preserve, strengthen and, perhaps, renew the structure to meet new challenges. This is as true in international life as it is in national life.

4. What steps in your opinion are the most vital
in bringing about such a peace?

One important step, as matters stand, undoubtedly is to maintain and strengthen support for the United Nations, with full understanding both of its limitations and of the purposes it can best serve at the present time. In a divided world the United Nations cannot be a policeman enforcing the law upon nations great and small. But because its worldwide membership transcends regional interests and meets on the common ground of the Charter, the United Nations can serve a policy of reconciliation. For the same reason it can, as I have pointed out, serve in many cases as the most effective instrument for concerting the actions of governments in support of the goals of the Charter.

The unremitting pursuit of efforts to achieve the peaceful resolution of conflicts that threaten peace is the greatest need today. Despite the inevitable setbacks and disappointments, the diplomatic processes of the United Nations tend to wear away many differences and to bring us in the long run to solutions in the common interest. These processes should be used more frequently in this spirit.

Recently we have also seen three important examples of ways in which the United Nations can serve effectively as an instrument for concerted action by governments. One is the establishment of the International Atomic Energy Agency, another the creation of the United Nations Emergency Force and the third the clearance of the Suez Canal. I believe we are only beginning to realize the potentialities of the United Nations for such constructive purposes.

*5. What in your experience have been the main
difficulties toward that end?*

The main difficulties in the way of making progress toward peace do not result from defects in the structure of the United Nations. They are caused by the tensions of an age of revolutionary change in the life of man and the relationships of peoples. Such developments as the conquest of atomic energy, with its immense powers to destroy or to create, the ideological conflicts, the renaissance of Asia, and the awakening of Africa, continue to create problems of adjustment more complex, more pressing, and more widely felt throughout the world than ever before. The United Nations reflects all these great changes and problems of adjustment. It is sometimes blamed for their existence. We should rather be thankful that the United Nations exists to help the governments and peoples in their efforts to avoid the dangers and use positively the great opportunities for progress our age presents.

*6. Do you believe that the big-power veto is an insuperable
barrier to effective functioning of the UN?*

No, I do not think it is an insuperable barrier. It is true that under the Charter of the United Nations the Security Council can order enforcement action only if the Council acts with the concurrence of all five permanent members. It is also true that all other substantive decisions of the Security Council are subject to this power of veto by a permanent member. However, there are other provisions of the Charter which enable Member Nations to act together in support of the maintenance of peace on the recommendation of the General Assembly where there is no power of veto. And the General Assembly, like the Security Council, can recommend terms of peaceful settlement although it cannot order enforcement action in the extreme cases where the Council is entitled to do so. Despite the divisions of the "cold war" and the unanimity rule, the Security Council has in the past been able to act on a number of important occasions in support of peace and I hope it will be able to do so increasingly in the future. The relative roles played by the

General Assembly and Security Council in such matters will, as always, reflect the political realities playing within the constitutional framework of the Charter.

7. The critics say that the small powers carry too much weight in the Assembly. Do you agree?

Some critics say this. There are others, especially in the less powerful countries, who say that the great powers exert too much weight in the General Assembly. Both criticisms, I think, tend to exaggerate the problem. No system of weighted voting, based either on power or population, seems politically conceivable at this time. The system of one vote for one nation is appropriate to an organization of states which the Charter declares to be "based on the principle of the sovereign equality of all its Members." Nor is the Assembly a parliament of representatives elected from constituencies. It is composed of delegates appointed to represent governmental policies and these policies are subject to all the influences that prevail in international life, both in the United Nations and outside it. Furthermore the Assembly can act on important questions only by a two-thirds vote.

8. Do you believe that the time has come to revise the UN Charter? If so, in what general direction?

The members of the General Assembly, meeting in committee of the whole earlier this year, unanimously voted to postpone consideration of the question of the time and place for a Charter review conference. As I indicated in the Introduction to my Annual Report a few days ago, I believe that the real limitations upon action by the United Nations do not derive from the provisions of the Charter but from facts of international life which are not likely to be bypassed by a different approach or surmounted by attempts at merely constitutional reform. I also believe that there are promising and practical opportunities for improving the practice of multilateral diplomacy in the United Nations under the Charter as it stands and that the pursuit of these opportunities is a more urgent task than revision of the Charter.

9. The charge is made that the UN is too much of a propaganda forum. What is your answer to that?

One of the functions of the United Nations is to serve as a forum where the hopes and fears of nations in all parts of the world may be freely expressed. Surely this is a useful function and an extension of democratic ideals to the society of nations. To attempt to use the United Nations for mere propaganda advantage and voting victories is to divert the Organization from its main purposes—the winning of consent to the peaceful and just settlement of questions in dispute and the winning of agreement to programs of action that will support the purposes of the Charter.

*10. If there were no UN, what would, in your opinion,
be the state of the world today?*

The world would be in a state where everybody would agree that such an organization had to be created.

Statement in the General Assembly on His Reappointment—for a Second Term

UN HEADQUARTERS, NEW YORK   SEPTEMBER 26, 1957

THE SECURITY COUNCIL met in private during the morning of September 26 and promptly announced that it had "unanimously decided to recommend to the General Assembly that Mr. Dag Hammarskjöld be appointed as Secretary-General of the United Nations for a new five-year term of office." [1]

That afternoon the Assembly interrupted the annual general debate to vote on the recommendation by secret ballot. The vote was 80 in favor, with one spoiled ballot. Because the meeting coincided with the Jewish New Year, the Israeli delegation was absent but the Assembly's President, Sir Leslie Knox Munro, read into the record a letter from Mrs. Golda Meir requesting that Israel's affirmative vote for Hammarskjöld be registered "by means of this communication." [2] Hammarskjöld then gave the acceptance speech that follows. The concluding paragraphs reaffirmed the understanding of the responsibilities of his office which he had given to the Security Council at the time of the Suez and Hungarian crises eleven months before, and further defined these in terms that clearly would give scope for independent initiatives in support of peace.

After the Secretary-General's statement a score of delegates came to the rostrum to express their confidence and pledge their support. Included were the representatives of France, the United Kingdom, the United States, the USSR, and China (which had abstained when Hammarskjöld was first appointed in 1953), and spokesmen for every group of the smaller Member states. The Foreign Minister of Denmark, Jens Otto Krag, expressed the general sentiment as well as anyone:

> Dealing always with the most difficult and controversial matters, and often walking untrodden paths and hoping against hope, Mr. Dag Hammarskjöld has succeeded in finding solutions where none seemed to be in sight. But even more, in so doing he has won our admiration and respect and, I might almost say, a universal confidence very rarely enjoyed by any man and certainly unique in the field of politics. May I say also that his high personal qualities, his friendliness, his patience in

General Assembly Official Records, Twelfth Session, 690th Plenary Meeting, September 26, 1957.

[1] Security Council Official Records, Twelfth Year, 792nd Meeting, September 26, 1957.

[2] General Assembly Official Records, Twelfth Session, 690th Plenary Meeting, September 26, 1957.

dealing with the most complicated Gordian knot, his quiet sense of humor even in the midst of battle, all this has added to the position he holds in our minds." [3]

It is with a deep awareness of the significance of the responsibility which your decision imposes on me that I accept the appointment as Secretary-General of the United Nations for a second term.

When, in the spring of 1953, I was elected to my present office, I felt that it was my duty to respond to the unexpected call. What I could hope to do was to serve the aims of the United Nations to the limits of my capacity. My only claim now is to have tried to do so. Whether my service has met the needs of this difficult period in the life of the Organization and, indeed, the world, is for others to decide. Whether the direction I have tried to give to the development of the Office of the Secretary-General is the best one, will have to be judged in the perspective of time. Your decision is in these respects an encouragement for the future and a highly valued expression of confidence.

Nobody, I think, can accept the position of Secretary-General of the United Nations, knowing what it means, except from a sense of duty. Nobody, however, can serve in that capacity without a sense of gratitude for a task, as deeply rewarding as it is exacting, as perennially inspiring as, sometimes, it may seem discouraging.

There are many reasons for such gratitude. Let me mention first the privilege of working, on terms of mutual confidence, with all the governments and their representatives in order to find ways through the many problems arising in international cooperation.

Let me mention also the gratitude a Secretary-General owes to his collaborators in the Secretariat from the third basement to the thirty-eighth floor. He is fortunate to profit in his work from a team spirit which renders him unfailing support. He can count on dedication, often to thankless jobs, necessary for the success of the joint effort. He can trust that a challenge will be met with a deep sense of responsibility, broad knowledge, and a truly international spirit.

The significance of what this Organization stands for, as a venture in progress towards an international community living in peace under the

[3] *Ibid.*

laws of justice, transforms work for its aims from a duty into a privilege.

Political factors, yet to be overcome or outgrown, may put narrow limits on the progress possible at a particular juncture. We may believe that the United Nations needs basic reforms. We may even share the view held by some that its task ultimately will have to be taken over by a body with a different structure. However, we cannot doubt that the main direction of the work of the United Nations, as determined by the purposes and principles of the Charter, indicates the path which the world must follow in order to preserve the achievements of the past and to lay a basis for a happier future.

Therefore, service of the United Nations guided by those principles is profoundly meaningful—whether it bears immediate fruit or not. If it paves one more inch of the road ahead, one is more than rewarded by what is achieved. This is true whatever setbacks may follow: If a mountain wall is once climbed, later failures do not undo the fact that it has been shown that it *can* be climbed. In this sense, every step forward in the pioneer effort of this Organization inevitably widens the scope for the fight for peace.

I have tried to present my views on the role of the United Nations in the Introduction to this year's Report to the General Assembly. Last year I explained in the Security Council how I feel that I should interpret the responsibilities of the Secretary-General. I have little to add here, and nothing to change.

In the multidimensional world of diplomacy, the Euclidean definition of the straight line as the shortest way between two points may not always hold true. For the Secretary-General, however, it is the only possible one. This line, as traced by principles which are the law for him, might at times cross other lines in the intricate pattern of international political action. He must then be able to feel secure that, whatever the difficulties, they will not impair the trust of Member governments in his Office.

I do not believe that the Secretary-General should be asked to act, by the Member states, if no guidance for his action is to be found either in the Charter or in the decisions of the main organs of the United Nations; within the limits thus set, however, I believe it to be his duty to use his office and, indeed, the machinery of the Organization to its utmost capacity and to the full extent permitted at each stage by practical circumstances.

On the other hand, I believe that it is in keeping with the philosophy of the Charter that the Secretary-General should be expected to act also without such guidance, should this appear to him necessary in order to help in filling any vacuum that may appear in the systems which the Charter and traditional diplomacy provide for the safeguarding of peace and security.

The many who, together, form this Organization—peoples, governments, and individuals—share one great responsibility. Future generations may come to say of us that we never achieved what we set out to do. May they never be entitled to say that we failed because we lacked faith or permitted narrow self-interest to distort our efforts.

Message to the Opening Meeting of the General Conference of the International Atomic Energy Agency

VIENNA, AUSTRIA   OCTOBER 1, 1957

THE SECRETARY-GENERAL'S message to the first session of the International Atomic Energy Agency (IAEA), which follows, reflected the great importance and high hopes he attached to the creation and future potential of this new member of the United Nations family. The draft agreement on the relationship of the IAEA and the United Nations was unanimously approved by the IAEA General Conference on October 23 and by the United Nations General Assembly on November 14.

The message was presented on the Secretary-General's behalf by Under-Secretary Ralph J. Bunche.

May I, at the outset, convey to you the deep regret of the Secretary-General, Mr. Hammarskjöld, that contrary to his plans and his desires, he cannot be here, owing to unanticipated developments requiring his presence at the United Nations Headquarters. Until quite recently, he had hoped to participate in person in the history being made through this important step forward in the peaceful use of atomic energy—an event of untold significance for the world.

The message of the Secretary-General is as follows:

This meeting here in Vienna of the first General Conference of the International Atomic Energy Agency is the culmination of a process of construction that began almost four years ago in the General Assembly Hall of the United Nations in New York. It was there that the President of the United States first suggested the creation of an international atomic energy agency in 1953. It was there that the General Assembly, one year later, unanimously called for the establishment of the agency. And it was in that Hall, on October 23, one year ago, that the representatives of eighty-one nations unanimously adopted the Statute of the Agency.

UN Press Release SG/617, September 30, 1957.

Wheh it was first proposed, the creation of such an agency as this seemed to many an almost impossible task in the prevailing political climate. The governments had sought in vain for years to reach agreements concerning atomic weapons and disarmament in general. Indeed, we know they have not yet succeeded in reaching even a first-step agreement in this field, though the effort still goes on, as it must, and will be taken up once more at the General Assembly in New York this month while you are meeting here.

The development of atomic weapons, as well as other armaments, has thus continued outside the control of any international authority. It is all the more remarkable, therefore, that agreement was reached in less than four years to create an agency in which nations representative of all the different political groupings and regions of the world are pledged to work together in a common program for the development of atomic energy for peaceful purposes.

Without the existence of an organization as representative as the United Nations, it would have been impossible to compose the many differences and reconcile the interests that were involved. The fact that it has been done constitutes, I believe, one of the most hopeful developments in international life since the United Nations was established twelve years ago.

This agreement upon an international program for the use of atomic energy for peaceful and constructive purposes is, in itself, a contribution to the lessening of tensions in international life. It should also strengthen our faith that agreements may in time be reached through the same United Nations processes to banish the threat of nuclear war from the world. Finally, the establishment of the International Atomic Energy Agency opens up possibilities for cooperative development of new sources of power of immense potential significance for future economic and social progress throughout the world and especially in the economically less developed regions.

To an even greater degree than other institutions in the United Nations family this is a pioneering and experimental venture. Your Preparatory Commission has been prudent in its recommendations for the initial program of the agency. But in a longer perspective it is clear that the program of this agency ought soon to become one of the most extensive and important of the programs undertaken through the United Nations family of agencies.

All the signs point to the likelihood that in the next few decades nuclear energy can become one of the principal sources of power in the world. We know also that the addition of this new source of power will be essential both to sustain an expanding economy in many of the most industrially advanced regions and to provide a sufficient power base for the economic development of the less industrially advanced regions, where most of the people of the world still live in conditions of poverty.

The report of your Preparatory Commission declares that "the agency's creation is the expression of common resolve that the development of atomic energy shall not accentuate, but rather diminish the differences in the technological advancement and standards of living of the different peoples of the world." It might be added that the hope of closing the gap by raising standards of living in the less developed regions and thus avoiding some of the evils that accompanied the first industrial revolution of the past century depends to a large degree upon the extent to which your agency is able to carry out in practice the purposes for which it was created. Indeed the program of the International Atomic Energy Agency in the next few years might be regarded as one of the most necessary and valuable forms of technical assistance—understood in the full meaning of the term—that can be provided through the United Nations family of agencies. It will be a severe challenge to provide this assistance on an adequate scale in the short time remaining before the general use of atomic energy as a source of power becomes economically, as well as scientifically, practical.

The United Nations and the International Atomic Energy Agency share several important continuing responsibilities in the international control and development of atomic energy.

Next year the Radiation Committee of the General Assembly will report on the results of a series of fact-finding surveys on the effects of radiation on human life and its environment. This report will be of special interest to your agency, since one of your principal concerns will be measures for the protection of health and safety from the hazards accompanying the peaceful uses of atomic energy. No technological development is entirely free of risk, especially for those most immediately concerned. Yet the hazards in the atomic field are so high that there is special need to pool all available knowledge in this field on a continuing basis.

The United Nations will also convene next year, in Geneva, the second Scientific Conference on the Peaceful Uses of Atomic Energy. The agenda for this conference gives promise of resulting in an exchange of advances in knowledge as important as that which took place at the first conference in 1955. Finally, the report of your Preparatory Commission recognizes the close relationship between continuing efforts toward disarmament by the United Nations and the increasing use of nuclear fuels for peaceful purposes through the agency when it stresses the importance "of a reliable system of safeguards against the diversion of fissionable material to military use."

One of the items on your agenda is the draft relationship agreement negotiated by your Preparatory Commission with the Advisory Committee on Atomic Energy established by the United Nations General Assembly. This agreement reflects the special status of the International Atomic Energy Agency under the aegis of the United Nations and the special need for a close working relationship between the two organizations. It also reflects the desire to ensure effective coordination of the activities of the agency with those of other organizations in the United Nations family. When this agreement is ratified by you, and by the General Assembly at its current session, the International Atomic Energy Agency will enter the United Nations family in the formal sense and become its newest member. I can assure you that the United Nations Secretariat, for its part, wishes to do all it can to develop a fruitful program of close and continuing collaboration on the basis of this draft agreement, just as it has sought to render all possible assistance during the preparatory stage in the establishment of the agency.

I have said that this day—the first meeting of the General Conference of the International Atomic Energy Agency—marked the culmination of a significant process of construction in the institutions created to serve the international life of our times. But the creation of this institution is also a beginning. The program which you will now inaugurate is a unique experiment in international cooperation that can result in greatly strengthening the prospects of peace as well as in great economic and social benefits to all nations. I would be the last to minimize the difficulties you face in bringing to fruition in the years ahead the hopes that the agency was created to serve. But I have faith that you will be sustained in your endeavors by the knowledge of how very much depends upon your success.

From Report to the General Assembly
on the UN Emergency Force

UN HEADQUARTERS, NEW YORK   OCTOBER 9, 1957

THE SECRETARY-GENERAL'S report to the General Assembly on the United Nations Emergency Force was mainly a historical and descriptive account of developments since his last report in March. Except for the problems of finance the report was drafted in such a manner as to play down or avoid raising questions likely to provoke controversy. Thus the deadlock with Israel over deployment on its side of the armistice line was given a passing mention as the "unresolved" issue of "the completion of UNEF's deployment" (paragraph 44 in following text). The question of how long UNEF should continue on the Egyptian side was left open. The Secretary-General simply observed that UNEF continued "to be today, one of the preconditions of quiet along the line between Egypt and Israel" and that such quiet was, in turn, "indispensable to fruitful effort towards the removal of the major obstacles to peace in the Near East" (paragraph 47). His budget requests assumed that UNEF would continue for part or all of 1958.

Action was requested and required from the Assembly only on approving the budget, on how the costs of maintaining UNEF were to be shared and how the required funds were to be obtained. The relevant paragraphs in the text below reflect the beginnings of the financial difficulties that have plagued United Nations peace-keeping operations ever since and, in cumulative effect over the years, came to threaten the solvency of the Organization itself (paragraphs 99–101). The Secretary-General expressed his own concern quite clearly in this report (paragraph 106).

The text that follows includes all those parts of the Report, including some narrative, which are relevant to questions of policy. The report also included a great deal of detail on such matters as organization, logistics, and administrative and financial arrangements which has been omitted here. A more definitive account of such matters is given in the 1958 summary study on the experience of UNEF which will be reproduced in the next volume of the Dag Hammarskjöld public papers.

General Assembly Official Records, Twelfth Session, Annexes, agenda item 65, Document A/3694, October 9, 1957.

Introduction

1. The present report on the United Nations Emergency Force submitted in pursuance of General Assembly resolution 1125 (XI) of February 2, 1957, undertakes to present, in addition to financial aspects, essential data about the Force and its functioning, particularly since the last report of the Secretary-General on this subject (A/3568) on March 8, when full compliance with General Assembly resolution 1124 (XI) of February 2, 1957, as to withdrawal was reported. Prior to that date, the Force had been concerned mainly with taking over from the foreign troops, following the successive stages of their withdrawals from the Suez Canal area, the Sinai Peninsula, and the Gaza Strip. Since March 6, the Force, interposed between the armed forces of Egypt and Israel, has concentrated on its basic function of maintaining quiet in the area through deployment and patrolling in the Gaza Strip, along the eastern border of the Sinai Peninsula, and in the region of Sharm el-Sheikh.

2. The three parts of the report deal, respectively, with organizational and operational matters, the role and functioning of the Force, and administrative and financial arrangements affecting it.

I. Organizational and Operational Matters

1. Strength and composition

3. The original estimate, by the Commander of the Force, of the manpower needs of UNEF to perform the tasks assigned by the General Assembly, was for the equivalent of two combat brigades, or about 6,000 men. This target was reached with the arrival in Egypt of the Brazilian contingent in early February 1957. Since then, UNEF has maintained an approximate strength of 6,000 officers and other ranks, comprising contingents from the ten contributing countries: Brazil, Canada, Colombia, Denmark, Finland, India, Indonesia, Norway, Sweden, and Yugoslavia.

4. The numerical strength of each national contingent on September 15, 1957, was as follows:

Contingent	Officers	Other ranks	Total
Brazil	44	501	545
Canada	113	1,059	1,172[a]
Colombia	31	491	522
Denmark	25	399	424
Finland	15	240	255
India	27	930	957
Indonesia	37	545	582[b]
Norway	71	427	498
Sweden	27	322	349
Yugoslavia	55	618	673
Totals	445	5,532	5,977

[a] Including personnel of the Royal Canadian Air Force stationed at Naples and El Arish (Abu Suweir prior to September 5).
[b] Withdrew on September 12.

5. The determination of the numerical strength of the Force and its components is based upon assessments of need by the Commander of the Force, which have been reviewed from time to time. The main considerations weighed in determining the size and composition of the Force have been: the needs of the Force on the basis of its functions and responsibilities, at first in the Suez Canal region and, later, in the Sinai Peninsula and the Gaza Strip areas; the desirability of balance in the Force with regard to considerations of both geographical distribution and military organization; the comparative utility, in the light of assessed needs, of the troops offered; and the relative availability and economy of transport for the troops offered, together with their essential gear and vehicles.

6. On the basis of the most recent appraisal by the Commander, a reduction before long in the size of the Force by some 400 officers and men may be anticipated. As in any military organization, though perhaps to a lesser degree in UNEF, a substantial part of the personnel is necessarily engaged in vital support functions, such as administration, signals, engineering, supply and transport, workshop, ordnance, medical, dental, postal, pay, provost, and movement control. Elements of the Force engaged in such activities, as the Commander has pointed out, are neither suitable nor available for patrol and guard duties. Thus, of the total force on September 1 of nearly 6,000, only seventy-four pla-

toons, each of strength varying from thirty to forty-five all ranks—a total of less than 3,500 officers and men—were at the Commander's disposition for the regular patrol and guard duties of UNEF. The departure of the Indonesian contingent in mid-September reduced the number of platoons for such duty to sixty-five.

7. The Commander has emphasized in his reports that, for the task it is called upon to perform, UNEF's ground deployment is "very thin," even with the present numbers. He urges that the Force be maintained at a strength permitting a minimum of seventy-one duty platoons, which takes into account necessary allowances for leave, rotation, sickness, training, and essential reserve. Through planned reorganization and adjustments in support units, however, it is expected that a force, reduced from its present total of 5,977 to about 5,600 officers and men, would permit this minimum need for deployment to be satisfied.

2. Organization

8. The national contingents are the components of the Force and each of them, under the commanding officer of the unit, who is directly responsible to the Commander of the Force, retains its identity and organizational unity. The demands of service made upon the Force, however, frequently require the deployment of elements of a contingent, whether companies or platoons, in separate sectors. The Danish and Norwegian contingents, by voluntary arrangement between them, constitute a single battalion, commanded in rotation by officers of the two nationalities. The Norwegian medical company, which serves the entire Force, is under exclusively Norwegian command.

9. The Chief of the Command, Major General E. L. M. Burns, who is Commander of the Force, was appointed by action of General Assembly resolution 1000 (ES-I) of November 5, 1956. The chain of command runs directly from the Commander of the Force to the commanding officers of each of the national contingents. The Force is subject to orders and instructions only from its Commander and, through him, from the Secretary-General of the United Nations.

10. The headquarters of UNEF is located in the town of Gaza. There is a Chief of Staff, who is also Deputy Commander; a headquarters staff, consisting of personnel, operations, and logistics sections, each of which is headed by a Lieutenant-Colonel; and a special staff, consisting of officers responsible for legal, provost, engineer, signals, air staff, and medical matters. The Chief Administrative Officer and his

staff are civilians, drawn almost entirely from the United Nations Secretariat. In addition, a number of locally recruited civilians are employed.

11. Communications traffic between United Nations Headquarters and UNEF stations in the area, which is of substantial volume, is efficiently handled by experienced United Nations Field Service communications personnel. The UNEF communications network is coordinated with the established United Nations communications system.

3. Air support for the Force

12. As of September 1957, air support for UNEF consists of two Royal Canadian Air Force flights, 114 and 115. The 114 communication flight, based in Naples, has four C-119 aircraft. It is responsible for the heavy lift of mails, priority cargo, and passengers between Egypt and Italy. In the early period of the operation, twelve C-119 aircraft were employed. The 115 communication flight is based at the UNEF air station at El Arish (which was at Abu Suweir prior to September 5) and has four Otter and two DC-3 aircraft. This flight provides reconnaissance, medical evacuation, and internal transport support for UNEF.

4. Deployment

13. The major deployment of UNEF is along the Egypt-Israel armistice demarcation line and along the international frontier to the south of the Gaza Strip. This involves a line of quite considerable total length which, for the most part, runs in rugged terrain. The perimeter of the Gaza Strip, from the Mediterranean Sea in the north to the international frontier in the south, is 60 kilometres long. The international frontier, extending from the sea southwards to the Gulf of Aqaba, measures 213 kilometres. UNEF is deployed, on the Egyptian side only, along these two lines, totalling 273 kilometres, and patrols them constantly. The distance from the northern end of the Gulf of Aqaba to Sharm el-Sheikh, where UNEF is also deployed, is another 187 kilometres.

14. The positions and assignments of units of the Force are changed from time to time. As of September 15, the deployment was as follows:

(*i*) Along the armistice demarcation–Gaza Strip line: Danish-Norwegian, Brazilian, Indian, and Colombian battalions, and a Swedish company.

(*ii*) 'Along the international frontier—East Central Sinai Line: one Canadian reconnaissance squadron; one Yugoslav reconnaissance battalion.

(*iii*) In the Sharm el-Sheikh and Ras Nasrani area: the Finnish company.

(*iv*) In Gaza town: UNEF headquarters staff, the Swedish battalion, except one company; the Norwegian medical company.

(*v*) At Rafah: Canadian and Indian administrative and other support units in the UNEF maintenance area; a Finnish guard detachment.

(*vi*) At Naples: a communication flight of the Royal Canadian Air Force, consisting of thirty-three officers and one hundred fifty other ranks; UNEF liaison staff and a movement control detachment.

(*vii*) At El Arish: a communication flight of the Royal Canadian Air Force, consisting of thirteen officers and forty-five other ranks; a small detachment of the Brazilian battalion for guard duty; twenty-one officers and men for movement control.

(*viii*) At Port Said: one platoon, on monthly rotation among contingents, as security guard, together with a permanent movement control and port detachment required for port clearance and storage.

(*ix*) At Beirut (Lebanon): a leave centre detachment of nineteen officers and men.

15. Resolution 1125 (XI) calls for placing the Force "on the Egyptian-Israel armistice demarcation line," but no stationing of UNEF on the Israel side has occurred to date through lack of consent by Israel.
. . . .

II. The Role and Functioning of the Force

1. Responsibilities vested in the Force

30. By mid-September 1957, UNEF will have completed ten months of duty, during which it has been called upon to undertake important responsibilities involving a considerable variety of tasks. The Command for the Force, established by General Assembly resolution 1000 (ES-I), was to "secure and supervise the cessation of hostilities in accordance with all the terms of General Assembly resolution 997 (ES-I)." The General Assembly, in resolution 1001 (ES-I), approved guiding principles for the organization and functioning of the Force, as set forth in the Secretary-General's report of November 6, 1956 (A/3302), whereby, as must follow from its status under the Charter, the Force

could not be stationed or operate on a country's territory without that country's consent.

31. The Force, which has an international character as a subsidiary organ of the General Assembly, as affirmed in its regulations, was not established to undertake enforcement actions. While UNEF has a military organization, it does not use all normal military methods in achieving the objectives defined for it by the General Assembly. As indicated in the Secretary-General's report mentioned above, the functions foreseen for UNEF, when the cease-fire was being established, were to enter Egyptian territory with the consent of the Egyptian government, in order "to help maintain quiet during and after the withdrawal of non-Egyptian troops."

32. In the case of each withdrawal operation, the Commander of the Force, in close consultation with the Secretary-General, negotiated the technical arrangements with the Commanders of the British, French, and Israel forces.

33. Since the withdrawals of Israel troops from the Gaza and Sharm el-Sheikh sectors on March 7 and 16, respectively, the activities of UNEF have centered on the fulfillment of General Assembly resolution 1125 (XI) of February 2, 1957. The resolution called for "the placing of the United Nations Emergency Force on the Egyptian-Israel armistice demarcation line." In partial fulfillment of that resolution, UNEF is deployed, on the Egyptian side, along the armistice demarcation line and the international frontier.

. . . .

2. *Arrangements affecting the operation of the Force*

35. The cooperation of the Gaza administration and an awareness of the people in the area that the mission of UNEF is friendly and has the support of the administration are essential to the effective discharge by UNEF of its responsibilities.

36. Information from the Commander of the Force is to the effect that the population of the Gaza Strip has been made to know that Egyptian policy is opposed to infiltration across the demarcation line. Egyptian regulations against infiltration, including penalties, have been put into force, and the people of Gaza have been made aware of the role of UNEF in the prevention of infiltration. The Commander has been informed that the CID (police) in Gaza has been instructed to act vigorously with the object of finding persons responsible for mining and

other serious incidents and to prevent recurrence. Moreover, Gaza inhabitants are forbidden to approach within 500 metres of the demarcation line during darkness, and the *mukhtars* (local headmen) have been warned that they are responsible for preventing infiltration in their areas. Severe sentences may be awarded against violators of regulations against infiltration.

37. There is an understanding whereby a unit of the Palestine Police would be assigned specific duty in the prevention of infiltration and would cooperate closely with UNEF in such function, particularly in acting on UNEF requests relating to actual or apprehended infiltration and the free exchange of information concerning actual or potential infiltrators. In practice, thus far, this has meant mainly that the Palestine police received from UNEF the persons apprehended in the zone near the demarcation line. Patrolling along the line is done by UNEF alone. The Commander is of the view that the absence of incidents, and, in recent months, particularly those with mines, reflects more effective local police and CID action. He also reports that a regrouping of the Force, so that battalion boundaries will generally correspond to administrative subdistricts in the Strip, which are also the police subdistricts, may facilitate police cooperation with UNEF at the battalion level.

38. UNEF is authorized to apprehend infiltrators, and the Commander reports that accepted practice is for UNEF to take infiltrators into custody in a zone extending 500 metres from the demarcation line and hand them over to the local police.

39. No serious difficulties are reported with regard to (*a*) the enjoyment by personnel and vehicles of UNEF of full freedom of movement in the Gaza Strip, and in the Sinai Peninsula between the bases and headquarters of UNEF and the elements of its troops deployed along the demarcation line; (*b*) UNEF aircraft flying freely over the Sinai and the Gaza Strip; (*c*) the manning of the Gaza Airport by UNEF.

40. The relations between UNEF and the local population are said by the Commander to be good, generally speaking. He finds that the presence of UNEF under its existing terms of reference, despite occasional minor difficulties, is accepted as a good development by the majority of the inhabitants of the Gaza Strip.

3. Incidents

41. Since the Force was deployed along the Gaza line and to the south of it, there has been a steady reduction in both the number and

the severity of incidents along that line. Indeed, as of September 15, no report of any serious incident had been received since July 14, when a UNEF patrol was fired at, without casualties. There have been no raids from either side, whether in retaliation or of the fedayeen type. Military elements of Egypt and Israel are never in sight of each other.

. . . .

4. *Effectiveness of the Force*

44. UNEF was designed to meet a particular need in an acute emergency. The authority given to it was limited, as it could only be. The demands upon it which might arise from specific situations could not all be foreseen. The basic purposes and role, however, as defined by the General Assembly, have been clear enough from the beginning, and the orders and directives of its Commander on its functions and authority are precise. It often has had to move and act swiftly, but has done so always with the restraint required by the very nature of its status and role. In the course of its functioning, many issues have arisen, for most of which satisfactory solutions have been found. A few issues are unresolved, but still open. These include the completion of UNEF's deployment; authority for UNEF to fire during darkness at infiltrators approaching the line from either direction, which would be somewhat broader than its unquestioned right to fire in self-defence—a right which it has, on occasion, exercised; and the idea of a protective fence along a part or the whole of the demarcation line.

45. Despite its limited authority and some unsettled questions, there would seem to be no good reason to doubt that UNEF has been effective. It has earned acceptance as a significant pioneering effort in the evolution of methods of peace-making.

46. The prevailing quiet and generally satisfactory conditions along the line, so far as UNEF is concerned, should not, however, as the Commander of the Force has warned, be considered as obviating the need to find, when the time is propitious, satisfactory solutions for the main unresolved issues noted above. The line under present conditions is vulnerable and the quiet, at any moment, could be abruptly broken.

47. Looking back to November of last year, it may be recalled that UNEF was, in the first place, a precondition set by France, Israel, and the United Kingdom for the cease-fire. Subsequently, it was a precondition for the withdrawals from Egypt of the Anglo-French and Israel

forces. Upon completion of the withdrawals, it became, and undoubtedly continues to be today, one of the preconditions for the preservation of quiet along the line between Egypt and Israel. Such quiet, in turn, is indispensable to fruitful effort towards the removal of the major obstacles to peace in the Near East.

III. *Administrative and Financial Arrangements*

. . . .

86. It is the Secretary-General's considered view, as indicated earlier, that, for the first six months (i.e., during what might reasonably be regarded as the initial emergency period), it would be in keeping with the intent of the General Assembly, and, therefore, within the scope of his present financial authority, for the United Nations to reimburse participating governments for any special allowances, as distinct from basic salaries, paid to members of their contingents as a direct result of their service with UNEF in its area of operations, provided that such allowances can be considered reasonable, having regard to the circumstances in which the troops have been made available and to legal and other obligations devolving upon the government concerned. Unless it should be the view of the General Assembly that no adequate authority in fact exists, and that no element of "extra costs" associated with pay and allowances can be accepted as a proper charge against the Special Account, the Secretary-General proposes to honour reimbursement claims presented in accordance with the foregoing formula and to adjust his budget estimates for UNEF accordingly.

87. On the basis of claims submitted and of data obtained directly from the field, it is estimated that for all contingents such "special allowances" involved, during the initial six-month period, an expenditure on the part of the governments concerned of approximately $330,000 per month. Reimbursement by the United Nations may thus be expected to result in an additional charge to the Special Account for the period in question of $2 million.

88. In the event, however, of a contingent serving beyond the initial six-month period or of a replacement contingent being made available, the Secretary-General holds that the United Nations should agree to assume financial responsibility for all extra and extraordinary costs which a government is obliged to incur in making forces available for UNEF service. Apart from the costs of equipment referred to below, accep-

tance of this principle would mean, in effect, reimbursement by the United Nations of expenditure incurred in respect of pay and allowances over and above those costs which the government concerned would, in any event, have been obliged to meet. It would not, of course, preclude any government, who chose to do so, from voluntarily assuming all or part of such expenses.

89. In commending this general principle to the General Assembly, the Secretary-General is conscious of the fact that those Member states which have been maintaining UNEF contingents for more than ten months are finding it increasingly difficult to prolong the period of service of their troops, or to make replacements available in the absence of any firm assurance that identifiable direct expenses thereby incurred will be borne by the United Nations. It would seem to the Secretary-General, moreover, that beyond a limited emergency period, any arrangement under which a few Member states carry a disproportionately heavy financial burden does not represent a sound or equitable basis on which to discharge a collective United Nations responsibility.

90. Pending the receipt of more complete and documented statements from some of the participating governments, it is difficult to furnish any reasonably exact estimate and analysis of the "extra and extraordinary costs" which, under the proposed new formula, would fall to be reimbursed by the United Nations. Assuming, however, that, apart from equipment costs, they would relate almost exclusively to pay and allowance expenditures which would not otherwise have been incurred, it would appear from the data available that the approximate current level of such expenditures (i.e., during the remaining period of eight months) amounts to some $575,000 per month (inclusive of special allowances). This monthly estimate may be expected to be somewhat reduced, perhaps to a level of $545,000, consequent on the anticipated readjustment in the strength and composition of the Force, following the withdrawal of the Indonesian contingent during September 1957. Since the status of the various contingents and the conditions of their assignment differ very widely (e.g., in some cases, they are regular units of the country's armed forces, while in others, they are comprised of volunteers specially recruited for UNEF service) and since their rates of pay and other benefits are in accordance with national laws and regulations, which in themselves reflect wide variations, any subsequent changes in the composition of the Force could have a significant bearing on the future level of reimbursement costs. For the purposes of the first

financial period, however (i.e., from November 1956–December 31, 1957), the financial implications of the two reimbursement principles formulated above are tentatively and provisionally estimated as follows:

	United States dollars
For the first six months:	
Reimbursement of special allowances	2,000,000
For the remainder of the period:	
Extra and extraordinary costs relating to pay and allowances	4,500,000
Total	6,500,000

91. It should also be pointed out that, because of the prolongation of the period of service, most of the participating governments are faced with unforeseen costs in connection with the equipment, material and supplies initially furnished to their contingents. The General Assembly has, therefore, also to consider whether the United Nations should assume financial responsibility for the replacement of equipment that is destroyed or worn out, and for such deterioration beyond that provided for under normal depreciation schedules as can be assessed at the conclusion of the total period of service of a government's forces. In view of the fact that the main burden of furnishing much of the heavy and expensive equipment needed for the operations of UNEF, as a whole, has fallen on a limited number of Member states, the Secretary-General believes that, in the interests of an equitable sharing of costs, some appropriate recognition by the United Nations of this obligation is called for. The task of estimating possible claims that may eventually be made in this regard presents obvious difficulties. Some indication of the maximum liability, which the United Nations would be assuming, will be possible when detailed schedules recently supplied by the governments concerned have been analysed and costs estimated.

. . . .

7. *Financial requirements*

99. At September 30, it is estimated that the expenses of UNEF for the fourteen-month period ending December 31, 1957, will total be-

tween $24 million and $30.5 million, depending on such arrangements as may be agreed or confirmed by the General Assembly for reimbursement of special allowances or other costs to governments providing contingents to UNEF. At this time, however, only $6,330,000 has been paid in cash into the UNEF Special Account, $5,744,000 of this total having been paid in connection with the initial assessment of $10 million, and the balance of $586,000 paid as voluntary contributions. A further amount of $3,213,000 has been pledged in voluntary contributions, but has not yet been paid in cash and, of this sum, $2.7 million is dependent on the receipt of matching contributions from other Member states.

100. The wide disparity between the financial needs for the current period and the cash resources thus far made available or pledged to the Special Account by Member states makes it imperative that the General Assembly, in addition to determining the nature and extent of costs to be reimbursed to governments providing contingents to UNEF, give urgent consideration to the three following problems.

101. The first of these relates to the authorization to be granted by the General Assembly to the Secretary-General to incur expenses for the maintenance of the Force; the second to the basis for financing UNEF costs, whether by apportioning or assessing the expenses among the Member states or by other means; and the third to assuring adequate cash resources to the Secretary-General to cover expenses.

(a) *Obligational authority*

102. Regarding the Secretary-General's authorization to incur expenses for the United Nations Emergency Force, it will be recalled that the General Assembly, in resolution 1090 (XI), authorized an amount of $16.5 million for that purpose in respect of the period to December 31, 1957. Although the amount authorized corresponded with the amount requested by the Secretary-General, subject to the reservations noted earlier, his request was predicated on covering expenses for a twelve-month period rather than a fourteen-month period as provided in the General Assembly's resolution.

103. However, developments in UNEF's operation and composition subsequent to the General Assembly's authorizing action (such as the necessity which was unforeseen at the time of the Secretary-General's request to provide for the transportation costs involved in the single or double rotation of all the UNEF contingents) have necessitated revised

and increased estimates of costs likely to be incurred to December 31, 1957.

104. On the basis of the latest estimates of financial requirements which are given in annex A to this report, and in the light of the decisions that the General Assembly will take on the question of costs to be reimbursed to governments providing contingents, the Secretary-General requests that the General Assembly authorize him to incur expenses for UNEF:

(*i*) For the period ending December 31, 1957, up to a total of $23,920,500, plus such additional amount as may be authorized or required to implement such arrangements as may be agreed or confirmed by the General Assembly with reference to reimbursements of costs to governments providing contingents;

(*ii*) For any 1958 period, not more than a total of $20 million, plus such additional amount as may be authorized or required with reference to reimbursement of costs to governments providing contingents, it being understood that, so long as UNEF continues on its present basis of operations, the expenses of maintaining the Force would not normally exceed $2 million for any single month.

(*b*) *Basis for financing UNEF costs*

105. Perhaps the most important single issue calling for urgent consideration and decision arises as a result of paragraph 4 of resolution 1090 (XI), under the terms of which the General Assembly decided that, at its twelfth session, it would consider the basis for financing any costs of the Force in excess of $10 million not covered by voluntary contributions. It will be observed from the figures cited above that, as of the end of September, the shortfall in contributions received and assured (in excess of the $10 million assessed) as against estimated costs through December 31, 1957, is of the order of $12.8 million, without taking account of the estimated cost of reimbursing "special allowances" during the first six months ($2 million) or, should the General Assembly so decide, of reimbursing all "extra and extraordinary" pay and allowance expenses during the balance of 1957 (estimated at $4.5 million).

106. The Secretary-General holds to the view which he has previously expressed to the General Assembly that decisions which are taken by the Assembly itself and which have important financial consequences carry with them an obligation on the part of all Member gov-

ernments to make available the requisite resources or other means for their implementation. In the light, however, of the extremely limited response to date by Member states to the appeal for voluntary contributions, and of the complexity and scope of the operations in which UNEF is involved, he is constrained to question whether it is either feasible or prudent to place any undue reliance for the future on this method of obtaining the necessary budgetary provision. The Secretary-General is bound to stress the grave risks inherent in the present inadequate and insecure basis of UNEF financing. Unless, indeed, the possibility of UNEF successfully completing its mission is to be seriously jeopardized, it is essential that this vital United Nations undertaking be assured of the same degree and certainty of financial support as afforded to other United Nations activities which have as their purpose the maintenance of security and peace.

(c) Cash requirements

107. Regarding the need for assuring adequate cash resources to cover the expenses of UNEF, the Secretary-General considers that the existing authorizations may not be sufficient to meet the requirements of the situation, unless they are broadly construed to permit loans from Member states and unless there is a reasonable expectation that these will be forthcoming when needed. He considers it essential, nevertheless, to retain the authority granted to him in resolution 1090 (XI), (a) to advance from the Working Capital Fund such sums as the Special Account may require to meet expenses chargeable to it; and (b) to arrange, where necessary, for loans to the Special Account from other appropriate sources.

108. The authority to advance sums from the Working Capital Fund has been constantly resorted to during the current year, and the amount of such advances, outstanding at September 30, 1957, totalled $3,775,000. It seems likely, however, on the basis of past experience, that, unless such advances to the UNEF Special Account are substantially reduced from their present level of $3,775,000 before the early months of next year, there will not be a sufficient balance of funds in the Working Capital Fund or in the Central Fund to cover the costs of the normal activities of the Organization.

109. While the necessity to arrange for loans to the Special Account from other funds under the control of the Secretary-General has been narrowly avoided up to the present time, it would appear that such

loans could, in any case, only provide temporary relief for limited amounts and should not be relied on as a means of assuring the financial solvency of UNEF's operations.

110. In view of the necessity to cover the shortfall between the estimated financial requirements and the cash resources of UNEF indicated above, the Secretary-General believes it will be necessary to appeal for advances from Member states which may be in a position to make funds available, pending receipt of assessed or other contributions.

8. Summary of decisions requested by the Secretary-General concerning the Force

111. Matters requiring action by the General Assembly in terms of the UNEF report may be summarized as follows:

(*i*) The method or methods by which the funds required for the maintenance of the Force are to be obtained;

(*ii*) The need for increasing the Secretary-General's obligational authority for the period ending December 31, 1957;

(*iii*) The provision of appropriate obligational authority in respect of any 1958 period during which the Force may continue on its present basis of operation;

(*iv*) The problem of assuring the availability of necessary cash resources, pending receipt of contributions or other payments to the UNEF Special Account;

(*v*) The Secretary-General's interpretation of his financial authority in the matter of reimbursement of special allowances paid by governments to members of their UNEF contingents for the first six months of service;

(*vi*) The proposed formula under which, in respect of any period subsequent to the first six months of service, the United Nations would assume financial responsibility for all "extra and extraordinary" costs incurred by a Member government as a direct result of furnishing a contingent to UNEF;

(*vii*) The proposal that, in respect of equipment furnished by a participating government to its contingent, the United Nations should be financially responsible for its replacement in the event of its being destroyed or worn out, or for such depreciation (beyond that provided for under normal depreciation schedules) as can be assessed at the conclusion of the total period of service of a government's forces;

(*viii*) Arrangements for payment of compensation in the event of injury or death attributable to service with the Force.

HAMMARSKJÖLD consulted carefully with members of the UNEF Advisory Committee and other key delegates among the major and smaller powers before completing his report. After it was issued he worked and planned with them on preparing the ground and on questions of timing and tactics before the Assembly began formal consideration of the report. He was aiming for the strongest vote he could muster in support of the principle of paying for UNEF by applying the standard scale in assessing the Members for all costs of the Force not covered by voluntary contributions and special assistance.

Although a majority of the Members supported this principle, strong resistance continued from diverse quarters. The Soviet bloc considered the creation of UNEF by the Assembly illegal under the Charter and refused to pay. Arab states considered that they should not be required to help meet an expense caused by the Anglo-French-Israeli attack upon Egypt. Some Latin American and Asian Members objected to being assessed on the same scale as the regular budget for special measures in support of peace and security; they considered that the cost of such measures was, under the Charter, a responsibility resting first of all on the major powers. Some of the spokesmen for these viewpoints also took the constitutional position that assessments voted for UNEF should not be regarded as obligatory under Article 19 of the Charter.

The size of the increase caused by UNEF in the appropriations required for the United Nations and concern in the treasuries of Member governments about its implications for the future reinforced these political and constitutional objections. The regular 1957 budget (excluding UNEF) was $53 million and the 1958 budget $55 million. The cost of UNEF to the end of December 1957 was estimated at $30 million additional and for 1958 at $20 to $25 million additional. Thus UNEF would account for about a 50 percent rise in the total costs of the United Nations over the two-year period.

Consideration of the Secretary-General's report was delayed into November as Hammarskjöld and his allies among the delegates sought to win over as many as possible to their point of view. Finally, the United States and United Kingdom governments, both strong supporters of assessing the costs of UNEF on the regular scale, offered substantial financial contributions of $12 million and $1 million respectively, in the form of "special assistance," for the period ending December 31, 1957, on the understanding that 1958 costs would be assessed. The offer was communicated to the Members by Hammarskjöld in a note on November 19 (Document A/3745). Together with the voluntary contributions previously paid or pledged the additional $13 million went far toward meeting the balance of 1957 expenses above the $10 million originally voted in December 1956 as subject to the regular scale of assessments (page 411).

The debate was now promptly scheduled for plenary meetings on November 22. A resolution was introduced by twenty-one middle and smaller Members: Brazil, Canada, Ceylon, Colombia, Costa Rica, Denmark, Finland, India, Indonesia, Iran, Ireland, Italy, Japan, Liberia, Norway, Pakistan, Spain, Sweden, Thailand, Uruguay, and Yugoslavia. It was a widely representative group and included all the members of the UNEF Advisory Committee and all those with contingents in UNEF. The text of the resolution was as follows:

The General Assembly,

Recalling its resolutions 1000 (ES-I) of November 5, 1956, 1001 (ES-I) of November 7, 1956, 1089 (XI) of December 21, 1956, 1125 (XI) of February 2, 1957, and 1090 (XI) of February 27, 1957, concerning the establishment, organization, functioning, and financing of the United Nations Emergency Force,

Noting with appreciation the report of the Secretary-General on the Force, dated October 9, 1957 (A/3694), and the effective assistance rendered by the Advisory Committee on the United Nations Emergency Force,

Mindful of the contribution of the Force to the maintenance of quiet in the area,

1. *Expresses its appreciation* of the assistance rendered to the United Nations Emergency Force by Members of the United Nations which have contributed troops and other support and facilities, and expresses the hope that such assistance will be continued as necessary;

2. *Approves* the principles and proposals for the allocation of costs between the Organization and Members contributing troops as set forth in paragraphs 86, 88, and 91 of the report of the Secretary-General and authorizes the Secretary-General in connection therewith to enter into such agreements as may be necessary for the reimbursement of appropriate extra and extraordinary costs to Members contributing troops;

3. *Authorizes* the Secretary-General to expend an additional amount for the Force, for the period ending December 31, 1957, up to a maximum of $13.5 million and, as necessary, an amount for the continuing operation of the Force beyond that date up to a maximum of $25 million, subject to any decisions taken on the basis of the review provided for in paragraph 5 below;

4. *Decides* that the expenses authorized in paragraph 3 above shall be borne by the Members of the United Nations in accordance with the scales of assessments adopted by the General Assembly for the financial years 1957 and 1958 respectively, such other resources as may have become available for the purpose in question being applied to reduce the expenses before the apportionment for the period ending December 31, 1957;

5. *Requests* the Fifth Committee to examine, with the assistance of the Advisory Committee on Administrative and Budgetary Questions and in the light of the present resolution, the cost estimates for maintaining the United Nations Emergency Force contained in the report of the Secretary-General, and to make such recommendations as it considers appropriate concerning the expenditure authorized under paragraph 3 above.[1]

The resolution was adopted at the conclusion of one day's debate by a vote of 51 to 11 with 19 abstentions. This was well over a two-thirds majority, but the number of abstentions was ominous. Chile and Ecuador voted "no," along with the Soviet bloc, and four more Latin American members —El Salvador, Guatemala, Mexico, and Panama—were among the abstainers, together with the Arab states and a scattering of Asians. In addition some of those voting for the resolution nevertheless later failed to pay their UNEF assessments. The majority, it should be noted, included on this occasion both France and Israel, as well as the United States and United Kingdom.

In December the Advisory Committee on Administrative and Budgetary Questions, acting under paragraph 5 of the resolution, recommended that the appropriation for the first period, ending December 31, 1957, be fixed at $30 million, that the budget for the first six months of 1958 should not exceed $9 to $10 million exclusive of the extra expenses approved by the Assembly for reimbursement, and that estimates for the entire year be prepared in time for review by the Advisory Committee at its first 1958 session. The Fifth Committee accepted these recommendations and they were approved by the General Assembly on December 13 by a vote of 45 to 9 with 10 abstentions.

---

[1] General Assembly Resolution 1151 (XII), November 22, 1957.

Final Report to the General Assembly
on Clearance of the Suez Canal

UN HEADQUARTERS, NEW YORK   NOVEMBER 1, 1957

MOST OF THE Secretary-General's report on clearance of the Suez Canal was a historical account of the operation. The only action requested of the Assembly was on Hammarskjöld's proposal that the loans advanced by various governments to pay for the costs of clearing the Canal be reimbursed by means of a 3 percent surcharge on Canal tolls.

Introduction

1. Following the approval by the General Assembly of the Secretary-General's report dated November 20, 1956, on arrangements for clearing the Suez Canal (A/3376), and the adoption on November 24, 1956, of resolution 1121 (XI) authorizing him on the basis of that report to proceed with practical arrangements and negotiation of agreements for the speedy and effective clearance of the Suez Canal, the Secretary-General appointed Lieutenant-General Raymond A. Wheeler, Engineering Consultant to the International Bank for Reconstruction and Development, as his Special Representative in charge of technical operations. The Secretary-General announced also that he had secured the collaboration of Mr. John J. McCloy, Chairman of the Board of Directors of the Chase Manhattan Bank and former President of the International Bank, to assist him in an advisory capacity on the business negotiations connected with the project.

2. General Wheeler was released on loan to the United Nations by the President of the International Bank on November 26, 1956, on which date he assumed his duties at Headquarters. Also provided on loan from the International Bank was Mr. John Connors, to serve as General Wheeler's deputy in charge of technical operations. The Dutch and Danish consortium of salvage engineers, comprising the firms of

General Assembly Official Records, Twelfth Session, Annexes, agenda item 64, Document A/3719, November 1, 1957.

L. Smit and Co.'s *International Sleepdienst* of Rotterdam and Em. Z. Svitzer of Copenhagen, with which the Secretary-General had entered into preliminary arrangements in early November for a first concentration of salvage craft, crews and equipment to undertake the operation, were requested on the same date, November 26, to dispatch craft and equipment, already assembled, to the Suez Canal area.

3. On December 4, 1956, General Wheeler left Headquarters to engage in technical consultations with Egyptian authorities in Cairo. These discussions began on December 8 and resulted in agreement for the conduct of an immediate technical survey by the United Nations of obstructions in the Canal, in the first place south of Port Said; a few days later this survey was extended to cover the damaged base workshops in Port Fuad. Consultations between General Wheeler and the Commander of the Anglo-French fleet took place concerning salvage operations conducted by Anglo-French salvage units in the Port Said harbour.

4. The basis of the understandings upon which the operational relationship between the United Nations and the Government of Egypt was premised was agreed in general terms during General Wheeler's initial discussions. These understandings, as subsequently formalized between the Secretariat of the United Nations and the Egyptian Foreign Office, were confirmed in an exchange of letters dated January 8, 1957, between the Egyptian Minister for Foreign Affairs and the Secretary-General. The text of these letters was circulated as an annex to the report of the Secretary-General to the General Assembly, dated January 10, 1957 (A/3492, annex 2).

5. On November 14, 1956, the Egyptian government had announced the presence of mines in the approaches to the Suez Canal. During his planning conversations in Egypt, General Wheeler was informed that further mines and explosive charges had been laid in the Canal south of El Cap. The withdrawal of the Anglo-French fleet was completed on December 22, 1956. On December 27, negotiations were finalized concerning the agreed disposition of the Anglo-French salvage units retained after the withdrawal. On December 30, General Wheeler received satisfactory assurances concerning the final removal of explosives from Canal waters so as to enable him to move United Nations salvage crews and vessels safely in Canal waters south of El Cap. The United Nations salvage operation proper commenced on December 31, 1956, although work was resumed by some Anglo-French salvage vessels in

Port Said on December 29 and three United Nations salvage vessels were piloted by Egyptian naval craft through mine fields in the southern end of the Canal and began operations there on December 28.

Assistance by Anglo-French savage vessels

6. A salvage fleet had been commissioned by the governments of the United Kingdom and France and many of its components were at work in Port Said from the first week in November 1956 onwards. As a result of its activity in that port, the amount of work which it fell to the United Nations to undertake was lessened.

7. In mid-November, during the Secretary-General's visit to Cairo, the Egyptian government had invited the United Nations to assist with the task of clearing the Canal immediately after the withdrawal of non-Egyptian forces from Port Said and the Canal area.

8. Early in November, the governments of France and the United Kingdom—which at a somewhat earlier stage had offered to assume the task themselves—expressed support for the Secretary-General's efforts to organize a salvage team under the auspices of the United Nations. On November 21, a representative of the United Kingdom declared in the General Assembly that his government would do everything in its power to help and was ready to lend its resources and to work in any way desired in the task.

9. Available Anglo-French salvage resources, either in or en route to the Canal, were reported to number more than thirty vessels or items of floating equipment, and were proposed for use as a composite whole. General Wheeler's technical assessment of need, made in early December in the light of the other resources available to the United Nations, suggested that six of these vessels should be selected to be manned by United Nations crews and to operate south of El Cap, and that, further, three Anglo-French manned vessels should be retained to complete work on specific wrecks upon which they were engaged in Port Said.

10. The proposed transfer from the Anglo-French salvage fleet of six vessels for manning by the United Nations was later reconsidered and, by December 22, 1956, the date of the withdrawal of the Anglo-French forces from the Canal, General Wheeler recommended, without prejudice to his clearance target objectives, a redisposal of available salvage resources. Under this revised plan, vessels of the United Nations salvage fleet, without the addition of any Anglo-French salvage vessels, were to

be used south of El Cap and eleven—subsequently reduced to nine—Anglo-French manned salvage craft, with four support vessels, were to be retained to complete specific tasks upon which they were engaged in Port Said harbour. This harbour was then to be cleared of remaining obstructions by United Nations salvage elements after completion of their assignments in the southern reaches of the Canal.

11. The revised plan was accepted by the governments concerned. The retained Anglo-French salvage vessels were brought under the United Nations flag and were accorded the same immunity by the Egyptian government as that attached to the United Nations salvage vessels operating under General Wheeler's authority.

12. The tasks to be completed by the retained elements of the Anglo-French fleet were: the finalizing of a survey, already almost completed, of a sunken wreck by one small British salvage craft; the recovery of a sunken crane jib comprising part of a wreck already lifted by British units; the lifting and dumping of a sunken dredger on which work had been commenced by British units in November; and the removal of a small tug upon which a French salvage vessel was engaged. Some of the retained Anglo-French vessels left the Canal in stages during the first three weeks of January 1957, as each had completed the work assigned, and all had phased out of the operations by January 24.

13. Other assistance furnished to the United Nations from Anglo-French resources was the transfer under contract to the United Nations of a French-owned floating crane for manning by United Nations crews, and the transfer by the British Admiralty of some miscellaneous salvage supplies on a reimbursable basis. In addition, arrangements were concluded whereby two German lifting craft and supporting tugs originally chartered by the British Admiralty were transferred under charter to the United Nations, and liability for a proportionate share of the cost to the Government of the United Kingdom for their hire and outward passage to the Canal has been assumed by the United Nations.

United Nations salvage resources utilized

14. The United Nations salvage fleet mustered for the operation and drawn from Dutch, Danish, Belgian, Swedish, German, Italian, and Yugoslav resources comprised a general total of thirty-two vessels and pieces of floating equipment (six ocean salvage vessels, six coastal salvage vessels, four lifting craft, three sheerlegs and two floating cranes—supported by ten tugs and several small diver's boats). In addition,

twenty-four refloating pontoons or camels, and necessary stores of supplementary salvage equipment and material, were available. The total lifting capacity of the fleet approximated 10,000 tons and the total crews employed numbered 479, including forty-five divers. Of these resources, twenty-two craft or pieces of floating salvage equipment had arrived in the Canal by the date of the commencement of the United Nations operation, or within four weeks after the adoption by the General Assembly of resolution 1121 (XI) on November 24, 1956; the balance arrived in stages during January and one in early February 1957.

15. The fleet was not maintained at constant strength, but was reduced in size as the completion of each phase of the work indicated that the retention of any vessels would be uneconomical and their release would not be prejudicial to the completion of clearance targets within the time limits prescribed. Towards the end of January, two United Nations vessels were released, three more in the first half of February and two in the second half of that month, and five were released during March. In all, twelve of the United Nations salvage craft were therefore dispensed with within three months of the commencement of the operation, and twenty were retained and released in stages during April, in which month the clearance was finally completed. Through this flexible control over the fleet's operation, considerable financial savings were achieved without any consequential delays in the clearance of the channels and harbourages.

16. Except for the death while off duty of one United Nations seaman by accidental drowning, a circumstance which is recorded with deep regret, the operation was carried through without loss of life or serious injury to the United Nations crews involved, and without loss or significant damage to vessels or equipment. One floating crane was, however, lost in heavy weather in the Mediterranean on its homeward voyage. The loss was covered by insurance.

17. The Secretary-General wishes to record his appreciation to General Wheeler and his staff and to the contracting firms and their staff and crews for the outstanding success of the operation and for the efficiency displayed by all concerned therein.

Organizational Arrangements

18. General Wheeler's first administrative needs in Cairo were served by the staff and facilities of the United Nations Technical Assistance Board's resident representative established in that city. The initial sup-

porting staff in the Canal area was composed of three members of the Headquarters staff of the United Nations Technical Assistance Administration, who accompanied General Wheeler to Egypt. This initial support was replaced in January by an executive field headquarters establishment, comprising a deputy in charge of technical operations and four additional officers, including a press officer, with a total of eight clerks, secretaries, and radio operators drawn from United Nations staff and some additional locally recruited general service personnel.

19. The technical management of the integrated United Nations salvage fleet was furnished under contractual arrangements by a self-contained management group supplied by the Dutch and Danish salvage consortium, Smit-Svitzer. The group operated under General Wheeler's overall executive direction. It comprised a staff of twelve, including technical supervisory officers, administrative officers, and secretaries and clerks, with some additional locally recruited general service assistance.

20. An initial team of fifteen salvage surveyors and technical engineers to provide first estimates of the needs and costs was furnished under contractual arrangements by the Smit-Svitzer salvage consortium and by the Ralph M. Parsons Company of the United States, which conducted a survey of the workshops. This group accompanied General Wheeler to Cairo on December 8, 1956, and had completed its work by January 7, 1957. Two engineers were subsequently furnished by the International Telegraph and Telephone Company to survey the rehabilitation needs of the telecommunications system, and two additional engineers from the International General Electric Company surveyed similar needs connected with the navigational lighting system.

21. In consultation with Mr. John McCloy, arrangements were concluded with the firm of H. Howell and Company of Washington for the establishment of a system of continuous operating accounting controls and audit programmes. The arrangements provided for day-to-day controls over expenditures at source in the field, as well as concurrent auditing, as affecting contractual arrangements, at the offices of the main salvor contractors in Europe and at Headquarters. Obligations incurred directly at Headquarters and all financial payments were handled in the normal manner by the Office of the Controller.

22. Prior to the appointment of General Wheeler, the Secretary-General had established, within his Executive Office at Headquarters, a unit to render assistance to the Suez Canal clearance operation in the field.

This unit remained as the coordinating point at Headquarters to service General Wheeler's operational requirements, and was responsible, in consultation with General Wheeler and Mr. John McCloy, for all contractual arrangements between salvor companies and the United Nations. It comprised two full-time officers, assisted by one part-time officer and three secretarial assistants.

The Clearance Operation

Plan of operations

23. The plan of operations provided for the clearance of obstructions from channels and ports and harbourages with priority given to the speedy opening of a temporary channel to permit the earliest possible passage of vessels of limited draft and the release from the Canal of transit vessels which had been marooned at the time of its closure. The plan took into account also the necessity for the rehabilitation of workshop installations to provide maintenance facilities for operational craft and equipment to the extent necessary for transit operations; the restoration of the inoperative navigational lighting system; repairs to the damaged telecommunications system; the assurance that dredging services would be adequate to provide uninterrupted and safe passage; and the availability of operational craft for the handling of convoys.

Scope and execution of the operation

24. It was established by on-the-spot surveys that forty-two obstructions of a significant character existed in the Canal proper.

25. Of these, two had been refloated and four completely and one partially removed from shipping channels in Port Said by Anglo-French salvage units prior to the assumption of responsibility for the operations by the United Nations. Subsequent to this assumption of responsibility, one further vessel and a sunken crane jib were removed from the channel by British vessels and one tug was shifted to shallow waters by a French vessel and was subsequently refloated by units of the United Nations fleet.

26. Two obstructions were moved by the Egyptian Canal Authority without United Nations assistance, and the wreck of one vessel which had been grounded for six years in the shallows of the eastern harbour

of Port Said was found not to constitute an obstruction to shipping and was therefore not included in the United Nations salvage objective.

27. Thirty-two obstructions, including the collapsed spans of the El Firdan bridge, were lifted and removed from the channels by the United Nations fleet.

28. Anglo-French salvage resources had, prior to December 22, 1956, moved five wrecks from the western channel in Port Said harbour in order to provide a limited passage through that harbour for ships of 25-foot draft. The United Nations plan conceived of the removal by early March 1957 of such further obstructions within the channel south of Port Said as would be required to provide passage throughout the length of the Canal for ships of similar limited draft. The plan provided further for the removal by mid-May of remaining obstructions in Port Said and in the southern reaches of the shipping channel proper in order to provide through transit for ships of maximum draft. The final phase of the work, which was estimated to require some weeks beyond the mid-May date, envisaged the clearance of all remaining obstructions from ports and harbourages. Sufficient elasticity within the operating plan was developed to permit work to be executed concurrently where this could be achieved economically and without prejudice to the earliest possible reopening of the waterway to limited draft vessels as a first target objective.

29. A governing factor in the execution of the early phase of the work was the time required for the removal of the cement-laden blockship *Akka* at km. 81.4 and the concurrent removal, *inter alia,* of the tug *Edgar Bonnet* at km. 74.2 and the frigate *Abukir* at km. 160.7. Although the general designated programme was finished several weeks ahead of schedule in the southern reaches, a first limited channel was not opened within the planned time limit because of the notification by Egyptian authorities of the existence of explosives aboard the two latter vessels. The blockship *Akka* was removed from the channel on February 14, 1957, but clearance to proceed with work on the *Edgar Bonnet* was given by Egyptian authorities only on March 12. Explosive charges on the *Abukir* were found to be largely inaccessible for underwater removal and the attempt was ultimately abandoned and salvage work resumed by United Nations crews on the vessel on March 22. It was finally raised and the remaining explosives removed to the surface on April 8.

30. Notwithstanding, however, the fact that the above delays prevented the opening to shipping of a first limited channel in early March, as would otherwise have been achieved, the delays in effect aided in an earlier completion of the overall clearance operation. Some slowing down of the final salvage work would have been inevitable had it had to be conducted concurrently with the passage of vessels in transit through the first limited channel. The impossibility of such passage in these circumstances, in fact, enabled the residual work to proceed unhampered, and the final clearance of the Canal in all its stages, including the opening of ports and harbourages, was completed on April 10, some weeks earlier than had originally been predicted for the full clearance of the main shipping channel only.

. . . .

Financing the Operation
Loan contributions received

38. By a letter dated December 25, 1956, the Secretary-General invited Member states to make available to him contributions by way of an advance of funds toward the discharge of his responsibilities in connection with the Canal clearance operation.

39. In response, loan contributions were received as follows:

States	*Approximative equivalent in U.S. dollars*
Canada	1,044,045.68
Sweden	772,201.00
Liberia	4,000.00
Ceylon	3,733.49
Australia	1,000,000.00
Federal Republic of Germany	1,000,000.00
United States of America	5,000,000.00
Italy	399,525.68
Norway	1,000,000.00
Denmark	500,000.00
Netherlands	503,947.37
Total	11,227,453.22

The advances were deposited with the International Bank for Reconstruction and Development, which acted as fiscal agent for the United Nations for this purpose.

40. Services and supplies, valued at $500,000 on a comparable basis for similar services and supplies provided under United Nations commercial contractual standards, were commissioned by the United Nations subsequent to its assumption of responsibility for the operation, from resources made available by the governments of the United Kingdom and France.

Expenditures

41. The following summary reflects the limit of expenditures and obligations incurred by the United Nations:

	U.S. dollars
Administrative and general expenses	357,093.57
Operating costs of United Nations contractors	6,306,368.63
Survey and rehabilitation costs of Canal base workshops, the navigational lighting system and the telecommunications system	962,580.67
Reimbursement for services and supplies provided by the governments of the United Kingdom and France at the request of the United Nations	500,000.00
Contribution to essential dredging services	250,000.00
Total	8,376,042.87

*Proposal for Reimbursement of the Costs
of the Operation*

42. After consideration of various possible alternatives for meeting the costs of the operation as reflected in paragraph 41 above, the Secretary-General would recommend that, subject to reduction by such resources as might become otherwise available, repayment to contributor countries be effected by means of the application of a surcharge on Canal traffic under which arrangement a levy of 3 percent on Canal tolls would be paid into a special United Nations account, the procedures to govern such payments to be negotiated with the Egyptian gov-

ernment and with the other parties to the payments. On the basis of the current level of Canal traffic, it can be estimated that by this method the costs would be reimbursed over a period of about three years.

THE ASSEMBLY took up the Suez report in plenary session on December 14. The following resolution was sponsored by Brazil, Iran, the Philippines, and Thailand:

The General Assembly,

Recalling its resolution 1121 (XI) of November 24, 1956, regarding arrangements for clearing the Suez Canal,

Recalling further that the Secretary-General, pursuant to that resolution, requested and received from various governments as advances funds necessary to proceed with the clearing operation,

Having received the report of the Secretary-General dated November 17, 1957 (A/3719),

Mindful that the clearing of the Canal is of direct and immediate benefit to all shipping and trade using the Canal.

Expressing its appreciation of the prompt and efficient manner in which the clearance operation was organized and completed,

Expressing its satisfaction that the Canal is again serving world trade and international shipping,

1. *Notes* the expenses and obligations that have been incurred by the United Nations in the clearing of the Suez Canal;

2. *Endorses* the recommendation of the Secretary-General that, subject to reduction by such resources as might become otherwise available, reimbursement of the advances made by contributor countries to meet the costs of the operations be effected by the application of a surcharge on Canal traffic and that, under this arrangement, a surcharge of 3 percent on Canal traffic would be paid by all shipping and trade using the Canal into a special United Nations account, the procedure to govern such payments to be negotiated with the Government of Egypt and with the other parties to the payments;

3. *Authorizes* the Secretary-General to take the necessary steps to put this arrangement into effect;

4. *Urges* the governments of Member states to cooperate fully with the Secretary-General under the present resolution in order that advances made to the United Nations for the purpose of clearing the Canal may be repaid.[1]

The debate elicited many congratulations for the Secretary-General and all those whose cooperation had brought about the clearance of the Canal

---

[1] General Assembly Resolution 1212 (XII), December 14, 1957.

rapidly and at less cost than originally anticipated. The Soviet bloc considered that the United Kingdom, France, and Israel should have paid the entire cost, while Australia, Denmark, and the Netherlands would have preferred that the costs be assessed against the Members in accordance with the normal scale. The resolution providing for the 3 percent surcharge was, however, adopted without a dissenting vote—55 to 0 with 19 abstentions.

The Linnaeus Tradition and Our Time
(Presidential Address at the Annual Meeting of the Swedish Academy)

STOCKHOLM DECEMBER 20, 1957

HAMMARSKJÖLD flew to Stockholm a few days after the adjournment of the twelfth session of the General Assembly to deliver the Presidential Address at the annual meeting of the Swedish Academy. The text follows. Especially in its concluding paragraphs the Secretary-General had some thoughtful things to say of great relevance to international trends. After the Academy's meeting Hammarskjöld flew to Gaza to spend Christmas with the soldiers of UNEF.

The plain lay green with Ceres, the sky was clear and the lark whirred in the air on that May morning when Carl Linnaeus, "25 years old but for one night," rode from Uppsala on his journey to Lapland "in order to illustrate the same in 3 Regna Naturae."

The November night in Tistedalen, 14 years earlier,[1] was far away. A conquest of the homeland had started, in art, and in science. A conquest of the homeland—but also the conquest, in the world of intellectual culture, of a position which genius, courage, and effort cannot alone create in the political world.

A nation seeks its image in fiction and in history. Seeks and forms. Finds and forms itself accordingly—or rejects. The man on the bier in Tistedalen, and the student who rode out on the long trail through the three realms of nature, have both been simplified in popular imagination and fiction, and turned into figures embodying what we have wished to view as essential features of Swedish character. But, to the present generation, one of them and his times have increasingly receded into a past obscured by "the shadows which have converged in their

UN Press Release SG/643, December 19, 1957.

[1] Refers to the death of Charles XII in 1718, which marked the end of Sweden's position as a great power in Europe.

wake." The other has come ever closer to us: a shining prince of the
land of summer—although his mind, also, was to turn toward brooding
and to get chilled by the needling winds whistling through the small-
town streets; a Swede whose disciples were sent to the four corners of
the earth and returned with their findings to the master who was—and
knew that he was—one of the foremost figures of European culture.

This year, 250 years after his birth, our nation has paid homage in
many forms to the memory of Linnaeus. Here, some thought may be
devoted to his contribution toward the development of values which it is
the task of this Academy to safeguard.

Linnaeus wrote to inform. "The style is very simple," and "I have
presented things quite briefly," he wrote about himself as an author. But
freshness and precision, enthusiasm without lyricism, an instinctive eye
for meaning and causality, raised the great travel accounts and his other
writings in Swedish far above criticism from those "Nightingales of
Pliny" whose disapproval he foresaw. Matter-of-fact poetry—this term
of Almqvist's for a faithful realism in the Strindberg manner, ennobled
into song—is a phrase which comes to mind in characterizing Linnaeus
as a portrayer of the Swedish land. From his own points of departure,
he found his tune and his language. Thus he became both a pioneer and
a paragon. As an observer and a name-giver, Linnaeus taught us to see
with insight, but freely as when "it is ten in the morning in head and
heart." With the creative power of the poet, he showed us how better to
capture and hold the elusive experience of the moment in the net of language. Along the lines which were Linnaeus', our literature has been
enriched by values as essential to our emotions as the nature they mir-
ror.

In his diaries, the botanist, physician, and economist amassed useful
and "curious" notes, which as a whole gave a detailed and vivid picture
of the country. In all this, he remained one of those for whom "nature
rejoices."

His scenery "resounded like a paradise of birds." "Everywhere in the
forest, there was the laughter of the grouse." "Picus played a creaking
bass in the tall dry trees. The black grouse cooed far away; the thrushes
chirped in the trees and the other little birds twittered each in its own
manner." With keener senses, he felt how "the forest, wide, received the
tepid rain."

It was also a world of color. The most magnificent is the famous description of Scania (Skåne). "Brown with sorrel lie the fallow fields.

Brightest blue Echium covers the slopes, as brilliant as you can imagine. Yellow and shining, Chrysanthemum adorns the plowed fields.—Red as blood with Viscaria, the hills. Snow-white with fragrant Dianthus, the sandy expanses. Multicoloured are the rims of the roads with Echium, Cichorium, Anchusa Malva."

Deep down, it was a world full of meaning. In Linnaeus, a glimpse appears of that "conspectus of varied sounds, of forms and garb" which Fröding considered the attribute of God, not of man. A great naturalist guided the author, but a great poet permitted the scholar to peer into the secret council chamber of God. The totality of his works, in this respect, is more eloquent than the fragments one may select as samples. It may be permitted, however, to recall one of many which come to mind.

"The spruce were now in full bloom and gave off a strong dust in the strongest heat as soon as the trees moved; their infinity of male flowers, once strawberry-like and vivid in color, were now pale and spent; the female flowers were few, of a bright red, reclining with opened hollow scales as if to spoon up the male pollen and lead it to the red lancet-like pistils."

In this experience of *sponsalia plantarum* on a dusty summer's day in the forest on the road from Norrköping, Linnaeus gives us a key to the secret of his view of nature. Here, man is no longer the center of the world, only a witness, but a witness who is also a partner in the silent life of nature, bound by secret affinities to the trees whose wedding celebration he is allowed to observe. In this way, to Linnaeus, the forest ceases to be just a scenic decoration around the adventure of man, a romantic sounding board for dreams and fears, or a material asset to use or abuse. In its own right, it is moved by him into Swedish poetry, given domicile there in all its opulence and with a life of its own, along with the meadow and the roadside, the arctic heath and the moor, the seashore and the plain.

Linnaeus' humility as an observer and a researcher did not exclude a strong self-confidence. In a less generous general setting his reactions sometimes would have had a petty ring. Until dignity became a burden and melancholy caught up with him, he was saved by his lively eye for those amusing features which are rarely lacking in even the most sombre situation. A little impressed himself—and perhaps not free of the desire to impress others—but at the same time with irony, he told of his tribulations in the high mountains, when he fell "one musket shot" and "almost ended the comedy." His description of an old Lapp woman whom he once met on the moors is a caricature, cruel in a way, in its seeming lack of feeling for the fate underneath the surface, but its point is turned also against the narrator and his pathetic position. The irony which he showed toward pretentious know-alls and the numerous charlatans of his day found expressions which did not conceal his sense of superiority, but conveyed a picture of retained perspective and freedom from professorial self-sufficiency. Before the eye under which he felt the whole of God's creation was living, everybody was, after all, to the Linnaeus of the travel accounts, both a wise man and a fool.

In his *Journey in Dalecarlia* he described how the cattle, chased by the innumerable gadflies of summer, "would rather let a rickety skeleton dance over hill and dale" than expose themselves to these tormentors. That was a facet of his drastic imagination which for a moment brightened a situation where, on reflection, he would look at the other side of the picture. To suppress this smile would have been hypocrisy, a tribute his seriousness was too genuine to exact or permit. Linnaeus' feeling for the right, certain word has often been attested to. He had access to a rich treasury of dialect, without caring about the restrictions imposed in those days on an author. Nevertheless, his style would hardly have found its freshness, had he not been guided by his sense for the striking and for the unexpected associations of humor. Thus, in his accounts he often relied on meaningful but unexpected similes where his choice of words, leaping between different impressions and ideas, was capable of giving to his style a spontaneous richness comparable to what later poets have achieved in endeavors undertaken with that very purpose in mind.

Wonderment at nature's proof of the Lord's omnipotence had made young Linnaeus write this comment on his first experience of the midnight sun: "Oh Lord, Thy verdicts are incomprehensible." Later, when his eye, guided by somber experiences, was directed towards the world of men, this wonderment was turned into fatalistic mysticism. A parallel has sometimes been drawn with Strindberg: against the summer of the senses in the travel books or in *Hemsöborna,* there stands *Nemesis* and the wintry world of the Powers. Similar comparisons could be made with others. One may seem to discern a pattern. But why labor similarities which after all cannot do justice to the personality and its development? Suffice it to say that Linnaeus, even in the darker reaches of his being, can carry out the role as one of those in whom the people of Nifelhem have wished to see their features reflected with particular clarity.

Even the notes on *Nemesis,* now all too inaccessible, belong to our living literature. Crime and retribution, misfortune breeding misfortune, the vanity of mundane aspirations—thus fate is linked to fate in this dance of death, where the style has the economy and dry precision of a woodcut. Linnaeus' introductory words, addressed to his only son, provide the motif of these pictures of life. "There was a time when I doubted that God cared about me; many years have taught me what I leave to you. Everyone wants to be happy, but few are able to be." Beside this, however, there is a poem where brooding finally gives way to the trust of a grown-up child.

> Thou sawest my happiness
> when I was still lying
> in darkness.
> Thou settest my clock,
> Thou cuttest my bread,
> So why, almighty Hero,
> shouldst Thou forget me now?
> My house I have built
> by the grace of God.
> Therefore, I sleep unafraid.

These lines reverberate with the happy humility before the mystery which from the outset gave his accounts their paean note. Life, to Linnaeus, became a *mysterium tremendum.* It remained, till the end, a *mysterium numinosum.*

Linnaeus' Swedish works have always been read, and are perhaps read to an increasing extent, even outside the circle of experts. Their position is certainly explained in part by the personality behind the works and its continuing appeal to interest and imagination. The fact that, for instance, the *Öland Journey,* has been able to find readers in low-priced editions demonstrates, however, that it responds to a need, determined by the direction developed by the Swedish feeling for nature.

The relationship of a nation—and a generation—to older literature tells something about the continuity of spiritual life. It can also give an idea about the conditions of writing and of the writer: What is the reader seeking, and why?

Outside the limits of belles lettres, the works of Linnaeus occupy a place of their own with us. Other books which still have much to offer are resting in oblivion on the shelves of libraries, or reach only the few in new editions. Among them are, for example, the account of Linnaeus' pupil Pehr Kalm of his voyage to America, and Petrus Laestadius' *Journal* with its experiences of years as a missionary in Lapland.

The situation is hardly surprising, if we consider how short our memory has been even when it comes to the greatest innovators of earlier periods. The poetry of a man like Bellman has remained the property of the people thanks to the music. But the baroque paintings of a poet like Stiernhielm, where the blood pulsates and imaginative language is flowering without crowding out even the purest lyricism, appear as dead museum pieces in the nebulous perspective of school-day reminiscences. The history of literature has done its share. Perhaps it is now up to the writers themselves to go exploring, more than they have done, with their eye and their dexterity trained in what last year's Bellman Prize winner called "the difficult school." Might they not count on finding an audience for their counsel and interest in their findings among the readers whom, happily, this school has attracted? Perhaps this might also narrow the gap to the immediately preceding generation of writers, a gap which, now as always, is threatening because of the illusion that the old order is dead as all is renewed.

There is one possible reason for the estrangement from the past that is disquieting. In a mass culture, where publicity, working in the interest of sales, is constantly harping on the idea that the latest must be the best, the book, in the view of many, becomes relegated to the ranks of disposable and rapidly aging consumer's goods. This may lead to an industrialization of literature, which pays attention to the indications about public taste in the best seller lists in preference to that which is essential and therefore vital. In a situation which for such reasons, and perhaps also for other and deeper ones, is characterized by the quest for novelty and by conformism, a weakening of the position of older literature would be natural. The risk is enhanced if at the same time the position of the written word as such is becoming more precarious.

The book now has to compete with the press, and jointly they must hold their own against new forms of expression and communication: the films, radio, and television. The need for personal contact with literature of quality reflects an acquired taste. A form of expression requiring less activity on the part of the recipient is favored by that law of least resistance which prevails in this as in other fields.

In the end, we are faced here by the question of the intellectual climate and what determines it. It would be presumptuous to try, here and now, to contribute to this discussion. It is a banality which need not be further developed in this connection, to say that the present has given unusual weight to material progress, and that this means that it has deflected interest from spiritual exercises and found ways of satisfying it by a thousand and one new inventions. Nor is it an original view— whatever importance it may have—that new generations in the Western world have broken out of the sets of problems to which *une littérature engagée* seeks the answers. Observers of the international currents of today may be tempted to name another tendency, although so far it has not made a very deep imprint in our country. It may be that the cult of amorphous spontaneity in art and of a philosophy of absurdity which is calling the tune in some quarters these days, will prove to be a transitory phenomenon. No matter what new paths it may open for creative writing, it contains risks of a growing estrangement from readers whose interest is a prerequisite for the continued life of a work of art.

Eliot has spoken of our era as one when wisdom has been forgotten for knowledge and knowledge for information. May we escape a situation where these words become more than an expression of frustration, and where beside an esoteric poetry—which will probably always have its practitioners—there is produced nothing but literature where realism has been changed into reporting aimed at filling the mental vacuum of increasing leisure without worry or effort for the reader.

In such a situation the dead writers would become definitely forgotten. To keep their works alive is also a means of making room for new, creative writing which, like that of the precursors, is begotten in earnest and often born in pain.

The mental climate here referred to is also influenced, and perhaps not least, by political factors. One of these deserves mention here. This generation has seen Europe lose much of the powerful position it occupied for centuries, and a wave of nationalism has swept the continents. The revolutionary events we witness have led many into a defeatism which, although unspoken, is revealed by its inseparable companions: fatigue, bitterness, and sterile self-assertion. In this development, there are traces of the life of nations in earlier periods of upsetting social change—however difficult it may sometimes be to recognize in the coexistence of nations the principles for which one has once fought in one's own country.

There are good reasons, and good chances, to offer resistance to such a reaction. The old is not so rotten, nor the new so immature as many seem to think.

Only those who do not want to see can deny that we are moving these days in the direction of a new community of nations, however far we may be from its full realization, however often we may seem to have chosen the wrong path, however numerous the setbacks and disappointments have been. Could it be otherwise, when no other road appears open out of the dangers a new era has created? That democracy of human rights, with equality for nations irrespective of race and history, which has come nearer with the rebirth of Asia and Africa and must form the framework of the international community of the future, may open the door for new spiritual contacts, impulses, and problems. To give it reality, much must be jeopardized and perhaps sacrificed, but this is the price of an evolution, the main direction of which we can agree with. It would be a sign of spiritual senescence if such a situation gave rise to destructive despair.

But we can feel the pressure of other forces of the times as a threat to the life we find worth living. If we were to falter in our resistance on these fronts, we should have cause for despair. Then the shadow would fall heavily over the future, be it that of humanity, of the West—or of literature. Then our sacrifices for the development of a community of nations, formed by faith in the value of every human being, would lose all their meaning.

In spite of the changes in its external position, Europe is certainly able, in these various contexts, to keep a place worthy of its traditions. What has been lost in power can be made up by leadership. One condition is that Europe understands how to develop and maintain the values which are the foundation of her spiritual greatness. In this, every nation has its role to play. This Academy has part of the responsibility for the way in which Sweden meets the demands placed on her.

When Linnaeus, after his years abroad, was tempted by most favorable offers to remain there, he declined them because "a higher urge pulled him towards his Fatherland." Sweden, to Linnaeus, was the country where he wished to round out his life's work. It was done as he willed it. The scholar, however, knew no national frontiers. He was a European and, as a European, a citizen of the world. Much has changed, but it is still possible to balance and reconcile home and world, heritage and task in this manner. This can provide an answer to even larger problems than those of the individual.

Linnaeus rode out of Uppsala one morning in May. Many years later, on an evening in August, he returned over the plain.

Ever since Fällingsbro, autumn had steadily appeared before our eyes. The forest, 'tis true, was green, but more severe than in summer. The pastures and the meadows, 'tis true, were green; but without flowers, for the cattle had gone over the former and the scythe over the latter. The plowed fields were full of yellow sheaves, and the yellowish stubble after the harvest was mixed with green weeds. The ditches were full of water after the wet summer, and the multitude of Bur Marigold made them yellow, the rims of the road were covered with *Persicaria acri,* which now began to redden and hang its ears. Everywhere, the farmers were out working: some of them were cutting the grain with the scythe, while their womenfolk, heads and arms all white, sheaved it, some carted home their rye, some threshed, some crushed the clods with the sledge, some evened the field with the iron harrow, some sowed winter rye, some harrowed down the seed, some evened the field with the roller, while cow-herding children sang and blew their horns for the cattle in the pastures, until the bleak evening wind began to whistle, and the bright sun sank below the horizon as we entered the Garden of Uppsala.

May this timeless picture of man's work and nature's rest form the tailpiece of these thoughts on the Linnaeus anniversary.

A Room of Quiet
(*The United Nations Meditation Room*)
DECEMBER 1957

HAMMARSKJÖLD gave a great deal of thought and personal attention to the creation of the United Nations Meditation Room. Only a small space off the public lobby of the General Assembly building had been set aside for the purpose and it was Hammarskjöld who found solutions to the problems of creating in this small space a room of dignity and meaning. The text that follows is from the leaflet that is given to those who visit the room. It was written by Hammarskjöld himself, based on extemporaneous remarks he had made in April 1957 to an organization of "Friends of the Meditation Room" in thanks for their gift of over $12,000 to help pay for the remodeling of the room. At that time the front wall was still blank. During the fall of 1957 Hammarskjöld's friend, the Swedish artist Bo Beskow, came to New York and did the fresco on this wall. The Meditation Room was reopened to the public in December and the leaflet revised slightly to include mention of the fresco.

This is a room devoted to peace and those who
are giving their lives for peace. It is a room
of quiet where only thoughts should speak.

We all have within us a center of stillness surrounded by silence.

This house, dedicated to work and debate in the service of peace, should have one room dedicated to silence in the outward sense and stillness in the inner sense.

It has been the aim to create in this small room a place where the doors may be open to the infinite lands of thought and prayer.

People of many faiths will meet here, and for that reason none of the symbols to which we are accustomed in our meditation could be used.

However, there are simple things which speak to us all with the same language. We have sought for such things and we believe that we have found them in the shaft of light striking the shimmering surface of solid rock.

UN Headquarters leaflet, April 1957, revised December 1957.

So, in the middle of the room we see a symbol of how, daily, the light of the skies gives life to the earth on which we stand, a symbol to many of us of how the light of the spirit gives life to matter.

But the stone in the middle of the room has more to tell us. We may see it as an altar, empty not because there is no God, not because it is an altar to an unknown god, but because it is dedicated to the God whom man worships under many names and in many forms.

The stone in the middle of the room reminds us also of the firm and permanent in a world of movement and change. The block of iron ore has the weight and solidity of the everlasting. It is a reminder of that cornerstone of endurance and faith on which all human endeavour must be based.

The material of the stone leads our thoughts to the necessity for choice between destruction and construction, between war and peace. Of iron man has forged his swords, of iron he has also made his ploughshares. Of iron he has constructed tanks, but of iron he has likewise built homes for man. The block of iron ore is part of the wealth we have inherited on this earth of ours. How are we to use it?

The shaft of light strikes the stone in a room of utter simplicity. There are no other symbols, there is nothing to distract our attention or to break in on the stillness within ourselves. When our eyes travel from these symbols to the front wall, they meet a simple pattern opening up the room to the harmony, freedom, and balance of space.

There is an ancient saying that the sense of a vessel is not in its shell but in the void. So it is with this room. It is for those who come here to fill the void with what they find in their center of stillness.

Index